From TRIANON to the first
VIENNA ARBITRAL AWARD

Charles Wojatsek

From TRIANON to the first
VIENNA ARBITRAL AWARD

THE HUNGARIAN MINORITY IN THE FIRST CZECHOSLOVAK REPUBLIC
- 1918-1938 -

INSTITUT DES CIVILISATIONS COMPARÉES,
INSTITUTE OF COMPARATIVE CIVILIZATIONS,
MONTREAL

ISBN 2-920285-00-9
Production & Distribution
Réalisation & Diffusion. 1981
    Éditions M. Kolbe Editions
    P.O. BOX 2058, succ. Jacques-Cartier Branch
    Sherbrooke, Quebec, Canada   J1J 3Y1

PREFACE

The aim of this work is to focus attention on some internal political problems of the first Czechoslovak republic, primarily investigating the legal position of the Hungarian nationals of that state. The first Czechoslovak republic in history, after a short twenty-year existence, disappeared from the political map of the sovereign states of Europe. Similarities exist in the formation of the first and second Czechoslovakia in 1938 and in 1945. This Central European republic, in which many other foreign peoples from the neighbouring countries were forced to live under Czech domination, came into existence by the dictates of the victorious allies of a non-existing state after two world wars. In both cases, several exiled Czechs organized national councils abroad and they were recognized by some states as an allied belligerent government. "Czecho-Slovakia was formed in October 1918, as a result of the efforts of Thomas G. Masaryk and Edward Beneš, whose Czechoslovak National Committee in Paris had been recognized as a co-belligerent in World War I. [...] it was carved entirely out of the old dual monarchy of Austria-Hungary."[1] On October 5, 1938 Edward Beneš, the former minister of foreign affairs and later the second president of the ČSR, resigned and escaped from Prague, via Rumania, to London; British authorities were not aware of his arrival. At the end of World War II, in 1945, Beneš returned to Prague from London, via Moscow. With the help of Soviet Russia, Beneš functioned again as head of state. Now Czechoslovakia was smaller in area than it had previously been between 1918 and 1938. "For his part, Edward Beneš voluntarily tied the fate and future of Czechoslovakia to the Russian star. No hue and cry was raised when Czechoslovakia ceded

I

Ruthenia to Stalin, thus the first time in history bringing the Russian frontier beyond the Carpathians into the plain of Danube."[2]

If one is willing to modify a view of a given period by using historical sources to explain political movements, then the behavior of some Czech politicians and political adventurers living in exile during the two world wars can serve as studies in political intrigue. These politicians, remaining abroad during the wars, tried to create a new state with the help of foreign government leaders but without the consent of the population of the territory they wished to rule. The first effective resistance against this oppressive Czech rule was organized in 1938 on an international scale.

This study further examines the fate of the Hungarian population in the first Czechoslovakia where it was condemned to live with curtailed rights in a state of oppression as a minority group in the newly founded so called democratic republic of the Czechs. The Magyars of Czechoslovakia were placed in that country without being given a chance for self-determination. They were compelled to live on the Czechoslovakian side of the border in the immediate vicinity of Hungary. During the period of 1938-1945 the larger part of the Magyar minority group in the ČSR was liberated and returned to Hungary. The borderline of the dictated peace treaty of Trianon of June 4, 1920 between Czechoslovakia and Hungary was revised by peaceful means on November 2, 1938.

TABLE OF CONTENTS

BIBLIOGRAPHY

ILLUSTRATIONS

CHAPTER I

BOHEMIA'S EASTWARD EXPANSION

The Czechs and Their Central European Neighbours

The history of the Czechoslovakian political turmoil in 1938 must be regarded as a reaction against Czech political and territorial expansion in opposition to the aspirations of other national groups. The existence and collapse of the first Czechoslovak republic cannot be seen only as a solitary fragment in the history of Bohemia with extended borders eastward, but also as an unbelievably fortunate period in Czech national expansion. The growth of an illusory Czech power-policy was made possible by the unreasonable behavior of the victorious allied and associated governments in 1918. The inflated, short-lived Czechoslovak state was condemned to extinction as soon as the military situation was to be changed in Europe. For twenty years the Czechs ruled the other provinces from Prague. The components of the newly formed state were captive nations degraded to the status of national minorities. The entente political leaders unilaterally, without consultations with the governments of the area, imposed territorial changes in Central Europe without a minimal semblance of serious statemanship.

With this act the Czech politicians wanted to perpetuate their rule over those non-Czech people who formed the majority of the population; and yet, they were subjugated to a Czech minority rule.

The emergence and even the unglorious disappearance of the first Czechoslovak republic, 1918-1938, was connected with the political activities of its first two presidents, Thomas G. Masaryk and Edward Beneš. Before we try to understand the apogee and fall of the Czech political manoeuverings in modern European history, it is proper to examine the Czech historical development. Since their settlement in modern-day Bohemia, the Czechs have been surrounded by German tribes. The Czech tribes were in the Carolingian Empire's zone of influence, the Christian successor in the Western European part of the once powerful ancient Roman Empire. The Germano-Roman emperors extended their political domination together with Christian missionary activity to the Slavic tribes, and widened their political and military influence eastward in the lands inhabited by Slavic tribes. As a result of this politico-religious activity, fourteen Czech noblemen were baptized in 845 at Regensburg. The Moravian tribes, east of the Czechs, wanted to counterbalance the Frankish political weight, and requested Emperor Michael II of the Byzantine Empire to send Slavic speaking missionaries to Moravia. These two centres of Christianity competed for religious influence in Central Europe, and their rulers for political authority. Missionaries from Byzantium arrived in 863 to the Morava and Danube rivers to diffuse religious-political ideas from the East. This project did not succeed, and Moravia remained in the Roman sphere of influence and under Germano-Roman imperial rule. Later a Bavarian-Hungarian alliance destroyed the Moravian state. The Magyar tribes arrived in 896 in present-day Hungary, and expanded their rule from the central plains to the foothills of the Carpathian mountains. In the northern part of Hungary, a Slavic tribe, the modern-day Slovaks, became the subjects of the Hungarian state for one thousand years when Hungarian control was stretched to the mountain peaks, the natural borderline between Poland and Hungary for a millennium. The predecessors of the Slovaks in that area were the Avars, Marcomanns, the Quads and the colonizing Romans. There existed no established Slovak state. Tribal ancestors of the Slovaks surrendered without resistance or war, and accepted the rule of the central Hungarian tribe as did the newly arrived Hungarian tribes.[3] The Czechs and Moravians started a new political existence in a state, called Bohemia, which was part of the Holy Roman Empire of the German Nation as it was later renamed by Charles IV, king of Bohemia and emperor of the Holy Roman Empire. The Czech dukes received on different occasions the royal crown from the Germano-Roman emperors as a reward for faithful services rendered to the emperors. The royal crown was given in 1085 and 1158 only for the lifetime of the dukes; and later, in 1212 it became inheritable in the first Czech national dynasty, the Přemysl House by the disposition of the Sicilian Golden Bull of emperor Frederick II. Bohemia and Moravia remained, for one thousand years, a member state of the Holy Roman Empire. The kings of Bohemia became office holders of the empire, imperial cupbearers, and held the distinguished title, one of the seven electors of the empire. Inhabitants of the kingdom of Bohemia enjoyed every advantage of Western civilization, offered by membership in the empire. The kings of Bohemia opened the frontier regions of their country for German colonists because they needed their higher skills in trade as well as their intellectual qualifications. They were the predecessors of the Sudeten German population of the twentieth century Czechoslovakia.

During the Middle Ages, for over five centuries, the Bohemian and Hungarian kingdoms played a decisive role in European history under the rule of their national dynasties, the Přemyslides and the

Árpáds. After the extinction of their native royal families, the Czechs and the Magyars at many occasions elected common kings from the Luxembourg and Jagiellonian dynasties, and the two neighbouring countries were joined in personal union by their common monarchs. When Louis II, the king of Bohemia and the apostolic king of Hungary, died in 1526 on the battlefield of Mohács fighting the Turkish invaders of Hungary, the Habsburg dynasty acquired the Bohemian and Hungarian crowns. The Habsburgs of Vienna wore the royal crowns of Bohemia and Hungary until the end of World War I. The Habsburg kings during their four hundred-year long rule equally pursued anti-Czech and anti-Magyar policy contrary to their coronation oath. There were many misunderstandings with the government of Vienna, including armed rebellions against its rule, but at the same time these small nations of Central Europe were able to withstand the incursions from powerful neighbours in the multinational Austrian Empire. During their common history a feeling of togetherness, a cultural affinity and shared citizenship developed among the eleven national groups in the empire of 51,390,223 inhabitants. Later in Austria-Hungary the road for cultural, economic and political progress and success was open to all component nations.

The historic kingdom of Bohemia lost its constitution and national independence after the battle of the White Mountain, at the beginning of the Thirty Years' War. After that fateful event, the Czechs were rather willing to serve the Habsburg dynasty rather than to oppose the centralized tendencies of the Viennese government. They were not openly in opposition to the Austrian empire but they resented the fact that they did not obtain a similar deal as the Hungarians in the compromise with Austria in 1867 concerning national independence. During World War I the Czechs were working, secretly at home and openly abroad, against Austria-Hungary and were waiting for the defeat of the common homeland. With external help they succeeded in founding a new state in 1918. The delimitation of the frontiers of Czechoslovakia surpassed the dreams of Masaryk and Beneš, and the republic absorbed numerically more national minorities than the entire Czech population of that area. The nationality problems of the now destroyed Austria-Hungary were inherited by the Czechoslovak republic. The multinational Central European monarchy, which was previously able to resist imperialist pressures from the East and West, fell pray to the hatred of its enemies. The Allied and Associated Powers partitioned the Austro-Hungarian Empire and mutilated Hungary in the peace treaties although the Hungarian government had been against the declaration of war on Serbia[4] after the assassination of the Austrian heir to the throne because Hungary had no territorial claims on the Balkan peninsula. With the dissolution of the Danubian empire a political vacuum was created in Central Europe.

The weak successor states had to face innumerable internal problems and these small states were unable to resist the imperialist expansion of Hitler.

A Fraudulent Trick: the Existence of a "Czechoslovak" Nation

During World War I Masaryk, Beneš and their political collaborators in exile in Western Europe deceived the political leaders of the entente governments with the fabrication of a legend that a "Czechoslovak" nation existed on the territory of Austria-Hungary. They added to their invention that this "nation" wanted to be united in an independent state with leadership from Prague, under the direction of the Czechs. It is necessary to ascertain the historical fact that a "Czechoslovak" nation never existed, and does not exist even today. In 1918 the Czech political emigration succeeded in founding a Czechoslovak state. The unsatisfied Slovaks, after twenty years of cohabitation with the Czechs in the same republic, created their own Slovak state at the first possible opportunity. In October 1938 they demanded from Prague full autonomy for Slovakia promised them by the Czechs in 1918. They established, for the first time in history in March 1939, their Slovak republic with the assistance of Hitler. The undemocratic Czechoslovak government in Prague disappeared as a political factor in Central Europe, partly as a result of the intervention of the National Socialist government of Germany, and partly under the pressure of the demands of the discontent autonomist front of the Slovaks, Sudeten Germans, Hungarians, Poles and Ruthenians.

According to the teaching of romantic historiography, when glorious non-existing national histories were written throughout Europe, an illusion emerged that the Czechs, Moravians and Slovaks formed one Moravian state in the ninth century. This is only a legend which does not correspond to historical fact. The short-lived Moravian state never extended control over the territory of Bohemia or over Northern Hungary, which is twentieth century Slovakia. The Czechs in the second half of the nineteenth century, in the process of their national rebirth, wanted to gather more strength for their struggle against the Habsburg hegemony, and they saw in the Slovaks, living in Hungary, a reservoir to supplement the lacking element of the Bohemian nation. The Czechs and Slovaks never lived under a common government until 1918. The Czechs in Bohemia were exposed to different cultural and social influences than the Slovaks in Hungary. Slovak Lutherans, about 20% of their nation, did not accept the Catholic Bible nor the Latin ecclesiastic language. For two centuries, they adapted the Czech Hussite Bible and church songs for their congregations until finally they were translated into Slovak and their own ecclesiastical language was formed. The Slovak Lutherans strongly altered the Czech ecclesiastical language by the linguistic characteristics and specific features of the Slovak language. The Catholics initially worked out among the Slovaks a literary language which was followed by a scholarly dispute among the linguists. Later, in the middle of the 19th century the central Slovak dialect was accepted as a modern literary language. Use of Czech as a liturgical language by a small minority of the Slovaks contributed later, during the era of nationalism, to a pro-Czech political orientation and an anti-Catholic stand among the Slovak Lutherans. This political and ideological disagreement remained a divisive force among the Slovaks at home and abroad until the present day.

For ten centuries, the Slovaks as well as the Magyars regarded Hungary — a multinational state with Latin as the official language of the Parliament until 1844 — as a common homeland. This feeling ripened under the influence of their common historic heritage, common fate and long struggles with the external enemies of both nations in the defence of their fatherland. This pro-Hungarian affection of the Slovaks was demonstrated in contemporary Slovak literature.

In the Habsburg empire the non-German peoples almost simultaneously turned against the Germanization program of emperor Joseph II. The Czechs, Magyars, Slovaks, among others, began to cultivate their national conscientiousness. The intellectual leaders, writers, poets of the component nations of the Habsburg monarchy were very anxious to create educational and scientific institutions and theatres for preserving their national language and culture put in peril by the Germanization of Vienna.

Fresh Contacts Between the Czechs and Slovaks

The development of philology gave a great impulse to the creation of literary and linguistic works in national languages in the Austrian empire. The energetic activity of Joseph Dobrovský, 1753-1829, the illustrious Czech philologist, author of the *History of the Czech language and literature*, opened a new era of linguistics. He was born in Hungary as the son of a non-commissioned officer of the Austrian imperial army and, after his departure to Bohemia, he followed with interest not only the Czech but also the Slovak philological publications. The Slovak linguists remained in contact with him and they exchanged with him the results of their research. Their topics were focused on the problem of grammatical systems, questions of comparative Slavic linguistics which allowed for the examination of the growing awareness of Slavic affinity on a scientific basis. Dobrovský, the Czech Catholic priest remained in scholarly contact with Slovak Lutheran ministers, teachers and printers in Hungary who had interest in philology, publications in literary journals and books or who were collectors of Slovak proverbs and folk songs. Philology was acknowledged as an authority to give scholarly explanations on cultural and linguistic relations among the Slavic nations, including Slovaks and Czechs. The old common Slavic tribal relations became exploited for divergent cultural and political ends. Scholarly cultivation of Slavistics obtained a new significance in the contemporary situation. In the Austrian monarchy, national movements came into existence, and the intellectual leaders of the Slavic nations developed the idea of Slavic reciprocity as a means of cultural self-defence against the policy of denationalization and Germanization of Vienna. Its result was the spread of comparative Slavic studies, promotion of cultural cooperation and meetings among the promoters of these ideas.

The writers of the small nations in Central Europe desired to raise the quality of their national literature to the standard of Western European literatures. Linguistic progress gave an impetus to the embellishment of Slovak literature as a first step towards political nationhood. Slovak language reform was delayed by the persistence of the Slovak Lutherans regarding the use of Czech liturgical language not only for ecclesiastical purposes but also in literary works. The use of the antiquated biblical language of the Czech Brethren in liturgy by the Slovak Lutherans and in their literary products — inserted with Slovakisms — was a unique phenomenon. It was neither a Czech nor a Slovak living language. It became a tradition in the Lutheran congregations without representing a Czechophile political orientation in the first phase of Slovak national development. By 1843 the Slovak literary evolution reached the point of culmination with the foundation of the rules for a literary language by which the Slovak national consciousness gained significant animation. The Slovak language became protected from Bohemianisms which threatened its purity. There are deep grammatical differences between the Czech and Slovak languages in accidence, structure, word formation, declension of nouns and adjectives, conjugation of verbs, grammatical agreements and phonetics. The Slovak Lutherans gave up the use of old Czech liturgical language but as a remnant of their long religious connections with the Czech Brethren, they transferred their former ecclesiastical links to the political field in the form of cooperation with the Czechs against the wish of their Catholic confrères.

Foundation of the Slovak literary language encouraged demands of a cultural and political nature from the Hungarian government during the decades of boiling national feelings, and caused conflicts of national character which disturbed the thousand-year old peaceful relations between Magyars and Slovaks. This controversy was artificially instigated by the Czechs for political gains. Establishment of the Slovak literary language also fundamentally afflicted the dreams of those Czechs who tried to strengthen their own national energies from the potential forces of the Slovak people. They saw in the literary movement of the Slovaks a clear sign of national identity, and even a possible separation of the Slovak

Lutherans from the Czech biblical language. The Slovak linguistic independence was directed against the Czech intrusion into the intellectual life of the Slovaks with their alien culture and divergent language. One does not have to forget that in spite of the existing affinity among the Slavic languages in general, it is true that should a Slav want to speak another Slavic language it must be learned as any other foreign language. The Czechs also attempted to extend their grip on the Slovaks from another direction. The Habsburg kings for political reasons developped to a high degree the industrialization of Bohemia to the detriment of Hungary. They wanted to penalize the Hungarian nobility for maintaining their exemption from taxation and for refusing to pay taxes to the imperial treasury. Furthermore, the Hungarian nobility dared to lead revolts on many occasions against the unconstitutional rule of the Habsburg dynasty. The industrial development was therefore reserved to the politically faithful parts of the Habsburg domains. The economic prosperity of the lands of the crown of St. Wenceslas was promoted by the Czech loyalty to the Habsburg house. With the surplus capital the Czechs started enterprises in Upper Hungary inhabited by the Slovaks. In their efforts for economic expansion and hegemony among the Slovaks, the Czechs emphasized their Slavic affinity. It was a propaganda tool to gain economic advantages. Meanwhile, the Czechs spread news of political offenses directed by the Hungarian government against the Slovaks in order to bring them closer to themselves. The Czech propagandists gained the understanding of many Slovaks with their literary and political appeals. The defeat of the Hungarian revolution against the Habsburgs of Vienna in 1849, and the brutal Austrian oppression of Hungary was felt by Slovaks and Magyars alike. Later the government of Vienna under the pressure' of external political events was obliged to grant concessions to the Magyars and to even conclude a political compromise with them. It resulted in the foundation of the Dual Monarchy of Austria-Hungary. Triumphant, the Hungarian government did not show much understanding for the linguistic rights and cultural demands of the Slovaks. Even the minimal national-cultural claims of the Slovaks were not recognized in Budapest, the very same goals for which the Magyars were willing to revolt against the imperial government in Vienna. In their struggle for cultural survival, the Slovaks received support from tsarist Russia and from Bohemia but not for altruistic reasons from any of them. Both Slavic nations demonstrated a keen interest in the political, cultural and linguistic strife of the Slovaks. Political events of the twentieth century proved that it was not for unselfish motives. Slovaks fell victim to the Czech politicians. In 1873, a commemorative festival was organized in Prague for the centennial of the birth of Joseph Jungmann, the leading figure, poet, translator, founder and designer of the revival of modern Czech literature and national rebirth. *Matica Slovenská,* a literary society, sent a three-member delegation to Prague, consisting of prominent Slovak cultural activators. Participants expressed in their speeches the necessity and importance of the conclusion of a literary accord with the Czechs in the hope for a better understanding between the two nations. The Slovaks wanted to strengthen themselves with the new contacts, however, in the long run they did irreparable damage to the Slovak cultural tradition and national cause. A systematic cultivation of literary relations began between the two centres, Prague and Turčiansky Svätý Martin — Túrócszentmárton. At that time, Czech literature glittered in a more advanced stage of growth. The Slovaks hoped to gain from these contacts, especially after the dissolution of the *Matica Slovenská* in 1875 by the Hungarian government as a hotbed of anti-Hungarian agitation. The Slovaks accepted this outside encouragement, although some brochures printed in Bohemia considered the Slovak language as a dialect of the Czech, and the writers of those articles advocated a common literary language for both nations. This approach was a much more dangerous way for the annihilation of the Slovak national values than the open administrative measures of the contemporary Hungarian government which was subject to changes after each parliamentary election or appointment of a new government. The Czechs attacked the existence of a separate Slovak language in its roots with the insistence on the identity of the two languages. Behind the imagined and fabricated linguistic unity of these two Slavic nations, there was also a political danger for the Slovaks through a legend of a Czecho-Slovak national unity which became the newest threat against the existence of a Slovak nation. The penetration of Czech publications among the Slovak readers began with some articles in Czech almanachs written by Slovak poets and writers. After 1875, the Hungarian government with an intolerant educational policy drove away many Slovaks for study in Prague. Some Slovaks from Upper Hungary went to university in Prague and some even completed high school in Bohemia. The reopening of the Czech branch of Charles University in 1882 — it became a bilingual institution — gave a new incentive for learning to the young Slovaks who chose Prague instead of Vienna or Budapest. In the same year the *"Detvan"*, a Slovak student association, was founded in the Czech capital to keep the countrymen together and to foster interest in their common tongue. This student club maintained friendly relations with similar Czech and Moravian organizations. These political actions did not remain under the guise of innocent student movements forever. A new social club was founded in Prague in 1896, named *Česko-Slovenská Jednota,* Czecho-Slovak Unity. This association studied and propagated the idea of national fusion but made limited inroads into the ranks of the Slovaks, who remained faithful to their homeland and looked with fear upon the advertised political union with the Czechs. There were elaborate plans for Czech penetration into different walks of life of the Slovak region of Hungary: investments in economy, trade, commerce and literary publication. Bohemia sent her agents to the Slovaks for preparation of the Czech domination of every facet of the Slovak life. At this time, Slovak leaders did not suspect any intricate nor coordinated attack against their national existence on the part of the Czechs.

Scholarships were distributed for the Slovak students from Upper Hungary for studies in Bohemia. In the last three decades of the nineteenth century, various Czech clubs participated in granting aid to lure young Slovaks to Prague and to gain their support for the new Czech national expansion. In 1879, professor Thomas G. Masaryk arrived in Prague from Vienna to teach philosophy in the Czech section of the university. He became more of a politician than a professor of philosophy, more of a fighting student leader and political figure who, with the publications of his political views, wanted to influence different segments of Czech national life. Masaryk gave inspiration to the realists who in 1886 started to publish a bi-weekly entitled "*Čas*". In 1891 the politician-professor became a deputy in the Imperial Parliament of Vienna and the following year a member of the Bohemian Provincial Diet in Prague. It is true that for personal reasons and political disagreement with the *Young Czech* leaders he resigned from his parliamentary positions. In 1907 he again became a member of the Viennese Parliament and remained there until his escape from Austria-Hungary in 1914.

While at the University of Prague, Masaryk supported the radical section of the Slovak students who in their journal the *Hlas* propagated the Czecho-Slovak national unity. Their activity in Prague provoked the reaction of the anti-Czech Slovaks who in their newspaper the *Národnie Noviny* attacked the Czech manipulations against the linguistic, literary, cultural, national and historical existence of the Slovak nation under the pretext of the fictitious "Czecho-Slovak" national unity. The *Hlas* was not long-lived but it started the fermentation of political views which remained alive in intellectual circles. "Later this group was attracted to the Russophile political orientation".[5] In 1909, another faction of the Slovak youth movement started a review *Prúdy* which survived for five years. Along with the Slovak weekly in Budapest, *Slovenský Týždenník* 1903-1918, edited by Milan Hodža, member of the Hungarian Parliament and later Prime Minister of Czechoslovakia in the days of her dissolution, the *Prúdy* continued bitter attacks against the Magyar political leadership. Masaryk used these political agitators in his hate campaign against Hungary.

Formation of an Artificial Mosaic State in 1918

Today it is well known, from the plethora of available literature in many languages, that the peace treaties after World War I were drafted in an emotionally charged atmosphere in which it was impossible to arrive at negotiated treaties by reasonable compromises based on incontestable and undeniable evidence. The peace arrangements concluded among the former belligerents therefore came under attack several years after their signature, for several reasons, by those governments which were not satisfied with the dispositions of the treaties. The victorious countries, in their shortsighted hatred, wanted the total annihilation of their former enemies, and to extend their own territorial limits at the expense of their neighbours.

It is impossible to separate the formation of the first Czechoslovak republic from the names of Masaryk and Beneš. These two Czech emissaries used their connections abroad for the realization of their political aims. Their antipathy for the Germans, Austrians and Hungarians found a favourable echo in the foreign ministries of Paris, London, Petrograd and Washington where the Czech exiles gained admittance through their acquaintances. These persons organized the Czech emigrants for their cause, encouraged the desertion of Czech soldiers from the Austro-Hungarian army and enlisted them in units — called Czech legions — in France, Russia and later in Italy.

Masaryk, the 64-year old university professor and Beneš, the 30-year old teacher at a commercial academy, met in Prague in September 1914 and they coordinated their political ideas which culminated in the foundation of a Czech state after World War I. In 1914 Masaryk escaped from Austria-Hungary, and Beneš slipped away abroad less than one year later. During the war, Masaryk travelled around the world and worked mainly in British, American and Russian circles. Beneš successfully put into action his French — mainly free masonic — connections which he cultivated as a former university student in Paris. Masaryk had been several times in the United States of America even before his escape from Prague where he was introduced by his American wife into university and freethinker circles.[6] During the war Masaryk returned to the USA several times where he immediately acquired supporters among the Czech immigrants who gave him financial help. Even some American Slovaks sanctioned his vaguely described objectives.

Years before the outbreak of hostilities, several plans were circulated for the dismemberment of Austria-Hungary among the politicians of the nationalities living in the Dual Monarchy, and among their adherents in foreign countries. Masaryk and Beneš added to those plans their own ideas, and propagated them in numerous memoirs favouring the creation of a democratic Czech national state. In a memorandum, submitted in the Foreign Office to Sir George Clerk on 15 April, 1915, Masaryk claimed Upper Hungary for the Czech republic in order that this territory constitute a corridor between Bohemia and Russia. Masaryk did not think that the independence of a Czech republic could be guaranteed in any other way but by Russia's military might.[7] Besides Czech emigrants and influential foreigners, Czech agents abroad skilfully used the

Czech legions for the realization of their political purposes. In Austria-Hungary the regiments were recruited on a territorial basis, therefore, Czech officers were able to direct entire detachments to the side of the enemies on different fronts. These deserters numbered about 1,000 in Italy, 1,600 in France, 5,000 in Serbia and 50,000 in Russia. In February 1916, national committees were formed abroad. The National Council of the Czech Lands, later renamed as Czecho-Slovak National Council, issued a declaration in Paris for the establishment of a Czecho-Slovak state. Its chairman was the leader of the Czech exiles, Masaryk, vice-chairman Josef Dürich, Milan R. Štefánik, and the agile Edward Beneš. This Czech national council devoted its energy to activities in the entente chancelleries, newspapers, periodicals, addressed memoirs to entente governments for the realization of an independent Czech state which would be an important and useful ally against Germany. This promise was especially emphasized before French leaders. The champions of the Czech political exile worked indefatigably in entente circles and among the nationalities of the Danubian monarchy. Masaryk was a successful lobbyist in Washington and among some leaders of the Slovak and Ruthenian immigrants from Austria-Hungary. Masaryk's first success was achieved among the American Slovaks in Cleveland where the Slovak League of America agreed to the union of the Czechs and Slovaks in a new federal state. He continued his aggressive campaign, and the masterpiece of his activity in the USA was the conclusion of the Pittsburgh agreement in his presence, as Chairman of the Czecho-Slovak National Council, with the representatives of the following Slovak and Czech organizations: the Slovak League of America, the Czech National Alliance and the Federation of Czech Catholics. The political program for the union of the Czechs and Slovaks in an independent state was approved by these private citizens in the USA. In their belief, the Slovaks were to have their own administrative system in the province of Slovakia — until then Upper Hungary — with their own Parliament and the Slovak as a second official language. A democratic constitution was promised for a future Czecho-Slovak republic. The seventeen Slovak and twelve Czech signatories — among them Masaryk — promised intensified cooperation among American Slovaks and Czechs.[8] In their initial enthusiasm they collected for Masaryk $800,911.00[9], or according to another version only $674,885.00.[10] Masaryk influenced even the leaders of the American Ruthenians, and promised their nationals in Upper Hungary autonomy if they would join a new Czech state.

The Ruthenians in Hungary lived in the mountainous North-Eastern part of the kingdom and for centuries demonstrated their strong loyalty to their Hungarian homeland. They spoke a dialect of the Ukrainian language and belonged to the Greek-Catholic Church. They were separated from the Ukrainians of Russia by religious, linguistic and historic background. There was a trend — represented by a minority group — among the American Ruthenians which favoured a political union with the Ukraine; but after the Bolshevik revolution in Russia, the entente governments were not willing to allow Russian penetration south of the Carpathian mountains. Masaryk, the ardent Pan-Slavist, was willing to extend the borders of the future Czech state even to the territory inhabited partly by Ruthenians. On 26 October 1918, in Philadelphia, he signed a private agreement with Gregorij Žatkovič,[11] leader of the American Council of Hungarian Ruthenians, for the national autonomy of Ruthenians living in Hungary. Masaryk, an Austrian citizen in self-imposed exile, and Žatkovič, a naturalized American citizen, acted without any mandate from the population whose fate was involved in the annexation of Ruthenia by Bohemia.

These private agreements of Masaryk together with the distorted reports and memoranda of Beneš to the Allied and Associated Powers during the war and after the signature of the armistice were taken into consideration by various committees at the peace conference. These private agreements and reports were recognized as binding treaties or acceptable documents by the peacemakers. The solemn declaration of the American president in which he proclaimed the right for self-determination of the nationalities of Austria-Hungary was simply forgotten. The Czechs, once in power, never granted autonomy voluntarily neither to the Slovaks nor to the Ruthenians. The private agreements with Masaryk ended in the political oppression of the Slovaks, Ruthenians and other national minorities in the ČSR starting in 1918. The Czech political exiles thought it simpler to ask for the creation of an independent state for one nation — even if a "Czechoslovak" nation did not exist — than to explain the complicated historical relations between the Czechs and Slovaks.[12]

The next step towards success of the Czech exiles was the recognition of the Czecho-Slovak National Council in Paris on 30 June, 1918 by the French government and on 9 August, 1918 by the British government as an official agency for the representation of the Czecho-Slovak cause. The U.S. government, traditionally badly informed on European affairs, went even further when on 3 September, 1918 Washington recognized the Czecho-Slovak National Council as "a de facto belligerent government, clothed with proper authority to direct the military and political affairs of the Czecho-Slovaks."[13] Encouraged by this success, on 14 October Beneš notified the entente governments that the Czecho-Slovak National Council was transformed into a provisional government.

At home in Hungary 105 Slovaks, 56 of them local persons, gathered in T. Sv. Martin (Túrócszentmárton) on 30 October, 1918. They agreed to join the Czechs for ten years in a new common state. At the end of that period, the stipulation said, they would have an opportunity to express themselves concerning their political association with the Czechs. Two weeks prior to this meeting, the proclamation of the emperor in Vienna announced the transformation of Austria into a federal state. This imperial decree came late and could not prevent the collapse of the Monarchy which had been decided earlier by the entente governments during the war. The nationalities with foreign encouragements rejected this plan and they wanted to take their demands to international forums. According to the Czech political leaders, the Slovak and Czech problem became an international question. On 28 October, 1918 the Czech National Council in Prague proclaimed the Czecho-Slovak republic. The Austrian government, in order to avoid bloodshed, did not intervene to prevent this manifestation of constitutional change. The Czecho-Slovak question remained an international problem even after the collapse of the first ČSR in 1938.

The Czech agents in exile did not concentrate their efforts exclusively on their own case. They were the moving force behind the congress of oppressed nationalities of Austria-Hungary, convened in Rome on 8 April, 1918, where beside the largest Czech group there were also present Serbs, Rumanians and Italians. The historical rights of Hungary were destroyed from abroad with the help of the Western democracies. The Czechs showed incredible tenacity in pursuing their political program. They invented the fiction of a Czecho-Slovak national unity and demanded a new state for it. Similarly the fictitious Serbo-Croatian national unity emerged to place the Southern Slavic people in a new enlarged state — Yugoslavia — under Serbian rule. These fabricated national unities did not work in practice, and Czechoslovakia and Yugoslavia fell apart in roughly two decades after their inception. With the encouragement of the entente governments, other national councils in Hungary followed the Czech example of self-rule. The Croatian Diet on 29 October, 1918 proclaimed the cessation of the thousand-year old constitutional connection with the Hungarian kingdom. The Serbs of Hungary met on 25 November at Újvidék (Novi Sad), and the armed Serb bands demanded the annexation of Southern Hungary to the enlarged Serbia together with the non-Serbian population of the area. The Rumanians at their meeting at Gyulafehérvár (Alba Iulia), on 1 December, demanded the union of Transylvania with Rumania regardless of the composition of the population of that Hungarian province. The non-Rumanian population was excluded from the deliberations. The unrepresented people of Transylvania at Alba Iulia had their own meeting at Kolozsvár (Cluj) and expressed their wish to remain in Hungary. The Magyarophile Slovaks held a meeting at Kassa (Košice, Kaschau, Cassovia) to manifest their loyalty to Hungary. In such an atmosphere the last meeting of the Hungarian Parliament took place on 23 October, 1918. The Hungarian deputies were willing to allow liberal concessions to the nationalities; however, the answer from the representatives of the ethnic groups was a refusal to the Hungarian initiative under pressure from the entente powers, and the neighbouring countries. The Hungarian government resigned on 31 October, 1918, but a week earlier, under the influence of radical demonstrations the Hungarian National Council was formed under Count Michael Károlyi. Hungary was now detached from Austria. In the following month, on 16 November, the Hungarian republic was proclaimed and the Parliament dissolved. Károlyi became the head of the new government. This change in government and constitution did not earn international sympathy for the democratic government in Budapest, and did not prevent the planned mutilation of the thousand-year old land of the crown of St. Stephen. The last document of the Dual Monarchy was the signature of the armistice treaty for all the fronts. The new governments of the would-be successor states in Belgrade, Bucharest, Prague and Warsaw were barred by the armistice agreement from indirect occupation or annexation of territories from Austria-Hungary. However, with French diplomatic help and thanks to the intervention of the entente military missions, the organization of new states on Austro-Hungarian soil soon began. After taking over the government, Károlyi went to Belgrade where he concluded a separate armistice or rather a military convention with the head of the allied mission, the French general Franchet d'Esperey. This convention left the northern demarcation line of Hungary open. Károlyi ordered the Hungarian soldiers returning from the battlefields to lay down their arms in a naively idealistic gesture, hoping that the enemy would follow suit after four years of warfare. This was an invitation for creating a fait accompli on the part of the neighbours for the occupation of the Magyar land. The Belgrade military convention delimited the southern line for Hungarian evacuation. It left the Northern demarcation line with the Czechs open for the peace conference. The armistice did not stop military operations from the enemies of Hungary. In Paris, Beneš negotiated a demarcation line with Marshal Foch for the future Czech state and he pressed for the occupation of certain strategically important points in Upper Hungary before the peace conference could make a decision in that matter, and to keep those Hungarian regions under Czech control. According to Lt. Colonel Vyx, the French liaison officer of the allied mission in Budapest, the Czechs were entitled to occupy the territory of Upper Hungary inhabited by the Slovaks. The Czechs themselves did not know how much territory they should claim from Hungary. Independently of Beneš, the Károlyi government negotiated with the envoy of the Prague government, Milan Hodža, a demarcation line between Hungary and the would-be Slovakia. This agreement gave less to the future Czechoslovak republic than the Beneš-Foch plan. The cities of Pressburg and Kassa and the lowland settled by Magyars were not included in the Hodža-Károlyi plan. The French government was very anxious to extend its zone of influence through its newly acquired protectorate, Czecho-Slovakia, and sent a diplomatic note to Károlyi on 21 December, 1918 asking for the evacuation of Upper Hungary according to the Beneš-Foch plan.

The Czechs succeeded in the annexation of the desired territory even before the peace conference began its discussion of the boundaries of the first Czechoslovak republic. After the Slovak declaration of 30 October, 1918 in T. Sv. Martin, Czech bands slowly infiltrated Upper Hungary, the new Slovak province of Czecho-Slovakia which was left unprotected without any armed forces by the Károlyi government. They moved into Kassa on 30 December, 1918, into Pozsony (Pressburg, Posonium, renamed Bratislava) on 11 January, 1919, into Ungvár (Užhorod) on 12 January, 1919, by the end of February they occupied Csallóköz (Gross Schütt, Velký Ostrov Žitný), Érsekujvár (Neuhäusel, Nové Zámky), Losonc (Lučenec), Rozsnyó (Rosenau, Rožňava), and according to the Vyx note of 20 March, 1919, they penetrated more deeply in Hungarian territory. In the spring of 1919 the Hungarian Soviet Republic tried to take back a part of Upper Hungary. The Czech armed bands retreated from the Hungarian red army units.[14] However, in Paris, the peace conference decided on the borderline. Beneš expounded the Czech wish at the peace conference on 5 February, 1919 based on purposely erroneous data and distorted moral principles.[15] The borderline between Czechoslovakia and Hungary was determined in Paris on 12 June. The occupation of Upper Hungary, ordered by the dictated peace, was completed by 24 July, 1919. The Czech armed bands from the first day of their appearance introduced a bloody terror in the Hungarian communities amidst the defenceless and unarmed population. With the annexation of Upper Hungary to the ČSR, the tribulation of the Hungarian minority began.[16] The territory in question was inhabited by 1,703,000 Slovaks and 2,860,000 non-Slovaks. The Hungarians attached to the ČSR lived along the border on a 40-50 km deep strip of land in the immediate vicinity of Hungary. Statistics of the Hungarian population on that territory, according to censuses taken in different years and state sovereignties, were as follows: in 1910 — 1,070,772; in 1921 — 738,517 and in 1930 — 681,460.[17] The rapid decline of the number of Hungarians in Czechoslovak statistics indicate complete unreliability and sinister intentions of the Prague government.

The temporary occupation of Upper Hungary during the armistice became a permanent occupation for twenty years. The American diplomacy was not able to secure the much publicized principles of Wilson for the self-determination of the peoples in Central Europe. America's untrustworthiness and ignorance of Central European affairs left the terrain open for the intrigues of Beneš and to the apparent interests of the French foreign policy which wanted to have a satellite state in Central Europe. Beneš remained in Paris and did not return to Prague on 14 November, 1918 upon his appointment as the first foreign minister of the new state. On the same day Masaryk was elected president of the republic. Beneš' presence was needed at the peace conference for political manoeuverings and secret deals. He wanted to persuade the French government to dispatch troops to Bohemia and Moravia for the protection of those provinces from a possible German attack and to assist in the occupation of Upper Hungary.[18] The German population in Bohemia and Moravia made known its wish to remain in Austria. Beneš requested French troops for the occupation of his own country, Bohemia and Moravia, to prevent the self-determination of the German population living in those provinces. He did not get French occupational forces but a French military mission went to Prague to train the would-be conquerors and to accept French military control over the nascent Czech army.[19] There was a second demarcation line drawn and handed over to the Károlyi government by Lt. Colonel Vyx on 19 March, 1919. This was more advantageous for Czechoslovakia than the previous one.[20] As a result of it, the Károlyi government resigned and, in the great confusion on 21 March, 1919, the Hungarian Soviet Republic was proclaimed, lasting for 133 days.

On 5 February, 1919 Kramář and Beneš submitted a report to the Council of Ten on the Czechoslovak demands. They asked for recognition of the three main lands of the Czech crown: Bohemia, Moravia and Silesia in their historic frontiers and some rectifications on the Prussian, Bavarian and Saxon borders, a part of Kladsko and Upper Silesia and a part of the Moravian Field. Bohemia was economically the strongest state of the former Austria-Hungary having on its territory 75% of the chemical industry, 92% of glass industry, 75% of woollen industry and c., 60% of iron works of the extinguished state.[21] Furthermore, they asked for the annexation of Upper Hungary, under the name of Slovakia and Ruthenia, to the Czech lands. They also requested the resolution of the question of the Sorbians in Lausitz, the protection of the Czech population in Vienna, and connecting Czechoslovakia with Yugoslavia with a corridor, as well as the internationalization of some main rivers and railway lines. The Council of Ten appointed a commission for Czechoslovak affairs which in one month fulfilled the Czech demands with a few exceptions: the question of the Sorbs in Lausitz and the corridor to Yugoslavia were refused.[22]

Besides the territorial demands, Beneš spoke of a three hundred-year Austrian oppression, of the existence of a Czecho-Slovak state in the teenth century, of the sentiments of the population in the involved area, and of their common language and religion. All of these words were pure inventions. The whole affair is without precedent in the history of peace conferences.[23]

The Paris peace conference was officially opened on 18 January, 1919 and Hungary and her neighbouring successor states were notified of their future borders on 13 June. Between those dates, in spite of the armistice or several armistices, the war continued on Hungarian soil. The invading Czechs intimidated the peaceful population by executing prominent citizens upon their arrival in Hungarian communities. Beneš wanted to persuade the French authorities that the Prague government represented an order and peaceful development, a return to industrial production and a bulwark against Communism in Central Europe. "At the beginning of 1919, the Czechoslovak propaganda instigated against the Jewish-Hungarian Communist state. When in Hungary the national and Christian trend arrived at power... the Jews, disillusioned, ran away from Budapest. Slovakia was filled up with refugees who started their anti-Hungarian activities."[24] France did not recognize the Károlyi government and refused to receive its representatives in Paris. Consequently, Beneš had the field reserved for himself. He influenced the peace conference when it dealt with the delimitation of the Hungarian-Czecho-Slovak border. It was a great personal success for a Czech dissident who, three years after his escape from Prague, sat together with the representatives of France, Britain, U.S.A., Italy, Japan, Serbia, Greece, Belgium and Portugal and played a role in determining the fate of Kaiser Wilhelm and Emperor-King Charles as well as participating in the planning of the political borderlines of post-war Europe. Beneš negotiated with Foch that frontier of Slovakia which cut deeply into the Magyar ethnic territory. This was not enough for the Czech imperialists but they also claimed Ruthenia. The Czech occupiers moved deeply into Upper Hungary until they did not meet any resistance from the Károlyi government which observed the armistice and laid down the arms. In Paris the French government circles and the agents of the national minorities of pre-war Hungary masterminded a forcible dismemberment of the Hungarian kingdom and the annexation of 3.5 million Hungarians. They organized an armed invasion and arbitrarily prolonged the war, what suited the French assertion to the inheritance of the Habsburgs in Central Europe. Under this pressure the Károlyi government resigned and in the great confusion the Communists took over the power. Beneš emphasized that the events proved him right because he always emphasized the red danger in Budapest and Vienna. The Czech invasion of Hungary forced the Communist government in Budapest to defend the country, and the Czech march was halted. The Czechs answered this move with terror and the minister appointed by Prague for the administration of Slovakia declared martial law for the entire territory of that province.[25] The borders of Slovakia at that time were not yet determined by the peace conference. French military missions in the newly formed states suggested a combined attack on the Hungarian red army.[26] The ill-equipped Hungarian army liberated the greatest part of Slovakia and cleared it from the Czechs. Clemenceau, the president of the peace conference and great supporter of Masaryk and Beneš, on 10 June, 1919 sent a diplomatic note to the Kun government in Budapest in which he assured him that Hungary would be invited to plead her case before the conference for just borders. At the same time Hungary was asked to cease the attacks against the Czechs, or face military measures by the entente governments. He demanded a reply in 48 hours.[27] The French policy makers did not want to admit that their allies did not respect the armistice. Hungary was obliged to fight on several fronts, and Kun had to agree to the cessation of hostilities. The French and Czech political ideas were in complete accordance for the domination of the

Danubian basin. The British and American representatives demonstrated complete apathy and impotence concerning this goal. Central,European ethnography, economics and history were unknown to the peace makers. They did not want to hear of the stabilizing force of the Hungarians in the Danubian basin area.

The Czechoslovak-Hungarian Frontier

At the Paris peace conference officially Kramář, the prime minister, led the Czech delegation but in reality Beneš, the foreign minister, was the spokesman. They benefited from the immense hatred of the French against Germany and Austria-Hungary and from the unpreparedness and surprising unfamiliarity of the entente and American representatives with the issues involved. Beneš preached of a democratic national state of the Czechs and Slovaks and was against a plebiscite on the claimed territory from Austria-Hungary. The would-be national state wanted to annex Sudeten Germans, Slovaks, Hungarians, Ruthenians and Poles. During the peace negotiations Andrej Hlinka, a parish priest, leader of the Slovak Catholic Populist Party, went to Paris through Poland and with Polish assistance to the peace conference. He was accompanied by Francis Jehlička, another Slovak political leader, to counteract Beneš, and demand autonomy for Slovakia according to the Pittsburgh convention and the declaration of T. Sv. Martin (Túrócszentmárton). Beneš with his excellent French connections had the Slovak representatives expelled from France as Habsburg agents. Hlinka upon his return to the ČSR was imprisoned for eight months in Moravia, Jehlička remained in exile and fought for the autonomy of Slovakia from abroad. France, the friendly supporter of Czechoslovakism, sanctioned the Czech expansionism thus adding more difficulties to the ethnic problems of the new republic.

The treaty of Trianon, signed on 4 June, 1920, mutilated the territory of the millenial Hungarian kingdom, and destroyed the ideal geographic and economic unity of the Carpathian basin. The political and military strength of the Austro-Hungarian monarchy disappeared from the European balance of power. Other nations, first Nazi Germany and later Soviet Russia, filled the political vacuum left on the ruins of the Dual Monarchy. Hungary was forced to accept the clauses of the dictated peace treaty. The plenipontentiaries of the victors were not willing to examine the ethnic composition of the Magyar land. They made their decisions on the declarations and falsified statistics of Beneš concerning the ethnographic, historic, geographic and economic formation of Hungary. Beneš had quick answers to the questions arising from the debates of the Boundaries Commission. According to Beneš, Slovakia was part of a Czecho-Slovak state long ago, but at the beginning of the tenth century the Magyars conquered that political structure. According to Beneš the historic frontiers of Slovakia extended from the Carpathian mountains to the Danube river and

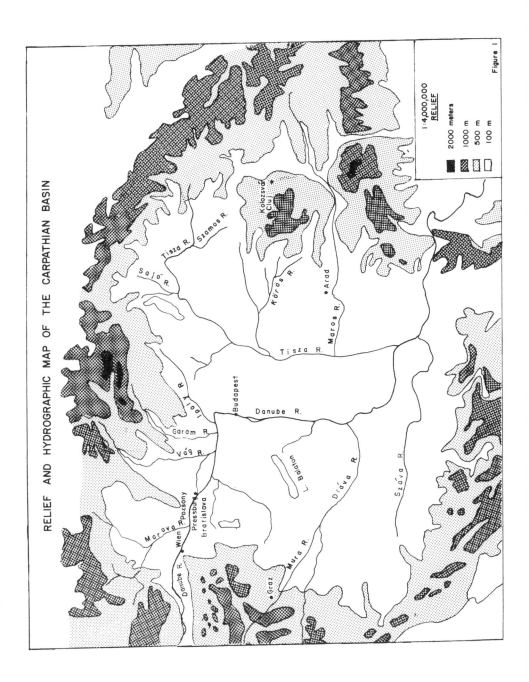

RELIEF AND HYDROGRAPHIC MAP OF THE CARPATHIAN BASIN

1:4,000,000
RELIEF

2000 meters
1000 m
500 m
100 m

Figure 1

19

HUNGARY BEFORE AND AFTER WORLD WAR I

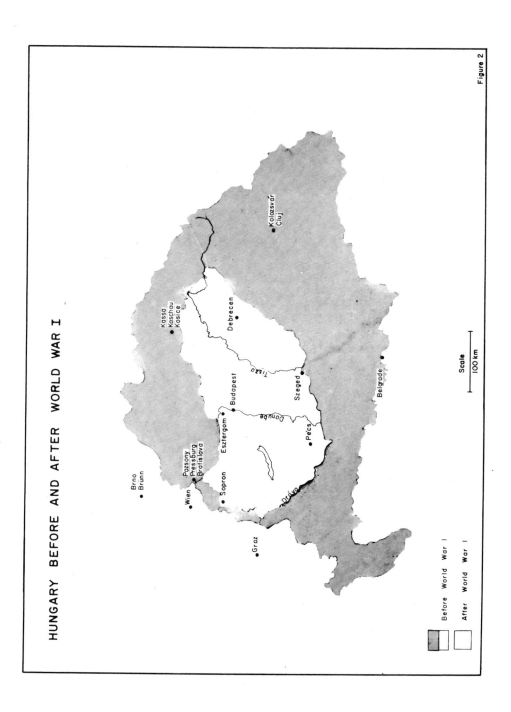

Scale
100 km

Before World War I
After World War I

Figure 2

20

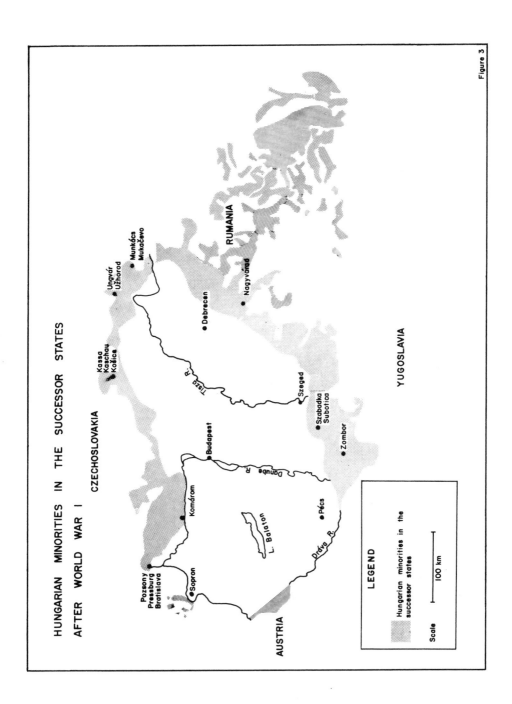

HUNGARIAN MINORITIES IN THE SUCCESSOR STATES AFTER WORLD WAR I

CZECHOSLOVAKIA

RUMANIA

YUGOSLAVIA

AUSTRIA

Kassa
Kaschau
Košice

Ungvár
Užhorod

Munkács
Mukačevo

Nagyvárad

Debrecen

Budapest

Komárom

Pozsony
Pressburg
Bratislava

Sopron

L. Balaton

Dráva R.

Pécs

Danube R.

Tisza R.

Szeged

Szabadka
Subotica

Zombor

LEGEND

Hungarian minorities in the successor states

Scale

100 km

Figure 3

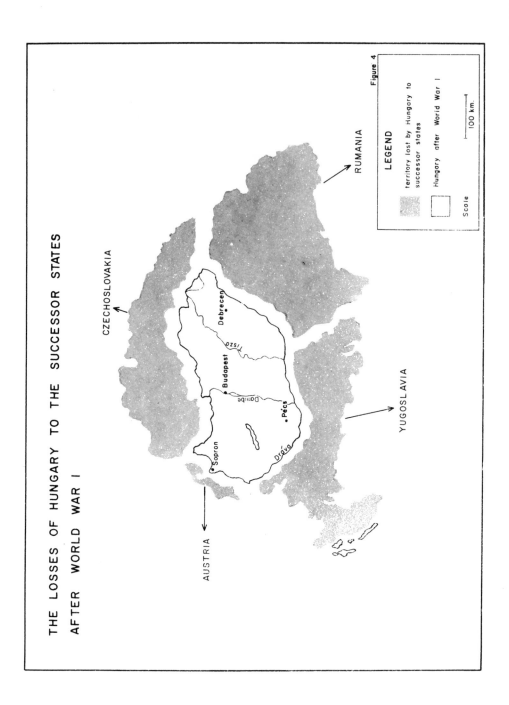

THE LOSSES OF HUNGARY TO THE SUCCESSOR STATES
AFTER WORLD WAR I

CZECHOSLOVAKIA

AUSTRIA

Sopron

Budapest

Debrecen

Tisza

Danube

Dráva

Pécs

YUGOSLAVIA

RUMANIA

LEGEND

territory lost by Hungary to successor states

Hungary after World War I

Scale

100 km.

Figure 4

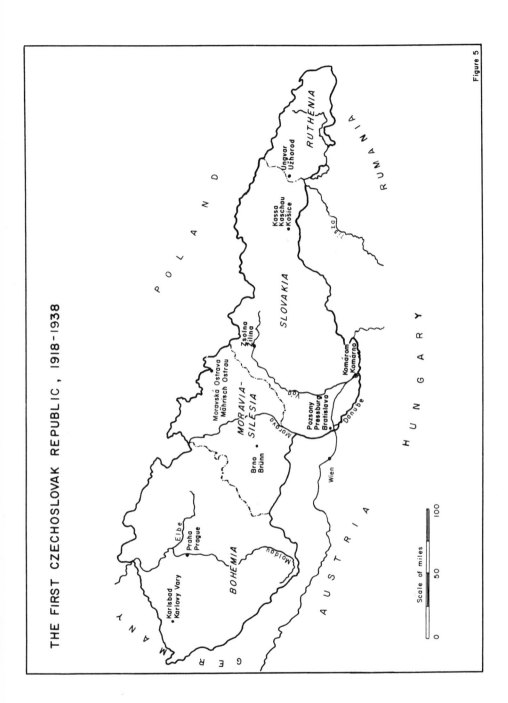

THE FIRST CZECHOSLOVAK REPUBLIC, 1918-1938

Figure 5

— in his opinion — it was necessary to take into account the common language, identical religious conditions — although the Slovaks were never Hussites — and moral affinity between the Czechs and the Slovaks.[28] Not a single word was true in this statement. It would take too much time to trace step by step through the boundary dispute. It has been discussed in many works and it would only be repetitious. The aim of the peace makers was in this case to satisfy the insatiable appetite of the Czechs and to create a great Czecho-Germano-Hungaro-Polono-Rutheno-Slovakia. A careful, precise, minutious, serious study of the ethnographic map of Upper Hungary was not important at all. The result of this unbelievably inimical attitude of the allied representatives toward the Magyars ended in the dismemberment of Hungary which country lost 71.5% of its territory and 63.6% of its population.[29] The treaty left 92,666 km² of the 325,411 km², and 7,606,971 of the total population of 20,886,487.

The extreme tragedy of Hungary can be illustrated in comparison with other smaller losses of land and population after different wars. In 1871 France lost to Germany 2.6% of her territory or 4,509.4 km², and 4.1% of her population or 1,579,219 persons.[30] Alsace and part of Lorraine did not constitute an integral part of historic France. Strassburg was occupied from the Germano-Roman empire by the forces of Louis XIV in peacetime, yet after the French defeat in 1871 many protests were filed against the harshness of the peace treaty which gave back to Germany parts of her earlier losses. After World War I Germany lost 13% of her territory and 9.5% of her population. The enclosed maps show the losses of Hungary to the successor states (Figures 1-5). In the support of their case the Czechs always referred to the historic borders of the mediaeval kingdom of Bohemia as natural boundaries. The Böhmer Wald, Erzgebirge, Riesengebirge, Šumava and the Sudeten Mountains surrounded Bohemia from three parts. The kingdom of Hungary could be compared with Britain, Spain or Italy as concerns the natural borders. The thousand-year old natural borders of the land of the Hungarian crown, the Carpathian mountains surrounded Hungary in a semi circular direction from north-west to north and to south-east. The natural borders of the Save and Danube rivers in the south were never questioned before the end of World War I.

The geopolitical and economic unity of Hungary was disregarded by the peace conference in Paris. It was unnatural to divide the lowlands from the highlands in the same basin. The rivers are the natural highways from the Hungarian Plains to the watershed of the Carpathian mountains. The mineral wealth of the mountainous regions and the agricultural lowlands ideally complement each other, resulting in a self-sufficient economic unity. Railways and roads were built mostly following the natural communication pathways and there were only two transversal railways in Northern Hungary. As a consequence of the Trianon treaty, the natural conditions were no longer in harmony with the political map of this part of Central Europe, including the successor states. The absurd border between the CSR and Hungary wanted to satisfy the Czech access to the Danube river and, by internationalizing it, in its entirety to the Black Sea. It could have been arranged by a commercial agreement. The former capital of the Hungarian kingdom, Pressburg for this reason was handed over to the new state; it was not justified on ethnic grounds. According to the 1910 census, the last before World War I, the county (comitat) of Pozsony, Pressburg, including its capital city had: 146,763 Hungarians, 39,488 Germans and 18,282 Slovaks.[31] The Boundary Commission was not interested in this. They listened rather to Beneš who asserted that previously the border of "Slovakia" had been the Danube river. The Czechs needed the Danube river as a frontier for strategic reasons. The Boundary Commission also found reasonable the Czech claim to the purely Hungarian Csallóköz (Gross Schütt), 180,000 hectares between the two branches of the Danube river, with 108,000 Magyars, 3,030 Germans and 1,170 Slovaks.[32] Furthermore, the Czechs demanded a section of the railway line between Pressburg and the Ipoly river north of the Danube. East of Pressburg, the new border divided purely Magyar regions, cutting off indigenous inhabitants from their own nation in Hungary, transgressing rivers, roads, railways, railway junctions, agricultural land and mines, paralyzing communities and separating landowners from their property on the two sides of the borderline. The Commission believed Beneš that the brook Rondva at Sátoraljaujhely was a navigable river, and it could be, therefore, an ideal dividing line between the two states for strategic reasons. The 800 km long border with Hungary did not give a defensible frontier to the Prague government. The terrain northward grew narrower towards the mountains which impeded the transversal — west-east — movement of troops in case of war. This territorial gain was still not sufficient for Masaryk and Beneš. They wanted to incorporate even Ruthenia. Before 1918 it was part of historic Hungary. The Carpathian mountains formed a natural border between Poland and Hungary; they descend gradually towards the great Hungarian Plains. The roads and railways follow a natural route, the valleys of the rivers. The large cities were founded at the meeting points of the lowlands and the foothills. The communication pathways connected Poland and Hungary through the mountain passes. The Ruthenians, descendents of the Ukranians, reached the Carpathian mountains in the thirteenth century and were settled by Louis the Great, the first Angevine king of Hungary. Relations between the Ruthenians and Hungarians were excellent during their common history. They were called *"gens fidelissima"* by the Magyar leaders because of their unquestionable loyalty to their chosen homeland. The Pan-Slavic propaganda, masterminded by Russian expansionism, tried to drive a wedge between these two friendly nations by using a small fraction of the Ruthenians in the service of the government of Petrograd. In 1918 the Hungarian Parliament passed a law on the autonomy of the Ruthenians for those four counties (comitats) where the Ruthenians had an absolute majority. At the beginning of March 1919, general secret elections were held and a government was elected for the Ruthenian region. On 21 March the short-lived Hungarian Soviet republic was proclaimed, and the danger it represented was the pretext for Beneš' demand to incorporate Ruthenia into the ČSR, and to prevent the spread of Communism from Russia through Hungary. On 8 May, 1919, Beneš told the peace makers that Ruthenia desired to form an autonomous state within the ČSR. In the USA Masaryk and Žatkovič signed a pact for this purpose. There were several Ruthenian councils formed in those days with different loyalties.[33] In Paris Ruthenia was transferred to the ČSR. The autonomy for Ruthenia was forgotten by Masaryk and Beneš. The Ruthenians were governed by Czech civil servants who did not speak their language and still constituted 72% of the public employees.

The Czechs did not need Ruthenia for strategic nor for economic reasons. It becomes obvious by a glance at the map that the narrow strip of land in the eastern end of Czechoslovakia simply could not have been defensible from Bohemia. Economically, the region is connected with the Great Hungarian Plains, and the two areas ideally complement each other with their products. There were no political reasons for the annexation of Ruthenia by Prague since the Czechs and the Ruthenians never had any previous historical ties, and their association in the same state never worked in an acceptable way for either group. The political union of Ruthenia with Bohemia hindered the economic and commercial development of the Ruthenians, caused for them an economic stagnation and depression. The possession of Ruthenia made the ČSR from a military point of view more vulnerable and more difficult to defend against external attacks.

In 1910, the four counties which later formed Ruthenia had the following population: Ruthenes: 44.8%, Magyars: 33.4%, others: 21.8%. In the cities, the Magyar and German population represented 90.4%, the Ruthenian 4.1% and the other nationalities 5.5%.[34] The number of Ruthenians living in the ČSR in 1921 totalled 459,364.[35]

The newly created successor states promoted French hegemony in Central Europe. There is a difference, however, between these political units and the Dual Monarchy. The Austro-Hungarian monarchy became a multilingual state through long historical development. Different nations and nationalities — eleven of them — lived there together for centuries. Contrary to this peaceful development, the Czechs forced to leave in 1919-1921 from their homes 56,000 Magyars according to their own statistics; but the Hungarian statistics exhibited 106,841 refugees.[36] In 1910 there were 7,468 Czechs in Upper Hungary, in 1921 the number of Czechs in Slovakia rose to 71,733, and in 1930 to 120,926.[37] The Czechs were able to hold the newly acquired foreign territories only with foreign support. Beneš, in 1919, betrayed the real Czech interests to the

French and later in 1945, to the Russians. He and Masaryk did not fulfill their promises to make a model democracy, an Eastern Switzerland, from the new state. They were vehemently opposed to a plebiscite because in that case they never could have had Czechoslovakia. The republic fell apart in twenty years because there were no equal democratic rights for all the citizens of the country. The peace treaty caused subsequent sufferings for millions. The ruining of the Danubian monarchy resulted in chaos and invited foreigh armed interventions in Central Europe.

The real fallacy was, that a real peace conference, at which the defeated would also have been present to demonstrate the limit of acceptable conditions, was never called together. In the extent of the territories taken from Hungary wrongs were perpetrated and gross injustices done.[38]

Footnotes

1. Glaser, *Czecho-Slovakia: A Critical History,* p. 3.
2. Helmreich, E.C., *West Europe: Sensitive Allies,* Current History, October 1953, p. 213.
3. Kővágó, J., *The Cities of the Hungarian Linguistic Territory in Slovakia,* p. 32.
4. Apponyi, A., et al., *Justice for Hungary,* p. 51.
5. *Problem Slowacki* (The Slovak Problem), Gazeta Polska, 24 May, 1938.
6. Beneš, V., *Masarykovo dilo v Americe,* p. 3.
7. Czakó, E., *La vérité sur les délibérations préliminaires du traité de Trianon,* p. 50.
8. Vnuk, F., *Slovakia's Six Eventful Months,* Slovak Studies, Historica 2, Cleveland-Rome, Slovak Institute, 1964, p. 22.
9. Lettrich, J., *Modern Slovakia,* p. 3.
10. Thomson, S.H., *Czecho-Slovakia in European History,* p. 291.
11. Macartney, C.A., *Hungary and Her Successors,* p. 215.
12. Gajanová, E., *ČSR a stredoevropská politika velmocí, 1918-1938.* Praha, ČAV, 1967, p. 16.
13. *Foreign Relations,* 1918, Suppl. I, p. 824-825.
14. *Felvidékünk-Honvédségünk,* p. 5 (Trianontól — Kassáig).
15. Csatár-Ölvedi, *A visszatért Felvidék adattára,* p. 28.
16. *Felvidékünk-Honvédségünk,* p. 28.
17. Balla, P., *A felvidéki magyarság külpolitikai tevékenysége,* p. 22.
18. Beneš, E., *Svetová válka a naše revoluce,* III, p. 500.
19. Gajanová, Op. cit., p. 31.
20. d'Olay, F., *Les frontières de la Hongrie démembrée,* p. 4.
21. Dobrý, A., *Kdo vládl v předmníchovské republice,* p. 5.
22. Gajanová, Op. cit., pp. 30-31.
23. d'Olay, Op. cit., p. 5.
24. Szvatkó, P., *A visszatért magyarok,* p. 30.
25. Milei-Smutny, *Dokumentumok a Szlovák Tanácsköztársaságról,* 1919, p. 38.
26. Ibid., p. 129.
27. Ibid., p. 114.
28. Czakó, E., *La vérité sur les délibérations préliminaires du traité de Trianon,* p. 27.
29. Ajtay, J., *La paix en danger,* p. 17.
30. Ibid., pp. 4-5.
31. Czakó, E., Op. cit., p. 32.
32. Ibid. p. 47.
33. Tarján-Falk, *Hungarians, Slovaks and Ruthenians in the Danube Valley,* p. 20.
34. Seeds of Conflict I, p. 11.

35. Kovács, E., *Szemben a történelemmel*, p. 11.

36. Macartney, C.A., Op. cit., p. 158.

37. Ibid., p. 125.

38. Magyar, Zoltán, *James T. Shotwell at the Paris Peace Conference,* The Hungarian Quarterly, Vol. IV, No. 4, 1938, p. 764.

CHAPTER II

INFRINGEMENTS UPON THE CIVIL RIGHTS OF THE HUNGARIAN MINORITY

Systematic Oppression of the Hungarian Minority

In 1919, the peace conference devised an artificial state consisting of a conglomeration of nations under Czech rule. A majority of the people, 54%, had to live in Czechoslovakia against their will. Monstrous damage was done to the Hungarian nation by an unjustified separation of the coherent Hungarian population and their land from the mother country by putting them as a frontier minority under foreign rule. The restoration of control by peaceful means over the former integral parts of Hungary was the aim of the subsequent governments in Budapest. The Allied and Associated Powers, the victors in 1918, tried to perpetuate the status quo after World War I, and — to avoid later difficulties — they put the guarantee of the rights of national minorities under the protection of the Council of the League of Nations in Geneva. The treaty signed on 10 September, 1919 at Saint-Germain-en-Laye between the Allied and Associated Powers and Czechoslovakia provided for the protection of national minorities. It was never honoured by the Czechs. Before the peace arrangements in Paris, Beneš stated in one of his numerous memoirs that the model of the Czecho-Slovak constitution would be the Swiss federal constitution and the new state would be a sort of Eastern Switzerland.[1] When in power, Beneš did not apply the Swiss constitution to the specific Czech conditions.[2,3] In agreement with the clauses of the treaty of Saint-Germain, Czechoslovakia had to recognize to all former German, Austrian and Hungarian nationals and/or their descendants the right of domicile which they had on the day of the ratification of the treaty, 16 July, 1920, on the territory which became or would be part of the ČSR based on the treaties already signed or in preparation.[4] There is contradiction between the stipulation of the treaty of Saint-Germain and Article 62 of the Treaty of Trianon of 4 June, 1920, which dictated the peace conditions to Hungary. The treaty of Trianon obliged Czechoslovakia to recognize for her citizens only those Hungarian nationals and their descendants who had the right of domicile on the territory which the ČSR received from Hungary prior to 1 January, 1920. The right of domicile was one of the necessary conditions for the acquisition of Czechoslovak citizenship. The granting of citizenship to those persons who received the right of domicile in communities only after that date, depended on the judgment of the government of Prague. The terms of the treaty of Saint-Germain concerning the guarantees of the minority rights could only be changed with the consent of the Council of the League of Nations. The Czechs had no right to change the minority rights unilaterally. With this action the Czechs wanted to deprive tens of thousands of persons of Hungarian origin of their citizenship and to treat them as aliens. They became foreigners on the land of their forefathers due to the intruders possessing foreign military and diplomatic aid. The Czechs also interpreted, in a restrictive way, the prevalent Hungarian laws. The Hungarian laws automatically recognized the right of domicile to a person who resided for four years without interruption in a community and contributed to the community taxes at least once during those four years. The Czech interpretation of the Hungarian laws required four years of uninterrupted sojourn in a community and payment of municipal taxes for the entire four-year period. In Hungary admission as a legal resident in a community became automatic or tacit after four years of residence, by descendance, or by marriage. It was not necessary to apply formally for the right of domicile or to receive a document to prove it. An application for Czechoslovak citizenship was processed only in that case if the applicant or his/her predecessor had received the right of domicile prior to 31 December, 1906 (when the ČSR did not exist yet), and it was proved by the minutes of the meeting of a municipality. Applications for Czechoslovak citizenship had to be mailed until 31 December, 1921. Late applications were not accepted. A Czech arbitrary decision further rendered more difficult the admission of the former resident Hungarian population to the citizenship of the new state by a decision of the Supreme Administrative Court of the ČSR, issued on 6 October, 1923. This did not recognize the tacit right of domicile. If a person wanted to acquire a document proving that right, he or she had to apply for it in a community.[5] This was an erroneous interpretation of the Hungarian law No. XXII/1886. This court decision invalidated, a posteriori, acquired rights.[6] The Hungarian law was not withdrawn or replaced by a new statute for Slovakia and Ruthenia in the new ČSR. Over twenty-six thousand people became stateless by losing citizenship in their native land. This number augmented by 1930 to 91,832 in Slovakia and Ruthenia.[7] Such degradation was a deliberate, malevolent step by the Czechoslovak internal administration. In the possession of this judicial weapon, the Ministry of interior and its police force could harass anyone they wanted to brand as an alien. An investigation of the right of domicile status of selected groups followed this court decision. Hungarians from all social classes, poor and rich, pensioners, widows, orphans, teachers, physicians, lawyers, workers, industrialists all alike were victims of harassment and deprivation of their rights. Many of them lost their livelihood or had to liquidate their assets and were forced to cross the border to Hungary as stateless persons. Their number was added to the already expelled 100,000 persons since 1918.

In the treaty of Saint-Germain, Czechoslovakia also accepted other legal obligations, towards her minorities. Sections 1 and 2 of Chapter I, and section 10 of Chapter II of this treaty were incorporated word for word into the Czechoslovak constitution.[8] Law 122/1920 of the language rights takes into consideration the appropriate chapters of the peace treaty. The official language of the state according to this was the "Czechoslovak" language. It must be noted that such a language never existed nor does it exist today, just as a Belgian, Canadian, or Swiss language does not exist. Such a fabricated language was the legal and official language of an invented nation. Law 122/1920 established guidelines for the language rights in the ČSR. In practice it meant that in Bohemia, Moravia, Silesia and Ruthenia the Czech language and in Slovakia the Czech and Slovak languages belonged to the official language category. The language law regulated the language rights of the minorities in the courts of law, administrative offices of the state and judicial districts. The use of the language of a national minority was permitted if according to the latest census at least 20% of the population belonged to other than the "Czechoslovak" language category, and the sphere of a judicial district was limited to that territory. Submissions in such districts had to be accepted and decrees issued not only in "Czechoslovak" but also in the language of the recognized minority. Legal entities were obliged to use "Czechoslovak" in their oral or written submissions. The law also regulated the language of instruction in the public education sector. In towns and districts Czechoslovak citizens other than Czech or Slovak speaking, if in considerable proportion, received instruction in their own language and managed their own cultural and charitable organizations. In spite of Law 122/1920 several million citizens of the ČSR, did not enjoy the most fundamental linguistic rights although the government of Prague was obliged by an international treaty to grant legal equality to all citizens. The government decree, No. 17 of 3 February, 1926, interpreted the application of the language law by using different derivates for the limitation or the extinction of minority rights in the republic. The minorities had to live in constant personal insecurity. The acceptance and declaration of granting equal rights did not mean the fulfillment of the obligations by Czechoslovak authorities.[9] One method for the quick diminution of the number of minorities in their counties was the falsification of the results of the census. In Slovakia and Ruthenia the enumerators completed the questionnaires, and there was no control over or legal recourse against their activities. A comparison of the 1910 Hungarian and the 1921 and

1930 Czechoslovak statistics shows a rapid official decrease of the Hungarian population of the republic.[10]

Province	Year	Magyars	%
Slovakia	1910	893,586	30.55
Ruthenia	1910	334,745	29.60
		1,228,331	60.15
Slovakia	1921	634,827	21.48
Ruthenia	1921	103,690	17.34
		738,517	38.82
Slovakia	1930	571,988	17.58
Ruthenia	1930	109,472	15.44
		681,460	33.02

"The aim of the census in the ČSR was something else than in other modern states. In Czechoslovakia it served not only social, economic, cultural and military aims, but it also had a crucial, importance for the ethnic affiliation. The census had to secure the domination of the Czech minority in the state. The census became the means of internal policy."[11] The oppression of the Hungarian minority, in exactly the same way as the other minorities, was a step towards the creation of a Czech national state. "When the administrative, judicial and c. districts of Slovakia were recognized in 1926, the boundaries of five judicial districts in which the Magyars were particularly strong ... were so remodelled as to bring the Magyar percentage below the statutory 20%."[12]

The Czechoslovak Land Reform

The appointed — not elected — revolutionary National Assembly passed Bill No. 251/1919[13] which set up the Land Office to implement land reform, or rather, the limitation of possession of land acreage by one landowner. The Czechoslovak land reform was in reality the confiscation of land from their owners without adequate compensation. It was politically motivated without social or economic purpose. A great part of the land in Bohemia, Moravia and Silesia was owned by Germans, and in Slovakia and Ruthenia by Magyars. The Czech revolutionary National Assembly passed laws and took away with the semblance of legality the land from the German and Hungarian landlords, and distributed it among Czech, Moravian and Slovak colonists in German and Hungarian districts. It was a political handout for those who were willing to support the policy of the new masters governing in Prague. The government seized the land through the Land Office, it was recorded in the Registry Office, and the Land Office disposed of such land. The land

34

could be distributed, rented or forced farming could be introduced on it. Such seized land was kept in limbo, in uncertainty, because the former owner could not cultivate it properly with the necessary investments for profitable farming.

The Land Office paid an average of 2,100 Kč (Czechoslovak crowns) per hectare when the average price was 10,500 Kč. The land purchaser had to pay to the state 4,000 Kč per hectare. The loss of the Magyar landowners was 3,500 million Kč.[14] The government made a net profit of 12 million Kč on 2.5 million hectares of land.[15] In Slovakia from the total land area of 10,713,533 cadastral yokes (1 cadastral yoke = 1.412 acres) of which 5,003,196 cadastral yokes were arable, the state seized 2,865,735.10 yokes = 26.7% of the total land. The arable land was 19.1%, or 956,213.03 yokes. The state returned to selected owners a total of 588,862.03 yokes of which 293,099.08 yokes were arable. During this operation the Hungarian population suffered serious losses: 1,836,137.05 or 80.7% of the total land, of which 528,743.12 or 79.8% was arable land. The losses of other nations were as follows: Germans: 4.5% arable land, Slovaks: 1.6% arable land.[16] (See Appendix No. 3). Compensation for the seized land was regulated by order-in-council No. 329/1920 and No. 53/1921.[17] The Land Office paid the 1913 and 1915 prices not in the old Austrian crowns but in the new Czechoslovak currency. Payments were made in non-transferable bonds bearing 3% interest with an amortization period of one-hundred years.[18] The aim of the land reform was the weakening of the economic power of the Germans and Hungarians in order to force them to forfeit their land in the frontier zones to the faithful political followers of the reactionary government of Prague disguised as democratic rulers. In Bohemia, Moravia and Silesia 72% of the estates were left in the possession of the owners; whereas in Slovakia and Ruthenia — formerly Upper Hungary — this percentage was only 28%. The land reform, which confiscated the arable land over 150 hectares or over 160 hectares in case of co-ownership, or non-arable land over 250 hectares, broke the homogenous Hungarian language territory in Slovakia by settling on the expropriated land Czechs, Moravians and Slovaks. These outposts of the Slavic element in Hungarian regions received all kinds of financial support, including long-term loans for the purchase of land, buildings and instruments, to ensure their successful farming. This forced transfer of property deprived about 50,000 Hungarian agricultural workers of their livelihood because they had to leave their homes located on the confiscated land.[19]

Another device for the distribution of land to government supporters was the creation of residual estates. Selected persons could receive land above the permitted level from the Land Office. This way, land could be obtained up to 1,000 cadastral yokes or 1,412 acres. Altogether 581 colonies were created in Bohemia, Moravia and Silesia, and 2,276 in Slovakia and Ruthenia.[20] It was characteristic of the operation of the Land Office that it never had to explain its manipulations, and for budgetary purposes it did not belong to any ministry during its 15-year existence, although it had to manage property worth billions of Kč. Its dealings were never controlled by the usual way of a parliamentary democracy. The land confiscation by the Czech "liberators" was a form of denationalization and economic destruction of the chauvinistic program of the government under democratic façade. Full compensation for the confiscated land was never provided to the landowners.

Capital Levy

A new tax, called capital levy, was enacted by the revolutionary National Assembly at the beginning of the existence of the Czechoslovak republic. This tax had to be paid on the property owned on 1 March, 1919. This tax was raised on movable and immovable property up to 30% of the value of one's possessions. The motive for the introduction of this tax was the accumulation of income, called war fortune. It had to be paid even if the property was not acquired during the war. Similarly to the seized land by the Land Office, this tax was recorded in the Registry Office; consequently, the property owners lived in complete uncertainty as to their title deed, and did not dispose of their property freely. This was a very high additional tax required by the new Czech rulers. The final sum of this tax was never determined during the twenty-year existence of the ČSR, and it left irreparable damages. This extra tax became even higher when it was collected. Due to the depreciation of the Czechoslovak currency, the retroactively levied capital levy tax reached three times its initial sum when it had to be paid.[21] If one adds to this sum the income, property and school taxes demanded at once for six years retroactively, it is clear that they were well beyond the means of the taxpayers, and consequently ruined many of them financially leading them into desperation. On 29 March, 1938 the House of Deputies in Prague discussed an amendment to the Land Reform Act and Capital Levy Act (of 1919). Two years prior to this amendment, Bill 129/1936, was supposed to regulate the problems connected with these laws but they were not solved until the projected date of 1938. The government introduced an amendment again in 1938 which deferred the final actions connected with these two laws for another two years.[22] In practice, it meant that these problems were never solved because the republic collapsed in the same year leaving behind the burdens created by the appointed revolutionary lawmakers.

Reimbursements of War Loans

During World War I loans were offered by the citizens to help the war efforts of the Austro-Hungarian government in the form of interest-bearing bonds and/or mortgages. The Czechoslovak government had also to assume the debts, not only acquire the assets, of Austria-Hungary. The exchange rate offered for the war loans caused another grievance to the population of Slovakia and Ruthenia. After passing Bill 216 on 30 September, 1924, there was a short time allowed for the redemption of these government obligations. In the Austro-Hungarian monarchy, taxes were allowed to be paid with war loan bonds.[23] The taxation offices in Czechoslovakia collected taxes for the years 1916-1918 when the republic did not yet exist. In the ČSR, claims for these war loans were limited to 25,000 Kč ($1 = 30 Kč), and they could be filed in the district taxation offices. The rigid application of regulations, the control, the revisions, the tardiness in connection with the redemption of the war loans caused hardships to lenders. Interest on the loans was not paid by the Czechoslovak authorities, and the mortgages could not be discharged without the approval of the Registry Offices. If the taxation officers wanted to delay the repayment of the loans or to release the mortgages, they checked and rechecked the eligibility of claimants or used several other delaying tactics. In some districts war loans were redeemed for higher rates than in others. The Czechoslovak crown (Kč) was taken at parity with the pre-war Austro-Hungarian gold crown when in reality the ratio was ten Kč to one gold crown. The Czechs were not the losers in this operation since they did not support the Austro-Hungarian government with their contributions during the war years.

The Fate of the Hungarian Banks in Slovakia and Ruthenia

The Hungarian owned banks, loan associations and credit unions suffered great financial damage due to the change of borders and the banking regulations of the new rulers. Some deficit occurred when many debtors of these financial institutions had to evacuate the new state and many credit claims could not be collected from beyond the frontiers. These losses forced many lenders out of business. The unfair treatment of the Prague government dwindled the branches of the Hungarian banks. The banking regulations permitted the increase of the original capital investment only to Czech and Slovak banks. The banking law No. 239/1924[24] supported the Czech and Slovak banks from the state treasury to help them to offset financial losses caused by political changes. This aid was given through discretionary power as well as by permits for establishing new branches. The government extended preferential treatment to selected Czech and Slovak banks but not according to the needs of economy. Politics governed this monetary policy in order to weaken the Hungarian banks to the detriment of the economy of the Magyar populated areas of the republic. The Prague government reached its objective: many banks owned by Hungarians had to close their doors for business. During the first ten years of the ČSR the number of Hungarian banks was reduced from

126 to 15 in Slovakia and to 5 in Ruthenia.[25] This procedure of constant pauperization of the population of Slovakia and Ruthenia was augmented by requiring paper money to be validated by government issued stamps. This was a method for controlling the circulation. With this procedure the money lost 55% of its value in Slovakia and 90% in Ruthenia.[26] Another study puts the shrinking of the Hungarian financial institutions in the ČSR from 177 to 37, their local branches from 52 to 27, their agencies from 29 to 7, their capital from 61.5 million gold reserves to 20.7 million, their reserves from 30.5 million to 12.2 million Kč.[27]

The Czechoslovak Taxation Policy

The taxation policy of the government was a political weapon hidden behind various sets of regulations valid for the Czech lands and for the former Hungarian lands. In practice they manifested themselves in arbitrary changes of figures on the income tax return forms completed by the taxpayers. Appeals against decisions had no delaying effects on enforced tax collections and led to the auctioning of properties and caused numerous bankruptcies among defenceless taxpayers. The general public was certainly not responsible for the slow work of the taxation officers or for the levying of taxes retroactively for six years together with retroactive interest charges. Arrears in tax payments had some side effects, too. Applications for passports were sent to the district taxation offices for verification of tax payment. Persons found to be in arrears could not receive passports unless a substantial collateral deposit in securities was made.

There were inequalities in tax rates.[28] Income tax on wages in Slovakia and Ruthenia was 10%, in Bohemia and in Moravia 2%. The Hungarian population of the republic was very much inconvenienced by this taxation policy. Flying commissions of the internal revenue offices terrorized the over-taxed Hungarian minority. Power of taxation in Slovakia was significantly curtailed with the de-industrialization of the province. The Czechs progressively destroyed the competitive industry built during the Hungarian sovereignty, and until 1934 they closed down 215 factories in Slovakia.[29] The taxation power of this province was weakened by this economic policy.

Pensioners

At the time of change in state sovereignty the retired persons suffered much as a result of the political events. The Czech authorities interrupted or completely withdrew the payments of pensions waiting for the outcome of citizenship applications or special investigations. This group found itself in the most grave financial situation. When the state wanted to escape from its obligations towards those of its subjects who for a lifetime had worked honestly as public servants, they were condemned together with their widows or orphans to a poverty stricken life of misery. In many cases the right to pension was not recognized. Some persons were forced into early retirement and received an income equal to the minimum required for bare survival when in fact rising consumer prices would have justified a more humane treatment.

Magyar Cultural Life

According to the international obligations undertaken by signing the peace treaties, the Czechoslovak government had the moral responsibility to grant equal rights to the national minorities. These principles were incorporated in the Czechoslovak legislation[30] but were not enforced: statistics speak for themselves. The systematic reduction of the schools of Magyar language instruction in the ČSR is proof of the cultural maltreatment of the Magyar minority. On the territory of Upper Hungary, the post-war Slovakia, in 1918 there were 3,298 Magyar elementary schools. In 1921-22 this number was reduced to 727. The Czechs had one high school for every 48,000 inhabitants, the Hungarians in the ČSR one high school for every 137,000 inhabitants.[31] The planned destruction of the Magyar elementary schools had a direct consequence on the number of the Magyar high schools since only those students were allowed to continue their studies in Magyar high schools who completed their elementary training in the same language. In 1918, sixty Hungarian high schools functioned in the territory which the peace treaty had detached to the ČSR. Under Czech and Slovak administrations this number was reduced to eight. Cities with an absolute Hungarian majority did not get high schools in the language of the majority. Law No. 189/1919 prescribed the establishment of schools in such communities where at least forty children could be found in a language group. This law was not enforced to satisfy the needs of the Hungarian school-aged children. Cultural oppression manifested itself through the entire educational system, not only at elementary level. The tendency of curtailing Hungarian instruction was continued in the classical, commercial, agricultural and vocational high schools. New schools were not opened even if the Hungarian parents asked for them.[32] Instruction at university level in Magyar language did not exist in the ČSR. The University of Prague and the University of Pressburg employed a part-time lecturer, the same person, for giving lectures on topics of the Hungarian literature. Studies completed and diplomas received at universities in Hungary were not recognized in the ČSR. University studies in Hungary were discouraged and were even regarded as a hostile act. The acquisition of passports for such purpose encountered enormous difficulties, and the receiving of Czechoslovak currency for studies in Hungary was simply impossible due to exchange regulations. There were no scholarships available for Hungarian students in the ČSR which was supposedly their state, and they had to be loyal citizens of the new republic.

In 1929 President Masaryk donated 1 million Kč for the foundation of a Hungarian scientific, literary and artistic association. It was put under the direction of Hungarian speaking individuals loyal to the ČSR, many of whom escaped to safety in the ČSR after the collapse of the Hungarian Soviet republic. The Czech democracy protected them and used their services to divide the solid opposition of the patriotic Hungarians.

Hungarian Theatres in the ČSR

Theatres play a great role in the cultural development of every nation and have an important function in the maintenance of the national spirit. It is therefore understandable that in many countries monarchs lavishly supported the national theatres by their donations. The Czechoslovak Republic also supported the theatres through the state budget with a sum of 20,660,000 Kč (1930) but the existing two Hungarian theatre companies received only 100,000 Kč of that sum instead of the minimal pro rated share of 1,770,000 Kč they were entitled to.[33]

The Hungarian theatre companies had to share on a territorial basis the buildings and stages of the Slovak companies. For Hungarian performances the buildings were obtained before or after the peak season. This added to the hardships of those companies which had to maintain themselves with the help of patrons and supporting benevolent associations in the towns of Slovakia and Ruthenia. Permission to function had to be obtained from the counties. Invitation of actors and actresses from Hungary was permitted only on exceptional occasions and with great difficulties. Under these circumstances no one could speak of equal support of the theatres of the Hungarian minority from the state budget.

The Hungarian Press in the ČSR

Article 113 of the Czechoslovak constitution declared freedom of the press. The Czech authorities, however, exerted constant pressure on the newspapers, journals and other publications of the Magyar opposition parties as well as on other non-Czechophile publications through censorship. This operation was covered by the Defence of the Republic Act No. 50/1923.[34] Printed material was silenced if it contained views defending the minority rights or the speeches of the Hungarian deputies in the Prague Parliament critical of the government's policy towards minorities. The introduction of censorship was a flagrant violation of the constitution worked out by the Czech revolutionary National Council. In the fourth year of the new republic even this method of control was abandoned and substituted with confiscations of publications critical of the minority or language policy of the Prague government. The severity of this measure can be understood from the frequency of the blank pages of the reprinted second editions of newspapers after the confiscation of the first editions. For instance, between 1 January and 1 October 1927, 1525 printings of newspapers were confiscated in Magyar, German and Slovak languages in Czechoslovakia. If the entrepreneurs did not want to face heavy financial losses and readership declines, the newspapers had to be reprinted but with blank spaces. In 1933 and 1934 the Prágai Magyar Hirlap (Prague Hungarian News), the official paper of the Hungarian opposition party, was suppressed for three months by the state censorship.[35] When the Magyar newspapers reported various abuses committed against Hungarians the publication of those papers was simply suppressed for months.[36]

The Czechoslovak government wanted to counteract the activity of the Magyar language newspapers loyal to their nation, and started to subsidize newspapers in Magyar language in the service of the state. These Czechophile papers were managed and manned by such Hungarian speaking reporters and journalists who sought asylum in the ČSR after the collapse of the Hungarian Soviet republic in 1919.

The importation of publications in any form from Hungary was banned. Only three or four selected newspapers were allowed a place on the newsstands in Slovakia and Ruthenia; otherwise, the Hungarian press was tightly excluded from the reach of the Magyar population in the ČSR.

Churches

The dismemberment of Hungary disrupted the work and administration of churches because several Roman Catholic and Greek Catholic dioceses were entirely or partially lost, and the Calvinist and Lutheran districts suffered damages for the same reason. These disruptions were worsened by the expulsion of Magyar bishops, parish priests and pastors from the occupied territory by the Czechs. Three Roman and two Greek Catholic bishops, as well as many priests and ministers were expelled from Slovakia and Ruthenia. When the autochthonous Hungarian population passed into the minority status, it was deprived of its religious leaders. The ecclesiastical institutions remained the focal point of the Magyar population in the defence of the language, culture and tradition of their ancestors. The Prague government in its anti-Hungarian harassment turned against the Calvinist ministers who helped preserve the true Magyar national feeling in their congregations. Their persecution appeared in the usual form. If the government disliked the activity of a priest or minister, it withheld the congrue guaranteed for them by law. Appeals against such administrative decisions remained unanswered for decades so the involved persons could not take their case to court. These grievances were presented to the League of Nations in Geneva by the Hungarian deputies in the Prague Parliament when legal redress could not be obtained in the ČSR.[37] For self-protection, the Hungarian minority had to form social, philanthropic and charitable organizations and help the underprivileged members of its group, many of whom fell into a degraded status in the ČSR.

Political Parties

Until 1918 the natural political centre for Hungarians was Budapest. After 1918, the northern frontier at the nearest point was only 40 km from the capital. The Trianon treaty debarred a large segment of the Hungarian population from contact with its own race. The new minority suddenly had to build up its own political organizations in the ČSR. The ideal solution would have been the formation of only one political party in Slovakia and Ruthenia for the protection of Hungarian interests. The Czech authorities did not give their approval for such a party.[38] In 1920 the Hungarian leaders were not allowed to form a single party, therefore, there were two parties, the Hungarian Christian Social and the National Smallholders Party, both in opposition to the government in Prague.

Government circles tried to divide the Hungarian voters and organize them into different sections of the Czech or Slovak political parties in order to rule them more easily. The primary concern of the national minorities in the ČSR was the preservation of their natural rights, and not the integrity of the improvised state. Their loyalty depended on the respect for the use of their own language, granting of citizenship, establishment of schools for their children and consideration of their property rights by the new rulers. The Magyars, faithful to their national heritage, never wanted to acquiesce in the Czech occupation of Upper Hungary. In the parliamentary elections, held on 18 April, 1920, the Christian Democrats sent four deputies, and the Smallholders one deputy to the Prague Parliament[39] from Slovakia for the defence of the interests of the Hungarian minority. In 1920 there were no elections in Ruthenia.

The two parties in opposition saw the necessity of harmonious work and coordination of their strategy. With this realization they set up a common central bureau for the Hungarian Parliamentary Club initially with headquarters at Losonc (Lučenec) in Slovakia. It was later transferred to Prague. The two Magyar parties in opposition defended the vital interests of their constituents and in 1935 the number of deputies in Prague was augmented to nine and of senators to six. The Hungarian leftist parties were represented by three deputies.

It must be noted that electoral constituencies were unjustly created. In the most exclusive Czech constituency of Prague, 19,469 votes were necessary for the election of one deputy. In the Slovak constituencies of T. Sv. Martin 21,000 votes, in T. Sv. Mikuláš 19,000 votes elected one deputy. In the Hungarian constituencies of Érsekujvár/Nové Zámky/31,000 and in Kassa/Košice/33,000 voters elected one deputy.[40] The increasing encroachment of the government in the political rights of the Magyar population forced the political leaders of the two parties to form only one Hungarian opposition party for a more effective fight within the limits of the democratic institutions. On April 21, 1936 the representatives of the Hungarian Christian Socialist Party and the Hungarian National Party, at their congress held in Érsekujvár/Nové Zámky/, declared the fusion of their parties in the United Hungarian Party.[41] With a renewed and younger leadership the united Hungarian opposition led the twenty-year desperate struggle against the Czechoslovak government to a successful conclusion. It was achieved by the unification of the larger part of the territory settled by Magyars in the ČSR with Hungary by peaceful revision of the border in 1938.

Footnotes

1. Young, E., *Czechoslovakia, Keystone of Peace and Democracy,* pp. 346-347.

2. Glaser, Op. cit., p. 39.

3. Schmid-Egger, B., *Der Völkerbund und die Sudetendeutschen Minderheitspetitionen der Jahre 1920-1926,* p. 6.

4. *Traité entre les Principales Puissances Alliées et la Tchéco-Slovaquie signé à Saint-Germain-en-Laye, le 10 septembre 1919,* Sbírka zákonů a nařízení Státu Československého, 21 Dec. 1921, p. 234.

5. Borsody, I., *Magyarok Csehszlovákiában,* p. 71.

6. La Question de la nationalité sur la base de l'indigénat de la minorité hongroise en Tchécoslovaquie, Mémoire à la Société des Nations, p. 10.

7. Ölvedi, J., *A magyar kisebbség Csehszlovákiában,* p. 280.

8. Sb. zák. a nař., 1920.

9. Macartney, Op. cit., p. 156.

10. *Narodnostní vývoj Československé republiky,* pp. 61-62, 88-89.

11. Winkler, W., *Der Wert der tschechishen Nationalitätenstatistik,* p. 9.

12. Macartney, Op. cit., p. 156.

13. Sb. zák. a nař.

14. Macartney, Op. cit., p. 172.

15. Public Record Office /PRO/, FO. 307, pp. 4-5.

16. Tarján-Falk, Op. cit., p. 39.

17. *A Csehszlovákiai Magyar Népszövetségi Liga Memoranduma a Népszövetséghez* p. 39.

18. Sb. zák. a nař., 1921.

19. Moravek, A., *Hungarians in Czechoslovakia,* p. 709.

20. Tarján, O., *The Ways of Czechoslovakia and its Magyar Minority,* p. 56.

21. Grosschmid, G., *Kisebbségi sors,* p. 328.

22. Prágai Magyar Hirlap/PMH/, 30 March, 1938.

23. *A Csehszlovákiai Magyar Népszövetségi Liga ...,* p. 15.

24. Sb. zák. a nař., 1925.

25. Tarján-Falk, Op. cit., p. 37.

26. Borsody, Op. cit., p. 60.

27. Macartney, Op. cit., p. 177.

28. *A Csehszlovákiai Magyar Népszövetségi Liga...,* p. 15.

29. Jehlicska, F., *Le problème slovaque,* p. 1.

30. Sb. zák. a nař., 189/1919.

31. Szvatkó, P., Op. cit., p. 187.

32. Grosschmid, Op. cit., p. 38.

33. Ibid., p. 249.

34. Sb. zák. a nař., 1924.

35. d'Olay, F., *La presse hongroise dans les états successeurs,* p. 6.

36. Balla, Op. cit., p. 18.

37. *Mémoire à la Société des Nations,* 1935, p. 27.

38. Borsody, Op. cit., p. 63.

39. *Statistická příručka Rep. Československé,* III, p. 280.

40. de Valous, G., *Le sort des minorités en Tchécoslovaquie,* p. 279.

41. Purgat, J., *Od Trianonu po Košice,* p. 97.

CHAPTER III

LEGITIMATE SELF-DEFENCE OF THE MAGYAR MINORITY AT INTERNATIONAL FORA

Petitions to the League of Nations

The ever increasing misuse of political power by the Prague government forced the representatives of the Hungarian parties to submit petitions on behalf of their constituents, and question the government in Parliament for the causes of ignoring their assumed responsibilities towards the national minorities, including the Hungarians. Due to insufficient, unsatisfactory or evasive replies from Prague, the major grievances were submitted for remedy to the League of Nations, the international organization which was commissioned with the supervision of the enforcement of the minority treaties. It was the duty of the League of Nations to seek redress of the accused governments for the complaints of the national minorities. The representatives of the Czechoslovak government, Karel Kramář, the Prime Minister, and Edvard Beneš, the Minister of Foreign Affairs, signed the treaty of Saint-Germain; however, the international obligations were never fulfilled by their government. Article seven of the Minorities treaty of 1919 guaranteed to all Czechoslovak nationals equal rights before the law, the enjoyment of the same civil and political rights without distinction of race, language or religion.[1] The Czechs were acutely aware of the methods and intricacies of handling the national minorities from their own experience in the Austrian Empire.

The pressing problems of minorities menaced the peace. It was one of the functions of the League of Nations to promote and preserve good international relations and understanding. This was a complex task since, during the 26-year existence (1920-1946) of the League, its policy depended not only on the attitude of its member states (between 63 and 44), but also on the behavior of its former members and non-members as well as on the domestic policies of different governments. The functions of the League were performed through its distinct organs: the Council, the Assembly, the Secretariat, several permanent and ad hoc committees. The Council was the main guarantor of the fair application of the stipulations of treaties concluded for the protection of linguistic, racial and religious minorities. The Minorities Section of the Secretariat was authorized by the Council to judge the receivability of petitions, subject to revision by the Council or by the Committee of Three to which the petitions of minority groups were referred. An annual report had to be sent by the Committee of Three to the Council on the number of examined petitions every year.[2] The assembly of the League discussed questions of principle related to the problems of the rights of the minority groups. Any member of the League could bring a dispute on minority questions before the Permanent Court of International Justice for advisory opinion.

Among the charges against the Czechoslovak government brought before the Committee of Three were: the declaration of martial law in the first year of the republic which curtailed every form of movement; censorship which forbade the Magyar language press to publish the minority grievances; the cases of dismissal of Hungarian civil servants on a large scale, deprivation of pensions and allowances to orphans and widows; removal by force of the Hungarian religious leaders; expulsion from Czechoslovakia of the politically non-desirable persons for the Prague government; expropriation of the estates of Hungarian landowners without adequate compensation; machinations with the results of each census that resulted in decreasing the number of Hungarians for statistical reasons, under 20% in many judicial districts; taking into preventive custody leading personalities of the Magyar minority; arresting persons wearing the Hungarian national tricolour, listening to the Hungarian national anthem on the radio, reading journals forbidden to import in Slovakia or Ruthenia, the heavy taxation and intimidation of the Hungarian population and not granting the promised autonomy to Slovakia and Ruthenia.[3] These serious grievances were presented to the Committee of Three of the Council of the League of Nations. Similar petitions were handed to the Committee of Three by all national minorities of the Czechoslovak republic. This committee examined the petitions. If it decided to act upon them, they were first sent in the case of the ČSR to the government of Prague for comments, evaluation and reply. Thus the accused government became the judge in a case levied against it. Some petitions were forwarded to the Council for action. The Council acknowledged their receipt, or recommended them to the special attention of the government involved and asked it to draw the necessary conclusions from them. Sometimes the Council requested the governments to conform with the stipulations of the minority treaties. In practice it meant that the petitions did not lead to any changes in the treatment of the minorities in the ČSR. Furthermore, it was known that Beneš with his interventions at the Committee of Three[4] prevented, on numerous occasions, the forwarding of petitions for discussion, thus to give them publicity.[5] The Minorities Section of the League consisted of employees from the following countries: Spain (President), Denmark, Columbia, Norway, Persia, Yugoslavia, Australia and Ireland.[6] The fate of millions, and a just settlement of their grievances, depended on conscientious examinations and acting upon them by this international forum. The director of the Minorities Section of the General Secretariat, Erik Colban, was the most important figure for the protection of the minorities and for the method of handling some petitions. Owing to the good relations between Colban and Beneš, the petitions of the minorities from Czechoslovakia were slipping with a great art into oblivion. Beneš was considered by Colban as a moderate politician and an expert on minority questions. Business was done secretly and in private conversations.[7] The minorities of the ČSR had to find other means for exposing their problems. The peace treaties made it possible for Beneš and the Czech minority to tyrannize the majority in the ČSR.[8] Statistics of the ČSR: 1) area: 142,375 km^2, 2) population: Czechs 42%, Germans 22%, Slovaks 21.87%, Magyars 6.25%, Ruthenians 2%, Poles 1.87%.[9] In 1921, at the meeting of the League of Nations, the delegate of the ČSR expounded the situation of their national minorities, and presented it as a model for the just treatment of minorities. He discussed the Czechoslovak democratic system of elections but remained silent on the flagrant injustices concerning the required number of votes for the election of deputies and senators in the Czech and non-Czech constituencies.[10] In December 1930 outside help arrived in the difficult struggle for the Magyars in the ČSR when the American-Hungarians in Cleveland, Ohio sent a petition to the League of Nations demanding the peaceful revision of the Trianon borders of Hungary. Five hundred signatures supported the petition (Appendix No. 4).

The concern of the League of Nations was only the preservation of the status quo reached in the suburbs of Paris in 1919, not the rendering of justice to those who went there with confidence in their hardships seeking the prevention of the violation of their rights. In fact, the minority problem was a very serious heritage of the dangerously imprudent settlements after World War I. In thirteen states of Europe with a total population of 106,280,000, there lived 26,780,000 people under the legal protection guaranteed to — but not adhered to — the minorities.[11] The League of Nations proved to be incompetent and inefficient in dealing with these problems. There was no mechanism for the enforcement of international agreements.

In the ČSR the legislative power in 1919-1920 was exercised by an appointed revolutionary National Assembly, an enlarged national council consisting of 216 Czechs (80%) and 54 Slovaks (20%). Other nationalities were left out although the Sudeten German Social Democrats demanded the participation of all nationalities in the deliberations. The systematic and purposeful oppression of the ethnic minorities in the ČSR began with the imposed constitution on them.

The legal source of the minority rights in the ČSR was the peace treaty of Saint-Germain-en-Laye of 1919. It contained the obligations of the Czechoslovak government for granting equality before the law to all nationals of the state. The Minorities treaty constituted international obligations and were placed under the guarantee of the League of Nations. However, the League formed an ideological group and was not devoted to the service of justice and equity.[12] Principles laid down in the treaty were subsequently changed in the formulation of the laws by the provisional National Assembly in Prague, where the national minorities had no representation. It was not a liberally debated constitution. The minority rights were not identical with the rights of the majority, i.e. with the rights and privileges of the Czechs. In the so-called democratic ČSR, the legislation, government decrees and instructions for the enforcement of laws, created a double standard for different segments of the populations. Ethnic groups, subjugated to the Czechs, did not become full-fledged citizens of the new republic but rather were diddled out of equal rights. The application of the laws and the decisions of the constitutional court slowly, but purposefully, took away the rights from the minorities assured for them in the peace treaty and the constitution. A comparaison, for instance, of article seven, paragraph three of the peace treaty with the Čsl. law No. 121/1920, paragraph 218, illustrates the evasion of international obligations accepted by the Prague government. The above paragraph of the peace treaty states that no Czechoslovak citizen could be limited in the free use of any language in private or business transactions, in religious or any other publications or in public meetings. The law, contrary to this, states that the citizens of the republic could use any language in private or commercial life, in religious matters, in the press and in any notices or public meetings *within the limits of the general laws.* Later the use of the language was limited by the language law to communities where a minority was represented by at least 20% of the population. In 1926 the cities of Pressburg, Kassa and Ungvár were annexed to the counties in their vicinity and the Hungarian population in them was artificially diminished for statistical purposes under 20%, consequently losing the use of their mother tongue in the offices of public administration and in the courts.[13] Similar examples could be quoted from different segments of life such as schooling, cultural institutions and state subsidies to chartered organizations. Granting autonomy to Slovakia, Ruthenia and Sudetenland and the recognition of minority rights would have strengthened the new state. Instead of introducing a democratic rule, the Czechs had chosen political oppression, and with that fatal step they helped to destroy their republic in twenty years. The Czechs were democrats among themselves in their customs and political views but they did not recognize the basic tenets of democracy for others such as equality before the law and the right of self-determination.

The Czechoslovak Alliance System and Hungary's Desire for the Peaceful Revision of the Borders

In 1919 the victorious allies believed that they had introduced a fair, even a superior, international political system. In the successor states, in fact, the contrary happened. There were continuously, year after year, many acts of injustices committed against innocent people who were persecuted in the ČSR because they were not Czechs. The latter were suddenly tossed unexpectedly into a situation of an ethnic minority and degraded into a discriminatory social and legal status on their own land. With a great deal of cynicism, the Czechs expected loyalty from those unfortunate millions. Czechoslovakia was a successor state thrown together in a make-shift way by mendacious statements and untrue statistics. The captive nations and nationalities in the ČSR wanted to escape from their sufferings and return to their mother countries surrounding the new republic. The Czechoslovak government could maintain its existence only with the financial and military help of the Western European governments, mainly France. "Our treaty with France is for us a real guarantee for the future; it covers us in our vital questions, leaving for us sufficient liberty for carrying out an independent policy with Germany, England and Russia,"[14] Beneš asserted in his political instructions to the Czechoslovak embassies. Masaryk and Beneš misled not only the Czechs but also their allies, first of all France, because they did not uphold the promised democratic principles of their government. This complete dependence on France became catastrophic in the pre-Munich days of 1938.[15] The Prague government and the executor of its foreign policy, Beneš, did not base the security of the newly born state solely on the maintenance of friendly political relations between France, England and the ČSR, but he surrounded his fragile state with a number of treaties. France, the mightiest and wealthiest country of the post-war years in Europe, was sufficient to keep the Weimar republic at bay. There was no immediate danger from Germany, exhausted and defeated. Beneš turned his attention to the encirclement of Hungary. All four of the Magyars' neighbours, even Austria, the former partner in the monarchy, received part of the territory and population of Hungary in the Trianon treaty. A plebiscite was allowed only in the city of Sopron and fourteen villages which voted 75% for Hungary after the delimitation of the border. The Czechs, Serbs and Rumanians had a common goal: to prevent the repossession of territories by Hungary taken away from her in the peace treaties. Beneš, already on 30 December, 1919, before the signing of the Trianon treaty, entered into negotiations with the Yugoslav government in Belgrade and on 5 January, 1920, with the Rumanian government in Bucharest, proposing the encirclement of Hungary to prevent her claims for the revisions of the borderlines. These preliminary talks paved the way for a treaty of defence and mutual aid alliance with Yugoslavia, signed on 14

August, 1920, and a similar treaty with Rumania was signed on 23 April, 1921. The encirclement of Hungary from three sides was completed on 7 July, 1921, with the Rumanian and Yugoslav treaty of alliance.[16] This triple alliance, called the Little Entente, with its army of 830,000 men was aimed against the 35,000 man army of Hungary, and the restoration of the Habsburg dynasty in Austria or in Hungary. The Little Entente, especially the Czechs, were so afraid of the return of Charles IV of Hungary to his throne that the three members of the newly formed military alliance forced Hungary to declare the Habsburgs dethroned as was voted by the Parliament of Budapest after the second apparition of the ex-king in Hungary from his exile in Switzerland.[17] Disarmed by the peace treaty, encircled by hostile neighbours, economically crippled by the peace makers, the Magyar race separated into four states from the fatherland, was completely at the mercy of the new political factor, the Little Entente, and its chief sponsor, France. The policies of the Hungarian government were closely monitored by Czechoslovakia, for the Czechs knew that the Magyars even in their desperate situation could not accept the territorial mutilation of their country and the political persecution of their blood-brothers on the other side of the frontiers of Hungary. In spite of their frustration and hopeless circumstances, the government of Budapest could not write off the losses in population and territory because changed political conditions could bring back what misfortune took away from the nation. The Ministry of Foreign Affairs was kept informed about the cracks in the Versailles system in order to escape from the death sentence pronounced over the nation at Trianon. The Magyar minorities could not expect any intervention on their behalf from the government of Hungary because the fatherland was economically destroyed, militarily disarmed, condemned to pay war reparations and was put under permanent military control of the entente powers from the summer of 1921 until the end of March 1927. A Control Commission of 52 members kept a strict surveillance on the disarming of the Hungarian army and the production of arms and ammunitions. The presence of this Commission hindered even the secret rearmaments when the well-equipped neighbours strengthened their armies. Britain supported the Hungarian request in the League of Nations, and after three years of deliberations on 31 March, 1927 the entente control was replaced with a less strict control of the League of Nations. Earlier the membership on the Commission was reduced to 11 in 1922. Interdiction of rearmaments was dissolved only in August 1938 when the balance of power changed drastically in Europe, and the League of Nations, France and the Little Entente lost their predominance in Central European affairs. It was clear before the Hungarian government that the peaceful revision of the borderlines and the reacquisition of the dispossessed territories could be done only with the assistance of powerful and friendly states.[18] The Little Entente was aware of the Hungarian efforts, and on the initiative of the ČSR they protested in Budapest against the revisionist endeavours of the Hungarian government.[19] In Budapest the nationality section of the Prime Minister's office dealt with the problems of the Hungarians living abroad, and was supported in this rescuing operation with a scant budget of 2 to 3 million pengő ($1 = Pengő 5) per year.[20] Hungary was mutilated and put under the financial control of the League of Nations which had to approve all loans or bonds the government negotiated on foreign money markets, mostly in London, Paris, Vienna and Rome. Britain and Italy wanted to break the monopoly of France controlling Central Europe. They took a great interest in granting loans to Hungary. In 1926, a balanced budget was produced; the Control Commission was disbanded in April 1927.[21] This financial control, while it existed, extended its sphere of authority to the examination of the fiscal and monetary policy, population statistics, industrial and agricultural production, external trade, commercial policy, and the system of taxation and budget. A sound economic policy helped to extract Hungary from her complete political isolation in which she was placed after World War I. For a long period, France was not able to maintain her dominant role in the League of Nations, nor among the members of the Little Entente. Britain and the United States of America, with their financial power, were breaking up the sole hegemony of France. Italy, the unsatisfied victor of the war, turned against the Versailles system together with crippled Germany. Hungary found understanding and financial backing in Britain, and political support in Italy. The nascent Czechoslovak state was afraid of the Italo-Hungarian rapprochement, and did everything to support the political and economic independence of Austria, signing a treaty of neutrality in case of conflict with Italy on 16 May, 1924. This treaty was not renewed when it expired five years later because of Italian opposition. Italy tried to replace the French influence in the Danubian basin, and this orientation in foreign policy led to the conclusion of the Italian-Hungarian treaty of friendship, cooperation and arbitration on 5 April, 1927 on the occasion of the visit of the Hungarian Prime Minister, Bethlen, to Rome. The goal of both countries was to change the Versailles and Trianon settlements, and satisfy their territorial claims. This treaty signified the end of Hungary's political isolation, and obtained for her valuable support in the League of Nations. At the same time the injustices of the Trianon treaty were brought up and debated in the British Parliament. This activity in foreign policy was backed on the home front with the foundation of the Revisionist League in Budapest which became the propaganda tool and moving force behind this movement. Under the auspices of an active foreign policy the Revisionist League was founded on 11 August, 1927 for developing the revisionist propaganda within and outside of Hungary. Thirty-four clubs took part in the establishment of this organization.[22] On 5 May, 1928 Mussolini supported Hungary's revisionist demands by stating that conditions of Hungary with half of the nations territory and nearly half of the Magyar inhabitants wrested from her, constituted a running sore, poisoning the whole atmosphere of Central Europe.[23] Prime Minister Gömbös, the successor of Bethlen, advocated the rights of the Hungarian minorities in the successor states.[24] Lord Rothermere's proclamtion of 15 March, 1931, on the national day of independence of Hungary, remembered the millions of Hungarians who were suffering under implacable foreign oppression. It was his firm conviction that the world's public opinion began to recognize the great injustices inflicted on Hungary in the peace treaty of Trianon, and that the revision of borders would develop into an international problem.[25] On 14 February, 1929, the Hungarian Upper House asked the Foreign Minister to take the necessary steps in an opportune moment at the League of Nations in the matter of the Trianon treaty.[26] Gömbös continued the cultivation of the Italian friendship, but for the realization of the revisionist goals his concept of foreign policy required collaboration with Germany, another antagonist of the 1919 treaties, and Italy. These two governments had diametrically opposing views on the Austrian independence. Gömbös successfully established closer links of political consultation and economic cooporation with Italy and Austria. His efforts culminated in the signature of the protocols of Rome on 17 March, 1934. They defined the political and economic ties among Austria, Hungary and Italy. In the framework of these agreements, Gömbös suggested the extension of closer relations with Germany. Mussolini was willing to cooperate with the Germans on the basis of the protocols of Rome for the solution of the problems of the Danubian basin.[27] The German support of Italy during the Abyssinian crisis was transformed into a military alliance between Rome and Berlin. The violation of the Versailles treaty by Hitler initiated the diplomatic recognition of Soviet Russia by various governments, and led to a military alliance between France and the Soviet Union on 2 May, 1935, and between the ČSR and the USSR on 16 May, 1935. Hungary's revisionist claims were supported by Italy and Germany, and they were counteracted by the ČSR and her French and Russian allies. With the growing military power of the axis states, the question of the border revision of the successor states emerged to an international level.

The peace treaties were also condemned by non-interested parties. The American Secretary of State, Robert Lansing, had declared that "the Versailles treaty menaces the existence of civilization," and two Popes had stigmatized that instrument. Benedict XV had condemned it for "the lack of an elevated sense of justice, the absence of dignity, morality or Christian nobility," and Pius XI in his encyclical *Ubi arcam Dei* (26 December, 1922) deplored an artificial peace set down on paper, "which instead of arousing noble sentiments increases and legitimizes the spirit of vengeance and rancor."[28]

Foreign Endorsements for the Territorial Aspirations of Hungary

The positive result of the official Italian support of the rightful demands of Hungary before world opinion encouraged the Bethlen government to announce publicly, in Parliament, two months later, the defence of the Magyar minorities living in the Little Entente states. At the beginning of the period of international backing of Hungary's revisionist claims, a segment of the British press upheld the Hungarian case. Germany, even in 1933, only partially endorsed the Hungarian claims for the restoration of the Magyar-speaking minorities to the mother country. It was emphasized in Berlin that this aim should be concentrated on the ČSR because Germany had certain interests in Rumania and Yugoslavia.[29]

On 21 June, 1927, the *London Daily Mail*, Lord Rothermere's paper, published an article "Hungary's Place under the Sun." This brave approval of the necessity to revise the treaty of Trianon by changing the borders in favour of Hungary was enthusiastically welcomed in Hungarian circles. The minority problems were included on the agenda of the March 1929 meeting of the League of Nations at Geneva at the request of the German Foreign Minister. Hungary's representative also submitted a memorandum asking for the enlargement of the existing authority of the Council of the League which should have protected the rights of minorities in accordance with the peace treaties. The enforcement of those articles did not prove to be satisfactory. The members of the Council were not willing to take upon themselves an additional task in disciplining the member states which violated their international obligations. It was decided, rather, to create a commission, the Committee of Three, for filing and processing the complaints of minorities demanding the amelioration of their fate under foreign rule. The Committee of Three did not live up to the expectations of the movers of that amendment. The attitude of Hungary was sober-minded, tactful but at the same time determined. The small, poor and defeated country, encircled by enemies, used the available legal means on the international stage for presenting its request. Article XIX of the Covenant of the League of Nations envisaged the peaceful reconsideration of the peace treaties by the Assembly of the League which have become inapplicable and whose continuance might endanger the peace of the world.[30] The authors of the Versailles and Trianon treaties did not want to consider any negotiations for peaceful alterations of the existing state of affairs. Possibilities for rapprochement among the states of the Danubian basin were improved by the change in world politics. In the new constellation of power, the most elementary human and national rights could not be denied any longer to the Hungarian minorities. Hungary was forced to break her isolation, and established commercial and political ties with friendly states. This ended the political monopoly of the Little Entente in the Danubian basin.

More weight was carried by voices raised abroad, depicting the tragic conditions that the peace treaties caused in post-war Hungary. The keepers of the spoils grabbed at Trianon, the Little Entente, tried to maintain the dogma of the inviolability of the peace treaties which they violated over and over again.

Italy's strengthened international position provided significant support to the revision of the Trianon treaty. On 5 June, 1928 in the Senate, Mussolini deplored the detachment of the territory and population from Hungary.[31] The main purpose of the Italian action was the enforcement of her position in continental Europe. This public pronouncement of Mussolini aided Hungary and the Magyar minorities more than the occasional references to the same problem by prominent Britons or certain French newspapers receiving grants from Budapest for propaganda purposes. Mussolini spoke out repeatedly on behalf of Hungary during the following ten years, demanding the alteration of the post-war status quo and suggesting the separation of the League of Nations from the treaty of Versailles. The balance of political forces was modified with the signature of the protocols of Rome on 17 March, 1934 by Mussolini, Dollfuss and Gömbös. The first protocol called for the maintenance of peace and the economic restoration of Europe respecting the independence of every state. The three governments decided to hold common consultations for considering the opportune course. Economic relations among the three countries were provided for in the second protocol. The third protocol announced the conclusion of a new commercial treaty between Italy and Austria within two months.[32] For a long period of time before this agreement, the Italians emphasized the necessity of examining the economic problems in the Danubian basin.[33] Prime Minister Bethlen welcomed the friendly inclination of Italy as a first step toward political cooperation. The Budapest government was deeply concerned with the problems of Magyar minorities in the neighbouring states. Beneš voiced the opinion that they had been definitively solved in the ČSR.[34] The Little Entente was solidly guarding the heritage of Trianon, and none of the three countries was willing to start individually a new political orientation in the question of territorial revision without consulting the other two members of the alliance. In February 1933, immediately after the acquisition of power by Hitler, Beneš propelled by his fear, asked the Little Entente to conclude an organizational pact against Hitler, and put it under the direct authority of the Permanent Council of the alliance.[35]

Hungary had to live in a dismembered condition until further changes in the military power structure of Europe offered an opportunity to free herself from the entanglements of the Trianon system. Meanwhile, the detached members of the nation were not forgotten or given up by the Budapest government in spite of the constant threat against revisionism by the Little Entente. The defiance of the Versailles treaty by Germany, the reoccupation of the demilitarized Rhineland, the unilateral declaration of rearmament, the annexation of Austria basically placed the ČSR in an untenable situation. In 1933 the Gömbös government started to develop contacts with Germany, also a revisionist power, and that line of policy was pursued by Prime Minister Darányi. Among others, the new Prime Minister said that Hungary was willing to regulate the pending questions with her neighbours on the basis of reciprocal agreements. The first step was to secure the rights of the minorities and to protect them by international law. Without a satisfactory settlement of the minorities problem normal relations could not develop between Hungary and the Little Entente.[36] Hungary could not continue to tolerate her mutilation and the constant threat by Little Entente around her. Darányi proclaimed the Hungarian standpoint in his speech at Győr. The ČSR reacted to those pronouncements. The great powers were silent when in 1935 Germany introduced obligatory conscription, violating the articles of the peace treaty. Nothing happened when Austria started to arm herself. A relatively large number of people were aware that Hungary had been arming herself for a long time. However, the situation of Hungary was different because it was in the interest of the Little Entente to check Hungarian revisionism. Darányi announced that Hungary is not willing to wait any longer. Afther this statement — in the opinion of Prague — the Little Entente could violate openly the articles of the peace treaties concerning Hungary. The ČSR could reject the protection of the Magyar minority by the peace treaties[37], it was stated in Prague.

Prague felt the pressure from Germany, Italy, Hungary, Poland and the majority of the Slovaks who were supposed to be a state-maintaining nation in the republic of the Czechs and Slovaks. With that political constellation a favourable moment arrived for the dissatisfied minorities to demand the abandonment of the oppressive policy practised by Prague toward them. The government of Prague was adamantly opposed to the revision of borders. Beneš, in his exposé on the international situation, declared in the Chamber of Deputies on 25 April, 1935 that "History shows that detachment of territories always started the most bloody wars, and I have no doubts that it would be again the situation according to today's international thinking and tension... It was possible to dispose of territories at the peace conference. From that moment when it is in the legal possession of this or that nation, it is simply absurd to want to require again the right of disposition. It is our standpoint and from that we do not give up anything."[38] Beneš' speech mirrored Bohemia's territorial expansion. To maintain this kind of a conglomeration of nationalities, the Czechs fortified themselves with treaties of alliances and lived in a false sense of security. During the peace negotiations in 1919, the Czech agents worked on secret deals behind the scenes. Nineteen years later, they entrenched themselves behind military alliances with the hope that international agreements would be sufficient to save the inflated

Bohemia which was called the ČSR. The Czechs prepared their own misfortune. They simply did not know how to govern a multi-ethnic mosaic state. They took cover under the ČSR-France and the ČSR-USSR military agreements. They did not know what to do with the golden opportunity to realize a democratic government in the centre of Europe to the satisfaction of the people who were compelled to live in the republic of the Czechs. It was impossible to perpetuate the maltreatment of the nationalities, the Germans, Hungarians, Ruthenians, Poles and the supposedly ruling Slovaks, by using the power of authority against them which manifested itself in passing laws for the defence of the republic, through censorship and military force. All of this was insufficient to prevent an open outburst of discontent of the majority against the Czech minority when favourable circumstances permitted it without the possibility of being molested or punished by the Czech state apparatus.

Footnotes

1. Frey, A., *A Danubian Chronicle,* The Hungarian Quarterly, Vol. IV, 1938, p. 181.
2. Aufricht, H., *Guide to League of Nations Publications,* p. 189.
3. *Question à la nationalité sur la base de l'indigénat,* Mémoire à la Société des Nations, p. 33.
4. Szvizsényi, Z., *Hogyan veszett el a Felvidék,* p. 22.
5. Truhart, H., *Völkerbund and Minderheitenpetitionen,* p. 170.
6. Vladár, E., *Mi is az a Népszövetség?,* p. 25.
7. Schmid-Egger, B., Op. cit., p. 64.
8. The Times, Feb. 17, 1938.
9. Czakó, E., Op. cit., p. 22.
10. Schimd-Egger, B., Op. cit., p. 16.
11. Truhart, H., Op. cit., p. 170.
12. Frey, A., Op. cit., p. 181.
13. Sziklay, F., *Kisebbségi magyar sors,* Magyar Szemle, No. 3, 1927, pp. 281-282.
14. Brach, R., *Francouzskýalianční systém a Československo na počátku roku 1924,* Čas. Vojenského Hist. Ústavu, Ročník 1968, p. 9.
15. Lvová, M., *Mnichov a Edward Beneš,* p. 11.
16. Werner, A., *Eduard Beneš der Mensch und der Staatsman,* p. 193.
17. Horthy, N., *Memoirs,* p. 129.
18. Szinai, M.-L. Szűcs, *Horthy Miklós titkos iratai,* pp. 68-69.
19. Ibid., p. 81.
20. Ibid., p. 32.
21. Horthy, M., Op. cit., p. 135.
22. Kis, A., *Magyarország Külpolitikája a második világháború előestéjén,* p. 18.
23. Villari, L., *Italian Foreign Policy under Mussolini,* p. 54.
24. Gajanová, A., Op. cit., p. 230.
25. Affari Esteri, No. 2433/248.
26. Gajanová, A., Op. cit., p. 244.
27. DGFP., C.I., p. 169.
28. Villari, L., Op. cit., p. 204.
29. Ibid., p. 340.
30. Czernin, F., *Versailles,* p. 156.
31. Pesti Napló, June 6, 1928.
32. Villari, L., Op. cit., pp. 116-117.
33. Lavoro Fascista, July 18, 1930.
34. Ibid.
35. Gajanová, A., Op. cit., p. 306.

36. Prágai Magyar Hirlap (PMH), March 6, 1938.

37. Národní Politika, March 7, 1938.

38. Leták, M., *V osidlech zrady,* p. 94.

CHAPTER IV

PARLIAMENTARY MANOEUVERINGS IN PRAGUE

The Nationality Problem in Czechoslovakia

In 1938 the Czechoslovak question once more became an international problem as it had been in 1918 and 1919, when the Czech political emigrants from Austria-Hungary insisted on making it an international affair. The political troubles of the Czechs in the nascent republic were created first of all by the "sister" nation, and a ruling partner nation, the Slovaks. The Slovak politicians who gathered on 30 October, 1918 in T. Sv. Martin (Túrócszentmárton), and signed the declaration of adhesion to a common state with the Czechs, did not know of the declaration of the Czecho-Slovak republic two days earlier in Prague. The Czech and Slovak political activists made an undesirable governmental organization for their people without sounding their opinions through a vote. It was an alliance without any semblance of consideration for the common good of both nations, not to speak of the other national minorities forced into that state. The Czechs could refer to the lands of the Crown of Saint Wenceslas in their quest for an independent state, however, the Slovaks lacked such a historical experience, and were ready to share political power with the Czechs. Once occupied by the Czech army units, the Slovaks were split in their political choice between Prague and Budapest. A small minority of them were willing to co-operate with the centralist Czech government in Prague, but the majority were the followers of the clerical Slovak Populist Party, led by Reverend Hlinka. This party was the rallying point of the autonomist anti-Czech Catholic Slovaks, comprising about 80% of their nation. When the Czechophile plenipotentiary minister for Slovakia, Šrobár, was not able to fulfill the aspirations of the Slovak clergy, and appoint some of its anxious and impatient members to higher ecclesiastical offices by removing the Hungarian bishops from the territory which then became Slovakia, those priest-politicians turned against Šrobár and the Czecho-Slovak regime he represented. It was an ideological as well as a political power struggle for influence in Slovakia.[1] Hlinka became the focal point of the Slovak separatists. The clericals were furious, and their anger was transferred against the Czech freethinkers, freemasons, Hussites, Czech Brethren and Czech sympathizers among the Slovaks. In the political arena, they left the T. Sv. Martin platform, and promoted a movement for the autonomy of Slovakia. A group of Slovak Catholic priests met at Rosenberg (Rózsahegy, Ružomberok), the hometown of Hlinka's parish: the outcome of the meeting was the convocation of the convention for formation of the Slovak Populist Party on 18 December, 1918.[2] There was another anti-Czech movement which on 30 October, 1918 formed a Slovak National Council at Eperjes (Prešov) in Eastern Slovakia, former Upper Hungary, and on 11 December it declared the independence of Slovakia at Kassa.[3]

A third group, the radically anti-Czech Slovaks were forced into exile. They organized a Slovak revolutionary government at Cracow on 26 May, 1921 under the presidency of Francis Jehlička and Francis Unger as Minister of Foreign Affairs.[4] The headquarters of the Slovak Council in exile were established in Geneva, conveniently located for presenting the grievances of the Slovaks in the ČSR to the League of Nations. In their memoranda, they demanded the annulment of the Pittsburgh agreement, and enumerated the causes of the Slovak dissatisfaction with the Czech government in Prague: the Czech immigration to Slovakia, employment of Czech civil servants, teachers, professors with salary bonuses in Slovakia. The revision of the treaty of Trianon was, according to them, not only an imperative, but the Slovak demands on the day of the revision presented to the Czechs would amount to 20 billion British pounds sterling, the approximate sum of the Czech loot taken away from Slovakia in the first 15 years of the republic.[5] This council was very active between the two World Wars and known for its anti-Czech and pro-Magyar stand. It is worthwhile to mention that the Plenipotentiary Minister for Slovakia in 1921 disbanded that Slovak National Council which in 1918 signed the declaration in favour of the ČSR.

The Slovak Populist Party was fighting on the home front the Czechoslovak government and demanded the federalization of the republic. Jehlička, the leader of the Slovaks in exile, in 1921, went to the United States of America. In his presence the functionaries of several Slovak associations from New York State and Pennsylvania accepted a resolution which declared the Pittsburgh agreement with Masaryk null and void and demanded independence for Slovakia.[6] At home the Slovaks based their demands for autonomy on the Pittsburgh agreement. Bills were introduced in the Prague Parliament for self-government in 1922 and 1930. Deputy Vojtech Tuka, in 1922, asked Prague to fulfill the promise in the Pittsburgh agreement and lead a satisfactory cultural and economic policy towards Slovakia.[7] The bills for Slovak autonomy were voted down in the Prague Parliament. In this seemingly endless conflict the Czechs changed tactics by taking some of the autonomist Slovaks and Sudeten German activists in the central government. The Slovaks were bought off for the establishment of a Slovak provincial Diet. This new approach worked for a while, and the Slovak Populist Party was represented in the government with two portfolios for two years, 1927-1929, and the German activists — Social Democrats, Agrarians, Christian Socialists — from 1926 to 1938, each with one cabinet member. The Slovak Populist Party left the government coalition after the trial which saw the sentencing of one of their deputies to a 15-year prison term for treason. After publishing an article in the *Slovak* on 1 January, 1928, entitled "Vacuum Juris", Tuka's parliamentary immunity was lifted, and he was put on trial. At the meeting in T. Sv. Martin (Túrócszent-márton) of the Slovak politicians on 30 October, 1918, a motion was presented which was discussed but not formally moved, se-conded and voted upon. For ten years Tuka wanted to experiment with the proposed political union in the Pittsburgh agreement with the Czechs in the envisaged common state. The T. Sv. Martin declaration was the cornerstone of the state.[8] In Tuka's opinion the Slovaks had the right to decide, after ten years of partnership with the Czechs, on the desirability of such a political association; therefore, he called the situation arriving on 30 October, 1928 "vacuum juris" a legal status in which the Czechoslovak republic had no longer any legal force over the Slovaks, who would be free to choose their political future. The Czech political, military, judicial, and police apparatus gave a heavy blow to the Slovak jurist for expressing his personal opinion and the aspirations of his nation. With his prison sentence, the Slovak separatists were silenced for ten years.

The Prague government surrounded itself with legislation against the non-obedient minorities with the Law for the Defence of the Republic introduced in 1923 and extended in 1933; also in 1923, laws were passed for censorship, and suspension or suppression of periodicals judged dangerous for the state and, likewise, laws were accepted for the dissolution of political parties dangerous for the government. It is interesting to note that the following quotation appeared in the restored Czechoslovakia after 1945: "In the second half of 1923 there was the first attempt made at the transition to a Fascist dictatorship. A new press law was promulgated which had to prosecute all publications hostile to the government. Furthermore, the offices of Masaryk's republic, which boasted itself as democra-tic, suppressed 38 periodicals, among them the *Rudé Právo* (Communist), for six months."[9] Among the newspapers repeatedly suspended from three to six months were the *Slovák* (Slovak populist), *Národnie Noviny* (Slovak Nationalist) and the *Prágai Magyar Hirlap* (Hungarian Opposition).[10] In addition to these laws, the government's main support was the army against the hostile nationality bloc which formed the majority of the population. Pragued used a strong hand policy coupled with intimidation. These measures did not help to consolidate the fragile state. On the contrary, it brought the Slovaks closer to the oppressed and dissatisfied minorities whose cooperation broke the Czech hegemony causing the collapse of the republic.

The Slovak Populist Party kept the pressure on the Czechs. In 1933, an opportune occasion arose for anti-government demonstrations when, at Nitra, the 1,100th anniversary of the consecration of the first Christian church built by Prince Pribina was celebrated in the presence of the representatives of the Prague government, foreign and church dignitaries and an immense crowd.[11] The autonomists received a wide publicity from this affair. The Slovaks went forward with their movement, and sought political cooperation with those parties which stood for the autonomy of Slovakia. This strong Catholic manifestation was directed against the Czechs, who, on 6 July, 1925, had demonstrated against Catholicism in Prague at the unveiling ceremony of the statue of John Huss, an early reformer, in the presence of the government, at which time the papal nuncio had been deeply insulted and had departed for Rome.[12]

The Sudeten German Question

In April 1920, the appointed Czechoslovak provisional National Assembly was dissolved upon completion of the constitution, and the first parliamentary elections in the ČSR took place on 18 May for the Chamber of Representatives, and a week later for the Senate. The Sudeten Germans sent five parties to the elections obtaining the following results: Social Democrats 31 deputies, the National Party and the National Socialist Workers' Party 15 deputies, Agrarians 11 deputies, Christian Socialists 10 deputies and the Democrats 5 deputies. Out of 281 deputies there were 72 Sudeten Germans elected, and of 142 senators, 37 belonged to the Sudeten German parties.[13] When the Chamber of Representatives met the first time on 1 June, 1920, the German deputies declared that Czechoslovakia was created against their will, and they did not renounce the right of self-determination.[14] Similar statements were made by the deputies of the Slovak Populist Party and the Hungarian opposition parties. Deputy Lajos Körmendy-Ékes stated in the Chamber of Representatives on 2 June, 1920, — two days before the signature of the Trianon peace treaty — that the Magyars in the ČSR were detached from Hungary against their will.[15] The declarations signed by the deputies and senators of the Sudeten German parties included also the Social Democrats. They rejected the peace treaty of Saint-Germain which stated that the Germans of Bohemia, Moravia, Silesia and Slovakia wanted to unite themselves with the Czechs to establish the Czechoslovak republic. The ČSR was, therefore, the outcome of a Czech decision. The Sudeten Germans never had been consulted and the result of the peace treaty can be regarded as an enforcement which never had been legally authorized. Injustice cannot become a law even by a thousand-year practice. The Sudeten

Germans demanded with all their power self-determination for themselves. This declaration was renewed on 18 December, 1925 on behalf of the German parties by Franz Spina, deputy of the Sudeten German Agrarians and Vice-President of the Chamber of Representatives in Prague, who protested against the violation of the right of self-determination of the German population in the ČSR. He declared again that the Sudeten Germans did not recognize the peace treaties of Versailles, Saint-Germain and Trianon as a source of law. The seven-year existence of the ČSR with its sytem of government was intolerable for the incorporated people. He further enumerated the grievances of the Sudeten Germans: the import of Czech public employees, enterprises, workers, business and agricultural colonists on the German speaking population. Parallel with these actions, the Sudeten Germans lost their employment. The government closed German schools, unnecessarily establishing Czech ones; through land reform it confiscated the land from the German proprietors and helped denationalize the German area by Czech newcomers. The state should be developed according to the requirements of the citizens. The Sudeten German deputies were determined to defend the free development of their constituents and eliminate the Czech ruling system.[16] In the meantime, in 1922, the German Social Democrats addressed a memorandum to the Congress of the Socialist Workers International held at Hamburg. It criticized the Czechoslovak government which ruled in a dictatorial way since the foundation of the republic: political meetings were dissolved, free associations inhibited and newspapers were seized. Politicians of the opposition parties were put on trial for high treason, there were no elections called in East Silesia and Ruthenia, military executions kept whole areas oppressed, citizens were shot down in the streets, all this on the pretext of the national state and its constitution.[17] After the 1925 elections the Sudeten German policy had partially changed. There were signs of differences in opinion regarding internal politics. After the second elections in the republic, the Sudeten German Agrarians and Christian Socialists, and later the Social Democrats, were ready for political cooperation with the Prague government by forming a coalition government with the Czech parties in order to gain some economic and social advantages. These three Sudeten German parties took an active part in the government between 1926 and 1938 each of them with one portfolio. On 14 October, 1926, Prime Minister Švehla had a historic meeting with German deputies and decided to open new relations with them in domestic policies as equals to equals in spite of the existing and known difficulties.[18] However, there were no changes in the internal policy of the Czechoslovak government vis-à-vis the national minorities due to this temporary cooperation between the Czech and German parties. On 7 October, 1933, the Prague government dissolved the Sudeten German National Socialist Workers' Party as a dangerous political association for the state. The abolition of the party took place within 24 hours after the decision taken by the government, and the activity of the local, district, county and national organizations ceased to exist in order to maintain the unity and inviolability of the state against anarchy, disintegration and revolutionary movement.[19] Extraordinary times demanded this from the government — said the official explanation.[20] The German National Party was also suppressed. The economic situation of the Sudetenland was extremely bad. Hundreds of thousands were without jobs and starving as a result of the Czech economic policy toward the Sudeten German industry. A few days before the elimination of the two German opposition parties, on 1 October, 1933 Konrad Henlein made a patriotic appeal to the Sudeten German population and announced the formation of the Sudeten German Homeland Front with a program for the protection of the cultural and economic interests of the Germans in the framework of a friendly cooperation with the other peoples of the state.[21] Henlein's movement united the Sudeten Germans. Six weeks prior to the May 19 elections in 1935, it took the name: Sudeten German Party. Upon his call, the dispersed Germans living in Slovakia formed the Carpatho-German Party, a united body for the defence of their interests.

Henlein displayed a great deal of courage when he entered politics in the camouflaged democracy of the Czechs. He was aware of the Defence of the Republic Act of 1923 which stipulated strict punishments for acts, speeches, articles and pictures used against the republic or its representatives; acts or threats against the ministers, deputies of the Parliament or its committees. For the intimidation of their political opponents, the authors of this law put into it 306 possible punishments. Furthermore, the adherents of the regime, the army was assured of 25% of the budget.

The Czechs created around themselves a false feeling of security with the adoption of these measures. Paragraph 1 of the Defence of the Republic Act lays down that a person who attempts forcibly to incorporate or detach a portion of the Czechoslovak republic in a foreign state is punishable by 5 to 20 years or life imprisonment.[22] In addition to the Defence of the Republic Act, on 13 May, 1936 Act No. 131/1936 said that unreliable workers, managers and directors must be dismissed.[23] Measures were taken to defend the state against any attack on its sovereignty, independence, integrity, constitutional unity, democratic republican structure and security. The Supreme Defence Council even in peacetime had wide powers. Frontier zones were established under military authority.[24] The Czech democracy slowly was turned into a dictatorship. The Defence of the Republic Act of 30 April, 1937 made Beneš a dictator in practice.[25] After his fall in 1938, Beneš denounced everybody who was not of the same opinion as he.[26]

The unsolved minority problem arose the interest of the British government. Their ambassador in Prague sent a report to London on 3 March, 1934 regarding the minorities question. He called the republic an unnatural creation. The distance between Prague and

London was less than between Prague and Ruthenia, and the republic with its awkward borders and a strong neighbour was in a difficult position. On the border strip of the state an unloyal population — rightly or wrongly — wished the disappearance of the state at the first opportunity. Only a rational internal political compromise with the minorities could solve the tension. A promise for the correct handling of the minorities was the basis for the creation of the republic. The ruling Czech group was not capable of fulfilling it. Remedy could come only from outside. The status quo of the ČSR could certainly not be maintained any longer.[27] After the May elections in 1935 the Sudeten German parties had the following representation in the Prague Parliament: Sudeten German Party (Henlein) 44, Social Democrats 11, Christian Socialists 6, Agrarians 5.[28] The Sudeten German Party received 66% of the German votes and two weeks after the elections the German Christian Socialists and Agrarians joined the SGP. The Sudeten Germans with 55 deputies became the strongest party of the Czechoslovak Parliament. In 1938 only the German Social Democratic Party did not join the United Sudeten German front for ideological reasons but it also gave up its participation in the government coalition. National self-conscience was growing and in this political process of transformation among the Sudeten Germans the smaller parties disappeared. The Germans in the ČSR did not want to become traitors of their national cause by splitting their political forces and they rushed to Henlein's party which closed the membership applications on 31 May, 1938.[29] In 1933, Henlein formed his *Heimatfront* (Home-landfront). He was for democracy but the party under the influence of events became more and more radicalized. The British government made contacts with the Sudeten German Party, and three months after the landslide victory in the 1935 elections, Henlein was invited to London by the Royal Institute of International Affairs. In his speech given to the members of the Institute, the Sudeten German leader emphasized that the German minority in the ČSR demanded only their rights and they were for the democratic constitution of the state but those rights assured in the constitution were not granted. This was the reason for his movement. It had nothing to do with Hitler's aim to unite, in one state, all Germans living around and outside Germany. He never saw Hitler, nor did he speak with him, nor had he any correspondence with him, and further, he never had contact with the German government of the day. According to Henlein, the territorial revision was not a solution to the problems. Pan-Germanism was as dangerous as pan-Slavism. The Sudeten Germans were loyal to the state and were ready for cooperation with the government as long as the German population was to receive a better treatment. His aim was to stop radicalism and promote the peaceful development of the German population.[30]

Soon after the Parliamentary elections in 1935, Henlein began his foreign travels. In that month he went to Switzerland to vacation for health reasons. In Geneva he had an excellent opportunity to meet several representatives of foreign governments accredited to the League of Nations.[31] At the end of 1935 the Sudeten German Party started a compaign in Western Europe against the foreign policy of the ČSR. In Paris they attacked the Soviet influence in the ČSR and the 36 air bases built around Prague and other points for the operations of the Soviet air force against Europe. The most significant action of the Sudeten German Party abroad was the establishment of contacts with British and French political circles. Henlein, during his 1935 visit in London and subsequent travels there, informed the British government of the real situation and complaints of the Sudeten Germans in the ČSR. In his interviews he always declared his loyalty to the state and his desire for securing equal rights for his people in the republic.[32] The Czechs replied to this with their remarks that the road to Prague from Sudetenland does not lead through Paris, London or Berlin. One may add to this that during World War I, the road from Prague did not lead directly to Vienna through Paris, London, Washington or Moscow used by the Czech political agents. Henlein visited London several times between 1935 and 1938 and gave interviews to newspapers. The Sudeten Germans opened permanent offices in London and Paris. In Paris the connection with the Ministry of Foreign Affairs was of non-official nature through the comte de Brinon.[33] The Sudeten German deputies also travelled to Switzerland, France, Britain, Sweden promoting their cause and attempting to gain sympathy for their struggle. Sudeten German solidarity was the response to the long Czechoslovak oppression. A Czech interpretation of the democratic principles was eloquently expressed by a former Czech cabinet minister, Rašin, who said during a conversation with a German Social Democratic deputy, Joseph Seliger, on 4 November, 1918: "The right for self-determination is only an empty phrase, but when the entente has won, power counts."[34] Under those circumstances the Sudeten Germans were determined to create an international affair from their domestic struggle. The Czechs created a German problem within the borders of the republic by not granting full citizens' rights to the Sudeten Germans and the other minorities. The British received first hand information of Czech internal problems from a successful Sudeten German political leader.

The Czechs became aware of the German political force within the borders of the state. Hence, the local organization of the Czech National Socialist Party at Liberec (Reichenberg), in the Sudeten district, passed a resolution at a meeting on 17 May, 1937 for the dissolution of the Sudeten German Party.[35] Although the demand was not granted, nevertheless the existence of such a motion demonstrated the fear of the Czechs in Sudetenland. The Sudeten Germans in turn made contacts with other dissatisfied minority groups: the Slovaks, Hungarians, Poles and Ruthenians. By September 1938 there was a united front against the Czechs which led to foreign intervention for settling the problem. On September 13 and October 20, 1935 Henlein's party had two important strategic sessions in order to give directives to the deputies of the party. Lawsuits were started against several members of the SG Party for anti-state activities and the party's journal *Rundschau* on 25 June, 1935 was suspended for six months.[36] In August Beneš reacted in the name of the government to the dynamic activity of the Sudeten German Party with a speech which was followed by similar declarations by other members of the government. Beneš delivered a speech on 19 August, 1936 in the capital city of Sudetenland, in Liberec (Reichenberg). The essential passages of his remarks did not admit the errors made by the government during the past eighteen years. He added that the national struggles, on all ethnic fronts, are natural and ineluctable, but that the two peoples had reached such a degree of maturity that it is impossible to denationalize them... There was a certain radicalization among the national minorities in every state, not only in the ČSR, and it was necessary to study it seriously. According to international law, the national questions, recognized in every state without exception, are internal political questions. Czechoslovakia adhered without any reservation to this principle. Not a single European state had the right to meddle in this question. The ČSR as a sovereign state was completely conscious of its dignity and of its rights. The only influence the ČSR was willing to accept and respect in these questions was the control of the League of Nations. He declared that in the ČSR no nationality was threatened neither in its existence nor in its culture.[37] Interesting thoughts from the President of the republic but they came too late. Until he directed the affairs of the state, the ČSR was not willing to alleviate oppressive political conditions of the national minorities and secure for them a life worthy of a democratic society. It was impossible to disregard the grievances of the minorities. Prime Minister Hodža announced in the Chamber of Representatives on 10 November, 1936 that the government wanted to solve the minorities problem in accordance with the demands of the activist ministers.[38] The government was willing to deal with handpicked persons and the traitors of the ethnic groups but not with the representatives of the majority of the minorities. Hodža dwelt with the German problem and with the demand of proportionality in the Senate on 7 December, 1936 and admitted that the government studied the numerical basis of the matter.[39] He acknowledged that in some branches of public administration the Germans were not appropriately represented but proportionality could not be realized without regard to the attitude of civil servants to the state. On 24 January, 1937 Hodža in his radio broadcast spoke of the perfection of the public administration and of the minority policy. The government has always extended full national justice and its stand has been against Bohemization or Slovakization of the minorities.[40] Beneš, in his radio message on Christmas 1937, promised a slow amelioration of the grievances of the nationalities. With this declaration Beneš admitted that discrimination had existed in the ČSR. The President and the Prime Minister knew that it was impossible to continue the dangerous play with the rights of the nationalities. Germany and on a smaller scale Poland and Hungary demanded the solution of the minority problem of the ČSR.

Foreign Interventions in the Internal Political Struggle

The nationalities, which formed the majority of the population in the ČSR, found a common denominator for their demands: it was called human rights. The successful result of their long and difficult struggle proved that the Czechoslovak republic never should have been established with all its component provinces. That state was not the result of a historical development or even historical forces struggling in a closed geographic area. Partly the mismanagement of the Prague administration, partly the natural attraction of the minorities for unification with their own peoples across the border disrupted the republic. In the permanent condition of conflict with the Czechs, the smaller nationality groups received enormous support for their objectives from the largest minority, the Sudeten Germans. The malcontents, with united forces internally and with external assistance, terminated the repressive use of Czech political power. Open interest in the Sudeten problem was stressed for the first time in Germany on 25 February, 1934. On that day Neurath, the Foreign Minister, told Mastný, the ambassador of the ČSR in Berlin: "Earlier those were the Poles, now they are the Czechs — unfortunately I cannot conceal it from you — against whom are directed the unfriendly sentiments in the people. It is the Sudeten German question — in my opinion — which on both sides, no doubts, worries us."[41] In soft diplomatic language it was a very serious warning for the Czechs. Henlein's movement had received the support of the Reich government, and a sympathetic reception in England and other European countries.

It was unreasonable to ignore any longer the grievances of the Germans and the claims of the other minorities. The nationalities could not loyally collaborate with the Prague government and support the development of the country in which they were not treated as equals. The mother countries of the Magyar and Polish minorities also watched closely the internal political events in the ČSR, and in an opportune moment demanded vigorously the rectification of their common borders with the ČSR. The charter of the League of Nations offered a possibility of correcting the injustices of the Treaty of Trianon, and Hungary could not abandon the likelihood of a peaceful change of frontiers, when millions of Hungarians lived for twenty years along her borders in the adjacent states. The disintegration of the Versailles system, and the strengthening of Germany's military position put the Czechoslovak government in a very delicate situation. Beneš, who built up his alliance system with the aim to help the French to encircle Germany, and with the Little Entente to enclose Hungary, found himself surrounded by the claimants of the territory of the republic on historical and ethnic grounds. Even his alliance with Soviet Russia did not help him. In 1938 the ČSR became isolated in her desperate efforts to maintain her impossible political structure. The Czechs, in order to save face, first tried to negotiate with the activists in the minority groups who in the past collaborated with the central government for the amelioration of the living conditions of the nationalities. Under the impact of events, the number of activists was diminishing, and drastic changes were needed to satisfy the demands.

The diplomatic history of the pre-Munich days is well known in every European language. It would be repetitious to mention here again the diplomatic exchanges and related events leading to the arbitration of the four Western European powers at Munich on 29 September, 1938, when Czechoslovakia had to give up the Sudetenland to Germany. The Czechs, holding their indefensible position, in spite of the advice of their allies, seemed resolved to provoke a European war for the maintenance of their political system. The official paper of the Czech legionnaires, the *Národní Osvobození,* on 31 May, 1938 commented on the return of the chairman of the Parliamentary Defence Committee from a month's visit to Soviet Russia, that the Soviet army would certainly come to the assistance of the ČSR if she were attacked. This of course was also duly noted in the Sudeten German press. Several similar declarations and organized mass meetings on the same lines misled the population. The allies of the republic in 1938 decided to follow a policy of peaceful settlement by negotiation and not by armed conflict. The British advised negotiations to the Czechoslovak government with Henlein after this latter's two visits in London in 1938. Prime Minister Hodža himself proposed to Paris the creation of an international commission if negotiations broke down. The British were thinking of offering a mediator as a sign of their interest in the fate of the ČSR, but Beneš still continued to evade the British advice.[42] Beneš made a remark to the French ambassador that he had begun to wonder whether France did not now feel that the ČSR was becoming a burden to the English and whether the French government did not contemplate abandoning the policy they had followed for twenty years towards this country.[43] The stage for a peaceful solution of the problem was set, and the Czechs had to call meetings first with the Sudeten Germans and later with the Hungarians, Poles, Slovaks and Ruthenians. The outcome of these long and painful exchange of demands altered the composition of the first Czechoslovak republic without resorting to a European war.

Contacts Among the Representatives of the Minorities

Before the nationality question arrived at its final stage, the Czechs had ample opportunity to solve the problem internally. On

April 3, 1930, eighty Sudeten German, Hungarian, Ruthenian and Polish deputies signed a petition in which they demanded the formation of a parliamentary committee for the regulation of the minority problem according to article 22 of the rules of the Chamber of Deputies. This motion was not discussed because of the resistance of the Czech parties.[44] The German Christian Socialist Party, one of the activist groups, submitted its demands on 26 June, 1936 to Prime Minister Hodža which contained political, religious, national wishes, equal arrangements for schooling, participation in the state administration, fair share in the economic life, ending the denationalization, reform of the census laws and demand for a German broadcasting station.[45] A similar demand was aired in a memorandum on 27 June, 1937 by all the German activist parties.[46]

The Hungarian opposition parties and the Slovak Populist Party demanded equal rights and autonomy for Slovakia. Autonomy for Ruthenia was still not granted by the Prague government in spite of pressures in this respect. President Beneš was not sincere in his Christmas radio speech of 1937 when he promised an improvement in the life of the national minorities and the elimination of the causes of grievances. Two weeks later, Dérer, a Czechophile Slovak cabinet minister, went as far in his hatred for the Slovak autonomists that he declared publicly that the collaborators of Hlinka were political snivelling brats and rascals.[47] The ruling class in Prague had no understanding at all for the views of their political adversaries who were forced in opposition because they were not willing to accept Bohemian domination. The minorities were the victims of the change in state sovereignty. They had to unite their actions against the conquerors who subjugated them not on the battlefields but with the help of their supporters at the negotiating tables around Paris in 1918 and 1919.

The Hungarian minority was in a weaker negotiating position than the Sudeten Germans. They were less numerous, and behind them there was a mutilated, disarmed Hungary, surrounded by the triple military alliance of the Little Entente on her borders. Consequently, it could give only a marginal external encouragement to the brethren living in minority status in the neighbouring countries. The ČSR, in her constant fear, was heading toward a military dictatorship to intimidate her minorities and neighbours alike by giving the impression of being a heavily armed camp. The government barricaded itself behind a well equipped army, border fortifications, and oppressive legislation. In 1937 a Bill was introduced in Parliament for national defence education. Reasons for the need of that Bill were given in the deterioration of the external political situation of the republic. Many laws of the ČSR deeply interfered with the private rights of her citizens, of their social life, and of the activities of social organizations.[48] Many laws were in contrast with democratic principles and human freedom.

The only path for achieving better relations between the government and the national minorities, and between the ČSR and her neighbours was the Czech recognition of the fatal mistakes and imprudent provisions of the peace treaties, the extension of full and equal rights to all citizens and above all the peaceful revision of the borders. The Czechs had based their political existence on the treaties of friendship concluded with other powers. In 1938 those arrangements were no longer functional. The interference of the great powers in the affairs of the Danubian basin had its dangerous concomitants. Foreign ideologies — in the case of Czechoslovakia the Soviet Russian, in the case of Hungary the German and Italian — started their penetration parallel with the various treaties signed with these governments. The military alliance of the Little Entente still existed against Hungary but the Hungarian government demanded equal military rights. This changed Hungarian position gave a more secure feeling to the Magyar minority in the ČSR. Even in Paris the protection of the Magyar minority by Hungary found more favourable response than in earlier times.[49]

The parliamentary elections of 1935 and the strengthening of the opposition gave a serious signal to the government of Prague to formulate new policy towards the national minorities. Although it was very dangerous from the standpoint of individual liberty to criticize the Czechs and their institutions as they were protected by laws, nevertheless, it was the duty of the Hungarian opposition parties to defend bravely, in spite of the envisaged heavy punishments, the interests and rights of the Hungarian population. President Beneš was forced to speak on internal political questions during his travels in the country.

On 11 September, 1936, Beneš invited the Chairman of the United Hungarian Party, count Esterházy, to his summer residence in Slovakia, and expressed his views on the general European political situation. Later he switched over to the internal problems of the ČSR, and mentioned that a coalition government was the only possible way of governing the country. He offered to consider the participation of the United Hungarian Party in the government of Prague to prevent the persecution of the Hungarian minority in the ČSR if there were a revolution or some other internal political changes in Hungary. In such a case, repercussions would be taken inevitably against the Magyars in the ČSR. It was a hidden menace by the President of the republic. Beneš was thinking of a ministry without portfolio with a certain budget of which the Hungarian minister would dispose freely. The minister would be able to develop the approved Hungarian cultural institutions with that fund. The Hungarian minister, furthermore, would have free access to the President, and could formulate demands. Beneš was thinking of Esterházy himself as a minister without portfolio. He was a courageous advocate of the Hungarian cause, and was not disturbed by the fact that there were many legal procedures pending against him. Those were originated by the Czechoslovak autorities. Beneš admitted that he knew of the errors which had been committed against the Magyars by the Prague government, and that they should be rectified. He checked a list presented by Esterházy to the President's secretary a few days earlier. Beneš added that he was against the revision of the borderline in favour of Hungary. Esterházy, avoiding the question of borders — it was dangerous because of the Defence of the Republic Act — told Beneš that the Hungarians did not want to serve the interests of their ethnic group in the framework of a Czechoslovak coalition government. The Magyars were not looking for opportunism. Such persons were not regarded as Hungarians who escaped to the ČSR after the defeat of the first Hungarian Soviet republic and who for financial compensation served the interests of the Prague government. Esterházy further explained to Beneš the policy of denationalization pursued by the government and its agencies. The Hungarian deputy did not believe that Hungary was nearing a revolution, and if the Magyar minority were persecuted in the ČSR because of internal events in Hungary it would be the duty of the Hungarian minority leaders to take the case to international forums. The Magyars in the ČSR did not accept the offer of a cabinet post in the Prague government and did not remain silent. Their economic, cultural and linguistic grievances did not find a favourable hearing or remedy. The competent Czechoslovak authorities had to show their benevolence and understanding before anything could happen concerning the proposals of the President. Beneš asked Esterházy not to disclose to the press that the meeting between them took place.[50]

It was not the first meeting of Esterházy with Beneš. Towards the end of 1935 the ill-health of the President demanded the election of his successor. Masaryk wanted to see Beneš in that high position, and negotiations were initiated with the representatives of political parties. Among the first deputies it was count Esterházy to whom Beneš explained the wish of Masaryk as well as the importance of the Hungarian votes for himself. He admitted that many injustices were committed against the Hungarian minority, but he was willing to remove them in exchange for Hungarian support. Esterházy could not give any firm commitments alone, and recommended the invitation of Jaross, another Hungarian minority leader. Several days later a Hungarian delegation went to Hradsin, the castle of Prague. Beneš promised them everything they asked for but the delegation wanted a written confirmation of his statements. Beneš hesitated to commit himself in writing. Finally it was agreed upon that the reception of the Hungarian demands would be confirmed by Beneš. Of those demands only one point was fulfilled, a donation of Kč 100,000.00 ($30,300.) on one occasion to the Hungarian Mensa Academica in Pressburg. The Hungarian minority leaders were tricked by the future president of the republic who broke his word after his election.[51] Two months later a new nationality policy was promised by the Prague government, and the deliberations were based on the cooperation of the activist parties.

Meanwhile there were changes even in the activist camp. In 1937 the German activists forwarded a common list of demands to the Hodža government which was then working on a new nationality policy which did not provide enough concessions to the minorities. Beneš himself wanted to take a more active part in the management of the state affairs. He himself went to Belgrade in April to the Little Entente conference, the first time since he became President and had to abandon the foreign affairs portfolio. He thought his presence was needed to gain international support for the ČSR in the internal difficulties. The Prague government decided to start negotiations with the minorities, and a new nationality policy was unveiled on 12 November, 1937 and Hodža began his deliberations with the Sudeten German party on 16 November.

The Question of Minorities: an Internal and External Problem of Czechoslovakia

President Beneš and Prime Minister Hodža were vehemently against any kind of substantial concessions or autonomy for the territories inhabited by Germans, Slovaks, Hungarians, Ruthenians or Poles, and even more so against the revision of the borders in the regions of the national minorities. Both of them held their offices since the end of 1935, the year in which the parliamentary elections strengthened the opposition. The cause of the nationalities gained momentum through internal and external actions, reaching its climax in 1938. Twenty years earlier, when Beneš negotiated the southern borderlines of the future ČSR in Paris with the aid of the French, Hodža tried to do the same with the Hungarians in Budapest. In 1938 the political constellation was different, and the same methods could not be applied again for the deliberate misrepresentation of facts. By the irony of fate, it was the role of these two men to negotiate in 1938, under pressure from their allies, new borders with Germany, Poland and Hungary in albeit altered conditions. In 1918 the degradation of Germany and Hungary was a triumph for Beneš, Hodža and their associates; twenty years later the humiliation of the ČSR, the overthrow of its President and the dismissal of its Prime Minister was a failure of both men and the political concepts they represented. Their democracy was a disguised dictatorship for the non-Czech part of the population. It missed the essential elements of a democratic system: equality before the law and respect for the human dignity of national minorities. The minorities reciprocated to the Czechoslovak government appropriately when the opportunity arose. In self-defence it was their duty to end the perpetration of injustices committed against them by the users of political power in Prague. The Czech politicians were so confident in the inviolability of their power base, protected by treaties of alliances, a modern well-armed army, strategically located line of fortifications, a gendarmery, a police force and laws for the defence of the republic, that every susceptible move or deed by the opposition to the democracy of the Czechs could be nipped in the bud. This ultra self-confidence or political blindness of the Czech leaders resulted in delaying tactics and intransigence which ultimately produced outside intervention and resulted in the reduction of the territory of the republic in favour of Germany, Poland and Hungary, and a forcible granting of autonomy to the Slovaks and Ruthenians. All of these steps came too late, and were insufficient to save the artificial borders from disappearing.

Signs of danger for the continued maintenance of the Czech domination appeared after the May 1935 parliamentary elections the results of which clearly indicated an increased dissatisfaction of a large segment of the population with the government. During the following years, Beneš toured the country delivering speeches while Hodža introduced a new nationality policy in 1936. It was not called a minority policy; perhaps it suggested a new outlook of the old problem. This innovation did not signify a benevolent attitude to the badly neglected and mismanaged question. It was just a new appearance of an agitated confusion camouflaging an unwanted policy imposed on the government by events at home and abroad. Neither Beneš nor Hodža were sincere in the extension of full citizenship on every subject of the republic and introduction of truly democratic system of government. They were compelled to pretend before the general public that a democratic transformation was taking place which would save the government by getting around the thorny and acute problem without changing anything in the old practice.

The diplomatic activity and international interest in the Czecholovak question which culminated in 1938 is recounted in a plethora of literature. Hundreds of books and articles have been published on this subject as well as on the Sudeten German portion of the problem. The status of the Hungarian minority in the republic and the demands of this national minority has until now received less publicity. The Magyars exerted less pressure on Prague than the German minority.

During the pre-Munich years and during the 34 days between the Munich agreement and the Vienna arbitration, the Hungarian government and the Hungarian minority in the ČSR behaved more correctly towards the Czechoslovak government than the other nationalities of the republic. The six coalition parties of the Prague government had to negotiate with the leaders of the minorities, first of all, with the strongest group of the Sudeten Germans. Prague had to come out with some concessions, some plans as they called them, to pacify the nationalities and to try to give a chance for the captive minorities to lead a bearable life. The Czechs made a great mistake by waiting so long with the solution of the minorities question. It was getting late for finding a satisfactory answer. Germany became a military power, and the right for military equality for Hungary was recognized by the signatories of the Protocols of Rome.

Hungary was willing to discuss economic matters with the Prague government on condition that her equality in rearmaments and the question of the Hungarian minority was settled. At the end of April 1936 a Polish government delegation visited Budapest. There the Czechoslovak difficulties were discussed, and the Poles did not indicate any territorial claims at that time from the ČSR. They rather expressed their interest in the coordination of their policy with Hungary concerning Ruthenia.[52] For one thousand years, there was a common and peaceful border between Hungary and Poland, and the Poles longed for a safe southern border. They were encountered in east and west by their centuries old enemies. During the next two years the Poles displayed vigorous diplomatic activity for the re-establishment of the former common Polish-Hungarian border in the Carpathians.

The Sudeten Germans sought to establish contacts with the Hungarian minority leaders in the ČSR and desired to gain encouragement for them from Budapest.[53] They planned to send emissaries to the Hungarian government already in 1936 but the visit was delayed for two years.[54] They thought that the Hungarian minority in the ČSR was not aggressive enough and perhaps they needed emboldening from Hungary for the common cause. The Czechoslovak government in its uncomfortable political situation hardened the traditional oppressive measures against the minorities, and tried to involve even the Little Entente by asking for the transformation of the existing alliance into a regional treaty which would invoke the *casus foederis* if any of the contracting parties should be attacked from any direction.[55] Rumania and Yugoslavia did not want to cover the Czech internal problems nor commit themselves for the armed defence of the ČSR. The two Little Entente partners of the ČSR first in the economic sphere, later on the political front, moved closer to the axis powers, and consequently their negotiations with Hungary concerned the treatment of their Hungarian minorities and they were conducted on a different basis against a different backdrop than that found in Prague. Meanwhile Mussolini had openly endorsed the Hungarian revisionist aims in his speech in Milan on 1 November, 1936.

The Czech treatment of the minorities started receiving international attention, and it was impossible to hide it by inaction. Prague first used the policy of intimidation which had been employed on countless occasions in the past. The national minorities in the frontier zones lived in constant insecurity and threat due to the Defence of the Republic Act which was used against them very frequently. Even their cultural life was hindered by Prague. In April 1936 a planned Sudeten German cultural week by the Henlein Party at Aussig (Ústí nad Labem) had been prohibited by the government, and the direction of the party was informed that its official daily, *Die Zeit,* and its weekly magazine, *Rundschau,* could be interdicted because of their frequent confiscations by the censors. After such an overture, the possessors of power, Beneš and Hodža, at the end of the month invited the representatives of the Sudeten German Party to discuss the future political attitude of the party,[56] It was a naive approach from these two senior experienced politicians to think that the Sudeten Germans would confide them their future plans and tactics. In Beneš' view, the minority problem did not exist any longer in the ČSR, the minorities had more rights than they were entitled to, and nothing should be changed. Beneš, in his powerful position, did not want to hear of the legitimate grievances of the minorities and of their rectification by legislation. Under those conditions, the two parties were too far from each other and a common ground for serious negotiations did not exist. At home, the subdued nationalities incessantly demanded their rights secured for them in the peace treaty. However, the movement of the national minorities was supported abroad by the press and by members of several parliaments in various countries in Western Europe. These unforeseen occurences of foreign support forced the Czech leadership to alter its old strategy in internal policy. A satisfactory conciliation and compromise with the national minorities was a pressing problem, but in spite of the gravity of the situation, Hodža was talking only of cultural concessions, more language rights, and perhaps the usage of the names of localities in the language of the minority on the inscriptions of post offices and railway stations. These proposals were ridiculous when it was very well known by the government that the minorities had more serious demands: adjustments in making up the economic losses since 1918, equal budget for schools, sharing the public employment, and the public works, and administrative autonomy for the regions inhabited by the nationalities. The strengthening of the opposition in the 1935 elections was not a sufficient sign for a needed policy change in Prague. The stubborn standpoint of the government embittered the situation to such a degree that two years later, after the Austrian Anschluss, the rearmanent of Germany and Hungary and because of the cooperation between Italy and Germany, the concessions demanded in 1936 by the minorities did not satisfy them in 1938 when the balance of power tilted against the ČSR. In 1936 the Prague government rather negotiated the eventual concessions destined for the minorities with the activist politicians who represented only a small fraction of the ethnic groups. This proves that Prague did not want to negotiate in good faith and did not want to consider long overdue demands. On 18 February 1937, Hodža signed an agreement with three German activist ministers without portfolio in his own government (Appendix 5). It was presented to the press and foreign correspondents as a great accomplishment for the internal peace of the state.[57] The activist politicians were satisfied with little, insignificant concessions but these would not stop further impoverishment and misery in the Sudetenland or in the regions of Southern Slovakia where the Magyar minority lived in a similar situation. The official press release was replete with promises for the future material well-being of the Sudeten German population by giving them a greater share in public works, investments, social care, state employment, government subventions for cultural purposes and the use of German in their contacts with the state authorities. After eighteen years in power, the Czechs finally started thinking of granting some rights and promoting better living conditions but only to the largest minority group, and even that only under external pressures. The Henlein Party, indeed was very soon ready with the repudiation of the plan prepared by the government and its activist German ministers. Henlein in his speech in Aussig (Ústí nad Labem) enumerated the demands of his party on behalf of the Sudeten German population. He wanted to officially transform Czechoslovakia, corresponding to reality, into a nationality state. His main points were as follows: autonomy which was not in contrast with the unity of the state; recognition of a national group as a corporate unit for securing its free development within the borders of the state; administration for the autonomous territory for the safeguards of minority rights and reparations for the damages done to the Sudeten Germans since 1918.[58] In addition, the program of the Sudeten German Party included the introduction of laws in the Parliament for the protection of nationalities, and, in case of their rejection by the Czechs and their allies, secure foreign support. A strong Sudeten German union around one party was the reaction to the Czech imperialistic nationalism which denied democracy to the minorities who were fighting for their national existence. Hodža responded to the move of Henlein, and asked for a one year period to work out the details of an agreement.

Time was almost running out for the Czech counter-propositions. After 12 March 1938, Bohemia was militarily in the grips of Hilter from three sides. His will to unify the Germans with the Reich added militancy and boldness to the Sudeten dynamism. Every peaceful agreement was made impossible by the Czech opposition to moderate demands. The Czechs were thinking of accepting or provoking foreign intervention on their behalf, perhaps by the repetition of the brilliant performance of Beneš abroad during World War I with influence-peddling and falsification of well-known facts. Czech illusions were placed in the hope of solidarity with France and Russia, but not creating acceptable conditions for the citizens of the state. On 18 February 1937, the government signed a document with the Sudeten German activists for the application of the principle of proportionality which promised them a certain degree of state employment (Appendix 5).[59] Hodža did not negotiate with the opposition parties. The first step was not followed up by legislation, and therefore it could not have beneficial results for the internal political settlement. It was not continued even by any administrative measures or the part of the government. In reality nothing was changed in the life of the minorities and their old grievances did not get redress. The government was unwilling to allow the introduction of any reforms, and the activists themselves saw a stand-off. They themselves were convinced of the futility of their cooperation concerning the solution of the minority question. Eight months after the February agreement, Jaksch, deputy of the German Social Democratic Party, an ardent supporter of the government, made the following declaration in the Prague Parliament: "The German policy of understanding has in many fields failed to find practical recognition of its vital necessities. It would do no service to the cause to deny that even the most loyal adherents to the policy of understanding in the German camp are dissatisfied with the pace at which the February agreement is being put into effect. The consequences of the failure of the honest efforts embodied in the agreement can be averted no longer by words, but only by facts. From this point of view I am compelled to describe the national-political side of the account as unsatisfactory."[60] Hodža was using various tactics but was unable to secure in the constitution even minimal rights for the nationalities. These citizens of the republic in their desperate situation had to turn for support to their blood relatives across the state boundaries, although every contact with them was extremely dangerous for their personal security considering the strict dispositions of the Defence of the Republic Act. The great threat to the individual freedom in the ČSR made the internal problems explosive.

The Magyar minority lived under the same civic restrictions as the other nationalities. The authorities arrested and sentenced hundreds of Hungarians for wearing the Hungarian tricolor, singing the Hungarian national anthem or listening to it on the radio if it was heard and reported to the police, for participation in balls in Hungary and noticed in the ČSR, for living in university residences in Hungary, for singing innocent military songs, for taking Levente (Cadet) cigarettes ornated with the tricolor across the Czechoslovak border from Hungary.[61] If the newspapers wrote about the complaints of the minorities, they were confiscated by the censors before their appearance on the news-stands. Complaints could not be aired; even the printed words menaced the existence of the state. This policy of intimidation created only brave fighters and many martyrs on the minority front.

Yet, there were some Czech voices in the Prague Parliament which did not approve the permanent obstruction of the minority question by the government and the President. Beran, the Chairman of the Czech Agrarian Party and chief opponent of Beneš, who tried to thwart the election of Beneš to the presidency, wrote an article in the newspaper *Venkov* (Countryside) in its New Years' Day issue, recommending the consideration of political realities and include the Sudeten German and Slovak Populist parties in the government by offering them portfolios.[62] This possibility of cooperation with the opposition for saving the republic was hinted to the President before Germany's annexation of Austria, a fatal incident not only for the independence of Austria but also for that of the ČSR. The article of Beran produced a sensation among the Czechoslovak politicians. They were not accustomed to such declarations. For them in the year of the twentieth anniversary of the foundation of the republic it was not desirable to accept all parties into the government, which disapproved the existence of the state. In Beneš' view more parties in the government would make governing more difficult. In Beran's view, even if more parties in the government made the task of governing more difficult, they lent proof to the strength of the government. In his opinion the relations with the minorities needed regulations. It was necessary to proceed in the direction which was expressed in the government's decision on February 18 of the previous year. There had to be an honest and worthy compromise with the Sudeten Germans. More than one-quarter million German voters gave confidence to the Sudeten German Party, and the necessary conclusions had to be drawn from it. They should recognize the ČSR and not keep dreaming over the borders. In communities and institutions where they form the majority, the leadership must be given to them with proportional representation to the Czech population. Similarly, they should share in the government of the country. Every German should not be regarded as a traitor because he belongs to the same party. It cannot be regarded as a heroic act if the Vice-Speaker of the Chamber of Representatives does not give a ticket to the gallery of the Chamber to the Chairman of that party which has received the largest number of votes at the elections. This is not the road towards an agreement. The policy makers have to proceed with dignity and responsibility. All the members of the minorities know that in time of danger the whole Czechoslovak nation which suffered for centuries wants to conclude a compromise with the citizens belonging to other nationalities. His wish is that the year of the jubilee might bring a tight cooperation with those nationalitites with whom until now there were many misunderstandings."[63]

The declaration of Beran carried much weight because in the same issue the *Venkov* published an interview with Henlein, who among other things, said the following: Let us remember the time of the origin of the state. The feeling of satisfaction filled every Czech and Slovak, but the Germans think back with depression and mourning to the year 1918. It is not the year of victory but the year of the German defeat, as it has always been emphasized from the Czech side. However, if we cast a glance at the past twenty years, one can see that in the Czech camp the minds start to clear up. Here are not only satisfied people but also dissatisfied Germans, Slovaks, Hungarians and Poles. If the twentieth year of the republic could produce such a feeling that this state is our state, then we could have a celebration which corresponds to the reality. We wish to all nations of the republic but first of all to the Czechs that they should dispose of such wisdom and self-criticism that they might have a successful year in 1938. In that year the ideological and power constellation is different from that of 1918. The Czech nation is older than this state, and its historic tradition lays an obligation on the Czech people. He would like to see that the Czechs think back to the Austrian times when they were in a similar situation as the Sudeten Germans in 1938. They have to understand the mood of the Sudeten Germans. The Czechs have the power to make offers for a better understanding.[64] Beran wanted to influence the internal and international relations with his article, and Henlein wanted to prepare the Czech public opinion for the next phase of the confrontation in the minority policy with the government.

The New Year began with a concentrated attack on the government of Prague not only by the Sudeten Germans but also by the Slovak and Ruthenian autonomists as well as by the Magyar and Polish minorities. The Sudeten Germans took over the leadership of the opposition, and prepared the formation of the minority front against Prague. A delegation of the Sudeten German Party went to the parish of Hlinka in Rosenberg (Ružomberok, Rózsahegy) on 8 February, 1938 to discuss the cooperation between the two parties, and to establish a liaison for harmonizing the basic principles of a common policy.[65] From Rosenberg, Kunzel and Frank, deputies of the Sudeten German Party, went to Budapest for an informal meeting with Pataky, Secretary of State of the Nationality Affairs in the Hungarian Prime Minister's Office, on the necessity for collaboration between the United Hungarian Party in the ČSR and the Sudeten German Party. They informed Pataky of their negotiations with the Slovaks, and the planned common Slovak-German-Magyar demonstrations in Pressburg on the occasion of the 20th anniversary of the Pittsburgh agreement. They also were received by Prime Minister Darányi, and Foreign Minister Kánya. Both of them assured the Sudeten deputies of their complete accord with the policy to be followed in the Czechoslovak question. At the expressed wish of János of Esterházy and Andor Jaross, leaders of the Hungarian minority in the ČSR, they also met the former Prime Minister, Bethlen, who already, in 1918 and 1919, tried to realize a cooperation between the Sudeten Germans and the Magyar minority.[66] The Slovak autonomists set out in 1938 with the motto: Attack in the New Year on Prague because Prague does not want to agree on anything.[67] Beneš had a meeting with Tiso of the Slovak Populist Party on 15 March but he did not want to hear of a Slovak administration of Slovakia, nor did he recognize the Pittsburgh agreement, and recommended that Slovaks become Czechoslovaks.[68] Under those auspices there could not be found a common basis for further negotiations between the Czechs and Slovaks under the leadership of Beneš.

The small (81,737) Polish minority in the ČSR also felt oppressed and wanted to live with their own race in Poland. The government in Warsaw in the early months of 1938 dealt with the Czech question. In Poland there was an interest not only in the fate of the Polish population in the ČSR but also in the realization of a common frontier between Poland and Hungary. If Slovakia and Ruthenia were detached from Prague they should have been prevented from falling under German domination.[69] Warsaw was pressing on international forums for a common border with Hungary on the old border lines in the Carpathian mountains with the renewal of the safe historical border between the two friendly states. This could have been achieved easily had Hungary granted autonomy to the Slovaks and Ruthenians, where they belonged before 1918. A segment in the Slovak Populist Party, led by Sidor, preferred Polish orientation. He was the emissary on the part of the Slovaks to negotiate an agreement with the Poles. Poland did not want to occupy Slovakia, the former Hungarian territory, and conducted long discussions with Budapest on the potential cooperation for a common border. The key to this question, due to later developments, was in the hands of the National Socialist government of Germany. The Poles tried to persuade several European chancelleries of the desirability of the re-establishment of the old border between Poland and Hungary to form a barrier against the German expansion eastward. These anti-German plans reached Berlin. The common Polish-Hungarian border was realized only in March 1939, after the Hungarian annexation of Ruthenia, with German consent. The north-south concept of the Polish and Hungarian foreign policy was not new. For centuries the north-south line of the Poles, Hungarians and Serbs proved to be a successful barrier against the invaders from the east and south. This political orientation was changed under the reign of Sigismund of Luxembourg, King of Hungary and Bohemia and emperor of the Holy Roman Empire (1387-1437) because of his involvements in the Czech, German, Italian and Church affairs which turned his attention to Western Europe from the burning problems in Eastern Europe. Beck, the Polish Foreign Minister, presented the idea of a third Europe for consideration, a bloc from the Baltic to the Aegean and Adriatic Seas for safeguarding the independence of the small nations in that immediate area. It had an anti-German and anti-Russian edge. The political vacuum remaining after the destruction of Austria-Hungary had to be filled with the people living in that region and not by foreign invaders. This was felt instinctively by the Polish and Hungarian statesmen. The Polish government was scrutinizing the developments in the ČSR, and Beck in his speech on 12 January, 1938 before the Polish Foreign Affairs Committee said that any decision made by the ČSR in favour of her minorities, if not applied to the Polish minority, would be regarded by Poland as an unfriendly act.[70] The Prague government reacted to this open manisfestation of support for the Polish minority, and the Czechoslovak ambassador in Warsaw told Beck on 4 May that the Polish minority would enjoy the concessions granted to any other minority.[71]

In February 1938, Horthy, Kánya and Csáky made an official visit to Warsaw coordinating their plans on the minority question in the ČSR.[72] In March the Polish government gave its accord to the cooperation of the Polish political parties in the ČSR with the United Hungarian Party. The Czechs made an unsuccessful attempt to divide the governments of Poland and Hungary by treating their minorities differently. Esterházy was consulted in Budapest on the Slovak affairs and had talks with the Slovak Populist Party concerning the future of Slovakia. There were constant high level negotiations on political and military questions between Poland and Hungary. The Poles were very much concerned with the standing of Hungarian-Slovak relations. They knew that there had been some contacts between them through the mediation of the United Hungarian Party in the ČSR, and that Hungary had offered autonomy for Slovakia in case of the change of the ČSR borders. The Poles regarded the future status of Slovakia and Ruthenia as members of Hungary, and in April 1938, according to instructions given to the Hungarian ambassador, Hitler did not claim Pressburg nor other parts of Slovakia.[73] Tiso, leader of the Slovak Populist Party, had a chance to talk to the Hungarian Foreign Minister, Kánya, on the occasion of the Eucharistic Congress in Budapest at the end of May, but there are no details available of this meeting.[74] The Slovaks had more confidence for negotiations in the Hungarians living in the ČSR than in those in Hungary, and had certain reservations concerning an autonomous Slovakia within Hungary. This was the explanation extended to Esterházy on his visit to the Polish Foreign Office in the course of preparations made for the case of the liquidation of the ČSR in June.[75] From the Polish and Hungarian point of view the concern was understandable facing the menace of placing the whole of Czechoslovakia under German control. In such an eventuality, the fate of Poland and Hungary, they thought, would be similar to that of the ČSR after the Austrian Anschluss. A secure border was vitally important for both countries. For this reason so much time and effort was spent in Warsaw and Budapest on Polish-Hungarian diplomatic contacts and on the nationality problem of the ČSR.

Footnotes

1. Kramer, Juraj, *Slovenské autonomistické hnutie*, Čsl. Časopis Historický, IX, 1961, 346.

2. Hoensch, Jörg, *Die Grundlagen des Programms der Slowakischen Volkspartei*, 320.

3. Dvortchak, Victor, *Aide-mémoire sur la Question Slovaque*, 6.

4. Ibid., 11

5. Jehlička, François, *Le problème slovaque*, 10.

6. Dvortchak, Op. cit., 7.

7. Hoensch, Op. cit., 334.

8. Mlynárik, Jan, *Slovenská národná rada a včelovanie Slovenska do Československého štátu, 1918-1919,* Čsl. Čas. Hist., VI, 1968, 513.

9. Jandera, A. A., *Kapitoly z dejín předmnichovské republiky,* Praha, Orbis, 1953. 201-202.

10. Jehlička, Op. cit., 11.

11. Macartney, Op. cit., 145.

12. Miksche, Op. cit., 32.

13. Burian, Peter, *Chanzen und Grenzen des sudetendeutschen Aktivizmus,* 135.

14. Chmelář, Joseph, *Le problème allemand en Tchécoslovaquie,* Prague, Orbis, 1936, 45.

15. Hoensch, Jörg, *Der ungarische Revisionismus und die Zerschlagung der Tschechoslowakei,* 19.

16. Ibid., 93.

17. Nittner, Ernest, *Dokumente zur sudetendeutschen Frage,* 90.

18. Ibid., 98

19. Chmelář, Op. cit., 125.

20. Nittner, Op. cit., 125.

21. Ibid., 124.

22. Public Record Office (PRO), FO. 371/21738, 205.

23. Macartney, Op. cit., 179.

24. Ibid., 180.

25. Miksche, Op. cit., 32.

26. Ibid., 36.

27. Nittner, Op. cit., 126.

28. Burian, Op. cit., 147.

29. Duff, Grant, *Europe and the Czechs,* 153.

30. Nittner, Op. cit., 128.

31. César, Joroslav — Bohumil Černý, *Politika německých boržoazních stran v Československu v letech 1918-1938,* Praha ČAV, II, 1962, 314.

32. Ibid., 315.

33. Private interview with Dr. Walter Brand, formerly of the Sudeten German Party, on 5 July, 1972 at Waldkraiburg in Bavaria

34. Schramm, Gottfried, *Češi a Němci v ČSR,* Dějiny a Současnost, 8, 1968, 15.

35. Leták, Miroslav, *V osidlech zrady,* Praha, S vobodné Slovo, 1965, 226.

36. César — Černý, Op. cit., 317.

37. George, Pierre, *Le problème allemand en Tchécoslovaquie, 1919-1946,* 53.

38. César — Černý, Op. cit., 391.

39. Ibid., 392.

40. Ibid., 393.

41. Vnuk, F., *Munich and the Soviet Union,* Journ. of Cent. Eur. Aff., XXI, Oct. 1961, 293.

42. PRO, FO. 371/21723, 3 June, 938.

43. Ibid., 341/21726

44. Jakabffy, E., *A szudétanémetek,* Magyar Kisebbség, 1936, 298-299.

45. Nittner, Op. cit., 148.

46. Ibid., 154.

47. Prágai Magyar Hirlap (PMH), 10 January, 1938.

48. Pesti Hirlap, 25 June, 1937.

49. Lidové Noviny, 27 May, 1937.

50. Ádám, Magda, *A müncheni egyezmény létrejötte és Magyarország külpolitikája, 1936-1938,* II, No. 32.

51. Čulen, Konštantin, *Po Svätoplukovi druhá naša hlava,* (Život Dr. Josefa Tisu), Middletown, Jednota, 1947, 169-170.

52. *Československá otázka v diplomatických spisoch Horthyovskéko Maďarska,* Hist. Čas., XIV, 1966, 626.

53. *A müncheni egyezmény...,* No. 11.

54. Ibid., No. 14.

55. Ibid., No. 40.

56. Ibid., No. 14.

57. Szvatkó, Pál, *A csehszlovák-szudétanémet kiegyezés kisérlete,* Magyar Szemle, XXX, May 1937, 71.

58. Ibid., 73-74.

59. *München eine offene Frage,* München, Ackermann, Heft 12, 1938, 10.

60. Survey of International Affairs, 1937, 457.

61. Balla, P., Op. cit., 25.

62. Venkov, 1 January, 1938.

63. PMH, 2 January, 1938.

64. Ibid.

65. D.G.F.P., Series D, II, 124-125.

66. Ibid., 135.

67. Ibid., 190.

68. Čulen, Op. cit., 193-194.

69. Cienciela, *Poland and the Eastern Powers,* 56.

70. Ibid., 60.

71. Ibid., 72.

72. *A müncheni egyezmény...* No. 135.

73. Ibid., No. 152.

74. Tilkovszky, Loránt, *A revizió és nemzetiségpolitika Magyarországon,* 22.

75. *A müncheni egyezmény...* No. 250.

CHAPTER V

ALLIANCE OF THE
DISCONTENT NATIONAL MINORITIES

Confrontations with the Representatives of the National Minorities

For twenty years, the Prague government excluded the elected representatives of national minorities from policy-making because they remained in opposition. Deals were made solely with fractional minority parties or subsections of Czech parties having bought up members of the minorities who were used as spokesmen for an entire ethnic group. The disregard for the interests of the nationalities dit not prove to be an adequate path in the promotion of the citizens' welfare. No political party received a clear majority during the existence of the first ČSR, except the Sudeten Germans in 1935. They, as well as the other ethnic groups, were a proscribed nationality in the democracy of the Czechs. The strongest Sudeten German Party was not invited to participate in the government, although, according to rule of the parliamentary democracy, the strongest party must be invited to form the government. Perhaps the Czech Agrarian Party tried to change old practices in 1938 and suggest a new political strategy by moving to the right of centre in the government coalition. President Beneš, and the coalition party leaders, caused political chaos by ignoring the majority representation of the nationalities in governing the country.

The rulers in Prague divided the minorities into two groups: deserving privileges or punishment. The privileged were those who accepted smaller or larger favours from the government. They increased the distrust of a large population segment in the government. For those few individuals a minority problem officially did not exist. The dissatisfied minorities, more than 50% of the population, waged a constant struggle with the overlords in Prague. The constitution secured rights for the minorities, but for twenty years those obligations were not met and the nationalities suffered significant losses in all walks of life. The dirigents of the republic missed an excellent opportunity in February 1937 to prove their goodwill and accept responsibility for a just compromise with the nationalities when the activist minority politicians asked for reforms and concessions. The government in its first nationality plan made some significant promises to the oppressed millions. These promises contained the use of the languages of minorities in the pamphlets, on the information sheets and on some buildings of the national railways and post offices. For the minorities it meant that they would have been able to read, in their language, the promotional material for tourism or the names of some railway stations. The realization of promises would have meant for the Magyar minority that bilingual publications or inscriptions would have appeared in those communities where they formed 50% of the population, according to Czechoslovak statistics. For the Polish minority a 20% presence was promised in the new definition of the language rights. The demands of minorities went beyond inscriptions on railway stations which should have been there from the very beginning of the ČSR's existence. Hungarians had a right to 24,000 positions in the national railway company and post offices based on their proportionate population, but only 7,000 Hungarians were employed by these state enterprises.[1]

There was widespread disappointment regarding the lack of seriousness in the approach of the government to urgently needed solutions of internal problems. The concern was expressed in a joint interview with the leaders of the autonomist opposition parties arranged by the managing editor of the *Slovák*, Sidor, on Sunday, 27 February, 1938. Sidor was one of the leading deputies of the Slovak Populist Party. The invited, among them Esterházy, deputy of the United Hungarian Party, Henlein for the Sudeten German Party and Pješčák for the Ruthenian Autonomous Agrarian Party, were ready to answer questions from reporters. One year had passed since the promised reforms of the government, however, the grievances of the minorities were not redressed. Slovak autonomists started the offensive in the press. In the year of the twentieth anniversary of the republic and of the signature of the Pittsburgh agreement, autonomy for Slovakia was not yet codified. All three opposition party leaders unanimously demanded autonomy for their minority groups, including a free national development guarantee in the constitution. Esterházy emphasized the thousand-year old common fate and goals of the Slovaks and Magyars.[2] The government was supposed to have eased the harsh treatment of the Magyars since February 1937. In spite of the promises, exactly one year after the announcement of better prospects for the future, the gendarmerie harassed members of the United Hungarian Party in the town of Királyhelmec (Královský Chlumec) who wanted to attend a meeting of the party by blockading the building and asking for personal identification cards from those intending to enter. Many of them were forced to leave the premises.[3] This occurrence along with similar incidents did not augur an era of undisturbed relations between the government and the minorities. Hodža still wanted to negotiate through the activists, but it only served to aggravate the situation, internally and abroad. The neighbouring states could not watch with disinterest or indifference the manner their brethren were handled in the ČSR. Internal tension grew incessantly, and the autonomist front, representing more than 50% of the population, was united in its demand. It was impossible to disregard the dissatisfaction of the autonomists; therefore, Prime Minister Hodža decided to negotiate with them neglecting consideration for the introduction of much needed reforms. The government wanted to side-step the minority problem rather than solve it.

Confrontations with the Hungarian Minority

From the beginning of 1938, the Prime Minister was involved in endless negotiations with the representatives of the opposition parties, activist groups, foreign governments and with the members of his own cabinet, until his resignation from office in September of the same year, concerning the nationality issue. There were rectifications needed in many purposeful anti-Hungarian actions of the government. Prague was aware of the grievances: the colonization of Czech, Moravian and Slovak farmers on the land confiscated from Hungarians and settling them among totally Hungarian villages; the forced denationalization; the anti-Hungarian school policy; the economic weakening of the Magyar minority; the deception in public opinion by misleading propaganda and the generally dishonest use of political means for maintaining a distorted image of the real face of Czechoslovak democracy. It was a great mistake on the part of the politicians in power to attempt the creation of a national state from a typical state of nationalities. There were very few counties in the ČSR where the language spoken by the various nationalities could not be heard. Hungarian political leaders informed the Prime Minister that they had a solidarity feeling with the Slovaks and other autonomists but they assumed their responsibility and were willing to negotiate with the government. An amended constitution could afford the Hungarian minority compensation for sufferings and grievances since the foundation of the republic. The latest offer for the extension of the language law to the inscriptions on some railway stations and post offices was not a satisfactory reform for the Hungarian opposition. The Magyars wanted to find the way to their prosperity in the ČSR. They were the autochtonous population in Slovakia, and were not the result of assimilation or Magyarization.[4] Esterházy, Jaross and Szüllő were the three leaders who were invited by Beneš, as Foreign Minister in 1935, and their votes were solicited for their support in the presidential election in exchange for promises eventually not honoured.

On 12 January, 1938 Jaross presented the demands of the United Hungarian Party in the Chamber of Deputies in Prague. On 5 April he presented them again in 12 points, demanding equal rights for the Magyar minority, reparation of damages since 1918 caused in the administration of justice, citizenship procedures, public administration, language laws, educational policy, census, and demanded autonomy for Slovakia and Ruthenia.[5] But the aim of the Czechs remained the denationalization of the Hungarians under their rule, the destruction of their national conscience, the impairment of their economic, political and cultural forces. For twenty years the Hungarians resisted the powerful pressure of the Czechoslovak government.

On 31 March, 1938, the deputies of the United Hungarian Party issued a manifesto calling for unity and solidarity among the Hungarians of the republic. They asked Magyar farmers, workers, tradesmen, public employees and university graduates to join a camp of courageous warriors for rightful Magyar demands.[6] That manifesto of the members of the Czechoslovak Parliament was confiscated in several counties. It happened not long after the meeting of those deputies with the Prime Minister for finding the path for improved relations between the two sides. There was a lack of sincerity on the part of the government. Its action was a bluff for internal consumption. In the same days, Hodža granted an interview to the foreign correspondent of the *Paris Soir*[7] demonstrating to the French that he was negotiating with the opposition on the solution of the problems, and wanted to save the state from a permanent crisis. The legitimate demands of the nationalities in the cultural and linguistic fields or in the proportionality of state employment, and economic advantages could be met within the framework of the liberal, democratic Czechoslovak constitution. The same reporter questioned the Sudeten German leader, Henlein, who intimated that the Sudeten Germans would like to assume responsibility in the leadership of the republic by becoming members of a government together with the Czechs and Slovaks. For this reason they asked for administrative and financial autonomy, and proportionality in public offices.

These were nice words from the Prime Minister, but the mortgages for capital levy and on the lands designated for confiscation by the Land Office had still not been released. Hungarian proprietors did not dispose freely of their holdings after twenty years of waiting. Another step was characteristic of the weaknesses and sinister intentions of the government. In May and June of 1938, communal elections were held in the ČSR. Already on 1 April, the Minister of Interior ordered the ban on all public and political meetings based on the decision of the government. The pretext was given for not disturbing the prevailing tone of the 20th year of jubilee. The real cause can be discovered in preventing the political parties from presenting their platform and program to the electors. Detailed information was sent to appropriate law enforcement agencies before the dates of communal elections were made public. Only the presidium of the political parties could conduct confidential meetings. Even such meetings were controlled by the police. A list containing the names of persons present had to be signed, and identification cards shown; the police obtained the name and address of every participant.[8] This kind of dictatorial method had been employed by the government against rival political parties. The government could not, and did not find remedies for the grievances of minorities without changing its policy. At the 1935 presidential election, confidence was given by the Hungarian opposition parties in advance to Beneš in exchange for his promises of a just minority policy. They were disappointed with his performance as president. Nothing transpired, only small, insignificant actions. Three years later the ČSR got into a very difficult political situation. The government of a state full of nationalities was thoroughly cognisant of the minority demands, but wanted to oppress them indefinitely and deprive them of their rights and remain unpunished.

In the April 8 issue of the *Prágai Magyar Hirlap,* the official newspaper of the Magyar opposition, the speech of deputy Jaross delivered three days earlier in the Chamber of Deputies was summarized. The United Hungarian Party demanded a change in the internal and external political orientation of the government: emancipation and autonomy for all nations in the republic, compensation to the Hungarians for all losses caused to date by inequality before the law; in the regions where Hungarians lived, hiring of civil servants in proportion to the population, and where they formed the majority, the direction should be in Magyar hands; in Magyar language schools and other institutions of education officials should be elected by the population, the demanded Hungarian schools should be opened and the schools of the *Slovenská Liga* in purely Hungarian regions should be removed because they had been established there to serve denationalization; freeing the agricultural production from the restrictions of the state monopolies and assuring of its competitiveness by customs agreements; the Czech, Moravian and Slovak colonies and residual properties in the Hungarian language belt should be distributed among Hungarian farmers; the establishment of the minimum salaries should be introduced; Hungarian workers should be protected by restricting the hiring of others than unemployed Hungarians; the use of Hungarian tradesmen in public works and a system of compensation for dismissed Hungarian public servants and pensioners; further demands were: establishment of national cadastres in every community for securing a complete equality among all nationalities, passing laws for the punishment of denationalization, autonomy for Slovakia and Ruthenia, termination of the military alliance with the Soviet Union and political agreements with the neighbouring countries. The efforts of all the nations of the republic should be used for the preservation of the state.[9]

At the end of March the Czech *Národní Politika* published an editorial in a similar tone.[10] It stated that nothing else was left but to acknowledge the failure of activism and to review the demands of the Sudeten Germans, whether they were compatible with the sovereignty of the state. It was important for all citizens, regardless of their language, to feel satisfied in the common fatherland and not to give them reason to look over the borders. In spite of such rare Czech voices, tempers were very high in those months, and incidents easily erupted over the most innocent comments made in public places or in the streets. People were detained by the police on the basis of Law No. 20, paragraph 2, which said: "Those who ridicule the name of the republic, its crest, its flag or the picture of the President or damage or remove them in order to lower the dignity of the republic or of the president of the republic, are punishable for that offense with a jail sentence from eight days to six months."[11] Under those conditions it was dangerous even to talk aloud in the streets or at public gatherings.

In such a charged atmosphere it should have been wise for the government to announce as soon as possible the promised nationality statute. It was delayed because the government was helpless and indecisive concerning the contents of the proposed concessions to the minorities. Advice was sought through diplomatic channels in Paris and London. In the ČSR the interested parties did not yet know anything of the reforms in the making; however, the *London Times* on 4 May[12] already had inside information concerning the main points of the nationality statute: change in the language law, that German would be recognized as equivalent with the Czech and Slovak languages; the recognition of cultural autonomy for all nationalities with its own budget; introduction of the languages of ethnic groups in cultural and educational matters; public service jobs in proportion to all ethnic groups; ombudsman for the enforcement of the language law. It was felt that the government could not postpone the negotiations with the nationalities for a long time. The United Hungarian Party handed to the Prime Minister on 9 March — that is prior to Henlein's proclamation of this eight Karlsbad points — the demands of the Hungarian minority elaborated in detail in eighty-one points. The memorandum contained the legal, cultural and economic grievances of the Hungarian population. In the view of the Hungarian deputies, the problem could be solved only by the revision of the constitution.[13] They demanded the participation of all nations of the republic in the work of the new constituent assembly which was not the case in 1918. On the economic front the memorandum demanded a Hungarian management of financial institutions, credit unions, the rebuilding of the dismantled industrial enterprises in the Magyar regions, a Hungarian agricultural chamber, a wheat board, reinstating the Hungarian landowners in their properties, urgent regulation of rivers, including the systematic dredging of the Danube, 10 million Kč for land improvement, change in railway tariffs for making the agricultural and industrial products of Slovakia competitive with those of the Czech historic lands.[14] The United Hungarian Party tried to obtain rehabilitation for the two-decade-old grievances. The Sudeten German Party took note of the Hungarian memorandum with Henlein asking Esterházy for closer cooperation on 9 April, after the Sudeten leader's visit to Hodža.[15] Since 1935, Henlein had made several trips to London. The British also wanted to obtain information from the original Hungarian source on the nationality problem in the ČSR. The Hungarian Committee of the House of Commons invited two Hungarian deputies of the Prague Parliament, Géza Szüllő and Andor Jaross, for a visit to London.[16] A list of the grievances and demands of the Hungarian minority was presented and explained to the British policy-makers leaving little doubt on the urgency of internal reforms in the ČSR. The visit took place in June because of communal elections at the end of May.[17]

The British government was examining the possibility and necessity of sending an observer to the critical territory. During the end of May and beginning of June, the British and French newspapers were reporting the travels of William Strang, chief of the Central European section of the British Foreign Office, to Paris, Berlin and Prague. London wanted to contact the interested and involved parties by sending their officials and members of the Parliament to the ČSR and to her neighbours, and inviting the representatives of the national minorities from the ČSR to London to explain the causes of their grievances and the reasons for their demands. Prague was in the forefront of international interest, and Beneš could not remain silent in such a situation. He granted an interview to the French newspaper *L'Ordre*,[18] in which he pronounced that the Czechs could face most grave consequences if they were not determined to apply necessary measures resulting in internal and external peace. The people would accept the fulfillment of those demands which were compatible with national security but would not cede any national territory to foreign governments without erecting brave defence. The Czech people had more confidence in their allies than in their nationalities but unexpected news started to pour in the ČSR. According to the information of the *Prager Presse*,[19] a message was sent to Prague from Paris through ambassador Osuský urging the most liberal statutes to the Sudeten Germans. This was emphasized since the government refused the eight Karlsbad points of Henlein after their proclamation in April. The French were afraid of provoking a crisis by Czech intransigence and wanted to advise caution and flexibility. It was difficult for the Czechs to accept the idea of satisfying the demands of the nationalities. In pre-war Hungary there was an autonomous county system for internal administration but it was changed in Slovakia, and an administrative monster was created throughout the republic. The counties elected their own officials. In the ČSR the autonomists had asked for it, too. Prime Minister Hodža, at the end of June 1938, decided to receive the leaders of the opposition parties at an audience including the Sudeten Germans, the Slovak autonomists, the Poles, the Ruthenians and the Hungarians. On 29 June the Polish opposition handed over the memorandum of the committee of Polish parties, and on the same day the Hungarian representatives were received by the Prime Minister. The official press release read: "On June 29 at 11:00 a.m. at the invitation of Dr. Milan Hodža, Prime Minister, on behalf of the United Hungarian Party Dr. Géza Szüllő, Andor Jaross, János Esterházy and Dr. Endre Korláth, members of Parliament, appeared at the Prime Minister's office. The Prime Minister was briefed on the written memorandum of the party, delivered some time ago, and on the implementation of the basic principles expressed in it. The members of the legislation had an occasion to inform the Prime Minister in detail of the vital requests of the Hungarians in Czechoslovakia."[20] The Prime Minister did not say anything to the representatives of the five ethnic groups regarding the nationality statute in preparation. This attitude of the government added to the uncertainty of the problem. The word "statute" was constantly used instead of "legislation" or "changes in the constitution." In other words, there were plans for lesser changes only through ordinances and not by legislation. The problem of the minorities could have been solved only by changes in the constitution which would have clearly spelled out equality before the law of all nationalities. Only such recognition would have ended the existing discrepancies and inequalities concerning the rights of citizens. There were no provisions in the constitution for the use of government statutes. Perhaps an order in council would have been equivalent to a statute, but in that case, the word statute would only have camouflaged the insincere intentions of the government. The interests and legal status of the minorities short of legislative changes would have been exposed to the caprices of governments and the composition of the Parliament. Rights ought to be secured in a constitution. The leaders of the nationalities had every reason to doubt the good intentions of the government when they saw the unnecessary delays in the publication of reforms concerning their fate. Such tactics would only serve to make permanent their lasting oppression in the democracy of the Czechs. On 20 July, Hodža received again the leaders of the United Hungarian Party, and outlined the planned Bills for the next parliamentary session. It suggested that the government had some legislation in preparation. For the following weeks, the Prime Minister indicated the completion of the definite text of the reforms, language law, and plans for autonomy. The Hungarian representatives could not comment on unknown bills, and asked for the remedy of the grievances by legislation.[21] The government's obstruction was obvious because the voluminous material of the proposals had to be studied before being presented to Parliament which, at that time, was on summer vacation. This meant that the government wanted to postpone the presentation of the bills to Parliament until fall and to gain time in avoiding an embarrassing confrontation with the minority leaders which would reveal the real face of the Czechoslovak democracy. The Czechs were not able to free themselves from the troubles caused by the creation of the republic. The problem became more and more burning daily. There was feverish diplomatic action in the background, and Prague was waiting for the outcome of such diplomatic bustling. The intervention of the great powers was a possibility in the case of a deadlock in the direct negotiations between the interested parties.[22] A proposal was made by the German ambassador in Britain that an international conference should deal with the Czechoslovak problem. It should consist of Britain, France, Germany and Italy. It would mediate between the government and the Sudeten Germans. France first approved the plan for a four-power conference, later disapproved it, stating that such an international conference would meet the opposition of the USSR, Poland and the Little Entente.[23] Behind the internal problems of the ČSR there were international bargainings which grew to proportions too large for an undisturbed internal agreement. Beneš, Hodža and the coalition government showed their unwillingness toward eliminating the conflict by understanding the minority demands. This could be the only reason for the inexplicable retardation of government proposals for months in lieu of confronting their proposals with boldness to the opposition. The British press, time and again, hinted in competent diplomatic circles for an international mediation with the participation of Prague, Berlin, London, Paris and Rome.[24] Britian did not want to be involved in armed conflict on behalf of a malfunctioning Czechoslovak government. London was rather willing to convoke an international conference of those parties which were interested in the Czechoslovak problem. Chamberlain announced, in the House of Commons, that Lord Runciman had been asked to play a role in the Sudeten German dispute with the consent of the quarelling parties. The mediator would consider the views of all the minorities.[25]

By the end of July, the long awaited nationalities statute, or the second plan of the four plans, which were produced hurriedly before the beginning of September, was completed. Parts of it were released very slowly through some ostensible leaks to the press. It contained arrangements of the decentralization of the government between the capital city and the provinces. The provincial assemblies would be transformed into Parliaments with some restricted legislative power. Within these Parliaments, there would be national curiae for the management of certain nationality affairs. Grievances would belong to the jurisdiction of distinct councils in each province. The nationality statute contained the minority laws in force, and proposals taken from the memoranda of the minorities were added to them. There was a suggestion, for example, for protection against denationalization and political intimidation. These crimes would be punishable with maximum imprisonment of five years. The principle of proportionality would be gradually enforced in the public service, public works and budget. The interests of the minorities would be looked after in the administration, agriculture, commerce, social services, cooperatives and education. County school boards would be divided according to the languages spoken by the population. The percentage granting the use of the language of minorities in the public administration and courts would be lowered below 20% but the proportion was not yet determined.[26] In the following days, there were additional leaks to the press. The newer particularities of the plan reaffirmed the principle of equality before the law for all citizens. The nationality statute represented but a framework which had to be filled along the process of negotiations with the desired contents. The plan repeated some of the paragraphs in the constitution and added to them provisions for peace among the nationalities. The adherence to a minority was to be determined by the mother tongue which could be changed at the age of 18 by a declaration to the county administration. The proportional employment of all nationalities did not apply to the gendarmerie, police, customs police, army, army suppliers, air defence system, state plants, railways, post offices nor to the employment in mines.[27] The chief of staff declared that the nationality code could not be observed in the army, in the border fortresses, defence production, commissioned and non-commissioned officer corps. The army had two conditions for employment: trustworthiness and knowledge of the official language. With this declaration, the chief of staff inadvertently admitted that the soldiers enlisted from the minorities were not reliable.

The Hungarian opposition party kept pressuring the government for more concessions, and on 24 July deputy Szüllő demanded self-determination for the Hungarian minority.[28] In Stockholm, Szüllő represented the Hungarian minority of the ČSR at the congress of national minorities, called for the study of the problem of ethnic groups. The representatives had a common goal, namely, the preservation of ethnic culture and economic power. It was emphasized at the meeting that the League of Nations, which was entrusted with the enforcement of international treaties for the protection of minorities, became the greatest adversary of the protection. It appears, therefore, that between 1929 and 1935, from the 852 submitted grievances, only two emerged to the stage of ruling. The problem of the national minorities in Europe could be solved only with the extension of human rights, not with concessions and treaties.[29]

Confrontations with the Sudeten German Minority

In general, the Sudeten German question stood at the forefront in the ČSR of 1938 because of the importance of its consequences to the solution of the minorities problem. Yet, there was also a Slovak, Ruthenian, Polish and Hungarian question, and the conditions of the smaller nationalities were more grave than those of the Sudeten Germans. It was sad for them to realize that only numerical abundance counted in a constitutional state. The rights of the people were never determined by equal standards in the ČSR. Nevertheless, internal peace required equality before the law. On February 3, 1938, almost one year after the promised, supposedly new minority policy of the Hodža government, Spina, the Sudeten German minister without portfolio, announced that the Prime Minister shortly would present new proposals to regulate the minority problem. It was later discovered that it was only a reaction to the submission of the Sudeten German Party's motion for a new nationality policy. The government did not extend the use of the language law to the railways, postal services and state monopolies, which would have meant for the minorities the use of their language in contacts with these institutions. The excuse of the government was that only the Parliament could change the language law through legislation. However, the government had not introduced bills to this end. The support of the government by activist politicians was futile for the Sudeten German population.[30] In 1926 the activists initiated a historic turning point with their entry in the government of Prague, and in 1938 they provided another direction to the historical development of the republic with their exit from the government. The minorities condemned the activists as traitors for their role in the government. Several days after Hitler's march in Austria, the activists started to resign from the government, with the exception of the Social Democrats. The former activists joined the Sudeten German Party and demanded autonomy for the Sudetenland. They suddenly realized that the Czechoslovak-German border had stretched from 800 km to 1200 km. The French-German border was only 300 km in comparison with the delicate situation of the Czechs after 12 March, 1938.

The government of Prague suddenly discovered the existence of the Sudeten German Party, the largest party of the Czechoslovak Parliament and on April 1, three of their deputies were invited by the Prime Minister to discuss political questions.[31] It was a belated move because twenty years after World War I, and after twenty years under Czech rule, the fate of the Sudeten Germans became connected with the German government. Neither the Germans nor the other minorities expected anything positive to emerge from the planned minority statutes because they did not guarantee any progress in the protection of minority rights. They were to be the codification of the existing laws and decrees without any new content. The twenty-year experience had shown that those clauses were insufficient and the relations with the nationalities needed improvement through reform.[32] The Sudeten German Party held its party day on April 24 in Karlsbad. In his speech at that meeting, Henlein, the leader of the party, summarized the known demands of the Sudeten German population: complete equality and autonomy (Appendix 6). The party had 800,000 members together with the 212,000 increase of membership in March. He emphasized, for the record, that until that date his three attempts for rapprochment to the government were ignored first in 1934 at Böhmisch Leipa, then after the 1935 elections, when 70% of the Sudeten Germans manifested the support of his party, and later during the debates of the nationality question. The Sudeten Germans showed three times that they were ready to take part in the building of the state. Their leader was not willing to repeat his declarations for cooperation because he did not want to be rejected again. In 1918 the Sudeten

Germans believed in the Wilsonian principles of self-determination. They never abandoned that belief, but they would never again turn to the League of Nations with their grievances. They submitted more than twenty-two grievances and memoranda but the League did not comply with a single demand. Later they were looking for solutions within the state. The Czechs thought that the Sudeten German Party eventually would disintegrate. In 1938 90% of the Sudeten Germans supported Henlein. The Czechs never wanted to win over the Sudeten Germans for the cause of the state. He had certain conditions for a friendly coexistence with the Czechs: revision of the so-called Czech historic myth; revision of the unfortunate concept that the mission of the Czech people is to create a Slavic fortress against the German pressure in an easterly direction. He announced the demands of the Sudeten German Party in eight points.[33] Henlein's speech accelerated the diplomatic activity of the British government for the settlement of the Czechoslovak problem. The ČSR owed its existence to the demand of self-determination for the Czechs; however, the Czechs, twenty years later, were opposed to the application of the same principle for the minorities of the republic. The Czechs did not want to agree to a plebiscite because the Sudeten Germans and the other minorities were expected to vote for separation from the ČSR. Prague did not show any willingness to give up the natural borders of Bohemia and the chain of fortifications in the border zones. The Czechs did not want to respond in the affirmative to the idea that there would be no minorities in the state. The Sudeten German Party handed over the government on June 7 a memorandum containing proposals in 14 points for national pacification.[34] They did this because the government had a meeting scheduled with them on June 15, but the contents of the planned nationality statute were still not disclosed to the negotiating team of the party. No one understood the significance of the great secrecy surrounding the plans of the government. The basis of the negotiations was meant to be the Karlsbad decrees and the nationality statutes of the government. In May, Henlein, after the meeting with the government, went to London for a visit. His travels clearly indicated the great importance of the developments in the ČSR for Britain. Meetings took place again in July between the Prague government and the Sudeten Germans, and after them Henlein immediately went to Berlin under the pretext of inspecting a handicraft exhibition. These travels of Henlein reveal that the real decision making centres in the development of the Czechoslovak crisis lay outside the ČSR. The foreign governments had no doubt about the nature and extent of the problem. They did not find it sensible on the part of the Prague government to offer the national minorities such a plan of reforms which they did not study together in detail, with the representatives of the concerned population. The London newspapers confirmed the news in connection with the mission of Lord Runciman, who would function as a councillor at the Czechoslovak-Sudeten German negotiations.[35] In diplomatic circles a relief was expected in the Czechoslovak crisis from international intervention. Prime Minister Chamberlain announced in the House of Commons that the Czechoslovak government and the Sudeten German Party gave their consent to the mission of Lord Runciman who would act as mediator and investigator. He would take into consideration the opinions of all nationalities under Czechoslovak jurisdiction.[36] As an overture to the mediation of Lord Runciman, the Sudeten German Party on the day preceeding his arrival in Prague, issued a pamphlet containing the rejection of the nationality statute. It was not suitable at all for the solution of problems. According to the pamphlet the new statute must be regarded as an experiment for the codification of the existing status of injustice. The underlying concept was that only the Czech people were the state forming nation; all the others were but second class citizens with curtailed rights. Previously, for these second class nationalities exceptional laws had been passed, and the recently completed statutes were the extension of those exceptional decrees. The pamphlet refused the idea of Czech supremacy in every segment of the national life, and asked for equal rights for all citizens.[37] Its publication was well timed, and intended to influence the views of the British delegation in the nationalities disputes. The publication of the nationalities statutes by the government coincided with the arrival of Lord Runciman and the Central European experts in his entourage in Prague. The British delegation received the statutes before its departure from London. The reaction of the other autonomist groups, Hungarians, Slovaks, Ruthenians and Poles, was the same as that of the Sudeten Germans. They also rejected the Czech domination in the state, and repeated their known demands which had been handed over to the government in forms of memoranda. Similarly to the Sudeten Germans, they claimed equal treatment before the law.

Confrontations between the Slovaks and the Czechs

In Czechoslovakia the Slovaks did not receive the conditions of an independent national life. Officially it was the national state of the Czechs and Slovaks. The Slovaks demanded autonomy for Slovakia, solemnly promised them by Masaryk who even signed an agreement with some Slovak immigrants in the USA during World War I to this end. It was a strange agreement of private persons living in the USA with a Czech exiled political agent. It guaranteed the requirements for a free democratic national existence of the Slovaks, citizens of Hungary for the preceeding thousand years, in a planned state, as members of the "Czechoslovak nation". During their twenty-year cohabitation in the first Czechoslovak republic bitterness built up on both sides of the invented nation. The Czechs and Slovaks became irreconcilable political enemies, with the exception of the Slovak activists, who served Czech imperialistic interests. Articles printed in the two newspapers of the Slovak Populist Party, the *Slovák* and the *Slovenská Pravda,* provide enough evidence of the animosity between the two "sister" nations. The empty censored pages of the second editions of these often confiscated newspapers, and fiery editorials, printed in red in the *Slovenská Pravda* and entitled "Do Živého" (Touch on the raw), give sufficient grounds for proving the non-enviable situation of the Slovaks in their own state.

The Slovaks realized that they were excluded from power by the Czechs and the dissolution of Czechoslovakia was the aim of the majority of them. They were partners in the combined, single "Czechoslovak nation". The Czechs were not willing to grant absolute parity to the Slovaks, as was indicated in the name of the state. However, the Slovaks were not willing to renounce their national characteristics, conscience and language for a fictive Czechoslovak name. In September 1937, one year before the critical phasis of the Czechoslovak internal problems, the Slovak Populist Party introduced a bill in the Parliament for a change in the wording of the language law to permit the use of the Slovak in the public administration, courts, army, gendarmerie the same way in Slovakia as Czech was used in Bohemia, Moravia, Silesia and Ruthenia. The bill aimed to eliminate the term "Czechoslovak language" from the language law. In those territories which formerly belonged to Hungary Slovak should be the official language, and Czech in areas which in the past belonged to Austria. The "Czechoslovak language" is a non-existent politico-juridical term. The Czech philologists did not confirm that Slovak is a dialect of Czech, on the contrary, Slovak and several other linguists are of the opinion that Slovak is a particular independent language.[38]

In a bitter debate, Hlinka, leader of the Slovak Populist Party, answered the charges of Ivan Dérer, the Minister of Justice, a Slovak activist, when the latter called the deputies of Hlinka's party "lousy, snotty brats". Hlinka noted that no one ever heard such words from a Minister of Justice, and added that in an ethnic sense he never had recognized the Czechoslovak nation. His collaborators, members of the Prague Parliament would find the appropriate occasion for personal satisfaction for themselves.[39] They decided to take Dérer to court. Like the other nationalities, the Slovaks also presented their demands in 33 points to Hodža. The Prime Minister used his customary tactics, inviting Hlinka for a meeting at the end of February, just as he held discussions with the Sudeten Germans, Hungarians and Poles. With renewed promises, he invited the Slovaks in the government with two cabinet posts: postmaster general and minister without portfolio. After the meeting, Hlinka was interviewed by the *Prager Montagsblatt* in which he explained that before an eventual entry in the Prague government, the autonomy of Slovakia must be included in the constitution, in the spirit of the Pittsburgh agreement. The recognition of the Slovaks as an independent and sovereign nation would make of them immediately a government party.[40]

In 1938 Czechoslovakia became the scene of diplomatic activity for internal and external reasons. In March, Hitler occupied Austria, and he was considering the possibility of offering Slovakia and Ruthenia to Hungary. In May, Tiso, using the chance given by the Eucharistic Congress in Budapest, talked to State Secretary Pataky on the regulation of the minority problem in the ČSR and on the conditions of an eventual autonomy for Slovakia within Hungary. The Slovaks were very cautious in these talks, as were the Sudeten Germans, Poles and Hungarians in the ČSR, due to their fear of the Czechs and the stipulations of the Defence of the Republic Act. In June another deputy of the Slovak Populist Party, the Polonophile Karol Sidor, conferred with Beck in Warsaw on a Polish-Slovak union. He went to the port of Gdynia in an official capacity to receive the Slovak delegation from the USA bringing the original copy of the Pittsburgh agreement with them in the ČSR. Sidor learned from the Polish Minister of Foreign Affairs that Poland was not interested in a liaison with Slovakia. Esterházy, of the United Hungarian Party, also talked with Beck of Slovak autonomy within Hungary, with a Slovak governor, Parliament and the army. Beck desired to become an arbiter between the Slovak deputies and the Hungarian government. According to Italian sources, in Warsaw Sidor received confidential information from the Poles concerning possible autonomy for Slovakia from Hungary under Polish guarantees. Sidor expressed his wish to review this question with Esterházy rather than with the Hungarian government.[41] On May 13 the Hungarian chargé d'affaires in Prague replied to the Italian ambassador's question that the Slovak Populist Party leaders had been confidentially informed that Slovakia, in case of reannexation to Hungary, would have the largest possible autonomous government.[42] These party leaders were afraid of the Czech counter-intelligence and did not explore deeply this situation. In their indecision and power struggle with the Czechs, after Munich they opted for several months of stay in Czechoslovakia. It is true that the Czechoslovak army kept Slovakia under occupation at that time, but the fate of Slovakia and the Populist Party showed that their choice was not in the best interest of the Slovak people.

The deputies of the Hungarian minority were constantly demanding autonomy for Slovakia and Ruthenia; for this reason the formal creation of an autonomist bloc against the Czechs could not wait for a long time. The Prime Minister, however, wanted to reach an agreement with the Slovaks before the nationalities statute was published. The satisfactory solution of the Slovak question became very urgent for the government for two reasons. Hodža, himself an activist Slovak, belonging to the minority Lutheran group among the Slovaks, tried to offer some credibility to the fiction of the Czechoslovak nation, and avoid embarrassment before the four-member deputation of the American Slovak League brought to the ČSR for the display of the original copy of the Pittsburgh agreement for the twentieth anniversary of its signature.

On March 24, the Hlinka Party announced the formation of an autonomist bloc which included all minorities of Slovakia. Under the influence of these events, Hodža reported through radio the regulation of the minorities question by a nationality statute.[43] The American Slovak delegation arrived in the ČSR and held political negotiations at Hlinka's parish. An immense crowd, and the deputies of the Slovak Populist Party, were waiting for them at the railway station. When the Warsaw Express arrived, the leader of the delegation, Dr. Hletko, was holding in his hand the case in which the original copy of the Pittsburgh agreement was kept. Jozef Hušek, an American journalist, who himself signed the treaty twenty years ago, confirmed the authenticity of the document. Hlinka made it known to the crowd that in 1929 he had received a letter from the former president, Masaryk, also a signatory of the treaty, that the Pittsburgh agreement was counterfeit.[44] It is well known that Masaryk, Beneš and their associates did not intend to extend autonomy to Slovakia. The American Slovak delegation visited Prague, where they had an audience with Krofta, the Minister of Foreign Affairs, and President Beneš. In a press release Hletko explained that love for the Slovaks and Czechoslovakia was the reason for their voyage, and that the Pittsburgh agreement was not against the republic but represented its strength.[45] The Slovak delegation from Prague travelled to Pressburg (Bratislava), where on June 4 and 5, the Slovak Populist Party held a congress during which the speakers demanded autonomy for Slovakia. Hlinka declared that it was the most beautiful day of his life. In his feeling, Prague should learn that it did not want to hear previously that Slovakia belonged to the Slovaks.[46] A crowd about 100,000 strong demonstrated for the autonomy of Slovakia. Esterházy sent Hlinka a telegram on behalf of the United Hungarian Party wishing victory for the Slovak nation in its struggle for autonomy.[47] In the capital of Slovakia Hletko had an interview with Hodža who was present at the congress of his own party.[48] He learned from the Prime Minister that it was impossible to include the Pittsburgh agreement in a Czechoslovak constitution. The American Slovak delegation after a month's stay in the republic took back to the USA the original copy they brought with them to the ČSR. Before leaving the republic, Hletko sent a farewell article to the Slovak newspapers to be released after his departure. In the press release he included the following: "We knew that we would find opposition from those who do not want to respect the Pittsburgh agreement. We had to see with great dismay the lies and suspicions with which we have been attacked every day. In our life we had not seen as much distortion of truth as we saw here in the newspapers. We take back the original copy of the Pittsburgh agreement and leave here in the archives of the *Matica Slovenská* a certified copy of it made by the Czechoslovak consulate in the USA. The day cannot be far away when your demands will be part of the constitution."[49]

The Czech answer to the autonomist Slovak manifestations was an anti-Slovak press campaign in the course of which Beneš remarked that the signature of the Pittsburgh agreement was a great mistake of Masaryk. The Czechs were supposed to share the rule of the republic with their "sister" nation. They responded to the Slovak autonomists by showing their political power, and suppressed the Provincial Office of Slovakia in Pressburg for three months.[50]

Confrontations with the Ruthenian Minority

The Ruthenian politicians felt that the time had arrived for the regulation of the question concerned with the autonomy promised for Ruthenia at the end of World War I. The peace treaty of Saint-Germain[51] of 10 September 1919, also paragraph 3, article 2-9 of the Czechoslovak constitution of the year 1920, granted autonomy for Slovaks and Ruthenians.[52] The Czechs always regarded the Ruthenians as backward, uneducated people, and delayed the granting of autonomy to them until the Munich conference in 1938. In that same year there were three organized groups of different political orientation among the Ruthenians: the Ukranian option under Vološin, the Ruthenian national movement under Bródy, and the Russian trend under Fenčik.[53] These groups also reflected the views of the Ruthenian population concerning their preference in the debate of the language of instruction. There were different fractions of political orientation and for the future status of Ruthenia: in Czechoslovakia, in Hungary or in a state together with all the Ukrainians living north and east of the Carpathian mountains in Poland and in Russia. Vološin wrote in the *Podkarpatske Hlasy* of April 20, 1938 that Poland and Hungary wanted to divide the territory of Ruthenia.[54] The Ruthenian autonomists joined the other nationalities in the autonomist bloc versus Prague on 27 February 1938, when the first opportunity to do so arose. On March 4 in Prague, the autonomist deputies from Ruthenia demanded the granting of autonomy for the province in accordance with the international treaties and the constitution, to assure the possibilities for free development in agriculture, mining, industry, trade and commerce. They protested against the composition of the appointed council for Ruthenia by Prague. They preferred a democratically elected governing council by the people. On the council, 14 members out of 24 served the interests of the Czechs. The council was set up only to mislead foreign countries to make them believe that the international treaties were obeyed. In reality, the autonomy for Ruthenia was neglected for 19 years. Although the Czechoslovak Parliament voted for Ruthenian autonomy in 1937 (Bill 172/1937),[55] governor Hrabár declared to the press that it did not necessarily signify the enforcement of such autonomy. The deputies from Ruthenia protested against the censorship of the newspapers printed in the province, and made it clear that they would be obliged to take advantage of the use of the American press in the Ruthenian language to underscore their criticism of the Czechoslovak government.[56] They proclaimed that they had received authorization for initiating discussions with the Prague government for the introduction of immediate total autonomy for Ruthenia.

The Ruthenians in the USA followed with great interest the fate of their brethren, and a delegation from the federation of the American Ruthenian cultural organizations arrived in the ČSR to study the living conditions of the Ruthenians. They did not go there to be involved in the solution of the constitutional problems but made notes and promised to give an account of their impressions on their next congress at Pittsburgh. Twenty years before on their part an agreement was signed in the USA with Masaryk for the annexation of Ruthenia to the ČSR, therefore, they felt a moral obligation to recognize that province. Many letters had urged the American Ruthenians to embark on a fact-finding trip to the homeland.[57]

The Prague government could not ignore this manifestation of benevolent interest in the political fate of Ruthenia under Czech rule. The Ruthenians had as many grievances as the other oppressed nationalities of the republic. In the Prague Parliament, their deputies protested on behalf of the Ruthenian autonomist union against the practice of the censor at Ungvár (Užhorod) who, according to them, without any serious cause, confiscated the newspapers of the Ruthenian autonomist union for criticizing the government and for enumerating rightful demands of the population. They also protested against the prohition of the freedom of assembly when it was the duty of the members of Parliament to have contact with their constituents.[58] The delegation of the Ruthenian National Council presented their demands to Hodža on May 30 in which they petitioned repeatedly for granting autonomy to Ruthenia. At the same time, a delegation of the American Ruthenians visiting the ČSR, went to the Ruthenian regions and participated in a meeting of the National Council of Ruthenia. Dr. Gerovský, the leader of the delegation, did not comment during his stay in the ČSR on the political conditions of Ruthenia.[59] The delegation had had great difficulties obtaining visas from the Czechoslovak consular authorities in the USA. Gerovský announced that after his return to the USA he would convoke the congress of the American Ruthenians, and they would take a position on the problems of Ruthenia. Further, they would ask President Roosevelt to intervene in the Prague government on behalf of granting autonomy for Ruthenia because the USA had participated in the process of peacemaking, and therefore should see the enforcement of the clauses of the treaty of Saint-Germain. In September they planned to send a memorandum to Prague urging autonomy for Ruthenia.[60] The Czechoslovak government was under attack from the Ruthenians who in the opinion of some Czechs were illiterate people and could not sustain self-government.[61] (Ruthenians in the ČSR: 549, 169; in Ruthenia: 446, 916; in Slovakia: 91, 079; in Bohemia and Moravia: 11, 174.)

The German government also tried to use the Ruthenians for its own goals. A Ukranian Fascist propaganda was initiated from

Berlin. A delegation from the Sudeten German Party was present at the inaugural ceremony of the House of Culture at Ráhó (Rachov) in Ruthenia on August 26, 1938 with an ostentatious demonstration for the Ukranian camp.[62]

Confrontations with the Polish Minority

The territorial dispute over Silesia is over one thousand years old. It dates back to the beginning of the national history of Poland and Bohemia. In 1918 the Czechs demanded, for their new republic, regions inhabited by Poles. The Czechs were against holding a plebiscite, and a conference of ambassadors incorporated, according to Polish sources, 150,000 Poles of Silesia to the ČSR. Before that conference the Poles expressed their wish to belong to the restored Poland after World War I, a country partitioned three times by its neighbours. In the ČSR the Polish minority received the same unjust treatment from the Czechs as the other national minorities of the state. The Czechs tried to denationalize the Poles which caused constant tension between the two Slavic nations. There were unprecedented persecutions, investigations, criminal trials of the Polish public figures, confiscations of property under fictitious pretexts, suppression of Polish publications and press, restrictions on public meetings, prevention even of objective criticism of the existing political system, hinderance of the cultural activities of the Polish institutions, closure of libraries and reduction of Polish schools.[63] The Poles defended their constitutional rights and loyally cooperated with the government. Due to the disadvantageous modification of the electoral law, the Poles were able to secure a seat in the Chamber of Deputies only by joining their forces with the Slovak Populist Party in a constituency.[64] The Polish government was against the detachment of Polish inhabited territory to the ČSR, and already in 1924 demanded the revision of the border in the Javorina region. The new minority policy of the Prague government, announced on February 18, 1937, did not bring any amelioration for the Polish minority, and therefore they decided to demand autonomy in a radical way. They wanted to restore the ethnic situation of 1920 by instituting self-government.[65] The Foreign Minister of Poland, Beck, in a speech before his Foreign Affairs Council said that any decision made by the ČSR in favour of one of her nationalities, if not applied to the Polish minority, would be regarded by Poland as an unfriendly act.[66] The status of the Polish minority was discussed between Beck and Slávik, the ambassador of the ČSR in Warsaw on May 7, 1938.[67] The Poles in Czech Teschen (Český Těšín) formed the Polish Association of Czechoslovakia at a meeting of historic importance. A united front of the Polish political and social organizations was aimed at securing their demands from the Czechs. They could not imagine a good relationship between the two nations as long as the Czechs were not willing to give up their policy of denationalization as they did with the Moravians.[68] The Poles demanded reparations for the losses they had suffered since the foundation of the ČSR, and a fair share in civil service, schooling, and economic life.[69] This action had clearly been copied from the Henlein Party.[70] The Polish political opposition was directed against the chauvinistic policy of the government of Prague. The answer in Prague was the persecution of the Polish population. The *Dziennik Polski* in Mährisch Ostrau (Moravská Ostrava), the official newspaper of the Polish opposition party, was confiscated 14 times between April 1 and 21, 1938 for writing on the Polish school situation in Czech Silesia, and the dismissal of Polish workers from Czech plants.[71] In May, before the community elections, the Czechs intimidated the Polish population, prohibited political and public meetings, beat-up office-holders of the Polish Associations. The Czech police started a criminal procedure against the leaders of the Polish associations, based on the Defence of the Republic Act. The only Polish deputy in the Prague Parliament was placed under house arrest. Later he escaped to safety in Poland. There he became the vice-president of the War Committee of the Trans-Olza Silesia in Katowice. The Committee of the Union of Polish Parties in Czech Teschen asked for the right of self-determination for the Trans-Olza Polish population.[72] All of them had to answer accusations for breaking the law. It was followed by numerous arrests of Poles in Czech Silesia.[73] The Polish Socialist Workers' Party in the ČSR demanded complete equality for the Polish population and remedies for their grievances.[74] Their newspaper *Robotnik Śląski,* was confiscated for publishing an article on autonomy for the Polish minority.[75] The Czechs introduced terror to keep the national feelings of the Poles in check. It did not prevent the population to cast their ballots for the party of their choice at the community elections. In Trans-Olza Silesia in 32 communities in May 1938 the Poles received 299, the Czechs 237 and the Germans 18 seats.[76]

The government of Poland strongly supported the Polish minority in the ČSR. It was Beck's view that the Czechoslovak government might try to postpone the settlement. The Polish press expressed fear for the hostile attitude of Prague. Poland was in constant communication not only with Prague, Berlin and Budapest, but also with Paris, London and the two other members of the Little Entente concerning the Czechoslovak problem and the fate of the Polish minority in Czech Teschen and Northern Slovakia. A possible alternative for Poland in case of a crisis was not clear in London. The consensus was, however, that in case of a successful German attack on the ČSR, Poland would occupy the Teschen area.[77] Poland under the impact of the events in the ČSR terminated the Polish-Czechoslovak treaty of 1925 because of the discrimination against the Polish nationals in the ČSR.[78]

The Czechoslovak government promised a new nationality policy and the codification of the minority laws but it did not have sufficient moral strength and political wisdom to break with the old policy. In Prague it was regarded a crime to defend the rights and culture of the minorities, consequently, under those circumstances a solution had to come from abroad.

Footnotes

1. PMH, Feb. 18, 1938.
2. Slovák, Feb. 27, 1938.
3. PMH, Feb. 27, 1938.
4. Ibid., March 11, 1938.
5. *Felvidékünk-Honvédségünk,* Op. cit., 16.
6. PMH, March 31, 1938.
7. Paris Soir, March 28, 1938.
8. Express, April 1, 1938.
9. PMH, April 8, 1938.
10. Národní Politika, March 29, 1938.
11. Die Zeit am Montag, May 2, 1938.
12. The Times, May 4, 1938.
13. PMH, May 10, 1938.
14. Ibid.
15. *A müncheni egyezmény...* No. 143.
16. PMH, May 19, 1938.
17. Affari Esteri, No. 12003/PR/C.
18. L'Ordre, June 1, 1938.
19. Prager Presse, June 11, 1938.
20. PMH, July 1, 1938.

21. Ibid., July 21, 1938.

22. The Times, July 23, 1938.

23. PMH, July 24, 1938.

24. The Times, July 25, 1938.

25. Venkov, July 27, 1938.

26. Lidové Noviny, July 26, 1938.

27. Prager Tagblatt, July 27, 1938.

28. PMH, July 24, 1938.

29. Ibid., Aug. 27, 1938.

30. Ibid., Feb. 3, 1938.

31. ČTK, April 1, 1938.

32. Neue Morgenpost, April 13, 1938.

33. PMH, April 26, 1938.

34. Die Zeit, July 20, 1938.

35. Daily Telegraph, July 26, 1938.

36. PMH, August 2, 1938.

37. Die Zeit, August 3, 1938.

38. Affari Esteri, No. 239753/1136/C.

39. Slovák, January 10, 1938.

40. Prager Montagsblatt, Feb. 25, 1938.

41. Affari Esteri, No. 3193/R.

42. Ibid., No. 2813/R.

43. Külpolitikai adatok az 1938. évről, 50.

44. Slovák, May 29, 1938.

45. PMH, June 2, 1938.

46. Slovák, June 6, 1938.

47. PRO, FO., 371/21578.

48. Slovák, June 8, 1938.

49. Ibid., Aug. 10, 1938.

50. PMH, June 19, 1938.

51. Wierer, R., *Das Nationalitätenrecht*, 144.

52. Sb. zák. a nař.

53. Koźmiński, M., *Polska i Węgry*, 144.

54. Ibid., 102.

55. Sb. zák. a nař.

56. PMH, March 5, 1938.

57. Ibid., June 2, 1938.

58. Ibid., April 6, 1938.

59. June 2, 1938.

60. Slovák, July 11, 1938.

61. PMH, Jan. 22, 1938.

62. Affari Esteri, No. 231099.

63. *Wolf L., La minorité polonaise en Tchécoslovaquie*, 3.

64. Ibid., 9.

65. PMH, March 31, 1938.

66. Cienciela, Op. cit., 60.

67. Gazeta Polska, May 10, 1938.

68. Ibid., March 28, 1938.

69. Dziennik Polski, May 10, 1938.

70. PRO, FO., 371/21564/9503.

71. Gazeta Polska, April 23, 1938.

72. Ibid., Sept. 7, 1938.

73. Ibid., July 15, 1938.

74. Ibid., April 3, 1938.

75. Ibid., July 12, 1938.

76. Ibid., May 31, 1938.

77. PRO, FO., 371/21723.

78. Gazeta Polska, Sept. 22, 1938.

CHAPTER VI

SOLUTIONS FROM ABROAD FOR THE CZECHOSLOVAK INTERNAL PROBLEMS

The Mission of Lord Runciman and the Dissatisfied Minorities

The radicalization of the internal political situation in the ČSR worried the British and French governments. Beneš, in confusion and desperation, lost his good judgment, and one day before the communal elections one class of reservists and some special units were called to intimidate the population, although, in reality, the government was apprehensive of outbursts of violence. The mobilization was accompanied with an anti-German press campaign. Germany answered this with a political counterstroke. Deterring the population was not necessary, revolution was not in the making. The use of force in peacetime produced a reaction in the elections, and the opposition augmented its seats in the municipal councils and mayoralties. A sober solution in such an overcharged climate must have come from other responsible sources. In Berlin the British ambassador made efforts to moderate the German press. In Prague the French and British ambassadors urged Beneš to come to a speedy and comprehensive settlement.[1] The idea of recommending a mediator appointed by the British government occurred to ambassador Newton in Prague. With such a step, Britain indicated her interest in the Czechoslovak problem, although Beneš continued to avoid his advice and observations.[2] Capt. Plugge asked the Prime Minister in the British Parliament whether he would consider calling a conference dealing with long-standing grievances of the Hungarian minorities in the countries surrounding Hungary, with a view of removing the cause of unrest since Britain signed the peace treaty of Trianon. No conference was planned but the view was expressed that the Hungarian minority and the Hungarian government were resolved to negotiate and not to resort to force in arriving at a just settlement. The Hungarian minority endured misfortunes unparalleled in history, and time had come to correct the injustices of Trianon by legal and peaceful means.[3]

The Anschluss gave Germany a preponderating economic influence on Hungary, but Hungary's sympathies were directed towards England. In spite of Hungary's well-intentioned plan for rapprochement with Western Europe she was left in the German political orbit, abandoned diplomatically by the West.

The Czechoslovak Ministry of Foreign Affairs had delivered a copy of the first plan of the nationalities statute to the British ambassador on 22 April, one month earlier than it was presented to the leaders of the autonomist parties. In his speech at Tábor, Bohemia, on 20 May, Beneš mentioned the preparation of a plan for a far-reaching solution of the minorities question based on the principle of equality among equals.[4] The government contemplated introducing certain changes but, according to the constitution — it was impossible to touch territorial integrity of the state. The following day a partial mobilization was ordered by those who were supposed to start negotiating in bona fide with the opposition. In such an atmosphere the Sudeten German Party refused to confer with the government unless its attitude showed an improvement.[5] The second Defence of the Republic Act 131/1936[6] included enactments against any kind of threat to the republic. Paragraph 138 of Section 7 described the creation of the highest state defence council with members of the government and the president. In exceptional circumstances this council could issue decrees with the consent of the president which in 14 days had to be presented to the Parliament. The law also included the punishments for offences against the law which gave dictatorial power to the government. Another law, 132/1936, dealt with the dissolution of political parties.[7] In July the British observers in Prague reported to London that there was a possibility of a military dictatorship in the ČSR. They regarded it as a weakness of Beneš' decline to accept an agreement with the Sudeten Germans in a false optimism regarding British and French support. There were reports of deliveries of Soviet aircrafts to the ČSR. Beneš of course, did not want to grant autonomy to any ethnic group. The Czech intransigence opened the way for Henlein and the Slovak nationalists to Hitler.[8] On July 6 ambassador Kennedy sent the following telegram from London to the Secretary of State in Washington "As to the Czechoslovak situation, the Czechs tell him they are making real concessions to the Sudeten, and the Germans tell him the Czechs are doing practically nothing. However, he is convinced that nothing is going to happen unless some unfriendly incident occurs such as the shooting of a couple of Germans or Czechs at the borders."[9]

The possibility of the services of a British mediator was mentioned to Beneš and Hodža on July 1, if the need for them should arise.[10] Beneš was informed that in the event of a deadlock the only British course would be to intervene with the proposal for a plebiscite with the object of detaching portions of the Sudeten areas from the ČSR on the German frontier.[11] Beneš was known in international diplomatic circles as follows: "He was the quickest and ablest man in words and formulae but he was also a gambler without a real sense of responsibility."[12] The Czech intransigence brought forth a Sudeten German patriotism. The British, given the Czech stubborness, did not lay idle and made preparations for the selection of a mediator should the Czechs and Sudeten Germans be interested in it. Lord Runciman accepted the role of an independent mediator if the above condition was met. He studied the problem, and on August 3, accompanied by Lady Runciman and his staff, arrived in Prague. At the railway station there was no official welcoming ceremony because the Lord did not go to Prague in an official capacity. The President, Prime Minister and Foreign Minister sent their representatives; and two Sudeten German deputies, the mayor of Prague and the staff of the British embassy were present.[13] The Runciman mission was the central interest not only in the Czechoslovak capital but also in other European chancelleries. The first task of the mediator was to reach a peaceful solution of the Sudeten German problem backed by a government of 70 million people. The Hungarian minority could not line up such a strong assistance. Yet, the Hungarian government expressed its willingness to establish normal relations with the ČSR and the other members of the Little Entente to secure an amelioration of the treatment of the Hungarian minorities. The efforts of the Hungarian foreign policy received a valuable recognition in the *Journal de Genève*. It praised the policy-makers of Hungary who succeeded in maintaining a balance of flexibility in a wise and temperate conduct of foreign policy between Rome and Berlin. The Axis did not exercise an exclusive influence on Hungary, and this careful line gained the sympathy of Britain for Budapest.[14] The Hungarian question in the ČSR was not among the priorities of the British delegation, because the relations between Czechs and Sudeten Germans caused more worries to the Czechs than those of the Magyars. The ideological direction of the Magyars was national and Christian. Both tendencies were on a collision course with the aims of the German government, and in spite of this, the question of the revision of the Hungarian borders without the support of Berlin would have been lost. The contacts with Italy were less dangerous because of geographic distance, and a less harmful possibility of the penetration of Fascist ideas in Hungary. As a result of the power politics, the Runciman mission occupied itself primarily with the Sudeten German question, although the Hungarian minority leaders were asking for the same concessions for their fellow countrymen as Lord Runciman was prepared to recommend in Prague for the Sudeten Germans. The Executive Committee of the United Hungarian Party, with nine deputies and five senators in the Prague Parliament, did their utmost to be received by Lord Runciman, and to be included in his schedule for discussing with him the demands of the Magyar population. The parliamentary caucus of the United Hungarian Party enclosed in its letter to the Lord a bilingual welcoming article published in the official paper of the party (See Appendix 7). They desired to make sure that it reached the members of the British delegation.[15] They did not know that the article, immediately after its publication, was read by all members of the British mission at their headquarters. In Prague, only the *Prágai Magyar Hirlap* had the courtesy to salute Lord Runciman with an article written in English. The delegation was emotionally touched by that gesture all the more because they received a silent and cool reception from the public in Prague.[16]

There was feverish activity behind the scenes in government circles, including negotiations and meetings with recently discovered individuals among the various nationalities. The first day of Lord Runciman's stay in Prague was very busy with official visits to the President of the republic, to the Prime Minister and Minister of Foreign Affairs. In the afternoon they gave a social get-acquainted reception to the negotiating team of the Sudeten German Party.[17] The British had to know the positions of the opposing parties before they started to negotiate with them. Yet, the key to the problem was in the hands of Hitler. The outcome of the mediation efforts depended on the political strategy of Germany. In the Sudeten German Party, several individuals had been found who seriously believed in an agreement with Prague, and did not want to become citizens of Nazi Germany. They, however, remained in the background. It was suspected that Hitler was not willing to accept any kind of solution in the Sudeten question until the Czechoslovak government renounced the treaty of alliance with France and the Soviet Union. He demanded the change of the foreign policy of the ČSR.[18] Under international pressure the government also initiated talks with the other nationalities. At the end of August, Hodža informed Esterházy, and even a member of the Hungarian Parliament, George Apponyi, that as soon as the Sudeten Germans had received the outlines of an agreement, he would start negotiations with the United Hungarian Party.[19] All the autonomists wanted to see Lord Runciman as soon as possible, and present him their plans for a just solution of their grievances. The Slovaks, the Poles, the Ruthenians decided to inform the Lord in detail of their situation.[20] Negotiations between the British delegation and the government constituted the main point of events. The government wanted to debate the issue initially on the basis of its plan, the nationalities statute, and later on some proposals. Negotiations with the British delegation were regarded confidential, and communiqués were not published on the discussed topics. In reply to the Hungarian request, Lord Runciman received the representatives of the Hungarian minority for the first time on August 12. After the meeting the bureau of the British mission issued the following press release: "Friday at noon Lord Runciman received the delegation of the United Hungarian Party, Dr. Géza Szüllő, Andor Jaross and János Esterházy, and talked over with them certain questions included in the memorandum which earlier had been handed over to him." The first meeting with the British delegation ended at 1:30 p.m. After lunch Szüllő was invited for a coffee by Lord Runciman. Lady Runciman had known Szüllő from international meetings of the League of Nations.[21] The minutes of this first meeting say that the United Hungarian Party received the Prime Minister's project in regard to reforms only about a fortnight before, but they were told that these were not final. Consequently, the party could not comment on the non-existing proposals. The well-known Hungarian complaints were discussed with the British mission: domination of Czech officials in the Hungarian districts and in their financial administration, excessive taxation, restriction of the use of the mother tongue in contacts with the courts and public administrative offices, and great difficulties in obtaining the citizenship papers, agricultural and industrial losses, requested compensations for damages suffered since the end of the war, lack of Hungarian administrators, Czech colonization in Hungarian districts, and the problem of education. Jaross added that the Czech majority formed a kind of dictatorship. It was impossible for the Hungarian minority to live forever in the ČSR; but the party was prepared to accept a *modus vivendi* for the present.[22] In the same month, a congress of national minorities in the Swedish capital studied the preservation of ethnic culture and economic power.[23]

During the intervening time the British delegation was engaged in talks with Prime Minister Hodža and the Sudeten Germans, because the latter submitted an answer of 14 pages to the proposals of the government which according to informed circles were qualified as sharp and demanded the renewal of the Karlsbad points. The British mission had to withstand a test of their mediation efforts. It was expected that the Sudeten German Party would reject the conditions of the government. The unsettled question was the British attitude towards the possibility of a German invasion of the ČSR if the Sudeten German demands were not granted. German troop concentrations along the Czechoslovak border could be regarded as an ill omen.[24]

The Hungarian opposition party was assured by deputy Frank that the Sudeten Germans would accept only such an agreement which would include the Hungarians, Slovaks and Poles.[25] The Budapest government observed the events with close attention. Prime Minister Imrédy and Foreign Minister Kánya discussed the relations between Hungary and Czechoslovakia and the Little Entente at their visit in Rome on 18 July with Mussolini and Ciano. According to the Italian leaders, the territorial gains of Hungary were in the interest of Italy, and they promised an intervention in Yugoslavia to restrain her government from attacking Hungary in case of an armed conflict between Hungary and the ČSR.[26] Hungarian diplomacy tried to divide the Little Entente by setting different conditions to the solution of the Hungarian minority problems in those three states. The Little Entente, at their conference held in Bled, Yugoslavia, recognized Hungary's right to rearmament, and declared the reciprocal renunciation of use of force between Hungary and the three states in question.[27] Several questions remained in limbo mainly because of the Czechoslovak crisis and the rights of the Hungarian minority in the ČSR. On 21 August, during the Bled conference, Horthy left for an official visit to Germany. He was accompanied by Prime Minster Béla Imrédy and Foreign Minister Kálmán Kánya. The Regent's wife christened in Kiel a new German cruiser the "Prinz Eugen." The trip of the Hungarian statesmen to Germany ended in a fiasco. During their stay in Germany, the communiqué from the meeting of the Council of the Little Entente was published simultaneously in Bled and Budapest, and its contents were discussed among Horthy, Hitler, Imrédy, Kánya and Ribbentrop. The Germans were uneasy in the belief that Hungary was looking for an agreement with the Little Entente thus thwarting the German plans against the ČSR. The Germans tried to persuade the Hungarian delegation to march into Slovakia when the German army entered Bohemia, and to cooperate with the German plans for the liquidation of Czechoslovakia. But the Hungarians refused to consider military cooperation emphasizing the weakness of the Hungarian army, and they did not want to fight simultaneously on three fronts. The rearmament of the Hungarian army had just started. Hungary wanted a peaceful revision of the Trianon borders. The news from Bled caused disappointment in Germany. Not only Hungary's right to rearmament was recognized by the Little Entente but also certain concessions to the Hungarian minorities in the three allied countries were promised. Hungary formally declined to deploy forces against the Little Entente. This did not mean that Hungary gave up her claim to the revision of her common borders with the neighbours. Hungary was not willing to participate in a military adventure with Germany against the ČSR, and therefore two months later she lost Germany's support for the repossession of territories from the ČSR. It was the comment in Prague after the Little Entente conference that Hungary had shown political independence from Germany at Bled.[28] In August 1938 Hitler was willing to give Slovakia to Hungary as a reward for a joint armed attack on the ČSR.[29] The result of the state visit in Germany was the loss of German support, and an objective German evaluation of the border problem between the ČSR and Hungary. In Prague, on 24 August, Lord Runciman requested a written reply from Esterházy concerning the views of the United Hungarian Party on the Bled agreement.[30] The relations between Hungary and the ČSR developed more slowly than with the other two neighbouring countries. A possible revision of the borders was rebuffed by the Czechoslovak government.[31] Lord Runciman's negotiations with the Sudeten German Party reached a deadlock. On 18 August, Beneš decided to take over the direction of the dealings with the Sudeten Germans.[32] He did not agree with the line Hodža was pursuing. Beneš was working on a third plan for the nationalities. Henlein had a long conversation with Lord Runciman on August 18, regarding the political and economic situation of the Sudeten Germans. They had to be defended against the formidable government sponsored Czech invasion of the Sudeten areas. The only remedy was the separation of the Czechs and Germans. Henlein wanted to achieve this by a negotiated settlement or through a plebiscite. He said, he was for peace and was determined to hold back his people in spite of Czech provocations. He was not absolutely committed to his terms pronounced in Karlsbad. Those terms were vague to allow room for compromise so that the frontiers of the republic would not be broken up. He was concerned with the high unemployment rate of the Sudeten population.[33] On 16 August, the riots in the industrial town of Brux demonstrated the tension which could erupt during a riot. The police gave permission to the Sudeten German Party to hold a rally on the installation day of the new mayor. Brux had a population of 30,000, two thirds of them German, the remainder Czech. About 5,000 Germans took part in the parade, and they were halted by about 1,200 Czechs on the market place. These were no shots fired, but a great deal of fighting and stone throwing took place resulting in 32 injuries on the same day, and 12 on the following day. The Sudeten Germans accused the police of complicity with their opponents.[34] A few weeks later, a more serious incident led to the breaking off of negotiations between the government and the Sudeten German Party.

This very difficult political situation was looming in the background when Lord Runciman received for the second time deputies Esterházy and Jaross who on 25 August, had first informed him of the Hungarian grievances and desires. The allocation of government posts in the Hungarian districts depended on political considerations; the Czechs used the Hungarian activists, and Hungarian language newspapers they published against the interests of the majority of the Magyar population. The Hungarian nationals desired to control their schools and wanted a redistribution of land. The appointment of teaching personnel was decided on three levels. University professors were appointed by the Minister of Education in Prague, high school teachers and principals by the provincial offices of education, and elementary school teachers by the local boards. There was no Hungarian language university in the ČSR, and even the chair of Hungarian literature was occupied in Prague and Pressburg by a non-Hungarian professor. The deputies admitted that the knowledge of Slovak was desirable but did not agree that Hungarian should be taught in Slovak. The Hungarian minority was also ready to accept that the ministries of foreign affairs, defence and finance should be left under the control of the central government.[35]

In London the Foreign Office informed the Polish ambassador that Lord Runciman made arrangements to receive the representatives of the Polish minority on 25 August. The Polish government informed London that it did not wish Lord Runciman to act as a mediator but rather to secure the equal treatment of the Polish minority with the Sudeten Germans in any eventual settlement. Assurances were given that this assertion would be brought to Lord Runciaman's careful consideration.[36] The political situation and the claims of the Polish minority were presented on 25 August at 11:00 a.m. by deputy Wolf. They were similar to those of the other nationalities. The Poles wanted to settle the problem of their minority in the ČSR in lines similar to the Sudeten Germans but independently of Hitler.[37] After the failure of the mission of Lord Runciman, the Polish government considered the demand of the border revision with the ČSR under the provision of Article XIX of the Covenant of the League of Nations. Poland was even determined to take the territories inhabited by the Polish speaking population from the ČSR by force.[38]

The British mission kept London informed of the proceedings in Prague, and one of their members was sent there to the meeting of the Council of Ministers. He informed Chamberlain of the attempt of Lord Runciman to work out a plan, and influence Hitler for moderation in order to break the deadlock of the Prague negotiations.[39] The third Czechoslovak plan recommended the restoration of the county system which existed in the ČSR before 1927 in lieu of a centralized government.[40]

The powerful silent partner in the negotiations with the Sudeten Germans was the government of Germany. Berlin had been kept informed by Henlein of the course of developments. Lord Runciman wanted to assist both sides in reaching an agreement; therefore, he asked Henlein to convey the message to Hitler that he would like to bring the Czechs and Sudeten Germans together on the basis of the Karlsbad points, and the proposals of the Prague government. He was anxious to get Hitler's approval for that direction of the negotiations. On September 1 and 2 Henlein talked to Hitler and Ribbentrop. No clear-cut answer was given to this plan, and Henlein had two alternatives: negotiate for an autonomy within the ČSR or ask for a plebiscite. During Henlein's visit in Germany, the representatives of the Sudeten German Party described to Lord Runciman their unsatisfactory conversation with Beneš. The President did not go far enough on the points discussed. Hitler sent a note to several European governments assuring them of his peaceful intentions; but if the settlement of the Sudeten question should be delayed for a long time, he could not do otherwise but give them aid with all possible means. There was increased diplomatic activity in connection with the Sudeten problem, and the committee of the coalition parties in Prague dealt with the solution of the nationality question of the republic.[41] Europe was expecting concessions from Beneš to alleviate the tense international situation and the serious internal conflict. There were no signs of change in the twenty-year old Czech obstinance, therefore, Britain decided to negotiate directly with Germany on the Sudeten German question which from then on was tightly connected with the events that took place in London and Berlin.

On August 28, the third plan of the Czechoslovak government was ready. It was not the final one, but the Czech tacticians wanted to ease the tension of their own creation. They came out with a third plan only because the negotiations were boken off with the Sudeten Germans. The third plan more closely resembled Henlein's eight Karlsbad points than the nationalities statute. It projected the organization of cantons (Gaue) with a state appointed representative and an elected president, increased German public servants and economic help to areas of chronic unemployment. The propositions were characterized as inadequate by the Sudeten German Party.[42] The demands of the nationalities requested their recognition as national groups within the ČSR with equal rights as a corporate body and a right to self-determination. The government did not regard these principles compatible with the integrity, unity and indivisibility of the state. The parties were diametrically opposed to each other on this issue, and the negotiations, in spite of Lord Runciman's mediation, were consequently interrupted. Another possibility was in the making, and a member of the British mission had a long discussion in the Swiss embassy at Prague, at the right source, concerning the Swiss constitution and cantonal system.[43] The government of the United States of America was also interested in the developments of the Czechoslovak crisis, and the American ambassador, Kennedy, had a long meeting with Chamberlain, and with the Czechoslovak ambassador in London, Jan Masaryk. Kennedy informed his government in a long report of the conflict.[44] It was assumed in London that Lord Runciman was prepared to draft an independent proposal if a great gulf should exist between the third plan and Henlein's counter-proposal. The third plan did not solve the tension. Beneš negotiated again with the Sudeten Germans and Lord Runciman. Hodža met the representatives of the United Hungarian Party and informed them of the third plan.[45] Agreement could not be found until the self-determination of the Sudeten Germans was accepted by Prague. The cantonal system of the third plan which proposed to divide the German district in four administrative units, did not satisfy the Sudeten German Party.

The Czechoslovak government was ready to prepare a fourth plan in case the third plan did not work. The Prime Minister called the Sudeten German representatives for a meeting on 6 September to present them the fourth and final plan of the government, and initiate with them further negotiations. The same day Henlein went to Berchtesgaden and from there to Nurenberg for the party day of the National Socialists as the personal guest of Hitler.[46] For several days there was speculation concerning the contents of the fourth plan which included the following points: appointment of public servants and policemen according to the proportion of nationalities and placing them in the counties of their own nationality; new language law based on complete equality; state subsidies to the Sudeten region in the amount of 700 million Kč in form of a loan from France and Britain; autonomy for the nationalities in those countries where they formed the majority; guarantees for the boundaries and the unity of the state; minorities departments in the central government which would control foreign affairs, finances and the army; protection of the citizens against denationalization; drafting of bills with the cooperation of the Sudeten German Party subject to the approval by Parliament.[47] The Sudeten Germans made their demands clear in the eight Karlsbad points, but Prague, instead of a definite plan, delayed its decision, testing tempers and causing diplomatic interventions. The western powers did not want to be involved in a conflict over the minority rights in Czechoslovakia. The negotiations were continued because of the presence of Lord Runciman. After the publication of the fourth plan, the reply of Hitler to the letter of Lord Runciman arrived in Prague and caused intensive diplomatic activity in Prague, London, Paris and Berlin. The contents of the letter were not disclosed but Hitler rejected the idea of armed intervention, and demanded further concessions from the Czech position which would correspond to an autonomy.[48] All parties continued the talks. On 3 September the British mission received Ignac Schulcz and George Csizmazia, representing the Hungarian Social Democratic group in the ČSR. They explained to the mediators that they did not want to see the destruction of the republic. They had obtained important social benefits from the Czechs, such as suffrage, unemployment benefits and a democratic way of life. Their main difference with the United Hungarian Party was ideological but in certain questions, e.g. language of education, all the Hungarians of the ČSR were unanimous regardless of party membership.[49]

After the publication of the fourth plan the Slovak autonomists expressed their displeasure with certain aspects of it, notably the division of Slovakia into administrative districts. Knowing the Slovak attitude, the Hungarian Social Democrats told the British that they would not like to be oppressed by the Slovak majority, if Slovakia were taken as a unit and given an autonomous legal status.[50] In their opinion the Hungarian minority question should be regulated by the central Parliament. The fears of the Hungarian Social Democrats were not unfounded. The city clerk in Pressburg issued a circular letter in which he prohibited the use of the Hungarian language in official contact with clients. Magyar taxpayers numbering 30,000 in Pressburg, the former capital city of Hungary (1541-1848), and the former coronation city of the kings of Hungary (1563-1830), were forbidden to use their own language when they went on official business to the city hall. That circular letter was issued in those days when the Prague government made promises for the restoration of the language rights of the minorities. The city clerk was paid by the taxpayers but he was a member of the *Slovenská Liga,* the association spearheading the denationalization of the minority groups. The city clerk went too far in his intolerance by issuing an ordinance and threat of criminal proceedings against the disobedient employees of the city. Deputy

Esterházy protested against that circular letter to Prime Minister Hodža. It was withdrawn, and the city clerk quickly went on vacation.[51] The remarks of the Magyar Social Democrats to the British mission were justified in connection with the wish of the Slovak Populist Party relating to the planned cantonal administration of Slovakia.

The Italian embassy in Budapest reported to Rome its frequent conversations with Esterházy of the United Hungarian Party in the ČSR who made numerous trips to Hungary, Poland, Germany and later to Italy. According to Esterházy's observations, the situation in the ČSR reached, on 29 August, alarming proportions because of the hostile demonstrations in Prague against the Runciman mission which found itself in a difficult position.[52] The same day the Italian counsul in Pressburg noted that the ship on which Regent Horthy returned to Budapest on the Danube passed by Pressburg at 8:00 a.m. Thousands of Hungarians were waiting for him from the early morning hours on the banks of the river. When the steamer reached the city the onlookers waved their hands and waved their handkerchiefs. The Regent, surrounded by his retinue on the deck, responded with several military salutes. Extraordinary measures were taken on the Czechoslovak shore (about 130 km) to keep the population of the nearby villages away from the river. The Czechoslovak authorities wanted to prevent pro-revisionist demonstrations among the Hungarian minority living in that area.[53]

The Slovaks, as the supposed ruling nation, for twenty years had been demanding autonomy for Slovakia. The British embassy in Prague prepared a memorandum for the Foreign Office on the position of the Slovaks in the ČSR. The main complaint of the Slovaks was that the Czechs had been tactless to them, treating them as an inferior race but their grievances included political, economic, cultural and personal questions.[54] The Czechs followed a short-sighted policy towards the Slovaks. Slovak activists, who belonged to a minority among the Slovaks, were used by the Czechs to serve the interests of Czech imperialism in Czechoslovak colours. The majority of the Slovaks lived under the influence of the anti-Czech clergy. The Slovaks also wanted to have an appointment with the Runciman mission to air their grievances. Two Slovak political parties sought interviews with Lord Runciman: the Slovak Populist Party, represented by its Vice-President, Josef Tiso, and the Slovak National Party, represented by president designate, Ján Pauliny-Tóth. According to the remarks of this latter politician, it was necessary to make the Czechs understand that the Slovak problem could be settled without shaking the unity and safety of the state.[55] He was received on 18 August by the British mission, and explained that the Slovak question should be settled independently from the concessions made to the Sudeten Germans. The problem between the Slovaks and Czechs could be solved if the Provincial Diet, and a proposed government for Slovakia, were to be given authority to make appointments in the civil service, to sign state contracts and have their own budget. The representation of Slovakia in the Czechoslovak Parliament in Prague should be increased from 70 to 88. The Czechs were against the increase of Slovak influence for fear that it might contribute to a possible disintegration of the ČSR.[56]

The autonomist Slovak Populist Party sent a letter to Lord Runciman and asked for an audience in order to inform him of the existence of the Slovak question and the necessity of its settlement. The British Foreigh Office had been sufficiently briefed on the Czech and Slovak relations, and the causes of the quarrels and discord among them. It was noted by the Slovak Populist Party that it had won 20 seats out of the 59 Slovak mandates, and was struggling with the Czechs for the equality of rights, for the national, cultural, political and economic development of the Slovak people.[57] The British delegation declined the request of the Slovak Populist Party, because Lord Runciman was invited to the ČSR by the government in agreement with the Sudeten German Party to assist bringing about a settlement in the difficulties between them. The British mediator was unwilling to undertake any kind of intervention between the Czechs and the Slovaks without the approval of the Czechoslovak government. During the interval of the exchanges of these two letters, the fourth plan of the Czechoslovak government was published, and the Slovaks were opposed to the cantonal system which, in their opinion, would have shared the administration of Slovakia with the Hungarian and German minorities. They wanted to rule Slovakia as the Czechs ruled Czechoslovakia. Although the Slovak autonomists were not received by the British delegation, they, nevertheless, submitted the problems of the Slovak nation in a thirteen-page memorandum.[58] Hlinka's Slovak Populist Party thought if the Sudeten Germans deserved autonomy, the Slovaks were equally worthy of it. Tiso sent a confidential memorandum to Lord Runciman in which he did not hesitate to present the Slovaks as a national minority. The Hlinka Party felt the the Slovaks were in a worse situation than any other minority which enjoyed the support of bordering states. Tiso referred to the Czech fiction of a "Czechoslovak nation" as non-existent, and said such a nation, just as a Russian-Polish, Czech-Polish, or French-Italian nation, did not exist. The origin of the Czechoslovak fiction is the Pittsburgh covenant which is the basis of the close association of the Czechs and Slovaks under the same laws. It resulted in the invasion of Slovakia's administration and cultural, spiritual and economic life by the Czechs. Tiso was against the subdivision of Slovakia into cantons because in some of them the Magyar population could have absolute majority.[59] Concurrently the Slovak Populist Party participated in meetings with the other nationalities and they formed with them a common autonomist front against the Czechs.

The supporters of the Ruthenians abroad also reminded the British delegation in Prague that the Czechoslovak government had not yet kept its promises of autonomy for Ruthenia enunciated in the treaty of Saint-Germain. They indicated that London had some moral responsibility in the fulfillment of that obligation as one of the co-signatories of that treaty.[60] The Runciman mission was advised from Rome that the secretary-general of the Carpatho-Russian Union of North America was on his way to Prague with a letter from Hodža on him to the effect that, if pressure was exerted on the Czechoslovak government by the British or French it would make it easier for Prague to grant self-government for Ruthenia.[61] Autonomy did not cover the fullest degree of independence. The Ruthenians wanted to become masters of their own territory as the Sudeten Germans, Slovaks, Hungarians and Poles wanted to see their own people elected to offices and not be administered by the Czechs. In 1938, the Ruthenians were not waiting any longer for a move from Prague. On September 1, the representatives of the Republican Party in Carpathian Russia, Senator Bačinsky and Mayor Bukovič, and Bródy, representing the Autonomous Union, visited Hodža and declared that the two parties concluded an agreement and demanded autonomy in accordance with the treaty of Saint-Germain, and early elections to the Ruthenian Diet.[62].

Some grievances of the minorities reached Lord Runciman directly. The Hungarians of Léva (Levice), who formed the majority of the population, asked the government, in vain, to re-open the Hungarian high school taken away from them in 1918. They offered classrooms and the expenses for furnishing the school but permission for the opening of a high school was not forthcoming from the Czechoslovak authorities. This negligence prompted the Magyars in Léva to send a memorandum to Lord Runciman with the request of intervention on their behalf to the Prague government.[63]

The delegations and representatives charged with the negotiations of the nationality rights suspended their work because of the fatal incidents in Mährisch Ostrau (Moravská Ostrava) between the Sudeten Germans and the Czech police. Lord Runciman invited Esterházy to his office and told him that he would be willing to make some arrangements in the Mährisch Ostrau incident if it was the wish of the Sudeten Germans. It was his impression that the remaining differences were bridgeable, and asked Esterházy to warn Frank, Vice-Chairman of the Sudeten German Party, about the dangers of interrupting negotiations. This would mean war, misery and communism.[64] Frank met Runciman the same day, September 8, and asked for the acceptance of the Karlsbad points.

In the Prague Parliament, the autonomists formed a common front. A press release was issued at the end of the conference. Under the presidency of K.H. Frank, the Political Comittee of the Sudeten German Party held a joint meeting with the Slovak Populist Party, the United Hungarian Party and the Committee of the Polish Union. It was pointed out that in the basic principles for the urgently needed reorganization of the state, and in the opinions concerning the regulation of the nationality question there was complete unanimity. It was decided that joint meetings would be repeated according to needs.[65] The autonomists were convinced that their demands could only be fulfilled with their complete cooperation for the transformation of the ČSR into a federal state.

Those days required serious deliberation on the part of the leaders of the republic. President Beneš spoke to the citizens of the ČSR on September 10. For twenty years — according to him — the republic had been a prosperous and tranquil state but the grave problems needed new methods for solution. He intended to settle them but the rapidity of world events demanded a faster tempo. He did not deviate from the old principles of the state but wanted to reach a degree of political justice which could be realized. In this spirit negotiations were started with all the nationalities, first with the Sudeten Germans. Reform plans had been published which assured free political, cultural and economic activities, and national rights for all the nations and nationalities of the state according to their numerical strength. The government was ready to make a sacrifice for the peace, and wanted to establish good relations with the strongest neighbour of the ČSR, Germany. A new climate was needed at home, a new understanding, a moderation of the press on all sides. These things could bring the much needed confidence to the peaceful task.[66] Beneš spoke prior to the congress of the National Socialist Party in Nurenberg, and of Hitler's sharp attack and treats on Czechoslovakia.

Slovák, the official paper of the Hlinka Party, in its editorial entitled "Our patience is also running out", reminded Beneš that in 1935 the Slovak Populist Party voted for him in the presidential election. Then the Czech press praised the political wisdom and maturity of the Slovaks. There were long, open and honest discussions with the new head of state on the Slovak question but without any results. He was warned verbally, in the press, in memoranda and in requests that everything was not in a satisfactory condition in Slovakia. As loyal citizens, the Slovaks used all possible means to induce the authorities to make the necessary steps for constitutional changes. Sometimes they received answers for their requests, other times they did not. The time for the fulfillment of demands of all nationalities living in the republic had arrived. The title of the Slovaks, as a ruling nation, was attractive. No one could live on empty titles. The Slovaks wanted their rights, liberty, employment, bread, existence, with one word: future. They did not believe in promises any longer. It was said that the Czechs went to the limits of their concessions. The twenty-year patience of the Slovaks reached the ultimate limits of human patience.[67] Five days later Beneš invited four representatives of the Hlinka Party for lunch. According to the press release, during the friendly conversation the Slovak deputies handed the President a memorandum containing the urgent demands of the party.[68]

Three members of the Runciman mission tried to find Henlein in his home at Asch (Aš) — a four-hour auto trip from Prague — upon his return from Nuremberg. A meeting was arranged between the Sudeten German leader and the British mission on September 15 before noon. Two days earlier the government proclaimed martial law in eleven counties. Henlein informed the Runciman mission that he declared the Sudeten German negotiating team dissolved in view of events of the preceeding 48 hours. In his opinion the conditions for the continuation of the negotiations ceased to exist in conformity with the original instructions. Henlein thanked the British mission for their kind efforts to solve the nationality problems. The news reached Prague late at night, and there was a meeting of the government held immediately upon the receipt of the news.[69]

A very interesting disclosure of facts was brought to the attention of the British delegation in Prague. Deputy Neuwirth, the legal counsel of the Sudeten German delegation revealed after the dissolution of the party, that on the Czech side the real power was in the hands of the army and the extremists, and Hodža was deprived of his authority. The Germans were in favour (95%) of union with Germany, and Henlein could not convince his followers to remain in the ČSR. Only a quarter of the Sudeten Germans constituted the revolutionary element which was responsible for the current turning point, the majority were apprehensive of war. In his view the chief advantage of the plebiscite would be that it would transfer the whole question to another plane from that with which Hitler's Nuremberg speech had dealt.[70]

There was an hour-long Czech radio transmission from Vienna every day, and a Prague radio replied in German in polemic language. The British embassy in Berlin warned the Foreign Office of the ominous tone of the German press which depicted the sufferings of the Sudeten Germans in Czechoslovakia. They were in reality defenceless against the Czech police, soldiery and communist mob. Under those conditions Germany should not have been blamed for supporting the cause of persecuted Germans.[71] The Czechoslovak government dissolved the Sudeten German Party and all its organizations, and the police occupied the offices of the party, confiscated the correspondence and other documents found therein. Court action was ordered against Henlein for the attempt to violate the territorial integrity of the state.[72] Similar actions had been taken against other organizations. The dissolution of the party was the result of Henlein's demand of September 15 for the cession of the Sudetenland to Germany.[73] After those events it was wholly out of the question for the Sudeten Germans to remain within the ČSR. One month earlier, there was a near breakdown in the negotiations after the Brux incidents on August 16 and 17. On September 15, after long and arduous work, Lord Runciman returned to London to give a report to the cabinet. (Appendix 8.) He went to Czechoslovakia as a mediator between the Czechs and the Sudeten Germans, and almost became a mediator between the ČSR and Germany. The last proposal of the Sudeten German Party was the inclusion of the Sudeten areas in the Reich.[74] On September 21,

Lord Runciman considered that there was nothing further for the members of his mission to do in Prague, and suggested their return to England.[75]

The Failure of British Mediation and Its Aftermath

After the rupture of talks between the government and the Sudeten German Party, the internal problems of Czechoslovakia were transformed into an acute international affair. The Hungarian minority also needed external help for obtaining their constitutional rights in the ČSR. That assistance could come first of all from the Hungarian nation and to a lesser degree from friendly governments. The Magyars could consider Mussolini as the most powerful supporter of Hungarian claims. The Italian Prime Minister decided to influence the protracted negotiations in Prague by writing an open letter to Lord Runciman. His suggestions were published before Chamberlain's visit with Hitler. His newspaper article was published in all German papers. In Rome the press reported that Chamberlain had a telephone conversation from Berchtesgaden with the Duce, about a four-power conference — Britain, France, Germany and Italy — to examine the Czechoslovak question and other European problems.[76]

On September 15, 1938, when an article entitled "Letter to Runciman" appeared in the *Popolo d'Italia,* Mussolini's Milan paper, it was not known that on the same day Runciman decided to break off his mediating role in Prague between the Czechoslovak government and the Sudeten German Party. The article was not signed but it was thought to have been written by the Duce. It claimed that some weeks earlier the world had no clear idea what Lord Runciman would do in Prague. Was his work only one of mediation or had it, at a certain moment, become one of arbitration? Lord Runciman had read dozens of memoranda and hundreds of letters, received dozens of people and conferred with the leaders of all concerned nationalities, for there was also a Magyar, a Polish, a Slovak problem, not only a Sudeten German problem. There were as many problems as nationalities which burdened the Czechoslovak republic at Versailles. The writer of the article assumed that Lord Runciman had reached the conclusion that a Czechoslovak nation did not exist. The components of Czechoslovakia were of diverse races and could not bear one another. They were animated by a centrifugal force and only a police force kept them together. The treaty of Versailles did not restore the historical Bohemia but it created a new and artifical state which from its birth contained in itself the elements of its own dissolution. The writer of the article believed that Lord Runciman had seen the situation in those terms, and should have simply proposed the plebiscite to Beneš not only for the Sudeten Germans but for all the nationalities which asked for it. He wished courage to the British Lord to propose plebiscites under international supervision. With such a bold move, the hotbed of disorder and anxiety in Europe could be eliminated. It was practically impossible for Italy to pursue a policy with Czechoslovakia; it would be possible with a Bohemia of tomorrow.[77]

A Polish newspaper, *Gazeta Polska,* reviewed an article written in a French weekly *Gringoire*. It represented one of the groups around the former Prime Minister Tardieu. Months before the British mediation, already on April 22, an article was published in the French paper entitled "Whether France is obliged to fight for the Czechs." It described the activities of those French who wanted to drag France to the defence of the Czechoslovak goverment. The analysis of the author concluded that a Czechoslovak nation did not exist, and Czechoslovakia was an artificial political creation without a possibility for life, development and defence. It was a state of Czechs, Slovaks, Germans, Ruthenians, Hungarians and Poles. The international situation of the ČSR was tragic if she could not even count on the help of France or the USSR. In spite of a seemingly democratic ČSR, there was a rule of a most autocratic small group of people. The sympathy of the French leftists for the ČSR was based on the links binding together the French and Czech influential politicians with Beneš at their helm who governed the republic in a dictatorial way. Beneš committed many political errors one after the other over the preceding twenty years. He hindered the restoration of the Habsburgs, blocked the shipment of ammunitions directed to Poland in 1920. He had much influence in the French Foreign Ministry and the press. Similarly, he was the patron of the pactomania which took France in the general direction in which she found herself. The article of the *Gringoire,* which was read by about 600,000 people, was not an isolated phenomenon in the French press, according to the summary of the *Gazeta Polska.*[78]

Mussolini again made comments about Czechoslovakia in his speech at Triest on September 18. London and Paris had been informed that Italy had resolved that the Czech problem should be settled entirely and definitively. France and Britain should not remain indifferent to the voice of the German and other nationalities in the ČSR or to the urgency of a decision. The situation needed plebiscites and swift action. Only plebiscites could satisfy the nationalities and the territorial usurpation of Czechoslovakia since the treaty of Versailles. The historical friendship towards the Hungarians and Poles dictated the policy of the Rome-Berlin axis he said — but a European responsibility demanded a total solution of the Czechoslovak problem. It has been proven that the Czechoslovak state was not a durable creation.[79] On September 21 Mussolini touched again the Czechoslovak problem in another pronouncement in Treviso. The ČSR lived through very critical moments. It would be better to call that state Czecho-Polono-Hungaro-Rutheno-Rumano-Slovakia. He urged the solution of the Czechoslovak political question initiated by the British Prime Minister, and to bring the small country in a peaceful port.[80] Three days later in Padova (Padua), Mussolini once more mentioned the Czecho-slovak difficulties. The new Prime Minister, General Syrový, was a great friend of Moscow, and his first act was to order the general mobilization of the army. The German answer was to allow Prague six days, until October 1, to reach a decision. It would be the greatest absurdity for millions of people to die to save the rule of Beneš. Mussolini wanted to call the attention to the responsibilities of Prague while there was time to localize the conflict and find a peaceful solution.[81] The following day, on September 25, Mussolini commented in Vicenza on the mistakes committed in 1919 at the conclusion of the peace treaties. Their untenability was proven already in 1921. It is human to make errors but to maintain them is diabolic. It would be the most tragic paradox of mankind to go to war for the ČSR and preserve a mistake for a longer period of time.[82] Mussolini continued his series of attacks on the ČSR in the course of which he recognized and appreciated the efforts of the British Prime Minister in order to provide a solution to the Czechsolovak problem. On September 26 at Verona he equally praised the patience of Germany shown in this question. It was evident that the Czechs must come to their senses, and not engage in a conflit, the outcome of which could not be doubtful. The triple problem, German, Hunga-rian and Polish, required a thorough solution according to the forces of history. Beneš and the Czech people should have been aware that only a few days were left for a pacific settlement of the controversy. Europe certainly did not need a number of charnel houses on the frontiers of different countries. There should have been an extraordinarily rapid succession of events in granting justice to the minorities in the ČSR and reconciliation among peoples. It would be useless to try to save the Europe of Versailles which was constructed in defiance of geography and history. Italy was not for that Europe.[83]

The visit of the British Prime Minister in Germany opened a whole series of international activities. In Roman political circles it was considered as a probability that the representatives of Britain, France, Germany and Italy would hold an international conference to discuss important European questions.[84] This news was the forerunner of the convocation of the Munich conference later that month. This idea had emerged more than three months earlier. The French ambassador in Berlin mentioned this to the British ambassador in Paris already on June 8, as a personal suggestion intended for Hitler.[85]

The Hungarian government intensified its activity in connection with the solution of the problems its nationals faced in the ČSR. The August state visit of Horthy to Germany left a strain on German-Hungarian relations because Hungary did not want to support the hard and dangerous German political and perhaps military course. The expected support from the British government for the equality of rights for the Hungarian minority in the ČSR did not materialize. According to British interpretation, the determination of the rights given to the Hungarian nationals in the ČSR was the task of the negotiations between the two interested states. The British government intervened in Prague on behalf of the Polish minority, which numbered about one tenth of the Hungarian minority, asking the Prague government to give formal assurances to Poland for granting the same rights to the Poles in the ČSR as to the Sudeten Germans. The British failed to extend their mediation efforts in favour of the Hungarians.[86] The British ambassador in Prague told Esterházy that the Hungarians would get much less than the Poles, and Lord Runciman's task was only the study of the German problem.[87]

The Polish ambassador in London reported that during the discussion of the Czechoslovak crisis with the British Foreign Secretary, the views of London were expressed that the treaties could be changed by three methods: by negotiations, by the threat of force, or by the use of force.[88] The Polish and Hungarian ambassadors in London informed each other of the territorial demands of their governments from the ČSR. Hungary wanted to regain that territory from the ČSR where Hungarians formed more than 50% of the population, and suggested a plebiscite for the mixed regions, and for the Slovaks and Ruthenians. The map published by the naval intelligence service confirmed the correctness of the ethnographic maps made in Hungary. The British government had understanding for the Polish demand of the Trans-Olza part of Silesia but expressed its hope that Poland would not do anything in the existing delicate situation that could increase the general crisis.[89] The unofficial judgment of the French government was that it would be better to apply the plebiscite for the Polish minority in the Teschen (Těšin) area. With it, the French wanted to prevent the take-over of Polish Silesia by Germany. Ten days later France persuaded Britain to allow the whole portion of Teschen-Silesia to come under Polish rule.[90] After the Munich conference, the Poles residing in Paris supplied this information for the occupation of that territory after 24 hours notice to Prague. The Polish ambassador told Bonnet that Poland had many complaints against France. In 1919 France intervened in the decision concerning the future of Silesia, and the administration of the district of Wilno. Later, France signed a treaty of non-aggression with Germany and Soviet Russia, and interfered with the evolution of Poland's relations with Lithuania. Beneš had to be persuaded to stop dreaming that the Czechs were the representatives of the fiction of Pan-Slavism, which led them to their present catastrophe.[91]

Although the Hungarian government lost the confidence of Hitler and Ribbentrop, who almost told them in August, 1938, that they must choose between Kiel or Bled in their revisionist claims, between the backing of Germany or cooperation with the Little Entente, Budapest was forced to adhere to Germany for the successful conclusion of the Magyar policy for regaining the territories and nationals lost to the ČSR in 1918. Kánya declared on

127

September 1, that Hungary would maintain her claims against the ČSR, and five days later Prime Minister Imrédy, in his speech at Kaposvár, dealt with the problem of Hungarian nationals in the ČSR whose treatment was an obstacle in the normalization of relations between the two countries.[92]

Upon the return of Chamberlain from Berchtesgaden, there were meetings of crucial importance for the Sudeten problem between Chamberlain, Halifax, Daladier and Bonnet. It was easier for the French to let Britain pressure Prague than to take the initiative in Paris. Joint British and French recommendations were expected in Prague in the sense that in case of surrendering the Sudeten district to Germany the four powers would guarantee the frontiers of the new Czechoslovak state.[93]

The German secret service intercepted several telephone conversations between September 14 and 28, 1938 which took place between Beneš in Prague and his ambassadors in Paris and London. Jan Masaryk in London was told that the ČSR was not ready to carry out the Anglo-French plan. Beneš gave instructions to Masaryk in London and Osuský in Paris to get in touch with the opposition in both countries and negotiate with them the overthrow of the British and French governments.[94]

In those decisive days the Regent of Hungary could not remain silent. He wrote a letter to Hitler on September 17, between the two visits of Chamberlain to Germany. According to the British press there was an intent to detach the German inhabited regions of Czechoslovakia, with or without plebiscite and annex them to the German Reich. In Horthy's view, that sort of settlement would fall short of the final regulation of the Czechoslovak problem. All the nationalities of the ČSR must have equal rights to decide by a plebiscite whether they would want to live under foreign domination or within their nation.[95] In that extraordinarily auspicious moment, Horthy considered it necessary to call Hitler's attention to that circumstance, and count on his support in his talks with the British Prime Minister. After dispatching his letter, Horthy was invited on a hunting trip to Germany, most likely by Göring. On September 20, Hitler sent an aircraft for Prime Minister Imrédy who in Obersalzberg explained the Hungarian territorial claims to the Chancellor.[96] The German Chancellor brought up those Hungarian demands during his scheduled second meeting with Chamberlain two days later in Godesberg. Hitler planned to lay the demands for the plebiscite in Sudetenland before Chamberlain. Göring recommended the application of pressure by Poland and Hungary for the realization of the plebiscite for the Polish and Hungarian minorities in the ČSR.[97] According to the Polish ambassador, Göring asked the Hungarian ambassador to his office, and encouraged him to direct more active demands against the ČSR.[98] The Italian ambassador forwarded to Ribbentrop Ciano's conversation with the British ambassador saying the fulfilment of the Polish and Hungarian demands were indispensable conditions for the regulation of the Czechoslovak question.[99] After these interventions, Hitler refused the proposition to sign the guarantee of the ČSR's borders without the participation of Poland, Hungary and Italy.[100] The Polish government wanted to gain the support of Rumania and Yugoslavia for the revision of the Czechoslovak-Hungarian border by giving Hungary back Southern Slovakia.[101]

In Czechoslovakia the government lost its good judgment, martial law was proclaimed for three months, and letters for abroad had to be mailed unsealed. The parliamentary caucus of the United Hungarian Party held a meeting in Pressburg, and issued the following declaration: The Magyar ethnic group in Czechoslovakia has been living on the territory of this state for twenty years as a consequence of the enforcement of the peace treaty of Saint-Germain-en-Laye but it never felt any doubts that it wanted its share in all rights which are due to all nations and nationals expressed in divine, human and moral laws. The Hungarian ethnic group for twenty years fulfilled its duties as one of the most disciplined nations of the republic, because it was convinced of the necessity of peace for healing the wounds caused by the World War. For twenty years the possessors of power in the state never took into consideration the interests of different ethnic groups, among them those of the Hungarians. With their legislative enactments, they served exclusively the idea of a Czech national state. It was an erroneous policy which created an international situation which became part of a European political concern and threat to world peace. The British mediation wanted to expand the conditions of the coexistence of the Central European nations on a new and secure basis. The Magyar ethnic group in the ČSR wanted to take the direction of its own future into its own hands, and obtain the right that was given in 1918 only to some nations, that is the right of self-determination.[102]

On the same day, the Hungarian government instructed its ambassador in London that Hungary would have territorial demands if the Sudetenland were ceded to Germany.[103] Warsaw, Rome and Paris also were notified of the Hungarian standpoint.[104] This was done on the advice of Göring given to the Hungarian ambassador in Berlin. Furthermore, the necessity of demonstrations, provocation of incidents, armed clashes, and strikes by the Hungarian population in the ČSR, and the intensification of the press campaign abroad was counselled by the German government.[105] The British government finally notified the Hungarian government that it completely understood the interest of Hungary in the fate of the Magyar minority in the ČSR, and the Hungarian point of view had been placed on record, and would receive consideration at the appropriate time.[106] The same day the Hungarian ambassador in Prague delivered a note to the Foreign Ministry in which the Hungarian government demanded equal treatment for the Magyar minority in the ČSR with the Sudeten Germans. It was made known in a memorandum in London by the

Polish ambassador that Poland requested similar solutions for the territories of the Polish and Hungarian minorities as granted to the Sudeten region.[107] The Polish envoy emphasized the same thing in Germany, and added the necessity of a common border between Poland and Hungary by the annexation of Ruthenia to Hungary as defence measures against the spread of bolshevism.[108] For the Sudeten German question a joint Anglo-French solution was recommended on September 19 to Prague. It contained the transfer of districts to Germany with absolute German majority without plebiscite, and international guarantee for the reduced frontiers of the ČSR. Two days later the ČSR complied with the Anglo-French demands. On September 23, at his second meeting with Chamberlain, Hitler demanded more territories from the ČSR by October 1, and handed a map to the British Prime Minister delimiting the territory to be occupied immediately, and the districts where holding of a plebiscite was required before November 25. Hitler also demanded self-determination for the Hungarian and Polish minorities. Total mobilization was the Czech reply, and the Hodža government resigned. The Parliamentary caucus of the United Hungarian Party sent a message to the Magyar population in the ČSR through its newspapers that every grievance should be announced to the secretariat of the party for possible protection of the Magyar interests due to the difficult situation caused by the extraordinary measures taken by the government.[109]

Beneš once again addressed a radio message to the population in which he asked for the preservation of calm and national unity. He had plans for every possible emergency, and wanted to reach an agreement leading to a general reconciliation among the powers and between the ČSR and her neighbours. If it is necessary, we fight, if it is necessary, we negotiate — he said.[110] He did not fight, and the Munich conference of the four Western European powers on September 29 drew a new borderline between Germany and Czechoslovakia by awarding the Sudeten German districts to Germany. The political position, the historical importance, and the humanistic principles of the ČSR were not that powerful that other nations would be willing to defend them. For the Hungarian minority the declaration attached to the Munich agreement was of vital importance. (Appendix 9) The heads of governments of the four powers declared that the problems of the Polish and Hungarian minorities in Czechoslovakia, if not settled within three months by agreement between the respective governments, would form the subject of another meeting of the heads of the governments of the four powers present in Munich.[111] It made possible the revision of the border the Hungarians waited for twenty years.

From the Munich Conference to the Arbitral Award of Vienna

Three days before the Munich conference Krofta called the Hungarian ambassador to the Foreign Ministry, and read him a declaration that the Czechoslovak government was ready to engage in friendly negotiations with the government of Hungary. He added that the Hungarian nationals in the ČSR would be granted the same rights in the nationalities statute that had been worked out with the Sudeten Germans.[112] The French alliance did not function in the most crucial moment, and in Geneva, Litvinov declared that the Czechoslovak-Soviet treaty of alliance of mutual aid lost its effect in consequence of the Czechoslovak acceptance of the Anglo-French ultimatum.[113] The new Prime Minister, General Syrový, a former Czech legionnaire in Russia, was a willing tool of Moscow, and, with Beneš, wanted to prevent the annexation of Sudetenland by Germany in the last moment at the cost of a European war. Soviet officers and bolshevik agitators arrived in Ungvár (Užhorod) in Ruthenia.[114] The ČSR had confidence in her fortifications and in her eastern ally which, indeed, did not intend to fight in her defence. The Czechoslovak defence plan was partially based on the border fortifications and on the army, which since September 23, had been fully mobilized. Its discipline became loose for many soldiers — even Czechs deserted to German territory in Austria.[115] The journal of the Association of Czechoslovak Army Officers, the *Dûstojnické Listy,* strongly attacked the Hodža government before its resignation for its stand on the minority question. The powerful army saw in it the weakening of the government's position.[116]

In Munich a new European balance of power was created. It took into consideration the right to self-determination of oppressed minorities. The League of Nations was not willing and was not able to apply the principle of self-determination. It did not initiate the peaceful change of the dictated borders after World War I. It is an irony of the human rights movement that the totalitarian dictatorships, the anti-democratic governments, forced the application of the ethnic principle in the redrawing of the Czech mosaic state frontiers. British and French statesmen were just assisting them in that process because of their military unpreparedness. Their attitude towards the minorities of the ČSR was not sincere. Recognition must be given to the British and French delegations at Munich for adopting the arrangements moved by Mussolini for the solution of the demands of the Hungarian and Polish nationals in the ČSR within three months by direct negotiations among the involved governments. On September 29, State Secretary Csáky was sent to Munich by Imrédy as an observer. He was equipped with statistics and a letter of accreditation from Horthy to Mussolini requesting the inclusion of Hungary's territorial demands in the agreement.[117] In Munich there was the last chance to include the situation of the Hungarian minority in the ČSR in an international treaty. Two days before the Munich conference, Dorothy Thomson, the famous American publicist in New York, supported the Polish and Hungarian claims for the territories inhabited by them in the ČSR which needed similar treatment as the Sudeten Germans.[118]

After the Munich conference Poland did not wait for the willingness of Prague to meet her demands. Warsaw sent an ultimatum to Prague and demanded, in 14 hours, the transfer of Teschen to Poland by noon of October 2, and the evacuation of the Frysztat district in 10 days. The demand was granted on October 1,[119] and by October 4 the Polish inhabited districts in the ČSR were occupied by Polish armed forces. Hungary did not imitate this course of action. She was waiting in a chivalrous manner, and hoping for the victory of justice and fair play, but soon had to learn with bitterness that in international politics justice did not count. Germany used threats in her demands for the acquisition of Sudetenland. Before the Munich conference the Hungarians were told by Berlin that they might be left out of the deal if they did not join an eventual military action against the ČSR on the side of Germany.[120] After Munich Germany did not want to support an excessive strengthening of Hungary.[121]

Imrédy told the Italian ambassador in Budapest that Hitler wanted a war against the ČSR for reasons of prestige; the Hungarian army was not ready to fight a war at that time.[122] After Munich when the Magyars needed Germany's pressure on the ČSR, Göring told Darányi, the former Prime Minister who visited Germany, that Germany had demobilized and could not offer any help to Hungary.[123] Germany, after the Munich conference, wanted to win over to her side Czechoslovakia, a former adversary, and changed her political strategy. Berlin was against such new frontiers which would include a common Polish-Hungarian border, presenting an obstacle in German expansion.[124] In October 1938 Hitler and Göring were ready to turn against the Hungarians.[125] In Budapest the government evaluated the Munich agreement from the point of view of the Magyar demands for the rectification of the borderline between Hungary and Czechoslovakia. The representatives of four powerful European states acknowledged the collapse of the Versailles system in Central Europe, and the failure of Czech imperialism. The Czechoslovak government was forced by external intervention to give up territories on which the population would not tolerate further brutal and extended political oppression disguised as democratic rule. Hungary wanted to obtain the same treatment for the Magyar nationals in the ČSR as the Sudeten Germans and Poles received. She proved several times her willingness to achieve her goals by peaceful means. The Western European democracies obeyed only the demands of a militarily-strong Germany. The Magyar nationals in the ČSR demanded only self-determination, simple ballots, not an award or arbitration from the more numerous armed nations of Europe. Hungary expected justice from the great democracies, but on the contrary, it was tossed into the arms of Fascist and Nazi governments. Hungary had to accept the support of the two totalitarian states, although she almost lost the active aid of Germany for not being willing to participate in a planned German war adventure against the ČSR. After Munich, Germany did not need Hungary's alliance against the common enemy, the Prague government, and what is even more strange, Berlin reproached Hungary for thinking of a safe, common border with Poland which was interpreted in Germany as a possible front against the Nazi government. Rendering justice and giving consent for the self-determination of the Magyars under Czech rule was expected in vain from the Western democracies or from the League of Nations which made only five decisions, out of 852 grievances brought before it, between 1929 and 1935.

Hungary had the support of Poland, for the rightful retrocession of the Magyar populated part of the former Upper Hungary. Mussolini supported the Hungarian claims for the reason of Italy's political and economic penetration in the Danubian basin. Stressing her case, the Hungarian government had to use, in addition to diplomacy for creation of tension, irregular bands on Czechoslovak territory to force action from the signatories of the Munich agreement for her territorial demands. The Czechoslovak army was still fully mobilized, and Budapest had to take similar counter-measures.

On October 1, 1938 a Hungarian note in Prague demanded the opening of the negotiations based on the Munich decision for the self-determination of the Magyar minority in the ČSR.[126] The same day at 11:00 a.m. the Czechoslovak Minister for Foreign Affairs notified the Hungarian ambassador in Prague that his government was ready to open negotiations to arrive at a friendly agreement concerning the Hungarian minority in the ČSR.[127] The Hungarian government was urging Prague to initiate the negotiations, but Beneš was still in office, and the old tactician once again talked of the nationalities statute and the extension of full citizenship rights to the Hungarian minority but not the granting of self-determination. The Magyar ethnic group wanted to rid itself of the Czechoslovak rule. As to the Slovaks, Hungary agreed to grant them the right for self-determination. The Slovaks themselves were undecided as to what course to take; they negotiated with the Czechs, Poles and Hungarians. Every political orientation had its followers in the small Slovak nation. Some of them would have remained in the ČSR with an autonomy, others would have have joined Poland, and yet others would have returned to Hungary. In 1918 they were not satisfied with Hungary, in 1938 they were not satisfied with Czechoslovakia, and in 1945 they were not satisfied with Germany which helped them create a so-called independent Slovakia. The Slovak Populist Party at the end of September held two cards in hand; one playing with Prague, the other with Budapest. The Slovaks, in case of joining Hungary, stated their conditions as follows: administrative and executive power for Slovakia with the use of the Slovak as official language; legislative power for internal affairs, education and judicial matters, their own budget. Hungary accepted those conditions and kept them secret to avoid possible persecution or assassination of the Slovak leaders by Prague.[128] On

October 3 Hungary directed diplomatic efforts through Prague for making preparations for a settlement by asking for these steps: the release of the Hungarian political prisoners, the discharge of soldiers who were Hungarian nationals, the setting up of local detachments for the protection of life and property, the transfer of two or three cities in the frontier zone of Czechoslovakia as a symbolic gesture for further territorial concessions, and occupying them by Hungarian troops. Six communities were named for this purpose. The suggested date, time and place for commencing the negotiations was: October 6 at 4:00 p.m. at Komárom (Komárno).[129] The dangerous three-month time limit determined in Munich was successfully reduced by the Hungarian diplomacy to one month. Twenty years after Trianon, the graveyard prepared for Hungary was opened. A twenty-year period of Czech occupation of Upper Hungary could not serve as a legal basis for the possession of Magyar land if a thousand-year old common historical past could have been disregarded in the treaty of Trianon doomed to failure.

The City of Komárom, divided by the Danube river, was chosen as the scene for the bilateral negotiations. In Trianon, the city was cut in half. Its northern part was given to the ČSR, the southern remained in Hungary. The headquarters of the Hungarian delegation were established on a steamer in the port of Komárom. The negotiations took place in the Hotel Central in the Czechoslovak part of the city. The radio stations in the ČSR informed the population of the exchange of diplomatic notes, and of the granting of the same treatment to the Magyar minority as the Sudeten Germans had received. The Rumanian and Yugoslav governments were notified of the decision by Prague.[130]

Ciano informed the Hungarian ambassador in Rome that Hungary could count on one hundred Italian fighter planes to defend Budapest with the requisite pilots due to the proximity of the mobilized Czechoslovak army.[131] The Italians were willing to support Hungary. In their evaluation a successful military action from the part of Hungary was impossible. The army was not sufficiently equipped, and there were two lines of fortifications on the Czechoslovak side of the border. One immediately close to the state border (3 km), and the second line extending from the Little Carpathian Mountains to Nagyszombat (Trnava), Nyitra, Léva, Losonc, Kassa.[132]

Csáky, from the Foreign Ministry, went to Warsaw at the beginning of October to talk over the problem of the common border with Poland. The Poles developed very intensive diplomatic activity for the renewal of the traditionally friendly border with Hungary. The Polish ambassador in Berlin described Hungary as a stabilizing force in the Danubian basin.[133] The Germans became suspicious of the Polish-Hungarian cooperation, especially after the occupation of Polish Silesia by the ČSR at the beginning of October. Ribbentrop noted to Ciano that the ambassadors of Britain, France and Italy in Warsaw should have prevented Poland from sending an ultimatum to Prague and regulate the Polish problem in the ČSR. Ciano said that many Poles were expelled from the ČSR and 240,000 Germans were forced out by the Czechs before the Munich conference.[134] The Germans themselves wanted to occupy parts of Silesia but the quick action of Warsaw prevented them from taking over the Polish population and the important railway centre of Oderberg (Bohumin).

Signs of easing the tension were shown by the decision of the police in Pressburg to return 15,000 radio receivers to their owners. The "enemies of the state" could not listen to the news from Budapest, Vienna, Berlin, Paris, London or Warsaw during the long political crisis in the ČSR. The possession of a radio receiver by a "non-reliable" citizen in the opinion of the Czechoslovak authorities put the republic in danger. The political leadership in Prague also saw the necessity of solving the Slovak problem. The negotiating team of the Slovak Populist Party found the concessions offered by the Czechs unsatisfactory, therefore, the national executive council of the party was summoned for October 6 to Žilina (Zsolna, Sillein) to report on the results of the negotiations, and ask for further recommendations.[135] The Czechs, with Beneš at the helm, were clinging to their position but the tactics for gaining time and creating a fait accompli did not always work. The Slovaks had to play a twenty-year waiting game for their autonomy until the nationality problem of the republic reached a decisive stage. The real obstacle of a peaceful internal political development, Beneš, had finally disappeared from the political scene. In the evening hours of October 5, General Syrový, the Prime Minister, fulfilled "the most difficult task of his life," and read on the radio, broadcasted by all Czechoslovak stations, the letter of President Beneš, informing the government of his decision to resign and the reasons leading to his decision. The historical events forced Beneš out of office. Defenestrations of politicians in Prague had occurred at different intervals: in the Hussite period, at the outbreak of the Thirty Years' War, and after the Communist coup d'état after World War II. Beneš accomplished his own moral elimination. In 1938 he did not wait for his physical removal from the Hradsin. The obstructionist of the harmonious political development of the state, the founder of the dictatorial government gave up his office. Then the Slovaks, autonomists and former anti-autonomists, dared to formulate their common demands: a wide autonomy with their own government.

After his resignation Beneš stayed in the ČSR for three weeks, and in the greatest secrecy escaped to London. He cautiously prepared his departure from Prague to London through Rumania. On October 22 two aircrafts arrived in Croydon from Rumania to camouflage the flight of the fugitive ex-President. The fear of Beneš was exaggerated but characteristic of his lack of courage. The ambassador of the ČSR, Jan Masaryk, had to extend his apologies to the British government for the late notification of the arrival of Beneš after his landing at the airport of London. The ambassador explained that Beneš was not able to see anyone immediately because he had been sick from his birth, and had always suffered from trouble of the tympanum.[136] Perhaps it was a diplomatic sickness to cover the embarrassment caused by his escape.

The Slovaks before their meeting at Žilina demanded the recognition of the legal personality of the Slovak nation, the official use of the Slovak language, and a Slovak Diet with ample administrative and executive power, except in the functions of finance, defence and foreign Affairs. After Žilina, the Slovaks formed their own government. At Zilina, three Slovak political parties met: the Slovak Populist Party, the Agrarians and the Slovak National Party. Even the Ruthenian representatives were invited to the negotiations.[137] A delegation, consisting of Czechophile Slovak politicians, was sent there by the Czechoslovak government. The fusion between the autonomist and centralist parties deprived the Czechs of their support in Slovakia. The Slovaks introduced a one party system in their new autonomous province, released the Slovak political prisoners retained by the Czechs, and ordered the arrest of their political enemies. On the order of the new Slovak Prime Minister, Mgr. Tiso, during the night of October 22 in Pressburg alone, about 30 persons were taken into custody. In many communities there were anti-Jewish manifestations.[138] There were also in Prague anti-Semitic demonstrations in the streets and public places. The first autonomous Slovak government dissolved the masonic lodges. In Pressburg alone there were nine lodges: two Jewish, one Czechoslovak, two Slovak, two Hungarian and two German. The most valuable part of the lodges was a historical museum with documents for the relations with masons in other countries. The Slovak Populist (Hlinka) Party and the Hlinka Guard installed their offices in the occupied temples.[139] The Slovak politicians, after the resignation of Beneš, were not afraid of their physical elimination or imprisonment: they then turned against their political opponents. On October 14, the presidents of the coalition parties in Prague had a meeting where Sidor represented the Slovak Populist Party. An agreement was reached in principle for the personal background of the candidates for the presidency of the republic. It was decided that the new president had to be a civilian, and in consideration for the Slovak Populist Party, should be Catholic. The new president of Czecho-Slovakia could not be a Socialist nor a mason.[140]

The Czecho-Slovak government used delay tactics[141] in starting the intergovernmental negotiations with Hungary, but with Beneš out of the picture, they agreed that their delegation would meet the representatives of the Hungarian government at Komárom on October 9 at 19:00.[142] Czecho-Slovakia was represented by Tiso, the newly formed autonomous Slovakia's Prime Minister, Ďurčanský, Slovakia's Minister of Interior, Párkányi, Minister of Ruthenian Affairs in Prague (he did not go to Komárom), and Krno, a diplomatic advisor.[143] Members of the Hungarian delegation were: Kánya, Minister of Foreign Affairs, Teleki, Minister of Education, Pataky, Secretary of State, Péchy, Secretary of State and several experts. According to Ciano, it was a great mistake on the part of Hungary to negotiate with the Slovaks rather than with the Prague government.[144] Since the Munich conference, only ten days earlier, the political constellation changed to the detriment of the Hungarian claims. The sublime ideas of national self-determination evaporated, and political interests superseded them. Germany had plans for the domination of the rest of Czecho-Slovakia, and she became the defender of the diminished Bohemia. The Germans found an ally in the Slovaks who wanted their own state without Czechs. Hungary was not satisfied with those new developments, and the Regent asked the British Prime Minister in a personal letter for his assitance in those hours of great importance for Hungary.[145]

The mechanism for the inter-state meeting was set up, and seeing the German and Polish examples, a similar solution was expected in Hungarian circles on both sides of the international border. The convocation of the conference was a sign of hope among the Magyar nationals in the ČSR. The legislators of the United Hungarian Party of the Prague Parliament and of the Provincial Diet of Slovakia at their meeting in Pressburg on October 7 decided to form a Hungarian National Council for the direction of the Magyars' fate in the ČSR. This message was broadcasted the same evening along with the declarations of the Slovak Populist Party by Mach, and by Halprecht for the Germans living in Ruthenia. On behalf of the United Hungarian Party Esterházy expressed his thanks to the signatories of the Munich conference who embraced the cause of the Magyar nationals, and helped their liberation. He predicted that in several days the Magyar minority would be united with Hungary but calmness was required to ensure the smooth progress of negotiations. Both countries would have minorities, it was impossible to draw the border on the exact ethnic line. Even if there was a frontier line between the Slovaks and Magyars, the two nations should cooperate under the changed circumstances. When Jaross stepped to the microphone, one of the employees of the radio station wanted to prevent him from reading the proclamation of the Hungarian National Council. After the incident, Jaross read the resolution which asserted that the United Hungarian Party, already on September 17, asked for the right of self-determination and plebiscite. Since then the events shook the foundation of the Czechoslovak republic. The annexation of German and Polish inhabited areas was in progress by Germany and Poland. The ČSR had notified Hungary that it was willing to negotiate the fate of the Magyar populated territory. The Hungarian National Council demanded the immediate handing over of the territory in question to Hungary, the evacuation of that territory by the Czechoslovak army, the cessation of billeting of troops with Hungarians, and paying of indemnity for the damages caused by them, the transfer of the control of administration to the United Hungarian Party, the restoration of the freedom of expression and assembly, and the free wearing of the Hungarian tricolour. The resolution was announced to the Czechoslovak and Hungarian governments, to Poland, and to the signatories of the Munich agreement.[146] The leaders of the Hungarian minority were too optimistic in their expectations because the retrocession of their territory to the fatherland was delayed for a month due to a new deal in store between Czechs and Germans on the one hand, and between Slovaks and Germans on the other. These factors were not present in the pre-Munich days, and hindered the smooth transfer of power of the claimed territory to Hungary.

In October the Slovaks took over the administration of Slovakia from Prague, and the former political brotherhood was changing between the Slovak and Hungarian autonomists. Finally, the Slovaks dared to say openly that they preferred their own political independence free from the Czechs, and the Magyars had the courage to declare that they wanted a border revision and return to Hungary. Until then both desires had to be kept under silence because of the Czechoslovak Defence of the Republic Act. The former alliance against the Czechs turned into a competition between the political concepts of the Slovak Populist Party and the United Hungarian Party. Esterházy, who had parliamentary immunity as a deputy, was stopped at the border, and was asked to hand over his passport to the border guards under the pretext that male persons between the ages of 12 and 60 were not permitted to leave Czecho-Slovakia. After arguments, he kept his passport but was forbidden to leave the country. Measures were taken against him to hinder his diplomatic activities on behalf of the Hungarian minority. In those emotionally charged days, the editor of the *Prágai Magyar Hirlap,* Paul Szvatkó, was also arrested by the Prague police. Persecution was a method of silencing the opposition.

The political transformation of Ruthenia also disrupted the tranquil atmosphere in the republic. The members of the Prague Parliament representing Ruthenia, the Russian Central Council and the Ukranian National Council, held a joint meeting on October 8 at Užhorod (Ungvár) to formulate the political demands of Ruthenia in the presence of Governor Hrabár, and the Ruthenian Minister in the Prague government, Párkányi. They decided to present a list of seven ministers to Prague, and request their appointments. After the confirmation of the new government for Ruthenia they wanted to take over the executive power of the province. Thereupon Hrabár announced his resignation, and Párkányi became his successor appointed by the Prague government.[147] The internal subdivision of the republic resulted in three governments with 30 ministers: 18 in Prague, 5 in Pressburg and 7 in Užhorod (Ungvár). The number of ministers rapidly grew as the territory of the republic diminished.

Against this background, the direct negotiations started at Komárom, the city divided between the ČSR and Hungary. After procedural discussions, an agreement was reached in the handing over of two communities on the border to Hungary as a symbolic confirmation of the willingness for greater territorial concessions. Ipolyság (Šahy) in 24 hours counting from October 9 at 24:00 o'clock, and the railway station of Sátoraljaújhely (Slovenské Nové Mesto) in 36 hours from the same date were occupied by Hungarian army units. The details were worked out by the military experts present. The next difficult point arose in the use of statistics. The Hungarian delegation based its demands on the 1910 census.[148] The Czecho-Slovak delegation argued that newer statistical data would be more favourable to them. The Germans used the 1910 census, in the case of the Sudetenland, as the most recent reliable data. As pointed out in a previous chapter, the Czechoslovak censuses served the political purpose of denationalization. Territories had been taken away from Hungary by the order of the peace conference without such elaborate discussions based on statistics, and with experts from different fields present. Hungary made an offer for plebiscite not only for the Magyar regions but even for Slovak and Ruthenian districts, because Hungary was not afraid of the outcome of a plebiscite. Before further examination of the dispute, a quick glance at the justification of the use of the 1910 census results would clarify its importance. It should be noted that the ethnic settlements in the disputed area of 1938 corresponded to the points of contact between the Magyar and Slavic tribes in the 10th and 11th centuries. There are numerous works published on this question based on the findings of archeology, linguistics, folklore and written historical sources before the Czechs succeeded in the occupation of Upper Hungary in 1918. The Hungarian government did not seek historical justice by claiming territories which had been detached without a scrupulous examination of the composition of every little community and of the wish of the population. The false statements of Beneš and the strong antipathy of Clemenceau were not supported by statistics at the peace conference in 1919. The Hungarian proposals were founded on the location of the known and existing Hungarian settlements. The territory in question was taken away forcibly from Hungary in 1918 and without confirming the ethnic principles. The last census before the mutilation of Hungary took place in 1910. It was necessary to use the statistics of that census to enable the return to the conditions of 1918. The first Hungarian census to distinguish between nationalities was taken in 1880.[149] "At the time of the establishing of the Hungarian rule, the ancestors of the present day Slovaks lived in loose tribal communities. There did not exist an established Slovak state. The conquering Hungarians, however, immediately established and organized a state which withstood the test of centuries. The Slovak tribes surrendered without resistance nor war, nor even a battle. No use of force against the Slovaks has been noted by history."[150] The Turkish occupation (150 years), and the wars of liberation destroyed the Hungarian population and, to replace the vanishing Hungarian element, Slovak settlers descended from the highlands to spread out later in all directions.[151] The former capital of Hungary, Pressburg, was established by German immigrants. In its population the Hungarian element never possessed a majority but neither did the Slovaks.[152] Pressburg was promised to Hungary by Hitler in 1938 at the beginning of the Czechoslovak crisis but later the Germans favoured the Slovaks for political gains.[153] The distribution of the nationalities did not change from the 18th century according to reliable documents and various sources. According to Petrov, the unbiased Russian statistician, the Hungarian-Slovak ethnic dividing line remained unchanged throughout the last 130-150 years.[154] This view was expressed ten years before the Czechoslovak crisis.

The new frontiers of the ČSR, according to the Munich agreement, could not be guaranteed without taking into consideration the right of self-determination of the nationalities of the ČSR. In 1918 there was no plebiscite either in Sudetenland or in Slovakia (Upper Hungary), because the population would have opted for Germany and for Hungary. After twenty years of constant degradation, the minorities of the ČSR wanted to live as free citizens in the states of their nations. In case of plebiscites under international supervision only those persons were given the right to vote who lived there in 1918, the year of the Czechoslovak dispute, or their descendants. The imported colonists and officials could not have the right to vote; on the contrary, the expelled persons and their descendants would have been eligible. The outcome of the free votes cast under such conditions was evident for the government of Prague. A plebiscite, which was promised towards the end of World War I, was repeatedly requested by Hungary to enable the Hungarian minorities abroad to decide where they preferred to live. In October 1938, the Slovaks and Ruthenians opted for autonomy in the ČSR. One must not forget that those decisions were taken when, in Slovakia and Ruthenia, a mobilized Czecho-Slovak army of 20 classes was ready to intervene on the order of Prague. For a period of four months, these two provinces remained parts of the ČSR.

The Hungarian delegation in Komárom, on the basis of the 1910 census, asked for the transfer of 14,150 km² with a population of 1,090,000 with Magyar majority. The territory included the cities of Nyitra, Kassa in Slovakia; Ungvár and Munkács in Ruthenia.[155] The area included 12 of 13 towns and 812 of 830 villages with Hungarian majority transfered to the ČSR in 1918, representing 77.9% of Hungarians.[156] The Czecho-Slovak delegation, instead of presenting counter-proposals, the following day tried to sidetrack the whole question of retrocession of the demanded belt of land. They talked of the economic, industrial and strategic importance of the area as well as the lines of communications and railway centres necessary for the ČSR. These delaying tactics were unacceptable to the Hungarian representatives. The Czecho-Slovak delegation asked for postponement of the talks. The Slovaks at the Komárom negotiations were influenced by Karmasin, editor of the German language newspaper *Grenzbote* in Pressburg. After the cession of the Sudetenland to Germany, he was the political leader, a small Führer of the Carpatho-German Party in Slovakia. Karmasin was present at Komárom as an observer, but in fact as a Nazi spy. He obtained an audience for Ďurčanský and Mach, two ministers of the new autonomous Slovak government, with Seyss-Inquart, the Reich's governor in Vienna, under the disguise of economic talks for the not far away Slovak independence. The Nazi governor of Austria, with his connections in Berlin, made an appointment for the Slovak emissaries with Göring for the day following their arrival in Vienna. The Slovaks asked Göring for the support of the Reich's government against the Hungarian demands.[157] The Germans saw a golden opportunity to interfere with the furthering of their expansion in Slovakia. Ďurčanský, fresh in his position in the Slovak cabinet and in the Czecho-Slovak delegation in Komárom, disclosed his real identity in the very first days of the existence of the Slovak autonomy. He was, together with other autonomist Slovaks, an implacable enemy of the Czechs, and yet, after the events at Žilina, they accepted the mandate to represent the new version of the Czecho-Slovak republic at an international conference. The Czechs themselves had no reason on any grounds to claim Hungarian territory, and they thought perhaps the Slovaks would like to have those territories for themselves which in 1918, with the aid of the protectors of Masaryk and Beneš, had been given to Czechoslovakia. The Slovaks plotted against the Hungarians with the Nazis. They forgot one important detail. No matter who penetrated the Danubian basin, and tried to partition it, the Slovaks and Magyars would have to live there as neighbours after the departure of the conquerors, and would have to find the conditions of a peaceful and prosperous life.

The Hungarian delegation at Komárom learned of the visit of the Slovak ministers in Berlin; where a deal was made for the retention of purely Hungarian areas in Czecho-Slovakia. After the occupation of the Sudetenland by Germany, and Polish Silesia by Poland, the Czecho-Slovak occupation of Hungarian territory was impossible, but an obstruction was staged by the Czecho-Slovak delegation at Kamárom. They offered a wide-degree of self-government for the Magyars living in the new autonomous Slovak part of the ČSR which was inconsistent with the earlier retrocession of Ipolyság and Sátoraljaújhely to Hungary as a symbol of more territorial concessions. Then they offered a 90 km long part of the purely Hungarian Csallóköz (Velký Ostrov Žitný, Grosschütt), an island between the two branches of the Danube river, between Pressburg and Komárom, an area of 1,840 km² with a population of 105,000. They wanted to keep in the ČSR several villages on the Csallóköz, in the vicinity of Pressburg. This did not satisfy the Hungarian delegation, and later it was modified to an area of 5,400 km² with 350,000 inhabitants. These Czecho-Slovak proposals did not follow the ethnic line but economic, strategic and transportation interests. The Slovaks were told that the basis of the border correction was the ethnic principle, the other aspects could be considered with mutual good-will. Since purely Hungarian districts would have remained in the post-Munich Czecho-Slovaco-Ruthenian republic, the Hungarian delagation, under instructions from Budapest, did not see reasons for staying longer in Komárom,[158] and declared that it would ask the arbitration of the four Munich conference signatories. On October 22 a third proposal was made for the retrocession of 11,300 km^2 with a population of 740,000 to Hungary.[159]

Several deputies of the United Hungarian Party from Slovakia and Ruthenia, among them Esterházy and Jaross, stayed in Komárom during the negotiations and played important roles as go-betweens for the two delegations. Their presence proved essential, especially in decisive moments. Many emissaries and delegations visited Komárom from those villages which lay in the racially mixed regions. They were expecting a plebiscite, and were troubling the assistants of the negotiators with their questions concerning their future.[160] No one was able to give them answers for those vitally important inquiries. The mood of the population was disturbed by the bilingual, Slovak and Hungarian, pamphlets dispersed by air which denounced the retrocession of territory to Hungary.[161] Before the interruption of the negotiations in Komárom, the Hungarian National Council in the ČSR submitted a memorandum to Tiso and Bačinsky in the Czecho-Slovak delegation, and to Kánya in the Hungarian one, in which the representatives of the Hungarian National Council in Slovakia and Ruthenia demanded their representation in the negotiations. They argued that the subject of the discussions was the territorial sovereignty and the rights of the Hunagrian minority. This memorandum was signed by the following deputies from Slovakia and Ruthenia: Szilassy, Esterházy, Jaross and Vozáry.[162] In the meantime, the retrocession of the two towns, Ipolyság and Satoraljaujhely, to Hungary took place with a solemn and enthusiastic reception of the Hungarian army and administration. The Magyars in the ČSR had waited for twenty years for their return under Hungarian sovereignty.

On October 14 the Czech press recognized in the comments on the Komárom conference that the Slovaks and not the Czecho-Slovak central government conducted the discussions on behalf of the ČSR. The press wrote that the Slovak counter-proposal implied the surrender of Grossschütt to Hungary, and the Hungarian counties south of the Slovak Ore Mountains.[163] The Italian consul in Pressburg had a conversation with the Vice-Premier of Slovakia, Ďurčanský, who returned from a trip in Germany. He was received by Göring who assured him that the Reich would not claim Pressburg as a gesture towards the Slovak nation. During the conversation Ďurčanský asked the consul to arrange a visit for Tiso and himself in Rome to clear the Slovak attitude towards Hungary.[164] The Slovak ministers were not given the chance to travel to Rome for it would have taken too much time and caused unnecessary delay in the solution of the Hungarian claims. A few days later Prime Minister Tiso told the Italian consul in Pressburg that he found a favourably disposed attitude in Germany for the Slovak cause, and would like to have some understanding from Italy. He sent Sidor to Warsaw and Mach to Zagreb to seek sympathy for the government of Slovakia.[165] It was the view in the consular corps at Pressburg that in the presence of the Czech police and army, the Slovaks were not able to express their views freely. The idea of a Slovak state, detached from Bohemia, originated with Ribbentrop. The German Foreign Minister brought up this possibility to Tiso at the latter's visit to Munich on October 19, 1938.[166] From a Slovak autonomous government the Germans created in March 1939 a Slovak republic which immediately became a German satellite. Hitler in that month scared the Slovaks with a Hungarian occupation when in reality he wanted to occupy not only Bohemia and Moravia but also Slovakia to encircle Poland.

In those historic days the Hungarians in Slovakia formed national unity by the fusion of different political trends. The Social Democratic Party of Slovakia and its affiliated trade unions accepted a resolution on October 10 according to which the Hungarian socialist workers joined the Hungarian National Council. They wanted to take part in the work for the Hungarian national cause. The Slovaks already had declared their right to self-determination and the same right belonged to all the autochtonous people of Slovakia without any distinction regarding language, nationality or religion.[167] On October 14 the Hungarian National Council issued a proclamation to the Magyar minority in the ČSR asking it that after the break in the talks at Komárom, the Magyars should keep their poise and self-discipline. They reassured the Magyar ethnic group that in those troublesome days the Hungarian National Council worked for its rights.[168] There was a great need for this announcement because tempers were flaring at that time in Slovakia resulting in demonstrations. The Slovaks could express their feelings and joy over their autonomy but the Hungarians were attacked either by the Slovak mob or the gendarmerie not only for demonstrating in favour of their union with Hungary but even for entirely innocent expressions of their national feelings such as wearing the so-called Bocskai neckties. (Bocskai was the leader of an uprising against the Habsburg king of Hungary in 1604.) The Hungarian National Council had to intervene with the new autonomous Slovak government for the liberation of arrested Hungarians of various communities. The life of the Magyars in the ČSR became extremely difficult because of the martial law in vigour in their region.[169] The political leaders of the Hungarian minority formed a national council and issued the following proclamation:

Proclamation of the Hungarian National Council[170]

Hungarians!

The negotiations between the Czecho-Slovak delegation and the Hungarian delegation were unsuccessful. (Here the censor erased ten lines.)

We call upon all Hungarian brothers and sisters to stand in closed ranks behind the Hungarian National Council faithfully as these serious times demand it, and to maintain their composure.

The Hungarian National Council works for the rights of the Hungarian ethnic group.

It is our firm conviction that in the Carpathian basin it is possible to create peaceful conditions for a long period of time if every nation can live in its state and can develop its proper cultural, economic and national strengths. We wish this for the Slovak and Ruthenian nations, but we want to secure our rights independently of their fate.

God be with us in our subsequent work.

Komárom, October 14, 1938

The Hungarian National Council

Footnotes

1. PRO., FO., 341/21426, 133.
2. Ibid., 251.
3. Ibid., 371/22372.
4. Lidové Noviny, May 21, 1938.
5. Die Zeit, May 23, 1938.
6. Sb. zák. a nař.
7. Ibid.
8. PRO., FO., 341/21436, 276-277.
9. Foreign Relations of the U.S.A., 1938, I, 57.
10. PRO., FO., 341/21426, 194.
11. Ibid., 211.
12. Ibid., 222.
13. PMH, August 4, 1938.
14. Journal de Genève, July 23, 1938.
15. PRO., FO., 800/306, 105-106.
16. PMH, August 5, 1938.
17. Op. cit., August 6, 1938.
18. Česká Výzva, August 6, 1938.
19. PRO., FO., 800/306, September 2, 1938.
20. PMH, August 6 and 10, 1938.
21. Op. cit., August 13, 1938.
22. PRO., FO., 800/306, 130.
23. PMH, August 27, 1938.
24. Daily Mail, August 18, 1938.
25. *A müncheni egyezmény...* No. 275.
26. Ibid., No. 269.
27. Ibid., No. 288b.
28. České Slovo, September 3, 1938.
29. *Memoirs,* Admiral Nicholas Horthy, 162-164.
30. *A müncheni egyezmény...* No. 299.
31. Affari Esteri, No. 724/105
32. *A müncheni egyezmény...* No. 297.
33. PRO., FO., 800/306, 141.
34. Ibid., 145.
35. Ibid., 108.
36. PRO., FO., 371/21564, 157.
37. Ibid., 208.

38. Ibid., 213.

39. Ibid., 108.

40. PMH, August 26, 1938.

41. Op. cit., August 27, 1938.

42. Bruegel, J.W., *Czechoslovakia Before Munich,* 240.

43. PMH, September 1, 1938.

44. Prager Tagblatt, September 1, 1938.

45. PMH, September 2, 1938.

46. PMH, September 7, 1938.

47. Prager Presse, September 8, 1938 & PRO., FO., 800/3-4, 370.

48. PMH, September 7, 1938.

49. PRO., FO., 800/306, 110.

50. Ibid.

51. PMH, September 9, 1938.

52. Affari Esteri, No. 12332/P.

53. Op. cit., No. 2411/259.

54. PRO., FO., 341/21564.

55. Ibid.

56. Ibid., 800/305.

57. Ibid., 459, 463.

58. Ibid., 364-376.

59. Affari Esteri, No. 232962.

60. PRO., FO., 800/306, 37.

61. Ibid., 341/21567, 154.

62. Ibid., 800/306, 58.

63. PMH., September 10, 1938.

64. *A müncheni egyezmény...* No. 322.

65. PMH., September 9, 1938.

66. Ibid., September 11, 1938.

67. Slovák, September 11, 1938.

68. Ibid., September 16, 1938.

69. PMH., September 15, 1938.

70. PRO., FO., 800/304-9316, 78, 80.

71. Ibid., 341/21465, 147.

72. PMH., September 18, 1938.

73. PRO., FO., 341/21438, 186.

74. Ibid., 341/21482, 115.

75. Ibid., 240.

76. Affari Esteri, No. 14761/PR, September 17, 1938.

77. Popolo d'Italia, September 15, 1938.

78. Gazeta Polska, April 23, 1938.

79. La Tribuna, September 19, 1938.

80. Ibid., September 22, 1938.

81. Ibid., September 25, 1938.

82. Ibid., September 26, 1938.

83. Ibid., September 27, 1938.

84. PMH., September 17, 1938.

85. PRO., FO., 371/21723, 30.

86. *A müncheni egyezmény...* II, No. 308.

87. Ibid., No. 309.

88. Nieopublikowane dokumenty, EE/MG/no.52/tjn/191, September 21, 1938, 33.

89. Ibid., AB/MR/no. 52/tjn/200, October 7, 1938, 451.

90. Ibid., No. 78, Nr. G.M.S. 2946, September 17, 1938.

91. Ibid., No. 83, Nr. G.M.S. 3071, September 22, 1938.

92. DGFP., D.V., 302.

93. Historický Časopis, Op., cit., p. 603.

94. PRO., FO., 341/21747.

95. Horthy Miklós titkos iratai, No. 35.

96. Historický Časopis, Op., cit., 603.

97. Nieopublikowane dokumenty, Nr. G.M.S. 2935, No. 118.

98. Ibid., 2950, No. 122.

99. Ibid., No. 133, 3088.

100. Ibid., No. 135, 3168.

101. Ibid., No. 128, 3168.

102. PMH., September 19, 1938.

103. *A müncheni egyezmény...* No. 351.

104. Ibid., No. 358 and 362.

105. Ibid., No. 361.

106. Ibid., No. 370.

107. Ibid., No. 378, 379.

108. Ibid., No. 377.

109. PMH., September 23, 1938.

110. Ibid., September 24, 1938.

111. DGFP., D, II, 1016.

112. *A müncheni egyezmény...* No. 395.

113. Új Magyarság, September 23, 1938.

114. Ibid., September 28, 1938.

115. Affari Esteri, 213684/C.

116. Gazeta Polska, August 14, 1938.

117. ADAP., II, 671.

118. Gazeta Polska, September 28, 1938.

119. *A müncheni egyezmény...* No. 448.

120. Ibid., No. 401.

121. Ibid., No. 425.

122. Affari Esteri, No. 4348/R., September 6, 1938.

123. Ibid., No. 17058/Pr/C., October 15, 1938.

124. PMH., October 21, 1938.

125. Čulen, K., Op., cit., 558.

126. *A müncheni egyezmény...* II, No. 432.

127. Ibid., No. 442.

128. Ibid., No. 403.

129. ADAP., IV, 26.

130. PMH., October 4, 1938.

131. *Ciano's Diary,* October 5, 1938.

132. Affari Esteri, No. 810/543.

133. Nieopublikowane dokumenty, p. 83-84, August 24, 1938.

134. Dokumenty z przededenia II wojny światowej, Nr. 4-8, October 1, 1938.

135. PMH., October 5, 1938.

136. PRO., FO., 341/21588, 463-464.

137. PMH., October 7, 1938.

138. Gazeta Polska, October 24, 1938.

139. Affari Esteri, No. 2768/302.

140. PMH., October 16, 1938.

141. Chászár, E., *Decision in Vienna,* 45.

142. *A müncheni egyezmény...* II, No. 477.

143. Ibid.

144. DGFP, Pol. IV, 7430.

145. Szinai, M. — L. Szűcs, *Horthy Miklós titkos iratay,* 180.

146. PMH., October 9, 1938.

147. Ibid., October 11, 1938.

148. *A müncheni egyezmény...* II, No 487, 488, 489.

149. Kővágó, J., Op., cit., 33.

150. Ibid., 32-33.

151. Ibid., 34.

152. Ibid., 36.

153. DGFP., Pol. V., 131.

154. Kővágó, J., Op., cit., 38.

155. DBFP., III, Vol. 3, 152.

156. Chászár, E., Op., cit., 39.

157. Hoensch, J., Op., cit., 136-137.

158. *A müncheni egyezmény...* II, No. 487, 493a.

159. 8 Órai Újság, November 13, 1938.

160. PMH., October 13, 1938.

161. Ibid.

162. Ibid., October 15, 1938.

163. Bohemia, October 14, 1938.

164. Affari Esteri, No. 5519, October 16, 1938.

165. Ibid., October 20, 1938.

166. Hoensch, J., *Die Slowakei,* 211.

167. PMH., October 15, 1938.

168. Ibid., October 18, 1938.

169. Ibid., October 20, 1938.

170. Ibid.

CHAPTER VII

THE PEACEFUL REVISION OF THE CZECHO-SLOVAK-HUNGARIAN BORDER

Prelude to the Vienna Arbitration

The Komárom negotiations broke down because the Slovak ministers representing Czecho-Slovakia did not bargain according to the conditions agreed upon by the Prague government. They did not have experience in international conferences, and wanted to keep territories for themselves which had been taken away from Hungary by the Czechs. During the conference, the Slovaks wanted to make a special deal with Hitler. In Komárom they presented irrelevant arguments for keeping as many Hungarians in Czecho-Slovakia, perhaps as hostages, as there were Slovaks living in Southern Hungary among the Magyar population. The Slovak settlers in Southern Hungary lived on their freely chosen land and had no desire to live in Czecho-Slovakia. In those perturbed months an expansionist mood dominated the minds of politicians. The German government was thinking of occupying several communities in Slovakia close to the Austrian border, including Pressburg.[1] The Germans also wanted to establish themselves in Ruthenia by placing German sympathizers in the new autonomous government to counteract the Polish-Hungarian drive for a common border by the retrocession of Ruthenia to Hungary.[2] Emphasis was put in Poland and Hungary on the defensive nature of the desired common frontier in the Carpathian mountains. In the French press, the anti-German role of the planned common Polish-Hungarian border was emphasized. It was duly noticed in Germany. After Munich the German government did not need the assistance of the Hungarian government against the ČSR, and Berlin hindered the Magyar efforts in Slovakia and Ruthenia. Those provinces were regarded as a German zone of interest. Bródy, the Ruthenian minister arrived late at Komárom and could not influence the outcome of the conference with his planned declaration concerning the cession of Ruthenia to Hungary.[3] Párkányi, the Ruthenian minister in the reorganized Prague government, did not go to Komárom. Bródy later was arrested on the order of General Syrový for his pro-Magyar stand in the Ruthenian question.[4] Under the impact of events Prague appointed the first Ruthenian government in Ungvár in October 1938.[5] The Hungarian delegation returned to Budapest and presented its report to the government on the Czecho-Slovak offers. Both sides initiated feverish diplomatic activity. Horthy wrote a letter to Hitler on October 13[6] in which he gave a brief account of the happenings in Komárom, and asked him to receive his emissary Darányi, the former Prime Minister, for an audience. After the fiasco of the state visit in Kiel, because of the agreement at the Bled conference between Hungary and the Little Entente, Imrédy and Kánya became *personae non gratae* in Berlin. The race for Hitler's diplomatic support began. The Czechs and Slovaks were hoping for his protection. Hungary notified the four signatories of the Munich agreement and Poland of the failure of direct negotiations with the ČSR. Simultaneously, the new Czecho-Slovak Foreign Minister, Chvalkovský, visited Hitler in Munich, and promised him a German orientation in Prague's external and internal policies.[7] The members of the Slovak autonomist government continued to visit Hitler, and serve the German interests in a servile manner. Five months later they obtained their reward, the expulsion of the Czechs from Slovakia, and the creation of the short-lived Slovak republic which lasted until the end of World War II. After Chvalkovský, the Slovak and Ruthenian ministers begged Hitler to give less to Hungary than she was entitled to on the basis of the Magyar settlements and the wish of the involved population. Already in April 1937, the German-Hungarian friendship became estranged because Berlin's propaganda developed among the Volksdeutsche in Hungary.[8] Darányi was dispatched to Munich to repair the damage done in the eyes of Hitler and Ribbentrop in August by Imrédy, Kánya and Horthy during their visit to Germany by defending Hungary's independent position taken at the Bled conference of the Little Entente. Darányi had to counterbalance Chvalkovský's cooperation with Berlin. He eased the tension when in the name of the Hungarian government a closer coordination of the foreign policy was offered to the Berlin-Rome axis, and the possibility of joining the Anti-Comintern Pact, and leaving the League of Nations.[9] Earlier Ribbentrop had promised his visitors from the ČSR that five cities: *Pressburg, Nyitra, Kassa. Ungvár* and *Munkács* would remain in the ČSR. These cities until Ribbentrop's intervention lay on the Hungarian side of a line of the map. Darányi also took a map with him delimiting the Hungarian demands. These demands included the retrocession of the pure Hungarian districts to Hungary, and a plebiscite under British control in the mixed areas, divided in the following eight districts: 1) between *Érsekujvár* and *Nyitra*, 2) around *Jolsva* (Jelšava), 3) the district east of *Rozsnyó* (Rožňava, Rosenau), 4) *Kassa* and the district west of the city, 5) the district *east of Kassa* up to Tőketerebes (Trebišov), 6) *Ungvár*, 7) *Munkács* and its immediate district, 8) the southern edge of Ruthenia north of the Rumanian border. In this last district a railway line became a contested issue.[10] From Munich

Darányi spoke with Imrédy by telephone, informing him that Ribbentrop already superficially drew a line on the map for Chvalkovský, leaving the five above-mentioned cities on the northern or would-be Czecho-Slovak side of the "Ribbentrop line."[11] Darányi presented the minimal Hungarian claims according to instructions received from Imrédy. Tiso and Ďurčanský for the Slovak autonomous government, and Bačinsky for the Ruthenian autonomous government also visited Ribbentrop and presented their demands.[12] Germany asked Darányi to drop the idea of a four-power conference, and accept the arbitration of Germany and Italy only. On October 22, the German ambassador in Budapest transmitted the proposed borderline, the "Ribbentrop line," to the Foreign Ministry as the basis for renewed negotiations between the ČSR and Hungary. Kánya was forced to look for support from Italy. Csáky, Chief of the cabinet in the Foreign Ministry, flew to Rome, and conferred with Mussolini and Ciano. He explained to them the Magyar territorial claims. He accused Germany of encouraging the ČSR against the Hungarian demands. Hungary was determined to test the dispute before a four-power conference, and Ciano notified the other three governments — Britain, France and Germany — to arrange the conference. He did not know that Ribbentrop was opposed to such a conference, and told Darányi so in Munich. The Germans preferred, once again, direct negotiations between the two countries involved. Ciano had to call off — with great displeasure — the planned conference, and accept the German approach.[13] When the note of the Ribbentrop line became known, the Hungarian ambassador to Rome told Ciano that the Czech proposal, which wanted to keep five cities, Pressburg, Nyitra, Kassa, Ungvár and Munkács, was unacceptable. The Magyars would be willing to give up Pressburg and Nyitra as a concession but definitely not the three other cities. Hungary would ask for an Italian-German arbitration in the western part of Slovakia, and for an Italian-German-Polish arbitration in the eastern part.[14] It is interesting to note that the Slovaks were also thinking of turning to a third power for mediation. Sidor, the Polonophile deputy of the Slovak Populist Party, was sent to Warsaw most likely for that purpose. A few weeks later, the sympathy of the Slovaks changed into a Polonophobia when the Poles wrested three small Polish speaking districts from Slovakia in the Tatra mountains.[15] The population in the disputed territory became impatient, and it was reported that on October 22, Ajka, a community on the left bank of the Danube asked Mussolini for retrocession of Pressburg to Hungary.[16] In Cleveland, Ohio the Hungarian-Americans asked Mussolini to use his good offices in exerting every effort to restore Northern Hungary to the motherland.[17]

Ciano urged Prague, at the request of Hungary, to make a concrete offer to Budapest. If the two governments could not agree, the two axis powers could function as arbitrators.[18] Ciano was briefed on the "Ribbentrop line" on the map of the Hungarian-inhabited strip in Southern Slovakia, and of the German Foreign Minister's wish to strike five cities from the Hungarian claims. All those five cities were earmarked by Ribbentrop for the ČSR. He did not apply the idea of national self-determination for the Magyars. Before Munich he wanted to persuade Hungary to join Germany against Czechoslovakia. After Munich he defended the Czechs and Slovaks with the same zeal as he had attacked them earlier. Hungary was willing to make some concessions around Pressburg and Nyitra, but was not ready to sacrifice the other three cities with Magyar majority.[19] Hungary did not trust Germany, for that reason Budapest wanted to include Poland among the arbitrators at least for the eastern part of Slovakia and for Ruthenia. The Germans, feeling a strong Italian support for Hungary, hinted a four-power conference which they had rejected eight days earlier.[20]

The British government also preferred a direct agreement between the two states in the frontier problem to avoid another four-power conference.[21] The Soviet Union showed understanding towards the idea of a plebiscite but still considered the Magyar procedure forcible because it was the outcome of the Munich agreement.[22] The Poles were still pressing for the realization of the common border with Hungary, on one section of the old common border, in Ruthenia. There was no hope for joining Hungary on the full length of the former common border because of the German support of Slovakia.[23] In order to obtain the approval of Rumania for its plan, the Polish government promised a railway line to Bucharest via Ruthenia. The immediate aim of the Polish Foreign Minister's trip to Rumania in the second half of October 1938 was to solicit the consent of the Rumanian government for the occupation of Ruthenia by Hungary. However, Germany blocked the realization of the restoration of the natural and former common border between Poland and Hungary in Ruthenia. The Rumanians did not want to hear of the repossession of Ruthenia by Hungary since the Rumanians had the largest Magyar minority among the successor states, and, in that case, they would have lost the common border with their Czech allies. Germany also wanted to weaken Polish prestige by opposing the common border with Hungary which lay as an obstacle in the path of German eastward expansion; furthermore, the two friendly neighbours were potential enemies of the Reich. The German counter-demand was the connection of Danzig and Prussia with Germany by extraterritorial railway and autoroute. Germany wanted to have unperturbed influence in the region. The Rumanians, however, had their own plans for the occupation of more Hungarian territory westward from the existing Hungaro-Rumanian border to the Csap-Kassa railway line.

The Polish view of the Slovak question was logical. The Poles were of the opinion that in order to prevent territorial disputes between the Magyars and the Slovaks, Slovakia should be given full autonomy, guaranteed by Poland, in the framework of the Hungarian state. That solution would eliminate all border disputes between the two neighbouring nations. Italy appeared favourable to the realization of the Polish-Hungarian border. The Italian government wanted to increase its influence in the Danubian basin but, after the Anschluss, Mussolini did not conduct an anti-German policy in Central Europe.[24]

The French press openly wrote of the Polish plan as an anti-German project. It was not wise on the part of Germany's enemies to extend wide publicity on the efforts of the Polish diplomacy which in reality was directed against German imperialism. It elicited a German reaction, and consequently, Italy also became opposed to the idea. Five months later, in March 1939, with the consent of Germany, Hungary occupied Ruthenia and restored the common historical border with Poland on the ridge of the Carpathian mountains. In 1938 Germany's condition for a consent to a common Polish-Hungarian border was a demand of a mile-wide extraterritorial road and railway link between Prussia and Danzig, a kind of cross-corridor across the Polish corridor to the sea which was refused by Poland.[25] In March 1939 Germany occupied the rest of Bohemia and Moravia which was left after the Munich conference for the Czechs. Berlin could not oppose the reoccupation of Ruthenia by Hungary in such an atmosphere.

The danger and threat of German expansion occupied the minds of the Hungarian statesmen who tried to restrain it through Italian friendship. The Hungarians could not renounce their claims based on the ethnic principle, and on the wish of the Hungarian minority in the ČSR to accomodate Slovak economic interests and German territorial expansion. After the Austrian Anschluss, the German government did not rectify one of the injustices committed against Hungary, and did not consider the restoration of the Magyar population in the province of Burgenland to Hungary as a friendly, anti-Trianon gesture.

In 1918 the borders were not delimited with experts holding precise documents, statistics and maps as at the Munich and Vienna conferences in 1938. Hungary expressed in Berlin her wish for the repossession of Pressburg[26]. Pressburg was a special case because in 1910 not a single nationality enjoyed an absolute majority there. According to the 1910 census, Pressburg had 78,223 inhabitants, broken down as follows: Germans 41.90%, Magyars 40.60%, Slovaks 14.90%, others 2.70%.[27] Pressburg was the seat of a Hungarian county (comitat) already during the reign of the first Hungarian royal dynasty, the Árpáds (1000-1301). It became an administrative, cultural and economic centre. The city flourished in the fifteenth century under the patronage of the Renaissance king of Hungary, Matthias Corvinus, who in 1467, with the consent of Pope Paul II, and under his own royal patronage founded a university at Pressburg, the *Academia Istropolitana.** Pressburg thereby joined the small group of new university towns in Central Europe. In 1526, after the death of Louis II on the battlefield fighting the Turks, the

* Istros for Danube in Greek.

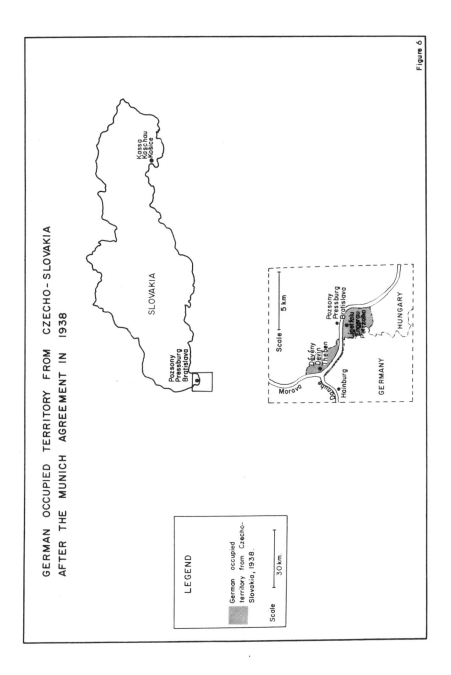

GERMAN OCCUPIED TERRITORY FROM CZECHO-SLOVAKIA AFTER THE MUNICH AGREEMENT IN 1938

Figure 6

Hungarian estates elected at Pressburg, in the church of the Franciscans, Ferdinand of Habsburg to be king of Hungary. When the Turks occupied Buda, the capital city, in 1541 and held it for 145 years, the seat of government was transferred to Pressburg, and remained there until 1848. The Hungarian Diet held its meetings in Pressburg for three hundred years. It became the coronation town. From that time well into the nineteenth century Pressburg was the centre of intellectual, spiritual, political and commercial life in Hungary. Many great poets and writers of Magyar literature lived in this capital, and many cultural movements originated within its limits. In 1825 at the meeting of the Hungarian Diet, Count Stephen Széchenyi offered one year's income to the foundation of the Hungarian Academy. When the capital was transferred to its old place, today's Budapest, the importance of Pressburg as a cultural centre remained. In 1914 the city again housed a university. At the meeting point of three languages and three cultures, Magyar, German and Slovak, close to Vienna, the former imperial city, Pressburg and its vicinity formed a much envied trilingual belt. It provided a good example for a peaceful and prosperous lifestyle to its residents. The ancestors of the Germans who immigrated to Hungary centuries before, and became assimilated to the Hungarian style of life, however, had preserved their customs, and were allowed to keep their schools and ancestral language. Pressburg was taken away from Hungary in 1918 because Beneš wanted to have an access to the Danube for the newly created ČSR. There were other options for granting privileges in the port of an international waterway or to a railway station than to donate cities to foreigners. On the basis of ethnic statistics Pressburg should not have been given to Czechoslovakia.

In 1938, after twenty years of Czecho-Slovak rule and persecution of the autochthon Magyar and German population, the vital statistics were changed but the twenty-year injustice could not serve for the sanction and prolongation of a foreign occupation of Pressburg. Hitler applied other principles for the Sudetenland where he demanded the recognition of the 1910 statistics. A plebiscite was not allowed in Pressburg in 1938 because the Germans of the city were considered "good Hungarians." Many centuries formed the traditions and spirit of the old Hungarian capital, and they survived the Czecho-Slovak period. There existed German and Slovak fears that the city in a free plebiscite would vote for Hungary. The Nazi government complicated the question of Pressburg by its aspirations for the city. A Slovak government delegation went to Vienna, and wanted to profit from the Hungarian-German controversy concerning the future of the city.[28] The Germans did not occupy Pressburg but the bridgehead of the city, on the right bank of the Danube, Ligetfalu (Petržalka, Engerau) was taken away from the ČSR by Germany on October 10, 1938 without any previous notification. It was a great shock for the four-day old autonomous Slovak government, but the Germanophile Slovaks did not dare to disagree with

Hitler. The Hungarian government expressed its disapproval of the German occupation of Ligetfalu which before 1918 belonged to Hungary. The protest, indeed, had to be withdrawn on German request. Hitler, accompanied by Marshall Göring, visited Engerau[29] on October 25. This was not the only community which the Germans took away from the Slovak part of the ČSR in 1938. On November 24 the German troops occupied, without incident and among the ovation of the predominantly German population, the zone of Devín (Theben, Dévény) on the left bank of the Danube at the estuary of the Morava River. It was considered a rectification of the borderline. (The Danube was the border at that point with Austria on the right bank.) As a consequence of this action, the waterworks of Pressburg fell in German hands 2 or 3 km from the city limits. The City of Pressburg requested that the government of the Reich rectify the borderline by several hundred meters to regain their aqueduct.[30] This was the same friendly German government which two weeks earlier had occupied Ligetfalu.

Another dispute arose between Hungary and the autonomous Slovak government of the ČSR for the possession of Kassa (Košice), the capital of Eastern Slovakia, formerly eastern Upper Hungary. Göring secretly promised Kassa to the Slovaks. Kassa is an old Hungarian cultural centre. In 1910 it had 44,211 inhabitants of whom 78% were Magyars. By 1930 the population grew to 70,000 as a result of immigration from Bohemia and Moravia, and from the surrounding Slovak districts of about 16,000 people.[31] The percentage of the Magyar population was artificially decreased in the falsified official Czechoslovak statistics. However, the secret ballots at the communal elections in May 1937 revealed the true ethnic character of the city in spite of the nineteen-year old Czechoslovak rule. The Italian consul in Pressburg sent the following report to the Foreign Ministry in Rome on May 25, 1937:

At the communal elections in Kassa (Košice) the United Hungarian Party received one third of the votes. It should be noted that the voters' registration was controlled by the Slovak minority of the city. In the 1930 census, Kassa, the largest city besides Pressburg, officially had only 18% Hungarians and consequently was deprived of the official use of the Hungarian language. (It was doctored under 20%). Besides the United Hungarian Party the Hungarian Socialists and Communists also received votes, and there was a Jewish Party which also received about 3,000 votes from the Hungarian-speaking Jews. The small German population also contributed to the victory of the United Hungarian Party. Kassa was inhabited in fact by a population with a Hungarian representation of fifty percent. The political importance of such a finding was that the Czechoslovak census policy was formulated to deny the minority rights to ethnic groups wherever the government wanted to reflect artificial population size in official statistics. The Czech government press ignored the whole affair in silence. The *Slovák,* an autonomist paper, denounced the scandalous difference between the official statistics and the results of the elections which revealed the Hungarian character of the city, and protested against the government which in a criminal way failed to slovakize the city. The Czech parties did not receive a single mandate.[32] The communal elections provided the Magyar population with free use of ballots to express their preference for the United Hungarian Party or for the Hungarian Socialists or Communists to represent their interests. The Slovak minority and the few Czechs in the city of Kassa did not vote for any of the Hungarian parties.

So, despite of two decades of Czechoslovak rule, the Hungarian character of Pressburg and Kassa could no longer be denied.

The conduct of the supposedly friendly German government during the preliminary discussions leading to the Vienna arbitration caused bitterness in Hungary. There were several exchanges of notes between Budapest and Berlin regarding the fate of the disputed cities, and Ciano approached Ribbentrop on behalf of the minimal Hungarian demands: Kassa, Ungvár, Munkács.[33] In case of an impasse, the Hungarian government was ready to accept the verdict of the arbitration of Germany and Italy with the participation of Poland for the eastern section of the republic. Ribbentrop was against the participation of Poland, but he himself wanted to avoid arbitration in order not to reveal his anti-Hungarian attitude.[34] Therefore, on October 22, 1938 the Foreign Minister in Prague transmitted to the Hungarian ambassador a proposal of his governement accompanied by a map. Hungary in her reply proposed the occupation of the non-disputable territories by her troops in three days starting from October 27; a plebiscite for the eight districts in question, except Pressburg, for which negotiations were proposed; and the realization of the right to self-determination for the Slovaks and Ruthenians under international control. If the note was refused, arbitration of Italy and Germany for the western, plus Poland for the eastern territories would be demanded.[35] Prague expressed its opposition to a Polish presence on the committee of arbiters. The Czecho-Slovak government remained silent on the Hungarian proposal for a plebiscite. In Prague there was no confidence in the loyalty of its own subjects. Prague was afraid of the results a genuine plebiscite would offer. Tiso even wrote a letter to Ribbentrop on October 25, saying he could agree to a plebiscite only if the Jews were to be excluded from voting.[36] The answer from Prague the following day stated if the October 22 proposal did not satisfy the Hungarian government, the Czecho-Slovak government would agree to submit the question to the arbitration of the two Munich signatories, Germany and Italy. If the two powers proceeded with the Hungarian proposal concerning Poland, the Czecho-Slovak government proposed likewise the inclusion of Rumania. The arbitration decision should fix the modalities and the time extension of the evacuation of the territories by the Czecho-Slovak troops, their transfer to Hungary, and their occupation by Hungarian troops.[37] Rumania, as member of the Little Entente, did not seem a natural partner for

Hungary. England and France regarded East-Central Europe as the zone of interest of the axis powers, and the British message was conveyed to Rome that London would be glad to see the settling of differences between the ČSR and Hungary by the Italian and German governments.[38] The behaviour of Germany was viewed with suspicion in Hungary.[39] The Germans not only conspired with the Slovaks but also started Ukranian propaganda in Ruthenia with the aim of realizing a Great Ukraine under German leadership from the territories of Ruthenia, the Ukranian district of Poland and the Ukraine. This was part of the German plans for penetration in Russia, therefore, the intervening states had to be under firm German control.

On October 24, 1938, at its meeting in Ungvár, the Ruthenian National Council demanded self-determination for the Ruthenians, and the delimitation of the Ruthenian-Slovak border. Ruthenia was still under Czech rule, and such demands put their movers in personal danger. Bródy, the Ruthenian deputy in the Prague Parliament, was put on trial by the Prague government, based on the Defence of the Republic Act, for his participation in pro-Hungarian movements.[40] After the Vienna award, Bródy was extradited to Hungary during the exchange of political prisoners. Under the energetic protest from Prague, Hungary revoked her demand for a plebiscite in Ruthenia.[41]

Ribbentrop then decided to go to Rome and talk with Ciano before a decision would be made in order to avoid any embarrassment.[42] The arbiters could not discuss territorial questions in the presence of the parties involved in the dispute. However, Ribbentrop had another sinister motive for his trip to Rome. On the eve of the arbitration he wanted to get something in exchange from Ciano for dropping the Czecho-Slovak demands, and accepting Ciano's pro-Hungarian stand. He tried to obtain Italy's immediate agreement for an alliance with Germany. The German plans for the conquest of East Central Europe had been ready. The idea of an offensive and defensive alliance was postponed but Ciano persuaded Ribbentrop to accept the Hungarian territorial claims without a plebiscite, drop the "Ribbentrop line," and give the disputed cities to the Magyars. Ribbentrop spoke with hostility not only of the Hungarian government but of the entire nation.[43] Csáky was waiting in Rome for the outcome of the conversations of Mussolini, Ribbentrop and Ciano. Meanwhile a new deputation, led by Esterházy of the United Hungarian Party from the ČSR, arrived in Rome to be briefed by Ciano on his conversation with the German Foreign Minister. Ciano wrote in his diary that he had known Esterházy from his visits to Budapest, and remembered him as an excellent dancer of the "csárdás," the Magyar national dance. Esterházy gave Ciano first-hand information regarding the problems, uncertainties and fears of the Hungarian minority in the ČSR under hostile foreign domination. Ciano understood the seriousness of the question and the desire of the Magyars in the ČSR to return to their homeland by drawing the borderline north at points some 30-40 km from the existing line along the Hungarian inhabited belt. Under German pressure, Hungary had to sacrifice Pressburg and its immediate vicinity. Even a plebiscite was not allowed there by the German "allies". With the support of Ciano, the Magyars wanted to obtain some villages around Nyitra where the Hungarian district reached north of the city. The Slovaks thought that, they could keep Nyitra (pop. 21,000), the seat of an old Roman Catholic bishopric, through the intervention of the Vatican.[44] Esterházy demanded for the Hungarian minority, which would remain in Slovakia after the arbitration, cultural and religious rights, guaranteed in an international treaty, and enforced by the Slovak autonomous government. He had a long and frustrating experience in the ČSR for securing the minority rights guaranteed in the peace treaty of Saint-Germain, and disregarded by the Prague government.

Following the visit of Ribbentrop to Italy, Ciano was informed by the German ambassador in Rome that the German Foreign Minister had agreed to give Kassa, Ungvár and Munkács to Hungary.[45] The Duce approved the strategy for the Vienna conference. With these preparations, Ciano was ready to defend once more in Vienna Hungarian interests based on the ethnic principle contrary to Ribbentrop's malevolent idea of using the conference as a vehicle to place the small nations in Central Europe under direct German control.

While the Axis governments formulated their positions, the two governments directly involved in the transfer of territory exchanged diplomatic notes. On October 28 Prague informed Budapest that it was ready to agree in advance with the decision of Germany and Italy, and proposed that within 24 hours the governments of Budapest and Prague would ask Germany and Italy to arbitrate their dispute.[46] The same day Chamberlain answered Horthy's letter of October 8, in which the British Prime Minister expressed his hope that the two interested governments would solve the problem by direct collaboration, and he offered his good offices if his assistance could be used for arriving at a solution.[47] The Budapest government asked the two powers for arbitration on October 29 and requested Prague to do likewise within 24 hours.[48] On the same day, Prague applied for the arbitration of Germany and Italy, and the following day replies of acceptance arrived in Budapest and Prague.[49] In those days, the Hungarian experts gave a detailed briefing to Ciano on the ethnic composition of the disputed zones. The Italian Foreign Minister could not promise in advance the securing of all demanded territories to Hungary but he was well informed of the existing situation, and was able to defend the Hungarian position against the Czecho-Slovak desires at Vienna. On October 31, Ciano had the opportunity to announce confidentially to the Hungarian ambassador in Rome, that Ribbentrop had given his consent to the retrocession of Kassa, Ungvár and Munkács to Hungary.[50] All par-

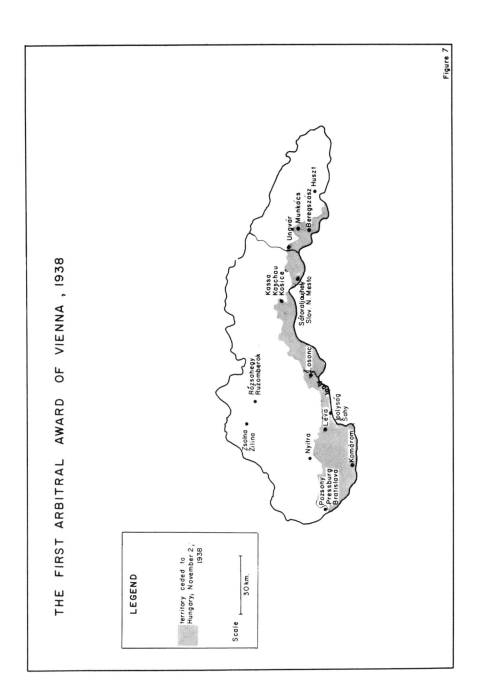

THE FIRST ARBITRAL AWARD OF VIENNA, 1938

LEGEND

Territory ceded to
Hungary, November 2,
1938

Scale

30 km.

Figure 7

162

ties involved in the process of arbitration were ready to travel to Vienna.

The First Vienna Arbitral Award

Belvedère Palace was the scene of the first Vienna arbitration dealing with the first revision of the treaty of Trianon of 1920, concluded between Hungary and Czechoslovakia, and dictated by the Allied and Associated Powers after World War I. The choice of the site was appropriate to the importance of the event, and it also had a symbolic meaning. The palace originally belonged to Prince Eugene of Savoy, the great seventeenth century soldier and commander-in-chief, who reconquered Hungary after a century and a half of Turkish occupation. In 1938 the conference at Belvedère Palace was the first stage in the peaceful reconquest of the lost Hungarian territories to the successor states after World War I.

On November 1, Ciano and Ribbentrop had a preliminary meeting at which the German Foreign Minister tried once again to keep Munkács in the ČSR as an important administrative and economic centre of Ruthenia. The ethnic principle was again ignored by Ribbentrop. Göring denounced the Hungarians in the presence of Ciano as unreliable people who promoted common interests with the Western powers.[51] At the end of September, the Germans demanded the recognition of ethnic settlements in Sudetenland at the drawing of the new border. On November 2, the two arbiters, Ciano and Ribbentrop, conferred again before they met the foreign ministers of Hungary and Czecho-Slovakia. Items discussed at the meeting and the working schedule are shown as follows:

The agenda for the Vienna conference on November 2, 1938

9:30 Preliminary talks of Ciano and Ribbentrop.

12:15 Beginning of the arbitral conference with the inclusion of the leaders of the Hungarian and Czecho-Slovak delegations to explain their standpoints.

14:00 End of the conference which was declared completed.

14:15 Lunch offered by Ribbentrop for all four delegations.

16:30 Final arbitration of Ciano and Ribbentrop in the presence of their close collaborators.

17:30 End of conference; the experts drafted the documents.

18:00 Acceptance of final draft; drawing of the map.

18:45 The Hungarian and Czecho-Slovak delegations arrived from their hotels to Belvedère Palace.

19:15 Announcement of the arbitration, signing of the minutes. Official statements.

19:45 The delegations left Belvedère Palace.[52]

The heads of the four delegations met in a joint meeting at 12:15 when once again each had the opportunity to express their views on the delimination of the ethnographic border between the ČSR and Hungary.

The complete list of delegations follows:

The German delegation: Göring, Minister President of Prussia; Ribbentrop, Woermann, Under-Secretary of State; Altenburg, Privy Councillor, Kondt, Councillor of Legation, Gaus, Department Head, Ambassadors Mackensen (Rome) and Erdmannsdorf (Budapest); Chargé d'Affaires Hencke (Prague); Doernberg, Chief of Protocol; and Minister Schmidt, interpreter.

The Italian delegation: count Ciano, Ambassadors Attolico (Berlin), de Facendis (Prague) and Gicliucci Vinci (Budapest), Magistrati, Councillor of Legation.

The Hungarian delegation: Kánya, Teleki, Minister of Education, Csáky, Chief of Cabinet, Pataky, Secretary of State, Ambassadors Villáni (Rome), and Sztójay (Berlin), Kuhl, Councillor of Legation. Sebestyén, Councillor, Szegedy-Maszák, Secretary of Legation, Ujpétery and Zilahy-Sebes, Draughtsmen.

The Czecho-Slovak delegation: Chvalkovský, Krno, Political Director, Masařik, Chief of Cabinet, Tiso, Prime Minister of Slovakia, Vološin, Prime Minister of Ruthenia, Teplanský, Economics Minister of Slovakia, Ďurčanský, Minister of Interior of Slovakia, General Viest and several experts.[53]

Ribbentrop in his welcoming address to the heads of the respective delegations mentioned that Hungary and Czechoslovakia requested the arbitration of Germany and Italy for the delimitation of the border between their countries. Germany and Italy fulfilled this request, and their task was now to find the final border on an ethnic basis. Hungary and the ČSR already had agreed on essential points but he deemed it advisable from their part to summarize their arguments to extend complete consideration. Ciano added that when the Berlin-Rome axis accepted the honouring role of arbitrators according to the wish of the governments of Hungary and Czechoslovakia, it was done with the aim of contributing to their efforts to rebuild Europe and to achieve peace.[54]

Kánya and Teleki defended the Hungarian proposal, the cities in question, including Pressburg (pop. 150,000) which in 1910 had a relative Hungarian majority. Chvalkovský and Krno submitted a Czecho-Slovak report. Tiso and Vološin were not admitted to the negotiating table at Vienna. The Prague government repeated its earlier argument that there would remain more Slovaks in Hungary — including those who lived for centuries far from the border-zone in Southern Hungary — than Magyars in Slovakia if the Hungarian proposal were accepted. Teleki argued that the principle of reciprocity was not involved in the present problems but rather the future of the Hungarian population in the border-zone of the ČSR adjacent to Hungary.[55] During lunch, offered by the German delegation, all members of the four delegations had opportunities for private conversations. Karmasin, the leader of the German minority in Slovakia, was given a chance to ask Ciano and Ribbentrop to leave Pressburg and the German enclaves of the border area in Slovakia. The final arbitration took place between 16:30 and 18:00 hours in the Golden Chamber of the palace with the participation of Ciano, Ribbentrop and their close collaborators. The Italian Foreign Minister dominated the meeting due to his preparation and knowledge of the problem. He was able to trace the new borderline easily, with the exception of several disputed zones, fulfilling the desired Hungarian claims.[56] Legal experts formulated the arbitral decision and the accompanying protocol.[57]

At the end of the first World War, the Western democracies did not request the opinion of the involved population when they delimitated the frontiers. Twenty years later the two dictatorships were willing to listen to the arguments of the involved nations regarding the correction of the borderline. In 1938 the Western democracies did not want to be involved in a diplomatic process of the peaceful revision of borders, preferring their own dictated peace treaties of 1918.

In Vienna Hungary received from her lost territory according to the ethnic settlements 12,700 km² of land and 1,030,000 persons including: 830,000 Hungarians, 140,000 Slovaks, 20,000 Germans, 40,000 Ruthenians and others.[58] In 1938 the ČSR gave up her districts populated by Germans, Poles and Hungarians, and contributed thereby to the easing of tensions. Its policy for twenty years was an eternal struggle to keep German, Polish and Hungarian territories. The positive aspect of the first Vienna arbitration for the ČSR was that there were no obstacles for the republic to achieve good neighbourly relations with surrounding nations. The Little Entente fell apart in Vienna. Hungary repossessed its nationals who for two decades were not abandoned by the mother country. A cabinet post was created in the Hungarian government for the administration and smooth integration of the returned territory to the fatherland. Many Hungarians and Germans were left several kilometers north of the Slovak side of the border. They would have preferred to live in Hungary. Telegrams were sent to Hitler from Mecenzéf (Nižný Medzer), Stósz (Štos) near Kassa, from Pozsony-püspöki (Biskupice nad Dunajom) and from other villages in the Csallóköz calling for adjustment of the border by the Mixed Commission in favour of Hungary.[59] Forty-seven villages from Verchovina, in Ruthenia, sent telegrams to Ciano and Ribbentrop after the Vienna decision demanding the annexation of their province to Hungary.[60]

The territory on the adjusted map had to be handed over, with unimpaired installations built there, to Hungary between November 5 and 10, the modalities of which were to be worked out by a joint Hungarian-Czecho-Slovak military commission. The reactions were different after the announcement of the outcome of the arbitration.[61] Kánya expressed his satisfaction to Magistrati, an assistent to Ciano; many Hungarians were moved, Villáni wept. The

Czecho-Slovak delegation was disappointed; Chvalkovský told Ciano: "I shall have to resign tomorrow. No government could survive such a blow."[62] In Vienna Kánya thanked Esterházy and Jaross for the generous work they did on behalf of the Hungarian minority in the ČSR. Jaross put into words the thoughts and feelings of those who on the retrocessed territory were liberated from two decades of Czechoslovak occupation and unjust treatment, thanks to the relentless diplomatic efforts of the Hungarian government.[63] In Budapest Prime Minister Imrédy, after receiving the news from Vienna, in his radio speech thanked the powers for taking on themselves the difficult and delicate task of arbitration. He emphasized that the conditions of peaceful coexistence had been created with the ČSR, and outlined the historical significance of the day. The Hungarians were overjoyed wherever they lived. Tiso also made a radio speech after his return to Pressburg from Vienna. He said that everything that could be retained for Slovakia was to be attributed to the Munich agreement because without it Slovakia would have been divided among its neighbours. He encouraged the Slovaks on the territory to be handed over to Hungary to stay there, not to opt for Slovakia. The intelligentsia was especially encouraged to remain and not to leave the Slovaks without any leadership in Hungary.[64] The Hungarian government officially expressed its gratitude to the Italian and German governments for the solution of the border question and the award.[65]

The Polish government used again, to its advantage, the border dispute of the ČSR as it had during the Sudeten German crisis. When the convocation of the Vienna conference became known through the news, Poland claimed from Slovakia the Polish-inhabited districts of Orava (Árva), Čadca (Csadca), the western part of the Javorina mountains and Zips (Szepes, Spiš).[66] On October 31, an ultimatum was sent to Prague and Pressburg for the transfer of these territories to Poland.[67] The ČSR accepted the Polish demand; the requested districts were placed under Polish control. The protocols of the transfer of territory were signed by the ČSR and Poland in the Polish resort town of Zakopane on December 1, 1938.[68] The area in question covered 221 km² with a population of 9,914. It is characteristic for the whole Polish — ČSR territorial controversy that each country used the local population to their advantage in census statistics. They are called Gurals, and speak a local dialect which is close to both the Slovak and Polish; it is not a literary language. On March 21, 1938, Beck, the Foreign Minister of Poland, in his interview with a correspondent of the *Daily Mail* declared that within the ČSR lived 250,000 Poles.[69] It was more than three times the actual number of the Polish nationals in all provinces under Czech control. The autonomist Slovaks were bitterly angry at the Poles for taking away from Slovakia the districts of Čadca, Javorina, Orava and Zips. The settlement of the Polish question was also part of the Munich agreement.

166

Solemn Reception of the Hungarian Army on the Receded Territory

Between November 5 and 10, 1938, Hungarian troops took possession of the former territory of the Hungarian kingdom awarded to Hungary in the first Vienna arbitration. The Regent, Horthy, and the Minister of Defence, Rátz, issued a general order to the army on November 4. They proclaimed that the home defence forces cross the Trianon border which had always been regarded in Hungary as temporary. One million of their brethren were waiting for them on the other side of the border. After two decades of grave sufferings, the Hungarian soldiers represented for them the fulfillment of their hopes. The land of Upper Hungary had many times been consecrated with the blood of the ancestors of the nation. The members of the armed forces had to enclose in their hearts all the inhabitants, Hungarians, Slovaks, Ruthenians and Germans, of the regained Hungarian soil. The Prince-Primate of Hungary, the Cardinal of Esztergom, with the consent of the conference of bishops, ordered the churches to toll the bells for half an hour from 10:00 A.M. on Saturday, November 5 when the troops started their solemn march into liberated Upper Hungary.[70]

On the northern side of the Trianon border, in the Hungarian populated belt of Southern Slovakia, the inhabitants were waiting joyfully for the arrival of the Hungarian forces. There were improvised public rallies organized for the reception of the Magyar army units. Triumphal arches were erected in many municipalities in a very short period of time between the departure of the evacuating Czecho-Slovak border police, and the arrival of the Hungarian soldiers. The reestablishment of the Hungarian state sovereignty went according to the arranged time-table worked out by joint military experts of both sides. In two cities, on November 6 in Komárom, and on November 12 in Kassa, joyous festivities took place on the occasion of the entry of the Regent, Admiral Horthy, on his famous white horse into the returned cities. According to Hungarian mythology, the pagan priest-magicians sacrificed white horses to obtain the favour of the Lord God of Hosts. In modern Hungarian history the white horse again became legendary when Admiral Horthy rode into Budapest in 1919 after the victory of his forces against the first Soviet republic on Magyar land.

The great enthusiasm with which the Regent was received at Komárom and Kassa could have persuaded the arbiters of Vienna that their decision was just. Both cities are sacred historical places to the Magyars. Komárom heroically resisted the troops of the Habsburg emperor-kings during the 1848-49 Hungarian fight for freedom; in the cathedral of Kassa are buried the remains of Prince Francis Rákóczi II, the 18th century leader of the fight for freedom against the oppression of the Habsburgs of Vienna. At Kassa the Regent with a gracious gesture greated the returned Slovaks, as equal partners, in their own language. It was greatly appreciated by the Slovak population present at the occasion. The cathedral of Kassa was the scene of an emotional ceremony commemorating the peaceful revision of the border. Present were the two houses of the Hungarian Parliament, the government and accredited diplomats. Lord Rothermere, the owner of the *Daily Mail,* and the first open supporter of the Hungarian revisionist claims a decade prior to the Vienna arbitration, sent a telegram to the President of the Hungarian Revisionist League, Francis Herczeg, the well-known novelist, and expressed his sincere joy on the retrocession of the Magyar Upper Hungary to the homeland.[71] Lord Rothermere was also invited to the ceremony at Kassa, and was seated in the diplomatic gallery. The Regent and Prime Minister Imrédy thanked Mussolini and Hitler; as Kánya did Ciano and Ribbentrop for their support of the Hungarian claims for redressing the wrongs of Trianon without bloodshed.

A Bill was introduced in Parliament which provided for the representation of the population returned to Hungary. This Bill recommended that the elected representatives who served in the Prague Parliament and became Hungarian citizens be invited by act of Parliament to become members of the Hungarian Parliament.[72] The deputies elected by the population living on the retroceded territory remained the representatives of their constituencies until the next elections. In contrast to this democratic solution, the newly created autonomist government of Slovakia introduced a one-party system. Elections were held in Slovakia for the only official ballot on December 18 which resulted in a 98% majority for the government. The Slovaks opted for a Fascist-type constitution. On December 31, the Slovak government ordered a census with an anti-Hungarian fury, followed by anti-Hungarian radio propaganda.[73]

In the series of border revisions affecting Hungary important changes occurred between 1938 and 1941. During that period Hungary partly regained the territories and population lost after World War I. In 1939, Ruthenia was retaken by armed intervention, and the desired Polish-Hungarian historic and amicable border was restored. In 1940, part of Transylvania inhabited mostly by Hungarians, was awarded to Hungary from Rumania by the second Vienna arbitration. In 1941, the Hungarian part of Southern Hungary, under Yugoslav occupation for 23 years, was reincorporated into Magyar sovereignty during the German-Yugoslav war. As an aftermath of World War II, the political map of Europe was drastically changed to the detriment of Hungary. Before touching upon this question, it is appropriate to examine the activities of the Czech master plotters in exile during the second World War, and the outcome of their intrigues concerning Hungary.

Footnotes

1. *A müncheni egyezmény...* II, No. 514.
2. DBFP, III, Vol. 3, 159.
3. Macartney, *History of Hungary,* 287.
4. PMH., October 13, 1938.
5. Ibid., October 14, 1938.
6. *A müncheni egyezmény...* II, No. 522.
7. ADAP, IV, 65.
8. Ciano, *L'Europa verso la catastrofe,* 162.
9. ADAP., IV, 72.
10. Ujság, October 25, 1938.
11. ADAP., IV, 72, 78.
12. PMH., October 22, 1938.
13. *Ciano's Diary,* October 14, 1938.
14. Affari Esteri, No. 12332/PR/C, October 21, 1938.
15. Gazeta Polska, October 15, 1938.
16. Presidenza del Consiglio dei Ministri, Fascicolo Nr. 5778/1938.
17. Pesti Hirlap, November 6, 1938.
18. Affari Esteri, October 17, 1938.
19. *A müncheni egyezmény...* II, No. 566.
20. Affari Esteri, October 22, 1938.
21. *A müncheni egyezmény...* II, No. 548.
22. Ibid., No. 553.
23. Ibid., No. 558.
24. Batowski, H., *Le voyage de Joseph Beck en Roumanie en octobre 1938,* 137.
25. *A müncheni egyezmény...* II, No. 583.
26. Ibid., No. 544.
27. Suddivisione etnica della populazione delle città sttentrionali nel 1910-1930, Affari Esteri, No. 489/1938, 4.
28. Affari Esteri, No. 166068/PR/C.
29. Gazeta Polska, October 26, 1938.
30. Affari Esteri, No. 3005/335.
31. Suddivisione etnica, Op., cit., 8.
32. Affari Esteri, No. 1602/126.
33. *A müncheni egyezmény...* II, No. 577.
34. *Ciano's Diary,* October 22, 1938.
35. *A müncheni egyezmény...* II, No. 578.
36. ADAP., IV, 99.

37. *A müncheni egyezmény...* II, No. 585.

38. DBFP., III, Vol. 3, 202-203.

39. *A müncheni egyezmény...* II, No. 588.

40. Affari Esteri, No. 5662, October 24, 1938.

41. Ibid., No. 574/I.R., October 24, 1938.

42. Ibid., No. 5519, October 28, 1938.

43. *Ciano's Diary,* October 28, 1938.

44. Hoensch, J., Op., cit., 193.

45. *Ciano's Diary,* October 30, 1938.

46. *A müncheni egyezmény...* II, No. 602.

47. Ibid., No. 603.

48. Ibid., No. 604.

49. Ibid., No. 612, 616, 617.

50. Ibid., No. 615, 618.

51. *Ciano's Diary,* November 2, 1938.

52. PMH., November 4, 1938.

53. Ibid., November 3, 1938.

54. Ujság, November 3, 1938.

55. ADAP., IV, 99.

56. *Ciano's Diary,* November 2, 1938.

57. *A müncheni egyezmény...* II, No. 621, 622.

58. Chászár, E., Op., cit., 55.

59. Affari Esteri, No. 2860/312.

60. Pesti Hirlap, November 6, 1938.

61. PMH., November 4, 1938.

62. *Ciano's Diary,* November 2, 1938.

63. Új Magyarság, November 3, 1938.

64. PMH., November 4, 1938.

65. *A müncheni egyezmény...* II, No. 625.

66. ADAP., IV, 98.

67. Ibid., V, 94.

68. BDFP., II, 381.

69. Hyndrák, V., *Polsko a československá krize na podzim 1938,* Hist. Vojenství, Vol. 8, 1938, 91.

70. Nemzeti Ujság, November 5, 1938.

71. Budapesti Hirlap, November 4, 1938.

72. Magyar Nemzet, November 4, 1938.

73. Külpolitikai adatok az 1938. évről, 46-47.

CHAPTER VIII

THE CONSEQUENCES OF AN
ABSURD CZECH IMPERIALISM

The Intense Agitations of Masaryk and Beneš for an Ambitious Czech Political Role

Masaryk's image has been propagated by Czech political writers as a great humanist and democrat. First of all it is necessary to note that he went into exile at the outbreak of World War I and succeeded with his foreign connections to help to undermine the Austro-Hungarian Monarchy. With the assistance of certain interest-groups he shaped a state for the Czechs. His private action cannot be called a democratic enterprise. It was not approved by the Czech voters. In the last prewar elections he received only 2% of the votes.[1] Before the creation of the Czechoslovak republic, he promised that equal rights would be incorporated in the constitution for all inhabitants of the new state. When he became President of the republic, he was no longer concerned with the protection of individual rights from an oppressive majority.[2] In Masaryk's view the Slovaks were really Czechs,[3] and should not have right to self-determination. Previously, he did not respect the constitutional provisions, and he made decisions on the advice of his selected but not elected politicians. Those motions were put to vote in the Parliament, and the party discipline was applied for their passage. Under those circumstances none can speak of proper democratic procedures. Under the rule of such a President the magnificent declarations about democratic principles remained only empty and meaningless words to cover the Czech oppression of other nationalities.

It was a great failure of the Czechoslovak internal and external policies that they were determined by Beneš in an authoritarian way. While in power, it was impossible to critize him openly. The Czechs had to bear the consequences of an enforced obedience. After his resignation and escape to England, at the beginning of November 1938, Senator Matoušek presented a Bill for creating a committee according to paragraph 54 of the constitution to investigate the causes of the national and governmental catastrophe. It was moved that the Permanent Committee of the National Assembly should conduct deliberations for instituting a special committee of investigation to determine the causes and establish responsibilities for the national tragedy. The committee of investigation would consist of four appointed members, among them one expert on international and one on constitutional law, and three members of the Chamber of Deputies and two senators. The Permanent Committee of the Chamber of Deputies would appoint three members of the committee of investigation which should report its findings to the Permanent Committee of the National Assembly in three months. Reasons given for the introduction of the bill were the avoidance of the political errors of the past, and charting a future line of foreign policy in conformity with the national interest. Documents found in the archives of the Council of Ministers and the Ministry of Foreign Affairs could furnish useful and decisive elements for a new foreign policy. Matoušek severely critized the conduct of the foreign policy of Beneš and his arbitrary decisions contradictory to the reports and recommendations of the ambassadors which resulted in a mistrust towards the ČSR in many countries.[4]

During those months in 1918 and 1919 in Paris when the ČSR was being created, the nascent state was subordinated to foreign interests. There was a lack of sufficient confidence in the strength and initiative of the Czech nation. Much consideration was given to the wish for future allies. Twenty years later the Czech view was the same. In September 1938 a Czech commentator wrote that the British government decides the fate of Europe on the basis of Lord Runciman's and Chamberlain's reports.[5] In international politics many interests cross each other but the moral power of a nation has to exercise its influence. The ČSR was artificially built in foreign chancelleries and its survival was tied to foreign help. Beneš was not cautious, he did not rely on the inner forces of the Czech people and disregarded the historic role of Bohemia. He did not take realistic decisions in times of trial. He counted on foreign intervention and compassion from others. In September 1938 the Czechs kept saying that they were not alone because France, Soviet Russia, Rumania and Yugoslavia were behind them. In 1919 Beneš alarmed France by pointing to a Communist menace for Europe from the Hungarian Soviet republic. This "threat" existed only for 133 days. In 1945 Beneš in exile went from London to Moscow and brought Soviet Russia to the Upper Danubian basin. The Czechs did not see the political errors in their own actions, they blamed others for the failures of their own making. They complained that their allies abandoned them in 1938. The Czechs did not demonstrate organizational or state maintaining skills when the golden opportunity presented itself. They cultivated megalomania and xenomania which destroyed them in 1938 and 1948. Their propaganda was based on obsession with the need of foreign intervention which finally led to the termination of Czech independence.

The Encircled Encircler

The year 1938 was of crucial importance for the fate of the ČSR. It fell into a state of economic, strategic and political encirclement. The political wizard of the republic, Beneš, successfully surrounded Hungary after World War I with a military alliance of the Little Entente that gave him a feeling of security besides the Franco-Czechoslovak and Soviet-Czchoslovak treaty of mutual assitance. In the twentieth year of the republic, the German, Hungarian and Polish territorial claims threatened this artificial state. These neighbours isolated President Beneš and his government from their supposed allies. The ČSR had a long common frontier with her unfriendly neighbours: 2,000 km with Germany, 1,000 km with Poland and 800 km with Hungary. The Czechs in their feeling of false security cheated, defrauded and oppressed those citizens of their state who were not Czechs. The nationalities fought a permanent life-and-death struggle with the happy possessors of the power of government. Czech internal policy was based on the oppression of the minorities which were more numerous than the oppressors. This was done with the blessings of the League of Nations, and the Western European democracies, the guarantors of the ČSR. All five non-Czech nationalities demanded the transformation of the republic in a neutral, federal state with equal rights for every citizen regardless of their language. The promised autonomy for the Slovaks and Ruthenians was not granted as long as Beneš stayed in office. Beneš was willing to provoke a European war in order to risk the survival of Czech hegemony in Central Europe. However, the existing military alliance did not work for rescuing the ČSR. After twenty years of existence, the Prague government sensed the danger and finally promised some rights to the nationalities which had been guaranteed in the peace treaties. Even during the crisis, Beneš and other Czech politicians delayed the necessary reforms and postponed for months the publication of the reform plans which contained insufficient concessions to the nationalities. When the Prague government came under pressure, it produced four consecutive plans only to exacerbate both internal and external relations. The mutilated Trianon-Hungary did not exert too much constraining force on Prague. It was the duty of the Budapest government to support the demands of the Magyar minority in the ČSR and call the attention of other friendly governments by diplomatic means to the sufferings of their brethren under Czech rule. Economic boycott, commercial isolation and communication ban by Germany, Poland and Hungary were not used to compel the ČSR to give concessions to the nationalities. The blessings of democracy existed only on paper in the ČSR. There was no equal justice, understanding or patience in the republic for every citizen. The non-Czech population lived in constant fear and subjugation. In 1938 the most blatant Czech injustices became exposed and unmasked. The Hungarian policy of revision of the Trianon treaty faced a crucial test. The public opinion of friendly states had to be rallied for the support of the rights of Hungarians under foreign domination.

A Czech national fantasy, an absurd imperialism and a harmful ambition tried to build a state without the necessary historical background, ethnic force and military accomplishments. Czech politicians during World War I succeeded in gaining territory from Austria-Hungary regardless of the ethnic composition of the population for the proposed state. They forced the Slovaks to recognize the fiction of a Czechoslovak nation, not admitting the historical, cultural, linguistic, religious, ideological and emotional differences between Czechs and Slovaks. During their twenty years in the same state, the Slovaks learned to dislike the Czech rule. The supposedly governing nation, the Slovaks were determined at the first opportune moment to assert their national demands against the Czech "sister" nation and shake off the repugnant idea of Czechoslovakism.

Prague eminently played the role of a great magician-tactician, and created the impression at the League of Nations in Geneva that the most democratic form of government was established in Czechoslovakia. They spread their propaganda in the press and through the private connections of Beneš and other politicians who wanted to maintain the status quo post bellum. Petitions containing the grievances of the national minorities of the ČSR never got to the League of Nations for open discussion. When the Versailles system tottered under the weight of historical changes, the Prague government started to wane. Its British and French supporters attempted to intervene in the internal affairs of the ČSR by sending there an independent observer. In the presence of a British mediator, one could not speak of the sovereignty of the Czechoslovak state. The Czechs needed an external intervention for solving their enormous problems which had accumulated during the twenty years of their statehood. As long as Beneš was among them in the ČSR, the Czechs were not willing to conclude an honest agreement with the nationalities and the autonomist Slovaks, the other "branch" of the invented "Czechoslovak nation."

The culture and civilization that the Hungarians created with their knowledge, skills and organizing abilities was exposed to systematic destruction for twenty years by the Czechs in Slovakia. The Magyars became a despised minority on their own native land. The former Hungarian system of public administration was altered to the detriment of the Magyars, their landed property was confiscated under the pretext of land reform, many of their schools were closed, some of their churches were taken away from them, their newspapers suppressed, and their literary publications censored. Under those circumstances no wonder that the national minorities wanted to return together with their land to their national states. In the changed military power structure the Czech primacy could not be upheld any longer. The Czechs became encircled by their political opponents. The Anschluss was more severe in its consequences for the Czechs than the attempted restoration of the Habsburgs that the Prague government prevented from happening after World War I. Germany encircled Bohemia from three sides, and beside the existing frontiers they established direct borders with Hungary, Italy and Yugoslavia. The penetration of the German influence in Central Europe affected the interests of the two other members of the Little Entente, too. The Czechs became the victims of the policy of Beneš whom they trusted for twenty years.

After more than ten years of the Czechoslovak crisis of 1938, some incriminating information was disclosed in the British Foreign Office against Beneš and Hodža. Documents, dated on 11 November 1938, revealed that Beneš and Hodža had privately deposited British banknotes and bank certificates in the value of two or three million British pounds in banks in the United Kingdom at the time of the Czechoslovak crucial days. The information was given by a man named, Samson, long resident in Britain. A personal friend of Mrs. Hodža, Mrs. Stern, from Czechoslovakia, went to see Samson, and asked him to put in his bank for safekeeping a box which she had received from Mrs. Hodža from Switzerland. The box contained banknotes of £ 50.00 and £ 100.00 together with bank receipts of fifty million pounds, sent out by Beneš and Hodža to be deposited in Britain. Inquiries were made at the Head Office of the Lloyds bank, and it was confirmed that Samson deposited three million pounds in one of the branches where he added verbally that other considerable sums were deposited on behalf of Beneš at various other banks.[6]

Beneš had a reputation from the years of his first exile and during his tenure of office as Foreign Minister that he did not perform his political activities according to the consistent rules of double-entry bookkeeping. The greatest worry of the displaced politicians from Prague was the transfer of funds in an illegal way from Czechoslovakia to Britain, France or Switzerland. Jan Masaryk, the ambassador of Czechoslovakia to Britain, contacted the Foreign Office for the transfer to his account in London of a sum of about £ 21,000.00 standing to his credit in Prague, thus evading the Czechoslovak exchange restrictions. He requested the use of the Czechoslovak Refugee Relief Fund of the Lord Mayor of London for his own personal purposes. He added that Beneš at that moment had sufficient money, and was to receive £ 15,000.00 from his publishers in advance for his planned book. Part of the money which Masaryk wished to transfer belonged to Beneš, as it was found out by the Anglo-Czechoslovak Bank.[7] The leaders of Czechoslovakia did not stay in their places when time came to give account for the conduct of their policy during their tenure of office. They escaped abroad.

The Political Activities of Beneš During His Second Exile

In Britain Beneš lived from the income of millions of pounds sterling and was watching from the background the political events. In April 1939 he formed a political directorium of Czech politicians living abroad. His presidency terminated by his resignation in October, and by the election of Hácha as new president in November 1938. After the outbreak of World War II in September 1939, Beneš created a Czechoslovak National Committee abroad which was recognized by the British and French governments. When in 1940 France fell to the Germans, the British recognized Beneš' group as a provisional Czechoslovak government in exile, and Beneš as president. A state council was established with displaced politicians at hand. Contrary to the wish of Beneš, those Czech politicians who escaped from Bohemia to Moscow became politically active.[8] This prevented Beneš from repeating his old political game from World War I of renewing Czechoslovakism according to his ideas.

The entry of the USSR into the war against Germany in June 1941 ended the isolation of Beneš from the Moscow based Czech refugees. Soviet Russia concluded a treaty of mutual aid against Germany with the Czechoslovak government in exile, and gave diplomatic recongnition to the Beneš group in London. At that time Russia also recognized the pre-Munich boundaries of the ČSR. The British government did not accept the idea of the legal existence and continuity of the pre-1938 ČSR. Beneš, however, experienced difficulties with Moscow. He was not able to influence the Czech politicians there and lead them in accordance with the concept of his political game. The Czech exiles in Moscow were put under Russian control. Beneš invited to his government in exile in London two Moscow-based Czech politicians but his offer was rebuffed.[9] The former president in exile reactivated his memoranda-writing activity and tactics of persuasion for reaching his political ends. The allies against Nazi-Germany listened to some of his proposals and the Munich agreement was declared null and void by its signatory, the British government, on 5 August 1942, and its was followed by the French government in exile in London with a similar declaration on 29 September of the same year.

When the fortunes of war started to change in favour of Soviet Russia, Beneš began to build his political future on Russian assistance. He arrived in Moscow on 11 December 1943.[10] Two days later he signed a treaty of friendship, mutual assistance and postwar cooperation. The exiled president and ally of the USSR received a red carpet treatment in Moscow, and promises for non-interference in the internal affairs of other states in the post-war period. This was put in a special clause of the treaty between the two parties.[11] The British government did not give its approval to the signature of the Russo-Czechoslovak pact. The conclusion of this treaty submitted Beneš to Stalin.[12] In a written agreement Stalin assured Beneš on 8 May 1944 that a civilian administration on the territories occupied by the Soviet troops would be transfered to the

Czechoslovak government.[13] Six years earlier in September 1938, after the receipt of the Anglo-French démarche, Beneš said that there was a third possibility: a close association with Russia. Beneš, in his vindictiveness against the French and British for their participation in the Munich agreement, turned for help to the Soviet Union, and, with Russian assistance, took revenge on Germany and Hungary. They were within his reach due to Russian advancement into German and Hungarian territory. His plan for the expulsion of the German and Hungarian population from their homes in the regions handed over to Beneš by Stalin, leaving behind them their possessions, came closer to realization. One of the greatest Czech chauvinists, who liked to glitter in democratic colours, wanted to revenge himself on the Sudeten Germans and Magyars for his own political misfortune. Already in 1942, he had turned to the British Foreign Office to obtain their consent for his plan of the deportation of three and a half million Sudeten Germans from Bohemia. In the British view there was no reason for such an action, and the Russians likewise rejected his plan in 1942 when the military situation was catastrophic on the Russian front. Beneš pursued his plan to the end. In June 1943, Beneš presented his project to President Roosevelt in Washington, and told him that Britain and Russia already had given their consent to the ejection of the German population from the territory of the former ČSR. It was told him in Washington that with regard to the concurrence of the two other allies, no resistance could be expected from the USA to his plan. Beneš returned to his London headquarters, and informed the Russian ambassador to his government in exile, that Britain and the USA had agreed to the expulsion of the German population from the pre-war Czechoslovak territory, and only Moscow opposed to it.[14] When it was communicated to Moscow that the British and American governments had already accepted the responsibility for the Beneš plan, finally the consent was given by the Soviets. On 8 August 1945 the Potsdam conference sanctioned it.[15] The liquidation of the international agreement provoked by the Czechs in 1938 received another favourable declaration for the Czechoslovak government in exile towards the end of the war. On September 27, 1944 the *Corriere di Roma* reported that the Italian Council of Ministers decided that the Munich agreement of September 29, 1938 and the Vienna arbitration of November 2, 1938 were null and void. Reason for this action was given only briefly: they were the results of the foreign policy of the Fascist government of Italy.[16] Neither detailed examination of historic documents nor demographic statistics were necessary for reaching a conclusion by the democratic Italian government. The standpoint occupied by the defeated Italy in this question was not a logical approach for the conduct of foreign policy. It was rather a hasty reaction in 1944 against the foreign policy of the government of Mussolini.

As the Red Army was approaching the borders of the former ČSR, Beneš wanted to make a deal with the Soviet government for the administration of that territory. For this reason, he went from London to Moscow. Once he was there he had to accept a Czechoslovak government appointed by Russia which was not exactly to his liking. He soon became aware of it: he had made an error when he trusted Stalin. Under the protection of the Soviet army he reached the capital of Eastern Slovakia, Kassa (Košice) on 5 April 1945, and was back in Prague on 11 May. He returned to his former capital with foreign military aid but without the consent of the population. During his stopover in Košice, he proclaimed the notorious "program of Košice." The program of the renewed Czechoslovakia contained the suppression of his political opponents, and the persecution of the non-Slovak, non-Czech and non-Slavic population of the new and diminished Czechoslovakia. The real character of Beneš was reflected in his dictatorship. The appointed members of the government, recruited from the six coalition parties, among them the Communist Party of Czechoslovakia and the Communist Party of Slovakia, accepted a program on Russian soil, dictated partly by Moscow and partly by Beneš. The formation of local national councils (soviets) was a Communist idea but the terrorization of the non-Slovak and non-Czech nationalities by those local councils was in the plan of Beneš. He issued orders for the expulsion of the enemies of the state from their homes, and for the confiscation of their property. The so-called unreliable persons were deprived of their citizenship. They became unemployable with this presidential decree and their livelihood was taken away from them. With the help of Moscow, the Slovaks to a certain degree avoided the wrath of Beneš. In spite of Beneš' protest, Slovakia received a provincial government beside the central government in Prague.[17] The Sudeten German communities were surrounded by armed Czechs who expelled the population from their homes, forcing them to leave all their belongings behind. Beneš, the coalition government and the local councils reserved the same treatment for that part of the Hungarian population which was put again under Czecho-Slovak rule. The army units of the "independent" Slovakia (1939-1945), which fought the Russians, suddenly became soldiers of the Czecho-Slovak army by putting the Czecho-Slovak tricolor on their old Slovak army uniforms. They were used for billeting in the Magyar communities and chasing the unprotected population into Hungary. Czech and Slovak democrats, Communists and Fascists equally took part in the confiscation of Hungarian property, unlawful detention of Hungarians and deprivation of their human rights. The Potsdam conference did not approve the plan of the Czechoslovak government for the deportation of the Hungarians from their villages and towns to Hungary. Beneš wanted to repeat his *fait accompli* tactics from World War I without waiting for peace negotiations. After the rebuff in Potsdam, the "democratic" Czechoslovak government tried to use other methods for getting rid of the Hungarians thrown for a second time in the twentieth century under Czecho-Slovak oppression. The

Prague government initiated negociations with the Soviet-occupied Hungary for an exchange of population. It was thought in Prague that the Slovaks living in Southern Hungary would be willing to relocate themselves in the state of the Slovaks and Czechs — at that time free of Russian occupation — and Prague could force an equal number of Hungarians to leave the republic. An agreement for the exchange of population was signed between Prague and Budapest in February 1946 but it backfired for the Czechs and Slovaks. An exodus of Slovaks from Hungary did not materialize. Rich Hungarian farmers from southern Slovakia were selected for transfer by the Czecho-Slovak authorities in exchange for mostly poverty-stricken Slovaks. The land evacuated by the Hungarian farmers was destined to the Slovaks willing to move under those conditions to the ČSR in 1946 and 1947.

The wrath of Beneš did not spare even innocent Magyar children. They could not go to school since it was prohibited to open schools with Hungarian language of instruction. This anomaly was changed in 1948 only after the elimination of Beneš from the presidency by a coup d'état. In 1949 the Communist Party ordered the reopening of the Hungarian schools in Slovakia.

In 1946 another method was practiced in the ČSR for the extinction of the Magyars. It was called re-slovakization, i.e., forced acceptance of the Slovak nationality. Between 17 June 1946 and 30 December 1947, during the savage period of denationalization, 135,317 applications were filed out of fear.[18] All the applications were not favourably accepted by the new conquerors and promoters of Pan-Slavism. 81,141 applications were immediately rejected. By 30 December 1947, 326,679 persons, including members of families, were recognized of Slovak nationality by the Central Committee for Re-Slovakization.[19] This procedure of forced slovakization, often with the use of gendarmerie, went against the inner convictions of the sacrificed persons. Even such Hungarians who did not speak Slovak were threatened and intimidated to a point that they sent in their applications to the committee in the hope of retaining their possessions or employment. It was not a voluntary desire on their part to become officially member of an alien nation. In their defencelessness they simply wanted to prevent the ejection of their families on 24-hour notice to Hungary.

The planned expulsion of the Magyars from the partially renewed ČSR after 1945 did not succeed completely. Between 1 April 1947, and 10 June 1948, there were 68,407 Hungarians forcibly transfered to Hungary from the ČSR. Since the end of the war in 1945 about 100,00 Magyars escaped to Hungary in order to avoid Czech and Slovak persecutions. In addition, 44,129 Magyars were forcibly evicted from their homes in Slovakia to the empty frontier regions of Bohemia from where three and a half million Sudeten Germans had been deported to Germany.[20] All this happened in the ČSR under the leadership of Beneš.

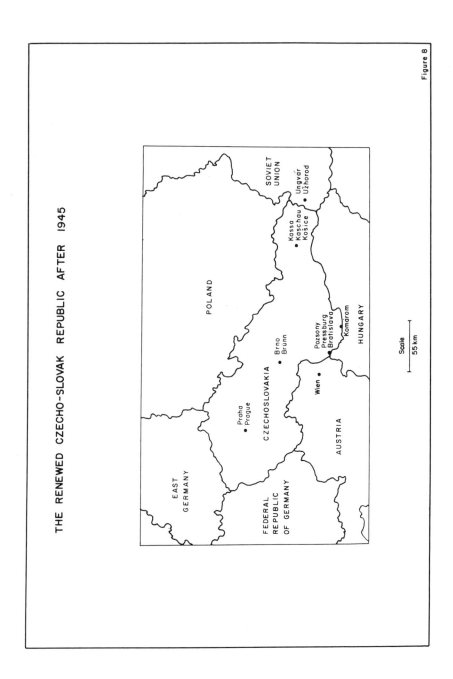

THE RENEWED CZECHO-SLOVAK REPUBLIC AFTER 1945

Figure 8

180

The Autonomist Slovaks and Beneš After 1945

In the disruption of the first Czechoslovak republic the Slovaks played a decisive role. Reverend Hlinka and his Slovak Populist Party began the Slovak opposition to the Czech rule already in 1919 at the Paris peace conference, and that struggle went on for twenty years. During that time the Slovaks unsuccessfully tried to remove the Czech influence from Slovakia. This goal was attained with the aid of Hitler in 1939 in the creation of a separate Slovak state. In 1945, after the collapse of the Slovak republic, the functionaries of the Slovak Populist Party, at home or captured on territories controlled by the victorious allies, were put on trial in the ČSR. The Peoples' Courts conducted the trials. In Pressburg Mgr. Tiso, President of the first Slovak republic in history, was sentenced to death by hanging. Beneš could not tolerate a second president in the same state. He was reelected in Prague on 19 May 1946. The following year he did not commute the death sentence of his rival. In April 1947 Tiso was hanged and with his execution the idea of a Slovak independent state received a mortal blow. The revenge of Beneš on his political opponents after his return to Prague from his second exile in 1945 resulted in the following court sentences: 362 executions, 420 imprisonments for life, 160,000 years of prison terms for 13,548 persons.[21] During the 1,000 years of common history, the Hungarians did not execute Slovaks for political reasons or send them to concentration camps as their "sister" Czech nation punished them during only twenty years of cohabitation in the same state.

Beneš received another surprise from the Slovaks. In September 1943 an illegal Slovak national council was formed in Pressburg composed of Communists and Democrats. This political movement produced unwanted effects on the plans of Beneš for the restoration of the Czechoslovak state. Independently of this Slovak initiative, General Čatloš, Commander-in-Chief of fascist Slovakia's army, still at war with the Soviet Union, made an attempt to save himself in case of Soviet victory. He sent a message to Moscow on 2 August 1944: "...the Slovak declaration of war on the USSR and the allies would be cancelled and simultaneously war would be declared on Hungary which would make the new regime at once popular. Overnight German military and civilian measures in Slovakia would be eliminated and possibilities created for big Soviet operations..."[22] Čatloš continued his message with these words: "...the national-political consequences would ensue after the end of the war, so that the Slovak political matters might be solved in accordance with the interests of the USSR..." There should be direct Slovak-Soviet contacts.[23] Čatloš, a rebel Lutheran, really did not fit in the Catholic Slovak Populist Party, and sooner or later it was inevitable that he revealed his true identity. The German protection of Slovakia was nearing its end, and the Slovaks, incapable by themselves of assuming independent statehood, were ready to place themselves under Soviet rule. A similar violent and hostile anti-Magyar Slovak nationalism was expressed in the attitude of the President of the Slovak republic (Mgr. Tiso). It was made public on the 14 and 15 January 1947 in the Peoples' Court of Slovakia in Pressburg at the trial of Tiso. He admitted in the presence of his former Minister of Defence, Gen. Čatloš, taken to court from his prison in Russia to testify against his former President, that the Slovak republic gave Croatia, a similar so-called independent state under German protection, supplies, clothing and armaments to equip and prepare the Croatian army to fight Hungary in alliance with Slovakia at the end of the war.[24] The Slovaks and Croats were encouraged to think of such action because of the German antagonism towards Hungary.

Beneš and Hungary After 1945

Back again in Prague, Beneš raised his demands against Hungary. The Czech reoccupation of Hungarian territory with Soviet assistance and the brutal persecution of the Hungarian population in the ČSR did not satisfy the democrat-dictator President. He demanded five villages from Hungary to widen the bridgehead on the left bank of the Danube at Pressburg. The reason given for this demand was the difficulty in supplying the city with food. It was an unexampled and unjustified demand. His wish was partially fulfilled by the peacemakers, and the ČSR occupied three additional villages from Hungary: Horvatjárfalu, Oroszvár and Dunacsuny, according to the Paris peace treaty of 10 February 1947.[25] The Hungarian population in the villages attached to the ČSR immediately became persecuted outcasts and augmented the number of proscribed subjects in the state of the Czechs and Slovaks. Beneš demanded additional territory from Hungary to the already occupied former Upper Hungary, although he knew very well that Britain and the USA did not intend to restore the pre-World War II boundaries of the ČSR. In his broadcast from London, Beneš stated on 26 July 1941, that in the renewed Czechoslovak state the borders of Slovakia and Hungary would be revised.[26] Beneš and Stalin, with the silent assistance of the victorious Western democracies, ruined Hungary to an even greater extent than the Trianon treaty.

After 1945 it has been forbidden in Hungary or in the successor states to even mention the peaceful revision of the borders or to complain against oppression, humiliation and degradation of the Hungarian minorities in the neighbouring states. The application of racist hatred by the Czechs and Slovaks against unarmed Hungarians handed over to them by the great powers demonstrates only the political immaturity, insecurity and monstrosity of the rulers of the ČSR.

Conclusion

Within twenty-seven years Hungarians were, for the second time in the 20th century, placed under foreign domination. Beneš succeeded twice in forming the most improvised, artificially built state in Europe. In 1938 his adroitness abandoned him, his own falsehood turned against him, and the state under his leadership staggered. After World War II, the second time in one generation, the Hungarian nation had to accept a verdict, originated from Beneš and Stalin, for territorial changes, with the concurrence of Britain, France and the United States of America. These three latter states liked to glitter as the occasional champions of human rights and democratic institutions. They threw millions of Hungarians into Czecho-Slovakia, Russia, Rumania and Yugoslavia. Beneš had the opportunity to fulfill a historic mission for the Czech people but, in the process, he became the destroyer of the Central European nations. Beneš misled the French by not keeping his promises for the respect of the obligations the ČSR assumed in the peace treaties after World War I. He could not delude the Russians who mercilessly removed him from the presidency in February 1948. The fallen political magician of the Hradsin Castle resigned from his high office for the second time in his life on 7 June 1948. Within four months he died on his private estate in Sezimovo Ústí. Following his disappearance from the political arena, the Prague Parliament did not order an investigation, as in 1938, to determine the causes, and the culpability for the loss of freedom and independence of Bohemia, Moravia, Silesia and Slovakia. The verdict will be pronounced by the examination of historical documents when they will be accessible for research. His ruthless and chauvinistic activities, together with his hatred for his political opponents, contributed much to the extinction of the independence of Bohemia and other East-Central European nations. The Czechs supported the war machine of Hitler, and the Slovaks totally collaborated with Hitler in their Slovak republic. At the Paris peace conference in 1946, the Hungarian delegation bravely defended in their carefully elaborated submissions the interests of the Magyar nation. Every effort was in vain, since the fate of the country and nation was in the hands of the Pan-Slavists, and the mutilation of Hungary at Trianon was repeated in Paris once again. The Czechs and Hungarians during their long national history lost the territory of their states partially or entirely to foreign invaders. They were occupied and liberated several times but every change in state sovereignty was accompanied by the deprivation of their freedom by conquerors and liberators alike. Foreign intervention has brought oppression to them, and has caused human tragedies.

It is interesting to note that almost four decades after the Munich agreement Chinese historians analyze the events from their viewpoint. They see Central Europe as a key point of imperialistic expansion in 1938 and also in 1968. In 1938 Nazi Germany started the weakening of the first Czechoslovak republic by annexing the Sudeten German population to Germany. The Chinese view does not mention that the annexation of Sudetenland was sanctioned by a four power agreement which ended the persecution of the German minority. Thirty years after Munich the government of Soviet Russia[27] ordered its troops to invade the diminished ČSR. In 1968 that occupation lacked the nicety and legality of an international agreement. The Chinesse authors emphasize that the Czechs were not invited to Munich[28] but at the same time forget to add for the sake of objectivity that the Hungarians were not admitted either to the 1918 negotiations in Paris when Hungary was mutilated. The Czech political exiles applied different tactics in 1945 from those in 1918. Their political alliance with the French in 1918 and with the Russians in 1945 ended in subservience to their supposed benefactors. Foreign dictatorships occupied Central Europe in 1939 and in 1945 as a result of the Czech political plots against the interests of the historic Bohemia and of East-Central Europe. The selling out of the Bohemian independence during the two World Wars proved to be a fatal mistake even for the originators of those disastrous alliances who temporarily had drawn personal advantage from their political actions.

The future free development of the peoples in East-Central Europe — among them of Hungary, Bohemia and Slovakia — can be secured only when the nations of that area once again could belong to their own zone of interest without the selfish interference of the great powers. The Polish political initiative called the "Third Europe" of 1938, or the medieval Polish-Hungarian-Bosnian north-south foreign policy concept of forming a wall against the intruders in a renewed, negotiated, modern form, could offer security and protection to the small nations in the Danubian and Carpathian areas against the undesirable interference and domination of the great powers. After so much suffering and political turmoil the psychological conditions have arrived for a true neighbourly cooperation and better understanding. The existing disputes could be settled on the basis of mutual respect and recognition of the basic interests of each nation without the intrusion of the neighbouring powers into that troubled region.

Footnotes

1. Szporluk, R., *Masaryk's Idea of Democracy,* SEER, XLI, 1962, 40.
2. Ibid., 35.
3. Ibid., 43.
4. Affari Esteri, No. 1724/1094.
5. České Slovo, 18 Sept., 1938.
6. PRO., FO., 432/21588, 492, 497, 498.
7. Ibid., 480, 485.
8. Miksche, Op. Cit., 36.
9. Táborský, Eduard, *Beneš and Stalin — Moscow, 1943 and 1945,* JCEA XIII, 1953, 181.
10. Ibid., 159.
11. Ibid., 162.
12. Miksche, Op. cit., 36.
13. Táborský, Op. cit., 271.
14. Wallace, William W., *The Foreign Policy of President Beneš in the Approach of Munich,* SEER, XXXIX, 1960, 133.
15. Miksche, Op. cit., 40, 41.
16. Corriere di Roma, 27 Sept., 1944.
17. Lastovička, Bohuslav, *Vznik a význam košického vládního programu,* ČČH, 8, 1960, 452.
18. Zvara, Juraj, *A magyar dolgozók részvétele a szocialista Csehszlovákia épitésében,* 211.
19. Botka & Assoc., *Magyarok Csehszlovákiában,* 239.
20. Ibid.
21. Forst de Battaglia, Otto, *Zwischeneuropa,* I. 12.
22. Čulen, K., Op. cit., 169.
23. Ibid., 170.
24. Ibid., 408.
25. Wagner, Francis S., *Hungarians in Czechoslovakia,* SNCE, 34, Separatum.
26. Lastovička, B., Op. cit., 452.
27. *Munich 1938 de la capitulation à la guerre,* 80.
28. Ibid., 50.

APPENDICES

APPENDIX 1

TREATY BETWEEN THE PRINCIPAL ALLIED AND ASSOCIATED POWERS AND CZECHOSLOVAKIA

Signed September 10, 1919

THE UNITED STATES OF AMERICA, THE BRITISH EMPIRE, FRANCE, ITALY, AND JAPAN,

the Principal Allied and Associated Powers,   on the one hand

And CZECHO-SLOVAKIA,   on the other hand (...)

Excerpts from the Treaty of Saint-Germain-en-Laye: The Minorities Treaty.

CHAPTER I

ARTICLE 1

Czecho-Slovakia undertakes that the stipulations contained in Articles 2 to 8 of this Chapter shall be recognised as fundemental laws and that no law, regulation or official action shall conflict or interfere with these stipulations, nor shall any law, regulation or official action prevail over them.

ARTICLE 2

Czecho-Slovakia undertakes to assure full and complete protection of life and liberty to all inhabitants of Czecho-Slovakia without distinction of birth, nationality, language, race or religion.

All inhabitants of Czecho-Slovakia shall be entitled to the free exercise, whether public or private, of any creed, religion or belief, whose practices are not inconsistent with public order or public morals.

ARTICLE 3

Subject to the special provisions of the Treaties mentioned below Czecho-Slovakia admits and declares to be Czecho-Slovak nationals *ipso facto* and *without* the requirement of any formality German, Austrian or Hungarian nationals habitually resident or possessing rights of citizenship (*pertinenza-Heimatsrecht*) as the case may be at the date of the coming into force of the present Treaty in territory which is or may be recognised as forming part of Czecho-Slovakia under the Treaties with Germany, Austria or Hungary respectively, or under any Treaties which may be concluded for the purpose of completing the present settlement.

Nevertheless, the persons referred to above who are over eighteen years of age will be entitled under the conditions contained in the said Treaties to opt for any other nationality which may be open to them. Option by a husband will cover his wife, and option by parents will cover their children under eighteen years of age.

Persons who have exercised the above right to opt must within the succeeding twelve months transfer their place of residence to the State for which they have opted. They will be entitled to retain their immovable property in Czecho-Slovak territory. They may carry with them their movable property of every description. No export duties may be imposed upon them in connection with the removal of such property.

ARTICLE 4

Czecho-Slovakia admits and declares to be Czecho-Slovak nationals *ipso facto* and without the requirement of any formality persons of German, Austrian or Hungarian nationality who were born in the territory referred to above of parents habitually resident or possessing rights of citizenship (*pertinenza-Heimatsrecht*) as the case may be there, even if at the date of the coming into force of the present Treaty they are not themselves habitually resident or did not possess rights of citizenship there.

Nevertheless, within two years after the coming into force of the present Treaty, these persons may make a declaration before the competent Czecho-Slovak authorities in the country in which they are resident, stating that they abandon Czecho-Slovak nationality, and they will then cease to be considered as Czecho-Slovak nationals. In this connection a declaration by a husband will cover his wife, and a declaration by parents will cover their children under eighteen years of age.

ARTICLE 5

Czecho-Slovakia undertakes to put no hindrance in the way of the exercise of the right which the persons concerned have under the Treaties concluded or to be concluded by the Allied and Associated Powers with Germany, Austria or Hungary to choose whether or not they will acquire Czecho-Slovak nationality.

ARTICLE 6

All persons born in Czecho-Slovak territory who are not born nationals of another State shall *ipso facto* become Czecho-Slovak nationals.

ARTICLE 7

All Czecho-Slovak nationals shall be equal before the law and shall enjoy the same civil and political rights without distinction as to race, language or religion.

Differences of religion, creed or confession shall not prejudice any Czecho-Slovak national in matters relating to the enjoyment of civil or political rights, as for instance admission to public employments, functions and honours, or the exercise of professions and industries.

No restriction shall be imposed on the free use by any Czecho-Slovak national of any language in private intercourse, in commerce, in religion, in the press or publications of any kind, or at public meetings.

Notwithstanding any establishment by the Czecho-Slovak Government of an official language, adequate facilities shall be given to Czecho-Slovak nationals of non-Czech speech for the use of their language, either orally or in writing, before the courts.

ARTICLE 8

Czecho-Slovak nationals who belong to racial, religious or linguistic minorities shall enjoy the same treatment and security in law and in fact as the other Czecho-Slovak nationals. In particular they shall have an equal right to establish, manage and control at their own expense charitable, religious and social institutions, schools and other educational establishments, with the right to use their own language and to exercise their religion freely therein.

188

ARTICLE 9

Czecho-Slovakia will provide in the public educational system in towns and districts in which a considerable proportion of Czecho-Slovak nationals of other than Czech speech are residents adequate facilities for ensuring that the instruction shall be given to the children of such Czecho-Slovak nationals through the medium of their own language. This provision shall not prevent the Czecho-Slovak Government from making the teaching of the Czech language obligatory.

In towns and districts where there is a considerable proportion of Czecho-Slovak nationals belonging to racial, religious or linguistic minorities, these minorities shall be assured an equitable share in the enjoyment and application of the sums which may be provided out of public funds under the State, municipal or other budget, for educational, religious or charitable purposes.

CHAPTER II

ARTICLE 10

Czecho-Slovakia undertakes to constitute the Ruthene territory south of the Carpathians within frontiers delimited by the Principal Allied and Associated Powers as an autonomous unit within the Czecho-Slovak State, and to accord to it the fullest degree of self-government compatible with the unity of the Czecho-Slovak State.

ARTICLE 11

The Ruthene territory south of the Carpathians shall possess a special Diet. This Diet shall have powers of legislation in all linguistic, scholastic and religious questions, in matters of local administration, and in other questions which the laws of the Czecho-Slovak State may assign to it. The Governor of the Ruthene territory shall be appointed by the President of the Czecho-Slovak Republic and shall be responsible to the Ruthene Diet.

ARTICLE 12

Czecho-Slovakia agrees that officials in the Ruthene territory will be chosen as far as possible from the inhabitants of this territory.

ARTICLE 13

Czecho-Slovakia guarantees to the Ruthene territory equitable representation in the legislative assembly of the Czecho-Slovak Republic, to which Assembly it will send deputies elected according to the constitution of the Czecho-Slovak Republic. These deputies will not, however, have the right of voting in the Czecho-Slovak Diet upon legislative questions of the same kind as those assigned to the Ruthene Diet.

ARTICLE 14

Czcho-Slovakia agrees that the stipulations of Chapters I and II so far as they affect persons belonging to racial, religious or linguistic minorities constitute obligations of international concern and shall be placed under the guarantee of the League of Nations. They shall not be modified without the assent of a majority of the Council of the League of Nations. The United States, the British Empire, France, Italy and Japan hereby agree not to withhold their assent from any modification in these Articles which is in due form assented to by a majority of the Council of the League of Nations.

Czecho-Slovakia agrees that any Member of the Council of the League of Nations shall have the right to bring to the attention of the Council any infraction, or any danger of infraction, of any of these obligations, and that the Council may thereupon take such action and give such direction as it may deem proper and effective in the circumstances.

Czecho-Slovakia further agrees that any difference of opinion as to questions of law or fact arising out of these Articles between the Czecho-Slovak Government and any one of the Principal Allied and Associated Powers, or any other Power a Member of the Council of the League of Nations, shall be held to be a dispute of an international character under Article 14 of the

Covenant of the League of Nations. The Czecho-Slovak Government hereby consents that any such dispute shall, if the other party hereto demands, be referred to the Permanent Court of International Justice. The decision of the Permanent Court shall be final and shall have the same force and effect as an award under Article 13 of the Covenant.

Treaty between the Principal Allied and Associated Powers and Czecho-Slovakia, Signed at Saint-Germain-en-Laye, September 10, 1919 London, H.M.S.O., 1919.

PROTOCOL PRESENTED BY DR. BENEŠ ON BEHALF OF CZECHOSLOVAKIA TO THE COMMISSION FOR THE NEW STATES AT THE PEACE CONFERENCE

Memorandum No. III

Paris, 20th May, 1919

1. The Czechoslovak Government intends to organise its State by taking as the bases of the rights of the nationalities the principles applied in the constitution of the Swiss Republic, that is to say, the Government designs to make of the Czechoslovak Republic *a sort of Switzerland,* while paying regard, of course, to the special conditions in Bohemia.

2. Universal franchise coupled with the system of proportional representation will be introduced — which will ensure to the various nationalities in the Republic a proportional representation in all elected organs (institutions).

3. The schools throughout the whole territory of the State will in general be maintained out of public funds, and they will be established for the individual nationalities in the parishes as soon as the necessity arises, on the basis of the number of children in the parish as fixed by law, to inaugurate a school.

4. All public professions (functions) will be accessible to the individual nationalities living in the Republic.

5. The courts of justice will be mixed courts in respect of the language employed, and the Germans will be able to bring their causes before the highest courts in their own language.

6. The local administration (local affairs of the parishes and districts) will be carried on in the language of the majority of the population.

7. The question of a person's religion will not be posed in the Czechoslovak Republic — there will be no difficulties in this connection.

8. The official language will be the Czech language, and the State for external purposes will be a Czechoslovak State. In practice, however, the German language will be the second language of the country, and will be employed on a basis of equality in the current administration, before the courts, and in the central Parliament. It is the intention of the Czechoslovak Government in practice and daily usage to satisfy the population in this connection, *but at the same time, of course, a special position will be reserved for the Czechoslovak language and the Czechoslovak element.*

9. Expressed in another way we can say that the present position (the Germans had a huge preponderance) in its broad outline will remain unchanged: *only the privileges which the Germans previously enjoyed will be reduced to their due proportions (for example, the number of German schools will be reduced where these schools shall be found superfluous).*

In general it will be a very liberal régime *approaching considerably to the Swiss régime.*

Miller, David Hunter, *My Diary at the Conference of Paris,* New York, Appeal Printing Co., 1924, XIII, 69-70.

APPENDIX 3

THE ENFORCEMENT OF THE LAND REFORM IN SLOVAKIA AFTER 1919

	Total Acreage in Slovakia				23 southern counties Hungarian Population between 22.55-94.73% — 1921 census			
	Arable land	%	Total land	%	Arable land	%	All land	%
A/Total Land Area	5,003,196.		10,713,533.		1,661,752.		2,600,031.	
Confiscated area	663,113.11		2,276,873.07		304,624.08		626,907.	
Losses of Hungarians	528,743.12	79.8	1,836,137.05	80.7	239,101.12	78.5	490,815.08	78.3
Losses of Germans	30,103.08	4.5	119,478.15	5.2	9,835.01	3.2	20,061.02	3.2
Losses of Slovaks	10,795.	1.6	61,886.05	2.7	643.08	0.2	1,160.08	0.2
Losses of Ruthenians	502.11	0.1	2,337.06	0.1	378.08	0.1	386.10	0.1
Losses of the ecclesiastical properties	74,447.05	11.2	207,723.06	9.1	54,633.10	18.0	112,682.15	18.0
Losses of others	18,521.07	2.8	49,310.02	2.2	32.01	0.0	1,300.04	0.2

The State retained for its own use 53.3%

	Number of cases	Acres	Average Acres
Land distributed in private property:			
Hungarians:	184,806	42,320.01	3.10
	11,502		

	Arable land	Total land
Losses of Hungarians:	489,028.02	1,793,817.04
Land received by Hungarians in %:	−75.8	
Hungarians should have received:	463,611.06 acres instead of 42,320.01	

* Source: *Magyar Statisztikai Hivatal Államtudományi Intézete Budapest, M. Kir. Egyetemi Nyomda, 1938.*

PETITION
FROM CITIZENS OF THE UNITED STATES OF AMERICA
TO THE LEAGUE OF NATIONS

The League of Nations, Geneva, Switzerland

We, the undersigned, citizens of the United States of America, respectfully petition for the revision of the Treaty of Trianon. In calling the attention of the League of Nations to the urgent necessity of peaceful reorganization among the nations of the Danube-Valley, we wish to emphasize, that we do not desire to jeopardize the interest of any nation, by we are guided by an idealistic intention, namely:

> to prevent a new conflict among the peoples of Europe and avert the outbreak of a new debacle threatening the possible annihilation of civilization.

Because of our favorable situation, we are able to descry the danger more clearly than those, who are living within the gloom of the events. For we perceive that the past world war means not only the dismemberment of a thousand-year-old country of Hungary, the bastion of the western civilization, the country of scientists, authors, artists and many millions of industrious people, of whom three-and-a half million of pure Magyar souls and two-third of the country's territory were handed over to unfriendly neighboring states; we discern that the world war meant not only the sacrificing of those many millions of people, who perished in same and uncounted generations to come, but it means also, that:

> the victorious states paid in blood and suffering the same amount and lost financially almost as much as the vanquished states, besides bearing the expenses of slow recovery in vain, because the new Europe is much more unsettled than the old one has been.

The last decade since the signing of the Treaty of Trianon demonstrates a terrifying experience. It indisputably discloses, that unbridled greediness created a number of succession-states with oppressed minorities, without having considered geographical, ethnical and economical entities thereby harboring the possibility of a new world-catastrophe.

It proved be impossibility of keeping within the boundaries of the newly created states, people of different language, culture and national character tied by natural, human and inseparable spiritual ties to their mother-country. These minorities broken off from their old mother-country, do not entertain any sympathy and loyalty for their new country, because of it being forced upon them and not only these minorities, but also the respective countries, whose unwilling subjects they are, are unhappy. The past ten years also prove, that the Treaty of Trianon was dictated so unfortunately, that though the tears of widows, orphans and war victims are scarcely dried:

> the people of Europe are divided into two groups, one consisting of nations enforcing the Treaty, the other favoring revision. These two opposing camps are bent on a new war and are ready to fly at each others throat at the least provocation.

Conditions indicate that the world is waiting in vain for the fulfillment of the promises as expressed in the preamble to the Treaty of Trianon. The Treaty of Trianon imposes on Hungary terms, causing indescribable misery and poverty, from which Hungary hardly, if ever will be able to recuperate, and the apparently victorious states are compelled to maintain immense armies for enforcing this Treaty of Trianon, thereby placing such a burden of taxation on its citizens that it borders on national disaster. It is an indisputable fact, that nations preparing for war, are likely to plunge into hostilities on the slightest pretext. It is the responsibility of the League of Nations to avert such fatal possibility, by creating an atmosphere of good-will based on the spirit of true democracy and self-determination for all people of this danger-spot of Europe. The hurriedly created succession-states should be reconstructed on the pre-war status-quo, thereby preparing the way for the unification of that Hungary, which for a thousand years was a geographical entity, acknowledged by the great Reclus and others, claiming that:

> Hungary is not a "made" country, but a "born" country, created by the profound wisdom of mother-nature. There should be a full equality between all nations and the security of one nation should not mean the permanent subjugation of a score of other nations. The stubborn denial of the rights, and systematic oppression of certain nations leads automatically to the most disastrous and deplorable outburst of the human energies now, as ever.

We gave the Wilsonian principles of self-determination to the world, which led to the termination of the war. It is our duty therefore to be the sentinels of the idealistic, but not applied principles in the case of Hungary. At the framing of the Treaty of Trianon people were not asked if they would consent to be torn off from their race and native country where they were born and raised; they were not asked if they wish to become a minority of a foreign country, not sympathetic to them. Therefore we earnestly pray, that:

> for sake of the most sacred ideals of mankind and for the sake of justice, the Treaty of Trianon be revised in such manner, that territories with compact Magyar population shall be returned to the mother-country, while territories with mixed population shall decide by plebiscite what disposition should be made of their territories.

In this manner only will it be possible to reconcile the small nations living in the Valley of Danube and in the region of the Carpathian mountains. This in turn would bring about an economic entente, that would serve mutually their and the world's best interest and would lead them on the road of progress, which at present is retarded by unnatural conditions.

The Senate of the United States of America did not ratify the Treaty of Trianon and we, the undersigned citizens of the United States, voicing the sincere desire of millions of our compatriots,

> appeal respectfully to the League of Nations, for the sake of the best interest of mankind, to render justice for Hungary and peace for the world!

In faith of this, we attach our signatures on the following pages, numbered from 1 — 510.

Chicago, Ill. Christmas, 1930.

TEXT OF THE AGREEMENT

Of February 18th, 1937, between the Czechoslovak government and the German "activist" parties

In a well-meant endeavour to make a permanent contribution to mutual understanding in nationality relations within the Republic and to climite all that is calculated to estrange from one another the people of this State at the crossroads of racial interests in Central Europe, the Czechoslovak Government has examined the present state of Minority Policy in Czechoslovakia, and, following the tradition of Czechoslovak democratic policy, has laid down further directives in this connection.

The Government is devoting very special attention and care to the economic situation of the areas affected by the world crisis in some branches of industry. If happens that these are areas inhabited for the most part by our fellow-citizens whose mother-tongue is German. The circumstance that the great bulk of State guarantees granted to industrial production have been allotted to German manufacturers is a proof that nothing can be more disloyal than to accuse the Government of lack of consideration for the economic situation of the German population. The Government is investing in public works and buildings in all parts of the State in due proportion to the needs of the particular areas and will see to it that everywhere — including thus the areas with a German population — local enterprise and local workers shall have first consideration. The central authorities that allocate contracts are enjoined to exercise strict supervision over all the organs subordinate to them in order that, among other things, this principle of economic justice shall be observed to the full. *The Government calls the attention of all organs in particular to their personal responsibility for the fulfilment of these instructions, and also calls attention to the consequences involved in any neglect of this official order.*

In carrying out its measures of social welfare and of health service the Government will pay due regard not only to the number of inhabitants but also to the degree of unemployment in the individual areas. In the sphere of social and health service for the young, the Government will — as heretofore — see to it that the members of the particular nationality concerned shall be entrusted with child-relief, and will do its utmost to ensure that the institution of child-relief shall be placed on a sound basis and further expanded.

In the matter of the acceptance of candidates for the State services the Constitution of the Czechoslovak Republic lays down in the second section of Clause 128 guiding principles in this matter to the effect that "differences in religion, belief, confession and language shall be no hindrance to any subject of the Czechoslovak Republic within the limits of the common law of the land, especially in the matter of entry into the public services, and offices, or of dignities". In addition to this constitutional principle, the Government acknowledges the permanent validity of another principle which it regards as its own and which has, at the sáme time, been adopted by all international authorities concerned, namely, the principle that *unconditional loyalty to the State is a natural and primary condition for the bestowal of rights upon racial minorities.*

The Government can, without the slightest bias, say that the moral force of the Czechoslovak State idea is increasingly proving its efficacy in bringing about collaboration among the nationalities. This fact and the steadily expanding knowledge of the official language enables the Government to take a further step in accepting members of the national minorities for the State services, and to pay ever increasing regard not only to general and regional interests and qualifications, but also to the interests of the Minorities so as to ensure them a just proportion of the posts in question.

In communications with public bodies and organs the language requirements of the racial minorities are guaranteed to the utmost practical degree by the constitutional law relating to language. The Government regards it as a simple behest of political morality and wisdom that the laws of the Republic should be unconditionally observed in all departments of public administration; in the matter of the prescription relating to the correspondence of the district and certain other authorities with the parishes where the majority of the population speak a different language, *the Government has ordered that translations in the language of the national minority in the parish shall be annexed to communications couched in the official language, and that this shall be done without waiting for a demand for it, and that no charge shall be made for the translation.*

The Government is prepared to amend the scope of language tests according to the real needs in view of the posts to which candidates will be allotted, and to contribute to the issue of appropriate textbooks.

The Budget Estimates will reflect the determination of the Czechoslovak Government that the democratic Republic shall regard it as its great political and moral task to support popular education and enlightenment to the very utmost of its financial resources, that is, to encourage not only the splendid traditions of the Czech and Slovak people in this connection, but also, in a spirit of due proportion, popular education and enlightenment among their follow-citizens and nations speaking another tongue, not only, therefore, the Germans and Magyars, but also all racial minorities. The Government also pays regard in this respect to fellow-citizens of Polish nationality. Now that no foreign influences intermeddle with our minority policy in this sphere, we are able, in conjunction with our Polish-speaking fellow-citizens, to solve all that may await solution in a spirit of justice and fraternity.

In the organisation of education regard is already paid in very special fashion to the cultural needs of the individual nationalities, and the Government does not in any way exclude the possibility of further intensifications within the framework of the organisation that has so far existed.

Wherever shortcomings or faults in local government administration shall be ascertained to the detriment of nationality interest or minority groups, the Government will see to their removal.

The Government consistently abides by its principles of a policy of strict justice to the minorities, and will develop that policy and accommodate it to the interests of the State and the national minorities.

Source: Young, *op. cit.*, 348-351.

THE CARLSBAD PROGRAM

The Carlsbad eight points put forward by Herr Henlein, leader of the Sudeten German Party:

1. *Establishment of full equality of rights and* of status between the German national group and the Czech people.

2. *Recognition of the Sudeten German national group as a legal personality* in guarantee of this equality of status in the state.

3. *Determination and recognition of the German-inhabited* territory.

4. *Setting-up of a German autonomous* administration for all departments of public life in so far as the interests and affairs of the German national group are concerned.

5. *Enactement of legal measures* for the protection of those citizens of the state who live outside the defined limits of the territory inhabited by their nationality.

6. *Removal of injustices inflicted* upon Sudeten Germans since 1918 and reparation of the damage suffered owing to these injustices.

7. Recognition and application of the principle: *German public officials in the German territory.*

8. *Full freedom to profess German nationality* and the German political philosophy.

Source: R.G.D. Laffan, *Survey of International Affairs 1938,* vol. II, Oxford University Press, London: 1951, 95.

PRÁGAI MAGYAR HIRLAP

XVII. évf. 190 (4819) szám [illegible] augusztus 4

A szlovákiai és kárpátaljai magyarság politikai napilapja

Előfizetési ár: évente 300, félévre 150, negyedévre 76, havonta 26 Kč., külföldre: évente 450, félévre 226, negyedévre 114, havonta 38 Kč. ● A képes mellékletlel havonként 2.50 Kč-val több. Egyes szám ára 1.20 Kč, vasárnap 2.— Kč.

Szerkesztőség: Prága II., Panská ulice 12. II. emelet. ● Kiadóhivatal: Prága II., Panská ulice 12. III. emelet. ● ● TELEFON: 303-11. ● ● SÜRGÖNYCIM: HIRLAP, PRAHA.

A Hungarian Welcome to Lord Runciman

The moment at which his Lordship sets foot on Czecho-Slovakian soil is one of extraordinary importance in the history of post-war Europe. The mission which brings him to this country — the role which he has undertaken, is entirely unprecedented.

In this part of Europe problems have literally piled up, on the solution of which depends the development of the coming years, the safety of states, the prosperity or decline of nations, and the peaceful and happy lives of the people — or their despair.

Twenty years ago it was believed to be possible to shunt off vital, effective historical forces, or to stifle them in their development. This cannot longer be maintained. The Peace Conference took into consideration only the two post-war extremes — victory or defeat. They forget that only s t a t e s can be temporarily defeated — not n a t i o n s.

The Czechoslovak republic was formed on the basis that the victory of the Czech, Slovak, and Ruthenian nations was recognised, while the German, the Hungarian, and the Polish nations living in this territory suffered all the moral and material casualties of the lost war. The activity of the statesmen in the course of twenty years, in building the state, aimed at one thing: to lay the foundations of the Czechoslovak national existence at the expense of the Germans, Hungarians, and Poles. This development is unhealthy and unnatural, and was bound to end in conflicts. To arrive at this, it had been sufficient to alter the balance of the Great Powers directing Europe's history. The events in March this year brought into clear light this altered balance, and thus the Czechoslovakian problem was cast up.

The world knows this problem as the German—Czechoslovak problem, but those who are living here, or who occupy themselves more thoroughly with the existing situation, must know that the setting out of the problem is not anything like so simple as that.

There is not only a German—Czechoslovak problem, but also a Hungarian—Czechoslovak problem, a Polish—Czechoslovak problem, and even a Slovak—Czechoslovak problem, and a Ruthenian—Czechoslovak problem.

The problem calls for absorbing consideration, involving extensive research. The noble lord is doubtless fully conscious of the fact that the task he has undertaken with such a degree of self sacrifice, is complicated and difficult. We can scarcely find in the course of history, that a statesman acting in his private capacity, has ever undertaken a task of such gigantic magnitude.

The Hungarian national community living in this state, lifts its hat with respect to, and salutes this noble son of the great British nation, who comes to us to advise the responsible leaders of this state and the representatives of the nations, and, as far as in human possibility lies, to untie this Gordian knot.

The noble Lord comes with the purpose of insuring peace within this state, and to lay the foundations of agreement between the various nations of Czechoslovakia, because British policy is set upon the establishment of this, as the key to world peace.

We know this, and we appreciate it respectfully. We Hungarians have lived for a thousand years our independent state life, in the most stormy part of Europe, which has been repeatedly stirred up by by Oriental barbarism. We have suffered and bled, and in the past of every Hungarian family, is the record of martyr-heroes, who gave their lives and blood for Christian civilisation, or Hungarian liberty and independence. The present generation of Hungarians living here, are the descendants of such ancestors. This generation can endure and can suffer — it cannot live in dishonour.

We have within us the feeling that twenty years ago, we were denied the right that President Wilson proclaimed with prophetic inspiration: the right of self-determination of the nations. Only this right can restore our life of honour, by giving equal conditions and equal possibility of development to every nation.

With reverence and deep honour, we salute Lord Runciman as he looks out upon this world which he wants, as an honourable, single minded man, to reform by bringing into harmony the contrasting conceptions and vital interests of nations. We wish him good luck in this great task.

We, for our part, desire nothing other than what issues spontaneously from the character of an English gentleman: the pursuit of justice in an unhampered, sincere way. In this we are ready to support loyally his efforts.

We believe deeply and unshakeably in the truth that we Hungarians have the right to live in liberty.

It is that which we wish clearly to convey, in all manly candidness to a statesman, a gentleman, and a Man, who has undertaken a great historical task.

Magyar üdvözlet Runciman lordnak

A pillanat, amelyben a lord Csehszlovákia földjére lép, a világháboru utáni Európa egyik rendkivüli pillanata. A küldetés, amellyel érkezik, a szerep, amelyet vállalt, uj és szokatlan. Európa e részében olyan problémák tornyosodtak föl, amelyek megoldásától évtizedek jövő történelme, államok biztonsága, nemzetek fejlődése vagy süllyedése, emberek nyugodt, boldog élete, vagy nehéz kétségbeesettsége függ.

Husz évvel ezelött élő és ható történelmi erőket képzeltek uj vágányra terelni, vagy fejlődésükben elfojtani. A békeszerződések a világháboru utáni nagy csatavesztés és nagy csatanyerés két szélső pólusát vették csak tekintetbe s elfeledkeztek arról, hogy csak államokat lehet legyőzni egy időre, de nemzeteket nem.

A csehszlovák köztársaság ugy alakult, hogy a cseh, szlovák és ruszin nemzet győztes voltát ismerték el, mig a német, magyar és lengyel nemzet, amely e területen élt, a háboruvesztés összes erkölcsi és anyagi terhét hozta magával. Husz év államépitő tevékenysége egyetlen célt ismert: a többség erejével megalapozni és kiszélesiteni a csehszlovák nemzet életterét a német, magyar és lengyel élettér rovására. Ez a fejlődés egészségtelen és természetellenes volt és konfliktusokhoz kellett vezetnie.

Nem [illegible] mint az európai történelmet irányitó nagyhatalmi erők egyensulyi megváltozása. Az idei március eseményei ezt az eltolódást [illegible] a nyomában [illegible] a csehszlovákiai probléma. Ezt a problémát a világ német—csehszlovák [illegible] ismeri, aki azonban itt él, vagy mélyebben foglalkozik az itteni helyzettel, látnia kell, hogy a tétel nem ilyen egyszerű. Nemcsak német—csehszlovák, hanem magyar—csehszlovák, lengyel—csehszlovák, sőt szlovák—csehszlovák és ruszin—csehszlovák probléma is van.

A kérdés sokszinü és sokrétegü tanulmányt és elmélyedést igényel. A nemes Lord bizonyára tisztában van azzal, hogy a föladat, amelyet oly személyi áldozatkészséggel vállalt, bonyolult és nehéz. A történelem folyamán alig találunk példát rá, hogy egy magánemberként föllépő államférfiu ilyen föladatot vállalt volna.

A köztársaságban élő magyar nemzetcsoport tisztelettel emel kalapot és köszönti a nagy brit nemzet eme nagy fiát, aki eljött hozzánk, hogy tanulmányozza a helyzetet, tanáccsal szolgáljon az állam felelős vezetőinek, valamint a nemzetek képviselőinek. A nemes Lord biztositani akarja az állam belbékéjét, meg akarja alapozni az ittlakó nemzetek együttélésének föltételeit, mert békét, mindenáron békét, világbékét kiván biztositani a világnak a brit politika.

Ezt tudjuk és tisztelettel értékeljük. Mi, magyarok ezer éven át önálló állami életet élő nemzet voltunk Európa egyik viharsarkában, melyet sokszor dult végig a keleti pogányság. Szenvedtünk és véreztünk s minden magyar család multjában ott állnak a mártir-hősök, akik a keresztény civilizációért, vagy a magyar szabadságért és függetlenségért adták oda életüket és vérüket. Az itt élő mai magyar nemzedék ilyen elődök sarjadéka. Tud tűrni, tud szenvedni, csak becstelenül nem tud élni.

Márpedig mi ugy érezzük, hogy husz évvel ezelőtt megtagadták tőlünk egy jogot, melyet oly prófétai ihlettel hirdetett Wilson elnök: a népek önrendelkezési jogát. Csak ez a jog adja vissza nekünk az egyenlő föltételek közt folyó, minden nemzetnek egyforma fejlődést biztositani tudó becsületes életet.

Tisztelettel és mély megbecsüléssel köszöntjük Lord Runcimant, mikor előzetesen körültekint abban a világban, amelyet becsületes uri igazságszeretettel kiván megjavitani és a népek ellentétes fölfogása, életérdeke közt a hidverés, sőt a hidbiztositás nemes föladatát vállalja. Szerencsét kivánunk neki ehhez a munkához.

[illegible] igazságkeresést [illegible]

[illegible] hogy nekünk, magyaroknak is jogunk van [illegible]

Ezt kivántuk elmondani [illegible] egy politikusnak, egy urnak, egy embernek, egy férfinak, aki nagy [illegible] föladatot vállalt magára.

A HUNGARIAN WELCOME TO LORD RUNCIMAN

The moment at which his Lordship sets foot on Czecho-Slovakian soil is one of extraordinary importance in the history of post-war Europe. The mission which brings him to this country — the role which he has undertaken, is entirely unprecedented.

In this part of Europe problems have literally piled up, on the solution of which depends the development of the coming years, the safety of states, the prosperity or decline of nations, and the peaceful and happy lives of the people — or their despair.

Twenty years ago it was believed to be possible to shunt off vital, effective historical forces, or to stifle them in their development. This cannot longer be maintained. The Peace Conference took into consideration only the two post-war extremes — victory or defeat. They forgot that only states can be temporarily defeated — not nations.

The Czechoslovak republic was formed on the basis that the victory of the Czech, Slovak, and Ruthenian nations was recognised, while the German, the Hungarian, and the Polish nations living in this territory suffered all the moral and material casualties of the lost war. The activity of the statesmen in the course of twenty years, in building the state, aimed at one thing; to lay the foundations of the Czechoslovak national existence at the expense of the Germans, Hungarians, and Poles. This development is unhealthy and unnatural, and was bound to end in conflicts. To arrive at this, it had been sufficent to alter the balance of the Great Powers directing Europe's history. The events in March this year brought into clear light this altered balance, and thus the Czechoslovakian problem was cast up.

The world knows this problem as the German — Czechoslovak problem, but those who are living here, or who occupy themselves more thoroughly with the existing situation, must know that the setting out of the problem is not anything like so simple as that.

There is not only a German — Czechoslovak problem, but also a Hungarian — Czechoslovak problem, a Polish — Czechoslovak problem, and even a Slovak — Czechoslovak problem, and a Ruthenian — Czechoslovak problem.

The problem calls for absorbing consideration, involving extensive research. The noble lord is doubtless fully conscious of the fact that the task he has undertaken with such a degree of self sacrifice, is complicated and difficult. We can scarcely find in the course of history, that a statesman acting in his private capacity, has ever undertaken a task of such gigantic magnitude.

The Hungarian national community living in this state, lifts its hat with respect to, and salutes this noble son of the great British nation, who comes to us to advise the responsible leaders of this state and the representatives of the nations, and, as far as in human possibility lies, to untie this Gordian knot.

The noble Lord comes with the purpose of insuring peace within this state, and to lay the foundations of agreement between the various nations of Czechoslovakia, because British policy is set upon the establishment of this, as the key to world peace.

We know this, and we appreciate it respectfully. We Hungarians have lived for a thousand years our independent state life, in the most stormy part of Europe, which has been repeatedly stirred up by by Oriental barbarism. We have suffered and bled, and in the past of every Hungarian family, is the record of martyr-heroes, who gave their lives and blood for Christian civilisation, or Hungarian liberty and independence. The present generation of Hungarians living here, are the descendants of such ancestors. This generation can endure and can suffer — it cannot live in dishonour.

We have within us the feeling that twenty years ago, we were denied the right that President Wilson proclaimed with prophetic inspiration: the right of self-determination of the nations. Only this right can restore our life of honour, by giving equal conditions and equal possibility of development to every nation.

With reverence and deep honour, we salute Lord Runciman as he looks out upon this world which he wants, as an honourable, single minded man, to reform by bringing into harmony the contrasting conceptions and vital interests of nations. We wish him good luck in this great task.

We, for our part, desire nothing other than what issues spontaneously from the character of an English gentleman: the pursuit of justice in an unbiassed, sincere way. In this we are ready to support loyally his efforts.

We believe deeply and unshakenly in the truth that we Hungarians have the right to live in liberty.

It is that which we wish clearly to convey, in all manly candidness to a statesman, a gentleman, and a Man, who has undertaken a great historical task.

PMH, 4 August, 1938

CORRESPONDENCE RESPECTING CZECHOSLOVAKIA, SEPTEMBER 1938

No. 1

Lord Runciman to the Prime Minister[1]

Westminster, S.W. 1,
September 21, 1938.

My dear Prime Minister,

When I undertook the task of mediation in the controversy between the Czechoslovak Government and the Sudeten German party, I was, of course, left perfectly free to obtain my own information and to draw my own conclusions. I was under no obligation to issue any kind of report. In present circumstances, however, it may be of assistance to you to have the final views, which I have formed as a result of my Mission, and certain suggestions which I believe should be taken into consideration, if anything like a permanent solution is to be found.

The problem of political, social and economic relations between the Teuton and Slav races in the area which is now called Czechoslovakia is one which has existed for many centuries with periods of acute struggle and periods of comparative peace. It is no new problem, and in its present stage there are at the same time new factors and also old factors which would have to be considered in any detailed review.

When I arrived in Prague at the beginning of August, the questions which immediately confronted me were (1) constitutional, (2) political and (3) economic. The constitutional question was that with which I was immediately and directly concerned. At that time it implied the provision of some degree of home rule for the Sudeten Germans within the Czechoslovak Republic; the question of self-determination had not yet arisen in an acute form. My task was to make myself acquainted with the history of the question, with the principal persons concerned, and with the suggestions for a solution proposed by the two sides, viz., by the Sudeten German party in the "Sketch" submitted to the Czechoslovak Government on the 7th June (which was by way of embodying the 8 points of Herr Henlein's speech at Karlsbad), and by the Czechoslovak Government in their draft Nationality Statute, Language Bill, and Administrative Reform Bill.

It became clear that neither of these sets of proposals was sufficiently acceptable to the other side to permit further negotiations on this basis, and the negotiations were suspended on the 17th August. After a series of private discussions between the Sudeten leaders and the Czech authorities, a new basis for negotiations was adopted by the Czechoslovak Government and was communicated to me on the 5th September, and to the Sudeten leaders on the 6th September. This was the so-called 4th Plan. In my opinion — and, I believe, in the opinion of the more responsible Sudeten leaders — this plan embodied almost all the requirements of the Karlsbad 8 points, and with a little clarification and extension could have been made to cover them in their entirety. Negotiations should have at once been resumed on this favourable and hopeful basis; but little doubt remains in my mind that the very fact that they were so favourable operated against their chances, with the more extreme members of the Sudeten German party. It is my belief that the incident arising out of the visit of certain Sudeten German Deputies to investigate into the case of persons arrested for arms smuggling at Mährisch-Ostrau was used in order to provide an excuse for the suspension, if not for the breaking off, of negotiations. The Czech Government, however, at once gave way to the demands of the Sudeten German party in this matter, and preliminary discussions of the 4th Plan were resumed on the 10th September. Again, I am convinced that this did not suit the policy of the Sudeten extremists, and that incidents were provoked and instigated on the 11th September and, with greater effect after Herr Hitler's speech, on the 12th September. As a result of the bloodshed and disturbance thus caused, the Sudeten delegation rufused to meet the Czech authorities as had been arranged on the 13th September. Herr Henlein and Herr Frank presented a new series of demands — withdrawal of State police, limitation of troops to their military duties, &c., which the Czechoslovak Government were again prepared to accept on the sole condition that a representative of the party came to Prague to discuss how order should be maintained. On the night of the 13th September this condition was refused by Herr Henlein, and all negotiations were completely broken off.

It is quite clear that we cannot now go back to the point where we stood two weeks ago; and we have to consider the situation as it now faces us.

With the rejection of the Czechoslovak Government's offer on the 13th September and with the breaking off of the negotiations by Herr Henlein, my functions as a mediator were, in fact, at an end. Directly and indirectly, the connection between the chief Sudeten leaders and the Government of the Reich had become the dominant factor in the situation; the dispute was no longer an internal one. It was not part of my function to attempt mediation between Czechoslovakia and Germany.

Responsibility for the final break must, in my opinion, rest upon Herr Henlein and Herr Frank and upon those of their supporters inside and outside the country who were urging them to extreme and unconstitutional action.

I have much sympathy, however, with the Sudeten case. It is a hard thing to be ruled by an alien race; and I have been left with the impression that Czechoslovak rule in the Sudeten areas for the last twenty years, though not actively oppressive and certainly not "terroristic," has been marked by tactlessness, lack of understanding, petty intolerance and discrimination, to a point where the resentment of the German population was inevitably moving in the direction of revolt. The Sudeten Germans felt, too, that in the past they had been given many promises by the Czechoslovak Government, but that little or no action had followed these promises. This experience had induced an attitude of unveiled mistrust of the leading Czech statesmen. I cannot say how far this mistrust is merited or unmerited; but it certainly exists, with the result that, however conciliatory their statements, they inspire no confidence in the minds of the Sudeten population. Moreover, in the last elections of 1935 the Sudeten German party polled more votes than any other single party; and they actually formed the second largest party in the State Parliament. They then commanded some 44 votes in a total Parliament of 300. With subsequent accessions, they are now the largest party. But they can always be outvoted; and consequently some of them feel that constitutional action is useless for them.

Local irritations were added to these major grievances. Czech officials and Czech police, speaking little or no German, were appointed in large numbers to purely German districts; Czech agricultural colonists were encouraged to settle on land transferred under the Land Reform in the middle of German populations; for the children of these Czech invaders Czech schools were built on a large scale; there is a very general belief that Czech firms were favoured as against German firms in the allocation of State contracts and that the State provided work and relief for Czechs more readily than for Germans. I believe these complaints to be in the main justified. Even as late as the time of my Mission, I could find no readiness on the part of the Czechoslovak Government to remedy them on anything like an adequate scale.

All these, and other, grievances were intensified by the reactions of the economic crisis on the Sudeten industries, which form so important a part of the life of the people. Not unnaturally, the Government were blamed for the resulting impoverishment.

For many reasons, therefore, including the above, the feeling among the Sudeten Germans until about three or four years ago was one of hopelessness. But the rise of Nazi Germany gave them new hope. I regard their turning for help towards their kinsmen and their eventual desire to join the Reich as a natural development in the circumstances.

At the time of my arrival, the more moderate Sudeten leaders still desired a settlement within the frontiers of the Czechoslovak State. They realised what war would mean in the Sudeten area, which would itself be the main battlefield. Both nationally and internationally such a settlement would have been an easier solution than territorial transfer. I did my best to promote it, and up to a point with some success, but even so not without misgiving as to whether, when agreement was reached, it could ever be carried out without giving rise to a new crop of suspicions, controversies, accusations and counter-accusations. I felt that any such arrangement would have been temporary, not lasting.

This solution, in the form of what is known as the "Fourth Plan," broke down in the circumstances narrated above; the whole situation, internal and external, had changed; and I felt that with this change my mission had come to an end.

When I left Prague on the 16th September, the riots and disturbances in the Sudeten areas, which had never been more than sporadic, had died down. A considerable number of districts had been placed under a régime called Standrecht, amounting to martial law. The Sudeten leaders, at any rate the more extreme among them, had fled to Germany and were issuing proclamations defying the Czechoslovak Government. I have been credibly informed that, at the time of my leaving, the number of killed on both sides was not more than 70.

Unless, therefore, Herr Henlein's Freikorps are deliberately encouraged to cross the frontier, I have no reason to expect any notable renewal of incidents and disturbances. In these circumtances the necessity for the presence of State Police in these districts should no longer exist. As the State Police are extremely unpopular among the German inhabitants, and have constituted one of their chief grievances for the last three years, I consider that they should be withdrawn as soon as possible. I believe that their withdrawal would reduce the causes of wrangles and riots.

Further, it has become self-evident to me that those frontier districts between Czchoslovakia and Germany where the Sudeten population is in an important majority should be given full right of self-determination at once. If some cession is inevitable, as I believe it to be, it is as well that it should be done promptly and without procrastination. There is real danger, even a danger of civil war, in the continuance of a state of uncertainty. Consequently there are very real reasons for a policy of immediate and drastic action. Any kind of plebiscite or referendum would, I believe, be a sheer formality in respect of these predominantly German areas. A very large majority of their inhabitants desire amalgamation with Germany. The inevitable delay involved in taking a plebiscite vote would only serve to excite popular feelings, with perhaps most dangerous results. I consider, therefore, that these frontier districts should at once be transferred from Czechoslovakia to Germany, and, further, that measures for their peaceful transfer, including the provision of safeguards for the population during the transfer period, should be arranged forthwith by agreement between the two Governments.

The transfer of these frontier districts does not, however, dispose finally of the question how Germans and Czechs are to live together peacefully in future. Even if all the areas where the Germans have a majority were transferred to Germany there would still remain in Czechoslovakia a large number of Germans, and in the areas transferred to Germany there would still be a certain number of Czechs. Economic connexions are so close that an absolute separation is not only undesirable but inconceivable; and I repeat my conviction that history has proved that in times of peace the two peoples can live together on friendly terms. I believe that it is in the interests of all Czechs and of all Germans alike that these friendly relations should be encouraged to re-establish themselves; and I am convinced that this is the real desire of the average Czech and German. They are alike in being honest, peaceable, hard-working and frugal folk. When political friction has been removed on both sides,I believe that they can settle down quietly.

For those portions of the territory, therefore, where the German majority is not so important, I recommend that an effort be made to find a basis for local autonomy within the frontiers of the Czechoslovak Republic on the lines of the "Fourth Plan," modified so as to meet the new circumstances created by the transfer of the preponderantly German areas. As I have already said, there is always a danger that agreement reached in principle may lead to further divergencies in practice. But I think that in a more peaceful future this risk can be minimised.

This brings me to the political side of the problem, which is concerned with the question of the integrity and security of the Czechoslovak Republic, especially in relation to her immediate neighbours. I believe that here the problem is one of removing a centre of intense political friction from the middle of Europe. For this purpose it is necessary permanently to provide that the Czechoslovak State should live at peace with all her neighbours and that her policy, internal and external, should be directed to that end. Just as it is essential for the international position of Switzerland that her policy should be entirely neutral, so an analogous policy is necessary for Czechoslovakia — not only for her own future existence but for the peace of Europe.

In order to achieve this, I recommend: —

(1) That those parties and persons in Czechoslovakia who have been deliberately encouraging a policy antagonistic to Czechoslovakia's neighbours should be forbidden by the

Czechoslovak Government to continue their agitations; and that, if necessary, legal measures should be taken to bring such agitations to an end.

(2) That the Czechoslovak Government should so remodel her foreign relations as to give assurances to her neighbours that she will in no circumstances attack them or enter into any aggressive action against them arising from obligations to other States.

(3) That the principal Powers, acting in the interests of the peace of Europe, should give to Czechoslovakia guarantees of assistance in case of unprovoked aggression against her.

(4) That a commercial treaty on preferential terms should be negotiated between Germany and Czechoslovakia if this seems advantageous to the economic interests of the two countries.

This leads me on to the third question which lay within the scope of my enquiry, viz., the economic problem. This problem centres on the distress and unemployment in the Sudeten German areas, a distress which has persisted since 1930, and is due to various causes. It constitutes a suitable background for political discontent. It is a problem which exists; but to say that the Sudeten German question is entirely or even in the main an economic one is misleading. If a transfer of territory takes place, it is a problem which will for the most part fall to the German Government to solve.

If the policy which I have outlined above recommends itself to those immediately concerned in the present situation, I would further suggest: (*a*) That a representative of the Sudeten German people should have a permanent seat in the Czechoslovak Cabinet. (*b*) That a Commission under a neutral chairman should be appointed to deal with the question of the delimitation of the area to be transferred to Germany and also with controversial points immediately arising from the carrying out of any agreement which may be reached. (*c*) That an international force be organised to keep order in the districts which are to be transferred pending actual transfer, so that Czechoslovak State police, as I have said above, and also Czechoslovak troops, may be withdrawn from this area.

I wish to close this letter by recording my appreciation of the personal courtesy, hospitality and assistance which I and my staff received from the Government authorities, especially Dr. Benes and Dr. Hodza, from the representatives of the Sudeten German party with whom we came in contact, and from a very large number of other people in all ranks of life whom we met during our stay in Czechoslovakia.

Yours very sincerely,
RUNCIMAN OF DOXFORD.

Miscellaneous No. 7 (1938) Correspondence respecting Czechoslovakia, September 1938. Cmd. 5847, London, His Majesty's Stationary Office, 1938.

1. Note — A similar letter was addressed by Lord Runciman to President Benes on September 21, 1938.

MUNICH AGREEMENT

(September 29, 1938)

I

Germany, the United Kingdom, France and Italy, taking into consideration the agreement, which has been already reached in principle for the cession to Germany of the Sudeten German territory, have agreed on the following terms and conditions governing the said cession and the measures consequent thereon, and by this agreement they each hold themselves responsible for the steps necessary to secure its fulfilment: —

1. The evacuation will begin on the 1st October.

2. The United Kingdom, France and Italy agree that the evacuation of the territory shall be completed by the 10th October, without any existing installations having been destroyed and that the Czechoslovak Government will be held responsible for carrying out the evacuation without damage to the said installations.

3. The conditions governing the evacuation will be laid down in detail by an international commission composed of representatives of Germany, the United Kingdom, France, Italy and Czechoslovakia.

4. The occupation by stages of the predominantly German territory by German troops will begin on the 1st October. The four territories marked on the attached map[2] will be occupied by German troops in the following order: the territory marked No. I on the 1st and 2nd of October, the territory marked No. II on the 2nd and 3rd of October, the territory marked No. III on the 3rd, 4th and 5th of October, the territory marked No. IV on the 6th and 7th of October. The remaining territory of preponderantly German character will be ascertained by the aforesaid international commission forthwith and be occupied by German troops by the 10th of October.

5. The international commission referred to in paragraph 3 will determine the territories in which a plebiscite is to be held. These territories will be occupied by international bodies until the plebiscite has been completed. The same commission will fix the conditions in which the plebiscite is to be held, taking as a basis the conditions of the Saar plebiscite. The commission will also fix a date, not later than the end of November, on which the plebiscite will be held.

6. The final determination of the frontiers will be carried out by the international commission. This commission will also be entitled to recommend to the four Powers, Germany, the United Kingdom, France and Italy, in certain exceptional cases minor modifications in the strictly ethnographical determination of the zones which are to be transferred without plebiscite.

7. There will be a right of option into and out of the transferred territories, the option to be exercised within six months from the date of this agreement. A German-Czechoslovak commission shall determine the details of the option, consider ways of facilitating the transfer of population and settle questions of principle arising out of the said transfer.

8. The Czechoslovak Government will within a period of four weeks from the date of this agreement release from their military and police forces any Sudeten Germans who may wish to be released, and the Czechoslovak Government will within the same period release Sudeten German prisoners who are serving terms of imprisonment for political offences.

Adolf Hitler
Neville Chamberlain
Édouard Daladier
Benito Mussolini

Munich, September 29, 1938

Annex to the Agreement

His Majesty's Government in the United Kingdom and the French Government have entered into the above agreement on the basis that they stand by the offer, contained in paragraph 6 of the Anglo-French proposals of the 19th September, relating to an international guarantee of the new boundaries of the Czechoslovak State against unprovoked aggression.

When the question of the Polish and Hungarian minorities in Czechoslovakia has been settled, Germany and Italy for their part will give a guarantee to Czechoslovakia.

Adolf Hitler
Neville Chamberlain
Édouard Daladier
Benito Mussolini

Munich, September 29, 1938

Declaration

The Heads of the Governments of the four Powers declare that the problems of the Polish and Hungarian minorities in Czechoslovakia, if not settled within three months by agreement between the respective Governments, shall form the subject of another meeting of the Heads of the Governments of the four Powers here present.

Adolf Hitler
Neville Chamberlain
Édouard Daladier
Benito Mussolini

Munich, September 29, 1938

Supplementary Declaration

All questions which may arise out of the transfer of the territory shall be considered as coming within the terms of reference to the international commission.

Adolf Hitler
Neville Chamberlain
Édouard Daladier
Benito Mussolini

Munich, September 29, 1938

Composition of the International Commission

The four Heads of Government here present agree that the international commission provided for in the agreement signed by them to-day shall consist of the Secretary of State in the German Foreign Office, the British, French and Italian Ambassadors accredited in Berlin, and a representative to be nominated by the Government of Czechoslovakia.

Adolf Hitler
Neville Chamberlain
Édouard Daladier
Benito Mussolini

Munich, September 29, 1938

British White Paper, No. 4, Cmd. 5848, London, H.M.S.O., 1938.

206

THE FIRST VIENNA ARBITRAL AWARD, 1938

No. 536, Protocol concerning the Arbitral Award establishing the Czechoslovak Hungarian boundary. Signed at Vienna, November 2, 1938

Entered into force November 2, 1938.[1]

Translation from 8 *Völkerbund* (1938), No. 3-4, pp. 54-55.

In pursuance of the request made by the Royal Hungarian and the Czechoslovak Governments to the German and the Royal Italian Governments to settle by arbitration the outstanding question of the areas to be ceded to Hungary, and in pursuance of the notes exchanged on the subject between the Governments concerned on October 30th 1938, the German Reich Minister of Foreign Affairs, Herr Joachim von Ribbentrop, and the Minister of Foreign Affairs of His Majesty the King of Italy and Emperor of Ethiopia, Count Galeazzo Ciano, have today met at the Belvedere Castle at Vienna and given the desired arbitral award in the names of their Governments.

For this purpose they have invited to Vienna the Royal Hungarian Minister of Foreign Affairs, M. Koloman von Kanya, and the Czechoslovak Minister of Foreign Affairs, Dr. Franz Chvalkovsky, in order to give them an opportunity in the first place again to explain the point of view of their Governments.

This arbitral award, together with the map mentioned in paragraph I, has been handed to the Royal Hungarian Minister of Foreign Affairs and to the Czechoslovak Minister of Foreign Affairs. They have taken cognizance of it and have again confirmed, on behalf of their Governments, the statement which they made on October 30th 1938 that they accept the arbitral award as a final settlement and that they undertake to carry it out unconditionally and without delay.

Done in the German and Italian languages in quadruplicate.

Vienna, November 2nd 1938.

V. Ribbentrop   Count Ciano   V. Kanya   Chvalkovsky

ANNEX

Arbitral Award of November 2, 1938

In pursuance of the request made by the Royal Hungarian and the Czechoslovak Governments to the German and the Royal Italian Governments to settle by arbitration the outstanding question of the areas to be ceded to Hungary, and in pursuance of the notes exchanged on the subject between the Governments concerned on October 30th 1938, the German Reich Minister of Foreign Affairs, Herr Joachim von Ribbentrop, and the Minister of Foreign Affairs of His Majesty the King of Italy and Emperor of Ethiopia, Count Galeazzo Ciano, have today met at Vienna and, after a further discussion with the Royal Hungarian Minister of Foreign Affairs, M. Koloman von Kanya, and the Czechoslovak Minister of Foreign Affairs, Dr. Franz Chvalkovsky, have given the following arbitral award in the names of their Governments:

1. The areas to be ceded by Czechoslovakia to Hungary are marked on the annexed map.[2] The demarcation of the frontier on the spot is confided to a Hungarian-Czechoslovak Commission.

2. The evacuation of the ceded territories by Czechoslovakia and their occupation by Hungary begins on November 5th and is to be concluded by November 10th. The individual stages of the

evacuation and occupation together with other details are to be fixed by a Hungarian-Czechoslovak Commission.

3. The Czechoslovak Government will take care that the ceded territories are left in an orderly condition on evacuation.

4. Individual questions arising out of the cession of territory, in particuliar questions relating to nationality and options, are to be settled by a Hungarian-Czechoslovak Commission.

5. Likewise, detailed provisions for the protection of persons of Magyar nationality remaining in the territory of Czechoslovakia and of persons of non-Magyar nationality remaining in the ceded territories are to be agreed upon by a Hungarian-Czechoslovak Commission. The Commission will take particular care that the Magyar national group in Pressburg is given the same position as the other national groups.

6. In so far as the cession of territories to Hungary involves disadvantages and difficulties of an economic or transport character for the territory remaining with Czechoslovakia, the Royal Hungarian Government will do everything possible, in agreement with the Czchoslovak Government, to remove such disadvantages and difficulties.

7. Should any difficulties or doubt arise in the execution of the arbitral award, the Royal Hungarian and the Czech Governments will immediately consult with each other. Should they be unable to reach an agreement on any question, such question will be submitted to the German and Royal Italian Governments for final decision.

Vienna, November 2nd 1938.

Joachim von Ribbentrop   Galeazzo Ciano

Source: *Washingtion, Carnegie Endowment for International Peace,* Vol. 8, 1938-1941, 210-202.

1. Not registered with the Secretariat of the League of Nations.

STATISTICAL DATA ON HUNGARY

Territory and Population[1]

I

	Territory in Square miles	Population in 1000
Hungary in 1914 (including Croatia)	125,649	20,886
Hungary in 1914 (without Croatia, but inc. Fiume)	109,223	18,264
Territory ceded in 1920 (Treaty of Trianon)	89,754	13,271
— To Austria	1,552	292
— To Czechoslovakia	23,798	3,518
— To Italy	8	50
— To Poland	227	34
— To Rumania	39,807	5,258
Territory remaining to Hungary	35,898	7,615
Hungary in 1920 (after Trianon)	35,938[2]	c. 7,900[3]
Hungary in 1938	35,938	9,129
Hungary in 1941 (within Trianon frontiers)	35,938	9,320
— Part of Northern Hungary regained in November 1938	4,605	1,062
— Sub-Carpathia (Ruthenia) regained in March-April 1939	4,657	694
— Northern Transylvania regained in August 1940	16,643	2,577
— Parts of Southern Hungary regained in April 1941	4,431	1,030
Enlarged Hungary in April 1941	66,274	14,683
Hungary in 1947 (after the Treaty of Paris)	35,916[4]	9,205[5]
Hungary on January 1, 1960	35,916	9,961
Hungary on January 1, 1967	35,916	10,197
Hungary on January 1, 1969	35,916	10,275

1. The main sources for these tables are: Information Hungary, edited by Ferenc Erdei and the Hungarian Academy of Sciences (Oxford: Pergamon Press, 1968); Jacob S. Siegel, The Population of Hungary (Washington: U.S. Government Printing Office, 1958); Statistical Year-book of Hungary, 1949-1955, compiled by the Central Bureau of Statistics from Statisztikai Évkönyv, Budapest 1957 (Washington: U.S. Joint Publications Research Service, 1958); and Magyar Statisztikai zsebkönyv (Budapest: Közgazdasági és Jogi Könyvkiadó, 1966).

2. Discrepancy is due to the slightly higher estimates by recent surveyors.

3. This sudden growth in population is due to the influx of refugees from the Succession States.

4. The difference of 22 square miles between the area of inter-war and post-war Hungary is due to the loss of three additional villages (the Bratislava [Pozsony] bridgehead) to Czechoslovakia.

5. Hungary's population on January 1, 1949. Data for 1947 is not available.

Source: Konnyu, Leslie, *A Condensed Geography of Hungary,* St. Louis, The American-Hungarian Review. 1971, 63-64.

BIBLIOGRAPHY

Published Documents

Ádám, Magda, *A müncheni egyezmény létrejötte és Magyarország külpolitikája, 1936-1938,* Budapest, Akadémiai Kiadó, 1965.

Das Abkommen von München, 1938, Tschecoslovakische Diplomatische Dokumente, 1937-1938, Praha, ČAV.

Akten zur Deutschen Auswärtigen Politik, ADAP, 1918-1945, Series D, 1937-1945, Baden, Baden, 1950.

Aperçu statistique de la République Tchécoslovaque, Prague, 1930.

Bethlen István titkos iratai, Budapest, Kossuth, 1972, (Szinai, M.&L. Szűcs, eds.).

British White Paper, No. 4, Cmd. 5848, London, H.M.S.O., 1938.

Carnegie Endowment for International Peace, VIII, 1938-1941, Washington, 1949.

Correspondence respecting Czechoslovakia, September, 1938, Miscellaneous, No. 7, Cmd. 5847, London, H.M.S.O., 1938.

Czechoslovak Sources and Documents, Vols. 1-4, New York, The Czsl. Information Service, 1942-1943.

Documenti Diplomatici Italiani, 7 Serie, 1922-1935, VIII, 1st. Poligr. St., 1972.

Documents on American Foreign Relations, Jan. 1938-June 1939, Jones Shephard S., Boston, World Peace Foundation, 1939.

Documents on British Foreign Policy, 1919-1939, (DBFP), London, H.M.S.O., 1946.

Documents Diplomatiques Français, 1932-1939, Paris, Min. des Affaires Étrangères, 1963-1968.

Documents on German Foreign Policy (DGFP), Washington, US Government Printing Office, 1951.

Documents on German Foreign Policy, 1918-1945, Series D, 1937-1945, Germany — ČSR, London, His Majesty's Stationary Office, 1950.

Documents on Hungarian Foreign Policy, (DHFP), Budapest, Akadémiai K., 1971.

Dokumente zur Sudetendeutschen Frage (DSDF), Nitter, E., ed. (München), Ackermann Gemeinde, 1967.

Dokumentumok a Szlovák Tanácsköztársaságról, Budapest, Kossuth, 1970.

Dokumenty z przededenia II wojny światowej, Polska polytika zagraniczna w świetle archiwów Wilhelmstrasse, 1937-1938, Sprawy Międzynarodowe, Nr. 4-8.

Le livre jaune français, Documents diplomatiques, Paris, Impr. nat., 1939.

Les données statistiques des enclaves homogènes hongroises et allemandes dans les états dits successeurs, Budapest, Hornyánszky, 1928.

Foreign Relations of the United States, Diplomatic Papers, 1938, Washington, US Government Printing Office, 1955.

Horthy Miklós titkos iratai, Budapest, Kossuth, 1972, Szinai, M.&L. Szücs, eds.

Hungary at the Peace Conference, Budapest, Min. of Foreign Affairs, 1947.

Külpolitikai adatok az 1938. évről, Budapest, Külügymnisztérium, 1939.

La Legislazione Fascista, 1934-1939 (XII-XVII), Vol. I, Pubbl. del Senato, Roma.

Nouveaux documents pour servir à l'histoire de Munich, Prague, Orbis, 1958.

Nové dokumenty k historii Mnichova, Praha, Nakl. Pol. Lit., 1958.

Sbírka zákonů a nařízení, (Sb. zák. a nař.), Praha, St. Nakl., 1921-1938, 1948.

Seeds of Conflicts, Series I, Hungary, Nendeln, Kraus Reprint, 1973.

Statistická Příručka Republiky Československé, III, Praha, SÚS, 1928.

Suddivisione etnica delle populazione delle città settentrionali nel 1910-1930, Affari Esteri, Roma, No. 489/1938.

Számjeltávirat valamennyi magyar királyi követségnek, Budapest, Táncsics, K., Karsai, E. ed., 1969.

Traité entre les Principales Puissances Alliées et la Tchéco-Slovaquie, signé à Saint-Germain-en-Laye, le 10 septembre 1919, in Sb. zák. a nař.

Ústav pro mezinarodní politiku a ekonomii, Dokumenty československé zahraniční politiky, 1945-1960, Praha, 1960.

Unpublished Documents

Documents from the archives of the Ministero degli Affari Esteri, Roma.

Nieopublikowane dokumenty, EE/MG/No. 52/tjn/191, August-September, 1938, Warsaw.

Public Record Office, London, Collected documents for the Czechoslovak crisis, 1938.

Books

Ádám, M., Gy. Juhász, L. Kerekes, *Allianz Hitler-Horthy-Mussolini*, Budapest, Akadémiai K., 1966.

Ajtay, Joseph, *La paix en danger*, Budapest, Hungaria, 1933.

Apponyi, Count Albert et al., *Justice for Hungary*, Review and Criticism of the Effect of the Treaty of Trianon, London, Longmans Green & Co. Ltd., 1928.

Arató, Endre, *A magyar-csehszlovák viszony ötven éve*, Budapest, Kossuth, 1969.

Atti del Parlamento Italiano, Vol. V, Discussioni dal 1 marzo 1938 — al 14 dicembre 1938, Roma, Tipografa della Camera dei Deputati, 1939.

Aufricht, Hans, *Guide to League of Nations Publications*, New York, Columbia Univ. Press, 1951.

Avon, The Earl of (Eden, Sir Anthony), *The Eden Memoirs, Facing the Dictators*, Boston, Houghton Mifflin, 1962.

Baker, James F., *The United States and the Czechoslovak Crisis, 1938-1939*, Tulane, Dissertation, 1971.

Balla, Pál, *A felvidéki magyarság külpolitikai tevékenysége*, Budapest, Fővárosi Ny., 1940.

Batowski, Henryk, *Kryzys dyplomatyczny w Europe, jesien 1938-1939*, Warszawa, Wyd. Min. Obrany Nár., 1962.

Batowski, Henryk, *Zdrada Monachijska*, Poznań, Wyd. Poznańskie, 1973.

Battaglia de, Forst, *Zwischeneuropa von der Ostsee bis zur Adria*, Teil I, Polen, Tschechoslowakei, Ungarn, Frankfurt a/M., Verlag Frankfurter Hefte, 1954.

Baumont, Maurice, *La faillite de la paix*, 1918-1939, Paris, Presses Univ. de France, 1945.

Beneš, Eduard, *Světova válka a naše revoluce*, Praha, Orbis, 1927-28.

Benns, F. Lee, *European History since 1870*, New York, Appleton-Century-Crofts, 1950.

Birdsall, Paul, *Versailles Twenty Years After*, New York, Freeman's Journal, 1938.

Bonnet, Georges, *Défense de la paix*, Genève, Ed. du Cheval ailé, 1946.

Bonsal, Stephen, *Suitors and Suppliants: The Little Nations at Versailles*, New York, Prentice-Hall, 1946.

Boros, Ferenc, *Magyar-csehszlovák kapcsolatok, 1918-1921*, Budapest, Akadémiai K., 1970.

Borsody, István, *Magyarok Csechszlovákiában*, Budapest, Az Ország Útja, 1938.

Borsody, István, *Magyar — szlovák kiegyezés. A cseh-szlovák-magyar viszony utóbbi száz éve*, Budapest, Officina, 1945.

Borsody, István, *Beneš*, Budapest, Athenaeum, 1942.

Borsody, István, *A felvidéki magyarság húsz éve, 1918-1938*, Budapest, Az Ország Útja 1938.

Botka-Csanda-Holotiková-Roják-Vigh-Zvara, *Magyarok Czehszlovákiában*, Bratislava, Epocha, 1969.

Bruegel, J.W., *Czechoslovakia before Munich: The German Minority Problem*, Toronto, MacMillan, 1974.

Bruegel, J.W. *Tschechen und Deutsche, 1939-1946*, München, Nymphenburger, Verlagshandlung, 1974.

Braunias, Karl, *Die Slovaken*, Stuttgart, W. Kohlhammer, 1942.

Brausch, G. *Deutschland — Ungarn,* Die diplomatischen Beziehungen vom Herbst 1937 bis zum Frühjahr 1939, Göttingen, Phil. Diss., 1956.

Burian, Peter, *Chanzen und Grenzen des sudetendeutschen Aktivizmus,* München-Wien, R. Oldenburg, 1919.

Celovsky, Boris, *Das Münchener Abkommen,* Stuttgart, Deutsche Verlags-Anstalt, 1958.

César, J.-B. Černý, *Politika německých borźoazních stran y Československu v letech 1918-1938,* Praha, ČAV, 1962, I, II.

Chászár, Edward, *Decision in Vienna,* The Czechoslovak-Hungarian Border Dispute, Astor, Danubian Press, 1978.

Chmelař, Joseph, *Le problème allemand en Tchécoslovaquie,* Prague, Orbis, 1936.

Ciano, Count Galeazzo, *The Ciano Diaries,* ed., Hugh Gibson, New York, Doubleday, 1946.

Ciano, Count Galeazzo, *Ciano's Diary, 1937-1938,* London, Methuen & Co., 1952.

Ciano, Count Galeazzo, *L'Europa verso la catastrofe,* Roma, Mondadori, 1948.

Cienciela, A.M., *Poland and the Western Powers,* Toronto, University of Toronto Press, 1968.

Čulen, Konštantin, *Po Svätoplukovi druhá naša hlava,* (Život Dr. Jozefa Tisu), Middletown, Jednota, 1947.

Csáky, Etienne, *Le pays et le peuple ruthène,* Budapest, Hornyánszky, 1938.

Csanda, Sándor, *Csehszlovák-magyar kulturális kapcsolatok,* Bratislava, Slov, Ped. Nákl., 1963.

Csatár, I. & J. Ölvedi, *A visszatért Felvidék adattára,* Budapest, Mahr, 1939.

Czakó, Etienne, *La vérité sur les délibérations préliminaires du traité de Trianon,* Budapest, Uno-Press, 1942.

A Csehszlovákiai Magyar Népszövetségi Liga Memoranduma a Népszövetséghez, Budapest, Hornyánszky, 1938.

Czernin, Ferdinand, *Versailles, 1919.* The forces, events and personalities that shaped the treaty, New York, Capricorn, 1964.

Czechoslovakia, Seeds of Conflict Series 7, Irredentist and Nationalist Questions in Central Europe, 1913-1919, Nendeln, Kraus Reprint, 1973.

Deák, Francis, *Hungary at the Peace Conference,* The Diplomatic History of the Treaty of Trianon, New York, Howard Fertig, 1972.

Delfiner, Henry, *Vienna Broadcasts to Slovakia, 1938-39:* A case study in subversion, New York, Columbia Univ. Press, 1974.

Deportation of the Hungarians of Slovakia, Budapest, Hungarian Society for Foreign Affairs, 1947.

Desbons, Georges, *Les Erreurs de la paix.* La Hongrie après le Traité de Trianon, Paris, Librairie des Sciences Politiques et Sociales, 1933.

Dobrý, Anatol, *Kdo vládl v předmnichovské republice,* Praha, St. Nakl. Polit, Lit, 1958.

Dreisziger, N.F., *Hungary's Way to World War II,* Toronto, Helicon Society, 1968.

Duff, Grant, *Europe and the Czechs,* Harmandsworth, Penguin Books, 1938.

Dvortchak, Victor, *Aide-Mémoire sur la question slovaque,* Paris, Le Conseil Slovaque, 1922.

Dvortchak, Victor, *La vérité sur le Traité de Trianon,* Paris, Par l'Auteur, 1933.

Dvortchak, Victor, *Prague la Rouge,* Paris, Chez l'Auteur, 1937.

Eubank, Keith, *Munich,* Norman, Univ. of Oklahoma Press, 1963.

Faust, Ovidius, *Ze starých zápisníc mesta Bratislavy,* Bratislava, Nákl. Ved. Úst. mesta Bratislavy, 1933.

Feis, Herbert, *Between War and Peace: The Potsdam Conference,* Princeton, Univ. of Princeton Press, 1960.

A felvidéki magyarság húsz éve, 1918-1938, Magy. Stat. Tság Államtud. Int., Budapest, Egyetemi Ny., 1938.

Felvidékünk — Honvédségünk, (Trianontól — Kassáig), Budapest, A Vitézi Rend Kiadása, Stadium Ny., 1939.

Fenyo, Mario D., *Hitler, Horthy and Hungary,* German-Hungarian Relations, 1941-1944, New Haven, Yale Books, 1972.

Ferdonnet, Paul, *La crise tchèque,* Paris, Éd. Baudinière, 1938.

Fierlinger, Zdeněk, *Ve službách ČSR: Paměti z druhého zahraničního odboje,* Praha, Svoboda, 1951.

François-Poncet, André, *The Fateful Years: Memoirs of a French Ambassador in Berlin,* New York, Howard Fertig, 1972.

Gajan, K. (ed.), *Germany and Czechoslovakia, 1918-1945,* Prague, Orbis, 1965.

Gajanová, Elena, *ČSR a středoevropská politika velmocí, 1918-1938,* Praha, ČAV, 1967.

Gastony, Endre B., *Revisionist Hungarian Foreign Policy and the Third Reich's Advance to the East, 1933-1939*, Dissertation, Univ. of Oregon, 1970.

Gathorne-Hardy, G.M., *A Short History of International Affairs, 1920-1939*, London, Oxford University Press, 1942.

Gatzke, Hans (ed.), *European Diplomacy Between Two Wars, 1919-1939*, Chicago, Quadrangle Books, 1972.

Gehl, Jürgen, *Austria, Germany and the Anschluss, 1931-1938*, London, Oxford Univ. Press, 1963.

George, Pierre, *Le problème allemand en Tchécoslovaquie*, Paris, Impr. Nationale, 1947.

Giolli, Filippo, *Come fummo condotti alle catastrofe*, Roma, Ed. Faro, 1945.

Glaser, Kurt, *Czecho-Slovakia: A Critical History*, Caldwell, Caxton Printers, 1961.

Goldmann, Rüdiger, *Die sudetendeutsche Frage auf der Pariser Friedenskonferenz*, München, Fides, 1971.

Gollanz, V., *Our Threatened Values*, London, V. Gollanz, Ltd., 1946.

Gromen, Richard J., *British Historians and Their Views of the British Policy of Appeasement in the Foreign Policy Crisis, 1931-1939*, Dissertation, Case Western Reserve, 1969.

Grosschmid Géza, *Kisebbségi sors*, Košice-Kassa, The Author, 1930.

Hankey, M.P., *The Supreme Control*, The Paris Peace Conference, 1919, London, Allen and Unwin, 1961.

Hedges, R.Y., *The Juridical Basis of Arbitration*, London, British Year Book of International Law, VII, 1926.

Henderson, Sir Nevil, *Failure of a Mission*, New York, Hodder and Stoughton, 1940.

Hitchins, K., *The Nationality Problem in Austria-Hungary*, Leiden, Brill, 1974.

Hoensch, Jörg, K., *Die Slowakei und Hitler's Ostpolitik*, Köln, Graz, Bohlau Verlag, 1965.

Hoensch, Jörg, K., *Die Grundlagen des Programms der Slowakischen Volkspartei vor 1938, München, Verlag R. Lerche, 1966.k*

Hoensch, Jörg, K., *Der Ungarische Revisionismus und die Zerschlagung der Tschechoslovakei*, Tübingen, J.C.B. Mohr, 1967.

Horthy, Miklós, *Ein Leben für Ungarn*, Bonn, Athenaeum Verlag, 1951.

Horthy, Miklós, *Memoirs*, New York, R. Speller & Sons, 1957.

Hóry, András, *Behind the Scenes of World War II*, Astor Park, Danubia Press, 1968.

Hořec, Jaromir, *Imperialisti proti československej samostatnosti*. Legenda o Wilsonovi, Bratislava, Slov. Vyd. Pol. Lit.,/955.

Hrušovský, Fr., *Slovenské dejiny*, T. Sv. Martin, Matica, 1940.

Hungarians in Czechoslovakia, New York, Research Inst. for Univ. Studies on Hungary, 1959.

International Legislation, Vol. 8, Washington, Carnegie Endowment for International Peace, 1938-1941.

Jaksch, Wenzel, *Europa's Weg nach Potsdam*, Stuttgart, Deutsche Verlag-Anstalt, 1958.

Jandera, A. & A. Mika, *Kapitoly z dějín předmnichovské republiky*, Praha, Orbis, 1953.

Jehlička, François, *Appel des Slovaques adressé à la nation française*, Vienne, Le Conseil Slovaque, 1933.

Jehlička, François, *Le problème slovaque*, Genève, Le Conseil Slovaque, 1935.

Jelinek, Yeshayahu, *The Parish Republic*, Hlinka's Slovak People's Party, 1939-1945, New York, Columbia Univ. Press, 1976.

Juhász, Gyula, *Magyarország külpolitikája, 1919-1945*, Budapest, Kussuth, 1969.

Kalvoda, Josef, *Czechoslovakia's Role in Soviet Strategy*, Washington, D.C. U.P. of Amer., 1978.

Kennan, George F., *From Prague after Munich*, Princeton, Princeton Univ. Press, 1968.

Kerekes, Lajos, *The Berlin-Rome Axis and the Annexation of Austria*, Budapest, Akad, Tört, Inc., 1962.

Kertész, S. D., *Diplomacy in a Whirlpool: Hungary between Germany and Soviet Russia*, Notre Dame, Univ. of Notre Dame Press, 1953.

Kertész, S. D., *The Fate of East Central Europe*, Hopes and Failures of American Foreign Policy, Notre Dame, Univ. of Notre Dame Press, 1956.

Kimminich, Otto, *Das Münchener Abkommen*, München, Fides, 1968.

Kimminich, Otto, *Stellugnahmen zum Münchener Abkommen in der deutschen Presse*, München, Collegium Carolinum, 1966.

Kirschbaum, Josef M., *Slovakia: Nation at the Crossroads of Central Europe*, New York, R. Speller & Sons, 1960.

Kis, Aladár, *Magyarország külpolitikája a második világháború előestéjén*, Budapest, Kossuth, 1963.

Kitsikis, Dimitri, *Le rôle des experts à la Conférence de la paix de 1919*, Ottawa, Presses de l'Univ. d'Ottawa, 1970.

Konnyu, Leslie, *A Condensed Geography of Hungary*, St. Louis, The American-Hungarian Review, 1971.

Kopecký, R., *Československý odboj v Polsku v roce 1939*, Rotterdam Jan Beran, 1958.

Kosáry, Dominic G., *A History of Hungary*, Cleveland, The Benj. Franklin Bibliophile Soc., 1941.

Kovács, Aloyse, *Au lieu d'un, trois états de nationalité*, Budapest, Pfeiffer, 1920.

Kovács, Endre, *Szemben a történelemmel*, Budapest, Magvető, 1977.

Kozeński, J., *Czechoslowacja w Polskiej Polityce zagranicznej w latach 1932-1938*, Poznań, Instytut Zachodni, 1964.

Koźminski, Maciej, *Polska i Węgry przed drugą wojną swiatową*, Warszawa, Polska Akad. Nauk, 1970.

Kővágó, József, *The Cities of the Hungarian Linguistic Territory in Slovakia*, Budapest, Inst. of the Letters and Arts, 1946.

Král, Václav, (ed.), *Politické strany a Mnichov*, Praha, Svobodné Slovo, 1961.

Krofta, Kamil, *The Substance of Hungarian Revisionism*, Prague, Orbis, 1934.

Kvaček, Robert, *Osudna mise*, Praha, Svobodné Slovo, 1958.

Kvaček, Robert, *Nad Evropou zatazěno*, Praha, Svoboda, 1966.

Laffan, R.G.D., Survey of International Affairs 1938, vol. II, Oxford University Press, London, 1951.

Lammers, Donald N., *Explaining Munich: The Search for Motive in British Policy*, Stanford, The Hoover Institute, 1966.

Leták, Miroslav, *V osidlech zrady*, Praha, Svobodné Slovo, 1965.

Lee, Dwight E., *Munich; Blunder, Plot or Tragic Necessity?* Lexington, D.C. Heath, 1970.

Lettrich, Josef, *History of Modern Slovakia*, New York, Praeger, 1955.

Ligue pour la révision du traité de Trianon, La lettre d'envoi et les commissions de délimitation, Budapest, Hornyánszky, 1928.

Lipski, J., *Diplomat in Berlin, 1933-1939*, New York, Columbia Univ. Press, 1968.

Lipták, L., *Slovensko v 20. storočí*, Bratislava, VPL, 1968.

Lombard, Paul, *Le Chemin de Munich*, Paris, Éd. de France, 1938.

Luža, Radomir, *The Transfer of the Sudeten Germans*, A study of Czech-German Relations, 1933-1962, New York, Unity Press, 1954.

Lvová, Mila, *Mnichov a Edvard Beneš*, Praha, Svoboda, 1968.

Macartney, C.A., *Hungary: A Short History*, Chicago, Aldine, 1962.

Macartney, C.A., *Hungary and Her Successors*, London, Oxford Univ. Press, 1937.

Macartney, C.A., *Independent Eastern Europe*, New York, St. Martin Press, 1966.

Macartney, C.A., *October Fifteenth, History of Modern Hungary*, Edinburgh, Univ. Press, 1956.

Mamatey, V.S., & R. Luža, *A History of the Czechoslovak Republic, 1918-1948*, Princeton, Univ. of Princeton Press, 1973.

Masaryk, Thomas G., *The Making of a State: Memoirs and Observations, 1914-1918*, New York, H. Fertig, 1969.

Mazon, André M., *La crise internationale de septembre 1938*, Paris, Ed. Jouve et Cie. 1938.

Mercier, M., *La formation de l'état tchécoslovaque*, Chartres, F. Lainé, 1922.

Micksche, F. (Oberst), *Donauföderation*, Salzburg, Forschungsinstitut für Fragen des Donauraums, 1953.

Mikus, Joseph, *Slovakia a Political History, 1918-1950*, Milwaukee, Marquette Univ. Press, 1963.

Miller, David Hunter, *My Diary at the Conference of Paris*, New York, Appeal Printing Co., 1924.

Mindszenty, Jozsef, Cardinal, *Memoirs*, New York, Macmillan, 1974.

Morrell, Sydney, *I Saw the Crucifixion*, London, Peter Davies, n.d.

Mourin, Maxime, *Ciano contre Mussolini*, Paris, Hachette, 1960.

Munich 1938 de la capitulation à la guerre, E 100 Petite Bibliothèque Chinoise, Paris, Éditions du Centenaire, 1979, Traduction.

Muralt (von) Leonard, *From Versailles to Potsdam*, Hinsdale, Henry Regnery, 1948.

München eine offene Frage, München, Ackermann Gemeinde, 1958.

Nagy, L. Zs., *A párizsi békekonferencia és Magyarország, 1918-1919*, Budapest, Kossuth, 1965.

Namier, L.B., *Diplomatic Prelude: 1938-1939*, New York, H. Fertig, 1971.

Les Négotiations de la paix hongroise, Compte rendu sur les travaux de la délégation, Budapest, Hornyánszky, 1920.

Noguères, Henri, (Transl. P. O'Brian), *Munich*, Peace for Our Time, New York, McGraw-Hill, 1965.

215

Nowak, R., *Der künstliche Staat*, Oldenburg i. Og., Stalling 1938.

Oddo, Gilbert L. *Slovakia and Its People*, New York, R. Speller & Sons, 1969.

Olay (d') François, *La Campagne de destruction contre les monuments hongrois 1918-1930*, Budapest, Athenaeum, 1931.

Olay (d'), François, *Les frontières de la Hongrie démembrée*, Budapest, Athenacéum, 1936.

Olay (d'), François, *La presse hongroise dans les états successeurs, 1918-1928*, Budapest, Athenaeum, 1929.

Paris Peace Conference, 1946, Washington, US Gov't. Printing Office, XX.

Perman, D., *The Shaping of the Czechoslovak State*, Leiden, Brill, 1962.

Peška, Zdeněk, *Kulturní samospráva národních měnšin*, Praha, Orbis, 1933.

Petrov, A., *Příspevky k historické demografii Slovenska v XVIII-XIX. století*, Praha, 1928.

Piloty, R. & O. Koellreutter, *Jahrbuch des offentlichen Rechts*, Band XI, Der Tschechoslowakische Staat, Tübingen, Verlag Mohr, 1922.

Presidenza del consiglio dei Ministri, Fascicolo Nr. 5778, Roma, 1938.

Pruuden, Salme, *Panslavism and Russian Communism*, Richmond, Foreign Aff. Publ. Co., 1976.

Purgat, Juraj. *Od Trianonu po Košice*, Bratislava, Epocha, 1970.

La question de la nationalité sur la base de l'indigénat de la minorité hongroise en Tchécoslovaquie, Mémoire à la Société des Nations, Prague, Club des Députés Hongrois, 1925.

Rabl, Kurt O., *Grundlagen und Grundfragen eines mitteleuropäischen Volksgruppenrechts*, Tübingen, Mohr, 1938.

Rabl, Kurt O., *Staatsbürgerliche Loyalität im Nationalitätenstaat*, München, R. Lerche, 1959.

Raisová, Eva. *Mnichov, 1938 a ako k nemu došlo*, Bratislava, Slov. Vyd. Plit. Lit., 1958.

Ránki, György, *A második világháború története*, Budapest, Gondolat, 1973.

Raschhofer, Hermann, *Die tschechoslowakischen Denkschriften für die Friedenskonferenz von Paris 1919/1920, Nationalität als Wesen und Rechtsbegriff*, Berlin, J. Springer, 1937.

Renzo (de), Felice, *Mussolini il Duce*, Roma, G. Einaudi, 1936.

Révay, S., *Die im Belvedere gezogene ungarisch-slowakische Grenze*, Budapest, Magy, Stat. Tság., 1941.

Ripka, Hubert, *Munich: Before and After*, New York, H. Fertig, 1969.

Rothermere, Harold S.H., *Warnings and Predictions*, London, Eyre and Spottiswoode, 1939.

Rotnagl, Josef, *Češi a Slováci*, Praha, Jos. R. Vilimek, 1945.

Roy, Douglas, *In the Year of Munich*, New York, St. Martin's Press, 1977.

Rystad, G., *Ambiguous Imperialism, US Foreign Policy*, Stockholm, Esselle Studium, 1975.

Sbírka zákonů a nařízení Státu Československého, Praha, St. Tisk, 1921-1938.

Schausberger, D., *Die sudetendeutsche Politik im Lichte der Parteien*, Reichenberg, Berlag F. Kraus, 1931.

Schindler, Dietrich, *Die Schiedsgerichtbarkeit seit 1914*, Stuttgart, M. Kohlammer, 1938.

Schmid-Egger, Barbara, *Der Völkerbund und die Sudetendeutschen Minderheitspetitionen der Jahre 1920-1926*, Freiburg, Staatsexamenarbeit, 1929.

Schuschnigg, Kurt von, *The Brutal Takeover: The Austrian Ex-Chancellor's Account of the Anschluss of Austria by Hitler*, New York, Athenaeum, 1971.

Sidor, Karol, *Slovenská politika na pôde pražského parlamentu, 1918-1938*, Bratislava, Knihtl. Andrej, 1943.

Simpson, J.L., *International Arbitration: Law and Practice*, London, Stevens & Sons, 1959.

Smith, Denis M., *Le guerre del Duce*, Roma-Bari, Ed. Laterza, 1976.

Sobota, Emil (transl. J. Kalfus), *Das tschechoslowakische Nationalitätenrecht*, Praha, Orbis, 1931.

Sréter, István, *Nem, nem, soha!*, Budapest Viktoria Ny., 1927.

Stanek, Imrich, *Zrada a pád: Hlinkovští separartisté a tak zvaný Slovenský stát*, Praha, St. Nakl. Pol. Lit., 1958.

Stercho, Peter G., *Diplomacy of Double Morality: Europe's Crossroads in Carpatho-Ukraine, 1919-1939*, New York, Carpathian Research Center, 1975.

Stuyt, Al. L., *Survey of International Arbitration, 1794-1938*, The Hague, M. Nijhoff, 1939.

Surányi, László, *La tragédie des peuples danubiens*, Budapest, Athenaeum, 1929.

Szinai, M. & L. Szűcs, *Bethlen István titkos iratai*, Budapest, Kossuth, 1972.

Szinai, M. & L. Szűcs, *Horthy Miklós titkos iratai*, Budapest, Kossuth, 1972.

Szulc, Tad, *Czechoslovakia Since World War II*, New York, Viking Press, 1971.

Szvizsényi, Zoltán, *Hogyan veszett el a Felvidék*, Budapest, Franklin, 1921.

Szvatkó, Pál, *A visszatért magyarok*, Budapest, Révai, 1938.

Tarján, Ödön, *The Ways of Czechoslovakia and Its Magyar Minority*, Budapest, Hornyánszky, 1935.

Tarján, Ö. & A. Falk, *Hungarians, Slovaks and Ruthenians in the Danube Valley*, Budapest, Hornyánszky, 1938.

Teichova, Alice, *An Economic Background to Munich: International Business and Czechoslovakia, 1918-1938*, New York, Cambridge Univ. Press, 1974.

Thomson, S. Harrison, *Czecho-Slovakia in European History*, Princeton, Princeton Univ. Press, 1953.

Thorne, Christopher, *The Approach of War, 1938-1939*, Toronto, Macmillan, 1968.

Tilkovsky, Lóránt, *A revízió és nemzetiségpolitika Magyarországon*, Budapest Akadémiai K., 1967.

Tilkovszky, Lóránt, *Teleki Pál, 1879-1941*, Budapest, Akadémiai K., 1974.

Truhart, Herbert, *Völkerbund und Minderheitenpetitionen*, Wien-Leipzig, Braumüller, 1931.

Turczel, Lajos, *Két kor mezsgyéjén*, Bratislava, Tatran, 1967.

Ullrich, Oskar, *Der grosse Irrweg der Tschechen*, Prag, Berlin, Volk und Reich Verlag, 1943.

Vallet, Francis, *The Peaceful Settlement of Disputes*, London, Dobbs Ferry, 1965.

de Valous, Guy, *Le sort des minorités en Tchécoslovaquie*, Paris, La Correspondance, Tome 28, 1922.

Vávra, F. & J. Eibel, *Viedenská arbitráž — Dôsledok Mnichova*, Bratislava, Osveta, 1963.

Villari, Luigi, *Italian Foreign Policy under Mussolini*, New York, The Devin Adair Co., 1956.

Vladár, Ervin, *Mi is az a Népszövetség?*, Budapest, Hellas, 1930.

Wagner, Francis S., *Hungarians in Czechoslovakia*, Reprint, New York, Res. Inst. for Minority Stud., 1959.

Wagner, Francis S., *A magyar kisebbség helyzete a szomszéd államokban*, Youngstown, Kat. Magy. Vasárnapja, 1975.

Wagner, Francis S., *Political Historiography and Its Bibliography in Post-War Central and Eastern Europe*, Separtaum, Studies for a New Central Europe, 1972.

Wallace, William V., *Czechoslovakia*, Boulder, Westview Press, 1976.

Weisskopf, Kurt, *Agonia della Cecoslovacchia*, Milano, Bramante Ed., 1968.

Werner, Arthur, *Eduard Beneš der Mensch und der Staatsman*, Prag, Verlag Morawitz, 1935.

Werth, Alexander, *France and Munich*, New York, Harper 1939.

Wetz, Wolfgang, *Selbstimmungsrecht der Völker und völkerrechtlicher Schutz nationaler Minderheiten von Versailles und St-Germain-en-Laye*, Freiburg-Breisgau, Bär-Bartosch, 1929.

Winchester, Betty J., *Hungarian Relations with Germany, 1936-1939*, Dissertation, Indiana Univ., 1970.

Winkler, Wilhelm, *Der Wert der tschechoslowakischen Nationalitätenstatistik*, Wien, aus dem Böhmerwald Jb., 1923.

Wheeler-Bennett, John W., *Munich: Prologue to Tragedy*, London, Macmillan, 1963.

Wiskemann, E., *Czechs and Germans*, London, Oxford Univ. Press, 1938.

Wolf, L., *La minorité polonaise en Tchécoslovaquie*, Varsovie, Comité d'Aide Culturelle aux Polonais en Tchécoslovaquie, 1936.

Wynne, Waller Jr., *The Population of Czechoslovakia*, Washington, D.C., U.S. Govt. Printing Office, 1953.

Young, E.P., *Czechoslovakia: Keystone of Peace and Democracy*, London, V. Gollancz, 1938.

Zinner, P.E. *The Diplomacy of Eduard Beneš*, Princeton, Princeton Univ. Press, 1953.

Zvara, Juraj, *A magyar dolgozók részvétele a szocialista Csehszlovákia épitésében*, Bratislava, Epocha, 1969.

Periodicals

Acta Historica (AH)
Acta Universitatis Carolinae Philosophica et Historica (AUCPH)
Annuaire Polonais des Affairs Internationales (APAI)
Bohemia (B)
Časopis Vojenského Historického Ústavu (CVHU)
Československý Časopis Historický (CCH)
Československý Přehled (CP)
La Correspondance (C)

The Central European Observer (CEO)
Current History (CH)
Danubian Review (DR)
Dějiny a Současnost (DS)
Der Donauraum (D)
East European Quarterly (EEQ)
Foreign Affairs (FA)
Foreign Relations (FR)
The Historian (H)
The Historical Journal (HJ)
Historický Časopis (HC)
Historie Vojenství (HV)
The Hungarian Quarterly (HQ)
International Affairs (IA)
Journal of Central European Affairs (JCEA)
Journal of Central European History (JCEH)
Journal of Modern History (JMH)
Katolikus Szemle (KSz)
Korunk (K)
Kulturbrief (KB)
Magyar Kisebbség (MK)
Magyar Szemle (MSz)
Merkur (M)
Monatshefte für Auswärtige Politik (MAP)
Národní Osvobození (NO)
Nouvelle Revue de Hongrie (NRH)
The Review of Politics (RP)
Revue Dějin Socializmu (RDS)
Slavic Review (SR)
Slavonic and East European Review (SEER)
Slovakia (S)
Slovak Studies, Historica (SSH)
Studies for a New Central Europe (SNCE)
Survey of International Affairs (SIA)
Századok (Sz)
Századunk (Szk)
Történelmi Szemle (TSz)
Vierteljahshefte für Zeitgeschichte (VHZ)
Wirtschaftliche Zeitschrift (WZ)
Zeitschrift für Osteuropäisches Recht (ZOR)

Essays in Periodical Literature

Ádám, Madga, *Madarsko a Malá Dohoda, 1937-38 v období před druhou světovou válkou*, ČČH, Vol. XI, 1963, 742-757.
— *Über die gemeinsamen Aktionen Hitlerdeutschlands und Ungarns zur Aufteilung der Tschechoslowakei*, WZ, Sonderband, 1964, 133-139.
Armstrong, Hamilton F., *Armistice at Munich*, FA, XVII, 1939, 197-290.
Bányai, László, *A német Mitteleuropa és a dunavölgyi összefogás*, K, 1938, No. 7-8, 676-683.
Batowski, Henryk, *Le voyage de Joseph Beck en Roumanie en octobre 1938*, APAI, 1959-60, 137.
Borsody, István, *A szudétanémetek belső politikája*, MSz, vol. 32, 1938, 909-319.
Břach, Radko, *Francouzský alianční systém a Československo na počátku roku 1924*, ČVHU, Ročník 1968, 3.
Bruckhardt, Carl, J., *Polen und die Tschechoslowakei zwischen den Kriegen*, M, 25-269.
Brügel, J.W., *Die Sudetendeutsche Frage auf der Potsdamer Konferenz*, VHZ, Jan. 1962, 56-61.
Celovsky, Boris, *The Transferred Sudeten Germans and Their Political Activity*, JCEA, XVII, 1957, 127-149.
Czuczor, László, *Csehek és magyarok*, K, No. 9, 1938, 723-739.
Fourré, Yann, *Les partis politiques en Tchécoslovaquie*, NRH, Mai 1938, 475-484.
Frey, Andrew, *Danubian Chronicle*, HQ, vol. IV, 1938, No. 1-4.

Garrai, Frigyes, A szudéta-német kérdés gazdasági vonatkozásaihoz, K, No. 10, 1938, 876-77.

Gasiorowski, Zygmunt J., *Polish-Czechoslovak Relations, 1918-1922*, SEER, vol. 36, 1956, 172-193.

Gooch, G.P., *European Diplomacy before the War in the Light of the Archives*, IA, vol. XVIII, Jan-Feb 1939, 77-102.

Gyulaffy, G., *Beneš és Titulescu az emigrációban*, MK, 1936, 592.

Halász, Miklós, *Csehszlovákia, 1918-1938*, SzK, 1138.

Helmreich, E.C., *West Europe: Sensitive Allies*, CH, October 1953, 213.

Hoensch, Jörg, K. *Účast Telekiho vlády na rozbití Československa*, ČČH, vol. XVIII, No. 3, 1969, 351-374.

Hyndrák, Václv, *Polsko a československá krize na podzim 1938*, HV, vol. 8, 1938, 91.

Jakabffy, E. *A szudétanémetek*, MK, 1936, 298.

Janišova, Milena, *Francouzská zahraniční politika a Československo v období příprav Mnichova*, ČČH, No. 5, 1963, 573-593.

Káňa, Otakar, *Těšinské intermezzo*, ČČH, XVIII, 1970, 397-410.

Kirschbaum, Josef M., *Facts and Events behind the Scenes of Slovakia's Declaration of Independence*, S, IX, 4, 1959, 1-7.

Kertész, S. *The Expulsion of the Germans from Hungary*, RP, vol. XV, 1953, 179-208.

Korbel, Pavel, *Národnostní menšiny v Československu*, ČP, vol. V, Feb. 1938, 20-27.

Kramer, Juraj, *Slovenské autonomistické hnutie*, ČČH, vol. IX, 1961, 346.

Křížek, Juraj, *Příspěvek k dějinám rozpadu Rakouska-Uherska a vzniku Československa*, RDS, V, 1958, 13-120.

Kvaček, Robert, *Československo — německá jednání v roce 1936*, HV, no. 5 1955, 721-754.

— *Zur Beziehung zwischen der Tschechoslowakei und den Westmächten vor dem Münchener Diktat*, AUCPH, 2-3, 209-233.

Lastovička, Bohuslav, *Vznik a význam košického vládního programu*, ČČH, vol. 8, 1960, 452.

Lockhart, R.H., *The Second Exile of Eduard Beneš*, SEER, vol XXVII, 1949, 39-59.

Low, Myron, J., *From Autonomous State to Protectorate: German Policy toward Slovakia*, H, vol. XXVI, 1964, 405-424.

Lvová, Mila, *K otázce tzv. objednaného ultimátu*, ČČH, no. 3, 1965, vol. XLII, 333-351.

Magyar, Zoltán, *James T. Shotwell at the Paris Peace Conference*, HQ, Vol. IV, no. 4, 1938, 764.

Marzari, Frank, *Projects for an Italian-Led Balkan Bloc of Neutrals*, HJ, vol. XIII, 1970, 767-788.

Megerle, Karl, *L'Allemagne et la fin de la Tchéco-Slovaquie*, Sepratum, MAP, Aug. 1939.

Mlynárik, Ján, *Slovenská národná rada a včelovanie Slovenska do Československého štátu, 1918-1919*, ČČH, vo. VI, 1963, 513.

Moravek, Andrew, *Hungarians in Czechoslovakia*, HQ, 1938, 709.

— *Magyar-szlovák-ruszin sorsközösség*, MSz, vol. 34, 1938, 220-229.

— *The Poles of Czechoslovakia*, DR, vol. 6, No. 2, 18-26.

Moseley, Philip, J., *The Occupation of Germany: New Light on How the Zones were Drawn*, FA, XXVIII, 1950, 58-604.

Odložilík, Otakar, *Eduard Beneš on Munich Days*, JCEA, vol. XVI, Jan 1957, 366-374.

Observator, *Struggle of Hungarians in Czechoslovakia*, DR, 5/2, 13-24.

— *Modern Czechoslovak Historiography*, SEER, vol. XXX, 1952, 366-92.

Olivová, Věra, *Československo — Sovětská smlouva z roku 1935*, ČČH, XIII, 477-499.

Ölvedi, János, *A magyar kisebbség Csehszlovákiában*, MSz, No. 3/31, 1938, 279-286.

— *Mit hoz a felvidéki magyarság?* MSz 3/35, 1938, 230-236.

Pichlík, Karel, *Die Entstehung der Tschechoslowakei*, VHZ, no 2, 1969, 160-180.

Puskás, A., *Adatok Horthy-Magyarország külpolitikájához*, Sz, vol. 95, 1961, 83-115.

Ripka, H., *Principles of Czechoslovak Policy, Past and Future*, CEO, vo. XIX, 1942.

Rouček, J. S.— J. Škvor, *Beneš and Munich: a reappraisal*, EEQ, vol. X, no 3, 374-385.

Schechtman, J.B., *European Population Transfer, 1939-1945*, RP, vol XV, 1953, 19-26.

Schmitt, Bernadotte E., *British Foreign Policy, 1919-1939*, JMH, 1949, vol. XXI, 320-326.

— *Munich*, JMH, XXV, 1953, 166-180.

Schoenfeld, F.A., *Soviet Imperialism in Hungary*, FA, XXVI, 1948, 558.

Schramm, Gottfied, *Češi a Němci v ČSR*, DS, 8, 1968, 15.

Schranil, N., *Der Versuch eines staatsrechtlichen Umbaus der Tschechoslowakei und ihr Ende*, ZOR, 5/1939, 542.

Sidor, Karol, *What led to the Proclamation of the Slovak Republic*, S, II, 3, 1952, 1-12.

Stanek, Imrich, *Vatikan, spojenec ľudáctva a tzv. Slovenského štátu*, ČČH, III, 1956, 82-110.

Sziklay, Ferenc, *Kisebbségi magyar sors*, MSz, 3, 1927, 282.

Skilling, Gordon H., *The Czechoslovak Struggle for National Liberation in World War I*, SEER, XXXIX, 1960, 174-197.

Szinai, M.L. Szűcs, *Príspevok k dejinám nemeckých a maďarských agresivných plánov proti ČSR v 1920-1939*, HČ, XIV, 1966, 595-607.

Szporluk, R., *Masaryk's Idea of Democracy*, SEER, XLI, 1962, 31-49.

Szvatkó, Pál, *A csehszlovák-szudétanémet kiegyezés kisérlete*, MSz, XXX, 1937, 71.

Táborský, Edward, *Beneš and Stalin — Moscow 1943 and 1945*, JCEA, XIII, 1953, 154-181.

— *The Triumph and Disaster of Edward Beneš*, FA, XXXVI, 1958, 669-684.

Temperley, Harold, *How the Hungarian Frontiers Were Drawn*, FA, VI, 1928, 432-447.

Tilkovszky, Loránt, *A német irredenta és Magyarország*, TSz, 3, 1970, 369-395.

Valenta, Jaroslav, *Polská politika a Slovensko v roce 1919*, HČ XIII, 1965, 403-422.

Vnuk, F., *Munich and the Soviet Union*, JCEA, XXI, 1961, 3, 285-304.

— *Slovakia's Six Eventful Months Oct. 1938 — March 1939*, SSH, II, 1964, 14-164.

Wagner, Francis S., *The Nationality Problem in Czechoslovakia after World War II*, SNCE 2, 1968/69, 73-82.

Wallace, William V. *The Making of the May Crisis*, SEER, XLI, 1963, 368-390.

— *The Foreign Policy of President Beneš in the Approach of Munich*, SEER, XXXIX, 1960, 133.

Weinberg Gerhard L., *Secret Hitler-Beneš Negotiations, 1936-37*, JCEA, XIX, 1960, 366-379.

Welisch, Sophie, S., *Czechoslovakia's Diplomatic Origins*, KB, III, 177.

Wierer, Rudolf, *Das Nationalitätenrecht in den Donauländern*, D. Jr. 2, 1957, 144.

Winters, Stanley, B., *The Young Czech Party, 1874-1914: An Appraisal*, SR, 1969, 426-444.

Wolfe (von) James H., *Roosevelt und die Sudetenfrage*, B, Band 9, 197-228.

Woytak, Richard, D., *Polish-Hungarian Relations and the Carpatho-Ukranian Question in October 1938*, EEQ, X, 3, 1976.

Zsigmond, L., *Ungarn und das Münchener Abkommen*, AH, 6, 1959, 261.

Newspapers — Press Agencies

Bohemia
Budapesti Hirlap
Corriere di Roma
Česká Výzva
České Slovo
Československá Tisková Kancelář — ČTK
Daily Mail
Daily Telegraph
Dziennik Polski
Express
Gazeta Polska
Journal de Genève
Lavoro Fascista
Lidové Noviny
Magyar Nemzet
Magyar Távirati Iroda — MTI
Národní Politika
Nemzeti Ujság
Neue Morgenpost
8 Órai Ujság
Pester Lloyd
Pesti Hirlap
Pesti Napló
Popolo d'Italia
Prágai Magyar Hirlap
Prager Montagsblatt
Prager Presse
Prager Tagblatt
Slovák
Slovenská Pravda

La Tribuna
Le Temps
The Times
Új Magyarság
Ujság
Venkov
Die Zeit
Die Zeit am Montag

INDEX

223

Bródy, András, 151, 160.

Brux, 115.

Bucharest, 14.

Budapest, 59, 75, 80, 82, 111.

Burgenland, 155.

Cantons, 117, 120.

Capital levy, 36,

Carlsbad, see Karlsbad.

Carpatho-German Party, 64.

Carpatho-Russian Union, 121.

Čas, 9.

Čatloš, Ferdinand, 181.

Censorship, 40, 46, 61, 78.

Census, 34, 139, 158.

Chamberlain, Neville, 93, 97, 116, 124, 128, 130, 161, 172.

Charles IV, of Hungary, 50.

Churches, 41.

Chvalkovský, František, 152.

Ciano, Galeazzo, 113, 137, 153, 160, 161, 163, 168.

Cleveland, 153.

Clemenceau, Georges, 17, 139.

Committee of Three, 46, 53.

Csáky, István, 81, 131, 153.

Csallóköz, 15.

Csizmazia, George, 118.

Czech, domination, I; rule, II; grip on the Slovaks, 7; penetration in Upper Hungary, 9; deserters, 11; national committees, 11; immigration to Slovakia, 60; political agents, 66; political blindness, 74; imperialistic nationalism, 77; opposition, 77; Agrarian Party, 78, 85, 89; historic land, 90; intransigence, 91; historic myth, 96; supremacy, 97, 110, 116, 117,

119; police, 121; oppression, 171; false security, 173; imperialism, 174; victims of Beneš, 175; Communists and Fascists, 178; and the war efforts of Hitler, 183.

Czecho-Polono-Hungaro-Rutheno-Rumano-Slovakia, 125.

Czechoslovak, National Committee, Paris, I; legend, 4, 12; statistics, 34; census, 34; Revolutionary National Assembly, 34, 38, 47, 48, 62; question, 59; government, 63; democracy, 87; problem, 93; - German border, 95; nation, 97; - language, non-existent, 98; government, 120, 124, 125, 128, 174, 175, 176, 178.

Czecho-Slovak, unity, 8, 13, 161, 164, 178.

Czechoslovak Republic (ČSR), first, I; co-belligerent, I; collapse of, 1; nationality problem, 3; formation of, 10; proclamation, 13; demands, 16; - Hungarian frontier, 18, 75, 85; statistics, 47; international obligations, 48; unstable situation, 55; - France, 55; - USSR, 56; isolated, 59, 64, 68, 69, 81, 82.

Czechoslovakia, successor state, 49; restored, 61, 62, 67, 114, 124, 125, 173, 178, 179.

Czecho-Slovakia (name used at the beginning of the republic and during Slovakia's short-lived autonomy), formation of, I, 138, 151, 163.

Daily Mail, 53, 166.

Danzig, 154.

Darányi, Kálmán, 55, 80, 152.

Rondva, brook as a "navigable river", 25.

Roosevelt, Franklin Delano, 102, 177.

Rothermere, Harold Viscount, 52, 53, 168.

Rumania, 75, 154, 172.

Runciman, Walter Viscount, 93, 97, 109, 110, 112, 114, 115, 116, 117, 118, 119, 120, 121, 123, 124, 172.

Russia, 77, 176.

Ruthenia, 16; in the ČSR, 26; population, 26, 69, 70, 75; autonomy from Hungary, 81; status of, 81, 99, 101, 121, 127, 151, 152, 159, 160, 168.

Ruthenian(s), 4; American Council of Hungarian Ruthenians, 12; gens fedelissima, 25; - Autonomous Agrarian Party, 86; autonomists, 97, 102; National Council, 102; - of the USA, 102; autonomy, 173.

Saint-Germain, treaty, 31, 62, 63, 101.

St. Stephen, crown of, 14.

St.Wenceslas, crown of, 59.

Sátoraljaújhely, 139, 142.

Schultz, Ignác, 118.

Self-determination, 15, 16, 48, 63, 66, 117, 129, 130, 131, 132, 133, 137, 140, 143, 154, 159, 160.

Serbo-Croatian, national unity, fictitious, 13.

Sidor, Karol, 86, 153.

Slavic, affinity, 5, 7.

Slovak, tribal ancestors, 2; republic, 4; literature, 6; - Lutherans, 6; peaceful relations with the Magyars, 6; cultural demands, 7; language, 8; students, 9; - League of America, 11; second official language, 11; declaration in 1918, 14; - Catholic Populist party, 18; separatists, 60; government, 60; - Council in exile, 60; National Council, 60; autonomy, 60; - Provisional Diet, 61; separatists, 61, 69; autonomists, 79, 80, 97, 98, 99, 133, 135, 137, 140, 143, 151, 152, 157, 158, 167, 171, 173, 178, 179, 181, 182, 183.

Slovak National Party, 119, 120.

Slovak Populist Party, 18, 59, 60, 61, 62, 70, 78, 82, 86, 89, 97, 119, 120, 133, 135, 136, 138, 153, 181.

Slovakia, 16, 17, 60, 82, 90, 97, 99, 100, 119, 120, 122, 127, 133, 136, 154, 166, 168, 184.

Slovakization, 67, 179.

Slovaks, reservoir of Bohemians, 4; victims of Czechs, 7, 59.

Slovenská Liga, 89, 118.

Slovenský Týždenník, 9.

Soviet, Russia, 52, 69; army, 69; - Union, 154, 172, 173, 176, 181, 184.

Stalin, Joseph, 178.

Sudeten German(s), 4; activists, 61, 62; grievances, 63; NSWP, 63; - Homeland Front, 64; United Front, 65; contacts with the Hungarian minority, 75; minority, 85, 94, 95, 96.

Sudeten German Party, 64, 67, 78, 80, 95, 96, 103, 110, 112, 121, 123.

Sudetenland, 67, 95.

Switzerland, Eastern, 27.

Syrový, Jan, 126, 131, 135.

Szüllő, Géza, 87, 91, 92, 94.
Szvatkó, Paul, 138.

Teschen (Těšín), 104, 127.
Third Europe, 81, 184.
Tiso, Joseph, Rev., 80, 82, 99, 119, 136, 143, 164, 166, 181, 182.
Transylvania, 168.
Trianon, treaty, I; revised, II; signed, 18, 24, 31, 42, 49, 51, 52, 53, 55, 63, 109, 114, 167, 182.
Tuka, Vojtech, 60.
Túrócszentmárton (T. Sv. Martin), 8, 12, 18, 59, 61.

Ukranian, 102.
Union of Polish parties, 104.
United Hungarian Party, 71, 80, 81, 86, 87, 88, 89, 90, 92, 112, 114, 115, 129, 130, 137, 138, 158, 160.
United States of America, 51, 60, 97, 102, 117, 119, 177, 182, 183.

Ungvár (Užhorod), 48, 102, 131, 138, 152, 153, 161, 163.
USSR, 93, 102, 176.

Vacuum Juris, 61.
Vatican, 160.
Versailles, system, 51; treaty of, 52, 53, 63, 126.
Vienna, 163, 165, 166, 168, 177.
Vološin, Augustin, 164.
Vyx, Lt. Colonel, 14, 16.

War loans, 36.
Warsaw, 14, 80, 82, 129, 132.
Washington, 12, 110, 177.
Wilsonian principles, 96.

Xenomania, 172.

Yugoslavia, 16, 75, 172.

Žatkovič, Gregorij, 12.

After World War I the allied entente governments in their political narrow-mindedness decided to liquidate the Austro-Hungarian Monarchy, a stabilizing force in Central Europe and, in the process, they dismembered the lands of the Holy Crown of Hungary. In the Treaty of Trianon they severely partitioned the millennial Hungarian Kingdom, destroyed the ideal geopolitical and cohesive economic unity of the Carpathian basin. With their action, they opened the road for foreign intrusions into the Central Danubian zone and its domination to the detriment of the population of the area.

THE HOLY CROWN OF HUNGARY
WITH THE COAT-OF-ARMS

Cover design by
Maquette de la couverture par *Claire Lalande-Couture*

Typographie: *Ateliers de Typographie Collette inc.,*

Achevé d'imprimer en juin 1981
à l'*Imprimerie HLN Inc.*
Sherbrooke, Québec

.

Wilson's publication of *Power, Racism, and Privilege: Race Relations in Theoretical and Sociohistorical Perspectives* (1973) is a transitional work which reflects his earlier interests in examining intergroup relations from an integrative power-conflict perspective. This is by far his most theoretical work (Noel 1975). However, this book did not generate much interest outside of sociology. Wilson shares that the sociohistorical and intergroup perspectives of race relations in the book, which were earlier developed at the University of Massachusetts, did not sufficiently appreciate class differences (W. J. Wilson, interview by author, June 16, 1997).

During these early years at the University of Chicago, the larger institutional environment, the graduate students, and firsthand observations of neighboring communities importantly influenced his scholarship. The professional norms of scholarship at Chicago encouraged "cutting-edge" theory and research methods; these challenged him intellectually to new levels. According to Wilson, at the University of Chicago, "the standard asked is, is it original and creative? The environment fostered an open mind." He noted further that faculty and graduate students challenged him to think about the broader forces affecting intergroup and intragroup relationships across class and race; they intellectually stimulated him to think more explicitly about larger macrosociological concerns. At the same time, observations of the neighboring communities within the south side Black metropolis led him to raise other questions. He added, "I would see differences on the south shore. The south side has Jesse Jackson's home and it has much of the poorest neighborhoods in Chicago" (W. J. Wilson, interview by author, June 16, 1997).

The Declining Significance of Race: Blacks and Changing American Institutions (1978) is characterized by a more complex analysis of the intersection of race and class that moves beyond the intergroup relations and racial conflict perspectives of *Power, Racism, and Privilege*. While this book maintains earlier sociohistorical interests, macrosociological interests in political economy become more explicit including analyses of changes in the modern industrial economy, government, and public policy. While largely examining the intersection of race and class, increased interests in the changing status of Blacks in cities are evident.

The writing, editing, and publication of the book that would become *The Declining Significance of Race* was characterized early by controversy. Through the invitation of Peter Rose, the general editor, Wilson was initially commissioned to write an undergraduate text on the African American experience for the Random House series entitled "Ethnic Relations in Comparative Perspective" (Rose 1993, 219). Although the manuscript submitted by Wilson was viewed by the general editor as laudatory and the most imaginative and controversial in the series, the managing editors assessed the manuscript critically and viewed it as more of a treatise. Because it had a definite thesis and had not followed the rough outline of the series, the managing editors at Random House recommended revisions that it conform more to the other books in the series. Rather than make the revisions, Wilson managed to get out of the Random House contract. The manuscript was then submitted to the University of Chicago Press where it was eventually published. Earlier drafts of this book were entitled *Black America* and *The Transformation of Race Relations* (Wilson 1979, 117). Wilson came up with the title "The Declining Significance of Race" assuming that the title would signal a new approach and "provoke people to read the book to see what I had in mind" (Wilson 1979, 118).

The public controversy preceding the sociological controversy appeared initially in the pages of *The Chicago Tribune* (Suro 1978). In an interview article entitled "Income, not race, to divide Chicago," Robert Suro, an editor, questioned Wilson: "What kind of place will metropolitan Chicago be in 1990?" In his answers, Wilson shared his argument that "Race will remain a very basic and important factor in some ways, but it is already of declining significance in the lives of individuals. Class differences, differences in education and income, are now the primary factors in determining how people will live" (Suro 1978, 1). Wilson noted that the growth of the Black middle class in Chicago and its movement into white-collar jobs and high-rise communities signaled the possibilities of integration (Suro 1978, 16). While he observed this upward mobility of the Black middle class as accompanied by "at least some shift in the racial balance of power," he also emphasized that with respect to the major institutions that run the city "there have been no basic changes in the distribution of power" (Suro 1978, 16).

Wilson predicted that with the shift from manufacturing to service-producing industries, the Black poor in central cities would be increasingly locked into unskilled and menial jobs, starvation, welfare dependency, and criminal hustling (Suro 1978, 16). The Black poor and working-class Whites would increasingly come into conflict over issues such as education, housing, and public space. Foreshadowing the future public-policy controversies on race and class, he underscored that economics, social class, and a history of accumulated disadvantages based on racial discrimination were the major barriers to the economic mobility of Blacks. And with respect to the tone of future public discourse he added: "I hope that Black leaders do not continue to focus on racism as a key problem because it obscures the more important economic issues" (Suro 1978, 16).

A *Chicago Tribune* editorial predicted "If justice is done, Prof. Wilson's book, "The Declining Significance of Race," (University of Chicago Press) will reach a wide audience and exert considerable influence" (*Chicago Tribune* 1978, 4). The editorial further noted: "His book is a confirmation of what many have realized rather than a novel statement. But the book can help reduce a damaging time lag, a tendency among Blacks and Whites alike, to act as if race were as significant in our society as it used to be" (*Chicago Tribune* 1978, 4). Although the *Chicago Tribune* editorial praised the book, Wilson felt that the commentary appeared to twist the tone of the arguments into a more conservative interpretation. This upset him.

The Declining Significance of Race generated the sociological controversy and visibility that were crucial for Wilson's emergence as a leading public intellectual and sociologist. This book received the Sydney Spivack Award from the American Sociological Association in 1978 for an important contribution in intergroup relations during the past five years. It is significant that this book received the Spivack Award in the same year of its publication (1978). However, its immediate honors and legitimation prior to scholarly reviews and debates were viewed as premature and problematic by some Black sociologists (A. Pinkney, interview by author, August 22, 1997). Following his receipt of the Spivack Award, the Association of Black Sociologists (ABS) issued a statement stating "it is the position of this organization that the sudden national attention given to Professor Wilson's book obscures the problem of the persistent oppression of Blacks" (Willie 1979, 177). The introductory portion of the "Statement of the Association of Black Sociologists" is provided:

> The Association of Black Sociologists is concerned that the book by Professor William Julius Wilson entitled *The Declining Significance of Race* was considered sufficiently factual to merit the Spivack Award from the American Sociological Association.
>
> The book clearly omits significant data regarding the continuing discrimination against Blacks at all class levels. It misrepresents facts presented in the volume, and draws inferences that are contrary to the conclusions that other Black and White scholars have reached with reference to the salience of race as a critical variable in American society.
>
> It is the consensus of this organization that this book denies the overwhelming evidence regarding the significance of race and the literature that speaks to the contrary. (Willie 1979, 177)

The questions, criticisms, and censure raised by the Black sociologists generated further controversy that increased his visibility in mainstream sociology and distanced him from many of these Black sociologists. In recent discussions, the perspectives of some of his harshest critics are categorically referred to by him as "racial chauvinism" and at other times as the "Black solidarity" school. Since the episode, Wilson has continued to retain friends, defenders, allies, critics, detractors, and enemies among Black sociologists.

The larger controversy accompanying *The Declining Significance of Race* symbolized the redefined political boundaries of liberals, neoliberals, neoconservatives, and conservatives. The sociological controversy brought to the surface other unresolved issues of changing race relations that emerged during the post-civil rights movement years of the 1970s. Interestingly, several of the toughest criticisms of the book did not appear in the mainstream media or mainstream sociological publications. One of the more thought-provoking and balanced appraisals was provided by the historian, Lerone Bennett Jr., who critiqued the "declining significance of race" school in its historical and sociological contexts (Bennett 1979). Bennett critiqued the class analysis as based on a vague and abstract use of the concept of class (Bennett 1979, 82). Bennett further noted that Wilson's historical interpretation followed conservative revisionist historiography and the sociological analysis failed to deal at length with systematic racial oppression (Bennett 1979, 81). Manning Marable pointed out that the most glaring weakness in historical interpretation centered on Wilson accepting the perspective of Blacks-as-objects-of-oppression rather than as active participants in their own history (Marable 1980, 211).

The controversy generated by *The Declining Significance of Race* also rapidly increased Wilson's recognition and reception outside of sociology in the larger public. Despite the continuing criticisms, Wilson loved intellectual debates and recognized that the attention given him through this sociological controversy was important to his professional mobility. To be criticized and misunderstood was better than being ignored. Through *The Chicago Tribune*'s early publicity for the book was found in an interview (Suro 1978), an editorial (*The Chicago Tribune* 1978), and a review by Andrew Greely (Greely 1978). In contributing to the public controversy concerning changing race relations, he took center stage alongside civil rights leaders and race commentators. In the controversy over this book, *The New York Times* featured a short interview with William Julius Wilson, and a response article by Kenneth B. Clark (1979). The exchange of Wilson and Clark in *The New York Times* and at a later conference on "The Declining Significance of Race" held at the University of Pennsylvania in 1980 not only exhibited Wilson's debating skills, but also symbolized Wilson's ascendancy as a successor to Kenneth Clark as a leading Black liberal voice in race relations.

Wilson's visibility was furthered in the media and during academic controversies. Hollie West would write a lengthy interview of Wilson in the *Washington Post* (West 1979). Bayard Rustin, the civil rights and labor leader, in severely critiquing Alphonso Pinkney's *The Myth of Black Progress* (1984) cited *The Declining Significance of Race* as an important contemporary analysis of class and race in substance and tone. Preceding and accompanying the "declining significance of race" controversy, was a larger neoconservative and neoliberal discourse of social class in the Black community that was largely propagated by White scholars.

The publication of *Power, Racism, and Privilege* (1973) and *The Declining Significance of Race* (1978) was accompanied by steady professional mobility, awards, and recognitions. Wilson gained promotion to professor in 1975, earned the endowed Lucy Flower Chair as professor of urban sociology, and served as chair of the University of Chicago, sociology department from 1978 through 1981. Soon after the Spivack Award, the Chicago Urban League awarded him the Beautiful People Award (1979), and the Chicago chapter of the A. Phillip Randolph Institute awarded him the A. Phillip Randolph Award (1981). The first of numerous honorary doctorates were received in 1981 from the University of Massachusetts-Amherst and Long Island University.

Compared to Amherst, Wilson appears to have worked more independently as a scholar in the sociology department during his early years in Chicago. There were no collaborative publications reflected in his first ten years at the University of Chicago. The new challenges of producing creative and original scholarship were more readily accomplished through book-length manuscripts that combined theory, research, and public policy than through collaborative or team research. The contentious quality of academic collegiality on campus was not as easily reflected in close social relations with colleagues off campus. Also, Wilson's increased integration into campus interdisciplinary programs and national public sociological controversies required greater independence. The sociological controversies, which thrust him as a public intellectual, were accompanied by increased periods of privacy and guardedness. His work style may be described as focused, tenacious, careful, and unrelenting.

In the transition from Amherst to Chicago, Wilson and his first wife, Mildred Hood Wilson divorced. In 1970, he married a former student and manuscript editor, Beverly Ann Huebner. His second marriage, an interracial one, has lasted more than thirty years. From this marriage he has a son, Carter and a daughter, Paula. The racially integrated Hyde Park community, where he lived, was an area in transition. It has been described as "a historic area where Black and White residents are accustomed to social contrasts" (Duneier 1992, 51).The upper-grade housing in Hyde Park is surrounded by low-income slums. It is a culturally diverse community with respect to educational, civic, and recreational activities. It is the sometime residence of Reverend Jesse Jackson, Muhammad Ali, Minister Louis Farrakhan, and the late Harold Washington.

Hyde Park is in some respects a fortress community. While it is in close proximity to the University of Chicago and the inner city social laboratory, it is well-policed, protected, and socially distant. Most of the residents, including many university students and staff avoid areas a few blocks from the campus (Duneier 1992, 51). Fear and social distance grew out of a history of strained relationships between the university and the nearby underclass neighborhoods. The middle-class community in Hyde Park provided a microsociological prism and island of interracial living amidst larger seas of hyperghettoization, racial segregation, and class antagonisms. Outside of occasional public lectures, Wilson's visibility and roots in Chicago's Black community were not deep.

REFOCUSING ATTENTION ON THE URBAN BLACK UNDERCLASS AND THE DISAPPEARANCE OF WORK

The controversy and criticisms generated by the *Declining Significance of Race* resulted in Wilson refocusing his attention on inner-city poverty and macroeconomic public policy. The first edition of the book did not address the policy implications and many reviews inaccurately associated him as a neoconservative (Wilson 1987, vii–viii). In *The Truly Disadvantaged*, he challenged both liberals, who were reluctant to discuss the urban underclass and conservatives, who were fixated on the culture of poverty. While appropriating the underclass discourse, integrating a research and public policy agenda, and going beyond both perspectives, the book importantly reframed the national debate by connecting the analysis of poverty with macroeconomic changes such as industrial decline and unemployment. The discussion of public policy critiqued the limitations in the visions of the civil rights movement and War on Poverty policies for addressing contemporary dislocations and urged universal rather than race-specific race policies to ameliorate these. The research findings in this book were preliminary. It is probably more significant that this book synthesized numerous studies, integrated competing macrosociological and microsociological perspectives, and introduced important sensitizing concepts that would become the basis of social science research. It is of more than passing interest that an earlier title proposed for the manuscript was *The Hidden Agenda*. This title called attention to the central strategy in his public policy approach.

The Truly Disadvantaged was reviewed and discussed widely. It is significant that the book was selected by the editors of the *New York Times Book Review* as one the ten best books of 1987, one of the winners of *Washington Monthly's* Annual Book Award (1988), and winner of the C. Wright Mills Award (1988) by the Society for the Study of Social Problems. In large part based on the book, Wilson was the winner of the prestigious McArthur Prize Fellowship. Subsequently, he was elected president of the Sociological Research Association (1987), the American Sociological Association (1989), and the Consortium of Social Science Associations (1993). *Time* magazine in 1996 named him as one of America's twenty-five most influential Americans.

Since this publication, Wilson has become increasingly visible in the national public policy debate on urban poverty. Based on the concepts of concentrated poverty and social isolation and several hypotheses that he introduced in the *Truly Disadvantaged*, the Social Science Research Council (SSRC) was influenced to create a new Committee for Research on the Urban Underclass. He has testified to the U.S. House of Representatives Select Committee on Children, Youth, and Families, participated in the Economic Conference of the President-Elect and Vice President-Elect, served as a member of Governor Mario Cuomo's Task Force on Poverty and Welfare, was an informal advisor to Mayor Harold Washington of Chicago, and participated in the "Twenty Years Since the Kerner Report" conference. Related honors include election as fellow to the American Academy of Arts and Sciences, the American Association for the Advancement of Science, the American Academy of Political and Social Science, and election as member to the National Academy of Sciences, the American Philosophical Society, the National Academy of Education, and the National Academy of Social Insurance. In 1998, Wilson was awarded the National Medal of Science "the highest scientific honor in the United States." He is only the second sociologist to have been awarded this honor.

At the University of Chicago, Wilson's responsibilities by 1990 were shared in the sociology department and the Irving Harris graduate school of public policy studies. His interests in researching inner-city poverty resulted in his founding and directing the Center for the Study of Urban Inequality. Through the Center, faculty and several graduate students became involved in a series of research projects that addressed the causes and consequences of high-neighborhood joblessness and concentrated poverty within Chicago. These studies include the Urban Poverty and Family Life Study (UPFLS), the Woodlawn and Oakland Neighborhood Study, and a study of the effects of high-risk neighborhoods on adolescent social development.

These studies of the Center have not only interviewed nearly twenty-five hundred poor inner-city residents and roughly one hundred ninety area employers, but also have made policy recommendations which are implemented in the Chicago metropolitan area.

Wilson's scholarly productions were greatest between the publication of *The Truly Disadvantaged* and *When Work Disappears*. Although Wilson continued to work independently, there are several collaborative publications. In academic governance, Wilson had a strong involvement in the University of Chicago policy committee, an interdisciplinary group that bridges departments outside of departments. His holistic and interdisciplinary interests were also partly accommodated in campus committees which focused on industrialization. To a greater degree than earlier, Wilson's audience extended beyond sociology and the academy to journalistic, governmental, nonprofit, and private sector audiences. Wilson consciously elaborates socio-logical concepts and hypotheses for these audiences. Though he continued to work independently, there are several collaborative publications accompany-ing the research on poverty and inequality. Among the scholars collaborating with Wilson were Kathryn Neckerman, Robert Aponte, Loic Wacquant, and Jolen Kirschenman.

Wilson's students remember him fondly as an exemplary scholar, teacher, and mentor. Not only is he remembered as being intellectually chal-lenging, rigorous, demanding, and thorough but also as approachable, sensi-tive, caring, and supportive. Intellectually, he had a contagious thirst for understanding and scholarship. Despite his national reputation, celebrity status, and aura, he attempted to reduce the hierarchy between himself as a faculty person and students. According to Robert Aponte: "When I first attended the University of Chicago, it didn't take long to see who I wanted to be like, who I wanted to emulate, and who I wanted to be mentored by." . . . "Wilson was someone who cared about the issues and someone who lis-tened to us." . . . "He was loyal to his students and took care of his students. He loved and respected and honored his students" (Aponte 1999). Mary Patillo-McCoy, who attended the University of Chicago with the specific intent of working with Wilson, noted: "he admonished his students not to simply research within the paradigm he has worked to establish, but to add to that body of knowledge, and indeed to challenge it" (Patillo-McCoy 1999, ix). His scholarly reputation was also reflected in his role as a dissertation chair and member on numerous doctoral dissertations. Margaret Andersen shares that "Bill's structural perspective and his insistence on strong empiri-cal evidence (without being overly abstract) has always been central to my thinking." Although not focused on gender, the social structural perspective that he brought to the study of race and class, was the framework Andersen first began to use in her scholarship on gender and society (M. Andersen, letter to author, August 31, 2000). During his years at Chicago, Wilson unquestionably had a greater impact on the graduate program and its stu-dents than any other faculty person.

In his seminars, Wilson encouraged students to study and engage the broader public debate on urban inequality and poverty. Students were expected to read and engage not only the academic controversies in sociology, but also the social policy perspectives of conservative authors such as Charles Murray and Lawrence Mead that might be often ignored. Leading journalists, who addressed poverty and welfare controversies, were also studied for their insights, framing of discourses, and public policy recommendations. In the research centers, lines of communication between students and community leaders were encouraged. On at least one occasion, a welfare mother from the community was brought into the seminar to share personal insights.

WILLIAM JULIUS WILSON AT HARVARD UNIVERSITY

In 1996, *When Work Disappears* is published. During the same year, Wilson relocated to Harvard University where he was appointed as a professor in the department of Afro-American Studies and the John F. Kennedy school of government. The transition to Harvard University coincided with Wilson's ascendancy as the leading national Black public intellectual. In the department of Afro-American Studies' W. E. B. Du Bois Institute, Wilson joined colleagues such as Henry Louis "Skip" Gates, Cornell West, Lani Guinier, and Orlando Patterson; they represented the most visible collection of nationally prominent Black intellectuals and what has been called by its Director, Skip Gates the "dream team." At the John F. Kennedy School, Wilson joined other scholars such as Christopher Jencks, George Borjas, Jane Mansbridge, and Katherine Newman. The combined interests of these scholars in issues such as labor markets, mobility, inequality, normative structures, and public policy closely converged with Wilson's interests. The move to Harvard University appeared to represent not only a continuation of his interests in urban inequality, but also it simultaneously was a refocusing of his scholarship on public-policy issues bearing on urban inequality in national and cross-national contexts. By focusing on cross-national problems of social and racial inequality in Europe, these will help inform the positions taken on domestic issues (Early 1996).

Wilson's theorizing on race, class, and urban inequality has been in continuous evolution. An understanding of Wilson's sociological theorizing and discussions importantly is connected with the sociological and public policy controversies and the changing institutional and professional situations that have helped influence his scholarly career. Nearly thirty years ago, the initial framing of his perspectives characterize his insights as a public intellectual in sociological controversies. In the context of the Black power movement of the early 1970s, Wilson reflects on the sociohistorical and theoretical contexts of contemporary race relations and political power. The societal or macrosociological analysis of race, class, and the postindustrial city, which will become a part of his sociological prism for analyzing the urban underclass, begins with his examination of industrialization, urbanization, and the changing class structure of Blacks. The possibilities and limitations of his analysis will not only influence his examination of the schism between the new Black middle class and Black underclass, but also pose continuing dilemmas for his policy prescriptions.

CHAPTER 2

INDUSTRIALIZATION, URBANIZATION, AND THE CHANGING CLASS STRUCTURE OF BLACKS

BACKGROUND

Industrialization is one of the salient macrosociological processes explaining the growth of cities and changes in the class structure. In classical sociology, theorists such as Karl Marx, Max Weber, and Émile Durkheim identified in industrialization a dynamic source of social transformation, resulting in complex changes in economic organization, the division of labor, class conflict, social dislocations, alienation, and the reorganization of society. Earlier in the twentieth century, Black scholars, examining the problem of the changing relationships among industrialization, urbanization, and the status of African Americans, frequently identified new structures of organization bearing on Black economic and social opportunity, social and cultural assimilation, and improved race relations while recognizing the structural downside of industrialization for Blacks with respect to disorganization, exclusion, marginalization, segregation, and poverty.

In response to the Great Depression of the 1930s, Black scholars at Howard University such as the economist Abram Harris, the political scientist Ralph Bunche, and the sociologist E. Franklin Frazier examined the historic development of racial stratification in the United States, offered theoretical explanations which gave importance to economic factors, and advanced social democratic solutions (Jackson 1990, 103). The increased significance of class in these analyses marked an important departure from W. E. B. Du Bois' race-based model. Outside the academy, A. Phillip Randolph, the Black socialist labor leader, saw in industrialization the possibilities of progressive industrial labor organizations and interracial coalitions bearing on the economic mobility of Blacks' and civil rights (Anderson 1973). Randolph's March on Washington Movement (1941) resulted in President Franklin Delano Roosevelt's issuing executive order 8802, which contributed

27

to the eroding of historic discrimination in employment against Blacks in industries receiving federal defense contracts and service employment in federal bureaucracies.

Several of these ideas on industrialization and the class structure became incorporated into the lengthy discussions of economics and inequality in Gunnar Myrdal's *An American Dilemma* (1944). Myrdal saw the World War II and post-World War II industrial expansion in northern and western cities, migration of Blacks to these urban centers, and federal fair employment policies as central to reducing the "vicious cycle" of discrimination and prejudice which limited the economic status of Blacks. Among the chapters focused on urban and industrial economics themes were: "Seeking Jobs Outside of Agriculture," "The Negro in Business, the Professions, Public Service and White Collar Occupations," "The Negro in the Public Economy," "Income, Consumption, and Housing," "The Mechanics of Economic Discrimination as a Practical Problem, "Pre-War Labor Market Controls and Their Consequences for the Negro," and "The War Boom—and Thereafter" (Myrdal 1944). It is instructive that in the framing and organization of *An American Dilemma* the focus on institutional questions of economics, politics, and justice are prominent and actually precede the discussion of social stratification.

Relatedly, the sociologist Oliver C. Cox anticipated in the industrial capitalism of the North, the increased worker solidarity, class consciousness, struggles, and the greatest prospects of social democratic movements among Black workers and White workers to erode institutional structures of race. Within the advanced industrial capitalism of the North, the problems of class were structurally the same between Blacks and Whites although more problematic in degree (Cox 1948, 583).

By the late 1960s and early 1970s, these theoretical interests in industrialization, urbanization, and the changing class structure of Blacks were continued by relatively few Black sociologists. The leading models used in sociologically examining race relations emphasized normative, functionalist, symbolic interaction, and power conflict perspectives that did not centrally incorporate the role of industrialization. In the power conflict perspectives, which accompanied the Black power movement, concepts such as internal colonialism and racial solidarity viewed racial groups as the key factor and downplayed the role of class (Carmichael and Hamilton 1967; Blauner 1972). With Frazier's death in 1962, Du Bois' decease in 1963, and Cox's passing away in 1974, a theoretical vacuum existed among leading sociologists in accounting for the changing postindustrial American institutions and Black urban communities.

One book, which critically grappled with the consequences of industrial decline and automation for Blacks in cities, was Sidney Wilhelm's *Who Needs the Negro?* (Wilhelm 1971). Wilhelm's conflict analysis of increased industrial and technological rationalization pointed in the direction of Blacks' heightened social dislocation, marginalization, and possible genocide. The nightmarish and pessimistic tone of these analyses went far beyond the discourses of assimilation, pluralism, and Black power. It also failed to anticipate the rational forms of integration that involved racial caste and resegregation. Although important in radical and critical sociology, Wilhelm was far outside the mainstream of sociology. In normative terms, advanced industrial capitalism could not solve these social dislocation problems based on his analysis. Despite its tone, Wilhelm importantly raised the question of the intersection between deindustrialization, social dislocation, and race relations.

The intellectual challenge facing a leading sociologist interested in interpreting the postindustrial city and Blacks would be one of recognizing the salience of industrial transformation and social dislocation as problems, integrating an analysis of changing institutional and group life, and resolving the separateness of assimilation, power-conflict, and racial solidarity perspectives in accounting for changing race relations. Wilson transforms the power-conflict and nightmarish themes of industrial dislocation and genocide, found in Wilhelm, into an analysis of industrial dislocation, the underclass, and economic integration.

At Chicago, Wilson importantly is influenced by the Chicago School traditions and particularly the scholarship of E. Franklin Frazier. Wilson incorporates several of Frazier's ideas into his research and analyses of industrialization, Black class changes, and inner-city poverty. At the same time, his earlier intergroup relations interests are increasingly refocused on the city. In refocusing intergroup relations on the city, he develops several theory sketches, implicit theories, and explicit theories based on functionalist assumptions. Finally, a stages model of industrialization and race relations fundamentally will integrate many more ideas. This will build in the logic of historical change.

E. FRANKLIN FRAZIER'S LEGACY

E. Franklin Frazier was a leading sociologist trained at the University of Chicago who taught at Atlanta University, Fisk University, and Howard University. Among his honors and recognitions, Frazier was the first Black sociologist to be elected as president of the American Sociological Association. Frazier brought to the Chicago School a sociological imagination that was informed by historical insights and political economy perspectives; he focused on race relations in national and cross-national contexts. As a public intellectual, he went beyond the conventional theoretical and research boundaries in sociology to address larger issues of social democracy.

Frazier's scholarship represents one of the most important early socio-logical attempts to address these complex relationships of industrialization and urbanization to changing Black institutional and organized life (Edwards 1974). In viewing the migration and urbanization of Blacks and their rela-tionships to the new industrial economic order early in the twentieth century, he saw these as potentially strengthening the patriarchal family structures destroyed during slavery. Frazier saw an accelerated occupational differenti-ation of Blacks in northern cities. In *The Negro Family in the United States*, he predicted that the growth of the Black middle class would depend on the increase of white-collar occupations in municipal and state governments and Black political power to compete for these" (Frazier 1966, 333). With respect to the Black working class or "Black proletariat," he recognized that "as the Negro worker becomes an industrial worker, he assumes responsibility for the support of his family and acquires a new authority in family relations" (Frazier 1966, 355). Elsewhere he noted: "As the Negro man has become an industrial worker and has no longer been dependent entirely upon domestic service and casual unskilled labor, he has become subject to a discipline that has affected his home life. The fact that he has received a higher and a more steady remuneration has enabled him to assume full responsibility for the support of his family" (Frazier 1968, 205).

Although Frazier clearly saw the unstable economic conditions of indus-trialization resulting in a larger segment of the urban Black community affected by folk, precarious, unconventional, and reactionary relationships of family life, he also viewed the increasing urbanization of the Black population, resulting in the emergence of a new middle class that was accompanied by the increased institutionalization of marriage and family (Frazier 1966, 207).

At the same time, the economic integration of the new middle class or "Black bourgeoisie" was characterized by increased cultural disorganization and conflicts. For Frazier, both this new Black middle class and Black intel-lectuals were alienated and marginal to both White and Black society. To the extent that Blacks escaped from the boundaries of their racially segregated status in the Black community, integration resulted in the Black middle class becoming more culturally isolated and exposed to the contempt and discrim-ination of White society (Frazier 1962). Furthermore, Black intellectuals were critiqued for embracing a largely integration and assimilation perspec-tive of Black socioeconomic and cultural conditions disconnected from a structural analysis of slavery (Frazier 1962). While Frazier viewed the urban-ization of Blacks during the 1930s, 1940s, and 1950s as directly correlated with the growth of a Black industrial proletariat and Black bourgeoisie, he recognized that the scale of this industrial urbanization had not significantly integrated large segments of the lower classes.

Frazier was the research director of *The Negro in Harlem: A Report of Social and Economic Conditions Responsible for the Outbreak of March 19, 1935* commissioned by Mayor Fiorello LaGuardia. In this, he connected an economic analysis of unemployment alongside institutionalized discrimination in employment, education, housing, and welfare to contextualize the riot as the result of "the smouldering resentments of the people of Harlem against racial discrimination and poverty in the midst of plenty." Frazier was particularly critical of discrimination in the privately controlled public utilities and recognized the importance of collective ownership in ameliorating these inequities (Platt 1991, 164).

CONVERGENCES OF WILLIAM JULIUS WILSON AND E. FRANKLIN FRAZIER

The concepts and hypotheses of industrialization and changing race relations derived from Frazier's research on the Black family and the changing institutions of Blacks in cities was a standard that would inform and inspire Daniel P. Moynihan's *The Negro Family: A Case for National Action* (1965) and be appropriated into public policy rationalizations. However, Moynihan's selective treatment of the historical and ecological structures of Black family adaptation take out of context important insights from Frazier. Wilson more significantly will bring Frazier's intellectual legacy, theoretical analysis, and "Frazier's ghost" back into contemporary sociological discourses.

While Wilson's work at the University of Chicago is generally focused on a macrosociological theory of race relations in postindustrial cities, it is specifically focused on the relationships between changing American social institutions and African Americans. Although there are several theoretical sources influencing his concerns, the theoretical and research convergences with E. Franklin Frazier are particularly instructive. Yet it is not clear whether these convergences are intentional or serendipitous. In *When Work Disappears*, Wilson briefly acknowledges Frazier's linking of the industrial economy, employment opportunities, and the assimilation of Black family structure (Wilson 1996, 17–18). Closer observation reveals that the theoretical arguments from Frazier's *The Negro Family in the United States* actually constitute a major part of the underclass analysis in Wilson's *The Truly Disadvantaged*. Related theoretical arguments in Frazier's *Black Bourgeoisie: The Rise of a New Middle Class in the United States* (1957), and other essays focused on race and culture issues inform his scholarship.

First, both scholars are concerned with the effects of industrialization on the stability of the Black family. In Frazier's analysis, the effects of industrialization in enhancing the role of the father as an industrial worker, structurally integrate the Black family. At the same time, the roles of ecological factors in the spatial, moral, and social bases of inner-city neighborhoods are treated in a larger context of Frazier's *The Negro Family in Chicago* and *The Negro Family in the United States*. By contrast, Wilson analyzes how deindustrialization and the loss of work undermined the stability of the poor Black family and the authority of Black men as fathers. In each of Wilson's major works, the importance of the economy and industrialization directly contribute to the growth of the urban Black community and related social problems. In his treatments of the inner-city underclass, lower-class family, and inner-city dislocations, Wilson has incorporated important insights and hypotheses from Frazier and extended these contemporaneously.

Second, both scholars view economic changes as contributing to class conflicts, alienation, and social distance which are partly reflected in the new Black middle classes. Frazier saw in industrialization, the changing division of labor, and urbanization, the basis for a "new Black middle class" at mid-century which was organizationally, politically, and culturally distant from the "genteel" Black middle class of earlier generations (Frazier 1957). Frazier's "new Black middle class" was also intellectually alienated from Black folk traditions and largely characterized by conspicuous consumption. Wilson sees within modern and corporate industrialism, the growth of federal government, and civil rights policies favorable to equality, a Black middle class that is increasingly economically bifurcated, socially alienated, and physically distanced from the Black underclass (Wilson 1978; Wilson 1986).

Third, both scholars in their examinations of industrialization, urbanization, and class changes are actually assessing the salience of competing sociological theories of assimilation, social class, and racial caste to account for the changing status of African Americans. Both will emphasize the traditions of Chicago School sociology and go beyond these to incorporate insights from other disciplines. Although both embrace liberalism and integration, there are critiques of assimilation alongside tendencies of cautious optimism. While Frazier draws from the ecological and race relations perspectives of Park and Burgess in examining the assimilation of African Americans, his socialist sensitivities led him to emphasize the primary role of economic integration rather than acculturation. For Frazier, the Black factory workers that cooperated with White workers had a consciousness that involved class and race. While Wilson draws from diverse assimilation and power-conflict perspectives within sociology for his holistic analysis of contemporary African-American assimilation, his macroeconomic analysis draws in part from controversies in public policy. The limitations of liberalism will result in Frazier incorporating aspects of social democracy, Black nationalism, and Wilson's integrating tenets of social democracy, neoliberalism, and neoconservatism.

Fourth, both scholars focus attention on the leadership dilemmas and service challenges facing the Black middle class. Earlier Frazier viewed the Black professional and business classes as having vested interests in racial segregation. These vested interests in maintaining the institutions and organizations of a segregated Black society were viewed as contradictory to larger economic changes that integrated the Black proletariat. He also viewed the new Black middle classes and Black intellectuals as alienated and marginal to both White and Black society. Wilson's discussion of the different opportunity prospects facing the Black middle class with respect to affirmative action and other discussions of the Black middle class in its social and residential mobility as abandoning the Black underclass underscored unresolved problems. To the extent that Black sociologists adhered to the limited models of the "Black solidarity" school and emphasized race rather than class, he viewed them as not addressing the important issues of inner-city poverty.

However, there are important differences in these analyses that grow from the different theoretical interests, research training, the objective historic conditions, and biographies in which their scholarship has been produced. While Frazier's sociology grows from history and social work administration, Wilson's sociology advances from theoretical and sociohistorical interests, which are influenced by his training in the philosophy of the social sciences.

Frazier's scholarship is that of a city person who is challenged to account for the changes in race relations growing out of the Great Migration, Harlem Renaissance, Great Depression, and the early post-World War II years. From his study of history and sociology, Frazier theorizes about African Americans' institutional and organized life. Although Frazier's dissertation is focused on Chicago, most of his research transcends this focus. His scholarship was largely written at Black universities in the South prior to the height of the civil rights movement. Social policy concerns enter but are not a major focus of Frazier's scholarship. Frazier's interests in linking larger historic, societal, and middle-level class characteristics and consciousness within the Black community with micro order role, interpsychic, small group behaviors, and sociocultural forces run through most of his scholarship.

Wilson's scholarship is one that becomes more urban and cosmopolitan over his professional career. His earlier ideals, sensitivities, and expectations of the individual and society come into greatest conflict within the complexities of postindustrial Chicago. His observations of class differences within the Black community will challenge earlier insights and conceptualizations. Drawing from the philosophy of social science and formal theory, he synthesizes these observations with empirical research, social history, and public policy concerns; he socially constructs these into big generalizations, characterizing African Americans in the post-civil rights years. Sociological theory and research are not easily distinguishable in this exercise. In explaining the changing prospects of Blacks in postindustrial cities, Wilson also initiates a discourse on what should be the public-policy concerns informing macro-economic policy, welfare, and civil rights in postindustrial America. Wilson's interests in linking macrosociological, intergroup, and microsociological concerns within the Black community are focused largely on structural forces and to a lesser degree, cultural factors. The important question for Wilson is as much a normative as empirical one of how to best link macrosociological changes in the economy, technology, and public policy with class changes and multiracial coalitions that bear on the inner-city underclass and race. Wilson's scholarship is written exclusively at northern universities.

Finally, it is significant that both Frazier and Wilson are characterized by changes in their public presentations of self that are reflected in symbolic changes of their professional names during career transitions. Following the condemnation of his article in the *Atlanta Constitution*, "The Pathology of Race Prejudice," which satirically analogized the behavior of race prejudice and insanity, the Frazier family was threatened with lynching and left Atlanta for Chicago. The earlier Edward Franklin Frazier became E. Franklin Frazier as a defensive and protective strategy. During his early years at Chicago and through the publication of *Power, Racism, and Privilege*, William Wilson did not use his middle name as an author. It is coinciding with the publication of *The Declining Significance of Race* and his entry into sociological controversy that his persona becomes William Julius Wilson.

RACE RELATIONS IN THE CITY—A NEW FOCUS OF INTEREST

Most important, for Wilson's interests in race relations in the city, is his adoption of a macrosociological perspective that accompany his years at the University of Chicago. During his years at the University of Massachusetts-Amherst, his theoretical explications were microsociological and more significantly influenced by intergroup relations, symbolic interaction, and functionalist-conflict assumptions. Although political-economy concerns entered his earlier analyses of race, these were not central and usually implicit. In fact, questions of industrialization, the state, and urbanization were absent.

Wilson's first systematic treatments of race and the city are produced in *Power, Racism, and Privilege* (1973); a book that represents a career transition between earlier race relations interests at University of Massachusetts-Amherst and later interests at the University of Chicago. In framing his arguments, he states: "I specifically wish to avoid a Marxian type of interpretation, namely, that discrimination results from a conscious, rational attempt on the part of elites to subordinate the minority to their own interests. The processes involved are certainly more complex than this, and usually much more subtle" (Wilson 1973, 9). This book is primarily concerned with developing a societal model of race relations that incorporates a dialectical relationship between integration and conflict processes and specifically avoids a Marxian interpretation (Wilson 1973, 6–11). Central to his theory is an examination of the dynamic relationships among power resource mobilization, systems of stratification, and racism. More specifically, he is interested in outlining and validating a model of how fundamental societal changes function to bring about shifts in systems of race relations from paternalistic to restrictive competitive or fluid competitive forms (Wilson 1973, 60–61).

Among the societal changes identified by Wilson as relevant to this problem are factors such as "beginning or growing industrialization, urbanization, internal migration and immigration, political changes resulting in internal or external pressures on the government, revolutions, and civil wars" (Wilson 1973, 61). As a consequence of these changes, Wilson notes that "racial groups may accumulate or lose resources and long-term effects in the balance of power between the racial groups may be produced." (Wilson 1973, 61). While arguing that the "more rapid the social change, the greater is the possibility that the social structure will loosen, thus making new resources available for either the dominant or minority group to use in order to extend or alter the balance of power in their favor, he also emphasizes that "absolute gains of minority groups may be further neutralized by the dominant group's ability to introduce new mechanisms of social control to preserve power advantage" (Wilson 1973, 61). Primary among the social forces identified is the role of industrialization in destroying established or traditional racial orders.

According to Wilson, there are intrinsic tendencies of industrialization that represent "structural requirements" and include factors such as: (1) emphasis on rational perspectives, (2) necessity of physical mobility, (3) primacy of contractual relations, (4) the requirement of an impersonal market, (5) the allotment of resources on the grounds of productive receipts, (6) the internal pressures that constantly activate the foregoing requirements (Wilson 1973, 62). In this discussion, he carefully summarizes and qualifies the conventional, functional perspective of industrialization and race relations by incorporating Herbert Blumer's critique and rebuttal (Blumer 1965). While viewing industrialization as a necessary factor in this shift from paternalistic to competitive race relations, Wilson qualifies this generalization by emphasizing that "we should expect to find little change in the racial order if the shift is not accompanied by political and social processes of sufficient magnitude to alter the racial alignment" (Wilson 1973, 64). Although recognizing political and social control processes, he does not go as far as Blumer in emphasizing the different responses of traditional orders to industrialization and in articulating the role of external managerial and governmental policies in changing race relations.

For Blumer, the societal reception of industrialization as a social change process in traditional societies takes place during the beginning of industrialization along nine "points of contact" and includes the structure of positions and occupations, the apparatus for filling positions, the new ecological arrangements, a regimen of industrial work, a new structure of social relations, new interests and new interest groups, monetary and contractual relations, goods produced by the manufacturing process, and patterns of income of industrial personnel (Blumer 1990, 58–75). Blumer emphasizes further that traditional orders may respond to industrialization in five ways: rejection, support, incorporation without resistance or disruption, separate development of industrialization growing alongside the traditional order, disruption (Strauss 1991, 171–172). Elsewhere, Blumer demystifies the functionalist assumptions of industrialization's axiomatic "disorganizational" consequences for traditional social orders and racial and ethnic hierarchies by arguing "that there is no fixed or locked relationship between the industrializing process and specific social happenings" (Strauss 1991, 174). Where industrialization is a factor in racial and ethnic competition and conflict, Blumer argues that the only place this is likely to occur is at points of contact between different subordinate racial groups (Blumer 1965, 236). For Blumer, in racially ordered societies, industrial imperatives do not naturally and impersonally move ahead to dissolve the racial factor but rather accommodate themselves to these societies (Blumer 1965, 238–239).

While Wilson shares most of Blumer's general propositions, there are important differences and changes in emphasis. First, Wilson treats industrialization as a progressive, rational force that is relatively independent of the racial order. Conversely, Blumer advances that "the apparatus and operations introduced by industrialization almost invariably adjust and conform to the pattern of race relations in a given society" (Blumer 1965, 240–241). Second, Wilson generalizes the role of industrialization as a factor subject more to quantitative variation and does not articulate the qualitative dimensions of variability except for his stages typology. Blumer identifies industrialization's quantitative variation as well as possible qualitative sources of variation such as type of ownership, managerial policies, kinds of occupations, levels of skill, concentration or dispersal of plants, diversity of products, and relation to markets (Blumer 1965, 239). Third, the "structural requirements" of Wilson's industrialization function to undermine traditional, paternalistic racial orders, promote conflict and conflict resolution, and decrease the significance of race. This more impersonal dimension of industrialization that appears in places of Wilson's analyses may be complemented or challenged, says Blumer, by nonindustrial factors of race, social class, religion, and familial background (Blumer 1965, 238). Social expectations, demands, and definitions of existing racial situations as influenced by "managerial policy" are salient. Fourth, Wilson's sociological theorizing of industrialization and urbanization advances selected hypotheses and deductively reasons from these the social consequences. The presentation of the empirical evidence is generally more illustrative, descriptive, and summarized. Blumer argues that the proper role of sociological theorizing should begin more inductively with empirical observations that might inform theories of the "middle range."

Contained in this work are background assumptions, conceptualizations, hypotheses, and implications of the role of industrialization and urbanization in social change that will reappear in later analyses of the *Declining Significance of Race* and *The Truly Disadvantaged*. Most of these will remain relatively intact. Others will be adjusted and reformulated. There is an implicit political-economy model of structural change that integrates the relationship between historic institutional and race relations changes that becomes increasingly explicated in later work.

Early on, industrialization appears as a progressive force and at different times acts as either a direct or indirect factor in restructuring changes in race relations. Later, the contextualization of macroeconomic changes in industrial decline and the formulation of macroeconomic policy to address these will be paramount. At the microsociological level, there are mobilization and intergroup power considerations of social change that will over time decline in significance. While these will be increasingly replaced by more conservative assumptions of social control, he will later address the concerns of mobilization through liberal and multiracial coalitions.

Accordingly, Wilson views urbanization as one of the direct causes of social transformation growing out of industrialization that promotes increasing power and competitive resources for minorities. As an opportunity structure offering increasing possibilities for integration into the society, the growth of cities is central to understanding the changing status of minorities.

> Although industrialization may not directly contribute to a realignment of the established racial order, it can contribute indirectly. We need only recognize that with the growth of industrialization comes the growth of urbanization. As expanding industry lures minority members to urban areas, they find themselves in a much better position to accumulate power resources. There are greater educational and occupational opportunities available in cities. The usual political, social, and economic imperatives of urban living provide greater opportunities to develop viable minority institutions such as schools, churches, political and labor organizations, and professional and business associations. The physical proximity of large numbers of minority individuals facilitates communication, ideological development, group identity, and collective action. Furthermore, in urban areas the minority

members are not as vulnerable to dominant attacks such as pogroms or
lynchings as they are in rural areas. For all these reasons, minority groups
concentrated in urban areas are in a far better position to mount an offensive against racial oppression and move into more fluid competitive relations
with dominant members. (Wilson 1973, 64)

Contained in this commentary is a macrosociological interpretation of
urbanization which is consistent with some of the classic sociological perspectives of the Chicago School, functionalism, and modernization. Also contained in this commentary is a macrosociological interpretation that
recognizes the role of intragroup mobilization, organizing, and institutions
that is consistent with a power conflict model. This interpretation is holistic
and largely builds into it adaptive, integrative, and functional assumptions of
urbanization. While the primary working model of urbanization in *Power,
Racism, and Privilege* is an intervening or mediating variable through which
industrialization facilitates the rapid growth of cities and the migration of
groups with implications for social mobility, there appear to be other places
in later work where urbanization is treated as an independent variable in its
own right, a dependent variable impacted by larger social structural forces,
and as a contextual variable.

Within this holistic theory, the dynamic of historical change appears
moved more by a cumulative evolution based on stages and ideal types than
a dialectic. This is particularly interesting considering some attempts by
Wilson to incorporate a dialectic at the level of intergroup relations. It is possible that these stages, when viewed cumulatively, represent a spiral of historical change. In later work, the earlier mobilization considerations of
intergroup change will be increasingly replaced by more conservative
assumptions of social control.

In his early work, the question of industrialization grows out of the
need for making a micro-macro linkage from race relations to the institutional order. In his later work, the question of industrialization in advanced
economies increases in significance as Wilson's sociological prism shifts to
accounting for the macro-micro linkages between changing political-
economy, industrialization, urbanization, and race relations. Rational factors
of economics and politics are primary. The noneconomic factors of culture,
race, and religion while descriptively and analytically treated in *Power,
Racism, and Privilege* and *The Declining Significance of Race* decrease in significance in *The Truly Disadvantaged*. Cultural and racial factors strategically
reappear in *When Work Disappears*.

In these earlier works, how he grapples with the role of the state in
social change and urban development is problematic for several observers.
This treatment of interconnections will identify macrosociological externalities of urbanization, race relations, and the quality of political relationships

during the modern period. Accompanying industrialization during modern race relations is the growth of the state, the expansion of corporate and government sectoral employment, and the growth of the Black middle class. Under the impetus of the increasing size of an Black urban population in the North, the mobilization of the civil rights movement, and its voting power, the federal government implemented policies designed to promote racial equality. The more variable record of local, state, and municipal governments, which are more autonomous to federal civil rights legislation, and which are increasing in significance during the "New Federalism," are not seriously incorporated into this assessment. Nor are the complexities of civil rights legislation in terms of human agency examined thoroughly. In this absence and vacuum, there is a deterministic, trickle-down scenario of the state in urban America that has neither accounted for nor resolved how government programs coming out of this period could be sometimes progressive and other times regressive in implementation. This conservative reading of history during the civil rights period and assessment of politics will have implications for his views on social policy and his role as a sociologist in this undertaking.

The substantive topics of relevance to Blacks in the city treated in Wilson's work resurrect a number of questions that have been of continuing concern in classical urban sociology and the new urban sociology. What are the changing relationships between dynamic social structural factors such as corporate capitalism, industrialization, and the bureaucratic state for the growth and decline of urban areas? How is the social structure of the larger society reflected and reproduced in the internal structure of the city in space? What is the salience of class, race, and place in the adaptation, assimilation, and structural integration of ethnic and racial groups? To what extent does selective migration and the human capital of groups explain the changing and persistent status of groups? How and why does the process of urbanism and demographic features of city size, density, and diversity have organizational and disorganizational social consequences for group life? The pioneering studies in this tradition began much earlier with W. E. B. Du Bois (Green and Driver 1978; Du Bois 1899). These questions have been addressed by scholars such as Robert Park, Ernest Burgess, Louis Wirth, Charles S. Johnson, E. Franklin Frazier, St. Clair Drake, Horace Cayton, Robert Weaver, Daniel Patrick Moynihan, Otis Dudly Duncan, Karl and Alma Taeuber, Reynolds Farley, Stanley Lieberson, Herbert Gutman, and Douglas Massey and Nancy Denton.

Wilson's directions in developing a more "societal" model of race relations raise and begin to address a number of questions that have been of continuing interest in sociological controversies of social change, political sociology, social movements, stratification, and race relations. These center

on the following: How and where do changes in the economy and government provide possibilities for affecting majority and minority group power
relationships and larger systems of racial and ethnic stratification? What are
the macrosociological and microsociological factors that explain the adaptation and assimilation of racial and ethnic groups into the metropolis and
larger society? How is the mobilization of minority group and social class
power resources reflected in different forms of social conflict and the change
of racism? What are the different outcomes of assimilation for Blacks in
racial and ethnic contacts and relationships? These questions have been central to the assimilation, pluralist, and power conflict models in the sociology
of race and ethnic relations. These are variations of age-old questions clas-
sically raised by Alexis de Tocqueville in *Democracy in America* (1969) and
Gunnar Myrdal in *An American Dilemma: The Negro Problem in Modern
Democracy* (1944).

Wilson's role as a scholar has primarily been a theoretical one of reviewing, analyzing, synthesizing, and reformulating the competing models of
racial and ethnic stratification. In both functional and symbolic terms, he has
become a leading interpreter of the African-American experience. Wilson's
concerns with the urban world of African Americans are partly shaped by theoretical interests. Complementing this are the observations, impressions,
research agenda, professional objectives, and personal experiences that have
interactively shaped Wilson's sociological imagination.

STAGES OF INDUSTRIALIZATION AND RACE RELATIONS

The presence of manufacturing in the Chicago of the 1970s had declined in
significance from the industrialization that Frazier described during the
1930s through the early post-World War II years. By the time Wilson arrived
in Chicago, the growing industrialization, which had inspired the classic theories of the city, had already experienced decentralization, suburbanization,
deindustrialization, and global shifts. It is through the sociological prism of
deindustrialization and urbanization in Chicago during the 1970s that
Wilson will refocus his earlier intergroup race relations interests and integrate a class analysis.

The salience of industrialization in his perspectives can be partly viewed
in his analysis of race relations history into three stages: preindustrial, industrial, and modern industrial (Wilson 1978). These stages roughly approximate antebellum slavery and the early post-Civil War era, the late nineteenth
century through the New Deal era, and the post-World War II period. In
each of these stages, macrosociological changes in the economy and state are
accompanied by changing patterns of race relations including the norms and
ideologies of racial domination that accompany racial stratification (Wilson

1978, 9–12). It is instructive that in 1973, Wilson used labels based on Pierre Van den Berghe's paternalistic, restrictive competition, and fluid competition concepts (Van den Berghe 1967) that described essentially the same eras. For Wilson, industrialization involves the transition from paternalistic to competitive race relations and the "progressive transition from race inequalities to class inequalities." Urbanization here is an intervening and contextual variable in the changing class structure.

Wilson's central argument in *The Declining Significance of Race* is "that different systems of production and/or different arrangements of the polity have imposed different constraints on the way in which racial groups have interacted in the United States, constraints that have structured the relations between racial groups and that have produced dissimilar contexts not only for the manifestation of racial antagonisms, but also for racial group access to rewards and privileges" (Wilson 1978, 3). In this thesis, Wilson has integrated an earlier typology of power relations in paternalistic and competitive systems derived from Pierre Van den Berghe's theory (Van den Berghe 1967) alongside a political-economy analysis (Wilson 1978, 54–55).

The economic history of the United States is focused on the changing "system of production" involving technology and "social relations of production" that include employment and property relations which have constrained race relations (Wilson 1978, 12–16). At the same time, historic changes in state policies and laws in response to changing political organizations and power resources have constrained and influenced race relations (Wilson 1978, 17–19). These relationships between the "system of production," "social relations of production," and state policies and laws are not deterministic as captured in traditional Marxian perspectives. To capture this dynamism, he integrates into his argument a Weberian assumption of the increased autonomy of the economy and state in the post-World War II years. Through the prism of industrialization, Wilson views the history of African Americans as the transition from paternalistic to competitive race relations and the "progressive transition from race inequalities to class inequalities." Urbanization becomes an important intervening and contextual variable in the changing class structure for Blacks in the industrial and modern industrial periods.

According to Wilson, the system of production in the preindustrial stage was a plantation economy in which slaveholders "relied on external markets for the reproduction of their labor force," and "the reproduction of slave labor was based almost exclusively on slave labor" (Wilson 1978, 27–28). The ideology of southern paternalism in race relations not only "justified slave labor as a legitimate exchange for the master's protection and direction, but also by the doctrine of reciprocal obligation simplicity acknowledged the slaves' humanity (Wilson 1978, 33). While racial separation was more a private concern than public policy in agricultural areas, in the urban south during slavery a more competitive pattern of race relations emerged, resulting in racial segregation.

With the rise of the White working class in the antebellum North and South, racial antagonisms resulted where Black competition in labor was eliminated through the growth of split labor markets, racial caste systems, and Black ghettos (Wilson 1978, chap. 3). Accompanying the period of Jim Crow legislation, Blacks were disfranchised, support for public education was reduced, and Whites systematically excluded Blacks from skilled occupations previously held during slavery (Wilson 1978, 58–59). In the South, the earlier political alliance between conservative White economic elites and Blacks was replaced by a coalition of White business elites, White labor, and White agrarian interests. In the North, the smaller Black population was more easily segregated and isolated.

The economies of cities from the turn of the century through mid-century are characterized by industrial expansion, Black migration, labor entry, and racial conflict. During this stage of industrial expansion, competitive race relations replace the paternalistic race relations of the preindustrial era. In the North, Black labor entry was based partly on management's use of Black workers as strikebreakers and as leverage against the demands of White workers for higher wages. Black alliances with industrial leaders in class conflicts between management and White workers resulted in a split labor market. Blacks entered northern industrial cities in low-paying, unskilled, and semiskilled work and more frequently in service work. In the South, a united White movement of White industrial, commercial, and agricultural leaders and the White working class resulted in the exclusion of Blacks from industry and employment in low-paying service and agricultural work (Wilson 1978, Chap. 4).

Wilson argues that across regions, Blacks did not develop the power resources that enabled them to compete politically. Blacks in the North were excluded from meaningful participation in White ethnic city political systems to the extent that Blacks did not compete for patronage jobs and government contracts (Wilson 1978, 85). In the South, disfranchisement, poll taxes, literacy tests, property requirements, all-White primaries, and intimidation are identified as politically excluding Blacks (Wilson 1978, 58–59). The class structure during the industrial stage is one where the Black masses are concentrated at the bottom of the occupational structure and a small business and professional class or "Black elite" serving the segregated Black community formed the apex.

Although a growing number of Blacks through the 1920s entered services, industry, business, and the professions, the prospects for advancement were limited and reversed during the Great Depression of the 1930s.

Through the Great Depression, Black entry into the expanding industrial order primarily was described by a split labor market, where Blacks were employed in northern industrial centers in low paying, unskilled, and semi-skilled work. The industrial growth, social class formations, and public policy changes accompanying the New Deal and World War II will be correlated with increasingly competitive (or modern) race relations.

Wilson synthesizes the orthodox Marxian theories to explain the first stage, the split labor market to explain the second stage, and a neo-Weberian analysis of the increased autonomy between the economy and state in contemporary race relations to account for the third stage. This synthesis is not only a theoretical exposition, but also appears to represent the evolution of earlier and more recent influences in his work. The materialist theories of economic structure in the first two stages appear replaced by an action theory in which modern capitalism is a rational system. Culture makes a difference in the structuring and development of society. The third stage will be made up of corporate liberal interventions that contribute to competitive race relations. In later scholarship, Wilson will further explicate the normative bases of these structural relationships in terms of public policy.

Underlying this analysis of the changing social relationships in the Black community is the "liberal expectancy" hypothesis. However, the growth of the Black middle class and Black urban underclass is not only an important focal point of this liberal interpretation but an anomaly that is not easily explained. In asking why did the position of poor urban Blacks deteriorate at the same time middle-class Blacks were experiencing unprecedented progress, Wilson responds that the emphasis on contemporary discrimination is a problematic explanation. Although historic discrimination was important, the new explanation for Black changes in the class structure will center primarily on different life chances due to changes in modern industrialization and corporate liberalism. This must go beyond race to incorporate social class and universal social rights. Modern industrial race relations represent progress only on the surface.

In outlining and validating the theoretical model of societal changes and the shifts in systems of race relations moving from paternalistic to competitive forms, it is significant that industrialization axiomatically involves the transition from paternalistic to competitive race relations and the "progressive transition from race inequalities to class inequalities." This axiom is the "iron law" that Wilson does not waver from.

Interestingly, the modern industrial stage takes on a number of characteristics of modernization perspectives with respect to race relations. Modernization perspectives see the development of postindustrial societies moving increasingly in the direction of rational and secular institutions in which the irrationalities of racism, discrimination, and privilege decline. In an increasingly deracialized society, social class, status, and civic solidarities are predicted to replace the salience of racial identities and solidarities.

This modern industrial transition will be characterized by both socio-economic opportunity and social dislocation. It is interesting that this macrosociological industrialization-opportunity argument is found a half century earlier in the analyses of E. Franklin Frazier, Gunnar Myrdal, and Oliver Cox. The changing patterns of race and social class, which reintroduce Frazier's controversy of the new Black middle class and the antithesis to the Black proletariat, grow out of this industrialization argument and are examined in the next chapter. These will go beyond macrosociological discussions and introduce the salience of neoconservative and neoliberal public policy perspectives.

CHAPTER 3

CHANGING PATTERNS
OF RACE AND CLASS

The Emergence of the New Black Middle Class
and the Urban Black Underclass

BACKGROUND

William Julius Wilson generated the greatest public discussion and controversy in his analyses of the changing class and race configurations of the Black
community in *The Declining Significance of Race* and *The Truly Disadvantaged*.
These focus on the emergence and growth of a new Black middle class and
the urban Black underclass. The explicated theories, implicit theories, and
theory sketches that inform these discussions appear to derive from several
theoretical and non-theoretical sources.

Since arriving at the University of Chicago, Wilson's theory moved
from an intergroup relations perspective based on the salience of race and
power resource mobilization to a new social stratification perspective which
emphasized the intersection of structural changes such as macroeconomic
growth and industrialization, social class, and race in the life chances of
Blacks. Relatedly, these societal perspectives of urban sociology and race
relations importantly drew from the traditions of the Chicago School and
traveled beyond these to incorporate insights from other sociological perspectives and social science disciplines. Ecological perspectives importantly
influenced his interpretations of urbanization and inner-city poverty.

Simultaneously, Wilson's discussions of changing race relations are
partly informed by neoconservative cultural discourses and public policy controversies that lie outside the boundaries of sociology but have frequently
entered its boundaries. In 1966, Irving Kristol argued in a *New York Times*
article "The Negro Today is Like the Immigrant of Yesterday." In his assessment, the experience of Blacks is not fundamentally different from White
immigrant groups, and Blacks can and will move up similar to the earlier
White immigrants (Kristol 1966, 50–51, 124–142).

During the 1970s, social scientists argued through journalistic and public policy arenas the liberal expectancy of Black progress and a new conventional wisdom. In, *The Unheavenly City: The Nature and Future of Our Urban Crisis* (1970), Edward Banfield would underscore that the force of prejudice and discrimination had lessened and the "movement of the Negro up the class scale appears as inexorable as that of all other groups" (Banfield 1970, 83). Banfield noted further that the number of middle-class and upper-class Blacks in many metropolitan areas was already sufficiently large to allow the formation of predominantly Black middle-class and upper-class neighborhoods in both cities and suburbs (Banfield 1970, 84). In response to civil rights policies and economic gains made by Blacks, Daniel Patrick Moynihan issued a new federal policy memorandum of "benign neglect." By 1973, Ben Wattenberg and Richard Scammon's "Black Progress and Liberal Rhetoric" through loose categorization defined most Blacks in the middle class (Wattenberg and Scammon 1973). Nathan Glazer, in his book, *Affirmative Discrimination: Ethnic Inequality and Public Policy*, argued that because no one was now excluded from broadest access, continuing Black problems were not to be explained by discrimination (Glazer 1975). Reflecting on these trends, Richard Freeman in, *The New Black Elite: The New Market for Highly Educated Black Americans*, noted: "Blacks moved up the occupational hierarchy rapidly, with highly educated Blacks breaking into previously 'closed' managerial and professional occupations" (Freeman 1976, 2). The unprecedented gains of contemporary college-educated Blacks is a theme.

It is instructive that conservative and neoconservative critiques of the civil rights movement, the War on Poverty, and related public policies to increase equality of opportunity will increasingly surface. Although liberals play a part in the expansion of equality of opportunity to several previously unprotected groups, there is also a liberal retreat from racial justice that is coded in policies of "benign neglect" and color blindness. Both neoconservatives and neoliberals converge in viewing the growth of the Black middle-class as particularly problematic. Although Wilson's Black middle class treatment will build on Frazier's treatment, these neoconservative and neoliberal analyses of civil rights and economic policies will more directly inform his interpretations, be appropriated by him, and critiqued.

This chapter addresses Wilson's handling of this controversy by reviewing his discussions of the contemporary Black social class changes, the theoretical and empirical critical appraisals of him, and his responses to these critiques. Out of several of these critiques, he will formulate new syntheses and refocus his models. Other important critiques will not be recognized or addressed.

MODERN INDUSTRIAL RACE RELATIONS: THE EMERGENCE OF THE NEW BLACK MIDDLE CLASS

Wilson views the Great Depression, World War II, and the post-World War II economic changes as related to the reorganization of the earlier Black class structure, its occupational differentiation, and the emergence of a new Black middle class. As a consequence of Franklin Delano Roosevelt's New Deal policies, legislation favorable to collective bargaining, fair employment practices, and the increased influence of the new industrial unions, the prospects of Blacks entering working and middle-class employment improved dramatically (Wilson 1978, 126–128). Building on Frazier's insights of the growth of a new Black middle class (Frazier 1957), he identifies the growth of Blacks in white collar, craftsmen, foremen, and working-class employment. During the 1950s and 1960s, the expansion of corporate industrial and government sector occupations resulted in particularly dramatic Black middle class growth (Wilson 1978, 129–130).

The post-World War II growth of the Black middle class is related to Blacks increasing power resources as reflected in the mobilization of civil rights organizations, enlarged voting, and gaining Black political control in central cities. Initially accompanying these class changes is the revival of the integrationist ideology focused on issues such as integrated education, open housing, and public accommodations (Wilson 1978, 134–135). Gains of Black political power in the cities resulted in "racial struggles of power and privilege" where conflicts with working-class Whites are sometimes expressed in ethnic terms (Wilson 1978, 116–117). Rather than providing economic and social mobility for Blacks, Wilson sees the significance of Black political control in central cities as heightening the racial antagonism and alienation with Whites over issues such as school busing and residential segregation (Wilson 1978, 120). Despite racial antagonisms, the prospects for the Black middle class appear on balance to be optimistic.

In 1974, it is instructive that Wilson's assessment of social-class developments among Blacks was more cautious and contingent. While he recognized the presence of educational, occupational, and income improvements taking place in Black communities, he emphasized the possible deterioration that these might have for upper-, middle-, and lower-income Blacks during cycles of economic decline (Wilson 1974, 150–151). At this time he also predicted the variable forms that White reactions to Black economic changes might take.

Four years later, he sees more deterioration in the Black lower class and underclass. He notes that with the growth of corporate industries characterized by advanced technology and productivity, the Black lower class is experiencing decreasing opportunities for higher wage employment and increasing unemployment (Wilson 1978, 96–99). In his identification of central city industrial decline, joblessness, and the urban Black underclass, Wilson correctly locates the reasons for the surplus Black labor force in the growth of the corporate sector, industrial technology, and management policies with respect to hiring.

The status of the Black middle class, however, receives a strikingly different assessment. As a consequence of corporate and government expansion and the influence of state intervention in programs such as affirmative action, talented and educated Blacks are viewed as experiencing unprecedented job opportunities comparable to Whites, for economic class is increasingly becoming more important than race in predetermining job placement and occupational mobility (Wilson 1978, 99–104). Wilson's discussion of the "declining significance of race," which is really intended to call attention to "the increasing significance of class," is partly an invitation to play up the economic class differences among Blacks.

In these efforts, he draws from the economist Andrew Brimmer's analysis of distributional changes in shares of aggregate family income and emphasizes that the inequality of incomes between the highest two-fifths and lowest two-fifths of families was greater among Blacks than Whites between 1969 and 1977. Based on these sociological facts, he concludes there is a "deepening economic schism" in the Black community (Wilson 1979, 13–14; Wilson 1978). This discussion also has an important convergence with an earlier essay by Daniel P. Moynihan entitled, "The Schism in Black America" (Moynihan 1972). Moynihan had argued that the effects of federal antipoverty programs, civil rights legislation, and related interventions benefited the younger more educated Blacks who increasingly reached economic parity with Whites. The poorest segments of the Black community including the unskilled, uneducated, and young persons in female-headed households were observed as worse (Moynihan 1972).

Wilson also argues that modern or corporate industrialization is a primary macrosociological variable affecting the economic schism between the Black middle class and Black underclass. He underscores the uneven distribution of economic resources in the social organization of urban Black communities is accompanied by differential political resources and social mobility. Yet, while the Black middle class through the 1970s was expanding and increasingly gaining entry into government, he also cautions that Black gains in urban politics are occurring at a time when the city as a base of political power is on the decline (Wilson 1978, 141–143).

Wilson's analysis of the post-World War II developments in government, influencing the upward status of the Black middle class makes two major points. First, the increased social mobility and economic resources of this new middle class are viewed as outcomes of increasingly liberal corporate employment practices and federal government policies of affirmative action that have favorably and differentially benefited educated and talented young Blacks. This integration would involve an increasing significance of what Milton Gordon has identified as corporate assimilation rather than liberal assimilation (Gordon 1981). Second, a substantial contribution of this new Black middle class formation and growth is dependent on federal bureaucratic employment and state and local government. The ascendancy of Blacks in federal and municipal activities occurs during the reorganization of national politics from a strong federalism with economic interventionism to a new federalism with economic deregulation and the reorganization of local government from strong city government systems to metropolitan-based power.

Wilson is especially on target when identifying the precarious and problematic nature of power resources in the urban Black middle class. However, the liberal expectancy hypothesis which advances that the Black middle class was generally experiencing greater integration than segregation in the economy is subject to controversy and different interpretations. As we shall see later, he does not fully develop the implications of this strong dependence of the Black middle class on the post-World War II growth of the state. There is a body of social science research that indicates greater segmentation and dual labor market outcomes among the Black middle class that he understates.

In this larger context of corporate industrialization, state growth, urbanization, and changing class structure, what sociological facts and evidence are used to substantiate the "declining significance of race" hypothesis? Wilson summarizes individual and aggregate educational and occupational trends through the early 1970s that show a convergence between Black and White patterns. Important are increased recruitment visits by corporate representatives to Black colleges and universities and the presence of affirmative action policies that accompany the improved status attainment. Crucial for his argument is another finding showing the highest relative incomes among young Blacks that are college educated. At the beginning of the 1970s, actual Black incomes for college-educated Blacks were less than White incomes for high school graduates and relative income for this group were roughly three-fifths the earnings for White college graduates.

Contributing more evidence to his argument of recent economic advances are findings cited from David L. Featherman and Robert M. Hauser's analyses of the 1973 "Occupational Change in A Generation Survey," which indicated similar effects of family background on educational attainment and occupational achievement for Blacks and Whites (Featherman and Hauser 1976; Featherman and Hauser 1978). Only a decade earlier, Peter Blau and Otis Dudley Duncan's research indicated that the discrimination effects in the labor market were so persistent that the socioeconomic characteristics of Black middle-class families factored significantly less than among White middle-class families (Blau and Duncan 1967).

There was also room for optimism if one selectively read the results from national public opinion surveys through the mid-1970s which indeed showed increasing favorability of White attitudes to general principles of equality of opportunity (Schuman, Steeh, and Bobo, 1986). Small reversals in the segregation scores among high-income Blacks and Whites through the decade, which were traditionally higher than segregation scores between low-income Blacks and Whites, though not mentioned by Wilson, are consistent with his argument.

WILLIAM JULIUS WILSON DEBATES CHARLES WILLIE AND KENNETH CLARK

The sociological controversy surrounding the changing significance of class and race initially appeared in the January-February 1978 and July-August 1978 issues of *Society: Transaction* magazine. The public controversy surfaced in the February 28, 1978 Op Ed page of the *New York Times* with an opinion by William Julius Wilson. An interview, which emphasized the primacy of social class in the future of Chicago, appeared two weeks later in *The Chicago Tribune* (Suro 1978). The journalistic reviews and editorials in the media were mostly laudatory. The reviews in sociological journals were mixed at best and critical at worse (Brewer 1978; Jorgenson 1978; Edwards 1979; Pettigrew 1979; Marrett 1980; Record 1980). Subsequent articles and opinions in the *New York Times, Washington Post,* and other mainstream journals would amplify, reappraise, and refocus the sociological controversy.

From the beginning of the controversy, there was considerable attention and contentious debate focused on the title of the book which had multiple and contradictory meanings. Wilson steered attention on his historic and structural analysis that was actually more concerned with the "increasing significance of class" than the "declining significance of race." Wilson argued that the socioeconomic and political changes have led to a deepening economic schism in the Black community during the last quarter of the twentieth century with the Black poor falling further and further behind middle- and upper- income Blacks (Wilson 1978, 152). He observed that while talented and educated Blacks were experiencing unprecedented job opportunities comparable with Whites with equivalent qualifications that are related to the expansion of white-collar positions in the corporate and government sectors, poorly trained and educationally limited Blacks in the inner city were increasingly restricted to the low-wage sector, with increasing unemployment and welfare (Wilson 1978, 151). Although Blacks were historically denied access through racial exploitation discrimination, and segregation, and these were reinforced by ideologies of racism, Wilson does not view these practices as providing a meaningful explanation of the current life chances of African Americans (Wilson 1978, 1). For him, the more meaningful explanation is one deriving from fundamental economic and political changes that have made "economic class position more important than race" and the growing intersection of economic class position and race. Wilson emphasizes that the current barriers to social mobility and integration are more impersonal and class-based rather than racial in origin.

Charles Willie views Wilson's analysis as isolating the "economic sphere from other institutions and social arrangements of society" (West 1979, 71). He also discerns Wilson's analysis as representing the perspective of the "dominant people of power" which emphasizes that stratification and mobility are largely a function of individual efforts and merit (Willie 1979, 145). In asserting that "the Black experience has moved historically from economic racial oppression experienced by virtually all Blacks to economic subordination for the Black underclass" Wilson has canceled out racial discrimination as a key cause of poverty (Willie 1979, 154). Willie argues that "racial discrimination is one of the major factors contributing to the economic deprivation among Blacks" (Willie 1989, 55), and "race has not declined but continues as a significant variable differentiating Blacks from Whites at all income levels" (Willie 1989, 86). Focusing on the aggregate and quality of life differences between Blacks and Whites, Willie sees significant evidence of institutional discrimination and oppression based on race. As a counter-hypothesis, Willie advances that race is especially increasing in significance for middle-class Blacks who are experiencing direct and extended contact with Whites as a consequence of desegregation and affirmative action (Willie 1979, 157). Willie's theoretical critique is focused on continuing institutional practices, macro-micro linkages, and implicit value premises. His counter-hypothesis is primarily group-based and microsociological.

Kenneth Clark considers the "declining significance of race" thesis as premature, seductive, and enticing. Clark views the historical and contemporary realities of American racism as "for the most part "democratic" in that all Blacks were perceived and treated alike." (Clark 1980, 100). While recognizing some signs of racial progress, he sees Wilson's analyses as leaving unanswered several issues of racial justice and equality. Through this discourse and analysis, Clark notes that "racial and color distinctions can now be masked by the assertion that class and cultural differences form the basis of continued, though more subtle discrimination" (Clark 1980, 100).

The "contemporary sophisticated racism" is characterized by more complex class-based and cultural-based "racism" rationalizations by White intellectuals, the increased presence of covert and repressed racial prejudices and discrimination, and the increased significance of tokenism as a measure of integration with respect to middle-class Blacks (Clark 1979). Clark's critique is focused on the sociological discourse underlying the "declining significance of race" thesis and the changing meaning of racism. For Clark, the similarities of racism experienced by African Americans are greater than the differences of social class. However, Clark does not address the particular macrosociological questions raised by Wilson.

Wilson responds to his critics who he views as emphasizing the narrow interpretation of "the declining significance of race." He notes: "Nowhere in my book do I argue that race is irrelevant or insignificant. It is not simply an either-or situation, rather it is a matter of degree" (Wilson 1978, 35–36). Interestingly, he does not disagree with Willie and Clark concerning the continuing presence of race and racial discrimination. The reasons offered by him for racial discrimination, however, are different. In response to Willie, Wilson counterargues "one of the legacies of racial oppression in previous years is the disproportionate Black representation in the underclass" (Wilson 1979, 170). Patterns of racial discrimination in the past, the accumulation of disadvantages passed on across generations, and macrosociological changes in the modern industrial economy and technology figure more prominently than contemporary racism. In response to Clark, he agrees that Black kids are kept segregated in inferior schools and "race not class creates this situation to persist" (Wilson 1980, 113). He emphasizes "the race factor remains extremely salient in social, community, and political issues" (Wilson 1980, 113).

Wilson does not disagree with Willie's counter-hypothesis of the increased significance of race among middle-class Blacks. According to Wilson, Willie's microsociological hypothesis does not refocus or invalidate his macrosociological argument because he views the negative consequences of racial discrimination interacting with economic changes adversely affecting lower-class Blacks more than middle-class Blacks. Despite some agreements, from his perspective Wilson sees the class and group differences in the Black community as generally obscured by both Willie and Clark.

In a *New York Times* magazine article entitled, "A Matter of Class," Carl Gershman advanced a more elaborate political argument of the growth of the underclass that later becomes incorporated into the analyses of Wilson's *The Truly Disadvantaged* (Gershman 1980). Gershman, who was a former research director at the A. Phillip Randolph Institute and then vice-chairman of the Social Democrats of America, argued that the Black political leadership that had emerged in the post-civil rights years was off course. This Black leadership was increasingly preoccupied with race matters such as Black power, reparations, and self-determination while the problems of underclass Blacks in the ghetto became worse. According to Gershman, the paradox of the schism between Black middle class improvement and Black underclass falling behind was politically explained by a racial accommodation politics in Black militant form. By denying that the conditions of lower-class Blacks were getting worse and emphasizing racism and racial victimization, the post-civil rights Black leadership had moved further from the analyses and policies in Kenneth Clark's *Dark Ghetto: Dilemmas of Social Power* (1965), Daniel P. Moynihan's *The Negro Family* (1965), and Bayard Rustin's "From Protest to Politics" (Gershman 1980, 92).

The conservative response to *The Declining Significance of Race* was largely receptive. Wilson's analyses of the civil rights movement and affirmative action policy converged and resonated with neoconservative and conservative intellectuals. The critique of Black power leadership and "Black solidarity" sociologists, which increasingly becomes a part of his public discourse, converges with those of an emerging cadre of Black conservative intellectuals during the 1980s. Following Ronald Reagan's election in 1980, Wilson received an invitation to personally meet with the president at the White House who was enthusiastic to meet with Black conservatives. However, Wilson turned down the invitation. Wilson mentions a *Chicago Tribune* editorial praising *The Declining Significance of Race* that in twisting his arguments into a conservative thesis upset and depressed him (Wilson 1979, 118). Conservative journalists and pundits selectively played on texts and bytes from the book that focused on the growth of the Black middle class and underclass and attempted to portray Wilson and his analysis as conservative. The appraisals of his scholarship by neoconservative and conservative intellectuals and their critiques of his critics will at times provide offensive and counteroffensive tactics.

The critiques of the critics will constitute an important part of the sociological controversy. These provide rhetorical, logical, coded, and rhythmic elements that become a part of the discourse that are subsequently appropriated by Wilson in responding to other criticisms. Wilson's responses to these and other criticisms are mostly rational with respect to addressing the issues of causal argument and evidence. Among the criticisms viewed as constructive and friendly, he uses these in revisions and elaborations of the arguments and discussions of the policy implications. Among the criticisms viewed as more challenging, unfriendly, and destructive, these are generally not acknowledged or can be evaded.

As a counteroffensive, Wilson and his defenders have advanced at least three principal lines of intellectual attack. First, because Wilson's scholarship is generally viewed as theoretically and empirically sophisticated, it is expected that acceptable criticisms should be based on empirical research of comparable scope and quality. For example, criticisms of his empirical research findings, that are focused on the controversies of the Black middle

class and underclass, which do not seriously grapple with the macrosociological contexts of changing economics and politics may not be considered persuasive. Second, based on the quality of questions and criticisms raised by
several of these critics it is possible for Wilson and his defenders to argue that
these critics are really not scholarly and in effect ideological and political.
Interestingly, criticisms based on neoliberal and neoconservative public
policy perspectives that are a part of the mainstream sociological controversy
and discourse are frequently immune from this characterization. The fact
that most of the toughest criticisms did not appear in leading mainstream
journals, but rather in specialized sociology journals, leaves this impression of
non-scholarly to many. His use of the category, the "Black solidarity" school
to characterize several scholars implicitly serves this function. Third, Wilson
has regularly viewed critics as misunderstanding, misrepresenting, and not
reading his arguments. To the extent these critics have misunderstood and
misrepresented his arguments and analyses, they are required to come around
to understanding Wilson's perspectives and arguments. This appeal to
authority is an exercise in discourse hegemony.

In a review of the book which critically analyzed its craftsmanship, Carl
C. Jorgenson notes: "By the title that the book was given, and by introducing
and summarizing the analysis in dramatic and somewhat overembellished
terms, Wilson achieves a policy impact far beyond the reach of the data and
sets the stage for his own 'misinterpretation.'" Jorgenson adds: "Wilson's
broad statements have such strong implications for public policy that his
more qualified analyses are frequently ignored" (Jorgenson 1978, 63).

The significance of the "declining significance" controversy derives in
no small part from the complex and multilayered meanings of race in contemporary American society that become constructed, clarified, reconstructed
and muddied in this ongoing "call-and-response." Wilson's supporters and his
critics sometimes selectively read his book in different ways.

THEORY AND RESEARCH ON THE NEW BLACK MIDDLE CLASS

There are three general perspectives that have competitively attempted to
account for the changing status of African Americans during the post-civil
rights movement years that inform *The Declining Significance of Race: Blacks
and Changing American Institutions* (1978). The first perspective emphasizes
the significant and unprecedented progress characterizing African Americans
in general and particularly the Black middle class. This interpretation, which
was most strongly associated with neoconservative and neoliberal intellectuals, focused selectively on recent improvements in social characteristics such
as education, income, and occupation and the returns to education associated
with college-educated persons. This more progress-based and optimistic

interpretation was less concerned with other social dimensions such as wealth, property, and housing. The second perspective underscored the deterioration and continuing racial inequalities, disadvantages, and exclusions experienced by African Americans in general as explained by the persistence of racism. This "continuing significance of race" perspective was most strongly associated with Black sociologists and liberal left thinkers. This more pessimistic interpretation usually focused on aggregate-level group changes without disaggregating these by social class and individual variations. When disaggregated by social class, the effects of race remain salient. The third interpretation viewed a growing polarization or schism within the Black community between the Black middle class and the Black underclass. This more cautious-optimistic assessment argues that a new Black middle class experienced unprecedented success and integration while the Black underclass experienced increased social dislocation and fell behind. This more centrist argument is a synthesis that emphasized the historic effects of race and the contemporary effects of social class.

Although the thesis and substance of *The Declining Significance of Race*, draws largely from the polarization/schism interpretation, the other interpretations are not absent. The symbolic capital of the title draws from the progress and optimism interpretation as well as several interpretations of the changing Black middle class. As we shall se, there are some interpretations and implications that converge with the increasing/continuing significance of race perspective. These, however, are discounted.

Wilson's "declining significance of race" thesis contains numerous assumptions, concepts, and hypotheses of the changing intersection of the economy, state, social class, and race in modern society. The interest in changing race relations is examined partly through racial ideologies—the norms, beliefs, and rationalizations of racial domination bearing on racial inequality. The thrust of his arguments is fundamentally macrosociological and historical. Microsociological analyses of social class and race are secondary.

THEORETICAL DISCUSSIONS OF THE NEW BLACK MIDDLE CLASS

Alongside the general arguments and research evidence bearing on the Black middle class are several underlying theoretical controversies. The theoretical controversies in the book have centered on the discussions of the following points. First, there are some that view Wilson's conceptualization of social class and class formation among the middle class as problematic. Although this begins with economic characteristics such as income and occupation, the linkages between these and a situation of Black class "crystallization" are ambivalent and premature. Second, despite the neo-Marxian convergence of his macrosociological analyses, Wilson actually incorporates a Weberian conception of "life chances" to call attention to the structural economic factors of shared "market situation" experienced by members of social classes. While the social characteristics of these are not fully specified, he focuses on human and social capital concerns of educational attainment and job attainment. Third, Wilson integrates a Weberian assumption of the autonomy of the economy and politics in hypothesizing that in the modern industrial (or post-civil rights era), the traditional racial struggles for power and privilege have shifted from the economic to the sociopolitical sector (Wilson 1978, 152). The decline of these racial antagonisms in the economy, as reflected in the growing job prospects of middle-class Blacks, are viewed as continuing rather than reversing (Wilson 1978, 153). Fourth, there is a historicist argument that specifies different cohort and period effects for those Blacks who entered the labor market during the late 1960s and 1970s. The life chances of the new Black middle class should be distinguished from persons in the older Black middle class, who experience the legacy of past discrimination and entered the labor market before the 1960s. Fifth, there are several structural imperatives which are fundamental to his interpretation of the progress of the new Black middle class such as the growth of high-wage economic opportunities in the corporate and government sectors, the growing Black accessibility to higher education and advanced technology, the interventionist role of the state in reducing the historic and continuing effects of discrimination, and the continuing mobilization of social movements against job discrimination.

It is important to underscore that Wilson does not explicitly argue that racial discrimination is generally on the decline or absent. While the title of the book plays to this interpretation, his argument is different. In fact, he indicates that there is continued White opposition to residential integration, public school integration, and racial discrimination against Blacks in public places that are all signs of "the unyielding importance of race in America" (Wilson 1978, 152). However, there is implicit in his discussion of the economy and social class being more important than race a liberal expectancy interpretation of the increased progress in modern race relations. The theoretical argument and hypothesis that class is more important than race becomes advanced as an objective historical and sociological fact.

With respect to the first point, Roy Bryce-Laporte indicates that it is unclear whether Wilson is addressing the formation of the Black middle class or its crystallization (Bryce-LaPorte 1979). Bryce-Laporte notes that the class analysis provided by Wilson neither examines the intersection of changing intergroup and intragroup effects of class and race nor does it elucidate the meaning of class (Bryce-Laporte 1979, 28–29). When examining the extent which the Black middle class is conscious of class, the degree which they affiliate with their class, and act on the basis of class affiliation and interests, Bryce-LaPorte notes that Wilson neither specifies the unit of analysis of class nor demonstrates a Black middle-class ideology of class and race. By not specifying a unit of analysis, the objective and subjective dimensions of class become confused. And by not demonstrating the presence of a Black middle-class ideology, only the emergence of this class, not its crystallization, can be demonstrated (Bryce-Laporte 1979, 29).

Thomas F. Pettigrew argues that independent of the evidence presented by Wilson, there is a zero-sum assumption of the logical relationships between class and race. Rather than seeing an interaction, he assumes that since class is increasing in empirical significance, race must be necessarily decreasing (Pettigrew 1979). If one is permitted an extension on this point, there is a very plausible interpretation that recognizes with increased class effects, there can also be increased race effects.

Considering the second point of a "shared market situation" and "life chances" within the Black middle class, these would require untangling the effects of macrosociological sectors and industries alongside the more microsociological human and social capital characteristics. Although Wilson seems to be arguing that within the most advanced corporate and government sectors, highly educated and talented young Blacks are becoming increasingly integrated. However, it makes a difference the degree which the new Black middle class is receiving its increased occupational and income returns to education from both the private and public sector. To the extent the government or public sector plays a disproportionate role in this growth and integration, these suggest dimensions of state growth, political class, and public interest group that go beyond the conventional market interpretation.

The third point of the increased autonomy of the economy and politics and the hypothesis that in the modern industrial (or post-civil rights era) racial antagonisms have shifted from the economic to the sociopolitical sector is problematic and has criticisms. George Wilson and Deirdre Royster (1995) state that while valid tests of this must examine racial inequality in the economic sector, in the absence of an explicit definition of this sector, the dimensions of economics must be interpreted liberally (Wilson and Royster 1995, 61). This liberal interpretation of economic progress is present in Wilson's analysis.

Other observers such as Charles V. Willie observe in Wilson's analysis of economic institutions in modern industrialization a logic that is characterized by the "error of particularism." Willie charges that in an attempt to isolate the economy from other institutions, Wilson has analyzed traits rather than the "serial patterns" of complex characteristics affecting Blacks (Willie 1978). Related criticisms such as Charles Payne's note an "interconnection fallacy" in his attempts to argue the autonomy of the political system from the economic system after World War II (Payne 1979).

It is possible that Wilson's distinction of the economy and government is meant to distinguish the direct (primary) and indirect (secondary) effects of discrimination on inequality. Although not specified, these imply a trend of centralized federal government. The secondary effects of inequality deriving from continued segregation in education and housing and discrimination in public places receive relatively little examination. Even when his argument is taken narrowly to mean economic opportunity, racial processes in education and housing discrimination have documented impacts on economic opportunity.

The fourth point of different period or cohort effects for middle-class Blacks entering the labor market during the late 1960s and 1970s distinguishes the effects of historic discrimination from the increased significance of class in contemporary race relations. The liberal expectancy in this hypothesis emphasizes that because younger college-educated Blacks are integrated more into the economic opportunity structure and have benefited more from affirmative action policies than other Blacks, the continuing discrimination should have more to do with social class effects than race effects. Although both objective and subjective bases of race and class enter here, Wilson is primarily concerned with the objective features of the economy.

Mark R. Warren explains that Wilson's assumptions of the contemporary differentiation of Blacks in social class lead to the conclusion that these class effects are unprecedented for the Black middle class (Warren 1995, 85). In order for racial discrimination to be significant, Warren sees in Wilson's logic the expectation that it should affect all Blacks equally. Built into his argument is the historic argument that the new Black middle class is "different in important ways from the one Frazier described: it is not restricted to certain occupations serving segregated ghettos and is more integrated into corporate America" (Warren 1995, 85). Because more privileged Blacks have always benefited from new economic opportunities, Warren questions whether this new differentiation of class and race among Blacks can be a prima facie argument against the continued significance of race (Warren 1995, 85).

It appears that Wilson's early criticisms of affirmative action and the Black middle class were based on its limited effects in ameliorating the conditions of the Black underclass. While this is correct, commentators argue that this line of interpretation is misleading. Orlando Patterson notes that the structuring of affirmative action was intended to be a top-down strategy to level the playing field for middle and working classes across race and gender; the underclass was not a target of this strategy (Patterson 1997, 155). Neil McLaughlin also states that Wilson's critique of affirmative action focuses almost exclusively on higher education and middle-class jobs and largely ignores the working-class jobs such as police, firefighters, civil service, and construction workers that have experienced the political backlash against affirmative action (McLaughlin 1993, 364).

Wilson's early critique appears to be an adaptation of neoconservative and neoliberal arguments against affirmative action. More recently, he has adopted a more liberal argument for "affirmative opportunity" that recognizes the utility of class-based affirmative action alongside flexible, merit-based standards in bringing Blacks into higher education. In these discussions, Wilson emphasizes that affirmative action programs based singularly on economic class would do little to sustain racial and ethnic diversity (Wilson 1999, 97).

With respect to the fifth point, Edwards argues that the structural imperatives that contributed to the growth of the new Black middle class had declined significantly by the late 1970s (Edwards 1979). Harry Edwards finds in the economic "stagflation" and rising energy costs, the "precipitous" decline in Black college enrollment and Black faculty and staff recruitment, the increasing scores of individual and class-action suits by Whites against affirmative action, the increased noncompliance of affirmative action, and the passage of Proposition 13 in California alongside the growing "tax revolt" nationally as evidence of this deterioration (Edwards 1979, 992). If an extension is permitted, the assumption of the continued growth of high-wage employment in the corporate and government sectors commensurate with the early 1970s and its translation into the growth of Blacks in high-paying administrative and professional occupations is undermined by analyses which show greater segmentation of the Black middle class in secondary labor markets and race-based occupations (Collins 1983). It is also questioned by national analyses of detailed census categories that show that the momentum of rapid growth ebbed and reversed during the 1980s (Wilson, F.H. 1995). Corporate downsizing and governmental reorganization accompanying the "new federalism" were also reflected in more intense economic competition between Whites and Blacks and reflected in "windows of opportunity" replacing "doors of opportunity" in discourses of social equality. Following the *Bakke v. Regents of California* decision (1978), Black enrollments in four-year colleges and universities decreased through the early 1980s. By the late 1980s, Black enrollment in higher education was proportionately lower than during the early 1970s.

RESEARCH ON THE BLACK MIDDLE CLASS

Empirical research on the Black middle class has not directly tested Wilson's macrosociological hypothesis of Black middle class emergence, growth, and crystallization and the hypothesis of the increased autonomy of the economy and politics in contemporary race relations. These have more directly examined the "life chances," period effects, and several microsociological dimensions of the Black middle class. These ask whether the economic gains described during the early 1970s were premature and to what extent the effects of cumulative past discrimination and continuing discrimination in the economy are understated.

Research validating the hypothesis of increased returns to education among the new Black middle class is found in some studies. Increased social class effects in the occupational status of Blacks are found in one study derived from the "Occupational Mobility of Black Men" surveys of 1962 and 1973 (Hout 1984). Based on the returns of occupational status and income of recent college-educated Blacks in the panel study of income dynamics, In Soo Son, Sue Moedel, and Gene Fischer (1989) found higher mean levels for Blacks. These studies validating the increasing significance of class were largely based on data through the early 1980s.

More mixed evidence and interpretations are found elsewhere. In the book *A Common Destiny*, the 1984 earnings of Black male college graduates were almost three-fourths (74 percent) of White male college graduates compared to only 52 percent in 1949 (Jaynes and Williams 1989, 301). Reynolds Farley and Walter Allen in *The Color Line and the Quality of Life in America* found that the probability of employment in executive, administrative, managerial, and professional occupations among Blacks with a college education was higher in 1980 than similar employment for Whites (Farley and Allen 1987, appendix table 9.1). On the other hand, these latter studies did not show income parity for Blacks (Farley and Allen 1987; Jaynes and Williams 1989) and Black men lagged behind White men in attaining high-level executive, administrative, managerial, and professional employment (Farley and Allen 1987). The probability of unemployment was greater for college-educated Black men and women than White men but less than White women (Farley and Allen 1987; appendix table 8.3).

More critically, the decades of the 1980s and 1990s provided changing social and economic conditions that provide the objective facts challenging Wilson's hypothesis of the increasing integration of highly educated and talented Blacks. Although recent social indicators indeed show a narrowing of the racial gap in college completion, this status attainment among Blacks has not necessarily resulted in increased returns with respect to employment and earnings. In 1990, census figures of college completion, for persons twenty-five years and older, showed 13.6 percent of Blacks and 24.8 percent of Whites attaining these levels (11.2 difference). For earlier college graduate cohorts represented in persons thirty-five years and older, the differential in 1990 was slightly larger at 13–15.5 percent Black, 28.5 percent White (U.S. Bureau of Census 1991, table 7). Unemployment ratios for Black college-educated persons have persisted around twice that of White college-educated graduates and have risen to 2.5 times the White unemployment (Wilson, Tienda, Wu 1995). Earlier convergence trends in incomes for the most highly educated and talented college-educated Blacks with Whites have reversed since the 1970s. In 1975, the median income of Black college graduates twenty-five years and older ($19,966) reached 90 percent of comparable White incomes; by 1990 the median income of Black college graduates twenty-five years older ($24,336) was 87 percent comparable to White incomes (U.S. Bureau of Census 1990, table 7). The greatest convergence in racial incomes since the mid-1970s is in the group that had completed some college (1–3 years). Between 1975 and 1990, these increased from 81 to 86 percent.

Trend studies on education indicate that while the racial gap closed with respect to Blacks high school completion and college enrollment during the 1960s and early 1970s, there was a widening gap in college completion beginning in the late 1970s that has been sustained through the 1980s and 1990s. Although current numbers of educated Blacks are larger than earlier, changing economic and political trends with respect to federal resources support is eroding earlier successes (Center for Budget and Policy Priorities 1988). Robert Hill noted earlier that while Blacks increased representation in the higher status occupations such as administrators and professionals during the 1970s, the proportion of Blacks with upper- and middle-income earnings actually decreased between 1970 and 1978 (Hill 1978). Bart Landry's research showed that during the 1973–75 and 1980–82 recessions, middle-class Blacks fared worse and lost ground to middle-class Whites. Between 1972 and 1983, the percentage of Blacks in all middle-class jobs increased nationally only 1 percent (Landry 1987, 194–195).

Racial segmentation in the formation of the Black middle class is addressed in Sharon Collins research (Collins 1983). In "The Making of the Black Middle Class," she emphasizes that employment opportunities since 1960 were generated by direct federal governmental interventions including: (1) Equal Employment Opportunity Commission, (2) Office of Federal Contract Compliance Programs, (3) federal contract set-aside programs, and (4) federally funded social welfare services. This "policy-mediated" rather than "market-mediated" situation in which the government increased the labor market demand for Blacks is related to the greater organization of the Black middle class in segregated as distinct from generalized markets (Collins 1983). Segregated market functions are directed at, disproportionately used by, or concerned with the distribution of goods and services that directly meet the needs of Black consumers and labor experienced Black concentration during the 1960s and 1970s. These included professional occupations such as personnel and labor relations, public relations, social scientists, and social workers. Black professional and administrative employees in city and state government in 1978 were disproportionately concentrated in sectors that served Blacks such as public welfare, corrections, hospitals, and health. In the private sector, Black entrepreneurs were similarly found in segregated markets of inner cities. Collins distinguished the employment of Blacks dependent on federal revenues as distinct from city and state resources that have more stable and generalized outcomes (Collins 1983, 375–376).

Marlese Durr and John R. Logan identified in the state-level governmental employment of Black managers other forms of segmentation. Although Black managers in the state government were found to have comparable pay to Black managers in mainstream employment, they were essentially segregated in racial (or minority) submarkets and received fewer benefits. These segmented Black state government managers were less likely to have civil service job protection, experienced limited upward mobility into mainstream, and experienced considerable job insecurity and dissatisfaction (Durr and Logan 1997).

Relatedly, secondary analysis of census data shows that the growth of the Black middle class during the 1980s was primarily accounted for by lower-middle-class administrative support and sales occupations and that the growth of Blacks in upper-middle-class executive, administrative, managerial, and professional occupations was connected to public employment and quasi-public services (Wilson, F. H. 1995). While upper-income and upper-middle income Blacks experienced a continuation of income gains during the 1980s, the income of lower-middle and working-class Blacks, which made up larger representations, slowed and reversed (Wilson, F. H. 1995, 31–32). When intergroup analyses of income across racial groups are examined, there is little to no evidence of relative improvements. In fact, the median income for the highest fifth of Black families was only slightly higher than the second fifth of White families. The recent integration of the Black middle class into the economy has been accompanied by its reorganization into segmented labor markets and specialized occupations that are structured by race.

James P. Smith's research provides compelling evidence of the changing tides of Black middle-class earnings since the 1970s that challenges the progress assessment (Smith 1993). During the early post-civil rights years of the 1970s, the implementation of affirmative action and equal employment opportunity policies were reflected in the narrowing of the income gap between Blacks and Whites addressed in *The Declining Significance of Race*. Since the 1970s, the racial income gap has stagnated and eroded. According to Smith:

> Among new college graduates, Black men earned 83 percent as much as comparable White men in 1967–68; by 1971–72 there was complete wage

parity. After 1971–1972, wage gains of young Black workers steadily eroded. For college graduates, this erosion marked both decades until we had come roughly full circle with a wage differential in 1990 little different than that which we started. (Smith 1993)

Over time, cohorts which entered the job market with wages exceeding those of comparable Whites by 2 percent were making only 75 percent as much as their White counterparts eighteen years into their careers in 1989.

Research on the subjective dimensions of the Black middle class has not substantiated the bases for the social class crystallization suggested by Wilson. There is a persistence of race in the social consciousness of middle-class Blacks and their experiences in public encounters. In examining the contribution of socioeconomic status on attitudes of economic well-being, political party identification, and identification with Blacks between 1964 and 1984, Cedric Herring found that independent of income, the attitudes of middle-class Blacks were more similar to other Blacks than those of Whites with similar income (Herring 1989, 278). In examining the General Social Survey from 1972 to 1984, Melvin Thomas and Mark Hughes found the effects of socioeconomic status on measures of social psychological well-being such as life satisfaction, trust, anomie, general happiness, and health showed Blacks with significantly lower scores than Whites (Thomas and Hughes 1986, 21).

The continuing significance of institutional discrimination for middle-class Blacks has been treated extensively by Joe R. Feagin (Feagin 1991, Feagin and Sikes 1994). In public spaces such as stores, hotels, amusements, streets, transportation, and contacts with police and in employment and home seeking, systematic and complex discriminatory practices of a coded and covert nature have replaced traditional de jure segregation.

Despite the attention given to the Black middle class in *The Declining Significance of Race* this is at best a secondary concern in Wilson's assessment of industrialization, urbanization, and the changing class structure of Blacks. He is more focused on the "sweeping" theoretical exercise of describing and explaining macrosociological changes in the economy, state, and their interconnections with race and ethnic relations. His theoretical interests in these larger questions frequently fall short in addressing the interrelations between social class and race that have complex and variable reproductions in urban Black communities. At the same time, his analysis of the social history of the Black class structure does not deviate from the industrialization stages framework. While this is useful in interpreting the experiences of Blacks in many northern cities, it is not clear that this generalizes to the Black class structure in most cities. Nor is there but passing concern with the intersection of urban history and culture in the changing Black class structure.

Despite the attention given to the Black middle class and underclass in his treatment of class and race, Wilson has curiously understated if not largely omitted the Black working class. This appears to grow from his use of a dialectical approach that is largely focused on the schism between the Black middle class and underclass. The omission or "invisibility" of the Black working class is striking considering its empirical reality, size, and dynamism. This "invisibility" of the Black working class is also significant considering Wilson's beginnings in a working-class community and family.

The theoretical discussions and the research literature on the new Black middle class have not influenced major changes in Wilson's concepts and framework. The latter appear more driven by the theoretical perspectives and dominant cultural beliefs characterizing the progress of the Black middle class that enter the public policy discussions. In later writings, Wilson is less directly concerned with the Black middle class and discusses this largely in the context of the underclass. At the same time, he does not usually address criticisms that fail to seriously address his premises. However, some of the criticisms do seriously address his premises. Compounding this, the socio-logical theory driving his analyses and discussions of the Black middle class are arrived at independently of most of the empirical research on the Black middle class.

It is instructive that Wilson resolves these controversies of the Black middle class in more subtle and symbolic ways. He responds to several criti-cisms in subsequent commentaries and essays by abandoning the theme of the "declining significance of race" and underscoring the "increasing signifi-cance of class" and the interaction between class and race. In a recent inter-view, he will also emphasize the importance of furthering affirmative action for the Black middle class alongside more universal policies. In other inter-views, he will share episodes of his professional career that indicate persistent challenges of race in the middle class. At best, Wilson's hypothesis on the growth and integration of the new Black middle class holds for the younger cohorts entering higher education and the professions during the late 1960s and the 1970s. There is much research that indicates more sober and less optimistic assessments. As a generalization for the subsequent post-civil rights years, it was premature and overstated.

MODERN INDUSTRIAL RACE RELATIONS: THE EMERGENCE AND GROWTH OF THE BLACK UNDERCLASS

In *The Declining Significance of Race: Blacks and Changing American Institutions*, Wilson sees the modern industrial period as characterized by decreasing eco-nomic opportunity for the Black lower class and underclass. The wartime and post-World War II economic improvements providing occupational entry and mobility for the Black middle class are accompanied by increases in Black unemployment for young and poorly trained ghetto Blacks, decreases in labor participation rates, higher welfare rates, and slower movement out of poverty (Wilson 1978, 129–134).

Nearly a decade later, Wilson views the macroeconomic changes in industrial decline and plant closings resulting in social dislocations that are reflected and reproduced in an increasing scale of concentrated poverty among inner-city Blacks in the largest metropolitan centers of the North and Midwest. At the same time, underclass behaviors such as family dissolution, welfare, and crime have increased in significance (Wilson 1987). He views the post-World War II civil rights reforms such as antidiscrimination policies in public accommodations, employment, housing, and voting rights legislation addressing the concerns of middle-class Blacks yet not sufficiently addressing the unique problems of de facto segregation and social class subordination confronting ghetto Blacks (Wilson 1978, 136).

THEORETICAL CONTROVERSIES ON THE URBAN BLACK UNDERCLASS

Wilson's theorizing on the emergence and growth of the inner-city Black underclass develops in stages. In *The Declining Significance of Race*, the concept of underclass appears synonymous with lower class. Neo-Marxian and neo-Weberian descriptions of class formation and the social relationships of class are integrated alongside a neoconservative interpretation of the growing class schisms between the Black middle class and underclass during the post-civil rights years. In *The Truly Disadvantaged*, he articulates several macrosociological-based hypotheses accounting for the growth of poverty that derive largely from changes in the economic opportunity structure and ecological changes affecting the social organization and quality of life within Black communities. While critiquing and building on the journalistic, public policy, and sociological controversies of the underclass, Wilson importantly refocuses these. While the role of economics and social class are salient, the interaction with race appears understated. Although Wilson has a structural and political-economy interpretation, there is no direct connection between his usage of the underclass and the original definition associated with Gunnar Myrdal.

In *The Challenge of Affluence* (1963), Gunnar Myrdal identified the emerging trends of social displacement among skilled and unskilled labor and the emergence of a class of unemployed and underemployed persons at the bottom of society (Myrdal 1962, 34). Myrdal viewed this "under-class" as economically useless rather than integrated into the society (Myrdal 1963, 35). This concept of "under-class" described a substrata class of unemployed and underemployed persons and families affected by deindustrialization who were socially differentiated. Although Myrdal originated the concept of "under-class" and this conception informs Wilson's structural analysis, it is interesting that Wilson has no acknowledgment or references to Myrdal in either *The Declining Significance of Race* or *The Truly Disadvantaged.*

By the early 1980s, liberals had largely avoided researching problems of inner city and using the underclass concept and discourse. Most civil rights leaders either critiqued the underclass concept or did not use it. One exception to this tendency is found in Douglas Glasgow's *The Black Underclass: Poverty, Unemployment, and Entrapment of Ghetto Youth* (1980) not only examined the economic structures and institutional discrimination in employment and wages bearing on unemployment, underemployment, but also blocked mobility among these poor persons. Glasgow's underclass concept identified a "permanently entrapped population of poor persons, unused and unwanted, accumulated in various parts of the country" (Glasgow 1980, 3). It is instructive that Glasgow's structural argument included market factors, institutional practices, and the legacy of racism (Glasgow 1980, 4). While Wilson's elaborations of the Black underclass converge with Glasgow, there is no reference anywhere to his scholarship.

In refocusing the questions of urban inequality bearing on the underclass, Wilson intellectually, inspirationally and symbolically draws from the sociological controversy generated by Daniel P. Moynihan's *The Negro Family: The Case for National Action* (1965). While Wilson's interests in connecting macroeconomic employment policies bearing on urban inequality and the poor converge with Moynihan's policy concerns, the theoretical analyses and concepts informing his arguments of deindustrialization and social dislocation derive more directly from Myrdal's *The Challenge of Affluence* and Frazier's *The Negro Family in the United States.* By appropriating the latter analyses and refocusing these, Wilson gives these new interpretations. In contrast to Myrdal who saw the emerging underclass as unintegrated and socially useless, Wilson views this class as integrated and potentially employable through transitional employment, training, and increased human and social capital.

Drawing from E. Franklin Frazier, Wilson appropriates the integration prospects of the Black proletariat under industrialization in the 1930s and 1940s and moves these forward to account for the employability of the underclass. Unlike Glasgow, Wilson's emphasis on economic factors will necessarily reduce the significance of racism and institutional discrimination.

There are at least two macrosociological theories of postindustrial economic transformation and urban inequality that are synthesized by Wilson. The descriptions of structural changes such as plant closings, joblessness, and disinvestment has similarities with the analyses in Barry Bluestone and Bennett Harrison's *The Deindustrialization of America* and *The Great U-Turn:*

Corporate Restructuring and the Polarizing of America (1988). However, the tone in Wilson's discussions stops short of critiquing corporate restructuring and its increased rationalization in the social dislocation. Bluestone and Harrison's research has identified a stronger interaction between disinvestment, plant closings, place, and race. More important for Wilson's theorizing of economic transformation is his integration of John Kasarda's hypothesis of structural transformation in the occupational hierarchy within urban areas and a deficit of Black human capital relative to the changing economy (Kasarda 1988; Kasarda 1989). The integration of concepts such as "mismatch" and human and social capital into the structural analysis of labor markets enables a more conservative, impersonal, and rational analysis.

There are alternative theories on the postindustrial economy and the underclass that attempt to identify the social class relationships underlying these social dislocations. Edna Bonacich argues that the "economic restructuring" identified by Wilson is only one of the surface dimensions derived from capital accumulation that is reproduced in inequality and poverty (Bonacich 1989). Bonacich notes "the biggest mistake that Wilson makes is to see class and race as somehow antagonistic or alternative models of social organization" (Bonacich 1989, 55). She emphasizes that racism is a part of the capitalist system that reproduces the Black poor through the continued systematic exploitation of people of color for profit and the demand that people of color must accommodate to the White man's cultural system (Bonacich 1989). Relatedly, William Darity argues that underlying the structural transformations, leading to increased joblessness, is actually the transformation from an industrial capitalism to a "managerial society" (Darity, Myers, Carson, and Sabol 1994). In the emerging "managerial society," the structural transformations of labor markets have resulted in the increased social unwantedness of superfluous labor and the institutionalization, imprisonment, and homicides of Black males (Darity, Myers, Carson, and Sabol 1994, 57). Furthermore, Ralph Gomes and Wanda Katz Fishman note that Wilson's analysis bearing on urban inequality focuses on the structural constraints accompanying the technological transformation of the labor force from a goods producing industrially based system to an information processing service-based system (Gomes and Fishman 1989, 87). However, Wilson does not specifically deal with the class relations of capitalism including the exploitation of labor, the accumulation of capital, and the technological revolution in production (Gomes and Fishman 1989, 87).

The stated agenda of Wilson's theorizing and research on the underclass is to explain problems of growing unemployment, poverty, and social dislocation within inner-city neighborhoods primarily through macroeconomic changes. The "hidden agenda" of this discourse is to rally support for the "truly disadvantaged" through universal policies such as employment, education, and health that cut across social classes and racial groups. Here Wilson challenges the conservative perspectives of the underclass that emphasize distinctively culture of poverty and pathological behavioral explanations. In challenging the conservative conventional wisdom, he will appropriate the underclass concept, develop a more holistic and structural explanation, and give it new meanings. Wilson converts the cultural variables from primary causal variables into intervening variables. In doing this, he accepts the premise that the effects of culture are real, but defines the ultimate causes as the structural forces that precipitate these cultural conditions among the minority poor. While there are also some convergences with more radical political-economy analyses, there is a conscious attempt to underscore the liberal tone.

Wilson's definitions of the underclass concept have undergone reformulation and elaboration. In *The Declining Significance of Race*, he used the term to refer to "those at the very bottom of the social class ladder" (Wilson 1978, 1). This economic definition implied the lowest of the lower class—the persistently poor. While the economic basis of the underclass has remained primary, he would soon append to this behavioral dimensions. Two years later, he would underscore that "the underclass embodies a reality that is not captured in the more general designation of "lower class" (Wilson 1980, 157). He noted that "in underclass families, unlike other families in the Black community, the head of the household is invariably a woman and the makeup of the underclass is also reflected in the very large number of adult males with no fixed address—who live mainly on the streets roaming from one place of shelter to another" (Wilson 1980, 157).

With *The Truly Disadvantaged: The Inner City, the Underclass and Public Policy*, Wilson combines the economic structure definition of underclass with an ecological definition of poverty concentration and social isolation. Most important for Wilson are weak labor force attachments that are reproduced in the environment of these inner-city neighborhoods. Included in this elaborated definition are "individuals who lack training and skills and either experience long-term unemployment or are not members of the labor force, individuals who are engaged in street crime and other forms of aberrant behavior, and families that experience long spells of poverty and welfare dependency (Wilson 1987, 8).

Important journalistic treatments of the underclass preceded and influenced his conceptualizations and discussions. One of the earliest articles, George Russell's "The American Underclass," appeared in *Time* magazine (Russell 1977). This article would identify a mostly Black underclass in the ghettos of northern cities. While discussing the loss of industrial employment as a factor, Russell emphasized as most important the deviant behaviors and values of the Black underclass (Russell 1977). In Ken Auletta's *The Underclass*

(1982), which were developed from his earlier articles in *The New Yorker*, morality and cultural were emphasized more than economic circumstances (Auletta 1982). His definition of the underclass, which included long-term welfare recipients, criminals, drug addicts, hustlers, and the homeless, is essentially a moral concept. Nicholas Lemann's "The Origins of the Underclass," which appeared in *The Atlantic Monthly* would help reintroduce the culture of poverty (Lemann 1986). He would locate the culture of the underclass in the culture of Blacks within the sharecropper South. A book by *The Chicago Tribune* entitled *The American Millstone* (1986) would move the discussion of the underclass from New York to the heartland and Chicago.

The political and public policy controversy bearing on the underclass was confronted head on by Wilson. In political terms, the larger underclass discourse initially had neoconservative and conservative meanings. In these discourses, which emphasized the culture of poverty and social behavior, there was hardly any mention of structural factors such as industrial losses and unemployment in the growth of the underclass. Early on, these neoconservative perspectives emphasized a cultural crisis traceable to the Great Society reforms of the 1960s, the ascendancy of an adversary and nihilistic culture, and an urban underclass seen as threatening larger societal institutions and norms of equality (Steinfels 1979, 58–62). During the 1980s, important books such as George Gilder's *Wealth and Poverty* (1981), and Charles Murray's *Losing Ground: American Policy 1950–1980* (1984), focused the conservative conventional wisdom of the underclass discussion on the perverse effects of the welfare system on Black unemployment and poverty, the lack of a hard work ethic among the Black poor, the withdrawal of Blacks from the labor market, and the growth of Black female-headed families (Gilder 1981; Murray 1984).

Wilson's elaboration of the underclass concept is structural and macrosociological. Although this meaning was explicit in *The Declining Significance of Race*, it appears that this conceptualization was a theory sketch to be filled in later. While the holistic and open-ended quality of the concept coincides to a degree with journalistic usages that refer to political, criminal, and behavioral underclasses, this apparently was not his intention. In *The Truly Disadvantaged*, he distinguishes his concept from the political, criminal, and behavioral underclasses that are prevalent in conservative perspectives. He further elaborates the underclass with both a meaning analysis and empirical analysis. In assessing the assumptions in the various meanings of the underclass, he arrives at two macrosociological concepts of underclass. In analyzing the growth of the underclass, there is a normative theory and concept that emphasizes the economic and industrial dislocation of the unemployed and working poor in cities. In setting the research agenda for underclass research, he operationalizes the underclass in terms of a spatial definition of concentrated poverty that is useful for targeting public policies to the most disadvantaged. Wilson argues that the ghetto underclass of families and individuals that remains in cities is collectively different and unprecedented. In *The Truly Disadvantaged*, he advances a liberal discourse of the underclass that challenges the conservative perspectives. Although Wilson retains the major macrosociological arguments of poverty, in response to Herbert Gans article, "Deconstructing the Underclass," he not only cautions and critiques the underclass's dangers as a planning concept and its negative implications (Gans 1990), but he also temporarily replaces the underclass concept with the concept of "ghetto poor" in his presidential address to the American Sociological Association (Wilson 1991). In *When Work Disappears: The World of the New Urban Poor*, the ghetto poor becomes the inner-city poor and jobless ghettos (Wilson 1996). The shift from underclass to ghetto poor signaled not only that the underclass term and debate were being abolished, but also represented a subtle shift from a designation of classes to one of individuals (Small and Newman 2001, 25).

Wilson's theorizing of economic restructuring, changing labor markets, and urban inequality attributes the high rates of Black joblessness in central cities to the decline of high wage, highly unionized manufacturing employment and the increasing spatial and social isolation of inner-city neighborhoods from mainstream economic opportunities. The *Multi-City Study of Urban Inequality Analysis Plan* has identified five principal hypotheses in the theoretical controversy for further empirical research (Browne, Farley, Johnson, and Tilly 1993). First, employment is directly influenced by local labor market conditions. Accordingly, persons in labor markets experiencing deindustrialization are more likely to be unemployed and underemployed than persons in labor markets experiencing rapid job growth in economic sectors that match skills requirements. Second, employment is directly influenced by neighborhood environment. Persons in poor inner-city communities which are geographically and socially isolated from mainstream economic opportunities are less likely to find jobs than persons in more affluent and geographically accessible neighborhoods. Third, employment is influenced directly by the type of school attended. As such, persons attending inner-city schools are less likely than persons attending suburban schools to acquire the required skills to compete for jobs in the postindustrial economy. Fourth, because employment is directly influenced by family background, persons growing up in lower-status, less-educated, and single-parent families are less likely to be employed than persons growing up in high-status, more-educated, and two-parent families. Fifth, employment is a directly influenced by individual human capital characteristics. Persons who are high school dropouts and have criminal records are less likely to be employed than persons who have completed high school and not had a "brush with the law" (Browne, Farley, Johnson, and Tilly 1993, 7–8). While the first three hypotheses are macrosociological, the latter two hypotheses are more microsociological.

Ronald Mincey has similarly identified in Wilson's theorizing the "deindustrialization" hypothesis that decreased central city industrial employment, reduced the demand for low-skilled workers, and in turn resulted in increased unemployment that most adversely affected inner-city Black men (Mincey 1994). Relatedly, he identifies two hypotheses of the growing underclass arising from macroeconomic and ecological changes (Mincey 1994). First, there is a marriageability hypothesis. Wilson hypothesizes that the high unemployment and decreased incomes that resulted in growing poverty among inner-city Black men negatively affected their marriageablity. As industrial decline resulted in less Black men working in employment that paid liveable wages, they were perceived by women as less marriageable and these conditions increased out-of-wedlock births and welfare dependency. Second there is the "demographic transition" theory. Wilson hypothesizes that the increased wealth, income, and consumption of the nonpoor Black middle-class and working-class persons enabled these Blacks to leave inner-city ghettos and move to more decentralized and suburban housing markets. Consequently, the out-movement of nonpoor Blacks from the inner city, which derived from civil rights policies such as affirmative action and fair housing, resulted in the increasing concentration and isolation of the Black poor.

There are two additional hypotheses of the underclass arising from the recent transformation of Black politics advanced in *The Declining Significance of Race* that are not treated in *The Truly Disadvantaged*. These center on the relationships among industrialization, racial stratification, and differential patterns of interclass political mobilization. In one hypothesis, Wilson suggests that the transformation of civil rights protests to Black community and ghetto issues during the 1960s increased lower-class Black awareness of racial inequality and the philosophy of racial solidarity. Growing out of specific ghetto Black grievances such as unemployment, inferior education, housing, and police brutality, ghetto revolts and poverty programs such as the Community Action Programs refocused attention on the Black underclass that was earlier centered on civil rights (Wilson 1978, 138).

In another hypothesis, he identifies the problem of social distance between the middle class and underclass in urban Black communities as an organizational consequence of modern or corporate industrialism. As such, he recognizes that the uneven distribution of economic resources by social class is accompanied by differential political resources and social mobility. While emphasizing that the Black middle class through the 1970s was expanding and increasingly gaining entry into government, he also cautions that Black gains in urban politics are occurring at a time when the city as a base of political power is on the decline (Wilson 1978, 141–143). In this analysis, he anticipates movements of metropolitan government, suburban political solidarity, "privatism," and tax revolts. He will return to this larger issue of urban and suburban politics in his public policy discussions in *When Work Disappears*. Implicit throughout Wilson's work is a theme of the precarious and problematic nature of power in the contemporary urban Black middle class.

Wilson's theorizing of economic restructuring, changing labor markets, and the urban inequalities experienced in Black communities and families due to the high rates of Black male joblessness provides a structural argument of the intersection of race, class, and gender that counters "femininization of poverty" explanations (Dill 1989, 73). However, gender scholars have criticized the particulars of his analysis for paying inadequate attention to the complex intersections of race and class in the lives of African American women (Edin 2000; Andersen and Collins 1998; Jarrett 1994; Hill-Collins 1990). The tone of the structural interpretation obscured and understated the continuing significance of racial bias, occupational segregation, and discrimination bearing on African-American employment, wages, and poverty. While discussing the deteriorating economic situation of poor Black families, he does not address the role that lower wages for Black women plays. Other research has elucidated differential adaptations (Jarrett 1994) and reasons for nonmarriage among single parent African American women (Edin 2000) that vary from Wilson's Black marriageability assumptions.

RESEARCH ON WILSON'S MACROSOCIOLOGICAL HYPOTHESES OF THE URBAN UNDERCLASS

Empirical research has generally supported the hypothesis that decreased central city industrial employment resulted in increased unemployment that adversely affected inner-city Black men. In Wilson's, *When Work Disappears*, the mismatch hypothesis of more rapid labor market growth in suburban manufacturing and commercial activities and the employment growth in central city labor markets having middle-class administrative, professional, and technical occupations, requiring post-secondary education and specialized training are illustrated by recent trends which show the deterioration in the educational and training levels of prospective inner-city workers (Wilson 1997). In Paul Jargowsky's *Poverty and Place: Ghettos, Barrios, and the American City* (1997), the effects of macro-level metropolitan economic opportunities (or income-generation variables) and economic segregation variables explained changes in neighborhood poverty and ghetto poverty during the 1980s (Jargowsky 1997).

The Multi-City Study of Urban Inequality series provides the most authoritative evidence of the effects of economic restructuring in local labor markets and racial bias and discrimination among employers (O'Connor, Tilly, Bobo 2000; Sjoquist 2000; Bluestone and Stevenson 2000; Farley, Danziger, and Holzer 2000; Bobo, Oliver, Johnson, and Valenzuela 2000; Moss and Tilly 2001). These studies examine not only the experiences of households in the labor and housing markets and their encounters with racial discrimination, but also examine how employers determine business location decisions, skills requirements, and recruitment, screening and hiring procedures. The general findings indicate that while the effects of economic restructuring, uneven growth, mismatch, and urban sprawl are important in each of the metropolitan areas, the effects of racial segregation and racial discrimination in labor markets continue to be significant.

There are two dimensions of the mismatch hypothesis that are reflected in empirical research informing Wilson's theorizing: spatial mismatch, skills mismatch. In spatial mismatch research, the decentralization of manufacturing and service employment from central cities to suburbs and the segregation of Blacks in central cities predict decreases in the employment and earnings of Blacks. These predict that increased Black suburbanization and access to transportation improves Black employment and earnings. In skills mismatch research, deindustrialization (or central city manufacturing losses) is predicted to explain increases in Black unemployment and increases in concentrated poverty within central city neighborhoods. There are studies validating spatial mismatch hypotheses (Popkin, Rosenbaum, and Meaden 1993; Bound and Holzer 1993; Hughes 1989). In comparing the effects of Gautreaux housing program in Chicago, participants who relocated to the suburbs were more likely to be employed (+13 percent) than those who relocated within the central city (Popkin, Rosenbaum, and Meaden 1993). Mark Alan Hughes found that manufacturing employment decentralization predicted growing ghetto poverty neighborhoods and these effects were increased when examining variables for northern metropolitan areas (Hughes 1989). With respect to the skills mismatch hypothesis, John Bound and Harry Holzer found that manufacturing declines explained as much as one-third to one-half of the employment declines among young Black high-school dropouts (Bound and Holzer 1993, 395).

According to James Johnson and Melvin Oliver, in central cities, where even service employment increased, the opportunities for young Black men to enter the job market tightened (Johnson and Oliver 1991).

There is other research that provides more negative evidence for the spatial mismatch hypothesis. In John Farley's research, Black male unemployment tended to be high relative to White males in metropolitan areas that had high percentages of Blacks, decentralized jobs, Black centralization, and educational inequities by race (Farley 1987). In David Ellwood's study, the proximity to jobs resulted in relatively little impact on Black adolescents' employment rates (Ellwood 1986). According to Samuel Cohn and Mark Fossett, discrimination and high unemployment appeared to explain the higher unemployment of Black males more strongly than spatial mismatch (Cohn and Fossett 1996). By comparing tracts with many employment opportunities with those with few employment opportunities, Thomas Cooke found no differences in the unemployment rates for Black men (Cooke 1993). Christopher Jencks and Susan Mayer provide an alternative to the mismatch hypothesis that advances the theory that racial segregation has reduced the demand for Black workers. In White areas, which are farther away from Black areas, it is less likely that employers will find Black workers based on consumer and employer preferences and discrimination (Jencks and Mayer 1990). In Black areas, they described the demand for Black workers as high (Jencks and Mayer 1990, 217). Interestingly, these older industrial areas appear to be the most probable locations for plant closings. These findings suggest the continuing roles of racial segregation, discrimination, and bias.

The hypothesis that high unemployment, decreased incomes, and growing poverty among inner-city Black men negatively affected their mar-riageablity has more negative findings. Although Wilson's argument that the two-parent family lost its appeal to Blacks, because more Black men earned less is persuasive; however, it is not empirically substantiated. Robert G. Wood's research finds that declines in the pool of "marriageable" Black men accounted for only 3 to 4 percent of the decline in Black marriage rates during the 1970s (Wood 1995). Other sociological research shows that roughly four-fifths of the decrease in marriage among employed Black males occurred independent of employment status changes (Jencks 1991; Mare and Winship 1991). There is evidence that the changing economic status of both men and women have indirectly affected broader cultural changes in norms relevant to changing social relationships between the sexes that have affected two-parent families. These center on changing norms of economic responsi-bility, fertility and contraception, and female work (Jencks 1991, 90–91).

More problematic is the hypothesis concerning the conversion of increased earnings, income, and occupational mobility among the nonpoor Black middle class and working class. While there is little controversy that Blacks in general are leaving inner-city ghettos and moving to more decen-tralized, outlying, and suburban housing markets, it is inaccurate to explain the increased concentration and isolation of the underclass in terms of this out-movement. The changing logic of housing markets and land in post-industrial cities do not necessitate the same degree of concentration of Blacks in inner-city neighborhoods as earlier. In several cities, the Black poor are experiencing tighter housing markets in concentrated poverty neighbor-hoods. Relatedly, Douglass S. Massey and Nancy Denton note that the pres-ence of high levels of racial segregation alongside large increases in Black poverty is more important than the "demographic transition" (Massey and Denton 1993).

The hypothesis of the increased social distance between the middle class and underclass in urban Black communities as an organizational consequence of modern or corporate industrialism is an important insight that has only been speculated on. One might extend that as the growth of the new Black middle class is to a large degree based on the growth of the public sector and administrative and professional activities which require the caretaking, differentiation, and the control of Black working and lower classes, the social distance between classes has political consequences.

As we shall see in other controversies, Wilson's most significant contribution with respect to questions of the changing status of African Americans focuses on how he has framed the debate and raised questions. Wilson's use of an industrialization context and his discussion of the dialectic between the Black middle class and underclass, moves the earlier race relations paradigm based on the moral dilemma, the contradictions of racial prejudice and discrimination, and a post-World War II liberal civil rights paradigm to a class-race analysis. His reframing of the underclass controversy, replaces the conservative "culture of poverty" paradigm with a more refocused liberal perspective, which emphasizes changing structural conditions, the environment, a class-based analysis of changing Black status conditions, and social democratic reforms.

The concepts and hypotheses identified by Wilson have become hegemonic in influencing the continuing theorizing and research on postindustrial economic transformation, urban inequality, and the underclass. The sociological controversies on the Black middle class and Black underclass are nested in broader sociological and public policy perspectives that address the underlying structure and reorganization of postindustrial society. The tone of the discourse and the descriptions of increasingly deracialized race relations provide previews of coming attractions. His eclectic intellectual strategy of framing controversy from the center necessitates that he uses at different times perspectives of the "outsider on the inside" and "the insider on the outside." Since his concepts and models are relatively open and holistic, they defy simple categorization and critique.

Reinforcing these macrosociological problems during the transition from industrial to corporate industrial social and economic conditions is the changing nature of Black population growth and its segregation in the city.

CHAPTER 4

━━━━━━

DEMOGRAPHIC AND ECOLOGICAL ANALYSES OF THE CHANGING URBAN BLACK POPULATION

BACKGROUND

Demographic and ecological studies have traditionally constituted an important part of the urban research program at the Chicago School. These were not separated from other parts of sociology, as they are at many sociology departments, but were an integral part of the entire research program. In these macrosociological perspectives, "ecological and demographic perspectives tend to merge with institutional and organizational analysis and with social-psychological concern" (Short 1971, xxiv).

The growth of the Black population, its redistribution through migration, and its reproduction through natural increase (the excess of births over deaths) has constituted continuing empirical and normative concerns in sociological theorizing of social problems. Whether these variables are examined singularly or simultaneously, patterns of migration, fertility, and mortality differentially affect the growth of the Black population and contribute to its quality of life. Social relationships of these primary demographic variables with secondary variables such as gender, age, income, occupation, education, and race enter social science and public policy discussions of "what is" and "what should be."

Although America has never had an official or explicit population policy, Gunnar Myrdal identified a general valuation in *An American Dilemma* of a quantitative goal in Black population policy where most Whites desire that there be as few Blacks as possible in America and where most Blacks preferred that the Black population grow as large as possible (Myrdal 1944, 167). Myrdal noted that among Whites this value was based on the "common belief that Blacks fare better and meet less prejudice when they are few in number" (Myrdal 1944, 168). The latter value continues to constitute a part of the dominant American cultural belief system.

Racial segregation and its role in the growth of the city and the differentiation of the city into natural areas has been a continuing concern in urban sociology and race relations. In Ernest Burgess's early essay, "Residential Segregation in American Cities" (1928), larger processes such as in-migration, Black population growth, the competition of groups for land and residence, and ecological processes of invasion, succession, and concentration were accompanied by the segregation of Blacks into Black ghettos near central business districts (Burgess 1928). Frazier noted that when examined internally, these Black ghettos could in turn assume the characteristics of a growing city with concentric zones where increased class and social status were correlated with decentralized geographic location (Frazier 1937). While there has been a continuing attempt to analogize the historic experiences of White immigrants in ghettos to the contemporary experiences of Blacks and to largely explain this segregation by social status and class (Glazer and Moynihan 1963; Kristol 1966), the liberal expectancy hypothesis has not been substantiated in the leading empirical research on racial segregation (Massey and Denton 1993, Taeuber and Taeuber 1965).

Wilson brings the insights of sociological theory and empirical research into his analyses of two demographic problems of Blacks in cities: (1) Black migration, population growth, and mobility, and (2) racial segregation and ghettoization. In these efforts, he has integrated into his theory sketches and implicit theories several hypotheses and summaries of empirical studies which inform his descriptions and analyses of historic and contemporary sociological relationships. At other times, there are normative discussions and explanations of what should be the changing demographic and ecological relationships of Blacks in their adaptation and assimilation.

In general, he synthesizes concepts, hypotheses, arguments, analogies, and evidence to support his generalizations. While he retains a functionalist interpretation of migration throughout, this moves increasingly from a functional conflict and organizational assessment in *Power, Racism, and Privilege* and *The Declining Significance of Race* to a more pessimistic, disorganizational, and racial caste assessment in *The Truly Disadvantaged*.

When viewed together, the evolution of his early and more recent views on migration and population growth constitute complex and dynamic dimensions of social organization (functionality) and disorganization (dysfunctionality). The tone of his analysis on Black social demography combines an optimistic vision, based on the historic integrative relationships of industrialization and Blacks competitive resources, and a pessimistic vision based on the tightening economic opportunities and "population explosion" among Black teenagers during the contemporary stage of modern or corporate industrialization.

Also contained in these discussions is an attempt to address the dominant cultural beliefs of Black population growth and contemporary racial segregation. At times, these cultural beliefs take the form of hypotheses and popular theories. While he extends some criticisms of these beliefs, Wilson's appropriation of neooconservative perspectives and liberal expectancy assumptions of racial progress constrain his analysis of these racial matters in the postindustrial city.

BLACK MIGRATION, POPULATION GROWTH, AND MOBILITY

Questions relating to the causes and consequences of Black migration in cities are recurring in classical and contemporary urban sociology. Sociological explanations of migration derive from numerous hypotheses which have attempted to account for the macro-level regional, metropolitan, and city differentials, group-level social class, status, gender, and age differentials, and micro-level network, kinship, family, life-style, and psychosocial factors affecting migration. With respect to African Americans, sociologists have usually viewed rapid and large-scale Black migration and population growth as sources of disequilibrium influencing urban social problems. Depending on the quantitative and qualitative character of Black migration, variable outcomes of disorganization, organization, and reorganization have been predicted for Black communities and the larger society.

During the early 1970s, Wilson taught a seminar at the University of Chicago on race relations that included lectures specifically focused on the urbanization of Blacks and the role of migration in group adaptation and assimilation. His early ideas on migration, which are presented in *Racism, Power, and Privilege*, provide a functional and ecological interpretation of intergroup relations that has complex outcomes. In this work, Wilson views the historic record and sees an integrative and progressive role that Black migration and population growth in the cities played during the Great Migration of the early twentieth century through the early post-World War II years in altering race relations. This functional-conflict interpretation of Black migration and mobility is consistent with classical urban ecological predictions based on the growing city. While he recognizes the racial antagonisms resulting from Black migration and population growth, these are ultimately integrative, resulting in Blacks' increased competitive resources and social mobility (Wilson 1973).

In his early work, Wilson is concerned with accounting for the movement from restrictive, paternalistic race relations to competitive race relations among Blacks (Wilson 1973, 52–59). Competitive race relations, that are usually associated with industrialization and urbanization, are accompanied by class differences becoming more salient relative to caste (Wilson 1973, 53). In accounting for the turn-of-the century Black migration, he advances the familiar hypothesis that Black migration to cities was accounted for by push, pull, and social agency factors associated with growing northern industrialization and southern agricultural decline. Despite beginning slowly, sharp labor shortages during World War I resulted in northern industrialists initiating campaigns with Black leaders, newspapers, and institutions to recruit large numbers of Black labor.

As a consequence of the increased size of Blacks in cities, the intense economic competition between Blacks and White immigrants was reflected in hatred and bigotry. According to Wilson, physical (spatial) segregation was introduced to protect the dominant group's status and minimize contact between the races (Wilson 1973, 53). Constrained by the ghetto, Blacks initially made little progress in terms of assimilation and consequently turned inward to racial consciousness and Black nationalism. Through the 1920s and the Great Depression of the 1930s, Black protest was largely restricted by institutionalized racism and segregation to the ghetto. Social and residential mobility for Blacks were largely constrained during this period (Wilson 1973, 105–108).

Beginning with the New Deal, Wilson argues that protective union policies of the Roosevelt administration, the increasing influence of the Black vote in cities, and federal initiatives to hire Blacks resulted in new movements of optimism, interracial cooperation, and civil rights protest. An important factor influencing these structural changes was the changed stance of industrial unions on race as represented by the antidiscrimination position of the Congress of Industrial Organizations (CIO). It is in the context of the Great Depression, agricultural modernization, early post-World War II industrialization and urbanization that the increasing wartime and post-World War II Black migration and growth of modern industrial race relations occur.

Although not emphasized by Wilson, the context of Black urban population growth, occurring during the early post-World War II decades of the 1940s and 1950s, was characterized by the largest actual volume of net Black out-migration from the South during the century. Compared to the Great Migration from the turn-of-the-century through the 1930s, the annual rate of Black out-migration from the South to northern and western cities during these early post-World War II years increased dramatically. In fact, the Kerner Commission Report emphasizes that more Blacks migrated from the south to the north and west during the 1940s (1,597,000) than migrated over the entire 1910–1940 period (1,541,000). As early as the 1960s, natural reproduction (the excess of births replacing deaths) had replaced in-migration as the primary demographic explanation of Black urban growth (National Advisory Commission on Civil Disorders 1968).

During this period of steady industrialization, Wilson advances that Black social mobility, deriving from the expanding employment, occupational improvements, and rising education, interacted with growing Black political resources. It is significant that in the North the employment growth of Blacks was accompanied by even more rapid economic growth among Whites that lessened the perception that Blacks were "threats." The industrialization that resulted in the increasing integration of Blacks in the economy was accompanied by their continued segregation into ghettos, which was eventually mobilized into protests and public policy reforms. Yet while this Black migration and urbanization partly contributed to the social organization, institutional differentiation, and political power of Blacks in cities, Wilson sees the competitive resources of Blacks and participation in urban politics through World War II as subordinated by party political machines and buffer institutions. Wilson argues that the subordination of the Black ghetto in city politics by White ethnic machines through World War II limited the historic occupational and status mobility of Blacks (Wilson 1973; Wilson 1978).

In *The Declining Significance of Race*, Wilson discusses the consequences of Black demographic growth and the prospects of mobility through political power. He emphasizes that during the 1960s and 1970s, when Blacks were making economic gains and gaining political control in some cities, the concentration of political power in metropolitan areas was shifting away from political parties to complex corporate bureaucracies (Wilson 1978, 78–87). Wilson is clear in noting that Black political power gains, which partly reflect the changing racial demographics of cities, are now augmented by broader macrosociological changes in power which involve a "politics of dependency" where the role of federal- and state-level funding and control in urban political processes is increasing (Wilson 1978, 139). This assessment of the prospects of Black social mobility through political empowerment and "plural but equal" strategies while necessary is not sufficient for Wilson. The challenge for Black social mobility and assimilation appears less a question of cultural and civic assimilation, and more a challenge of structural integration in the economy.

These discussions of Black migration and population growth are concerned not only with social mobility (integration), but also residential mobility (desegregation). In his theoretical formulations, the dynamics of Black migration, population growth and social mobility are largely moved by macrostructural economic and political changes that are both national and localized. Wilson's formulations of the intersection between Black urban migration, population change, and residential mobility draw largely from assumptions and concepts of urban neighborhood racial change that grow out of assimilation and ecological perspectives. While conflicts between racial groups are explicit in earlier work, these are understated in more recent discussions.

In more recent work, Wilson is less concerned with the integrative intragroup consequences of in-migration and population growth for Black competitive resources and mobility. Instead, his interests in population questions are increasingly focused on accounting for the Black underclass. Raising questions concerning the relationships between migration flow and mobility he hints at more regressive consequences of this phenomenon in contemporary cities (Wilson 1987, 34–35). In this revision, he becomes more interested in the "population explosion among minority youth" in cities and the consequences that these have for the age structure and future of cities (Wilson 1987, 36–39).

Examining the same Black urban migration that was earlier interpreted as functional for social organization, institutional differentiation, and mobility, Wilson now asks whether many current problems of the ghetto poor are "partly the result of the heavy Black urban migration that occurred throughout the first half of this century." To the extent that Wilson is constrained to understate the continuing significance of race, demographic factors are considered as alternative explanations. In essence, the growth rate and age structure of populations in urban Black communities have played important roles in the development of the underclass.

Wilson's primary argument emphasizes that the arrival of large numbers of Blacks during a short time span in the Great Migration of the industrial city "made it much more difficult for Blacks to follow the path of both the Europeans and Asian Americans in overcoming the negative effects of discrimination by finding special occupational niches." This historic mass migration appears characterized as an "in-migration of the poor." However, Wilson is aware that the "in-migration of the poor" hypothesis has weak empirical support and goes on to summarize the evidence which invalidates the in-migration of the poor hypothesis: (1) research showing higher rates of employment, income, and education among migrants vis-à-vis non-migrants, and (2) studies showing that recent Black migration to cities is relatively small and decreasing. At the same time, however, he apparently leaves open a related question of whether the size of the historic Black migration that continued several decades after the cessation of European and Asian immigration is directly associated with contemporary Black urban poverty.

Wilson hypothesizes that the "discontinuation of large-scale immigration from Japan and China enabled those Chinese and Japanese already in the United States to solidify networks of ethnic contacts and to occupy particular occupational niches in small, relatively stable communities" (Wilson 1987, 141). Does this mean that the lower contemporary status of African Americans vis-à-vis Chinese and Japanese Americans is to be largely explained by the cessation of historic immigration? Or might changes in the selectivity of Asian-American immigration, since the Immigration Reform Act of 1965, more adequately explain their increased status? Unfortunately, Wilson's generalizations gloss over the details of Chinese- and Japanese-American immigration histories.

A careful reading of these immigration histories would show the following sociological facts that contextualize these group histories and race relations. First, this explanation glosses over the role of international migration in the status upgrading of both Japanese and Chinese Americans during this period and particularly since the 1965 immigration reforms (Hart-Cellar). Compared to all immigrants and the native born American population, Asian immigrants were in relative terms more frequently represented in professional backgrounds prior to immigration (Wong and Hirschman 1983, 395–397). Second, this explanation obscures the reality that large segments of Asian populations in the United States are far from the "success story" and prosperity of the "niche" hypothesis. The immigration histories of Chinese and Japanese Americans in the United States indicate that their changing social and economic status has had less to do with the discontinuation of large-scale immigration that enabled the solidification of ethnic niches, networks, and enclaves. More important have been occupational preferences built into immigration reform laws, selectivity, settlement, and human capital factors.

Without this context, we are left with another version of the "Asian success myth," which has incorporated the hypothesis that decreasing or smaller migration flow is axiomatically an upgrading and selectivity factor in a group's social and economic status. At the same time, there is zero-sum logic of the relationships between in-migration and assimilation. Are we to believe that if groups have large scale and increasing in-migration, then the consequences for community life will with high probability involve increasing poverty and social dislocation? Conversely, if groups have small-scale and decreasing in-migration, then the consequences for community life are more promising and will involve relatively decreasing poverty and social integration.

The historic record indicates that the relationships between in-migration, size of population, and social and economic status are more variable and complex than presented. At the beginning of the twentieth century, urban Blacks that were established in business and professional activities experienced dislocations independent of and prior to the mass migrations. Between the turn-of-the- century and World War II, the volume of Black international migration by decades was among the most restrictive. Even during more rapid periods of migration, the contribution of Black immigration to overall Black population growth has usually been less than 15 percent.

One of the unintended consequences of Wilson's analysis of contemporary Black population growth is the policy implication of "smaller is better" through less Black migration. This has international, national, and local level dimensions. Although immigration of Blacks from the Caribbean and Africa remain among the currently most selective, opening these up would be problematic and destabilizing based on the arguments presented.

It should be noted that Wilson's policy prescriptions are more directly concerned with the redistribution of inner city Black populations to other places in the metropolis to improve their quality of life. Alongside macroeconomic changes, the redistribution of Black populations from the inner-city ghetto, in terms of commuting to suburban employment or residential movements to other neighborhoods is an important strategy of integration. The Gatreaux housing experiments in Chicago offer the possibilities of reintegrating the poor outside of the concentration of public housing.

Contained in the underside of these discussions are at least two popular theories or cultural beliefs appropriated by Wilson that in retrospect emphasize the failure of Black migrants in inner cities to adapt and assimilate—last of the immigrants theory, and the southern origins theory. The "last of the immigrants theory," emphasized by neoconservative perspectives of the 1960s, advances that Blacks are the most recent unskilled and low-income migrant group to reach the city (Banfield 1970). The "southern origins" theory, emphasized by Nicholas Lemann (Lemann 1986; Lemann 1991), argues that cities have historically attracted Black migrants who in turn have imported poverty and other forms of social disorganization.

Carole Marks argues that this "failure of Black migrants to assimilate" explanation does place the question of mobility in the structural context of industrial development and concludes that, in general, some times are better than others to migrate and that Blacks in particular, migrated at the wrong time (Marks 1989, 155). Although this line of reasoning represents an advance over traditional explanations such as the "legacy of slavery," or "racial oppression," Marks notes such theories leave unexplained why Black workers, residing in northern cities during the expansive period of the 1890s, experienced little social mobility in a society that had open doors of opportunity for immigrants. Marks notes further that "this perspective assumes that there was a better time for Black migration but begs the question of when that time would have been" (Marks 1989, 156). The "southern origins" theory has long been invalidated as tenable sociological theory (Tilly 1970). Compared to residents of northern cities, Black migrants have usually had lower rates of poverty and higher rates of two-parent families. Rates of crime and delinquency among migrants are generally lower than among residents (Tilly 1970, 158–160).

Wilson's interests in population growth become refocused in *The Declining Significance of Race* and *The Truly Disadvantaged* on the disorganizational consequences of the rapidly growing Black teenage population. Here, his discussions of the population explosion of young Blacks does not appear to grow directly from his initial analyses of economic opportunities conducive to historic urban migration and population growth accompanying industrialization but rather derive from concerns of deindustrialization and the growth of the underclass. There is a convergence here between Black population growth and the Malthusian theory of population (Malthus 1985). While comparing the growth of central city Black teenagers and White teenagers during the 1960s, in his book *The Declining Significance of Race*, Wilson highlights a 75 percent to 14 percent growth rate (Wilson 1978, 93). This unprecedented increase, which is associated with high levels of joblessness, high school drop-outs, juvenile delinquency, and crime exacerbates the "urban crisis."

In *The Truly Disadvantaged*, he attempts to account for the increase in Black unemployment among Blacks in general and Black teenagers specifically. Wilson argues that structural changes in employment (the lack of higher paying manufacturing jobs), an economic slowdown, and the rapid growth of Black teenagers are central. While recognizing that overall Black marital and non-marital fertility rates have fallen substantially since the 1960s, he underscores that Black out-of-wedlock births and particularly teenage births have increased "precipitously" (Wilson 1987, 66–71).

To his credit, he primarily accounts for the changing fertility and family structure in terms of increasing male joblessness. Macrosociological rather than microsociological factors are primary. Yet in another context, he draws from James Q. Wilson's discussions in advancing that the relative increase in minority young people, which has been actually slowing down and decreasing since 1970, may have reached a "critical mass" creating an explosive problem in the amount of crime, addiction, and welfare dependency (Wilson 1987, 38). Wilson's prescriptions for this "population explosion" are missing and left for other experts to frame. The Malthusian framing of the population problem here is less an objective problem than a subjective one. It would appear that the structural conditions explaining these developments in crime and addiction are similar to those explaining the changing fertility and family structure—increasing male joblessness. Built into the "population explosion" and "critical mass" concepts is a j-curve assumption of increased crime and deviance that is disconnected from human agency and progressive reforms in public policy. Although Wilson doesn't propose or intend institutionalization, the policy implications for the latter move by default in a direction of increased policing, prisons, and social control that contrast with the macroeconomic reforms that are actually advanced by him.

RACIAL SEGREGATION AND GHETTOIZATION

One of the most difficult sociological questions centers on the persistent racial residential segregation of Blacks, its causes, and consequences. Wilson's discussions of racial segregation and ghettoization are shaped by two broader concerns. A first concern is that of developing a stages theory of the history of race relations between Blacks and Whites in the United States. A second concern is that of linking hyperghettoization with deindustrialization and macroeconomic changes. Both of these concerns influence how he has examined racial segregation. While both of these concerns involve making macrosociological and microsociological linkages of institutional, urban community, and intergroup relations, he will introduce shifts in his conceptualizations and hypotheses over time that are characterized as increasing impersonality, rationality, and deracialization.

The urban ecological interests, while descriptive in his earlier work, become more theoretically explicit in later work. Where he is not principally concerned with urbanization or urban structure, he is continually required to account for its role in facilitating competitive race relations in general and the status of Blacks specifically. Out of this concern with urbanization is derived a discussion of segregation. For Wilson, what role(s) does urbanization play in the dynamics of segregation? How do the dynamics of segregation affect urban spatial structure?

Wilson views segregation as a social structure and process providing both possibilities and constraints for Black social, economic, and political movement. Historically and situationally, segregation has had both organizational and disorganizational consequences for Black communities.

HISTORIC SEGREGATION

In discussing the preindustrial stage of race relations, Wilson outlines the relationships between paternalistic race relations and Black-White contact in the cities during slavery. During slavery, he notes that the social distance between Blacks and Whites within cities was challenged by the high degree of physical contact and imperatives of a system of urban slave labor whereby slaves worked in their masters' businesses and were hired out. Under these conditions, the racial concentration of Blacks was minimized by norms discouraging geographic segregation and encouraging indirect supervision. Consequently, slaves lived side by side with their masters and other Whites and slaves who "lived out"; free Blacks, however, were scattered throughout the city (Wilson 1978, 37–39). In contrast, the social distance between races and the system of status inequalities was wide on the plantations and farms of the Deep South and was relatively unchallenged by close physical contacts. He hypothesizes that the segregation that developed in cities was a spatial social relation that created social distance where there was physical proximity (Wilson 1978, 39). This racial segregation was a symbol of racial caste, a form of racial control, and a dimension of the transition from paternalistic to competitive race relations. These patterns of racial segregation and other manifestations of competitive race relations in cities of the antebellum South, according to Wilson, "were never anywhere as harsh or developed as in the postbellum South or even the late antebellum North" (Wilson 1978, 39). Wilson views the emergence of the Jim Crow segregation laws as directly paralleling the rise of the White working class to its political power in the labor reform movement and its eventual alliance with the ruling class. He argues that in the North during industrial expansion, Blacks were initially "invisible" and not perceived as an economic threat (Wilson 1978, 63). This would soon change with the Great Migration.

In *Power, Racism, and Privilege*, Wilson identifies the historic reversals in discrimination and residential segregation that accompanied the Black migration and urbanization north at the turn of the century. During the era of industrial race relations or "Jim Crow Segregation and Biological Racism" (1890s–1930s), Black migration to northern cities was accompanied by increasing segregation and restriction (Wilson 1973, 104). Informed by the seminal analyses of Stanley Lieberson's research (Lieberson 1980), he argues that although initial levels of Black segregation were lower than those of some European immigrant groups, from 1890 on Black residential segregation became more concentrated and distinctive.

Why is this the case? Wilson offers the following hypotheses to account for this: (1) the increased competition, hostility, and tension between Blacks and immigrant groups in adjacent neighborhoods and Black "spillover," (2) the role of landlords in playing Blacks against Whites in raising rents, and (3) the role of White violence as a social control (Wilson 1973, 106–108). In this discussion of racial segregation, Wilson largely explains its historic patterns in terms of institutional, community, housing, and intergroup relationships that bring together classic ecological and social history interpretations. Here, there is no specification of the independent effects of class and race as variables. They are clearly interactive. There is little suggestion of the primacy of social class explanations of segregation consistent with liberal expectancy and neo-Marxian perspectives. Earlier dimensions of macro-level power conflict, evident in his discussion of preindustrial segregation during the industrial stage, have shifted to the community.

CONTEMPORARY SEGREGATION

Although the economic prosperity at the turn-of-the century through the 1920s improved the employment opportunities for Whites, these improvements had relatively little effect on Blacks through the 1930s. Accompanying the era of modern industrial race relations or "Competitive Race Relations and the Proliferation of Racial Protests" (1940–1970), Black migration and urbanization in the North and South are characterized by most Blacks experiencing social, economic, and political gains. He is careful to note that this social and economic advancement was heavily dependent on national economic growth and governmental policies associated with the New Deal, World War II, and the post-World War II years.

Despite structures of racial discrimination and segregation that restricted Blacks in the ghetto, there were organized consequences. At the same time that economic growth and governmental reforms occurred, the mobilized social action and leadership protesting these conditions in Black communities became steadily more resistant and militant. The competitive resources gained by Blacks in these industrial cities were more economic and political.

It is instructive that in *Power, Racism, and Privilege*, Wilson noted that "economic factors played a relatively minor role in the physical separation of Whites and Blacks" (Wilson 1973, 143). Drawing from the seminal research by Karl and Alma Taeuber (Taeuber and Taeuber 1965), he underscored: "Continued economic gains are not likely to alter substantially the prevalent patterns of residential segregation" (Wilson 1973, 143). Improved competitive resources derived from economic and class integration did not translate into desegregation.

It is during this stage of "Competitive Race Relations and Racial Protests" (1940s to the 1970s) where he argues that biological arguments of racism give way to cultural racism. In *Power, Racism, and Privilege*, Wilson hypothesizes that during the competitive race relations of the post-World War II years "the most effective way that the society of the United States is able "to maintain inequality while at the same time acknowledging as legitimate subordinate groups demands for more is through the pervasive and persistent practice of institutional discrimination" (Wilson 1973, 142).

Further, he notes: "Even though racist norms that directed the systematic exclusion of Blacks from full participation in stable, patterned, and organized procedures are no longer fervently supported, the fact that many features originally based on these norms continue to persist is testimony to the lasting influence of institutional racism" (Wilson 1973, 142). This concept of institutional racism appearing in this earlier work will not merely decline in significance in later work but will disappear as a concept altogether. The same concept is replaced by "effects of historic discrimination" in subsequent work. Wilson's articulation of the concept of institutional racism is largely normative and "value-added."

Although earlier arguing that competitive resources derived from economic and class integration did not translate into residential desegregation for Blacks, Wilson later plays to the "declining significance of race" thesis in his forecasts for the social and residential mobility of middle-class Blacks in Chicago (Suro 1978). In responding to the question of "How do you see the relations between Blacks and Whites evolving between now and 1990?" Wilson predicted, as more middle- and upper- class Blacks move into White areas of Chicago, these areas will be peacefully and successfully integrated. He did not see the rapid racial turnover of the past occurring but noted "people who share a level of affluence are finding ways of living together despite racial differences" (Suro 1978, 16). This prediction was based on trends affecting relatively small populations within the Black upper and middle class and spatially expressed in the North Side high-rise communities (Suro 1978, 16).

Despite the sweeping tone of these statements, Wilson does not explicitly state a dominant pattern of racial segregation for Blacks in *The Declining Significance of Race* (1978). One might expect, that the earlier conclusions concerning the persistence of racial segregation independent of economics and social class might still hold. In the absence of this, the implications for movement from the ghetto become more class-based. At some points, there are suggestions that larger trends of decentralization and suburbanization might be fundamentally altering historic patterns of segregation as in his discussions of Black middle-class movements from the ghetto in *The Declining Significance of Race* and *The Truly Disadvantaged*. At other places, such as in *The Truly Disadvantaged*, there are suggestions that segregation may in fact be continuing (if not increasing) for the ghetto poor and underclass. These different analyses of racial segregation grow out of a class-based conceptualization of the structural features of discrimination. Racial caste assumptions remain for the underclass.

Wilson's treatment of segregation in discussions of the urban underclass are captured by "social isolation," "concentration effects," and "hyperghettoization." In contrast to his earlier concerns with symbolic, social control, and caste dimensions of racial segregation, Wilson increasingly focuses on ecological and distributional dimensions of "disproportionate concentration" that characterize the most disadvantaged urban Black population (Wacquant and Wilson 1989; Wilson 1987). In these discussions, segregation remains a spatial relationship of social and physical distance reflecting macrosociological and intergroup relations. However, it appears driven more by structural forces of joblessness than racial discrimination. By the 1980s, mutually reinforcing spatial and industrial changes converged through class and racial exclusion and marginality to undermine the traditional ghetto for the poorest (Wacquant and Wilson 1989, 11). Primary among these industrial changes are the decentralization of industries, the deconcentration of metropolitan economies and turn toward services, and flexible forms of corporate organization. The Black ghetto of earlier becomes the jobless ghetto. Secondary to this exclusion and marginality is racial discrimination. These deracializing conceptualizations of segregation, while recognizing urban Black poverty as problematic, shift traditional concerns of racial discrimination and segregation to the effects of discrimination and the "hidden agenda."

AN APPRAISAL OF WILSON'S PERSPECTIVES OF SEGREGATION AND GHETTOIZATION

Wilson's perspectives of historic segregation synthesize important insights from social history, human ecology, and race relations. His societal analysis makes important linkages between different stages of race relations, the social and spatial forms of segregation, and accompanying ideological systems of racism. In hypothesizing racial segregation as a dominant form of racial caste and control in the transition from paternalistic to competitive race relations, he has correctly identified it as a historically specific sociological fact that became most developed in the postbellum South and the industrial North. His hypothesis for the emergence of the Jim Crow segregation laws, as directly correlated with the rising political power of the White working class in labor reform movement and its alliance with the ruling class, is informed by Marxian and split-labor market insights. His discussion of the organizational consequences of racial segregation for the mobilization of the civil rights movement is well-documented.

Wilson's handling of racial segregation in *The Truly Disadvantaged* can be characterized as an attempt to discuss the ghettoization and social isolation of the inner-city poor, using the growing city model of segregation and the integration of the new Black middle class into the opportunity structure, alongside an increasingly deracialized discourse. He wants to discuss racial segregation without reference to the persistent institutional contexts of racism. The logic of segregation derives from a growing industrial city earlier in the century. Although he recognizes that racial segregation continues to exist, it appears less central in the contemporary emergence and growth of the underclass than historically. To the extent that macroeconomic changes are primary and segregation has become more class-based, new sensitizing concepts of the underclass discourse such as poverty ghettos, hyperghettoization, and jobless ghettos replace racial segregation and institutional discrimination.

His discussions of post–World War II and contemporary racial segregation are less explicit and more problematic than his analyses of historic segregation. While recognizing the formation of historic ghettos and changes in current ghettos, he does not integrate insights that address the reorganization and persistence of racial segregation. Unlike the preindustrial and industrial stages, he is not definitive in articulating a dominant spatial pattern of segregation for the current Black community in general. By implication, segregation appears to vary by social class. At some points, there are suggestions that decentralization and suburbanization might be fundamentally altering historic patterns as in his discussions of Black middle-class movements to the suburbs in *The Declining Significance of Race*. At other places, such as in *The Truly Disadvantaged*, there are suggestions that segregation may in fact be increasing for the ghetto poor and underclass. These different analyses of racial segregation grow out of a class-based conceptualization of the structural features of discrimination.

In an early review of the *Truly Disadvantaged*, Adolph Reed noted that "by overlooking codified segregation, Wilson has overlooked the most central issue in Black life and how these are products of conscious human action and in turn create contexts within which people fashion specific agendas" (Reed 1988, 168). According to Reed:

> The transformation of postwar industrial cities was not driven by some abstract historical force but by a combination of private reinvestment decisions and state action. The impetus was centered around an urban renewal policy that along with explicitly segregationist policies in Federal public housing policy—cut off minority communities, displaced large sections of these communities and concern treated them between expressways, office complexes, stadiums and civic centers.
> There is the source of Wilson social isolation. (Reed, 1988)

The most systematic theoretical and empirical critique of Wilson's treatment of racial segregation is contained in Douglas Massey and Nancy Denton's *American Apartheid: Segregation and the Making of the Underclass* (1993). They argue "residential segregation is the principal organizational feature of American society responsible for the creation of the urban underclass" (Massey and Denton 1993, 8). While agreeing with Wilson's main thesis that macroeconomic dislocations negatively impacted inner city Black communities, they emphasize the interaction of racial segregation with poverty. They add "in the absence of segregation, these structural changes would not have produced the disastrous social and economic outcomes observed in inner cities during these decades" (Massey and Denton 1993, 8). The "hypersegregation," which is experienced by Blacks, and is reinforced by racial prejudice and discrimination, further builds deprivation into the residential structure of Black communities to such an extent that "When the rate of poverty is increased under conditions of high segregation, all of the increase is absorbed by a small number of neighborhoods" (Massey and

Denton 1993, 12). Massey and Denton's findings and generalizations draw from several empirical studies (Denton and Massey 1988; Massey and Eggers 1990; Massey 1990; Eggers and Massey 1991; Massey, Gross, and Shibuya 1994).

Paul Jargowsky's *Poverty and Place: Ghettos, Barrios, and the American City* (1997) provides comprehensive empirical evidence of changes in neighborhood poverty which more strongly validates Wilson's class-based hypotheses while critically appraising several of the racial segregation effects and conclusions identified in Massey and Denton's research. Jargowsky notes that with respect to the "demographic transition" hypothesis, the key empirical issues center on whether the out-movement of middle-class Blacks was large enough to measurably impact ghetto poverty and the importance of Black middle-class flight relative to other explanations of neighborhood poverty (Jargowsky 1997, 132–138). Jargowsky provides extensive demographic data documenting how Black middle class out-movement in United States metropolitan areas during the 1980s resulted in increasing concentrated poverty (Massey 1997, chaps. 1–4). Jargowsky finds evidence for changes in economic segregation among Blacks, explaining the changes in ghetto poverty and the overall level of economic segregation, helped explain ghetto poverty in 1990 (Jargowsky 1997, 183). Simultaneously, Jargowsky identifies evidence of economic segregation among Blacks in a cross-examination of the data and models used by Massey (Massey and Eggers 1990; Massey and Denton 1993; Massey, Gross, and Shibuya 1994).

With respect to the effects of racial segregation, Jargowsky notes that it is the interaction between high levels of racial segregation and poverty that explains the growth of neighborhood poverty rather than segregation in isolation as the key factor (Jargowsky 1997, 143). Relatedly, he questions how racial segregation can explain much of the recent increases in ghetto poverty since it has been declining (Jargowsky 1997, 143). However, he does acknowledge that racial segregation has indirect effects on Black income distribution that has consequences on capital accumulation (Jargowsky 1997, 183). Jargowsky also acknowledges that these alternative hypotheses of poverty change, such as Black economic status and economic segregation, may well turn out to be functions of past or current racial segregation (Jargowsky 1997, 142). The theoretical arguments of "the origins of the underclass" and continuing racial segregation based on Massey and Denton's analyses remain persuasive.

Insights from urban history also might inform this discussion of changing post-World War II segregation. Kenneth Jackson's *Crabgrass Frontiers* has broadly identified the historic federal housing initiatives of the Home Owners Loan Corporation (HOLC), the Federal Housing Administration (FHA), and the United States Housing Administration (USHA) and changing macrosociological bases of post-World War II suburban growth and ghettoization. For example, the Home Owners Loan Corporation (HOLC) by initiating a systematic rating criteria that undervalued central city neighborhoods that were dense, mixed, or aging, generated a formal and uniform practice of distributing home mortgages that largely excluded Blacks. Also, the Federal Housing Administration (FHA) through "redlining" helped turn the building industry against the inner-city and minority housing market and its policies supported the income and racial segregation of suburbia (Jackson 1985).

Relatedly, Arnold Hirsch in *Making the Second Ghetto: Race and Housing in Chicago, 1940–1960,* provides a useful analysis of the macrosociological dynamics underlying post-World War II segregation informing Wilson's examination (Hirsch 1983). Hirsch argues that the post-World War II government involvement in slum clearance, urban renewal, and public housing not only reinforced earlier patterns of segregation, which were limited to judicial interpretations of restrictive covenants, but also dynamically institutionalized new forms of de facto segregation. While federal legislation provided some statutory recognition that might have challenged racial segregation and discrimination, the discretion provided local officials permitted evasion of mandatory requirements and the overlooking of constructive approaches.

Hirsch goes further to explain the presence of high concentrations of Blacks in the public housing and the inner city as the consequence of complex forces including business, political machines, redevelopment agencies, universities, and ethnic communities (Hirsch 1983). Single-site and high-density building in central area land as opposed to scattered-site and low-density building in relatively more outlying land are seen as the outcomes of actual decision making and policy formulation rather than "concentration effects." Furthermore, historic attempts at urban redevelopment and managed integration in the Hyde Park community area, which border the University of Chicago, limited the expansion of Chicago's Black community to the east and west while constraining its southern movement (Hirsch 1983, 255).

The empirical research examining the changing distributional and segregation patterns of Blacks in cities and metropolitan areas since 1970, does not validate the broad outlines of Wilson's segregation hypotheses. It is possible that Wilson's interpretations of what had changed with respect to the residential segregation of Blacks between *Power, Racism, and Privilege* and subsequent writings went through more rapid transformation than what was actually occurring. Several ideas of the dominant cultural belief system of Black progress, which are reflected in leading conservative policy perspectives and journalistic discussions, enter these interpretations.

It seems ironic that the Chicago metropolitan area would form the context, social facts, and impressions that would lead Wilson to the sociological generalization that Blacks are leaving the ghetto or that there is an increasing class polarization and social distance between middle- and lower-class Blacks. Until recently, the Chicago metropolitan area has experienced relatively limited Black suburbanization and been statistically described as one of the more hypersegregated metropolitan areas nationally (Massey 1989). It is even more ironic that Wilson has not critically examined the question of racial segregation in his later work considering his earlier directions and the importance of this problem in urban ecology. His use of the concepts "social isolation" and "concentration effects" attempt to capture these traditional concerns of racial segregation in terms of class segregation.

As a counter-hypothesis, it can be argued that recent movements of Blacks into more decentralized, outlying, and suburban racially changing Black communities within postindustrial metropolitan areas have been accompanied by the persistence of high levels of racial segregation and institutional discrimination which suggests the reorganization of the traditional inner-city ghetto into the contemporary metropolitan ghetto. Contemporary Black suburbanization is generally characterized by the higher centralization of Blacks in inner suburbs where they remain locationally closer to other Blacks than Whites. Outlying upper and upper-middle class Black communities are frequently "gilded ghettos," which are contiguous or nearby lower-middle class and working-class Black communities.

Although there are vestiges of the historic urban development factors such as the concentration of inner-city Black poor in private renter apartments and low-income single-site public housing (or "projects"), since the 1970s macrosociological changes in the economy and housing market have increasingly put into motion a reorganization of the internal spatial structure of the central city and residential movements affecting inner-city ghettos. As cities make the transition from commercial and industrial centers to postindustrial administrative and service centers, there is greater centralization of activities involving corporate decision making, financing, government, and conventions in the central business district and nearby areas, and the emerging presence of new downtown construction, gentrification, and apartment conversions in central area neighborhoods. As land, construction, and financing costs have risen more rapidly than household incomes, the rental housing markets within central cities are caught in a "vicious cycle" where the supply of lower-priced housing has decreased. This tightening of the housing market, coupled with the increasing concentrated poverty in inner cities is resulting in a more marginal group of households subject to displacement, homelessness, and "emptying-out" as a complex function of racial segregation, redlining, disinvestment, abandonment, arson, and the deterioration of housing.

While a disproportionate share of minorities and poor people still live in central cities, increasingly, more decentralized and outlying neighborhoods within central cities, rather than inner-city neighborhoods, are becoming the new residences of the poor.

The reorganization of historically specific racial segregation in the postindustrial city suggests that the growth and concentration of the Black poor in the inner city are transitional or temporary processes. Inner-city neighborhoods, while segregated by race and class, are transitional areas. Interestingly, Wilson will integrate important elements of these critiques including the role of segregation, urban renewal, gentrification, and housing abandonment into his descriptions and analyses of *When Work Disappears* (1996).

CHAPTER 5

THE SOCIAL AND MORAL ORDER OF THE BLACK COMMUNITY
Social Isolation, Concentration Effects, and Disorganization

BACKGROUND

One continuing controversy in urban sociology has centered on how to best explain the complex forms of social organization and patterned behavior of life in urban communities. Early on, classical Chicago School sociologists recognized that macrosociological factors of commercialization, industrialization, and the division of labor were accompanied by the increased scale of demographic and ecological factors such as population size, density, and diversity that contributed to urbanism as a way of life and the cultural differentiation of groups by neighborhoods (Park, Burgess, and McKenzie 1925; Burgess 1925; Wirth 1938). While this cultural differentiation contributed to the integration of groups in the division of labor, it simultaneously resulted in their segregation and social isolation. Consequently, heightened racial segregation and social isolation were disorganizing conditions of nonassimilation.

The theme of the disorganized social and moral order of urban Black communities, which has grown out of social isolation and segregation, and has resulted in the nonassimilation of Blacks is a generalization which is influenced by social science insights and cultural beliefs coming out of public policy controversies. In *The Negro Family in the United States*, E. Franklin Frazier viewed within the racial segregation of urban Black communities an internal class differentiation where Black families were variably assimilated to mainstream American culture by social class. Middle-class Black families that were most integrated into the industrial economy and division of labor generally experienced greater sociocultural organization within the constraints of racial segregation. Lower-class Black families, that were the most weakly

97

integrated into the industrial economy and division of labor, experienced greater disorganization in their adaptation (Frazier 1966). Gunnar Myrdal, in *An American Dilemma*, saw within racially segregated Black institutions of the family, church, education, and voluntary associations the bases for a pathological form of community (Myrdal 1944). Myrdal concluded that social relationships of isolation, poverty, and ignorance created by slavery and urbanization resulted in Black cultural forms that were significantly different from mainstream American culture (Myrdal 1944, 927–956). In St. Clair Drake and Horace Cayton's *Black Metropolis* (1945), large statistical variations in social characteristics of the Black community such as poverty, family relief, illegitimacy, women employed in domestic and personal services, juvenile delinquency, disease, and mortality were analyzed as normative deviations and social disorganization (Drake and Cayton 1945, 174–214).

Themes of the segregation and social isolation of Black urban communities were appropriated in leading public policy analyses and discourses of Black poverty during the War on Poverty. In Moynihan's *The Negro Family*, the complex forces of the legacy of slavery, Black migration and urbanization, and Black male unemployment resulted in a self-perpetuating "tangle of pathology" reflected in the breakdown of the Negro family in urban ghettos (Moynihan 1965). Elsewhere, Edward Banfield in *The Unheavenly City* explained the poverty of urban Blacks by a distinctive patterning of attitudes, values, goals, and modes of behavior (Banfield 1970, 56). This ghetto-specific life style was seen as present-oriented, attaching no value to work, sacrifice, and service to family, friends, and community (Banfield 1970, 235).

During the 1960s, sociological perspectives that recognized the importance of social institutions, power-conflict, and social action situated the segregation and social isolation of disorganized Black communities in larger societal contexts. In *Dark Ghetto*, Kenneth Clark emphasized that the self-perpetuating pathology of the ghetto as a "colony" was a function of larger institutional externalities (Clark 1965). Clark noted that the "invisible walls" of the ghetto that were created by White society and people of power confined these inhabitants and perpetuated their powerlessness (Clark 1965, 11). In Stokely Carmichael and Charles Hamilton's *Black Power: The Politics of Liberation in America*, the disorganization and poverty of Black communities were analyzed as political and economic colonization that was explained by broader structures of underdevelopment (Carmichael and Hamilton 1967). Although not based on a colonial analysis, community action programs such as Mobilization for Youth, the Woodlawn Project, and other action organizations such as George Wiley's Welfare Rights Organization viewed the social isolation and disorganization of the Black poor as fundamentally linked to powerlessness that might be affected by political mobilization and collective action. Since then, the weakening of the Black power movement and the derailing of community action programs have been accompanied by the declining significance of power-conflict analyses.

By the early 1980s, the leading perspectives explaining the social isolation and disorganization of the Black poor were conservative and these were largely decontextualized from macroeconomic and sociological contexts. Macrosociological factors such as changes in industrialization, the division of labor, the organization of population in central city and suburban communities, and racial segregation were rendered invisible in these analyses. At the same time, there was an unrelenting attempt to explain the growth of Black poverty by the excesses of civil rights movement and Great Society social policies. According to George Gilder's *Wealth and Poverty* (1981), poverty resulted from the demoralizing impact of public policy and in particular a perverse social welfare system that "erodes work and family and thus keeps poor people poor" (Gilder 1981, 153). Charles Murray argued that due to increased social welfare spending, there was a growth in poverty, antisocial behavior, an increased withdrawal of Blacks from the labor market, and more female-headed families (Murray 1984). These perspectives, which resonated with the New Federalism of the Reagan administration, became the conventional wisdom.

Black conservative discourses which also surfaced during the 1980s emphasized that escalating Black poverty resulted from the growth of civil rights and welfare state policies (Sowell 1983; Loury 1985), federal regulations and minimum wage policies that have undercut job creation (Williams 1982), the erosion of intermediary structures in Black communities such as families and neighborhood groups (Woodson 1987), and patterns of internalized victimization that has morally and psychologically constrained Black human potential (Steele 1990). In sociologically explaining the persistence of poverty, these were likely to emphasize microsociological human and social capital themes of inherited poverty from Black parents to Black children in the form of lower material resources and educational opportunities (Loury 1981).

In *The Truly Disadvantaged*, Wilson challenges the conservative conventional wisdom that attempted to explain the social and moral order of Black poverty in terms of welfare and the culture of poverty. While appropriating some of the arguments of conservative perspectives, he refocuses these into macrosociological and urban contexts. He identifies a new dimension of the urban crisis during the 1980s in the increasing rates of social dislocation in ghetto neighborhoods that are signified by joblessness, teenage pregnancy, out-of-wedlock births, female-headed families, welfare dependency, and serious crime. While recognizing that ghetto neighborhoods experienced high rates of poverty through mid-century, he argues that these earlier inner-city communities exhibited features of social organization including a sense of community, positive neighborhood identification, and explicit norms and sanctions against aberrant behavior. Consequently, the groups currently left behind are collectively different from earlier (Wilson 1987, 3–4).

Wilson's treatment of "social isolation" and "concentration effects" is an attempt at integrating a microsociological analysis of the causes and consequences of the underclass to his primary macrosociological explanation of economic restructuring and social dislocation. It also represents an attempt to link the culture of poverty to a structural analysis of poverty. He defines social isolation as "the lack of contact or sustained interaction with individuals and institutions that represent mainstream society' (Wilson 1987, 60) and concentration effects refer to "the different experiences of low-income families in inner-city neighborhoods compared to other urban neighborhoods" (Wilson 1987, 58). As ecological concepts, social isolation and concentration effects include spatial, demographic, and social organizational dimensions.

The concepts of social isolation and concentration effects, which are used to describe and analyze the social problems of poor Blacks living in the inner city, incorporate the ecological perspective in general and numerous assumptions of the "growing city" in particular. In illustrating the role of social isolation and concentration effects in the internal structure of families, life-styles, and groups in this Black community, Wilson addresses most directly the intersection between social structure and culture. This enables him to critique the culture of poverty perspective and simultaneously bring it into his more situational and holistic perspectives. The social isolation and concentration effects, which are associated with social and cultural disorganization, provide a microsociological framework.

The primary cause of the "desertification" of the ghetto is the continued out-movement of Black middle-class and working-class persons from the ghetto to suburban communities. This "class flight" has been generated in part by the civil rights policies of affirmative action and fair housing. The problematic consequences of this "demographic transition" for the internal structure and culture of the inner-city ghetto are at least threefold. First, the loss of the Black middle and working classes remove important social and economic buffers and sources of leadership with respect to the Black community's organizations and institutions. Second, the loss of the Black middle and working classes leaves a vacuum with respect to role models, social networks, and various sources of human and social capital that enable vertical integration. Third, in the absence of significant integration with Black middle and working class persons, the Black lower class and underclass that remain increasingly adapt a "ghetto-specific" culture that is focused on non-mainstream norms and values.

The contextualized and multilayered treatment of the social and moral order of the inner-city Black ghetto is primarily a response to the conservative public policy perspectives which have emphasized the "culture of poverty." It is a refocused sociological perspective that brings culture under the framework of social structure. While the racial segregation bearing on social isolation is described, the interaction effects are understated. More often the effects of social structure interacting with culture are examined through the internal relationships of group social structure.

These are illustrated in his discussions of the traditional and current ghetto and the numerous social problems that have accompanied the emergence and growth of the underclass.

This treatment of the social and moral order of the inner city has several interrelated layers. It is a critical response and appropriation of conservative and neoconservative discourses that have emphasized the excesses of the civil rights and Great Society programs, the role of welfare, and the culture of poverty. Simultaneously, Wilson's discussion of the social and moral order is partly inspired and influenced by the concepts and hypotheses of classical Chicago School sociologists such as Robert Park, Ernest Burgess, Louis Wirth, E. Franklin Frazier, St. Clair Drake, and Horace Cayton. The underlying assumptions of the growing city, internal structure, residential mobility, and racial segregation become incorporated into his analysis. Also, the manner in which Wilson treats ghetto life builds on the ethnographic and community studies of poor Blacks while moving beyond and refocusing these. In his attempt to move beyond the traditional liberal perspectives in which culture and racial isolation were primary factors explaining the moral and social order, his structural interpretation will draw importantly from the insights of human and social capital perspectives. Overall, his approach generally suggests more dependent effects than independent effects of culture with respect to social and economic organization. It also appears that the concepts of "social isolation" and "concentration effects" are part of an attempt to discuss the intersection of class, race, and culture in an increasingly deracialized and de-cultured discourse. The analysis of moral and social order eventually moves in the directions of social economics and social action theory.

The microsociological examination of the inner-city ghetto includes a formal analysis of these complex social relationships that are delimited, clearly presented, and meaningful. The possibilities of this approach derive from the generalizations and its bringing together of disparate concepts and hypotheses that interpret the norms, values, and cultural orientations of the inner city Black poor in the context of the larger social environment. There are also discussions that play to the cultural beliefs of mainstream social science and the dominant American belief system with respect to painting a picture of an authentic and pathological Black culture.

For purposes of this discussion, Wilson's treatment of the inner-city ghetto in *The Truly Disadvantaged* is largely focused on the microsociological argument and the related research. These mainly center on Wilson's treatment of the following: (1) bringing the analysis of ghetto culture into a structural perspective, (2) the comparison of the traditional and current ghetto, (3) the analyses of the decline of Black ghetto families, and (4) the integration of human and social capital perspectives.

BRINGING CULTURE INTO A SOCIAL STRUCTURAL THEORY

Wilson recognizes that the insights provided by the Chicago School theorists, revisions of these theories, and systematic social science research provide a more useful starting point for understanding the intersection of culture and social structure within inner-city poverty compared to conservative and revisionist Black solidarity perspectives. While conservative perspectives emphasize the importance of liberal social policies as increasing the culture of poverty, Black solidarity perspectives emphasize the adaptability and strengths of Black families. Wilson notices that both of these perspectives miss the important linkage of economic structure and culture.

His discussion of the dislocation among ghetto Blacks is an attempt at appraising and synthesizing two competing models—the culture of poverty model, and the situational model of poverty. The culture of poverty model argues that a permanent and pathological culture of poverty through ghetto-specific value orientations and norms function to increase the probability of social isolation, disorganization, and anomie thereby leading to mutually reinforcing deviant behavior, inability to take advantage of economic opportunity, social deprivation, and residence in poor neighborhoods. Accordingly, the ghetto-specific culture of inner-city Blacks differs significantly in substance from mainstream culture.

By contrast, the situational perspective advances that the value orientations and norms of ghetto Blacks are not significantly different from middle-class and working-class culture. Through economic dislocation and deprivation, the societally approved goals of mainstream society shared by the poor are increasingly blocked, which result in variable adaptations. Because the economic and power resources of the ghetto poor were limited to begin with, and have been more dramatically and rapidly reduced than other groups in contemporary American society, this situation of economically "falling behind" explains the increased breakdown of community, family, interpersonal and personal relationships, and their residence in poor neighborhoods. Under a different situation of economic growth, improved employment prospects, educational opportunity, and job training the chances of ghetto Blacks improving their socioeconomic and residential status would be more optimistic and upbeat.

Wilson argues that the social and moral order of inner-city poverty is primarily a situational consequence of two changing structural relationships—decreased high-paying employment, and the out-movement of the middle class from these neighborhoods. To the extent that work is increasingly disappearing in these neighborhoods, the traditional norms and beliefs bearing on hard work, school, and family are also eroding. To the extent that the nonpoor middle and working classes have left these neighborhoods, the earlier Black community institutions, vertical class integration, and role models that served as a "social buffer" to lower classes are absent. Accompanying the decline of employment, community institutions, and vertical class integration, the sense of community, positive neighborhood identification, and explicit norms against aberrant behavior have also declined.

He notes that "the concept of social isolation does not mean that cultural traits are irrelevant in understanding behavior in high concentrated poverty areas: rather it highlights the fact that culture is a response to social structural constraints and opportunities" (Wilson 1987, 61). The microsociological consequences of life in environments where work has disappeared is reflected in the weak labor market attachments, lack of access to dominant institutions and social networks of people with stable jobs, social orientation, and low perceived feelings of self-efficacy. Persons experiencing "social isolation from stable work relationships and persistent unemployment face constraints in developing organized community life."

Although his descriptions converge with conservative perspectives, unlike these perspectives, he does not generally view the pathology and disorganization as permanent. Wilson views culture as a dependent variable effected by social structure. He emphasizes "as economic and social situations change, cultural traits, created by previous situations, likewise eventually change even though it is possible that some will linger on and influence behavior for a period of time" (Wilson 1987, 138). While not ruling out that some cultural traits might become self-perpetuating and constraining (Wilson 1987, 138), he underscores that the growing emphasis on social values deflects attention from the major source of social dislocation—changes in the nation's economy.

Although the ghetto-specific culture of the Black poor is not clearly explicated, there are suggestions of what this ghetto-specific culture might mean. There are suggestions in *The Truly Disadvantaged* that the norms and values that have emerged among the poor are in essence coping norms that the poor have adapted. The sources of these norms and values include the disappearance of industrial employment, working adults who serve as role models, and work ethics. At the same time, alternative norms and values have emerged from the welfare system, illegal drug trade, prostitution, and other forms of crime and deviation. There are other suggestions that the ghetto-specific culture is limited to the most intractable elements of the lower-class families and persons that have experienced several generations of joblessness. For the most part, the elements of adaptation and coping in these conceptualizations have largely conservative implications with respect to cultural and human agency.

Wilson stops short of identifying a distinctively African American or Black culture in the ghetto. The assimilation assumptions of Blacks with respect to cultural and structural assimilation are strong. Because Blacks and the Black poor are essentially Americans culturally, there is assumed to be no distinctive African-American culture. There is the strong implication that the Black poor share fundamentally the same values of the mainstream society. The interactions of racial segregation, discrimination, and dominance with culture are largely isolating. Disorganization within the Black ghetto is also decontextualized and distanced from the colonization and power conflict contexts. Although it is possible that contained within the deviation and crime of the ghetto are cultures of opposition and resistance, these are not hinted at.

THE TRADITIONAL AND CURRENT GHETTO

Based on the neighboring Chicago community areas, Wilson compares the traditional and current ghetto to account for the changing social relationships of the contemporary ghetto. This comparison identifies the specific historical and cultural conditions of the changing inner city and clarifies the most important empirical variables. The traditional ghetto appears inspired by St. Clair Drake and Horace Cayton's *Black Metropolis* (1945). The current ghetto is an examination of the same neighborhoods based on the Urban Poverty and Family Life study. The descriptions provided are designed to help illustrate why the contemporary social problems concentrated in the inner city are much more difficult and intractable than earlier. While this is a simple comparison of a set of neighborhoods over time, the analysis of the traditional and current ghetto also leaves the impression that he is making a historic comparison of the Black community.

His most seminal hypothesis views earlier inner-city communities as relatively stable, vertically class-integrated, and containing middle- and working-class families that served as a "social buffer" to lower classes. These earlier inner-city communities, or "traditional ghettos," grew out of the racial segregation associated with preindustrial and industrial race relations and were organized both internally and externally. Internally, these ghettos were organized as relatively autonomous communities containing truncated institutional and class structures, providing basic if not minimal resources for social control and mobility. Externally, these ghettos were dependent on externalities of the larger White society such as industries, commerce, corporations, real estate, politics, organized labor, and public services. Although the traditional ghettos may have contained problems such as family dissolution, educational failure, crime, and housing deterioration, these were not intractable (Wacquant and Wilson 1989). In the traditional ghettos there were more jobs and more people working.

The current ghetto, or "hyperghetto," that is a consequence of advanced capitalist economies and industrial transformation is characterized by heightened disorganization or breakdown. Physically, the disappearance of industries, businesses, and housing in these communities are conducive to social deterioration, loss of hope, and the succession of drugs and criminal activities. Wilson indicates that the Black church and press have little influence in these communities. To the extent that middle and working classes have left these communities, there is an absence of indigenous community institutions and resources for social control and mobility and ghetto residents become increasingly dependent on external institutions and services. Particularly absent are the mainstream role models that "help keep alive the perception that education is meaningful, that steady employment is a viable alternative to welfare, and that family stability is the norm, not the exception" (Wilson 1987, 56). In the current ghetto, problems such as family and community dissolution, educational failure, crime, and housing are subject to "concentration effects" and are viewed as intractable.

It should be extended that the organization of the traditional ghetto was the consequence of external and internal integration that was partly based on racial segregation and social isolation. Whatever disorganization existed in the racial segregation of traditional ghettos was significantly organizational. With growing industrialization replaced by deindustrialization, the reorganizing logic of the economy and the community left behind is increasingly disconnected, devastated, and uncertain.

Wilson's discussion of the transition from the traditional to current ghetto serves at least two functions. First, it is a recasting and synthesis of classical urban ecological and urban ethnographic theories. Second, it represents either a historic comparison or a set of ideal types to guide his analysis.

Accompanying this discussion, Wilson introduces numerous concepts and hypotheses that resurrect the sociological controversies on urban minority communities that are specifically informed by Louis Wirth's "Urbanism as a Way of Life" (Wirth 1938) and post-World War II critiques and reformulations of the urbanism theories (Gans 1962; Fischer 1975). Through his concepts and hypotheses, he refocuses the following questions on contemporary discourses of the postindustrial city in general and the inner-city ghetto in particular. First, through what social relationships does racial and class segregation, or what Wilson calls " social isolation," enter into the social disorganization and reorganization of the Black community? Second, to what extent are urban life-styles in the inner-city ghetto mediated by demographic-ecological factors of size, density, and diversity as opposed to sociocultural factors of social class, status, and life cycle stage. Third, to what extent can the inner-city ghetto, which is partly based on ecological social relationships, become transformed and integrated into the larger society?

In addressing how racial and class segregation influences the social relationships of disorganization and reorganization among inner-city Blacks, Wilson focuses largely on the "concentration effects" or hypersegregation. This hypersegregation is a pathological outcome of the deteriorating opportunity structure of employment and education and the out-movement of middle and working classes that provided cultural integration and stability. Interestingly, these neighborhoods are not made up of the working poor who constitute the majority of the poor nationally, but the nonworking poor. The intersection of race and social class, which has lowered their life chances, is reflected and reproduced in strained social relationships of families and neighbors and prevalent feelings of despair, hopelessness, and pessimism. Because these poorest of the Black poor have become increasingly isolated in their daily interactions from mainstream social networks, role models, and behavior, they can only draw from themselves. However, there is little or nothing in terms of stable social and cultural organization that can be based indigenously on the resources of these persons.

Because the microsociological relationships of social isolation and concentration effects are situational, they are not necessarily permanent or intractable. This reintegration is dependent largely on factors outside the ghetto and will require the inner-city poor to become more culturally and economically integrated. There are also implications that enabling the inner-city poor to move outside these neighborhoods into mixed socioeconomic neighborhoods would relatively increase their social and cultural contacts with mainstream culture although it would eventually involve forms of resegregation. These possibilities of the poor moving into housing outside the ghetto are exemplified in the Gatreaux program in Chicago.

The urban life-styles captured in Wilson's descriptions of the inner-city poor in Chicago come closest to the "swingers," "street corner men," and "street families" life-styles identified in Ulf Hannerz's research more than thirty years ago (Hannerz 1969). It is instructive that while Hannerz identifies the "street families" as largely composed of women and children with boarders and transients that contributed to family resources, the inner-city neighborhoods studied reveal relatively little in augmented or extended family household relationships. Also virtually absent are the "mainstream families" among the poor that approximated the two-parent families with children and characterized by middle-class norms and values. The lower levels of Black population size, density, and diversity has contributed to a lower moral density. Most problematic are the unemployed men and single-parent families who generally lack work experiences and orientations.

Because these residents perceive themselves as physically and spiritually trapped in the ghetto, and do not have memories of the earlier community, there is little sentiment and symbolism to socially construct a more viable and organized community. Although recognizing the role of both demographic-ecological and sociocultural factors in mediating urban life styles, these are almost exclusively disorganized. While residing in the city, there is little suggestion outside of their embracing of the mainstream goals of economic success and work, that the inner-city poor are culturally a part of the urban scene with the exception of the most pathological and pejorative elements. Of course, there are criminal and underground economy elements existing in the inner-city ghetto. Yet unlike St. Clair Drake and Horace Cayton's research that investigated the intricate relationships of the criminal and underground economy of illegal numbers (or "policy") in the Black Chicago of the 1940s alongside more legitimate business, political, and community institutions, there is little suggestion of the thin boundary between legitimate and illegitimate activities in these life-styles.

There are suggestions that the inner-city ghetto can be reorganized spatially into the larger metropolis. Although Wilson does not directly address this in his writings, there are hints that the inner-city ghetto is a series of neighborhoods experiencing uneven decline and growth. The declining neighborhoods, which are actually seas of decay, disinvestment, and displacement, coexist with other neighborhoods of renewal and gentrification. Despite the images of growth and succession suggested by the concept of "concentration effects," these inner-city neighborhoods are in more transition than depicted. Over the long run, one could safely predict more of these Chicago inner-city neighborhoods will experience out-movement and displacement of the poor and the increasing upgrading of these through demolitions, gentrification, and higher-rent apartment conversions into mixed socioeconomic and middle-class neighborhoods. Wilson's concerns with the restructuring of the inner-city ghetto is primarily focused on integrating the poor into these nonpoor socioeconomic neighborhoods where there are greater economic, housing, and social opportunities bearing on social capital.

Let us come back to the comparison. In making the comparison between traditional and contemporary inner-city Black communities, Wilson paints an idealized and "golden age" of community life during preindustrial and industrial race relations and segregation. The current ghetto is a "hyperghetto," which appears to be a worse case scenario of social isolation and concentration effects. The "hyperghetto," which was coined by his former student, Loic J. D. Wacquant, is a socioeconomically segregated section of the inner city characterized by "depacification" of everyday life, "desertification" of organizations and institutions, social "dedifferentiation," and "informalization" of the economy (Wacquant 1994). The community left behind is devastated.

While the descriptions are rich, insightful, and useful in calling attention to the current problems of joblessness and poverty, the generalizations simultaneously provide a misleading analysis. The new ghetto is a social construction that apparently is arrived at "from the armchair." It is a microsociological concept of community which derives from the isolation of select group characteristics.

The transition from the traditional ghetto to the current ghetto calls attention to the macro-level institutional, organizational, and social-class changes bearing on the micro-level moral and social order. This is not to argue whether important social changes have occurred. What is at issue is whether this perspective captures the most salient structural sources of this transformation and to what extent this comparison is the prototype model for an analysis of Black communities or one model among several. This treatment raises the following concerns.

First, the ghetto unit-of-analysis changes empirically over time. In the traditional ghetto, Wilson is describing a historic Black community sui generis. Within the boundaries of racial segregation, it is vertically integrated and culturally diverse. In discussing the current ghetto, Wilson appears less concerned with a holistic analysis of the larger Chicago Black community. Instead he analytically isolates several of the poorest and transitional community areas from the larger system of Black communities in the metropolis. Of course, the latter would provide much of the vertical integration and class diversity lost. The analytical isolation of these inner-city neighborhoods will enable him to use the concepts of "economic ghetto" and "jobless ghetto."

Second, it is questionable to what extent the social dislocations bearing on the loss of moral and social order identified in the inner-city ghetto are derived from the loss of manufacturing employment. At least for two decades, low-paying service employment rather than industrial employment in these neighborhoods has constituted the principal opportunity structure. In the past, it was not unusual for heads of household to work multiple jobs at menial wage scales. Wilson argues that the supply of these jobs, their wage scales, and the social capital of Black inner-city employees are insufficient.

Third, the eroded institutional bases of community associated with the out-movement of the Black middle class and working class is identified in the decline of Black business, the Black church, and the Black press. Although there is little question that the decline of Black business in inner city and other neighborhoods has affected the quality of life, strong arguments can be raised concerning the role of the Black church. To an extent, the older and more established Black churches have left inner-city locations as their members have moved out. Yet Black churches remain one the most persistent institutions within the inner-city Chicago ghetto and other central cities. Simultaneously, Black churches represent one of the most indigenous sources of community leadership training, business development, housing, and social renewal. It is possible that Wilson is responding to the growth and succession of evangelistic and store-front churches in these neighborhoods and the fact that the religious leadership, outreach, ministries, and services in these and other churches are not commensurate with the social problems. This hypothesis is implicit and not articulated.

Interestingly, there is no suggestion that public institutions such as schools and recreational programs existed in these neighborhoods or continue to operate. Although usually experiencing inequities, the closing of many of these inner-city public schools has meant the loss of an important community resource. Since the late 1980s, "community control" based schools have operated in several of these Chicago neighborhoods including the study area. The presence of public recreational programs for youth and young adults is partly based on the maintenance of viable educational institutions. These relationships of the state on the microsociological order are not elucidated.

Fourth, there is little indication in the descriptions and generalizations of the traditional and current ghetto that the primary institutions of Black businesses, churches, and the press coexisted with a range of secondary and tertiary institutions based on personal consumption, recreation, and amusements. These include institutions such as barber shops and beauty salons, fraternities and sororities, sporting events, theaters, jazz and blues clubs, juke joints, dance halls, liquor establishments, eateries, and poolrooms. The role of these institutions in the increased secularization and alienation of urban Blacks must be considered a necessary part of this analysis. These institutions not only have competed with the primary institutions, but but they also often have intersected with these in important activities, and in several respects represented alternative sources of cultural orientations, values, norms, and leadership. These institutions are intermediate with the primary institutions and the more "underground" criminal institutions.

THE DECLINE OF FAMILY AMONG THE INNER-CITY BLACK POOR

During the 1960s and 1970s, the discourses informing the social structure of Black families were importantly influenced by "Black matriarchy"—models based on the history of slavery and discrimination (Moynihan 1965), and "strengths of Black families"—models which drew from structural functional analysis and rational adaptation interpretations (Billingsley 1968; Ladner 1971; Hill 1972; Stack 1974). In discussing the declining status of two-parent families among inner-city Blacks, Wilson is careful to steer clear of the "Black matriarchy" and rational adaptation interpretations which entered much of the earlier sociological theory, research, and public policy controversies. Both of these frameworks have been selectively appropriated into conservative analyses and have been utilized in rationalizations to decrease support for the poor. Wilson's interpretations of changing social structure and culture reintroduce the discussions of both Frazier's *The Negro Family in the United States* (1939) and Moynihan's *The Negro Family: A Case for National Action* (1965). Following the thesis of the industrial growth conditions that Frazier had earlier predicted would increasingly structurally integrate the Black proletariat, the contemporary loss of these conditions has contributed to a severe situation of social and moral disorganization. Similar to Moynihan, the disappearance of work among the Black poor has contributed to a "tangle of pathology."

According to Wilson, the social dislocation caused by plant closings, deindustrialization, and the relative lack of well-paying employment for Black men has resulted in the relative growth of Black children born to unmarried mothers who are poor. Underneath this structural argument are at least four implicit microsociological hypotheses. First, there is a hypothesis that the weakened economic status of Black men and particularly those with steady jobs has decreased their potential marriageability among Black women. As such, there is a changed rational calculus of marriage and family that is more pronounced among the inner-city poor. Second, there is the hypothesis that Black poor men and women expect to marry and raise children in two-parent nuclear families. The norms of these two-parent nuclear families are expected to be more salient than extended families and single-parent families. Third, there is the hypothesis of changing expectations concerning sex, reproductive behavior, and the relative increase of out-of-wedlock births among Black women accompanying Black male unemployment. Accompanying the male joblessness and absence of marriageable men, an alternative ghetto-specific culture has emerged that valorizes the underground economy, drugs, underachievement, and early sexual activity. Fourth, there is the policy hypothesis that economic growth and the restoration of well-paying and stable employment will improve the social and economic status of low-income Black men and their marriageability prospects among Black women and in turn improve the norms of male responsibility and family.

The "Black marriageable male pool" hypothesis, although intellectually persuasive, has at best mixed empirical support (Stokes and Chevan 1996; Rolison 1992; Hess 1990). These are definitive in showing stronger effects of employment than welfare in predicting female-headed families (Hess 1990). Invalidating this hypothesis is Robert G. Wood's research, showing that declines in the pool of "marriageable" Black men accounted for only 3 to 4 percent of the decline in Black marriage rates during the 1970s (Wood 1995). Related sociological research shows that roughly four-fifths of the decrease in marriage among employed Black males occurred independent of employment status changes (Jencks 1991; Mare and Winship 1991).

It should be noted that Wilson emphasizes that his discussion of structural changes and cultural adaptations among Black poor families within inner-city Chicago are not to be generalized to Blacks of other social classes. However, it is more ambiguous to what extent the concepts and hypotheses, based on the inner-city poor in Chicago, are to be the basis for generalizations of the poor in other cities.

Because both two-parent families and family incomes are lowest among the Black poor, Wilson reasons from this correlation that the norms, values, and beliefs concerning lower-income Black men as prospective husbands have diminished. While the logical facts and reasons offered by him are correct, these have been taken out of context and can be misleading. It is instructive that while poor Black families have the lowest percentages of husband-wife families, the decreases in husband-wife families among the Black poor in recent decades are similar to those among middle-class Black families (Jencks 1991). Alongside economic changes such as unemployment and decreased earnings that directly explain the lowered marriageability, the indirect effects of economic changes on changing solidarities and group associations should have a value-added effect on changing expectations of marriage. Ethnographers have argued that changes in cultural norms, values, and beliefs might act as independent and intervening variables in helping explain these changes. These suggest stronger interpretations of culture.

Other reasons for the decreased marriage behavior among the Black poor might be found outside of it within the Black middle class and the larger society. While the increased education and income among individuals in the Black middle class are directly correlated with increased levels of marriage and family, this stronger economic integration in the postindustrial economy is precarious. One can hypothesize that accompanying the increased economic integration and status attainment are competing expectations of individualism, narcissism, and conspicuous consumption that may reduce family formation and contribute to family strain. At the same time, the increased economic integration among Blacks can come with several alternative non-family life-styles. Although the Black inner-city poor may attempt to emulate these middle-class behaviors to the best of their ability and resources, it is also possible that they have seen the contradictions in these materialist and individual values, have rejected many middle-class behaviors, and attempted to negotiate others. The moral authority of the Black middle class with respect to the inner-city poor is questioned at length by Mitchell Duneier (Duneier 1984).

Third, the hypothesis of the proportionate increase in out-of-wedlock births among teenaged Black women accompanying Black male unemployment attempts to call attention to differential fertility by family structure and neighborhood that bear on the Black poor. Wilson is calling attention to the racial differences in fertility during the late 1980s that were greatest among teenagers and the fact that these accounted for a growing proportion of Black births. However, the proportionate increase in out-of-wedlock births or "illegitimacy" is a sociological fact that is partly a statistical artifact. Wilson is aware that these rates among Black teenagers and other ages have dropped substantially since 1970 (Ventura, Curtin, and Matthews 1996; Farley and Allen 1987, 79). The much more rapid decrease in Black marital fertility at other ages explains this artifact. The trends in lowered Black teenage fertility through the late 1980s and 1990s is what should be expected under depressed economic circumstances. Compared to earlier, the access to contraception is higher. During the 1990s, decreases in the rates of Black teenage fertility have been greater than any other population (Ventura, Curtin, and Matthews 1996).

In suggesting that the increase of out-of-wedlock births among young Black women has been caused by increased Black male unemployment, Wilson is arguing a variation (and the worse case scenario) of the liberal expectancy hypothesis. The sociological facts indicate that increased unemployment among Black men was accompanied by decreased not increased illegitimacy. Black female unemployment, which also increased during the 1980s and early 1990s, might be expected to further depress these birth rates.

A more serious omission centers on how he treats the role of culture, which influences family formation and norms of motherhood and fatherhood. Wilson emphasizes that mainstream economic and work norms are salient in community, family, and interpersonal social relationships.

In the absence of regular work, one should expect the most accentuated disorganizing features of social isolation and concentration effects. By emphasizing these disorganizing patterns, the adaptations with respect to assimilation are viewed as problematic. In Carol Stack's *All Our Kin: Strategies for Survival in a Black Community*, Black teenaged women's expectations of marriage were formed independent of the employment status of Black teenaged men. Not only were these norms not influenced by the employment or unemployment status of Black men, but Black teenaged men were not usually culturally defined as marriageable (Stack 1974). Underlying these are extended family, caring and support systems, and sharing networks that cut across nuclear families (Stack 1974). Even assuming that young males regularly work in the growing low-paying service and temporary jobs sectors of the contemporary postindustrial economy, it is questionable to what degree these persons are viewed favorably as potential marriage prospects. In an increasingly rational, materialistic, and consumption-based economy, the continued marginalization of Black males challenges traditional economic roles of fathers and providers. To the extent that this marginalization of young Black males is translated into the increased incarceration and unpaid labor within the growing prison industries, these contemporary institutional contradictions undermine the liberal expectancy assumptions of economic integration.

Fourth, the hypothesis that improvements in the employment and income prospects of low-income Black men will increase their marriageability prospects represents for Wilson the moral higher ground with respect to social policy. This optimistic expectation appears to be long-term rather than short-term and grows out of the structurally determinist relationships between the economy and culture. Contained in this hypothesis is a materialistic assumption of the relationships between changing macroeconomic structure and cultural norms, values, and beliefs. There is a "trickle-down" assumption that over the long run the combination of sustained economic growth and the mobilization of the multiracial liberal coalition and its agenda into American politics will contribute to a more equitable redistribution of income and universal social democratic policies and be accompanied by race-specific policies. While these universal social democratic policies have "common ground" with most middle- and working-class Whites, they are also favorable to the increased integration of poor Black men and women in the economy. These universal reforms would actually necessitate cultural reversals in norms with respect to family, individualism, and consumption.

How much these macroeconomic growth factors will singularly contribute to these improvements in Black social and economic status is subject to question. In response to critics, Wilson's discussions of liberal, multiracial coalitions and the universal rights agenda underscore a necessary social movement and human agency to accompany recent globalization and economic growth. The increasing inequality of wealth and income between the highest and lowest social classes and the contraction of the middle classes which has accompanied a growing assault on welfare state policies such as Social Security, Medicare, and Aid to Families for Dependent Children (AFDC) are some of the institutional contradictions that compel the mobilization of liberal, multiracial coalitions. Accompanying the trajectory of

postindustrial economic growth, there will need to be other social movements, struggles, and public policies centered on more radical and progressive issues such as the growth in the prison-industrial complex, the
disproportionate sentencing policies deriving from the War on Drugs, the
increased institutionalization and criminalization of Black men and women,
the political disfranchisement of Blacks, resulting from these institutionalization processes, and the continued economic and political underdevelopment
of Black communities. Even assuming that macroeconomic changes will
induce changes in cultural orientations, this is not automatic. Critics have
argued that cultural changes in attitudes, values, and norms do not immediately follow the economic changes and might lag for generations.

HUMAN AND SOCIAL CAPITAL AND THE GHETTO POOR

In explaining the microsociological context of ghetto poverty, Wilson provides an alternative interpretation to the culturally determinist and ghetto-
specific culture of poverty models. At the same time, this alternative
interpretation, which is consistent with the cultural beliefs and logic of the
declining significance of race, provides a much weaker role of racial inequality. The new interpretation that replaces the traditional liberal perspectives is
found in the relationships of human and social capital.

According to human capital theories, the complexity of human behavior is analogized and reduced to income production and human capital essentially consists of those social and economic characteristics that individuals
have relevant to generating earned income (Becker 1962; Becker 1993).
Derived from neoclassical and microeconomic theories, human capital perspectives generally argue that a society's endowment of educated, trained and
healthy workers determines how productively the classical economic factors
of land, labor, and physical capital can be utilized (Woolcock 1998, 154).
Inspired by neoclassical economists, sociologists and other social scientists
have proposed the concept of social capital to broadly address the complementary social relationships, networks, norms, and information that contribute to a society's integration.

In the original treatment of the concept, Bourdieu defined social capital as "the aggregate of the actual or potential resources which are linked to
possession of a durable network of more or less institutionalized relationships of mutual acquaintance or recognition" (Bourdieu 1986, 248). Bourdieu viewed social networks as socially constructed through investment
strategies that enable actors to gain access to "economic capital" and simultaneously increase "cultural capital." While Bourdieu emphasized that the
outcomes of possessing social or cultural capital are reducible to economic
capital, the processes that bring these about are not reducible. Relatedly,

Alejandro Portes notes that social capital captures both the age-old socio-logical question of how "involvement and participation in groups can have positive consequences for the individual and the community" (Portes 1998, 1), but is increasingly coming to stand for "the ability of actors to secure benefits by virtue of memberships in social networks for other social struc-tures" (Portes 1998, 2). While social capital is intangible and emerges from social relationships, it is derived from "consummatory" and instrumental sources (Portes 1998).

Loric J. D. Wacquant and William Julius Wilson use the concept of social capital to describe and account for the depressed status of the inner-city poor and the weakened vertical integration of the poor in the contemporary ghetto. Although their discussions are partly inspired by Pierre Bourdieu and they cite his scholarship, their discussions also appear influenced by larger sociological controversies that have addressed broader and contradictory usages of the concept. On one level, sociologists have used social capital to focus on the differential access to opportunities among minorities as a conse-quence of intergenerational poverty, weaker social connections in the labor market, and the relative lack of information concerning economic opportu-nities. At another level, social capital calls attention to how social capital is relevant to the development of human capital. Or how is the integration of actors into social structures, organizations, groups, and networks translated into education, training, and health?

Wacquant and Wilson nominally incorporate social capital dimensions from Bourdieu focused on resources linked to the possession of durable social networks of institutionalized resources that have a bearing on investment and economic capital. Their discussions appear more focused on the outcomes than the processes of social capital. The role of cultural capital, which is asso-ciated with social capital in Bourdieu's work, is not broached. Simultaneously, Wacquant and Wilson's discussions converge with rational action conceptu-alizations that are limited to the role of social capital in the development of human capital. With respect to the Black poor, their analysis like Loury's emphasizes the intergenerational poverty passed on by poor Black parent's lack of wealth and educational resources, weaker relationships of young Black males to the labor market, and the lack of information concerning jobs and economic opportunities (Loury 1977).

Wacquant and Wilson's discussion is also influenced by James Cole-man's rational choice analysis (Coleman 1994; Coleman 1988). Similar to Coleman's analysis of social capital that introduced the concept to main-stream sociology, their discussion acts to heighten its visibility. In providing an alternative interpretation to the culture of poverty and, emphasizing how the losses of industrial employment, employable Black men, and middle-class families from the inner city have resulted in a "desert" of social capital resources, the deficits of the culture of poverty are now replaced by the deficits of the Black inner-city poor social capital. The weak vertical integration of the Black poor in social networks that are isolated to the ghetto helps explain the poverty.

Through numerous illustrations, Wacquant and Wilson describe how the ghetto social isolation and concentration effects are associated with disproportionately lower levels of social capital. In economic and financial terms, they note that ghetto-poor Blacks in Chicago are characterized by deficits in nearly every dimension identified. They illustrate this by showing in 1986 that one-half of the households had annual incomes of less than $7,500, only one-third owned a working automobile, one-fourth reported financial assets, one-ninth managed personal checking accounts, and one-tenth were home-owner households (Wacquant and Wilson 1989, 20–21).

The social integration of ghetto-poor individuals into solidary groups, networks, or organizations is a form of social capital providing identity development, education, information, emotional support, material resources, and networks of opportunity. This social capital is described by nearly half of the residents lacking a current marriage, live in, or dating partner. Yet even where ghetto-poor marriages and friendships exist, these are more frequently than other low-poverty and Chicago residents to involve less education, greater unemployment, and welfare assistance. Ghetto social isolation leads to low membership in formal organizations such as block clubs, community organizations, political parties, school-related associations, sports, fraternities, and sororities. In church membership, ghetto residence depresses attendance and religiosity. Black women in particular are least likely to know their neighbors (Wacquant and Wilson 1989, 22–24).

Although the concept of social capital and the sociological facts used to illustrate the deteriorating economic situation are accurate, these interpretations are incomplete and misleading for at least three reasons. First, the particular usage of social capital is decontextualized from important economic institutional factors and hence understates these. Second, the rational action and social network resource interpretation has an a priori assumption of deficits which does not necessarily extend to all of the microsociological relationships of the ghetto poor. Third, this usage does not identify the racially discriminatory networks of social capital (or "negative social capital") that emerge from competitive relationships between groups.

With respect to the first point, there is a relatively conservative definition of social capital that is focused on the social resources and networks that integrate individuals into families, solidarity groups, and organizations in the economy. Underlying this analysis of the inner-city poor, social capital deficits are assumptions that these are largely the consequence of individual, rational choice, and voluntary actions. Within this free market, the social controls or constraints of predatory economies within the ghetto, which require the poor to pay relatively more for consumer goods, housing, and check cashing, are neither examined nor hinted at. It is significant that in recent decades, several savings and loan institutions in inner-city neighborhoods have closed and other central city financial institutions have discouraged savings by low-income individuals by instituting minimum deposit policies. The deficits interpretation does not call attention to practices of insurance and homeowner redlining in inner-city neighborhoods that have functioned as disinvestment policies. At the same time, the more extended role of government intervention and social control in these neighborhoods through public welfare, housing assistance, and policing have often functioned to limit the possibilities of dense social networks and families.

With respect to the second point, it does not necessarily follow that because poor Blacks are low on economic characteristics such as education, employment, and earnings that they have low social capital. This is an over-rationalized rational choice interpretation. In contrast to the rational choice interpretations, there are other sociological perspectives which view social capital as normative resources used to define the boundaries of groups and the nonrational features of social relationships. For groups that are highly differentiated by cultural and racial characteristics and experience a high degree of discrimination with limited economic opportunity, Portes hypothesizes a high degree of social capital. This social capital of intragroup networks and relationships is expected to be high because prejudice and discrimination limit the probability of access to mainstream social networks and intragroup communication experiences contribute to unique rewards (Portes 1992). One might generally expect under conditions of adversity, that the Black poor are adaptable and creative in finding group sources of solidarity, emergent norms, and resources that derive from social networks. One can also expect under conditions of adversity, other forms of exchanges such as barter and noncontractual agreements. There will also be more coercive and predatory forms of exchange that emerge indigenously and from externalities of the political and criminal justice systems. This is not to suggest that these more conflict-based sources of social capital are preferable to the rational action characteristics earlier discussed. But to ignore these factors and focus the discussion of social capital strictly on the lack of integrative rational action properties among the ghetto poor is not culturally or sociologically sensitive. In proposing to integrate Blacks, it would make sense to recognize the group-related cultural elements and adaptations that have contributed to a group's stability and persistence and possibly build on these.

With respect to the third point, the tone of the social capital discussion in terms of unit-of-analysis is focused largely on intragroup social characteristics while neglecting solidarity and exclusion processes deriving from intergroup competition. To the extent that dense networks of social capital becomes the standard relevant to the development of human capital, these function to undermine the individualistic, rational, and meritocratic assumptions of achievement in status attainment models and the dominant American belief system. It is the in-group, solidarity forms of social capital that are the basis of social class and status group exclusion bearing on racial discrimination. Although there are forms of in-group social capital that are relevant on continuing discrimination, these are not hinted at.

Several of these points concerning the role of racial inequality have already been made with respect to decontextualized discussions of human capital. While the social resources and networks that integrate individuals into families, solidarity groups, and organizations in the economy is a beginning explanation of the inner-city's poor depressed condition, these do not go far enough in clarifying social class and racial group intersections. Critical theoretical analyses of conventional human capital theory have emphasized that these have usually explained the lower economic status of Blacks by analyzing their lower investments in relevant human capital characteristics such as education, training, skills, and work experiences. Because Blacks as rational individuals and an aggregate group are assumed to have acquired lower wages and are unemployed more, they are assumed to have acquired less human capital characteristics through rational choices of education, training, work, and careers. To the extent that human capital perspectives view the economic status of Blacks as largely rationally determined by their lower investments in themselves, these reflect Blacks' limitations. Conventional human capital perspectives are conservative in viewing racial discrimination as a minor or negligible part of the Black-White differences in economic status (Darrity 1982, 90; Franklin 1991, xvii).

The economist Gunnar Myrdal cautioned about human capital concepts in economics that were restricted to investments in education, training, and information (Myrdal 1968, chap. 29). Myrdal noted that these human capital approaches assumed that education was a homogeneous variable, ignored issues of education mix, wastage, and miseducation, and treated institutional economics and prevalent attitudes as inconsequential (Myrdal 1968). Also, Myrdal critiqued these human capital conceptualizations as bypassing social and economic inequality and the factor of a population's health (Myrdal 1968, 1547–1548).

William Darrity notes that while the early human capital approaches contained domain assumptions that argued Black and White workers have equal abilities and productivity, revised theories since the 1970s have increasingly dropped the assumption that Blacks are on average equally productive (Darity 1982, 77–78). These assumptions persist, despite empirical evidence that shows Black workers, who share the same social and economic characteristics with Whites, typically earn less and more frequently are jobless (Darity 1982, 90). In explaining inequality, Darity notes that human capital perspectives place primary emphasis on the acquisition of human capital characteristics such as education rather than on job and employment experiences. As such, human capital theory does not adequately explain income inequality (Darrity 1982, 84). Darrity urged that conventional human capital explanations of Black-White earnings differences should be relinquished (Darity 1982, 90). In essence, human capital minimizes the realities of racial discrimination in contemporary society.

Wilson's incorporation of human and social capital concepts to make sense of the microsociological order of inner-city poverty is an attempt to provide an alternative to the ghetto-specific culture-of-poverty paradigm that bolsters the declining significance of race theory. Simultaneously, the introduction of social capital into sociological discussions of poverty reduces the intellectual distance between sociology and economics while refocusing the attention of policymakers to the importance of noneconomic solutions to social problems. This convergence of social and human capital explanations also represents a continuing dialogue to consider redefining the traditional boundaries between sociology and economics in a "new economic sociology" (Swedberg 1990).

In making these adaptations toward mainstream economic theory, sociological perspectives of race relations can be expected to integrate new assumptions of the irrationalities of prejudice, discrimination, and racism in firms and labor markets that potentially understate the continuing significance of race. These social and human capital perspectives in many ways represent a retreat from the sociological analyses of the traditional civil rights and Black power movements. Yet in incorporating a social capital analysis that moves beyond strong racial discrimination explanations, Wilson will eventually be forced to adjust and abandon this formulation of social capital that is fundamentally in tension with his macrosociological analysis, public policy proposals, and more recent research findings.

OTHER REFLECTIONS ON THE MORAL AND SOCIAL ORDER OF THE GHETTO

Wilson's microsociological discussion of the moral and social order of the ghetto is important in moving the public-policy controversies on the underclass from a pejorative culture of poverty interpretation, to a structural interpretation emphasizing changing institutions and the social environment. It is a holistic examination that is informed by situational, ecological, and ethnographic perspectives. In providing a structural analysis of culture, Wilson systematically criticizes the culture of poverty and traditional liberal perspectives and identifies through a complex series of adaptations and coping responses the consequences of "social isolation" and "concentration effects." While the structural contexts of "social isolation" and "concentration effects" are larger than the ghetto, Wilson argues that the cultural adaptations that are intergenerationally transmitted among the inner-city poor are problematic to their integration. The human and social capital concepts and perspectives used, which replace traditional cultural insights, imply a more conservative interpretation.

The "demographic transition" hypothesis, which represents the most seminal ideas buttressing the microsociological arguments of the decline of the Black community and Black family are further elaborated in Elijah Anderson's ethnographic research (Anderson 1990). Anderson's, *Streetwise: Race, Class, and Change in an Urban Community*, provides the most cited research on the urban life-styles and "ghetto-related culture" emerging from economic dislocations, unemployment, low-wage service employment and the coexistence of Black middle-class flight, gentrification, and a drug economy. In the "Northton" community the loss of traditional jobs and the competition of an underground drug economy and culture have eroded the traditional buffers and informal sources of social control (Anderson 1990). Anderson indicates that at an earlier time, mentoring relationships between male "old heads"—older men whose acknowledged role was to teach, support, encourage, and in effect socialize young men to meet the responsibilities with regard to work ethics, family life, the law, and decency—and young boys "offered support to both the local and wider systems of social stratification and inspired boys to negotiate them through legitimate means" (Anderson 1990, 69–72). Female "old heads," often called "Mama," "Big Mama," "Moms," and "Mis'" traditionally augmented the relationship between parent and child (Anderson 1990, 73–76). These expectations changed with the large scale introduction of drugs. Replacing the old role models were new role models of the drug pusher, pimp, and illegal hustler, who give the appearances of being able to obtain big money more easily, glamorously, and in effect appear more successful (Anderson 1990, 77). It is instructive that Anderson later shows that in the inner city, there are more traditional (or "decent") families that encourage school and spiritual values including church attendance. While mainstream values are present there is also an inner-city street code that sanctions an oppositional culture and various forms of violence (Anderson 1997).

Jay MacLeod's *Aint No Making It: Leveled Aspirations in a Low Income Neighborhood* (1987) examines the reproduction of culture in a working-class community dominated by single-parent families and welfare recipients. By studying two comparable groups that differed in their occupational aspirations, MacLeod identified the variable forms that situational adaptations in poverty might take. Among the Hallway Hangers there existed a streetwise and communitarian cultural values that emphasized "being bad" and working in the drug economy; this attitude rejected traditional norms such as doing your best in school and holding down a job. The "communitarian" values were reflected in closer relationships with each other than with their families. Simultaneously, the Hallway Hangers had other cultural values that emphasized masculinity, physical toughness, and street smarts; they formed a distinctive culture. By contrast, the "Brothers" were influenced by their parents to embrace mainstream cultural values such as working hard, having a job, and raising a family. As conformists, the Brothers did their best in school, had steady girl friends, and spent their time doing things they valued as important. Underlying these differences in occupational aspirations were factors of family upbringing (Hallway Hangers had absentee fathers and brothers who were in trouble with the police while the Brothers had male authority figures and older brothers and sisters who did well in school), labor market experiences (Hallway Hangers worked in the illegal drug economy while brothers worked in regular jobs), and experiences in the school system (Hallway Hangers rebelled against the academic and social norms and were in trouble while the Brothers were well integrated into the school (MacLeod 1987).

Robert Sampson's research, which shows a direct relationship between high levels of joblessness and the weakening of neighborhood organization bearing on social control, validates Wilson's hypothesis (Sampson and Groves 1989; Sampson 1992, Sampson 1997). Sampson has shown that neighborhoods with weak levels of organization, social participation and unsupervised adolescents are more likely to emphasize macho values, sexuality, and violence (Sampson and Wilson 1995). Relatedly, Lauren Krivo and Ruth Peterson find that neighborhoods, experiencing structural disadvantage, experience significantly higher rates of violent crime (Krivo and Peterson 1996).

Probably the most important research bearing on these hypotheses are derived from the three studies that Wilson directed at the Center for the Study of Urban Inequality at the University of Chicago. These studies include the Urban Poverty and Family Life Study (UPFLS), the Woodlawn and Oakland Neighborhood Study, and the study of the effects of high-risk neighborhoods on adolescent social development. These findings will be discussed at more length in the next chapter. Extending the findings beyond Chicago is the "Multi-City Study of Urban Inequality" series focused on Boston, Detroit, Atlanta, and Los Angeles.

This is not to argue that the structural analysis of the "demographic transition," "social isolation," and "concentration effects" is entirely or mostly wrong. There is much here that is useful and insightful. However, the substance and tone of the concepts and hypotheses used in these interpretations do not go nearly far enough in addressing the complexity and diversity of the contemporary experiences of Black communities in general and inner-city communities specifically.

It is possible that in his attempt to provide a more objective and structural analysis and avoid a "Black solidarity" or "strengths of Black family" interpretation, Wilson has erred in the other direction. In identifying the micro-order of disorganization and breakdown in the inner-city ghetto, he makes clear that all is not well. Yet the most glaring omission in this analysis directly derives from the nature of the structural and group organization interpretation. The delimited and narrow examinations of the inner-city poor are largely examined in terms of their dysfunctional social patterns and do not seriously grapple with the social organizational, human agency, and culture matters that emerge indigenously from the Black community. The structural argument of culture while necessary is not sufficient.

There are some recent analyses that suggest the possibilities of bringing culture, agency, and indigenous factors in. Contained in the images, symbols, discourses, language, and various forms of popular culture are means to organize, restructure, and resist social disorganization. Robin Kelly in, *Yo mama is disfunctional: fighting the culture wars in Urban America* (1997), provides some clues to this cultural and human agency in his discussions of how the contemporary urban working class is mobilizing within low-wage service industries, organizing around community-based issues, and Black youth are reconstructing culture through forms such as "Go Go" and "Hip Hop" (Kelly 1997). Michael Eric Dyson notes: "The values and memory of social criticism connect it [rap] to a powerful history of African American cultural resistance, rebellion, and revolution" (Dyson 1993, 280). This resistive hip-hop music expresses an oppositional culture toward perceived oppression by White society and recommends a course of action to be taken directly or indirectly (Lott 1992). Stephen Nathan Haymes has identified in the struggles of urban Blacks to construct self-definitions, consciousness, and public space, an important basis of social organization and community (Haymes 1995). The language, symbols, and values expressed in these struggles around employment, racism, and displacement resurrect symbolic interaction discourses.

Mitchell Duneier has provided a most insightful critique of the hypothesis of the moral density and authority of the Black middle class vis-à-vis the Black working and lower classes (Duneier 1992, 130). Duneier argues that "social theory about urban poverty fails to recognize that the working poor are moral beings that can provide their own role models, at least on moral grounds" (Duneier 1992). Duneier's analyses questions the tone of the relationship between middle-class behavior and purportedly mainstream norms of responsibility, family, and work.

More critical are William Darity and Samuel Myers who view the Black middle class as not providing the mediating cultural influences that help curb the pathological behaviors of the urban underclass (Darity, Myers, Carson, and Sabol 1994, 57). Members of the Black managerial class, administering local government and welfare bureaus, are viewed as having ambivalent views toward the poor and vested interests in the increased control and institutionalization of unwanted inner-city residents. Rather than providing the mainstream role models, norms, and values favorable to the assimilation of the inner-city poor, they hypothesize that the Black middle class is directly associated with their increased marginalization and social isolation (Darity, Myers, Carson, and Sabol 1994, 158).

Contemporary Black urban communities are complex and diverse integrations of institutions, organizations, social classes, life-styles, groups, and individuals in continuous social transformation. Black lower-class communities, including underclass neighborhoods represent the most studied yet least understood invisible social relationships of postindustrial cities. By focusing on the situational adaptations to joblessness and "ghetto-specific" cultures, Wilson's discussion of the contemporary moral and social order of the inner-city ghetto appears to be primarily a reaction to the conservative perspectives which have stereotypically, perniciously, and pejoratively derogated Blacks in the ghetto. Although the middle class might contribute to the restoration of social order, there is hardly any suggestion that there are indigenous to these places identities and social relationships bearing on the renewal and reorganization of these inner-city neighborhoods.

One useful starting point in refocusing research on the moral and social order of urban Black neighborhoods would extend the examination of the ethnographic and community studies of joblessness into the broader context of social transformation within Black communities. One strategy would begin with more holistic community studies that cut across the institutional and organizational diversity and class and racial boundaries. These would also emphasize regional and cross-national continuities and discontinuities. These would explicitly examine the intersection of economic changes, power, and culture. To the extent that larger societal cultural orientations of materialism, rationalization and social dislocations are related to the underemployment and joblessness of Blacks, it is important to examine whether rationalization and materialism have a bearing on other social problems such as institutionalization, criminalization, incarceration, and the prison-industrial complex, the proliferation of drugs, guns, and violence, the underdevelopment of Black human and social capital in public education through greater placement of Black youth in non-college curriculums, high school certificate (less than the diploma) and special education programs, the disproportionately large presence of HIV/AIDS and other public health conditions, environmental racism issues such as heightened wastage dumping and pollution in Black communities, and "housing poverty" and homelessness. How are Black communities nationally and cross-nationally organizing with respect to these issues? Are the issues of economic justice viewed as related to these other issues (or are these other issues viewed independently)?

The classic community studies, represented by W. E. B. Du Bois's *The Philadelphia Negro*, the Atlanta University studies, and St. Clair Drake and Horace Cayton's *Black Metropolis*, might inspire a new generation of studies bearing on inequality or holistic community studies in their own right. Alongside macroeconomic change, these would draw from historical and sociological insights of changing social structure that open up the conservative assumptions in interpretations of Black human and social capital. These would focus on how post-civil rights policies in urban development, transportation, housing, public education, and environmental protection (and the resistance and refocusing of these policies by local decision makers) have contributed to both the reinvestment and renewal of some urban Black communities and the disinvestment and disorganization in other urban Black communities.

Another research strategy would examine the continuities and discontinuities between the group specific cultures of the inner-city underclass, the lower class and other classes in the Black community, the larger American society, and larger global society with respect to the assimilation and reproduction of so-called ghetto expressive culture such as music, dance, clothing, sport, and "styling." Rather than being socially and culturally isolated, these norms, values, beliefs, and symbols are predicted as becoming increasingly universal. Similar to the jazz, blues, and soul cultures of earlier generations, the so-called contemporary ghetto cultures are capturing and redefining the meanings of American expressive culture and the African-American experience while being transformed by those groups and individuals who appropriate it.

CHAPTER 6

THE WORLD OF THE NEW URBAN POOR

Jobless Ghettos, Fading Inner-City Families,
and the Changing Significance of Race

INTRODUCTION

Wilson's, *When Work Disappears: The World of the New Urban Poor* (1996), is a continuation of the issues raised in *The Truly Disadvantaged*. In this effort, he brings together evidence from three studies he directed at the Center for the Study of Urban Inequality at the University of Chicago to address the causes and consequences of high neighborhood joblessness and concentrated poverty within contemporary inner cities. These studies include the Urban Poverty and Family Life Study (UPFLS), the Woodlawn and Oakland Neighborhood Study, and the study of the effects of high-risk neighborhoods on adolescent social development. The data from these studies are used to test hypotheses about joblessness. Theoretically, "This book attempts to demonstrate that social structural factors are important for understanding joblessness and other experiences of the inner-city poor, but there is much these factors do not explain" (Wilson 1996, xiv). Similar to his earlier *The Truly Disadvantaged*, he identifies the primacy of macroeconomic, ecological, and public policy factors in the growth of poverty. Unlike earlier, the holistic explanations advanced here also include more extensive articulations of racial, cultural, and social psychological factors and their interactions with social structural factors.

The stated purpose of *When Work Disappears* is to inform the public and social policy debates and refocus the attention of social scientists and policy-makers on the powerful and complex role of the social environment in shaping the life chances of inner-city ghetto residents. In writing this book for a general audience, he also shares an aim of consciousness raising in attempting to affect a national dialogue on the need for both short-term and long-term programs to address public policies on employment, education-to-work transitions, and welfare reform (Wilson 1996). In this effort, Wilson underscores the urgency of social scientists, emphasizing the important and complex roles of the social environment in their research to policymakers, given the reemergence of conservative genetic endowment arguments in Richard Herrnstein and Charles Murray's *The Bell Curve: Intelligence and Class Structure in American Life* (1994). Furthermore, liberal policy-based research and commentary that has sometimes denied the existence of culture will be urgently necessary to identify and address the blocked opportunity structures of the poor, including the presence of culturally destructive behavior and attitudes (Wilson 1996).

In this book, Wilson rehashes, reformulates, and elaborates earlier discussions of economic restructuring, the out-migration of Black middle-class families from ghetto neighborhoods, and the role of concentration effects and social isolation in poor neighborhoods. However, the discussion of social policy is more extensive. This book is rich in descriptions which capture the hard times and depression of the Black poor living in jobless ghettos. The following issues are central: (1) the place of work in organizing the ecological, cultural, and sociological life of inner-city neighborhoods and the microsociological life of individuals; (2) the changing significance of race as examined through employer's views of Black workers; (3) the analysis of the American belief system of individualism as an ideology, and its implications for public policies such as employment, welfare, and poverty; and (4) a cross-national comparison and assessment of the American belief system with other advanced industrialized nations. While the first two issues are addressed by the research studies coming out of the Center for the Study of Urban Inequality at the University of Chicago, the latter two issues are addressed utilizing public opinion, social surveys, and policy arguments.

THE DISAPPEARANCE OF WORK AND JOBLESS GHETTOS

Compared to an earlier ghetto, Wilson indicates the current economic and social conditions are unprecedented. He defines the "new urban poverty" as "poor segregated neighborhoods in which a substantial majority of the individual adults are either unemployed or have dropped out of the labor force" (Wilson 1996, 19). In operationally defining jobless, Wilson uses a sensitive measure which takes into account both official unemployment and non-labor force participation (employment-to-population ratio). In contrast to earlier "institutional ghettos," the new urban poverty is a spatial phenomenon of "jobless ghettos." At the same time, these neighborhoods have low levels of social organization such as friendship ties, social cohesion, resident participation in political organizations and informal voluntary associations, unstable formal organizations, and weak informal social controls (Wilson 1996, 20).

The high joblessness and low levels of social organization are in turn reflected and reproduced in other neighborhood problems such as crime, gang violence, and family life problems. In discussing the social organization of neighborhoods, Wilson refers to "the extent to which the residents of a neighborhood are able to maintain effective social control and realize their common goals." There are three main dimensions of neighborhood social organization: (1) the prevalence, strength, and interdependence of social networks, (2) the extent of collective supervision that the residents exercise and the degree of personal responsibility they assume in addressing problems and (3) the rate of resident participation in voluntary and formal organizations (Wilson 1996, 20).

The cultural and psychological adaptations growing out of joblessness are addressed in the chapter, "Ghetto-Related Behavior and the Structure of Opportunity." According to Wilson, these cultural and psychological adaptations of inner-city poor are "constraints," which combined with restricted opportunities in the larger society, lead to ghetto-related behavior and attitudes" (Wilson 1996, 52). He is careful to emphasize that the disappearance of work is a function of a number of larger structural changes beyond the control of inner-city neighborhoods such as the new global economy, the decline of the mass production system, and the growing suburbanization of jobs (Wilson 1996, 54). Drawing from the UPFLS research, he underscores that "the total culture of the inner-city ghetto includes ghetto-related elements, but it also contains a predominance of mainstream elements" (Wilson 1996, 67). He hypothesizes that "in stable neighborhoods, people who are economically marginal and are struggling to make ends meet are more strongly constrained to act in mainstream ways than are their counterparts in high jobless neighborhoods" (Wilson 1996, 70). Varying with the individual's involvement in networks of friends and kin, he distinguishes elements of culture which are rational, "situationally adaptive," accidental, and unconscious (Wilson 1996, 71).

This discussion of culture appears to be partly a response to conservative perspectives, such as James Q. Wilson, which emphasize that underclass behavior is a significant consequence of "habituation" processes where people have acquired unconscious ways of behaving which are impulsive, unreflective, and self-indulgent (Wilson 1994). Although he does not dwell on this point, Wilson seems to be emphasizing that the rational and "situationally adaptive" elements of culture are predominant over the accidental and unconscious. Even where these cultural adaptations are unconscious and unreflective, these are primarily rational adaptations to larger structural factors of constrained opportunity. The ghetto-related behaviors, attitudes, and elements, in this discussion, appear to be limited to the most intractable and intergenerational patterns.

There is an analysis of changes in family structure in "The Fading Inner City Family." Currently, he notes that within the inner-city ghetto of Chicago, only one-quarter of Black families with children are husband-wife families and within concentrated poverty neighborhoods (at least 40 percent poverty) only 16.5 percent of the Black families with children are husband-wife families (Wilson 1996, 87). Although these are viewed as part of the national trend, affecting all racial and ethnic groups, the disappearance of African-American families in the inner city contrasts with Mexican American, Puerto Rican, and White American families. In explaining this phenomenon, Wilson notes that the scientific evidence does not substantiate the claim that AFDC plays a significant role in contributing to out-of-wedlock births. Concomitantly, he acknowledges that the scientific evidence for the Black male joblessness hypothesis, based on national studies, is mixed. While some research indicates that increased joblessness is unrelated, others indicate that changes in employment and income status account for a small proportion of the declines in Black marriage. It is instructive that because these nationally based studies do not strongly support Wilson's hypothesis of economic dislocation, joblessness, and inner-city dissolution, he feels that these do not directly inform his discussion (Wilson 1996, 96). He then proceeds to discuss the results of the UPFLS survey that include ethnographic data.

Drawing from this ethnographic data, Wilson advances several microsociological hypotheses bearing on marriage and family. These derive in large part from his earlier theorizing. Wilson argues that "both inner-city Black males and females believe that since most marriages will eventually break up and since marriages no longer represent meaningful relationships, it is better to avoid the entanglements of wedlock altogether" (Wilson 1996, 104). He hypothesizes "inner-city Black single parents, unlike their Mexican immigrant counterparts, feel little pressure to commit to a marriage" (Wilson 1996, 105). Accompanying the deteriorating labor market conditions that no longer sustain the "male breadwinner family," a new set of orientations has emerged that places less value on marriage and rejects the dominance of men as a standard of a successful husband-wife family (Wilson 1996, 105). It is the higher dislocation, joblessness, and concentrated poverty among inner-city Black men and the perceptions among many single mothers that the fathers of their children are limited financially and unreliable which primarily explains these behaviors. Simultaneously, there are weak norms supporting traditional husband-wife families that grow out of antagonistic and distrustful relationships between Black men and women. Despite these jobless conditions, sexual relations among inner-city Black teenagers are active, uncommitted, and influenced by peer pressures. Furthermore, in jobless ghettos the socialization to these ghetto-related norms across generations creates a "vicious cycle" and "tangle of pathology."

Wilson notes that Black children are less likely to be socialized into traditional expectations of family and work because: (1) mothers accept welfare
over low-wage employment (when child care and health insurance are not
provided by the latter); (2) fathers, who do not assume family responsibilities and experience restricted employment, become increasingly idle
(Wilson 1997, 107). Marriage is not a dominant part of the minds, hearts, or
spirits of the inner-city jobless.

Throughout this analysis, he compares the differences in joblessness
and poverty between African Americans and Mexican Americans and
attempts to explain why inner-city Blacks have much greater social isolation
and concentration effects despite the fact that Mexican Americans are more
recent immigrants to the cities. He argues that Mexican immigrants are more
economically integrated into the labor market; they emphasize traditional
norms of family and kinship (Wilson 1997, 106). Even where extramarital
relationships exist among Mexican Americans, there is greater group pressure
for marriage. Also, Mexican-American women with children draw from more
family, extended family, and friendship resources in providing child care
(Wilson 1997, 93). Wilson, however, is careful to interpret these patterns
among Mexican Americans as partly a situational consequence of social structural realities. He notes that marriage among Mexican immigrants "will very
likely decline the longer they remain in the United States and are exposed to
United States norms, patterns of behavior, and changing opportunity structures for men and women" (Wilson 1997, 106).

The disappearance of work alongside neighborhood ecological
processes of social isolation and concentration effects, which have reduced
traditional norms of marriage, family, and kinship, have resulted in the loss of
family among the inner-city poor in Chicago. Comparisons with Mexican
Americans indicate that these Blacks are significantly less integrated into the
labor market and less connected to traditional norms of family and extended
family. As a consequence of depressed economic situations, the inner-city
poor are socialized into ghetto-related culture. Although the structural economic changes are primary in explaining the loss of family, the discussion
provided by Wilson suggests that these economic factors are not sufficient.
As has been indicated earlier, the disappearance of traditional two-parent
families is a development that has occurred across social classes among
Blacks. While the levels of marriage and family are lowest among the poor,
the scale of losses is relatively similar for working and middle classes.

The social dislocations caused by Black unemployment and marginalization in labor markets have broader sources in social policies that have patterns of racial bias. Wilson argues that the loss of inner-city jobs not only has
decreased the supply of marriageable men, but also has resulted in norms
which are conducive to the acceptance of welfare over low-wage work and

the loss of traditional male parental responsibilities. The growth of crime, drugs, violence, and the "underground economy" are consequences of jobless ghettos.

Contemporary social policies neither have been favorable to the formation of Black families among the poor nor the marriageability of young Black males and females in general. These stateways interact to further depress the employability of Black Americans. As an extension, it should be emphasized that instead of increased employment and economic integration, there are recent signs that increased institutionalization, criminalization, meanness, and marginalization are predictable. First, the recent growth in prison industries and the increased incarceration of young Black men (18–30 years of age) in the criminal justice system are replacing the factories, technical training, and higher education of earlier post-World War II years. According to the United States Department of Justice, more than one-fourth of Black men (28.5 percent) are admitted to prison at least once and this rate is six times more likely than non-Hispanic White men (4.4) (Blumenstein 2001, 22). In some cities, the rate of Black males in their twenties under control of the criminal justice system exceeds 50 percent (Miller 1996). Second, recent reforms in the criminal justice system are reflected in sentencing disparities that have devastated the urban Black community. Accompanying the War on Drugs, racial profiling and disproportionately higher sentences for crack cocaine usage among poorer and working-class persons in contrast to powdered cocaine (an upper-class and middle-class drug), have removed the most visible cultural symbols of violence, crime, and drugs. Drug offenses, which account for racially disproportionate sentencing, find Blacks making up nearly 50 percent of all drug arrests. Interestingly, the sentencing disparity in the United States is the highest among advanced industrial nations. Third, the initiation of "welfare reform" policies while designed in principle to encourage work, has not been accompanied by commensurate increases in employment. There are indications that the "welfare reforms" provide fewer opportunities for educational improvement than earlier policies. Although these "welfare reforms" have been successful from the level of saving and redirecting public dollars, the shifting of these policies from the federal government to the states and local areas suggest uneven and punitive social programs for the Black poor.

THE CHANGING MEANING AND SIGNIFICANCE OF RACE AMONG EMPLOYERS

In *The Truly Disadvantaged*, Wilson understated the interaction of racial discrimination, segregation, and the concentrated poverty of inner-city Blacks. Consequently, the primary explanation of joblessness focused on structural dislocations caused by the loss of manufacturing jobs, the growing spatial mismatch between the suburban location of employers and inner-city workers, and the lack of human and social capital among Blacks. Critics of Wilson have charged that he had to a large degree left out the continuing role of race and cultural factors. He attempts to address these concerns in "The Meaning and Significance of Race."

However, "The Meaning and Significance of Race" is carefully delimited to examining the interaction between the changing world of work as seen through the eyes of employers and inner-city workers. It further elaborates the place of work in organizing the ecological, cultural, and sociological life of inner-city neighborhoods and the microsociological life of individuals. In this chapter, Wilson presents the results and interpretations of a survey focused on employers perceptions of inner-city workers' work ethics, job skills, basic skills, dependability, attitudes, and interpersonal skills drawn from the city of Chicago and Cook County. Here, he examines the demand-side of the employment question to ask "how employers view inner-city Black workers." Based on the 170 employers who provided comments in this survey, 74 percent expressed negative views of inner-city workers, describing the environment, neighborhood influences, family influences, and personal characteristics that inner-city workers bring to the work place (Wilson 1996, 112). In general, the levels of education and training brought to jobs by these inner-city workers, alongside the negative perceptions related to social-class behaviors, language skills, and mathematics skills are presented as the sociological facts leading to the reluctance of employers to hire inner-city Blacks or retain those who have been employed. Some employers interviewed shared concerns about these workers' honesty, cultural attitudes, and dependability.

Among the observations given by employers for why inner-city Black males cannot find or retain jobs, the two main reasons center on their lack of skills (38.5 percent) and lack of work ethic (36.9 percent). Other factors such as bad attitude (17.3 percent), lack of dependability (16.8 percent), lack of job skills (11.7 percent), and lack of interpersonal skills (8.9 percent) accounted for less weight. Interestingly, the role of racial discrimination is mentioned by less than one in seven employers (13.4 percent) (Wilson 1996, 118; table 9.1). When these observations of inner-city Black males are extended to Black employers, he finds that 80 percent offered negative comments in comparison with 74 percent of White employers. Because the statements concerning overt racial discrimination are not recognized as a significant factor in the employment of inner-city Blacks by most of the employers, and the statements of Black employers concerning the qualifications of inner-city Blacks, which do not differ significantly from White employers, Wilson infers that race discrimination does not appear to be a primary or salient factor. Consequently, he raises the question of how race interacts with other factors

(Wilson 1996, 136). While recognizing the continuing presence of discrimination, he underscores that the reduction of race in the labor market to a strong interpretation of racial discrimination is problematic. In reinterpreting the negative attitudes and actions of employers, he asks: "To what extent do they represent an aversion to Blacks per se and to what degree do they reflect judgments based on job-related skills and training of inner-city Blacks in a changing labor market?" (Wilson 1996, 136). As an alternative hypothesis, Wilson states that in the changing economy, employers are looking for workers with a broad range of abilities that are in short supply in inner-city schools. He asks: "If employers are indeed reacting to the difference in skills between Black and White applicants, it becomes increasingly difficult to discern the motives of employers: are they rejecting inner-city Black applicants out of overt racial discrimination or on the basis of qualifications?" (Wilson 1996, 136).

This alternative hypothesis is a variation of the mismatch hypothesis. At the same time, he identifies in these observations the presence of "statistical discrimination" in several of the selective recruitment strategies that employers use to screen out workers such as informal networks or referrals of employees, avoiding placing adds in city and ethnic newspapers, and passing over applicants from the public schools, welfare programs, and state employment service programs. Wilson's refocused discrimination explanation appears to grow out of the constraints of a slack labor market in which the demand for unskilled Black inner-city workers is low and their supply is high. Despite the disproportionately higher structural unemployment and underemployment among Black workers in general, it appears difficult for Wilson to interpret this disadvantage as strong employment discrimination. Indirect sources of discrimination, such as the unequal schools that inner-city workers attend, are usually found in the research to be a greater source of structural disadvantage. The deficits in human and social capital among inner-city workers and the discomfort and social distance among employers to hire them with weak discrimination appears to be interpreted as rational choice and practical.

It is also possible that short of antidiscrimination and active attempts to recruit inner-city workers, even those trained and qualified persons who happen to live in the inner city will have high probabilities of being unemployed. In asking "to what extent are they [employers] rejecting inner-city Black applicants out of overt racial discrimination or on the basis of qualifications," Wilson appears to be hinting that the latter explanation is stronger than the former. Overt racial discrimination would require conscious intent and in an increasingly rational marketplace would be noncompetitive, intolerable, and unusual. A situation of nondiscrimination, where all applicants are assessed on the basis of qualifications, would necessitate the elimination of both class and race discrimination. Although this would be more open and democratic, this apparently must also be rejected in a class and racially stratified marketplace. Wilson's discussion of discrimination is an attempt to elaborate an explanation that recognizes the complexities existing in the gray area between unconscious forms of systematic discrimination and nondiscrimination. The discussion of statistical discrimination appears to be an attempt to address institutional discrimination. Yet simultaneously, in denying the existence of institutional racism and giving credibility to deficits in human and social capital (as approximations of the culture of poverty), some observers view Wilson as embracing theoretical assumptions of rational discrimination (Steinberg 1997, 5).

While it is difficult to distinguish between the motives of employers and the consequences of employment practices, this mismatch hypothesis explains much less than it appears to. One alternative to the mismatch hypothesis would argue that racial segregation interacting with changing labor markets has reduced the demand for Black workers or diversity in general. In the most isolated White central city, suburban, and rural nonfarm areas, which are most spatially, socially, and culturally distant from central city Black areas, it is less likely that employers will find Black workers based on consumer tastes, employer preferences, and discrimination.

A second alternative to the mismatch hypothesis would argue that the low employment outcomes of Black men are in no small part a consequence of employer attitudes and stereotypes of the work ethic and employer's perceptions of the reliability and dependability of prospective Black male employees. Individual Black men, who are members of groups that have experienced the greatest employment discrimination and unemployment, are the same individuals that employers have the most negative attitudes and stereotypes. One might expect these employer's political and religious views, contacts with other racial groups, and degree of social and economic security (or insecurity) to enter these attitudes. The interaction between these racial attitudes, labor markets, and discrimination is more indirect and covert than direct and overt. Joleen Kirschenman and Kathryn Neckerman research on Chicago employers (Kirschenman and Neckerman 1991) validates this argument.

It is interesting that the nonrecognition of overt racial discrimination as a significant factor in the employment of inner-city Blacks by most of the employers and the statements of Black employers concerning the qualifications of inner-city Blacks do not differ significantly from White employers leads Wilson to the conclusion that race discrimination does not appear to be a primary or salient factor. Based on the data presented, there is no way of determining whether these attitudes and stereotypes of inner-city Blacks by Black and White employers are reflected in similar employment patterns.

(One should expect higher rates of inner-city employment among these Black employers simply because they have more contact with them.) Methodologically, one can raise several questions whether micro-level attitudinal data can adequately capture institutional discrimination that is more systemic in nature.

It is also possible that these attitudinal data address a dominant belief system or ideology concerning the decreasing significance of racial discrimination. Considering the labor market conditions and the lack of human and social capital among Black males in the inner city, it is difficult for employers (or for that matter the general public) to be empathetic or sympathetic for the inner-city disadvantaged.

Although there is little suggestion of strong racial discrimination, there is a discussion of the "selective recruitment" practices used by these Chicago employers that in effect significantly reduce the numbers of inner-city applicants in jobs (Wilson 1996, 133–136). From the perspective of employers, these practices are rational, practical, and efficient and contribute to a higher quality of applicants. Among the practices identified are those where employers limited recruitment to selective neighborhoods, avoided placing ads in Chicago newspapers, and passed over applicants from Black Chicago public schools. Interestingly, the subjective tests of job productivity used in employment interviews were more biased and yielded lower proportions of Black workers in entry level jobs than employers who used more objective skills tests . Alongside the "statistical discrimination," these "selective recruitment" practices constitute more rational, impersonal, and covert forms of discrimination.

Wilson has brought race back into the national discussion. However, while identifying contemporary patterns of "selective recruitment" and "statistical discrimination," any suggestion of strong racial discrimination and institutional discrimination are of secondary and declining significance. The lack of job-related skills and training among inner-city Blacks in the labor market figure more prominently than discrimination. What becomes clear is that the rational reasons provided by employers for not hiring inner-city Blacks are nested in nonracial and cultural factors. There is an implicit recommendation built into this analysis. Rather than emphasize racial discrimination, it appears more practical for the disadvantaged to strengthen their human and social capital resources and become more integrated and adaptable to mainstream presentations of self, interpersonal behaviors, and the technical skills favorable to assimilation.

In the Multi-City Study of Urban Inequality series, the principal findings show that while literacy, computer, and social skills are important to the integration of inner-city workers in the changing postindustrial labor force, race continues to interact with mismatch processes. In several cases, the effects of race are independent of the relationships predicted in mismatch hypotheses. Harry Holzer found that when controlling for "hard skills" requirements and the racial makeup of applicant pools, Blacks continued to be significantly underhired (Holzer 1996). Although skill requirements for suburban jobs were generally lower than for central city jobs, the hire rates for Blacks in the suburbs were much lower than in the inner city. Holzer also shares that "discriminatory employers may deliberately choose locations for their firms that make them inaccessible to Blacks" (Holzer 1996). Also, Phillip Moss and Chris Tilly found that some employers prefer to recruit immigrants rather than Blacks, even when Blacks have significantly higher skill levels and when immigrants live further away than the local Black population (Moss and Tilly 2001). These findings suggest a stronger role of current discrimination and bias.

THE AMERICAN BELIEF SYSTEM OF INDIVIDUALISM

The "Social Policy Challenge" outlines several elements of American culture and social structure that constitute Wilson's assessments of social change. There are chapters on "The American Belief System Concerning Welfare and Poverty" (Chapter 7) and "Racial Antagonisms and Race-Based Social Policy (Chapter 8) in *When Work Disappears: The World of the New Urban Poor.* For Wilson, American beliefs in individualism are a source of cultural values and norms that worsen rather than lessen contemporary inequalities. The crux of the problem is the following: While the objective social facts of unemployment, poverty, and welfare are primarily explained by structural factors such as global-level economic and industrial restructuring and rapid technological changes that bear on increased inequities between the highest and lowest paid labor, Americans in their social consciousness remain disposed to the idea that individuals are largely responsible for their economic situations. Drawing from public opinion polls and social surveys, he reveals that individualistic explanations for poverty such as lack of effort, lack of ability, poor morals, and poor work skills were given disproportionately more frequently by the American public than structural explanations such as lack of jobs, schooling, and low wages (Wilson 1996, 159). Drawing from the Kluegal and Smith survey (Kluegal and Smith 1988), he notes that the items most frequently cited by Americans centered on the lack of thrift and proper money management skills, "lack of effort," "lack of ability or talent," "attitudes from one's family that impede social mobility," "failure of society to provide good schools," and "loose morals and drunkenness." Simultaneously, Americans considered structural factors such as "low wages," "failure of industry to provide jobs," and "racial discrimination," least important (Wilson 1996, 160). As a public issue, Wilson notes that Americans are more concerned about the social obligations of the poor and particularly the welfare poor and less concerned about their social rights as American citizens.

Despite systematic social science research, which undermines the assumption that welfare negatively affects individual initiative and motivation, Wilson notes there is a paradox. Accompanying recent trends of continuing high poverty at a time of high prosperity, he explains that a dominant American belief system emphasizes "it is the moral fabric of individuals and not the social and economic structure of the society" that is taken up to be the root of the problem (Wilson 1996, 164). Wilson extends further that it is these beliefs, which formed the consensus for recent federal welfare reform initiatives, which are the basis for persistent stereotypes. At the same time, he locates within the social science research the evidence that Americans want to support those in poverty. He is sensitive that several meanings of welfare in the American belief system have associated racial feelings. He interprets these racial antagonisms as situational outcomes of economics and politics rather than as deep-seated and primordial relationships. The historically specific contemporary changes in metropolitan areas between central cities and suburbs that are further reflected in racial divides of Black and White are not insurmountable. Wilson challenges and critiques political leaders who have actually increased racial tensions by divisively encouraging racial groups to turn on each other and utilize arguments that blame the victims (Wilson 1996, 192–193).

To the extent that public issues such as unemployment, welfare, family break down, and inner-city crime are explained within the American public by individual failings, they are easily reinforced by the American belief system. In this context, he again emphasizes that race-based polices cannot solve the problems of the jobless poor. Nonracial factors, based on changing economic organization and the division of labor, figure more importantly than structures of racism, discrimination, and prejudice in the contemporary inequalities experienced by Blacks. While he recognizes that race, as a structural and cultural relationship, is a continuing feature of American society, the concept of racism is ambiguous. Generally speaking, public discussions of inequality, which are based on racism, tend to be divisive and polarizing. Most importantly, arguments based largely on racism fail to distinguish between the historic and current effects of racism on the changing status of the Black population and are much less likely to be heard, acknowledged, and legitimated in public policy. Wilson underscores that "during hard economic times, it is important that political leaders channel the frustrations of citizens in positive and constructive directions." (Wilson 1996, 192). It makes a difference, in Wilson's assessment, whether policy programs are based on nonracial vis-à-vis racial factors.

The discussion of "Racial Antagonisms and Race Based Social Policy" is both analysis and social policy prescription that attempts to clarify how the interaction between politically based policies and economic and social processes directly and indirectly affect racial antagonisms in urban America. Because the dominant American belief system, as reflected in White public opinion, associates poverty and welfare with individual shortcomings and overwhelmingly objects to government programs to address discrimination, policies that are perceived as benefiting only Blacks and racial minorities have been resisted, challenged, and overturned (Wilson 1996, 203).

Within these constraints, universal, social rights, and opportunity enhanced policies, which address issues such as job training, school reform, child care, and national health care, have potentially broad-based coalitions and constituencies that cut across the divides of cities and suburbs, social classes, and racial groups. Over the long run, analyses and policies that focus on improving the social and economic status of all groups rather than the most disadvantaged, will result in greater equality that will ultimately benefit Blacks. By contrast, race-specific and targeted policies and more controversial demagogic leadership that are focused on racially divisive issues are more likely to heighten existing racial antagonisms.

THE AMERICAN BELIEF SYSTEM IN CROSS-NATIONAL CONTEXTS

Wilson compares the American belief system of poverty and welfare with beliefs in other industrial democracies such as Britain, Canada, France, Germany, Italy, and Japan. In this discussion of the continuities and discontinuities among advanced industrial nations, he is asking to what extent might Americans learn from the economic, educational, and welfare initiatives of these nations and simultaneously how might these nations learn from the United States. This chapter is a framework for discussing the "appropriateness of long-term solutions to the jobs question in the United States" which specifically addresses the underlying structural relationships of employment, education, and family support systems and the structural relationships between cities and suburbs (Wilson 1996, 208).

With respect to employment, education, and family support systems, Wilson emphasizes that the United States can learn from nations such as Japan and Germany that have developed policies to increase high performance standards for secondary school graduation and strengthen the transitions between training and the workplace. These reforms are urgent because among the industrial democracies, he identifies the United States as having the weakest system of school to work transitions. Nations that have universal family policies, such as preschool child support and national leave programs, may inform the United States (Wilson 1996, 215). As an example, he highlights the French system of universal family policies which include extensive infant care, nursery schools, paid leave for newborn parents, child support enforcement, children's allowances, welfare payments for single mothers, and universal health care is highlighted (Wilson 1996, 215).

Capturing the discontinuity he underscores: "Among industrialized countries the United States is alone in having no universal preschool child-support, or parental leave programs" (Wilson 1996, 215). The cross-national comparison with European nations also offers lessons on city-suburban integration and cooperation along the lines of metropolitan politics, metropolitan planning, and regional authorities (Wilson 1996, 219). Wilson is aware that the governments in these nations have made more proactive and concerted attempts to plan and control urban development than the United States through their greater preservation of historic urban cores, greater public subsidization of housing construction and public housing, support of public mass transit, and a greater commitment to social welfare services that reduce inequality. Among the reforms identified in city-suburban cooperation in the United States are metropolitan tax base sharing.

However, it is instructive that Wilson stops short of advancing the "Europeanization" of macroeconomic policy and the social welfare policies of these social democracies in the United States. He emphasizes that the United States should "learn from the approaches used in other countries and adapt the best aspects into our own homegrown solutions" (Wilson 1996, 220). While applauding the universal policies and social rights of European nations, he recognizes the high costs and limitations of these. In Europe, the high levels of unemployment benefits received by lower skilled European workers has translated into an unwillingness to accept the lower-paying jobs that lower-income workers in the United States are forced to take (Wilson 1996, 220–221).

At the same time, Wilson recognizes that there are constraints to importing the social policies of European nations based on their different histories and cultures in addition to increasing strains being placed on the welfare state. He notes that many of the problems of race, unemployment, and the concentration of urban poverty that earlier characterized the United States are increasingly present in European nations (Wilson 1996, 221). Wilson recognizes that the economic and social changes in cities of Europe have created situations favorable for the growth of anti-immigrant antagonisms and the demagogic mobilization of racism. He has noted elsewhere that the heightening of racial antagonisms are exemplified in the looting of African and Asian asylum centers in Germany, attacks of Africans in French and Italian cities, and riots within Black neighborhoods in Britain (Wilson 1993c, 2).

To the extent that immigrant workers are disproportionately represented among the unskilled, jobless, and publicly identified in the debate over the maintenance of the welfare state, Wilson is conscious of the increased possibilities that changing economic and labor contexts in Europe will be politically mobilized and reproduced in ideological racism, discrimination, and segregation. Before the post-World War II years, European political parties, social movements, and policies associated with social democracy and universal rights were not significantly challenged by domestic issues of racism and race.

While Wilson emphasizes that the industrial democracies of Europe might inform the possibilities of social democracy in the United States, he is aware that the higher unemployment rates, larger unemployment benefits, and stronger unionization are not likely to be integrated into the United States economy in the near future. It is more likely that European nations might incorporate the lower unemployment, right to work laws, and free market privatization strategies from the United States.

The broader vision for economic integration combines the policy proposals of Sheldon Danziger and Peter Gottschalk (1995) and Micky Kaus (1986, 1992). Because structural shifts and demands in the economy have shifted from low-skilled workers, and the private sector is less willing to use low-skilled workers, Wilson anticipates that the public sector will be expected to create minimum-wage public service jobs modeled after the New Deal WPA type jobs (Wilson 1996, 232–233). Wilson emphasizes that the jobs created will not be high-wage jobs but with universal health care insurance, a child care program, and earned income tax credits attached, they would enable workers and their families to live at least decently and avoid joblessness and the problems associated with it (Wilson 1996, 234).

These continuities between the United States and the advanced industrial democracies and the possibilities of employment growth inspired by the New Deal WPA represent, however, only part of the structural challenges of social democracy confronting this analysis of inner-city employment in an increasingly postindustrial global society. Domestically, the political consequences of Black joblessness have a bearing on the interpretation and operationalization of the thirteenth and fifteenth amendments to the Constitution, the future of civil rights, and universal social rights.

Cross-nationally, the continuities among African Americans in the Diaspora and people of color within the southern hemisphere nations of the Third World may also inform the issues of racism, inequality, unemployment, and the concentration of poverty in the United States. Although the universal norms and values of advanced-industrial nations remain most explicit in our comparative analyses, the experiences of poverty and racism within countries such as South Africa and Brazil may inform the less articulated challenges of inequality and social and human rights bearing on African Americans in the United States. In the long run, it will be the fate of peoples and nations in Africa, Asia, and Latin America that will decide the fate of the rest of the world, both morally and economically.

COALITION POLITICS AND *THE BRIDGE OVER THE RACIAL DIVIDE*

In Wilson's most recent book, *The Bridge Over the Racial Divide: Rising Inequalities and Coalition Politics* (1999), he refocuses his analyses of rising economic inequality in American society with prescriptive arguments for a progressive, multiracial political coalition to combat inequality. Accompanying recent trends of globalization and economic inequality, upper- and upper-middle classes and working classes and the poor are becoming increasingly fragmented along racial lines and as a consequence do not see the possibilities of mutual political interests that cross the racial divide. As a counterveiling strategy he argues: "A large, strong, and organized political constituency is essential for the development and implementation of policies that will reverse the trends of rising inequality and ease the burdens of ordinary families" (Wilson 1999, 1). The book is a theoretical discussion of "how a broad-based multiracial constituency can be created, sustained, and energized." This book is dedicated to the labor and civil rights leader, Bayard Rustin who advanced a liberal-labor electoral coalition based on economic populism and universal social policies (Rustin 1971; Anderson 1997). More importantly, the book is explicitly defined as a new public rhetoric (Wilson 1999, 43).

Wilson argues that the creation of a multiracial coalition will depend on an adequate understanding of the conditions that cause racism to flourish and subside including the conditions that have contributed to rising inequality. Underlying his analysis is a situational perspective that locates the nature, dynamics, and consequences of racism as interrelated with social, economic, and political conditions. Racism, as defined by Wilson, is an ideology of racial domination which features: (1) beliefs that a designated racial group is either biologically or culturally inferior to the dominant group, (2) the use of such beliefs to rationalize or prescribe the racial group's treatment in society and to explain its social position and accomplishments (Wilson 1999, 14–15). Wilson recognizes that while the more categorical forms of biological racism and beliefs that "Blacks should be denied equal rights and privileges" have declined in significance, some institutional arrangements and practices continue to be guided by implicit racist assumptions, especially cultural racist assumptions" (Wilson 1999, 16). This "institutional cultural racism," which continues to be present in public and private institutions, impedes the progress of Blacks and other minorities and ultimately reinforces individual cultural racist beliefs about their traits and capabilities (Wilson 1999, 18).

Analyzing the forms of individual racial ideology that are prevalent in public opinion and racial attitude surveys, he emphasizes that the traditional White American attitudes favorable to principles of racial segregation and discrimination have been replaced by a mild form of cultural racist ideology (or "persistent subtle racism"), which combines its opposition to governmental programs with stereotypes about Black cultural traits. For purposes of a multiracial coalition, he underscores, "it would be a mistake to focus on this new form of racial ideology, however widely endorsed when discussing the willingness of Americans to work with other racial groups in a progressive coalition." (Wilson 1999, 23).

Economic anxiety, which has accompanied changes in the global economy and increasing social inequality, has been played on by highly visible demagogues who have heightened racial tensions. From the results of national public opinion polls, Wilson advances the possibility of a new alignment in support of a comprehensive social rights initiative that underscores the need for economic and social reform that benefits all groups. This multiracial coalition not only will have a broader vision of American race relations that acknowledges the existence of racial ideology and its past and present impact on the lives of minorities, but also would recognize other important race-neutral economic and social processes. In this more holistic perspective of the African-American economic experience, nonracial factors such as international competition and technological changes related to information-based systems and microcomputers and the expansion of free trade have reduced the importance of manufacturing and unskilled labor, resulting in increased joblessness and decreased wages among African Americans.

Wilson's recent discussions of racism in *The Bridge Over the Racial Divide* draw from an earlier distinction between biological and cultural racism developed in *Power, Racism, and Privilege*. This discussion is informed less by sociological considerations than political constraints. While he brings racism back into the discourse, he does so in a relatively limited manner. Several theoretical dilemmas and problems reappear. First, racism is analyzed as an intervening variable rather than an independent (or causal) variable (Early 1996). As such, larger social conditions such as the state of the economy and public policy figure more crucially. Second, the notion of racism is reduced to an ideology consisting of beliefs, assumptions, and values. While acknowledging that racism is present in institutions, his discussion is largely focused on the operationalization of these ideologies in public opinion and racial attitudes. Third, as a consequence of the public rhetoric and the multiracial politics coalition strategy focusing on universal nonracial issues, the challenge for organizing becomes focused on the issue of individual racism rather than institutional racism. Fourth, the discussion of the replacement of traditional biological racism by contemporary cultural racism has assimilation implications that race has declined in significance. Biological racism, which is more easily translated categorically, has given way to cultural racism that is more sensitive to propensities of individual minorities to assimilate. Fifth, there is the assumption that changes in racial inequality follow in large part from larger economic struggles for social rights and equality and political structures such as coalitions. Although there is little disagreement over the premise of a necessary relationship between political coalitions and larger struggles for social rights and equality, the form and composition these coalitions and social movements may take are complex, diverse, and open to controversy.

The current conventional wisdom, which is shared by conservatives, neoconservatives, neoliberals, and liberals stresses that the form of citizenship and political participation that most strengthens democratic institutions should emphasize universal norms and values that address the interests of all Americans. Group-specific coalitions that emphasize the politics of identity, race, ethnicity, gender, and sexual orientation are viewed as divisive and "balkanizing." Over the long run, there is little question that democratic coalitions, embracing social rights and equality, emerge from multiracial politics, whether involving integration, interracial cooperation, or pluralistic alignments.

Wilson appears to be arguing the primacy of multiracial politics in which racial minorities are integrated into majority group White political coalitions. While it is based on rational interests, it is also driven by assumptions of Anglo-American conformity. This argument, which is largely taken from Bayard Rustin (Rustin 1971), assumes that the interests of liberal, labor, and reform groups are identical with the interests of African Americans. In a racially segregated and divided society, there are several lessons from history that suggest that African Americans at the local and national levels might frequently "close ranks" and become empowered before forming national multiracial coalitions. As Stokely Carmichael and Charles Hamilton noted in these liberal coalitions the political and social rights of African Americans "have been and will always be negotiable and expendable the moment they conflict with the interests of their allies" (Carmichael and Hamilton 1967, 62–63). One can also critique whether the proposed labor coalitions between African-Americans and majority group White American workers derive from an analysis that recognizes their fundamentally different economic interests. As Sidney Wilhelm has forcefully argued in contemporary America, "the working class is divided not only because of racism, but also because of objective economic realities that necessitate divergent economic needs along racial lines" (Wilhelm 1980, 107). While the struggle for White Americans is increasingly a struggle against temporary joblessness, underemployment, and low wages for African Americans, the struggle is against permanent unemployment, temporary employment, persistent poverty, and expendability (Wilhelm 1980, 107). The class analysis in *Bridge Over the Racial Divide* views the high levels of unemployment among African Americans as a situational consequence of globalization and deindustrialization rather than as a permanent feature of the postindustrial economy.

As alternatives, one could easily argue that: (1) minority coalitions may initially close ranks around political interests that grow out of group-specific issues and reflect local situations prior to becoming parts of a national multiracial coalition; (2) simultaneously organize national political coalitions across and within racial groups. A. Phillip Randolph's 1941 March on Washington Movement (MOWM), which resulted in Executive Order 8802 and the dismantling of discrimination in industries receiving defense contracts, was organized as an independent Black social movement for both strategic and symbolic reasons. The history of the southern civil rights movement is filled with numerous localized movements that grew out of indigenous Black social institutions, organizations, and their mobilized resources (Morris 1984).

These questions aside, *The Bridge Over the Racial Divide* may have another message that goes beyond historical and sociological analysis. As the nation enters the twenty-first century, Wilson recognizes that existing social policies are not addressing the problems of ordinary families across race such as decent wages, affordable housing, quality education, and health care. The multiracial coalition that he envisions builds on and is informed by preexisting campaigns such as the national Coalition Campaign for Jobs and Income and the Living Wage Campaign.

OTHER REFLECTIONS ON *WHEN WORK DISAPPEARS*

When Work Disappears represents both sociological analysis and public discourse on the changing economic and social fortunes of inner-city Blacks in the postindustrial city at the close of the twentieth century. As a sociological analysis, it addresses the causes and consequences of joblessness on the microsociological structure of community, family, and social networks and attempts to explain why African Americans in comparison with newer minority groups are less assimilated and structurally integrated into mainstream American society. The historically specific conditions of plant closings and the emergence of a new service economy are accompanied by a situation in which Black labor is increasingly viewed as socially marginal and expendable. The analysis of the deficiencies in Black human and social capital alongside the employer's perceptions of inner-city Black workers' failings enables an interpretation where racism and discrimination are essentially nonracial.

As a public policy discourse, which is designed to draw attention to the more macroeconomic policies bearing on employment, training, and education in an increasingly information-based postindustrial society, Wilson's discussions are explicitly concerned with consciousness raising and the longer term political strategy of framing a public rhetoric and political coalition that will bring about universal social democratic rights. These discussions of public policy are importantly concerned with issues and themes that have been pervasive throughout his scholarly career—the roles of ideology, values, and cultural beliefs in race relations. While identifying a contradiction between universalistic American cultural beliefs of equality and the American ideology of individualism that represents a challenge to the liberal expectancy, Wilson pragmatically stops short of the larger underlying structural forces. While identifying a direct correlation between the growth of economic anxiety and racial antagonisms, the moral higher ground selected is one where issues such as economic growth, full employment, stronger school to work relationships, and transitional jobs preclude racially divisive issues centered on racism and discrimination. The substance and symbolism of this discourse in tone suggest not only enlightenment and pragmatism, but also suggest that as public discourse, race has declined in significance.

Both the sociological analysis and the public policy discourse are intertwined in the refocused liberal perspective of changing American institutions and race relations that were earlier elucidated in *The Declining Significance of Race* and *The Truly Disadvantaged*. The assimilation and integration assumptions in this recent work are strong in suggesting that the postindustrial technological revolution and economy that has led to large-scale social dislocations among inner-city Blacks might be addressed by social democratic reforms and the increased adaptation of African Americans to mainstream culture.

The analysis of deindustrialization and joblessness represents the fusion of sociological analysis and cultural myth. The cultural myth of Blacks in the industrial economy is derived in part from the liberal expectancy hypotheses of the idealized relationships between the growing industrial economy and the integration of Blacks into the society and the role of neoliberal policies. The cultural myth takes a historic interpretation of Blacks in the post-World War II economy that emphasizes greater structural integration than racial segmentation within the changing division of labor and opportunity structure. This myth generalizes the market experiences of Blacks in the most advanced corporate industrial sectors to the Black population in general. Some critics have suggested that lower-class Blacks were never represented as significantly in the industrial economy as hypothesized but were more represented as service workers (Steinberg 1997; Fainstein and Nesbitt 1996).

While Wilson's analysis is correct in identifying an economic situation in which Blacks are less integrated into the industrial economy and manufacturing employment than earlier, the descriptions of these contemporary economic contexts may be more accurate than the historical and sociological analyses.

Relatedly, in prescribing a policy solution to inner-city dislocations, Wilson takes the logic of economic growth and transitional jobs based on the experiences of the Works Progress Administration (WPA) forward to reintegrate Blacks into the postindustrial economy. The tone of this discussion provides an optimistic assessment that the government might play an enlightened and pragmatic role in addressing this heightened unemployment and joblessness. Yet it is also possible that in not frontally assaulting institutional discrimination, the presence of "transitional jobs" in the long run will be accompanied by persistent racial and class inequality that will hit the Black poor the hardest.

One of the underlying messages of *When Work Disappears* centers on how it prescribes the incorporation of African Americans into a changing postindustrial society. At the beginning of the twentieth century, leaders as diverse as Booker T. Washington, W. E. B. Du Bois, Marcus Garvey, and A. Phillip Randolph debated and attempted to actualize the most appropriate strategies for empowering and improving the social and economic conditions of African Americans. Although there were competing emphases of integration and Black nationalism in their objectives, the most successful leadership combined aspects of both approaches. Wilson's policy prescriptions grow out of a sociological analysis of the changing relationships between industrial economic growth and opportunity that converges symbolically with A. Phillip Randolph. With the emphases on economic growth and liberal labor coalitions, the substance of these policy prescriptions is closer to Randolph's disciple, Bayard Rustin. This is the post-civil rights Rustin who was unwavering in his arguments for liberal coalitions between organized labor and Blacks; he frequently criticized affirmative action for splintering these relationships.

The diversity of the African American experience has historically and contemporaneously been accompanied by other strategies of incorporation. As we are reminded by John Sibley Butler, Blacks who have historically emphasized the education of their children, encouraged entrepreneurship, home ownership, and self-help have also developed the social institutions, organizations, and leadership that have enabled adaptation and achievement. Rather than focusing on the integration of the Black poor into "transitional jobs," Butler emphasizes that in a changing postindustrial informational society, Blacks should focus on how to educate their children while providing important values. While the policies accompanying these efforts should emphasize building social incentives and nondiscrimination, racism does not have to be frontally assaulted (Butler 1991; Butler 1997).

As Rod Bush reminds us, there has also been a continuing role of radical Black nationalist movements among the oppressed that is a necessary part of challenging the institutional contradictions and social dislocations of globalization and deindustrialization (Bush 1999). Radical Black nationalism has included an antisystem analysis that connects capitalism, colonialism, racism, and classism while advancing redistributional programmatic objectives (Bush 1999, 238). These radical Black nationalist movements are critical of the sociological analysis and program objectives of liberal universalism which it views as a strategy of integrating and co-opting upper strata minorities.

When Work Disappears provides a macrosociological analysis of joblessness and poverty that importantly brings social structure into the center of the national debate. Its assessment of Black social and economic conditions is a necessary and substantial improvement over the pernicious and pejorative interpretations of morality and culture-of-poverty in conservative perspectives. At the same time, these discussions are less than sufficient in addressing the continuing racism, discrimination, and exclusion that characterize contemporary labor markets for Blacks. The objective conditions of Black joblessness are largely seen through the subjective sociological prisms of employers.

CHAPTER 7

WILLIAM JULIUS WILSON AND THE PROMISE OF SOCIOLOGY

BACKGROUND

William Julius Wilson's perspectives of changing American institutions, race, class, and the postindustrial city represent an important contribution of the use of sociology in public policy controversies. Wilson's perspectives bring together sociological prisms of theory, research, public policy, and cultural beliefs. As a public intellectual, his scholarship has challenged academic sociologists to engage the world outside of the university. Most importantly, Wilson's social democratic arguments for addressing urban inequality urge the development of economic common ground across the racial divide.

In this chapter, Wilson's scholarship on questions of race, class, and the postindustrial city, public policy discussions, and his role as a public intellectual will be discussed, assessed, and reflected upon. While he is best known for the sociological analyses of urban inequality contained in *The Declining Significance of Race* (1978), *The Truly Disadvantaged* (1987), and *When Work Disappears* (1997), these are only parts of a more complex intellectual attempt to place sociology strategically in the national public policy agenda. As I have pointed out earlier, these concerns have developed from his formal and pragmatic approaches to sociological theory and a continuing attempt to develop a holistic or societal model of race relations. The synthesis of theory, research, and public policy discussions provided in this scholarship represents an important social and cultural commentary. The letter, spirit, and action dimensions of William Julius Wilson in the American and sociological conscience are larger than the sum of the parts.

Wilson's contributions to the public understanding of sociology are broadly recognized. These contributions have influenced the public, private, and nonprofit arenas. President Bill Clinton has mentioned that William Julius Wilson's books "made me see race and poverty and the problems of the inner city in a different light" (*TIME* 1996). It is significant that Wilson participated in the Economic Conference of the President-Elect and Vice

President-Elect, served as a member of two Presidential Commissions, and was regularly consulted by President Bill Clinton and First Lady Hillary Clinton. His public service expertise is partly exemplified by memberships on New York Governor Mario Cuomo's Task Force on Poverty and Welfare (1986–87), the United States Department of Labor Commission of Work-force Quality and Labor Market Efficiency (1988–90), and Chicago Mayor Richard Daley's Youth Development Task Force (1993–95). Senator Bill Bradley of New Jersey informed Wilson that *The Truly Disadvantaged* illumi-nated his and other senators' understanding of the problems of ghetto poverty, raised their consciousness, and increased their awareness of the need for effective public policy to address these problems (Wilson 1993b, 9).

Nobel Prize winning economist, Robert Solow, has noted that Wilson's scholarship has influenced the tone of the argument on the pathology of poverty in central cities by bringing "careful observation and fieldwork to bear on a set of issues that have generally excited buzzwords, ideology, and polemics." "In shifting the policy debate from the culture of poverty and indi-vidual responsibility to the realities of the labor market," Wilson has made a convincing link between the "sociological aspects of ghetto life and the more narrowly economic factors of wage levels and the supply and demand balance for unskilled male labor." Solow adds that several of the hypotheses empha-sized by Wilson such as the lack of adequate job opportunities for Black males in inner-city poor areas, the flight of the middle class from urban ghetto areas, leaving an absence of role models, and the problems arising in the Black community from the absence of eligible husbands have clear public policy implications (R. Solow, letter to author, September 9, 1997).

Wilson's analysis and clarification of underclass concepts and hypothe-ses in their social structural contexts in *The Truly Disadvantaged* and *When Work Disappears* and the integration of his scholarly concerns into leading public policy and social science research institutions represents an important refocusing of the uses of sociology. While earlier sociologists have attempted to bring the imagination and insights of sociological theory and research into public policy controversies, Wilson probably more than any scholar helped reformulate and shift the national debate on poverty and the under-class during the 1980s and 1990s from the conservative perspectives empha-sizing the culture of poverty and individual responsibility to structural and environmental causes. There can be no doubt that the clear, dispassionate, and persuasive style of Wilson's scholarship has helped make the types of problems raised concerning the inner-city ghetto visible and acceptable to a large audience.

The moral and symbolic value of Wilson's role in sociological contro-versies has been partly related to his status as a leading African-American scholar who has taken on the most disputed questions of race and class in postindustrial America. In these sociological controversies, he has intellectu-ally challenged and debated successfully the nation's leading scholars. Accord-ing to Herbert Gans: "Wilson's work is the work that everyone has to answer to, one way or another" (Remnick 1996). Gans also credits Wilson with uniquely bringing sociology into public policy and increasing the public's understanding of sociology. Relatedly, Douglas Massey notes: "Wilson has helped refocus the attention of the discipline [sociology] to social structures. . . . During the 1960s and 1970s, the field of sociology became data driven. Much of this became focused on questions of individuals as much as social structures" (D. Massey, interview by author, August 10, 1997).

In response to *The Declining Significance of Race* controversy, Nathan Glazer notes: "Wilson's book looks at the present and future. These are not things that haven't been said before. It is the first time a Black social scientist has said them with such strength" (West 1979, 3). In his handling of the con-troversy in *The Declining Significance of Race*, "Skip" Gates shares

> For Wilson to publish that thesis he had to be willing to say, This is how I looked at the evidence. I've thought about it, and this is the way I think it is. I know everybody's going to beat me on my head, but I have to be willing to hang tough. To me, you're in the wrong profession if you don't have that kind of courage. You're not running for the president of the Black Nation; you're running for a kind of immortality, and it's contingent upon a kind of honesty. (Banks 1996, 231)

Critics appraise differently the substance, moral, and symbolic value of Wilson's scholarship. These center on the cultural and political functions of his analyses and social policy prescriptions. Douglas Massey underscores that Wilson "offered a vision of urban problems that Democrats found comfort-able. This didn't require them up front to deal with race. At the same time, Republicans felt that it legitimated their ideas" (D. Massey, interview by author, August 10, 1997). Adolph Reed emphasizes that Wilson's analyses and policy recommendations are "liberal accommodationism" that embraces the conservative right's frame of reference as a means of demonstrating credibil-ity (Reed 1996). According to Reed, Wilson's appropriation of "Black pathol-ogy" and "ghetto-related behavior" interpretations provided the legitimation for conservative welfare reform policies. In reincarnating Moynihan's analy-sis and public policy prescriptions, Stephen Steinberg views Wilson as legit-imizing the "retreat from race" (Steinberg 1995, 126). Steinberg notes that in repudiating race-based politics and social policy, Wilson has been immune to charges of racism (Steinberg 1995, 125). In retreating from an analysis that recognizes the contemporary presence of institutional racism, Steinberg views Wilson's analysis of deficient Black human and social capital giving cre-dence to rational discrimination among employers (Steinberg 1997). Charles

Willie notes that the interpretation of race and class offered by Wilson is the "perspective of the dominant people of power." "With respect to the role of how social change comes about, there is little Black self-determination in this assessment" (C. Willie, interview by author, June 23, 1997).

In Wilson's scholarship, the promise of sociology draws primarily from its role in formulating public issues and policy research. It represents the union of sociological theory and political sociology. Sociological and public policy controversies are the vehicles for this enterprise. Driving this promise of sociology is a recognition that the future of sociology will increasingly be based on the extent which sociological theories, hypotheses, and concepts are used in the formulation and discussion of public policy issues and the extent which sociological research broadens its domain of policy relevant scholarship and becomes more pragmatic, flexible, and accessible. There is an activism and political sociology contained in this promise.

Through sociological controversies, Wilson has been influential in refocusing contemporary race relations by synthesizing macrosociological perspectives of American institutions, organizations, and cities alongside diverse social order and power conflict perspectives of race relations. Throughout his career, sociological controversy and discourses are used to develop dialogues among competing theoretical perspectives in sociology and social policy. From the competition and contradiction between perspectives emerges a synthesis that is more holistic.

The syntheses in Wilson's discussions are evolutionary. Wilson's earliest formulations emphasize societal factors such as industrialization and urbanization and incorporate dynamic relationships among politics, power resource mobilization, systems of stratification, and racism. Early on, race relations are examined through intergroup relations and situational perspectives where functional conflict in race matters is primary. In subsequent formulations, he gives more significance to the macrosociological factors of industrialization, urbanization, and systems of stratification and at the same time incorporates an intragroup analysis of changing class and race intersections in his analyses of the Black middle class and urban underclass. Contained in the synthesis, which constitutes his holistic theory, is a primarily normative approach of addressing social problems.

Wilson's approach of theorizing has syntheses that fuse his observations, impressions, and generalizations with the theoretical controversies, empirical research, and public policy discussions of other sociologists and social scientists. Simultaneously, he has explicated the meanings of various concepts, hypotheses, theory sketches, and theories and integrated them into a societal or holistic framework. The possibilities of this theorizing are based in part on the sociological perspective constituting a starting point or center for the assessment of changing American institutions. Accordingly, this theorizing focuses on the generalizations, the linkages between macrosociological and microsociological structures and relationships, and the connections with public policy. In this enlightened approach, he brings together both complexity and simplicity in his analyses.

Also, the promise of sociology is found in a refocused liberal analysis of postindustrial capitalism that brings economics and politics into center stage. In both *The Truly Disadvantaged* and *When Work Disappears*, there is the attempt to explain the objective social facts of unemployment, poverty, and welfare primarily by social structural factors such as global-level economic and industrial restructuring and rapid technological changes that bear on increased inequities between the highest and lowest paid labor. Contained in this liberal analysis is a critique and reformulation of existing macroeconomic policies such as unemployment and underemployment, income inequalities, monetary policies, education-to-work transitions, child care, and health. The liberal analysis and social reforms provided are part of a moral and long-range vision.

The limitations in this approach derive from its strengths and are in large part found in the syntheses and generalizations. There is significant ambiguity in his approach that grows from the competing philosophical, theoretical, and ideological assumptions that are integrated in the syntheses. No doubt, part of this ambiguity reflects the holistic intellectual tendencies of theoretical eclecticism and pluralism that attempt to bring together competing and frequently contradictory canons of social science and practice. In contributing to the public understanding of sociology, there is ambiguity reflected in the blurring of his contributions as a sociological theorist and social researcher. There is the failure to distinguish the normative and empirical orientations in his analysis of social problems. This appears to be a latent function of the multiple roles that Wilson is expected to play as a sociological theorist and public intellectual both inside and outside the academy.

Relatedly, there is considerable ambiguity in his approach that grows from the competing politics and policy perspectives addressed. The dialectical reasoning in Wilson's discussions moves back and forth between pessimistic, conservative analyses and optimistic, liberal analyses. While the objective analyses of social structure and social change are variably characterized by relationships of integrative conflict and social control, the prescriptive vision of macroeconomic reforms, an urban Marshall Plan, and universal social rights draws strongly from his normative assumptions of liberal and social democratic politics. The possibilities afforded by the analyses of refocused liberal, social democratic, and race-neutral politics also constitute the constraints in his analyses of Blacks in cities.

The promise of sociology is found less in the empirical research that he has directed and interpreted. For most of his professional career, the theoretical research approach used by Wilson has not involved primary or secondary empirical research. The methodology and data manipulation used in his studies are generally descriptive and basic. The insights and generalizations derived from these studies are not really new or innovative. The historical and sociological observations and insights of Blacks in cities provided by Wilson, were developed earlier by scholars such as W. E. B. Du Bois, Robert Park, Ernest Burgess, Charles S. Johnson, E. Franklin Frazier, Allison Davis, St. Clair Drake, and Horace Cayton. The underlying conceptual model for examining contemporary changes among the Black inner-city poor is derived from an ecological perspective that earlier in the twentieth century predicted the growth and differentiation of groups that are isolated and concentrated by processes of invasion, succession, and segregation.

The Urban Poverty and Family Life Study (UPFLS), the research project that was designed to test Wilson's hypotheses, has been critiqued. Douglas Massey indicates that despite its generous support and funding, the Urban Poverty and Family Life Study has not influenced social science commensurate with its size and scope (Massey 1997, 416). Although the UPFLS study has been used extensively by scholars inside the project, relatively few studies using the data have appeared in leading social science journals and the data has not been used by researchers outside the project. Furthermore, Massey notes that *When Work Disappears* makes sparing use of the UPFLS data in "a decidedly nonanalytical way." In general, the data are not used to critically test explanations or to evaluate theories (Massey 1997, 416). The tabulations of survey results are presented to illustrate points and the quotations from the ethnographies are used to buttress arguments (Massey 1997, 416).

The uses of sociological controversy, consciousness raising, and cultural interpretation constitute the promise of Wilson's sociology that is partly inspired by C. Wright Mills. In *The Sociological Imagination*, C. Wright Mills identified the important consciousness and cultural meaning roles that sociological thinking might serve in formulating personal troubles into public issues that were situated in changing institutional contradictions (Mills 1959). Mills recognized that standing between the consciousness and material existence of people in modern society was communications (Mills 1951, 151), and sociologists in a democracy were challenged to increase social consciousness while developing the public understanding of social issues (Mills 1959, 192). Among the intellectual and political challenges facing sociologists were those of clarifying the values of truth, reason, and human freedom and politically actualizing these as philosopher kings, advisors, and independent intellectuals (Mills 1959, 179–181). Changing post-World War II American institutions, challenged Mills to critically examine the consequences of these as crystallized in *The Power Elite* and the new middle class in *White Collar: The American Middle Class*. Mills saw the bureaucratization and professionaliza-

tion of knowledge in academia, resulting in the growth of increased requirements of adaptability, technical precision, and routinization that constrained
sociologist's intellectual roles of clarifying the values of truth, reason, and
human freedom.

William Julius Wilson's attempts to connect sociological theory and
research with public policy, and develop a more important political role, illustrate one direction of the promise of sociology as outlined by C. Wright
Mills. Underlying this promise of sociology is an intellectual approach that
has continually clarified the meanings of truth, reason, and freedom and
clearly articulated what sociology is and should be. It is also significant that
Wilson's humanistic sociology challenges sociology to abandon the excesses
of its empirical precision and routinization and embrace a higher calling
based on its intellectual imagination and social consciousness. The promise
in William Julius Wilson's sociology contains an ongoing critique of the
retreat from this promise and a resolution that sociologists should complete
to actualize this promise.

For purposes of further discussing this intellectual approach and
reviewing the "promise of sociology," there are several important features in
Wilson's sociology which include (but are not limited to): (1) the complexity
and kaleidoscope of images growing from his sociological controversies, (2) a
holistic perspective of the sociologist and social policy, (3) his refocusing the
normative approach to the analyses of social problems, and (4) his refocusing
the liberal perspective. An attempt is made to also identify the challenges,
constraints, and problems facing his intellectual exercise.

A KALEIDOSCOPE OF IMAGES

William Julius Wilson's books have commanded the nation's attention on
race and class controversies due in no small part to the complex layers of the
multiple realities that define the parameters of African-American existence in
the United States. The complex layers of his analyses derive in part from the
diverse perspectives he has synthesized from sociological theory, sociological
research, and social policy. These have explicit, implicit, and serendipitous
meanings that become clarified in the discussions and appraisals of his work.
At the same time, there are complex meanings of William Julius Wilson the
scholar and man in terms of sociological traditions and political ideologies.
These symbols, images, and meanings have been conferred and projected on
him by honors, reviewers, defenders, and critics.

A radical image was associated with some of his structural analyses of
capitalism, the government, and the changing relationships between social
classes and racial conflicts in postindustrial society. To the extent that the
problem of race for Wilson was a complex one informed by Marxian and

neo-Marxian concepts and perspectives, it appeared on the surface to be radical and revolutionary. Many of the his analyses of social inequality and historical change, based on *The Declining Significance of Race*, were radical with
respect to the implications for social reform and social policy. These radical
implications, however, were not explicated. Although the problem and analyses converged with Marxian and neo-Marxian perspectives, Wilson was careful to distance most of the substance and tone of his interpretations from
these. The historic and comparative analyses of industrialization and class
formation were informed more by Weberian than Marxian notions. While he
retains political economy concepts and assumptions of the structuring and
reorganization of the society initially inspired by these classic thinkers, these
political economy perspectives become more conservative over time. The
historic analyses of changing institutions and social classes which were
prominent in both *Power, Racism, and Privilege* and *The Declining Significance
of Race* become increasingly focused on describing and explaining the changing socioeconomic and residential patterns of Blacks in the larger context of
the changing division of labor. The movement toward social control, ecological structure, and a moral order is more Durkheimian in tone.

Social democrat images and meaning are connected with the associations, coincidences, and convergences of his work in substance and spirit with
socialist thinkers. Social democratic values of democracy, egalitarianism, and
integration are central in his analyses. Among some, Wilson has been identified as the contemporary successor to Gunnar Myrdal, the Swedish economist. Myrdal's *An American Dilemma* provided the leading interpretation of
race relations in the Untied States that would influence post-World War II
civil rights policy reforms. Myrdal's analyses of international inequality and
poverty in *Asian Drama* (1968) and *The Challenge of Affluence* (1963) continue
to provide the standard for cross-national examinations. It was Myrdal who
first coined the concept of under-class to capture the consequences of structural inequality and social dislocation. In 1995, Wilson gave the Gunnar
Myrdal lecture at the University of Stockholm, Sweden. However, it is
instructive based on the citations and references in his scholarship, there is no
acknowledgment of Myrdal's treatment of the underclass until *When Work
Disappears* (1996). Michael Harrington, a leading socialist writer in the
United States and author of *The Other America: Poverty in the United States*,
has acclaimed *The Truly Disadvantaged: The Inner City, the Underclass, and
Public Policy* as "a pathbreaking book, critically important to our current
public and political debate as well as to social theory" (Wilson 1987, cover).
Wilson has affirmed his political perspectives and sentiments as a social
democrat and at other times as a liberal. Wilson has been listed on the
National Advisory Council of the Social Democrats, USA.

Interconnected with the social democratic persona are images and symbols that associate him with the history of the civil rights movement and labor movement organizations through his association with the A. Phillip Randolph Institute. Bayard Rustin, the socialist labor leader, civil rights leader, and founder of the A. Phillip Randolph Institute valorized *The Declining Significance of Race* in a scathing critique of Alphonso Pinkney's *The Myth of Black Progress*. Wilson's *The Bridge Over the Racial Divide: Rising Inequality and Coalition Politics* (1999) is dedicated to the memory of Bayard Rustin. The similarities between Wilson and Rustin's ideas of liberal coalition politics within the Democratic Party are not coincidental (Rustin 1971). Wilson was recognized by the Chicago chapter of the A. Phillip Randolph Institute and received the Chicago Urban League's Man of the Year award. Wilson was the most important and recognizable scholar who participated in the Twenty Years Since the Kerner Report Conference (1988). He has also been on the boards of the Joint Center for Political and Economic Studies and the Urban League.

The image of liberal derives from his attempt to refocus liberalism into contemporary social policy discussions, his politics, and his underlying intellectual approach. In both spirit and symbol, Wilson's intellectual strategy particularly requires him to reclaim and refocus the public intellectual legacy of Daniel Patrick Moynihan. Through his policy positions in both the Johnson and Nixon administrations, Moynihan was at the center of domestic policy prescriptions such as increasing the entry of Black males in the military, the guaranteed minimum income, and "benign neglect." Moynihan's strategy for focusing the nation's attention on the economic and employment problems of Blacks was a normative argument focused on the legacy of slavery, the declining lower-class Black family, and the tangle of pathology. Moynihan has unquestionably been the leading nationally elected public official, who is a public intellectual and champion of employment, income, and family legislation and issues.

Wilson views Moynihan's writings and public involvement as providing "a model for those who want to use social science research and knowledge to address issues of public policy" (Wolfe 2000, A17). According to his assessment, Moynihan was the first social scientist to recognize that poverty had become primarily an urban problem and the first to call attention to the increasing gap between middle-class African Americans and those living in poverty (Wolfe 2000, A17). Moynihan's intellectual craft of raising questions, dramatizing issues, setting agendas, and understanding real world conditions are instructive. Moynihan, in both spirit and letter, provides Wilson with a pragmatic strategy of how to frame an agenda as a conservative liberal and liberal conservative.

Wilson is unapologetic of his liberal perspectives and reincarnation of Moynihan. His social policy prescriptions on balance are liberal. More so than Moynihan's writings, his policy prescriptions such as New Deal and Marshall Plan transitional public works projects, welfare reforms, education-to-work transitions, and universal social rights derive from larger liberal and social democratic agendas. The agency for translating these into action, a liberal coalition of labor, women, and minorities is not new. The intellectual universe for Wilson is largely a liberal one where he is clarifying the values of truth, reason, and political freedom and politically actualizing these as a public intellectual. In this effort, his framing of the national debates are relevant to his bringing sociological concepts, perspectives, hypotheses, and research findings into public controversies. In making use of leading journals, newspapers, television, and interviews, he has utilized a strategy of bringing sociology into the public understanding of issues that was initiated by Robert Park.

There are neoconservative and conservative images that grow out of the convergences, coincidences, and appropriations of these analyses with his perspectives. Although Wilson has publicly embraced a social democrat and liberal persona, in his syntheses he has embraced several concepts, hypotheses, policy arguments, and domain assumptions from conservatives. In *The Declining Significance of Race*, his analyses of the schism in the Black community between middle-class and underclass Blacks, the "progress" appraisal for educated and talented Blacks, and his interpretation of the role of affirmative action were essentially neoconservative interpretations. In more recent writings, his holistic perspectives incorporate conservative insights in discussions of Black population growth and social problems, comparisons of Blacks and other minorities, social structure and culture, and human and social capital. Part of this conservatism appears influenced by a moral conservatism that runs through his ideas. While his politics and policy perspectives are acknowledged as liberal, the implications of several of his analyses provide legitimation for more conservative perspectives. However, Wilson has been careful to distance his analyses and policy perspectives from Black conservative intellectuals.

Wilson also represents a continuing tradition of African-American scholarship that has critically examined the intersection of capitalism, social class, race relations, and culture. This critical theory tradition, which has provided the antitheses and syntheses to mainstream race relations, has usually been segregated and isolated to the margins of mainstream discussions and made invisible. It is primarily during crises, when mainstream perspectives are unable to provide adequate answers, that the questions raised and perspectives offered by these critical scholars gain in legitimacy. Among the post-World War II theorists, Oliver Cox and Harold Cruse figure prominently in his early work. Cox who is best known for *Caste, Class, and Race*

(1948), provided one of the most systematic and exhaustive critiques of pre-World War II race relations perspectives, the fallacies in the caste paradigm, and Myrdal's *An American Dilemma* (1948).

Although Cox's scholarship was initially ignored by most sociologists, it is from Cox that Wilson is provided a systematic, historic, and comparative examination of the variable relationships of the economy, state, social class, and race. Oliver Cox, who Wilson once recognized as "the master" provided the theoretical foundations for his critique and reformulations of race relations theory. Harold Cruse, who is best known for *The Crisis of the Negro Intellectual* (1967), provided more focused assessments of the historic dialectic between integration and nationalist perspectives among African Americans and a social history of the dilemmas and challenges facing Black intellectuals. Cruse provides Wilson a critique of assimilation theory and a cultural analysis.

In his theorizing on the Black middle class and urban underclass, Wilson's thesis is informed by E. Franklin Frazier's observations in *The Negro Family in the United States* (1966). Frazier's predictions of the structurally integrative possibilities of industrialization and public employment for the "brown middle class" and "Black proletariat" anticipates and informs Wilson's interpretation of the post-civil rights progress. The discussion of the urban underclass represents the antithesis of the industrialization and opportunity argument and draws from Frazier's chapters on "The City of Destruction."

The kaleidoscope of images is functional in contributing to the range, complexity, and mystique of this scholar. With so many images and dimensions, it is not surprising that competing political camps and public policy perspectives would draw selectively from both the substance and symbolism of these analyses. The complexity in the sociological controversy, addressed by Wilson, is frequently blurred by both his critics and defenders who have not acknowledged the possibilities and limitations of his perspectives.

THE SOCIOLOGIST AND PUBLIC POLICY

Wilson's sociology does not stop with what he describes and analyzes as a problematic urban world. Intertwined with the academic role of sociological analyst is a prescriptive and interventionist role that involves subtle and complex relationships for the sociologist in public policy formulation. This current role was not always so. In his early work through *Power, Racism, and Privilege*, sociologists constituted an almost exclusive reference group and audience. The controversies generated by *The Declining Significance of Race* will sensitize him to the importance of policy implications and formulations. By *The Truly Disadvantaged* and *When Work Disappears*, Wilson becomes more concerned with the pragmatic task of addressing social science to a wider public-policy audience of governmental, industrial, and corporate leaders. Although sociologists will continue to constitute a primary audience, there are competing constraints to move beyond disciplinary boundaries.

As sociologist, Wilson views his task as primarily one of enlightenment. For sociologists, he develops, tests, and clarifies a system of hypotheses that will lead to systematic generalizations and social science knowledge. In this "search for truth," Wilson develops generalizations and sensitizing concepts that are as directly relevant to policymakers and journalists as academic social scientists. In developing these models of institutional change, Wilson incorporates an intellectual craftsmanship that provides answers and possible directions of social control. Although this sociology has concerns with Blacks in cities, its logic and vision are driven more directly by macrosociological and formal interests. As a social policy expert, Wilson is challenged to account for changing conditions of capitalism, industrialization, state bureaucratization, urbanization, and race relations by formulating a new policy agenda, consensus, and constituency. This challenge will increasingly involve a holistic approach that relates issues of race and poverty to broader questions of societal organization (Wilson 1987, 132). This new undertaking is necessary due to limitations of Black solidarity visions of race relations, the War on Poverty visions of joblessness based on environmental and behavioral measures, and contemporary conservative visions based on group values and individual initiatives. For the public, he is concerned with using existing theories and theoretical frameworks to influence the public discourse and the ways that policymakers think about social issues.

In his vision, Wilson sees the development of a more comprehensive policy framework as an attempt to relate problems associated with race to broader issues of societal organization. This sociologically driven vision of societal organization is "best described" by macro-institutional dimensions of the economy, state, and education that represent the social, normative, and cultural orders and technological dimensions such as stages of industrialization and degree of urbanization that "represent the material outcomes of systematic and goal-directed social relations and action" (Wilson 1987, 133). The more micro-level stratification of racial and ethnic groups with respect to benefits and privileges, and group differences in behavior, norms, and values reflect and amplify the constraints of larger societal organization and intergroup relations (Wilson 1987, 133). Wilson's policy agenda of economic and social reform grows directly from his analyses of the limitations in the traditional liberal and conservative conventional wisdom. His analyses conclude that race-specific policies such as affirmative action are limited and will require nonracial (universal) policies such as full employment, balanced economic growth, manpower training, and education. These universal reforms are in essence "a macroeconomic policy designed to promote both economic growth and a tight labor market" (Wilson 1987, 151). In principle, his diagnoses of the problems of Black joblessness, crime, out-of-wedlock births, single-parent families, and welfare dependency are functional consequences of his macrosociological model of institutional and technological change. There is a liberal and indirect role of expert called for in his work that challenges the sociologist to persuade policymakers through enlightenment more than direct participation in policy research, advocacy, and activism. The prescription is a "hidden agenda" where the social and economic conditions of the "truly disadvantaged" will be moved by widely supported and accepted universal programs in employment, job skills, comprehensive health care, public school reform, child care legislation, and crime and drug abuse prevention (Wilson 1991). He later adds to these programs addressing education-to-work transitions and urban policies.

There is also a more activist political sociology role. In "Race Neutral Programs and the Democratic Coalition," Wilson prescribes a "new political strategy for the 1990s that appeals to a broader coalition and addresses problems afflicting minorities that originated in racist practices but will not be solved by race-specific remedies" (Wilson 1990, 74–75). Because race-specific policies for past discrimination by Blacks are viewed as divisive and eroding the biracial class-based coalition that spearheaded progressive reforms, these are in need of restructuring. Arguing that race-specific policies based on principles of equality of individual opportunity and preferential group treatment are not sufficient for affecting the status of less advantaged Blacks because of past discrimination and contemporary structural changes in the economy, Wilson proposes a progressive new political strategy within the Democratic Party that consists of full employment policies, job skills training, comprehensive health care legislation, education reforms in public schools, child care legislation, and crime and drug abuse prevention programs (Wilson 1990, 79). Although these would benefit poor minorities, these "social justice" programs are to be presented as universal strategies that help all groups across racial and class solidarities. While Wilson initially defined this coalition as a biracial one between Blacks and Whites, in more recent discussions he has redefined this as a "multiracial coalition" that would increasingly reflect the diversity of Latino Americans, Asian Americans, and Native Americans as well as White Americans and African Americans. He has suggested that another layer of this coalition on the local level is the strategy of metropolitan politics initiated by Myron Orfield (Orfield 1997). This "metropolitics" would urge the building of coalitions between central cities and inner ring suburbs which are experiencing similar processes of industrial decline and social dislocation.

This new political strategy is necessary, argues Wilson, because: (1) as economic conditions have worsened for working and middle classes there is greater resistance to affirmative action and poverty programs; and (2) public opinion shows strong support for government labor market strategies that expand employment and training. Wilson distinguishes these race-neutral programs from neoconservative critiques of affirmative action and government intervention in social welfare.

Wilson has urged sociologists to play an increased role in public policy by arguing for a broader conception of the use and application of policy relevant sociological data, an increase in the role of sociological theoretical ideas, hypotheses, and concepts in national policy debates, and more consideration of ways to communicate the insights from sociological data, concepts, and theory (Wilson 1993b, 7). He emphasizes that sociologists have usually avoided entering the policy arena due to sentiments against the practical application of research and norms of waiting for the accumulation of sufficient data (Wilson 1993b). For Wilson, the extent that sociologists can provide concepts and perspectives that raise the consciousness and concern of policymakers and increase their awareness of the need for effective policy figures strategically in the future of the discipline.

More recently, Wilson has extended this raison d'être of sociology by addressing the strategies that sociological dialogue might take in engaging the public through the media (Wilson 1998). He urges sociologists to be pragmatic in focusing on issues that are high on the public agenda and in developing clear, creative, and thoughtful arguments that engage both academic and nonacademic audiences. The craft of writing should be focused on clear communication and intellectual sophistication while eliminating academic and technical jargon. He urges sociologists to increasingly make use of university public information offices, develop press releases, and write op-ed articles in newspapers. These are interests that converge with Robert Park, who was interested in the role of journalism and the press and his mentor Maxwell Brooks, who was interested in the Negro Press.

REFOCUSING NORMATIVE SOCIAL THEORY ON SOCIAL PROBLEMS

Since its inception, sociologists have been concerned with the social construction of knowledge relevant to changing social inequality and urban social problems. Sociological theorists have made both direct and indirect contributions by studying the issues, identifying and clarifying the arguments and analyses, and providing policy recommendations and research agendas.

Accompanying Wilson's formal and pragmatic approach is an attempt to bring both normative theory and political liberalism to center stage in the analysis of social problems. The excesses of empirical research orientations, which have constrained sociologists from playing the required roles in public policy, are tempered by normative orientations that are more adaptable. The inability of traditional liberalism and conservatism to adequately address the contemporary problems of urban inequality will necessitate a refocused liberal (or neoliberal) analysis.

The relative importance of empirical and normative theories in understanding social problems is a continuing debate that reflects the diverse positivist, pragmatist, and social ethical traditions from philosophy that integrate sociology. This debate partly reflects the diverse opinions concerning the relative value of closed, open, and negotiated relationships between academic sociologists and the larger society. The importance given to these orientations also varies across different graduate training centers and schools, social science networks, individual sociologists, and the complex integration of each of these in the larger division of labor involving social science research and theorizing.

Empirical orientations, which are based on positivist assumptions of social science borrowed from the natural and physical sciences, view the development of theory as proceeding inductively, normally, and incrementally from the accumulation of systematically observed and interpreted sociological facts and hypotheses which attempt to accurately reflect the realities of the objective outside world. Empirical theory is characterized by measurement, quantification, and tendencies toward structural explanations. Empirical-based theory is the capstone of normal social science.

Normative orientations, based on philosophical assumptions of the ethical systems, ideologies, values, and agencies of action, view the development of theory as proceeding deductively, directly, and systematically from general principles. Normative-based theory is characterized by its attention to ultimate questions, essences, meanings, and tendencies toward broad, grand, if not sweeping generalizations. Normative theories identify how the social world should be most appropriately viewed, what social institutions, structures, and groups need particular targeting, and how policymakers might control these problems and plan for the future. Normative theorizing proceeds from assumptions, premises, concepts, and hypotheses of sociological questions that may be logically validated by some combination of philosophical, historical, sociological, authoritative, public opinion, and anecdotal evidence or illustration. Normative theory is the capstone of consensus building and policy science.

While both normative and empirical orientations are necessary in Wilson's sociological theorizing of social problems, the normative orientation appears increasingly primary. The holistic, formal, and pragmatic aims of his theory are accompanied by a theory of human action and intervention. Wilson's normative theory proceeds deductively from concepts, premises, and hypotheses of a macrosociology that appear more directly concerned with consensus building and public policy than the measurement, quantification, and structural explanations associated with normal social science. Empirical-based theory and research play a secondary and supportive role in this exercise. This explains why when Wilson uses empirical research, he uses it more to describe facts and illustrate points than to statistically analyze the competing theories.

In identifying the social institutions of the economy, education, and welfare and targeting the "social isolation" and "concentration effects" of the inner-city Black poor as problematic, Wilson has focused an agenda of what should be the future direction that social scientists and policymakers might take. As a normative theorist, the concepts, hypotheses, and models that he uses to describe and analyze these problems contribute to understanding and consciousness raising, the mobilization and building of coalitions, and are ultimately concerned more with value imperatives than objective historical and sociological facts. Also, Wilson recognizes that the tone of his discussions and arguments should be accessible to mainstream cultural beliefs, public opinion, and decision makers and at the same time influence these.

Traditionally, the leading sociological theorists have usually given primary emphasis to normative arguments rather than empirical orientations in initiating sociology theories of social problems. Only during the past three decades have empirical research and empirical-based theories, with their more inductive and delimited orientations, come to challenge normative orientations in the formulation of theories of social problems. Wilson recognizes that a large part of empirical research in sociology is oriented toward specialized audiences, is more concerned with technical precision and rigor than communicating meanings, and does not reach those important audiences that might influence social policy. Consequently, the implications of this empirical research for both social theory and social policy are frequently unclear and unconnected. These are the empiricists whose scholarship Robert K. Merton identified by the motto, This is demonstrably so, but we cannot indicate its significance (Merton 1968, 139).

Wilson recognizes that the significance of his theorizing is found in its intellectual imagination, clarity, and scope. By redefining and refocusing attention on what should be the most important social institutions, social structures, social relationships, and social policies bearing on urban inequality and poverty, he has distinguished the "big picture" (or the macrosociological) from the "little pictures" (or the microsociological). The normative orientation derives from his values and the formal, pragmatic, and human action objectives of his theorizing.

The challenges for Wilson's normative theorizing focus not simply on the liberal values that have pragmatically assimilated conservative and neoconservative values and are in steady conflict. In advancing what is essentially a social order (or social control) model of society, the generalizations in Wilson's discussions are ultimately concerned with value imperatives. Wilson advances this social control model in order to gain the ears and acceptance of leading policy makers and the public so that he can make his structural arguments. As such, sociological theories, research, and facts are not ends in their own right but rather the means of bringing sociology into the public understanding of social issues. These tasks represent challenges not only for Wilson, but also dilemmas for sociology and sociologists as they attempt to build on these directions.

A critical appraisal must recognize his contributions to the public understanding of sociology but also explore several contradictions that bedevil the macrosociological analysis used by him. These challenges focus on the normative basis of his theorizing, the unexamined value assumptions of social structure and social change, and his synthesis that attempts to fuse objective and normative orientations.

The first challenge in assessing Wilson's theories is to recognize these as primarily normative arguments. Although these make an important contribution, it appears that the values in his theorizing are frequently not identified by him and most social science audiences and as a result pass for empirical generalizations. While the ambiguity of these contributions is useful in political and cultural discourses, these can be problematic and misleading as sociological facts. This blurring of his roles and contributions as a sociological theorist and researcher appears to be a latent function of the multiple roles Wilson is expected to play as a sociologist and public intellectual both inside and outside the academy. As a sociologist, the role of theorist and empirical researcher emphasize academic canons and scientific values while the role of public intellectual emphasizes the craft of raising questions, dramatizing issues, and setting agendas that reflect ultimate values and politics.

A second challenge centers on the unexamined domain assumptions and value premises of social structure and social change that guide his analysis of race relations. While his earlier formulations of race relations and society were dialectical and recognized the functionally integrative roles of intergroup conflict in contributing to social order, the more recent formulations are increasingly integrative and focused on social control and intervention. The existential question of conflict becomes controlled, quiet, and "invisible." At the macrosociological level, this normative theory has underlying domain assumptions of enlightenment, optimism, and progress for the future that derive from the rational and pragmatic intervention of national economic and political leaders that are sensitized by the rational persuasion of important intellectuals and energized by the mobilization of liberal and multiracial coalitions. For Wilson, the recognized conflicts of structural dislocations and blocked opportunity may be ameliorated through economic growth and social reforms. In his recent scholarship, power conflict is embraced more in historic analyses of social problems and reduced in contemporary problems.

A third challenge grows out of the synthesis with its competing aims of integrating an objective structural analysis of society which identifies the sociological facts on the one hand and a normative analysis concerned with clarifying meanings and values on the other hand. Accompanying the objectivity in this normative orientation, Wilson is also required to assimilate, correspond with, and summarize the beliefs and professional expectations that are associated with a specific value consensus. In this discourse among the social democratic perspectives, the neoliberal or refocused liberal perspectives, the traditional liberal perspectives, and conservative perspectives, Wilson's clarification of concepts and hypotheses draws from the most visible and important meanings that are used by national public intellectuals. In articulating the conceptual space of these perspectives, there are relatively few social scientists that are acknowledged or cited whose analyses deviate from mainstream liberal or conservative perspectives of social order and assimilation.

There are more than isolated examples where the concepts, hypotheses, and generalizations in his normative theorizing are insulated and immunized from competing theoretical perspectives and empirical research findings to the extent that they are not part of his paradigms. Associated with these paradigms are the "significant others" and "generalized others" that constitute his audiences in sociological controversies. This should not suggest that his sociological descriptions and analyses are not objective. In his analyses and attempts to frame the underlying discourse on the nature of race relations and social class in postindustrial American society, rather than simply describing or explaining them, Wilson can be selective with the theoretical perspectives and research evidence utilized.

The requirements of activism and political sociology, contained in this enterprise, can compete with the normal science theoretical and research requirements. In sociological controversies and debates that enter the public arena, the normal academic canons of discourse can be replaced by more politicized and revolutionary canons. In these situations, attempts at enlightenment and clarity can contest with authority and hegemony. Expectations and appeals of hegemony and authority in discourses can contend with the "search for truth." One consequence of these counterveiling intellectual pressures is that normative arguments can come close to ideology and serve ideological functions. In not explicating many of the value premises and cultural beliefs in his analyses these often pass as grounded sociological theories and hypotheses or the results of empirical research. The public discourse used by

Wilson becomes most explicit in *The Bridge Over the Racial Divide: Rising Inequality and Coalition Politics* (1999).

The type of discourse used with respect to class, race, and the post-industrial city is much larger than Wilson's sociological perspectives, the critics' responses, and his rebuttals to his critics. It is a condition that reflects the discourse on the current state of economic and political institutions in general and the cultural institutions of communications, education, and entertainment that help shape the dominant American consciousness, understandings, and beliefs concerning the continuing significance of racism and race. To the extent that comfort, escapism, and denial become more valued than sociological facts, it is possible that information and entertainment can become fused into infortainment.

REFOCUSING THE LIBERAL PERSPECTIVE ON SOCIAL PROBLEMS

Behind Wilson's theorizing is an attempt to integrate the conservative and liberal perspectives, which constitute the mainstream value consensus in social science and public policy discussions of society and social problems. These conservative and liberal perspectives do not simply capture the competing political orientations within the mainstream political culture but offer different sociological visions of the possibilities and limitations of changing institutions, group relationships and individual life in contemporary American society. Wilson recognizes that each of these perspectives offer incomplete answers to the current problems of urban inequality. When fused organically as the refocused liberal perspective, these offer the most comprehensive and pragmatic strategy for addressing social problems. This refocused perspective must focus on the "common ground" of the center and not the diversions of the margins.

Traditional conservative perspectives emphasize the free market as a source of political and economic freedom, the role of competition among individuals, groups, and institutions in contributing to the integration of community and society, and the limitations of government action in reference to the free market. For traditional conservatives, social problems derive from short circuits in the free market and competition that derive from the growth of the state and governmental actions that coerce individual freedom. These traditional conservatives view governmental intervention in support of equality as anathema, because it undercuts individual rights and reinforces unproductive behavior such as individuals not taking responsibility. Cultural conservatives emphasize primary rights as embodied in the family, church, and property in structuring community and society. Cultural conservatives expect social relations to be characterized by historical continuity as reflected in the "persistence of structures, communities, habits, and prejudices generation after generation" (Nisbet 1986, 24). For cultural conservatives, social problems are dysfunctional behavioral patterns, resulting from cultural deficits in intermediary institutions such as the family and church that are viewed as the principal structures through which socialization to core values occur. For direction, conservatives generally look backward to the past for a "golden age" of a moral community and society.

Related to the traditional and cultural perspectives are neoconservative perspectives that view the contemporary United States in a crisis of authority where the legitimacy and stability of government is threatened by the "overload" of an adversary culture (Steinfels 1979). This crisis is viewed as primarily a cultural crisis of values, morals, and manners that originated in the "New Frontier" public policies of the 1960s such as civil rights and the War on Poverty. As a consequence of value-added factors of increasing equality of opportunity, the growth of the 1960s welfare state, a revolution of rising expectations, and the emergence of a "new class" of professionals and a permanent urban underclass there are excessive demands on government (Steinfels 1979, 53–63).

Traditional liberal perspectives recognize the individual as primary and coming before society, institutions, and social structures. The freedom and autonomy of the individual with natural rights from the traditional restraints of the church, state, and elites was socially structured in the separation of constitutional powers among the executive, legislative, and judicial branches and freedom in the marketplace. Classical liberal perspectives, which are based on rational and utilitarian assumptions of human action, where social relations are fundamentally organic, indivisible, and evolutionary, are characterized by expectations of increased enlightenment, equality, and inclusion among represented groups. For liberals, the expansion of civil liberties and religious tolerance without government interference are expected to strengthen democracy.

During the twentieth century, liberalism has adapted its principles to the changing realities of a growing industrial society and the movements from rural and small town communities to city and metropolitan area communities. In response to the Great Depression of the 1930s, New Deal liberalism came to embrace principles of interventionist government, macroeconomics, pragmatic experimentation, and federal government centralization. Government became a broker for adjusting conflicting group interests of political parties, labor and economic organizations, the church, and voluntary associations. The affirmative role of government, symbolized by Keynesian economics and the welfare state, was a response to the high unemployment of the Great Depression, industrialization, and the existence of the New Deal coalition. During the 1960s, the earlier economic liberalism of the New Deal was augmented with the social liberalism of civil rights and redistribution policies.

More recently, neoliberal perspectives have attempted to establish a middle ground between the strong reliance on government intervention and spending that characterized New Deal and New Frontier liberals and the rejection of government regulation, federal centralization, and increasing equality embraced by conservatives. Caught between the proverbial "rock and a hard place," neoliberals recognize that contemporary postindustrial society does not offer the same possibilities for actualizing the New Deal notions of liberalism. In place of the New Deal visions of social democracy, neoliberals increasingly have a vision of society in which individual and social freedom ultimately result from economic growth and this is derived from new investments in appropriate technology, entrepreneurship, military reform, human capital, national service, and industrial innovation (Rothenberg 1984).

It is from the neoliberal perspective that Wilson attempts to develop a discourse among the social democratic, traditional liberal, neoliberal, neo-conservative, and conservative perspectives and synthesize these into his refocused liberal perspective. The macroeconomic growth and investments in appropriate technology, which are the central tenets of refocused liberal-ism, are accompanied by the freedoms of universal social rights. It is impor-tant for Wilson that the notions of economic growth and freedom, embraced by neoliberal perspectives, are consistent with and reinforce traditional Chicago School sociological perspectives of the city that predicted growth, competition, opportunity, and mobility. The vision of economic growth and public transitional employment, based on the New Deal experiences of the 1930s and the post-World War II Marshall Plan, influences his long-range optimism of integrating the urban inner-city poor into the postindustrial economy.

Liberals have traditionally viewed social problems as deriving from aberrations or normative conflicts associated with the actualization of free-dom, justice, and equality in the economy and government. Historic political movements and factions which emphasize elitism, strict constitutionalism, states rights, and ethnic chauvinism pose moral conflicts and are anathema, because these limit the possibilities of democracy and civic culture. Generally, moral conflicts result from less than adequate forms of enlightenment and civic culture among its citizens such as public education and political partic-ipation. Liberals view African Americans along with other groups as sharing a common human nature and history that is universally assimilable. Because African Americans are essentially Americans in culture, there is assumed to be no distinctive African-American culture (Myrdal 1944; Glazer and Moynihan 1963). In Gunnar Myrdal's *An American Dilemma* (1944), the historic problems of discrimination reflected ever raging moral conflicts between universal values of the American Creed and democracy and particularistic community, group, and individual expectations of conformity, prestige, and prejudice. The liberal expectancy is optimistic in viewing race relations as indivisible, organic, evolutionary, and progressive. The liberal expectancy anticipates the increased enlightenment of the government, public policy, and the progressive inclusion and equality of minorities into American society. Another perspective of liberalism in sociology emphasizes multiculturalism and the diversity of racial and ethnic group experiences that fall short of universal assimilation and social integration. With respect to policy, these emphasize corporate pluralism in which racial and ethnic groups are formally recognized and transitional and compensatory measures are used to address historic discrimination (Gordon 1981).

Wilson's analysis of social problems views these as deriving from structural and normative conflicts associated with the actualization of opportunity in the economy, workplace, and education. He has adapted the traditional liberal assumptions of social problems, which emphasize the normative conflicts that derive from less than adequate forms of enlightenment, political integration, and civic culture among its citizens such as public education and civic participation, and refocused these on economic and social opportunity. Robert K. Merton's classic essay "Social Structure and Anomie" (1968c) is the seminal inspiration for this analysis. Like Merton, Wilson views all Americans (including the poorest of the poor) as embracing the mainstream cultural orientations of materialism and work. Where there are social problems among these groups, it is not the deficits in their embracing of mainstream culture or ghetto-related culture that largely explains these. Rather, it is the conflict between the structure of economic opportunities leading to situational cultural adaptations which in turn further hampers opportunity. Once these structural changes occur, these will ameliorate the social dislocations that have contributed to unemployment, poverty, welfare, crime, and violence. Wilson is aware that there exist among the poor those persons who reject the dominant cultural orientations of materialism and work and others among the poor who are developing alternative cultural orientations. These forms of retreatism and rebellion are the aberrations.

In refocusing liberalism on social problems of race and urban inequality, there are both pragmatic and moral challenges. Wilson recognizes that the civil rights policies of the 1960s did not sufficiently address the economic justice issues bearing on inequality and poverty. He is aware that liberally sponsored legislation to address employment, such as the Humphrey-Hawkins bill that was neutralized, is an unfinished agenda. In both *The Truly Disadvantaged* and *When Work Disappears*, he forcefully and persuasively argues for employment growth among the poor and universal social rights. The moral challenge is one of forcefully and honestly addressing these issues while being heard. In providing a bigger picture and more compelling answers to the problems of the underclass than conservatives and traditional liberals, he has analytically and strategically stayed near the mainstream. In the conservative "mean season" political climate of the 1980s and 1990s, the social democratic analyses and policy prescriptions he has advanced can be viewed as progressive and compassionate. Compared to other advanced industrial nations, these policy prescriptions may be viewed as cautious.

CHAPTER 8

THE SIGNIFICANCE OF SOCIOLOGICAL PRISMS AND CONTROVERSIES

BACKGROUND

William Julius Wilson's sociology has diverse philosophical and theoretical influences. His sociological discussions are ranging and draw from a broad reading and understanding of sociology, history, economics, political science, and philosophy. At the center of his macrosociology is a continuing attempt to bring the insights of classical theories such as Karl Marx, Max Weber, Èmile Durkheim and the Chicago School into a contemporary dialogue. Accompanying this macrosociology, with its interests in capitalism, industrialization, technological change, government, and urbanization is a microsociology of competing assimilation-based, ethnicity-based, class-based and nationalist-based perspectives of racial and ethnic relations that are historically and sociologically situated.

At Chicago, Wilson attempts to explain the historic institutional contradictions of post-World War II deindustrialization, government, and urbanization and the changing intergroup conflicts of race and social class that are connected to sociological controversies and symbolized in his biography. At the same time, the sociological perspectives or "prisms" that have developed through his observations, experiences, scholarship, and sociological controversies influence his complex analyses of race relations and larger societal factors that provide the possibilities for his refocused and holistic vision of macroeconomic reform.

Wilson's concerns with developing a societal model of race relations, that challenge him to integrate his sociological theory interests with sociological controversy and social policy concerns, provide the connective threads that organize his examination of the experiences of Blacks in cities. Central to his theorizing at Chicago are his incorporation of a political-economy framework for the changing institutional order, a dialectic of functionalist and conflict perspectives of racial and ethnic relations, and the integration of urban ecological concepts of metropolitan-level and community-level changes.

The development of his primary interests of Blacks in cities such as industrialization, urbanization, and the changing class structure, Black migration, population growth, and mobility, racial segregation and ghettoization, and the social and moral order of the Black community grow out of his holistic theoretical interests. While informed by sociohistorical and empirical perspectives, his theorizing is primarily driven by a normative orientation. This normative orientation is pragmatic and increasingly open, adaptable to, and informed by sociological controversies and public-policy discourses. The dialectical reasoning, which is the basis for his discussions of competing sociological perspectives, subsequently becomes the dialogical approach or discourse.

The syntheses or resolutions to these competing and frequently contradictory directions are found in the liberal center. From this middle ground or "vital center," Wilson as an intellectual can substantively and symbolically challenge the conventional wisdom and status quo. In framing and refocusing the national debate on the urban underclass, there is a liberal critique of contemporary corporate capitalism. Through the objectivity and independence of his analyses, he attempts to transcend the segmented solidarities of social class, political party, and racial group that characterize polarized public policy and sociological controversies.

The significance of the sociological perspectives in his early training and writings are seminal in understanding his later writings. Throughout his scholarship, the social construction of reality largely grows from a theoretical starting point that informs and is informed by the competing sociological and public-policy perspectives that are part of his discourses. As such, the formulation and reformulation of concepts, hypotheses, and models in Wilson's sociological discussions do not singularly grow out of the objective historic and social conditions of changing race relations and urban inequality in American society at the end of the twentieth century. The philosophical and theoretical considerations in his analyses, evaluations, and critical appraisals of these competing sociological perspectives influence the "big questions" he raises.

Through this dialectic of theoretical discussions and critical appraisals, Wilson selects the most appropriate concepts, hypotheses, and generalizations to describe and explain the problems of race, class, and the postindustrial city. Simultaneously, these sociological controversies influence his changing observations, perceptions, and sensitivities. Also, the changing situational contexts of his biography, professional and collegial networks, and "significant others" in national social policy arenas enter his interpretations.

The holistic perspective, which represents an important part of Wilson's sociological prisms, derives in part from a philosophy of social science orientation. At the same time, the holistic perspective draws from a discourse approach that makes use of sociological controversies to arrive at generalizations and syntheses. This chapter addresses three aspects of Wilson's sociological prisms which undergird his analyses and continues to inform his discussions: (1) the formal approach to sociological theory, (2) the symbolic language of action, and (3) the use of sociological controversies in constructing the holistic perspective.

THE FORMAL APPROACH

Accompanying the complex layers of normative orientation and refocused liberalism in his sociological approach to social problems, Wilson's sociology is nested in a formal approach that is influenced by his early studies in the philosophy of social science. These writings address the issues of the social construction of scientific inquiry, the formalization of scientific theory with respect to explanations, concepts, and evidence, and the evaluative criteria to assess these (Wilson, Sofios, and Ogles 1964; Dumont and Wilson 1967; Wilson and Dumont 1968). This formal approach informs how he has grappled with other issues such as the nature of sociological knowledge, the relationships between sociological theory and sociological research, and the values of truth, adequacy, and validity. It should be underscored that Wilson's sociological writings after Washington State University and the University of Massachusetts-Amherst are not explicitly concerned with these formal interests. However, the logic, tone, spirit, and rhythm of subsequent analyses continue to draw from these.

In his early essays, Wilson addresses from a philosophy of social science perspective the evaluative criteria most appropriate for the assessment of sociological theory (Wilson, Sofios, and Ogles 1964). In this formal analysis, the language of social science theory is differentiated into observational language, theoretical language, and correspondence rules. Structures of explanation, concepts, and evidence represent the principal areas of this formal analysis (Wilson, Sofios, and Ogles 1964, 75).

With respect to the structures of explanation, Wilson distinguishes between experimental laws that are common in the physical and natural sciences and other theories that are more common in history and the social sciences (Wilson, Sofios, and Ogles 1964). He recognizes that the experimental laws which have "determinate" empirical content and are connected directly to experimental procedures do not capture the essence of sociological theorizing. Theoretical statements in social science are not directly subject to experimentation and generally refer to unobserved procedures and conditions. However, these limitations of direct observation are not problematic in social science theorizing. The theoretical capability of explaining diverse experimental laws that are dissimilar substantively provides a value-added insight (Wilson, Sofios, and Ogles 1964).

In clarifying the formal properties of concepts, Wilson distinguishes between explicit and implicit definitions. While explicit concepts are rigorous and denotative in describing terms that are directly observable, implicit concepts are defined through the context of the postulate network and the connection of some of the terms by rules of correspondence to observational terms and the empirical meaningfulness of the observational terms (Wilson, Sofios, and Ogles 1964, 75). In evaluating the meanings of concepts, Wilson argues that the rigorous criteria of using singular meanings for key concepts be replaced by pluralistic criteria that examine the various meanings of key concepts in the different contexts used. This more reasonable and contextual strategy of evaluating concepts permits sociologists the flexibility of evaluating the various meanings of the same concepts without denying their empirical significance (Wilson, Sofios, and Ogles 1964, 78). This contextual approach will provide Wilson with several possibilities in articulating the conceptual space of meanings while examining macrosociological and microsociological relationships and in synthesizing social order (functionalist) and conflict perspectives.

With respect to evidence, Wilson recognizes that direct evidence, which is common in the experimentally driven empirical research, does not characterize the development of sociological theory. Indirect evidence, which is derived from the theories that are derived jointly from a general theory, provides an alternative strategy. In evaluating evidence indirectly, Wilson suggests the use of an "inference chain of analysis," which indicates those statements that are strongly supported by the data, statements that are progressively weaker, and other statements that are speculative. Included in the latter are inference leaps and evidence-inference gaps. Wilson's formal approach contains a pragmatic approach. In this practical program of sociology, Wilson suggests bases or standards for the selection, evaluation, and utilization of concepts in sociological theories (Dumont and Wilson 1967).

Furthermore, there is a continuum in Wilson's formal approach to sociological theories that run between implicit and explicit construction. What distinguishes these explicit theories from implicit theories is the presence of "epistemic and constitutive significance where concepts are connected either directly or indirectly, with observables by rules of correspondence that have been empirically justified" (Dumont and Wilson 1967, 987). Implicit theories are characterized by isolated abstract concepts, have an ambiguity and openness of meanings, afford no clear specification to the sources of their derivation, and do not provide a definitive rationale for the use of indicators. The theory sketch—"a more or less vague indication of the laws and initial conditions considered as relevant to be later filled out into a full explanation"—falls between implicit theories and explicit theories. In the theory sketch, "the connection between the observable concepts and theoretical concepts is only presumed to represent an empirical relation." Explicit theories contain concepts with epistemic and constitutive significance alongside rationales for the use of correspondence rules. Explication consists of both meaning analysis and empirical analysis. Meaning analysis involves surveying the literature to "cull out the most basic assumptions inherent in various meanings of concepts." Empirical analysis refers to submitting meaning analysis to direct empirical test (Dumont and Wilson 1967, 988–990).

Wilson's formal approach to theorizing synthesizes the sociological approaches based on grand theory, abstract empiricism, and the new causal sociology. While he shares some concerns of addressing the broad and diverse questions of grand theory, his theorizing is closer to empirical research. While he shares some concerns of abstract empiricism in incorporating hypotheses and generalizations that derive from empirical research, his approach is more deductive than inductive.

Wilson's open system approach to sociological research appears to be informed by Myrdal's distinction of the two stages of social science research: the theoretical and practical. For Myrdal, theoretical research is "directed toward ascertaining facts and causal relations between facts" and practical research is the "logical procedure of relating value judgments to factual situations and to actual trends of change and, from their combination, deriving scientific plans for policies aimed at inducing alterations of the anticipated social trends" (Myrdal 1944, 1059). While Myrdal saw "theoretical research" as primarily concerned with the historic development and current situation, "practical research" is more concerned with policy choices that might be influenced by social planning.

Simultaneously, Wilson's approach to sociological theory converges with Robert Merton's "theories of the middle range." Merton described "theories of the middle range" as those [theories] which lie between working hypotheses in research and the systematic efforts to develop a unified theory to explain all of the observed uniformities of social behavior, social organization, and social change (Merton 1968a, 39). By simultaneously working between theoretical statements and empirical abstractions, Wilson can bring a retroductive approach that is continually sensitive to the problems of concept clarification, explanation, and evidence and that over time will be increasingly concerned with paradigm-building. This paradigm-building will contain the controversies of race and class in postindustrial America, the continuing concerns of University of Chicago sociology, and broader social science and public-policy debates of an interdisciplinary nature. The formal approach continues to influence how he has selected questions and concepts, grappled with the values of truth, adequacy, and validity, and worked through the relationships of concept, explanation, and evidence.

Also contained in Wilson's formal sociology is a humanistic sociology. It is an analysis of the meanings of human action that are grounded upon systematic theoretical explication and empirical research. This sociology of human action is primarily based on an idealistic and humanistic orientation that is ultimately concerned with identifying and clarifying normative systems and values. This helps explain why when he discusses macrosociological processes such as industrialization, growth of the state, urbanization, stratification, and micro-level questions of community and race relations, he is generally using normative lenses for defining and interpreting these relationships and their implications. This converges with what Gunnar Myrdal called "theoretical research." Wilson's formal sociology is secondarily based on a scientific orientation that is concerned with understanding empirical social problems that have grown out of the growing body of knowledge coming out of social science and social policy research. While the appropriate objective of investigation in his sociology is human action, the proper units of analysis are not necessarily "real humans" but frequently forms, processes, and outcomes of social structure. Wilson's use of sociohistorical perspectives while grounding and contextualizing his examination of contemporary socioeconomic conditions of Blacks, are constrained by needs of summarizing these into theory sketches, typologies, and stages. The details and complexities of history and sociology do not necessarily inform these analyses.

Wilson's formal theoretical interests in race relations are focused on change and persistence in racial and ethnic stratification. In accounting for the persistence of systems of racial and ethnic stratification in advanced industrial society, he notes that the consensus framework that stresses values to the exclusion of interdependence and coercive power provides only a partial explanation (Wilson 1980, 234-235). Drawing from Morris Janowitz, he notes that the "capacity of a social group or society to effect self-regulation consistent with a set of basic value principles is decreasing in advanced industrial society, because of the difficulty of legislative institutions to mediate conflicting group interests and resolve social and economic conflicts. "Because advanced industrial societies are characterized by interdependence even where value consensus is absent, he notes that the integration of these contemporary societies rest on a holistic framework of social control incorporating economic, technological, ecological, and institutional dimensions of social organization (Wilson 1980, 235). The systems approach advanced by Wilson involves a multivariate account for the normative order "but this hardly dictates a normative theory of macrosociology" (Wilson 1980).

It is instructive that the formal and substantive concerns in Wilson's early sociology are arrived at from the "library and office armchair" and "car window." There is little indication in Wilson's theorizing through *The Declining Significance of Race* that the implicit theories and theory sketches of Blacks in cities are derived directly from empirical research or systematic observations. In *The Truly Disadvantaged* and *When Work Disappears*, Wilson develops a research agenda and program that will ground and contextualize these hypotheses.

THE SYMBOLIC LANGUAGE OF ACTION

The philosophy of social science orientation and formal approach, which influence Wilson's discussions, are strong in emphasizing macrosociological structures of explanation and in clarifying concepts. Macrosociological relationships such as industrialization, urbanization, community, stratification, and public policy represent important variables in the empirical analysis of contemporary race relations and the normative symbolic language of action. With respect to the latter, the images, symbols, and rhetoric in his urban sociology provides not only descriptions and analyses of social institutions and structures, but also dramatizes and targets particular urban neighborhoods in need of intervention.

The perspectives of social structure, social change, and public intervention in Wilson's scholarship can also be sociologically understood as a type of symbolic explanation associated with historically specific situations. These are what C. Wright Mills called "situated actions" and "vocabularies of motive." According to Mills, the explanations current in sociology at different periods of history reflect the social experiences and social motives of American sociologists. Mills noted that before the 1940s, the typical vocabulary of explanation in mainstream sociological analysis was singular and these motives expressed a small town or rural bias (Mills 1963). He viewed the sociological vocabulary of the post-World War II period as a symbolic expression of a bureaucratic and administrative experience in life and work (Mills 1959).

Mills' insights inform us how the language in Wilson's perspectives of the inner-city underclass and the social and moral order of the ghetto represents a refocused liberal perspective of the sociology of social problems which attempts to (1) synthesize the public policy values and norms of neoliberalism and pragmatic conservatism; (2) integrate the domain assumptions and concepts of social control and social isolation which derive from the rational-legal bureaucratic *ethos* of modern corporate industrialization; and (3) integrate the cultural myths of the idyllic rural and small town past as manifest in the decline of community and the transition from the traditional to the current ghetto.

Refocused liberalism is adaptable to the ideas of both neoliberal and pragmatic conservative politics. Both neoliberals and pragmatic conservatives recognize an explicit role of the federal government in public policy. While neoliberals anticipate a stronger role of the federal government in articulating national urban policy, pragmatic conservatism recognizes the importance of urban programs and policies within deregulated and localized civic communities. With respect to interventions and social reforms, mainstream sociologists have usually followed these latter politics more than the politics of the radical left and radical right. While refocused liberalism provides some criticisms of macroeconomic policies and institutional arrangements, it is essentially incremental in its interventions and reforms. The assumptions of economic growth, with its possibilities for an improved opportunity structure, undergird Wilson's discussions of what is necessary to integrate (and reintegrate) the inner-city poor.

The rational bureaucratic *ethos* of modern corporate capitalism, with assumptions of increasing social control and integration, are reproduced throughout his analyses. This "corporate liberalism," with its economic, political, technological, ecological, and institutional dimensions of social organization, offers the possibilities for reintegrating the Black urban poor into the society. These are contained in the policy proposals of macroeconomic growth, transitional work programs, improved educational standards, child care programs, and universal social rights that will ultimately improve the human and social capital of Black poor.

Behind Wilson's use of the concepts of macrosociological change, "social isolation," and "concentration effects" are earnest attempts to refocus the nation's attention on the difficulties among the most dispossessed. The macrosociological perspective of change identifies complex economic, political, technological, and ecological factors that are more salient in explaining urban inequality than cultural and moral factors. At the same time, macrosociological change calls attention to historically specific developments of globalization, deindustrialization, and innner-city social dislocations that are objective in nature. The concepts of "social isolation" and "concentration effects" are attempts at identifying how larger macrosociological changes in the global society, nation, and metropolitan area are reflected in structural changes of inequality within urban neighborhoods. Although there are several sources of this social change in neighborhoods, these concepts examine the social consequences of poor populations left behind.

In his major writings, the rhetoric of social reform is mostly integrative in emphasizing the structural sources of social change, social dislocation, and reintegration more than the underlying institutional contradictions, power conflicts, and group struggles. For a society that has been generally unwilling to have an honest national debate on social class and racial inequality, these concepts represent an indirect attempt to address the conditions of class polarization and racial segregation.

The discourse of macroeconomic growth is explicitly delimited to questions of how increasing production is reflected in changing social relationships of work. The "grand design" and policies of macroeconomic change are largely national, system-level, and top-down. While the transformation of cities from industrial to service economies represents the primary economic change characterizing postindustrial cities, it does not explicitly address the economic transformations affecting the poor that are related to dynamics of urban redevelopment, real estate, and housing. In using the discourse of "concentration effects" and "social isolation," Wilson is not only targeting inner-city neighborhoods in need of intervention, but also through the images and symbols of decline, implying that the current neighborhoods are undesirable. With these images and symbols, urban redevelopment, gentrification, displacement, disinvestment, and abandonment are probably more likely consequences for these inner-city neighborhoods and residents in the "short run" than their reintegration in the economy. Real estate actors and governmental policymakers have used the language of decline, slums, and social concentration to legitimize the clearance of older housing through urban renewal.

As human ecological concepts, "social isolation" and "concentration effects" refer to the social disequilibrium and problems caused by the increased size, density, and homogeneity of the inner-city poor. While these are descriptive and sensitizing concepts, that capture and dramatize the problems of joblessness for a specific group and place of the poor, the symbolic language of action also decontextualizes the Black poor in these neighborhoods from other dynamics of institutions. It is not only deindustrialization and the disappearance of work that has led to the misery and despair of the inner-city poor. There are complex forces of disinvestment and disfranchisement among the political, housing, educational, welfare, health, public transportation and other institutions servicing the poor in these neighborhoods that have accentuated the "vicious cycle."

In this sense, "social isolation" and "concentration effects" are also mystifying concepts that obscure the objective historic and contemporary social control factors that have contributed to these problems and the institutional actors that might intervene in the future to exploit these. Behind the concepts of "social isolation" and "concentration effects" are actually cautious views of the possibilities of enlightened government intervention, on behalf of the poor, through conventional politics and civil rights policies. It is only on the surface that questions of power conflict in the social construction of public policies appear externalized and invisible. Wilson's recognition of the necessity of a "hidden agenda" strategy on behalf of the poor, which presses primarily for universal social rights policies while recognizing flexibility in racially targeted programs, presumes more heightened racial and class conflicts in the ghetto and American society than are usually explicitly discussed. It should be noted that these concepts of "social isolation" and "concentration effects" have already been used in policy rationales for breaking up inner-city neighborhoods and public-housing projects in Chicago. It is also theoretically possible that these concepts may be used in policy rationales for closing schools, streamlining social services, and increasing police protection in the inner city.

While there is no explicit mention of the myths of the idyllic rural, small town, and small urban community past anywhere in his discussions, the tone of the discussions that are based on the classic concepts of social disorganization and reorganization enter his interpretations of the decline of community and the transition from the traditional to the current ghetto. The Black ghettos of the past, that were vertically integrated, offered greater possibilities of community and social control than the contemporary inner-city ghettos which lack these resources. Racial segregation traditionally was accompanied by an enriched quality of life. While racial segregation continues, the interaction with economic segregation in inner-city ghettos is accompanied by the "desertification" of institutions and organizations. According to Wilson, a more ideal Black community would have greater social class and racial integration of the Black poor without the heightened racial segregation and social class isolation. Outside of small communities, or cities where Blacks are small populations, these idyllic patterns are unusual. The symbolic language of action here appears to be based on either resurrecting the "golden past" of the Black ghetto, which is present in some of the urban gentrification ventures, or increasingly integrating the Black poor in other neighborhoods outside the ghetto.

The refocused liberalism, in Wilson's universal policies, is viewed by some critics as representing a retreat from democracy. When the symbolic language of action is critically examined, the pragmatic politics are problematic. Stephen Steinberg argues "the notion of a "hidden agenda" contradicts Wilson's claim that racism is of "declining significance." Indeed it is because of racism that Wilson feels compelled to hide his agenda in the first place" (Steinberg 1997, 124). In an exhaustive discussion of his policy implications, Bernard Boxill argues that the focused liberal strategy in the "hidden agenda" is "justice through subterfuge" (Boxill 1992, 229–236). Boxill emphasizes that it contains elitist and paternalistic perspectives rather than democratic perspectives of how American society should be governed. At the same time, this enlightened manipulation goes against a dominant tradition in African-American political thought that policy-making involves the publicity requirement (Boxill 1992). Ira Katznelson notes Wilson's discussions of the universal policy goals discuss little the connections to Black political action and the mobilization of the Black poor (Katznelson 1997). Without these discussions, the political initiative for implementing these programs is handed over to middle-class Whites and is ultimately contingent on their good will, which is unlikely (Katznelson 1997).

Other critics have noted that the revisionist neoliberal interpretation buttressing his analyses and public-policy strategy is based on a fallacious reading of the changing relationships among the civil rights movement, organized labor, and the domestic social policy coming out of the New Deal, World War II, and post-World War II years. The universalism, which is advanced in his social policies, does not appreciate the integration objectives within the class- and race-based policies of previous civil rights movement organizations. For example, Richard Cloward and Frances Fox Piven indicate that the political coalition shaping the social legislation of the New Deal was made up primarily of southern congressmen and republicans (Cloward and Piven 1991, 737–740). This New Deal coalition defeated the more progressive income support programs and thereby gave the states and local areas authority over eligibility and benefit levels. Cloward and Piven note further that when Blacks became a political force in the democratic coalition during the civil rights movement of the 1960s, they in fact made demands for universal programs. Instead of the universal programs such as integration in jobs, education, and housing, Blacks received race-specific ones by national democratic politicians to neutralize conflict with organized labor and the White working class (Cloward and Piven 1991, 739). Relatedly, Charles Hamilton and Dona Hamilton identify a history of universalistic public policies advanced by civil rights organizations such as The National Association for the Advancement of Colored People (NAACP) and The National Urban League (NUL) that were complemented by race-specific policies (Hamilton and Hamilton 1986).

Jack Niemonen points out that Wilson's theoretical analysis of the state is focused on the federal level and is "quintessentially" liberal (Niemonen 2002, 38). In Wilson's claim that state intervention in the modern industrial period promoted racial inequality, his analysis was limited to federal legislation and excluded state and local decisions on social welfare, criminal justice, urban planning and zoning, and housing (Niemonen 2002, 40).

The challenges facing Wilson in refocusing liberalism on problems of race and urban inequality are both pragmatic and moral. These are reflected and reproduced in his discourses and the symbolic language of action. Because the liberalism of the 1960s and 1970s did not sufficiently address the universal and economic justice issues bearing on the Black urban underclass, it is practical to embrace this agenda. At the same time, the neoconservative analysis of civil rights policies and the progress of the Black middle class initially forms a part of his refocused liberalism.

Although there are several analyses and implications in *Power, Racism, and Privilege* and *The Declining Significance of Race* that lead to more progressive and radical policies, Wilson in his language is constrained to stay clear of strong social democratic policy reforms. The practical course is a continuing public-policy agenda focused on full employment, welfare reforms, education-to-work transitions, metropolitan government, and a Marshall Plan to rebuild declining cities. The moral challenge is one of honestly and forcefully addressing these issues while being heard. In balancing these different virtues, the importance of public visibility should not be alienated by excessive honesty and force. Acknowledgment and legitimation appears to necessitate the avoidance and distancing of polarizing and radical perspectives. The moral challenge is also one of bringing the expectations of social democracy into a postindustrial economy.

THE HOLISTIC PERSPECTIVE: CONTINUING POSSIBILITIES AND CHALLENGES

The theoretical possibilities of Wilson's holistic perspective and discourse are found in its syntheses and adaptability. Wilson's model of society is an organic, open system that pragmatically incorporates macro-level factors such as industrialization, state growth, technological change and urbanization alongside micro-level relationships such as racial and ethnic group adaptation and assimilation, immigration, mobility, power conflicts, and mobilization. Although the underlying assumptions of social structure are functionalist and normative, this is a functionalist model of societal organization that initially recognized the integrative consequences of social conflict in intergroup and institutional dynamics. Later it will integrate social control assumptions that recognize coercive power. Wilson's larger paradigm contains a complex integrating of domain assumptions, concepts, hypotheses, and sociological facts that are influenced by his formal concerns, interests, intellectual reference groups, and role in academic controversies. It incorporates a dialectical intellectual process of steady conceptual construction, de-construction, and reconstruction that amplifies and reflects larger existential realities.

From the sociology of knowledge perspective, Wilson's use of sociological controversies provide the structure that enables him to move beyond the normal boundaries of sociology, bring into dialogue competing sociological perspectives, bring sociology into dialogue with other social sciences, and simultaneously bring the sociological perspective into the public understanding of social problems. This is both an exercise in sociological theory and political sociology. There are possibilities and challenges in this enterprise.

First, his formal approach to the requirements of sociological theory and research combines what Thomas Kuhn in *The Structure of Scientific*

Revolutions has defined as the normal science and revolutionary science conceptions (Kuhn 1970). It initially has characteristics that approach a more revolutionary science conception of social scientific discovery and paradigmatic change. Through the use of academic controversies such as "The Insiders-Outsiders" controversy, "The Declining Significance of Race," and "The Underclass and The Truly Disadvantaged," Wilson systematically explores the anomalies of competing models of societal organization and race and ethnic relations for the purposes of clarifying issues, solving puzzles and ultimately developing a new paradigm. The possibilities of this intellectual strategy are manifest in: (1) the eclectic nature of this holistic analysis with its ability to clearly and parsimoniously link macrosociological and microsociological processes; (2) its analytical power to intellectually assimilate diverse conceptualizations, hypotheses, and paradigms which in normal science activities of the academy are usually segmented, bureaucratized, and disparately researched; (3) its heuristic value in calling attention to what problems in contemporary American society need research investigation; and (4) while articulating a core of substantive interests germane to the sociological perspective, there are important interdisciplinary directions which suggest stronger relationships of sociology with economics, political science, and history. While Wilson's formal approach converges with some of the requirements of a more revolutionary science in his exploration of anomalies and articulation of paradigmatic predictions, he stops short at this date of developing a fundamentally new paradigm of society.

In the normal science phases of his scholarship, Wilson becomes an intellectual and social organizational leader who organizes a research and training program and frames a research agenda. At the University of Chicago, his development of the Center for the Study of Urban Inequality, the Urban Poverty and Family Life Study, the Woodlawn and Oakland Neighborhood Study, and the Study of the Effects of Neighborhoods on Adolescent Social Outcomes in High Risk Areas and the University of Chicago-Northwestern University Consortium are part of this legacy. At Harvard University, the Joblessness and Urban Poverty Research Program, which Wilson directs, continues these directions. Other projects such as the National Research Council's Urban Underclass Database and the Multi-City Study of Urban Inequality in Atlanta, Boston, Detroit, and Los Angeles have utilized sensitizing concepts, hypotheses, and interdisciplinary methodologies advanced in part by Wilson. The National Commission on Cities and *The Kerner Report Twenty Years Later* (Harris and Wilkins 1988) has policy recommendations and interpretations based strategically on Wilson's concepts and perspectives.

Second, the pragmatism in Wilson's social construction of the complex relationships among industrialization, technological change, urbanization, race and the underclass exemplifies political strategy and diplomacy in research. This pragmatic political strategy and diplomacy involves: (1) principal and sensitizing concepts that are defined both explicitly and implicitly; (2) an a priori theory of stages of growth and progress in the hypotheses of pre-industrial, industrial, and modern industrial race relations; (3) underlying domain assumptions of rationalism, enlightenment, and optimism in modern economic and political development that accompanies progress; and (4) a top-down approach to theorizing, research, and public policy.

The possibilities of this pragmatism rest as much in what it clarifies as in what it obscures. Wilson's utilization of concepts and assumptions such as imperatives of industrialization, declining significance of race, the autonomy of the polity in modern industrial race relations, and underclass are arrived at theoretically, not empirically. The selective use of historical and social science evidence, that reinforces these generalizations, suggest that they may not be easily subject to empirical verification or refutation. The a priori assumptions of historical institutional change derive from a functionalist model of cumulative causation where the strategic factors of economic and technological change are illustrated. The presentation of institutional history is a teleological approach where historical fulfillment is an inevitable sequence of events that reduce greatly the range of human action in the past and present. Not surprisingly, Wilson's pragmatic approach can evade those details of public policy that contradict his conclusions.

Third, Wilson's substantive concerns with relating macrosociological changes such as industrialization, the growth of the state, and urbanization and microsociological changes in class and race focus renewed attention on the city, which converges with the larger debate in academic sociology over the possibilities of a distinctive urban sociology. Based on his analyses through *The Truly Disadvantaged*, Wilson sees problems of race in cities as ultimately nested in larger macrosociological or institutional concerns. Similar to classical European sociologists such as Karl Marx, Max Weber, Èmile Durkheim, and Georg Simmel, Wilson is fundamentally interested in the social, economic, and political implications of the development of capitalism. Similar to Robert Park, Ernest Burgess, E. Franklin Frazier, and Louis Wirth, Wilson is interested in how ecological processes of growth, competition, density, and diversity influence the assimilation and segregation of Blacks. Converging with the leading contemporary urban ecologists such as Amos Hawley and John Kasarda, Wilson views the social isolation and concentration effects of the ghetto poor as illustrating the disequilibrium of changing population, social organizational, environmental, and technological relationships that are nested in structural-functional explanations. Wilson's structural analyses of contemporary urban change converge with political-economy perspectives that emphasize deindustrialization and uneven development.

Unlike the turn-of-the-century Chicago sociology, that attempted to develop a distinctively urban sociology with city-level interventions of planning and control, there is not an explicit or distinctive urban sociology in his scholarship. Wilson sees external factors to cities such as macroeconomics, technology, and national social policy as primary. The "burning question" for Wilson centers on an analysis that transcends the city and race—economy, politics, and society. Accordingly, his prescriptions for social intervention go directly to the area of macroeconomic reform. These are not immediately concerned with the idiosyncrasies of regional-, metropolitan-, and city-level governmental forces. Wilson is correct in seeing cities and their social consequences as problems to be explained by larger economic externalities. Yet, one limitation in Wilson's societal paradigm centers on what some critics view as his deterministic treatment of the role of the state, power mobilization, and decision making in contemporary American society within recent work. It is instructive that within Power, Racism, and Privilege Wilson developed a paradigm of race relations that was partly based on a social power and mobilization perspective. By *The Truly Disadvantaged*, this becomes a more impersonal, hidden hand of the marketplace variable of power that is not explicitly articulated.

Fourth, in a continuing attempt to remodel his system of concepts and theories with a more dynamic institutional framework, Wilson's social prisms remain adaptable and open to interdisciplinary perspectives and insights. From economics, Wilson incorporates in his societal model a dynamic viewpoint of institutional change and intervention, economic growth and employment, and in later work a microsociological human and social capital explanation of ghetto poverty that brings the culture-of-poverty into social structure. From political science, Wilson's public policies are informed by public opinion and the perceptions of social inequality and social rights that are informed by dominant cultural beliefs and political ideologies. His more recent concerns with metropolitan and regional political coalitions follow debates in this discipline. From social welfare and education controversies, there is the identification of welfare reform, universal child care, higher educational standards, and stronger school-to-work transitions in his policy discussions. From human ecology, Wilson integrates in his hypotheses of social isolation and concentration effects, spatial mismatch explanations of the underclass that understate the persistence of race in modern urban society.

The model of macrosociological change, which is informed by Myrdal (1944), is complex, interdependent, and characterized by cumulative causation. In analyzing the problems of urban inequality, Wilson emphasizes that macrosociological changes such as globalization, deindustrialization, the shift toward a postindustrial service economy, government public policy, and the "social isolation" and "concentration effects" of the inner-city poor are inter-connected in a "vicious cycle." Wilson's optimism of the possibilities of pro-gressive social change derives from a vision that recognizes that cycles of depression, despair, and pessimism may be positively affected and reversed by macroeconomic growth and enlightened social action. There are also enlightenment beliefs in rationality, justice, social democracy, and individual-ism that influence the roles that sociologists might play in influencing the solution to social problems such as unemployment and poverty.

Although there is a continuing concern with social justice and race in his perspectives, these vary situationally. At the University of Massachusetts-Amherst, when Wilson's scholarship was not focused on policy concerns, the implications of his scholarship were relatively more radical, liberal, inde-pendent, and critical. At the University of Chicago, Wilson's refocused lib-eral perspectives become more fused with conservative perspectives. It is significant that the adaptation of these perspectives in his Chicago scholar-ship and policy perspectives are accompanied by his professional ascendancy. Since arriving at Harvard, Wilson has continued the public debate and research focus on urban inequality and joblessness. There are early signs that the tone and focus of his scholarship will probably be more national, lib-eral, and independent.

The possibilities of his sociological perspectives at Chicago rest on their greater appropriation of the classical traditions of Chicago School sociology, the dominant American cultural belief system, and public policy controver-sies. Wilson's holistic aims for the future of sociology have emphasized it becoming more interdisciplinary, combining macro- and micro-level data, integrating quantitative and qualitative methodologies, and pursuing contro-versial research that resonates with policymakers and the media (Wilson 1988, 89). The limitations and dilemmas, that accompany his intellectual remodeling of society, center on what structural issues of political, economic, and urban change are identified and selected. There is a clear movement away from those sociohistoric questions that earlier grappled with the power conflict contexts of racial inequality and its resolution. Although there is a continuing concern with inequality and social justice, these are viewed as sec-ondary to macroeconomic growth and reform.

CHAPTER 9

THE CONTINUING SIGNIFICANCE OF RACE AND RACIAL PRISMS IN THE SOCIOLOGY OF WILLIAM JULIUS WILSON

BACKGROUND

During the post-World War II period, the leading sociological theories developed to explain the continuing significance of race in the United States have been challenged to account for the changing institutions, social structures, and cultural beliefs bearing on the status of African Americans. William Julius Wilson's *The Declining Significance of Race*, *The Truly Disadvantaged*, and *When Work Disappears* are contemporary classics of race relations that represent leading statements and as such transcend the usual criteria of sociological theory and research. As a continuing discourse, which makes a holistic analysis of the changing institutional contradictions of changing post-World War II economy, workplace, government, and the changing intergroup conflicts of race and class, Wilson has used sociological controversies and theories to develop a "middle range" perspective that addresses social scientists and the American public in general to these new issues of urban racial inequality. Simultaneously, sociological controversies and theoretical discussions are the structures used by him to focus the observations, impressions, and sensitivities of his biography on this social construction of reality. In these theoretical discussions, the manner in which he has become the most important public intellectual in sociology speaks as much to Wilson's scholarship on race relations and urban inequality as the changing role of mainstream sociology and American cultural institutions in addressing cross-national and national issues of race and poverty. From a microsociological perspective, Wilson's discussions are an attempt to identify, clarify, and resolve the sources of intergroup, interpersonal, and personal conflict and success which have influenced his biography of upward mobility beginning from the poverty of a rural, nonfarm community to his current position as Geyser University Professor at Harvard University.

Wilson's theoretical construction is complex with multiple layers and undergoes reformulation and refocusing following sociological and public policy controversies. At the highest or universal level, Wilson is attempting to address and reframe the national discussions on race relations and poverty that go beyond sociology. This will draw from his appraisal of the leading post-World War II liberal perspectives on race relations such as Myrdal's *An American Dilemma*, Moynihan's *The Negro Family: The Case for National Action*, The Kerner Report, and recent neoconservative and neoliberal perspectives which become part of the refocused liberal perspective and are illustrated in *The Truly Disadvantaged* and *When Work Disappears*. Wilson is most concerned here with sociological knowledge which informs the public understanding of social issues and is importantly informed by public policy, political perspectives, and the use of journalism.

At the next or intermediate level, Wilsons interests are specifically informed by an attempt to bring a holistic and pluralistic discourse to the competing sociological theories and research in race relations that are usually fragmented, separated and polarized. These address a diversity of assimilation and power-conflict perspectives and are informed by sociohistorical insights. Intergroup and intragroup concerns of competition and power mobilization are also a concern here. His early articles, *Power, Racism and Privilege* and *The Declining Significance of Race* illustrate these concerns.

At the microsociological level, Wilson's observations of race relations are centered on intergroup dynamics that are informed by symbolic interaction, small group, and personal observations. These microsociological interests are reflected in some of his Amherst writings and more recent interviews and discussions.

More recently, Wilson has refocused the declining significance of race in *The Bridge Over the Racial Divide: Rising Inequality and Coalition Politics* (1999).

THE MYRDAL PROBLEM AND THE CONTINUING AMERICAN DILEMMA

Gunnar Myrdal's *An American Dilemma: The Negro Problem in Modern Democracy* represents the quintessence of the liberal perspective of race relations in both form and substance. Myrdal saw the significance of race as ultimately a moral contradiction between theory and practice. This was a contradiction between universal values of the American Creed—the doctrine embodied in the Constitution and Bill of Rights, high-Christian precepts, and the golden rule—and the particularistic discriminatory practices in Black and White relations that resulted from regional doctrines, local customs, conformity pressures, and individual prejudices of White Americans (Myrdal 1944). Over the long run, Myrdal predicted that the contradiction between American universal values and racial discrimination would be resolved in a direction consistent with these universal cultural values of the American Creed. At the same time, he emphasized that the increased role of the government and social-policy reforms, that dismantled the vicious cycle of de jure discrimination, would be necessary in improving the depressed social and economic conditions of Blacks and their quality of life. From Myrdal's perspective, the American dilemma was essentially a White problem and its resolution challenged the consciences, hearts, and minds of White America. Black Americans were seen as more secondary, passive, and reactive in responding to the dominant White majority and Black culture was assumed to be a product of social pathology.

Myrdal identified the role of values in sociological research and the importance of making explicit the value premises used in *An American Dilemma* and other sociological research for purposes of logical clarity and avoiding the hidden valuations that can lead to biases. Myrdal noted: "All social study, even on the theoretical level where facts and causal relations are ascertained, is policy-directed in the sense that it assumes a particular direction of social change to desirable" (Myrdal 1944). He emphasized that these value premises are not to be arbitrarily selected but should reflect the actual values held by people who are concerned with the problems being studied. These value premises are significant in that they resonate with people influential in the making of social policy.

An *American Dilemma* was not original in scholarship but rather a synthesis of social science knowledge on race relations through World War II. Among the Black scholars whose work is represented in *An American Dilemma* were Black social scientists such as Ralph Bunche, Abraham Harris, E. Franklin Frazier, and Doxie Wilkerson. The importance of Myrdal's contribution to knowledge is more normative than empirical. In identifying the problems of racial discrimination and "color caste" in the United States, he provided conceptual models and enlightened rationalizations that enabled the progressive post-World War II social policy reforms and state interventions in the desegregation of the military, public education, employment, and the extension of voting rights. Not only did *An American Dilemma* represent the leading sociological explanation of race relations relevant to the status of African Americans from the late 1940s through the late 1960s, but over time its ideas resonated with federally initiated executive actions, legislative reforms, and Supreme Court interpretations during these years. Martin Luther King's beliefs and tactics of active, nonviolent resistance, which were borrowed from Gandhi, and combined with his appeal to the moral conscience of White America draws from a sociological analysis informed in part by Myrdal. Although King and other civil rights leaders advocated a more proactive role of the government in enforcing antidiscrimination policies and practices, Myrdal's earlier arguments gave an important force to these.

As the ideas of *An American Dilemma* increasingly became a part of the American belief system, public policy, and the sociology of race relations, Myrdal had more cautious optimism of how race relations and civil rights were being played out in the United States. Myrdal saw his liberal expectancy predictions of progress and conflict resolution exemplified in the southern civil rights movement and the social-policy reforms enacted during the 1950s and 1960s. As urban civil disorders and rebellions emerged in northern cities during the late 1960s, many observers questioned whether the poverty, slums, hopelessness, and rage in these urban ghettos presented the historical and sociological contradictions to Myrdal's predictions. Some Black leaders, who analogized the civil rights, Black power, and community empowerment movements with decolonizing movements cross-nationally, saw the political control of Black communities and Black nationalism as alternatives to integration. The civil disorders and rebellions, that prompted the nation to reexamine the racial dilemma, were now symbolized in President Johnson's initiation of the National Advisory Commission on Civil Disorders or Kerner Commission Report (1968). The Kerner Commission Report refocused *An American Dilemma* on the continuing problems of racial inequality existing in the large cities of the North. In refocusing the hearts, minds, and conscience of the nation on the problem of White racism, the Kerner Report issued a strong challenge and indictment which the nation might take on, deny, or retreat from. In the context of warning of increased racial polarization, and the growth of two Americas "one Black which was increasingly in the central cities and one White which was increasingly in the suburbs" the Kerner Report recommended a policy of integration to improve the existing inequities. The Kerner Report recognized that the future of a racially integrated society would require greater national commitments and resources. While recommending integration as a policy choice, it also recognized that "enrichment" and "conservative" policies were competitive and might undermine the prospects of continued integration (National Advisory Commission on Civil Disorders 1968, 406–407).

The new American dilemma of race relations in the post-civil rights decades of the 1980s and 1990s is less crystallized than the moral contradiction between universal values of the American Creed and democracy and particularistic discriminatory practices. While the universal values of democracy and equality prohibiting de jure discrimination have become more unified, national, and codified, the values and cultural beliefs concerning economic justice, work, and social rights in the hearts and minds of Americans remain contradictory. American values of individualism, materialism, and group conformity compete with these more universal values. The dismantling of institutional discrimination as federal social policy has been replaced by the retreat from racial social justice.

According to Wilson, the increasing crystallization of wealth and income between the haves and have-nots in the Black community and the growing social isolation of the inner-city poor constitute the new American dilemma. Increased economic growth, universal social rights, and multiracial coalitions that are mobilized advancing racially neutral policies represent the beginning of a new resolution. Economic common ground rather than racial division is the normative starting point.

Myrdal treated at length the underlying value assumptions concerning "the Negro" growing out of the dominant American belief system that should be explicated in theory and research. Myrdal recognized that the explication of these value assumptions helped control biases in research and enabled the articulation of public policy goals in theorizing. Accordingly, social scientists should introduce explicitly stated, specific, and sufficiently concrete value premises from the outset of a study (Myrdal 1944, 1043). Finally, he urged social scientists to probe their own unexamined stereotypes and "opportunistic beliefs" and account openly for the value premises on which they based their research and the steps of reasoning used (Myrdal 1944, 1043).

Wilson is aware that his sociological perspectives on race relations and African Americans are not to be singularly judged on the merits of the theoretical and research insights provided by his scholarship and the policy arguments. Relatedly important is the degree that these descriptions and analyses resonate with a complex of several value assumptions deriving from the dominant American belief system in general and the sociological belief system in particular.

Depending on the extent that these value assumptions present possibilities of integration as opposed to conflict for consciousness, social solidarity, and professional mobility, these may be subscribed to differently by him and other sociologists. Although these value assumptions are expected to be explicit, these value assumptions are frequently implicit and hidden. These remain intertwined with the dominant cultural beliefs. These race relations values also interact with truth values. How these values of the dominant cultural belief system are embraced may constitute both theoretical and personal dilemmas.

Myrdal illustrated several of these value premises and cultural beliefs in the underside of race relations that continue to have relevance for sociologists. These provide the cultural boundaries and possibilities that influence leading sociological discourse of race matters. These have a bearing on understanding and appreciating the significance of Wilson's interpretations. These are discussed in "Biases in the Research on the American Negro" (Myrdal 1944, 1035–1041). Other extensions of these discussions with respect to contemporary race matters are provided.

First, Myrdal identified an expectation that optimism and progress should characterize matters of race relations over the long run. This value premise is associated with a bias for sociologists to overstate, accentuate, and play up sociological facts of progress and integration. Conversely, sociologists that emphasize social indicators of continuing discrimination and "falling behind," are expected to understate and obscure these sociological facts. Because there are dominant cultural beliefs of optimism and progress, sociologists in the mainstream take these as givens. Even when important institutional problems of racism exist, these are to be seen as capable of being ameliorated. Sociologists who provide analyses of social problems of race that conflict with the domain assumptions of progress and optimism are not only "swimming against the mainstream" but also must carry the major burden of proof in presenting theoretical arguments and research evidence.

A second value assumption identified by Myrdal emphasized that issues of race relations should be ideally viewed within the societal or macrosociological contexts of American economic, political, cultural, and social institutions and at the intergroup-level within the comparative stratification contexts of social class, status groups, and race and ethnicity (Myrdal 1944, 1039). By extension, this means that in an increasingly global, multiethnic, and diverse society, sociologists analyses of race should resonate with these more universal and cross-national contexts. Analyses at the regional, metropolitan, and local level should also interface with themes of globalization and diversity. The more that the status of African Americans is examined and integrated into these contexts, the more favorable and valid it should be evaluated. Studies of African Americans which are more holistic, indigenous, organization-based, and deviating from the aforementioned characteristics are generally devalued on principle.

Third, there has been a liberal expectancy value assumption that sociologists who study race relations examine these as outcomes of historic and environmental factors that are socially determined. To the extent that racial discrimination, segregation, racism and other related racial problems exist, these are seen as social constructions of reality which can be understood and controlled through social action and social reforms. The liberal expectancy assumption is egalitarian in expecting the historic inequities of race to be improved with increasing levels and movements of social class. In empirical research, the effects of race and other socially conditioned factors such as education, occupation, and income are to be statistically controlled to measure the effects. Under the liberal expectancy, the effects of social class and status over the long run are expected to be greater than the injuries of race. With respect to human potential and abilities, the liberal expectancy has a strong assumption of individualism. Individual differences within groups are viewed as greater than differences across groups.

Fourth, there is the value assumption that the most significant scholarship on race relations should be of the highest scientific rigor, integrity, and objectivity. Because even scholarly matters of race are often highly controversial and polarizing, these should at least address the aforementioned values of optimism, progress, historical and environmental causality, and societal contextualization. Formally, these should be of the highest theoretical and methodological rigor. Additionally, it is believed that values of integrity and quality are partly enabled by having significant scholarship on race relations reflected, reproduced, and favorably reviewed in the leading mainstream publications. This is a complex system of publishing houses, journals, editors, reviewers, critics, and executioners. Although in principle publishing in race relations is a competitive process of mobility for most sociologists, this has political implications. To the extent that scholarship in race relations is one of the most controversial subjects in sociology, it also has been one of the most controlled areas of scholarship. Mainstream journals have generally resisted the most controversial theoretical interpretations and research studies. There have always been alternative routes of sponsored mobility and books and non-mainstream publications are often more sensitive to new and controversial perspectives than established journals.

Fifth, Myrdal uncovered the cultural belief that the tone and sensitivity of race relations scholarship should be rational, dispassionate, and unbiased. The rational, dispassionate, and unbiased tone is enabled in part by balancing cultural sensitivity and social contextualization with physical and social distance. While the merits of cultural sensitivity and contextualization are to be lauded, the values of physical and social distance from Blacks are more problematic. Sociologists have frequently translated physical and social distance as values in their own right. As such, significant race relations scholarship can be derived from theoretical generalizations and empirical research that are not grounded in the existential realities of African Americans (Myrdal 1944, 1036–1037).

Compounding these are other value assumptions related to race relations and Blacks in cities. These have in part grown out of the antiurban bias that has accompanied American cultural beliefs and mainstream urban sociology. While these have long romanticized the rural, small town, and suburban ways of life and depreciated the urban, these biases continue to be associated with contempt and fear of the existential realities of Blacks in cities. When the contemporary realities of Blacks in cities are recognized, there is an underlying cultural comfort level which constrains and defines the problems and by whom. Problems of race and class, that involve power conflicts and structural inequalities, are generally minimized and made invisible.

There are ranging value assumptions concerning African Americans that are socially constructed and reproduced through contemporary racial stereotypes. The traditional stereotypes, that earlier focused on the biological, moral, and cultural inferiority of rural Blacks, folk Blacks, and Black migrants recently arriving in cities have been increasingly replaced by demonizing, sinister, and pernicious images of danger, moral decadence and "otherness" that continue to draw on alleged "physicality," moral, and cultural differences. In the popular culture, Black males are commonly viewed as the basketball players, hip hop artists and rappers, sexual studs, high school dropouts, drug hustlers and crack heads, killers, criminals, and menaces to society. Black females are portrayed as the matriarchs, quota queens, "sistas with attitudes," exotic divas, welfare hustlers, baby machines, and crack whores. The functions of these stereotypes, as rationalizations that accompany actions of continuing economic exploitation, political disfranchisement, and cultural subordination of Black Americans, are hidden and denied.

While Blacks are at this specific point in history one of the most highly urbanized groups in the United States, and are experiencing the institutional contradictions and social dislocations of changing economics, politics, and culture at a more heightened pace than other groups, mainstream sociologists are not expected to be acutely sensitive to these problems. These contradictions and dilemmas can be much more challenging for Black sociologists who are generally expected to be invisible. For Black sociologists who have grown up in cities, continue to live in cities, and have an identification and connection with urban-based issues that intersect with race and social justice, the possibilities for intervention center on how these scholars refocus their research and teaching for service and activism and in these efforts provide more engaged and dynamic social relationships of scholarship.

There are two other dominant cultural beliefs that confront sociological analyses of race and the city at the beginning of the twenty-first century: (1) the belief in an increasingly deracialized society, and (2) the belief in the decaying and dangerous inner city.

The first cultural belief represents the traditional liberal expectancy in the forms of multiculturalism and neoconservative class analysis. This analogizes the experiences of earlier European immigrants in cities to African Americans. Elsewhere, it anticipates that the growing demographics of the "minority majority" will erode traditional structures of race relations favorable to increased integration in the future. This prediction does not consider the adaptability of new forms of racism and racial categories in continuing racial stratification and social control.

The second cultural belief takes the antiurban bias, the stereotypes of urban Blacks, and needs for social control in the War Against Crime and recasts these into a new myth. None of the dominant cultural beliefs recognize that the urban growth, renewal, and dislocation within contemporary postindustrial cities have had particularly problematic consequences for Black communities. Nor do these cultural beliefs that have replaced rational analysis, recognize that the social consequences of racial segregation and social isolation that bear on poor Blacks in the inner city are like "ripples on a pond" that potentially might extend to other groups across race and social class.

It is significant that Wilson provides a rational analysis of changing race relations that is socially contextualized and environmentally determined. In his cultural discourses of race, class, and the postindustrial city, it is clear that he has also embraced the dominant American cultural beliefs of optimism, progress, and liberal expectancy. Underlying the logic of this race-class analysis are the cultural beliefs of an increasingly deracialized society that is manifest in the growth and mobility of the new Black middle class. In some discussions of contemporary Black population growth and the moral and social order of the inner-city ghetto there are allusions to disorganized and dangerous Blacks. For the most part, the rational, dispassionate, and unbiased tone in his analyses are enabled by his sensitivity to the problems of social dislocation among the urban underclass and their structural basis in economic changes and unemployment. The societal contextualization of modern or corporate industrialization and urbanization represents the starting point for reexamining race and class.

Similar to Myrdal, Wilson's scholarship is a synthesis of existing scholarship rather than original research. This is a synthesis of post-civil rights social science perspectives on the progress of middle-class Blacks and the falling behind of lower-class and underclass Blacks. Although this synthesis draws from the insights of sociological theory, social research, public policy, and cultural beliefs, the whole is much greater than the sum of the parts. In identifying the problems of the urban underclass, Wilson provides concepts, hypotheses, and arguments that are nested in macroeconomic structure and structural reforms in the economy, education, and social welfare. The significance of Wilson's contribution to knowledge is theoretical, policy-oriented, and cultural. In spirit, substance, and tone, his refocused liberal perspective is much more normative than empirical. Wilson's analyses draw from the diverse insights of critical and mainstream perspectives. His social policy recommendations represent a synthesis or hybrid of traditional liberal, neoliberal, neoconservative, and conservative perspectives. While *The Declining Significance of Race* represents a leading sociological explanation of changing race relations in the late post-civil rights years of the 1970s, its interpretation of the contemporary progress in race relations is not original. It draws significantly from preexisting neoconservative perspectives. In an attempt to clarify the refocused liberal assumptions in his arguments and policy perspectives, Wilson wrote a revised edition of *The Declining Significance of Race* and elaborated on the thesis of the underclass in *The Truly Disadvantaged*. Although there is a synthesis of conservative and liberal perspectives in these analyses, Wilson is explicit in criticizing the conservative conceptualizations of the underclass and the abandonment of the underclass concept altogether by liberals. *When Work Disappears*, is relatively more liberal in its social democratic policy prescriptions and implications than earlier work. The research on the inner-city ghetto, the declining family, and the significance of race among employers are more conservative in interpretation and remain closer in tone to *The Truly Disadvantaged*.

In identifying the post-civil rights progress and integration among the Black middle class and the falling behind and intractability of the Black underclass, Wilson recognizes that the normative requirements of clear and well-articulated concepts, hypotheses, and arguments figure more strategically than the simple results of empirical research and sociological facts in bringing the insights of sociology to the public understanding of social issues. In his selection of concepts, hypotheses, and frames of arguments, these should also be couched in value assumptions and implications that converge with the perspectives of significant political decision makers, policy analysts, and journalists. The craft of sociology required is not only one of masterful theoretical research, but also has political sociological requirements of diplomacy and statecraft. The additional requirements of the sociologists as political advisor and public intellectual are adapted and integrated into a holistic theoretical approach, which is partly based on human action and amenable to pragmatism. Among the leading scholars whose works are influential and acknowledged, Daniel Patrick Moynihan figures most prominently as the spirit and symbol, inspiring his use of sociological controversy to examine social policy issues.

The historical significance of William Julius Wilson's sociological perspectives of race relations is inseparable from the changing institutional contradictions of a specific period in United States history—the years of the Great Depression, New Deal, World War II, and post-World War II Cold War. The economic history of this period is initially characterized by Keynesian norms of government economic intervention and management focused on achieving increased levels of labor, productivity, and demand. Through the early post-World War II years, the growth of the welfare state was based on Fordist norms of production that was generated by a military industrial complex. Since the 1970s, the Keynesian model of economic growth has decreased as post-Fordist, deindustrialization and public policies based on deregulation, privatization, and the New Federalism have increased in significance. The United States government, during the early post-World War II years, was characterized by enlarged federal centralization and bureaucratization of the executive branch based on functions such as international diplomacy, military defense, and social welfare planning and provision. This growth of the federal state was accompanied by increasingly pragmatic and liberal visions of federal power and responsibility, democratic political participation, idealism, hope, and expectations of progressive inclusion in social reform. Accompanying the decline of Keynesian economic policies has been the ascendancy of a post-Keynesian state based on individualist and conservative visions of federal power and responsibility, republican political participation, cynicism, caution, fear, and expectations of regressive individualism in social reform.

The post-civil rights intellectual divide between Black and White sociologists is the starting point or "vital center" for Wilson's bringing into a refocused liberal dialogue the possibilities of social democratic equality and a socially engineered society. During these years, the intellectual dialogue between Black and White sociologists has generally been separated, polarized, and uneven. The intellectual social processes that influence the conversations and reflections of sociologists, including the internalized audiences and collective ideas that should be accepted, rejected, discarded, and reformulated, are circumscribed by cultural beliefs that intersect with race.

INTERGROUP PERSPECTIVES OF RACE RELATIONS

Wilson's sociological theorizing has an intergroup relations perspective. In *Power, Racism, and Privilege*, he initially views the nature of race relations as nested in "dimensions of power and their relation to dominant and minority group contact that cannot be completely understood if treated independently of the phenomenon of racism" (Wilson 1973, 5). He argued that a comprehensive account of race relations "must deal with the dimensions of power and their relation to dominant-group and minority-group contact" and "the dimensions of power cannot be treated independently of the phenomenon of racism" (Wilson 1973, 5). He uses the concept of racism to describe the experiences of subordinate racial groups that suffer from forms of exploitation that are directed by racist norms or racist ideologies of the dominant group (Wilson 1973, 7) and the concept of power to generally account for group oppression and the continued association of specific racial groups with particular positions of class or caste (Wilson 1973, 7). Taking issue with those sociologists who treat prejudice and discrimination in intergroup relations without context, he recognizes that "the frequency and degree of discrimination and other manifestations of prejudice against racial minority groups reflected the power of the White majority to dominate," and he emphasizes that resources and power potential are necessary to translate prejudice into discrimination (Wilson 1973, 7).

While viewing the importance of power conflict in race relations, Wilson cautions that the exclusive use of the power-conflict model as well as the integration-consensus model can be restrictive and problematic. In most cases of race relations, Wilson notes, intergroup contact involves a dialectical relationship characterized by "compounded and overlapping processes of conflict and integration, antagonistic cooperation, peace in feud, integrative functions of conflict, and forms of accommodation" (Wilson 1973, 8). Drawing from Richard Schermerhorn (1970), he defines integration not as an end state of interracial cooperation and reciprocal participation but as a "process whereby units or elements of a society are brought into active and coordinated compliance with the ongoing activities and objectives of the dominant groups in that society" (Wilson 1973, 8).

In *Power, Racism, and Privilege*, Wilson views the historic intergroup relations between Blacks and Whites in the United States as power contests where a dialectical relationship between integration and conflict has existed. Examining the complex and differential power relationships, he identifies a group's active power—the actual exercising of influence (Wilson 1973, 15)—and power ability (or resources) as the properties determining the extent of a group's ability to influence behavior such as social status, reputational power, capability to bear arms, political office control, control of mass media, wealth, land ownership, and social movement organizations (Wilson 1973, 16). The power resources of groups focus on "properties that determine the scope and degree of the group's ability to influence behavior" (Wilson 1973, 16).

Historically viewed, the differential power relationships in contacts between racial groups in the United States are identified by Wilson as (1) slave transfers associated with plantation economies, rigidly stratified occupational structures, and tight social control; (2) colonization involving the control of a territory by a nonindigenous racial group including the control and submission of indigenous groups' social, economic, political, and cultural institutions; and (3) voluntary migration in which immigrant racial groups move of their own free will and establish separate and autonomous communities (Wilson 1973, 21). With respect to racial stratification, he identifies two prevalent types of race relations—paternalistic, and competitive. This conceptualization draws significantly from the scholarship of Pierre Van den Berghe (1967).

Paternalistic race relations power systems, which accompany the preindustrial economy during the slave transfers and colonization stages, are characterized by subordinate groups lacking control of sufficient power resources to challenge the racial order and the dominant group's position approaching absolute control (Wilson 1973, 54). The economy, controlled by an aristocracy of the dominant group, has wide discrepancies between dominant and subordinate power groups resources; these gaps reflect racial divisions that are crystallized in a caste system that prohibits mobility except within castes (Wilson 1973, 52). To the extent that minority groups resist racial subordination, these are largely limited to constraint or pressure resources. Under paternalistic race relations, the chances of subordinate groups, using constraint or pressure resources, is low because the dominant group's controls are so extensive and strong that few entertain the possibility of successfully effecting change (Wilson 1973, 54–55).

Competitive race relations, that characterized the industrial and urbanized society, are accompanied by class differences becoming more significant relative to race (Wilson 1973, 53). These vary from the most restrictive competition through the more fluid and open forms of competition. In the former, Blacks were theoretically free to compete with Whites, yet extensive policies of discrimination and segregation reduced Blacks' chances of competitive resources. Organized resistance against racial stratification more typically took forms of nationalistic and separatist movements representing retreats rather than attacks. During this stage, Wilson sees the use of activist resources by subordinate groups such as protests or riots against property as unlikely (Wilson 1973, 56). In the more fluid competition, Blacks increasingly gain power resources that enable the use of persuasion and inducement and decrease the use of constraint resources (Wilson 1973, 57). It is instructive that with increased economic competition between Blacks and working-class and lower-class Whites, spatial segregation is introduced to separate groups and protect the dominant group's status.

Macrosociological perspectives of the changing linkages among the economy, state, technology, ecological organization, and their intersection with class and race are more developed in *The Declining Significance of Race* and *The Truly Disadvantaged*. His focus in these works shifts from the microsociological and intergroup concerns with power in majority-minority relationships to the articulation of macro-micro linkages bearing on his elaboration of the class divisions among Blacks in the modern industrial stage. In his theory of the preindustrial and industrial race relations, he has synthesized hypotheses of the orthodox Marxist and split labor market perspectives to account for the historic class conflicts bearing on race relations. During the preindustrial age, he argues that Marxian predictions of the capitalist class maximizing profits through controlling workers' demands and promoting divisions including racial divisions are valid.

The thesis of *The Declining Significance of Race* is essentially an exercise of synthesizing competing economic class theories of race relations and integrating these into his schema of different stages of industrialization. Wilson sees in the orthodox Marxist, the neo-Marxist split labor market, and the modern industrial relationships of class conflicts and race the bases for his arguments that (1) patterns of Black and White interaction in the United States do not consistently conform to the propositions of the first two perspectives (Wilson 1978, 8); and (2) the historic patterns of interaction between industrialization and norms and ideologies of racial domination are an expression of different systems of production, changing policies of the state, management interests, and workers' power resources (Wilson 1978, 11–12).

Wilson sees the propositions of orthodox Marxist theories, which predict that in the profit maximization motives of capitalists, the power of workers will be weakened by the promotion of divisions which include racial divisions, prejudices, and ideologies of racial exploitation, as more valid for the early industrial stage. This shows the early influence of Oliver C. Cox. During the next transitional stages of industrialization, a labor market split along racial lines develops where cheaper-priced Black labor is subject to exclusion movements and/or "caste" labor systems where higher-priced White labor monopolizes skilled positions and political resources (Wilson 1978, 7). This shows the influence of Edna Bonacich. During these first two stages of history, Wilson emphasizes "racial belief systems were quite explicitly based on assumptions of the Black man's biological and cultural inferiority, and therefore, have been appropriately identified as ideologies of racism (Wilson 1978, 9).

While acknowledging that industries conform to racial practices in established racial orders, Wilson sees variations from these in the modern or corporate industrial stage. To the degree that norms of exclusion play a salient role in describing and prescribing racial behavior, industries perceive little/no economic losses by adhering to racial norms, and the power of dominant group workers to protect their economic interests from minority group competition is decreased. Assuming the continued growth in the economy and norms of racial inclusion, these are consistent with the contemporary reorganization of racial practices. However, there is also, contained in the structural argument of changing economic and labor conditions, the implication that these variations may be short of growth or progress. Alongside progress, stability, inertia, and regression in racial equality are predictable during the modern industrial stage.

Wilson sees in the challenging of traditional racial norms of exclusion by the federal government, a rational economic interest on the part of industries to retreat from racial norms of exclusion and avoid economic losses, and the decreasing power of dominant group [White] workers as bearing on the increased variation of race relations during the contemporary period. The contemporary labor market for Blacks is a segmented structure where "Blacks are either isolated in relatively nonunionized, low-paying basically undesirable jobs of the noncorporate sector, or occupy the higher-paying corporate and government industry positions in which job competition is either controlled by powerful unions or is restricted to the highly trained and educated regardless of race" (Wilson 1978, 16).

It is instructive that paternalistic and competitive race relations are hypothesized to be stages in the dialectical relationships between conflict and integration. The competitive race relations appear to largely characterize his analyses of contemporary or corporate industrial society. The increased power resources gained by Blacks through labor struggles, the civil rights movement, and Black power mobilization alongside the increasingly interventionist role of the federal government in civil rights and the increased corporate liberalism of the private sector are evident. Wilson's emphasis on the "increased fluidity of competition" and the increasing significance of persuasion and inducement among leaders during the modern stage has liberal expectancy assumptions of greater interracial cooperation, accommodation, and assimilation. However, it is less clear that the emergent and dominant patterns of social interaction in the post-civil rights corporate industrial society and the norms and ideologies of racial domination reflect the uniformity of the earlier policies characterizing the post-World War II federal government.

In *The Declining Significance of Race*, Wilson noted that the most problematic area for labor market conflict in the modern industrial period would be related to affirmative action programs associated with civil rights (Wilson 1978, 16). Accompanying the growth of the corporate and government economic sectors, alongside the effectiveness of affirmative action programs, Wilson predicted decreasing racial antagonisms for the Black middle class. The successes of affirmative action for middle-class Blacks did not "trickle down" to poor Blacks. By *The Truly Disadvantaged*, the racial antagonisms related to affirmative action and a slack economy are increasingly salient in his analyses, discussions, and policy prescriptions. Viewing both the individual equality of opportunity and group-based equality of opportunity as insufficient in addressing the economic inequalities experienced by the Black underclass, Wilson proposes universal programs based on a "principle of equality of life chances" and economic class disadvantages (Wilson 1987, 117). In the more recent *Bridge Over the Racial Divide*, he argues that class-based affirmative action policies are not a substitute for race-based policies and would fail to maintain anywhere near the levels of racial and ethnic diversity attained in the last several years (Wilson 1999, 96).

This holistic approach to race relations and its formal and substantive concerns grows directly from his philosophy of social science orientation. In a continuing attempt to develop a societal model of race relations in modern industrial society, he consciously avoids the Marxian political economy perspectives evident in power conflict analyses and the reductionism of examining race relations as an intergroup problem sui generis as in traditional approaches. His cautious optimism which is articulated with respect to the possibilities of African Americans' assimilation in modern industrial race relations is predicated on value premises coming out of modernization paradigms, the possibilities of indirect, enlightened intervention, and a declining significance of race. This vision is arrived at through a theoretical synthesis of competing race relations models rather than through empirical research. Wilson's picture of the Black middle class, entering the mainstream of contemporary American society and an "intractable" Black underclass, which is socially isolated within inner-city ghettos, represents an attempt to bring together the conventional assimilation and racial caste paradigms utilizing an economic class-based logic. To the extent that racial discrimination and segregation are no longer official ideologies in postindustrial race relations, the "separate nations" language of the racial caste model, pluralistic themes of corporate liberalism, and ethnic solidarity should be avoided. It is instructive that in recognizing the possibilities and limitations of the ethnic-based and nation-based paradigms of race and culture questions in his early work, he comes close to nearly avoiding these in later work.

The intergroup relations perspective developed in *The Declining Significance of Race* and *The Truly Disadvantaged* is more specifically focused on the changing linkages among the economy, government, technology, ecological organization, and their intersection with class and race. There were class and race intersections in *Power, Racism, and Privilege* yet these were more explicitly concerned with power relationships and social conflict. Both *The Declining Significance of Race* and *The Truly Disadvantaged* are more complex, macrosociological perspectives on race in postindustrial urban America and must be examined from both empirical and normative lenses. The empirical perspective appears in his observations, descriptions, and analyses of the objective historical and sociological facts that enter into the social structures and relationships that influence the changing contexts of race. The normative perspective appears in discussions of the most appropriate paradigms and discourses for analyzing race and his universal prescriptions for social policy.

One of the major points that Wilson has attempted to emphasize is that nonracial factors, based on changing economic organization and the division of labor, figure more importantly than structures of racism, discrimination, and prejudice in the contemporary inequalities experienced by Blacks. While he recognizes that race as a structural and cultural relationship is a continuing feature of American society, the concept of racism is ambiguous. He views arguments based largely on racism and discrimination as failing to distinguish between the historic and current effects of racism on the changing status of the Black population. Moreover, these are much less likely to be heard, acknowledged, and legitimated in public policy.

This synthesis of competing race relations perspectives is one of the important and forgotten contributions of Wilson's theoretical work in sociology. In examining the competing theoretical perspectives of race relations, he recognizes the primacy of integration, assimilation, and social order perspectives in accounting for the changing status of African Americans. Yet behind his view of integration is not a simple functional, consensus, or stable social order. From the beginning, he recognizes the importance of historical change and social conflict in bringing about the continuous realignment and reorganization of social institutions, organizations, social movements, and racial and ethnic groups.

Based on the theoretical openness and pluralism of this societal approach, he emphasized the importance of power-conflict perspectives in providing necessary insights without abandoning the primacy of functionalist assumptions. The functionalist-conflict dialectic initially used in the sociohistorical interpretation, recognized the situational and human action qualities of intergroup struggles and contacts. His incorporation of the variable of power in analyzing racial and ethnic group mobilization and competition grows in part out of his interests in reconciling the possibilities of Carmichael and Hamilton's *Black Power: The Politics of Liberation in America* (1967), and the limitations as advanced in Lewis M. Killian's *The Impossible Revolution: Black Power and the American Dream* (1968). His scholarly writings on race relations through *Power, Racism, and Privilege* are written from the perspective of the "outsider" to political power and social movements. There is the increased presence of social democratic, social control, and liberal coalition assumptions in *When Work Disappears* and *The Truly Disadvantaged*.

Wilson's rational analysis primarily situates the contemporary problems of urban inequality in macrosociological institutions of the economy, education, and governmental public polices. The role of the environment in structuring social relationships and culture is central. Rational and impersonal aspects of social structure figure more importantly than the irrational and humanistic characteristics. Accordingly, the framework for interpreting contemporary problems of race and class intersections draws from corporate liberal assumptions of rationalization based on industrialization. While integrating a macrosociological context of changing institutions, his analysis of race relations remains primarily a microsociological one focused on racial group adaptation, assimilation, immigration, mobility, power conflicts, and group mobilization. It is instructive that while race enters into his analyses of *When Work Disappears*, it is not necessary for him to articulate the most invidious forms of race as structures of racism, racial formation, or institutional racism. Although he recognizes and describes the continuing significance of race, he generally understates this in his analysis. Because racial prejudice and discrimination are perceived as less significant in White public opinion and racial attitude surveys than earlier, a frontal assault against racism is viewed as problematic and unnecessary. Consequently, system-level and institutional relationships of discrimination and segregation are described and analyzed through larger impersonal and rational processes.

Behind Wilson's concepts and assumptions of "the declining significance of race" are liberal expectancy hypotheses of increased integration and assimilation. These embrace assumptions of racial progress and deracialization. The germinal ideas were most clearly identified in Robert Park's "race relations cycle," which anticipated increased accommodation and assimilation and Gunnar Myrdal's "theory of the vicious cycle," which predicted that the government by enabling social reforms and improvements in the quality of life could decrease the consequences of racial discrimination. Wilson clearly wants to distance his analyses and vision from the "separate nations," "Black solidarity," and "decolonization" themes found in 1960s classics such as the Kerner Commission Report (1968) and Carmichael and Hamilton's *Black Power* (1967). In "the declining significance of race" expectancy, the realities of persistent power conflict in racial stratification such as expressions and structures of racial separatism, racial caste, and apartheid are acknowledged and subordinated as objective facts. In *The Truly Disadvantaged*, he synthesizes the hypotheses of increased integration and assimilation to account for mobility of the new Black middle class and reintroduces the racial caste hypothesis to account for the growth of the Black inner-city underclass. Over time, the bringing together of neoliberal and pragmatic conservatism are reflected in a stronger embracing of consensus and social control perspectives underlying contemporary race relations. Earlier, he would view these race relations as dialectically related and characterized by competing processes of conflict and integration, antagonistic cooperation, peace in feud, integrative functions of conflict, and forms of accommodation (Wilson 1973, 8). The externalization of racial conflict in more recent analyses, represents an attempt to treat race as a given rather than treat it head on.

Wilson's recent discussions of racism in *The Bridge Over the Racial Divide* are informed as much by sociological analysis as political considerations. While he brings racism back into the discourse, he does so in a relatively limited manner. Not only is the notion of racism reduced to an ideology consisting of beliefs, assumptions, and values, but also his discussion is largely focused on the operationalization of these ideologies in public opinion. As a consequence of the public rhetoric and the multiracial politics coalition strategy focusing on universal nonracial issues, the challenge for political organizing becomes more focused on the issue of individual racism rather than institutional racism. The declining significance of race is manifest in the replacement of traditional biological racism by contemporary cultural racism.

In *Power, Racism, and Privilege*, Wilson argued that while ideological racism in its biological form was a part of traditional, patriarchal, and preindustrial social orders, the increased competition and contacts between racial groups in industrial and corporate industrial social orders, resulted in cultural ideologies of racism, replacing the more invidious and primordial forms.

This distinction between the biological and cultural forms of racism anticipated the contemporary discourses on neoracism (Winant 1994). While recognizing the presence of cultural forms of racism in postindustrial society, he underestimates their adaptability and persistence. It is instructive that while race enters his descriptions and analyses in *When Work Disappears*, he does not engage the more subtle forms of racial formation and exclusion.

The contemporary problems of racism, institutional discrimination, and segregation bedevil his analysis and challenge his vision of economic change and opportunity structure. While there are expectations of strong government intervention and spending that partly enable the economic growth and improvement of the opportunity structure, the continuing problems of race are viewed more as a consequence of "historic effects" and the "accumulation of disadvantages" rather than as the persistence of contemporary racism. While this is accurate in terms of some levels-of-analysis, it is misleading in obscuring more complex and rational forms of racial inequality. Consequently, the hidden injuries of race are reduced and decontextualized. It is with respect to the problems of contemporary race relations that the refocused liberal perspective becomes increasingly conservative. Wilson appears to share the liberal expectancy assumptions that view African Americans, along with other groups as sharing a common human nature and history that is universally moving toward assimilation. Because African Americans are essentially Americans in culture, there is assumed to be no distinctive African-American culture. There are rational and pragmatic reasons for this interpretation.

While it should be underscored that Wilson at no time argues that there is a "declining significance of race," the logical implications and substance of his theoretical analysis in general move in this direction. In his continuing efforts to develop a societal or macrosociological interpretation of contemporary race relations, it becomes clear that the imperatives of the postindustrial economy and the contemporary reorganization of the city are rational, impersonal, and integrative. Yet in locating the contemporary problems of the inner-city poor within the contexts of social isolation and concentration effects, Wilson wants to address the "invidious distinctions" of racial inequality by playing down race. His institutional analysis views industrial and corporate capitalism as systems of action that are more important and rational than racism that is viewed as an ideological and belief system of racial privilege. Because racial prejudice and discrimination are viewed as less significant than earlier in public opinion and racial attitude surveys, a frontal assault against racism is unnecessary and problematic. The adopted Marxian and Weberian assumptions of stratification constrain him to view social class, rather than racial group and ethnic group experiences, as accounting for the adaptation and assimilation of African Americans in the long run.

Wilson's concept of racism is a delimited one that enables him to understate and neglect institutional racism in contemporary race relations. According to Robert C. Smith: "Wilson does not define the concept of racism that he dismisses, and one almost gets the sense that he believes that no such concept can be unambiguous enough to capture the complexities of the post-civil rights era Black predicament" (Smith 1995, 106). Smith argues that alongside the cultural or ideological form of racism is a neglected institutional dimension. This discounting of racism as a cause of urban inequality and poverty stems as much from political expediency as from empirical evidence (Smith 1995, 106). Because macroeconomic forces are the primary causes in his analysis of urban poverty, it follows that universal economic programs, rather than race-specific programs, influence his definition of racism. Furthermore, in focusing on ideological racism, Wilson's cultural definition directly leads to analyses and discussions in the sociopolitical arena that are centered on the public rhetoric, cultural beliefs, norms, and public opinion related to race relations. To the extent that racism grows out of the competition between different racial groups for power, status, and privilege, it becomes essentially an intergroup rather than institutional process.

Finally, Wilson's analyses of contemporary race relations during the modern industrial stage take on a number of assumptions of modernization perspectives with respect to race relations. The "declining significance of race" draws from modernization perspectives which see the development of postindustrial societies moving increasingly in the direction of rational and secular institutions in which the irrationalities of racism, discrimination, and privilege decline. In an increasingly deracialized society, the salience of racial group identities and solidarities is to be replaced by social class, status, and civic identities and solidarities.

MICROSOCIOLOGICAL AND PERSONAL PERSPECTIVES

Although most of Wilson's writings are focused on the societal or macrosociological questions of race relations, there also is found a concern with microsociological questions of intergroup race relations and personal observations of race that are captured in writings and interviews. His microsociological perspectives are theoretically informed by insights coming from symbolic interaction and small group behavior perspectives. Wilson is concerned with accounting for (1) how the attitudes, feelings, and actions of persons across different racial groups are influenced by the interaction of skin color and socioeconomic status; and (2) how commitments to beliefs of racial integration and racial solidarity derive from microsociological contexts.

In an early essay entitled "The Significance of Social and Racial Prisms," he argues that "Blacks and Whites of the general public tend to view American race relations through different eyes, but it is likewise true that within each racial group perceptions vary according to income, occupation, education, and place of residence" (Wilson 1973, 395). His analysis views the "constant competitive struggle" of racial groups for the control of scarce resources as situationally influenced by complex and changing historical, economic, political, and sociological conditions and the extent which there exists "a belief in-group claims to certain rights and privileges have been (or will be) jeopardized or threatened by the specific actions of out-group racial members" (Wilson 1973, 409).

In this constant competitive struggle, Wilson recognizes that while Whites have historically subordinated Blacks through the economic exploitation of their labor through slavery, exclusion, and discrimination and the political neutralization of Blacks' power resources through disfranchisement and urban machine politics, the Black protests of the 1950s and 1960s represented important challenges to Whites' privileges, power, and competitive resources. In responding to the essays by Black and White scholars in the anthology *Through Different Eyes: Black and White Perspectives on American Race Relations* (1973), Wilson provides numerous discussions that illustrate his situational perspectives of racial group competition and conflict. The basic arguments from this essay remain relatively unchanged in his impressions over the past three decades.

Wilson hypothesizes that the extent of racial animosity among Whites is related to their socioeconomic status and their perceptions that Black entry and encroachment will decrease (or not decrease) their rights and privileges. He recognizes that upper and upper-middle class Whites, who do not directly compete with Blacks, can retain an abstract identification with the struggles of Blacks and perceive the least resentment and animosity. While middle-class Whites traditionally identified with the civil rights movement, there is emerging a class division where upper-middle class Whites have retained a less competitive perception and the increased contacts and competition between Blacks and lower middle-class Whites are reflected in increased hostilities. These hostilities are even more heightened for interracial contacts between Blacks and working class and poor Whites (Wilson 1973, 395–397).

Wilson views Black perceptions of racial animosity as explained by the "ways Blacks perceive both their inferior status and the efforts of Whites to keep them in subordinate positions" (Wilson 1973, 400). Black hostility to Whites has deepened he argues because of the heightened awareness and sensitivity to race exploitation created by the Black protest movement despite the fact that the racial subordination in recent decades is no greater, and in many ways is less than the oppression of previous decades (Wilson 1973, 400). Years later, Wilson will expect the Black middle class to experience less subordination and resentment relative to Whites than the Black working class and Black poor (Wilson 1978).

Wilson's microsociological perspectives of contemporary Black responses are based on a historical interpretation that sees a dialectic or struggle between two competing patterns of beliefs to the subordination and injustice experienced by Blacks—integration, and racial solidarity. Wilson views integration as characteristic of periods of optimism and hope where there are beliefs that the system is vulnerable to organized protest and there is the large scale use of pressure tactics which will force the dominant White group to share the resources they control. Integration is a response based on beliefs of rationality, interracial cooperation, and coalition building to improve the quality of life for Blacks. Racial solidarity is a response characteristic of periods of Black resignation, despair, and hopelessness where it is believed that political struggles and organized protest to promote integration are pointless and closing ranks is primary. Black solidarity movements, which grow out of racial segregation, place a premium on controlling Black institutions, developing Black consciousness, and establishing Black communities. Solidarity is a response based on beliefs of nationalism, racial cooperation, and group empowerment to improve Black quality of life. At the same time, racial solidarity decreases contact and interaction with Whites.

Over time, Wilson views the beliefs and responses of integration as more consistent with the universal cultural orientation of assimilation and individual achievement mobility. However, the degree that these cultural beliefs are embraced among individual Blacks varies by social class and status. Integration beliefs and responses are expected to be more strongly characteristic of older, higher and middle status, and secure Blacks. By promoting separation and group rights, Wilson views racial solidarity as undermining the liberal values of individual achievement and mobility. The Black nationalist and separatist beliefs are more consistent with the particularistic orientations of exclusion, segregation, and pluralism. Accordingly, these Black solidarity cultural orientations are expected to be characteristic of younger, lower status, and less secure Blacks.

Also, these general beliefs of integration vis-à-vis Black solidarity have relevance for the Black scholar in the academy. Wilson appears to view the Black scholar, having greater intellectual accessibility to racial integration in institutional contexts, professional associations, social networks, and inter-personal contacts, as illustrating more the ideal possibilities of universalism and assimilation than the Black scholar who remains isolated and segregated in Black institutional contexts, professional organizations, and groups. The universally oriented and racially integrated scholar is best situated to have the complex analysis which addresses the "common ground" of American society. Although there may be pluralist and racial solidarity perspectives that are negotiated by Black scholars in addressing the diverse and crosscutting audiences, over the long run the integration orientation appears more necessary than the latter.

Wilson's journey as a sociologist exemplifies the complex orientations of integration and universalism. As a public intellectual, his legacy as a scholar defies easy and simple categorization. His professional associations and networks have diverse relationships that cut across the intellectual communities of both White and Black scholars. Accompanying this liberal expectancy of integration is a dualism that has complementary pluralism dimensions in practice. Although Wilson's scholarship is primarily focused on the larger, more universal, and macrosociological questions that bear on changing American institutions, urban inequality, social policy, and mainstream White cultural beliefs, there is also significant substantive and symbolic evidence in his role as public intellectual as a leading interpreter of contemporary race relations and race matters. As an expert, his intellectual role includes advising not only leading institutions and agencies within the larger society, but also several Black institutions and organizations. Wilson's media interviews and appearances have appeared in *The New York Times*, *The Washington Post*, C-SPAN, ABC News, PBS, Black Entertainment Television (BET), *Essence*, and *The Progressive*. A careful reading of Wilson's scholarship during the Chicago and Cambridge years reveals a scholar whose sociological perspectives and opinions have had a broad reach and have significantly contributed to the public understanding of sociology.

It is not coincidental that the post-civil rights intellectual divide between Black and White sociologists is one starting point or the "vital center" for Wilson's bringing into a refocused liberal dialogue the possibilities of his microsociological perspectives of race relations. During these years, the intellectual dialogue between Black and White sociologists has generally been separated, polarized, and uneven. Wilson attempts to cross and transcend the racial divide. On the other hand, he views the insights of "Black solidarity" perspectives as turning inward and backward.

Symbolic interaction and cultural dimensions undergird this public intellectual role. It is not only objective social conditions that concern him, but also the appropriate symbolic dimensions of sociological discourses including the concepts, perspectives, language, and the public presentation. The intellectual social processes, that influence the conversation and reflections of sociologists, including the internalized audiences and collective ideas that should be accepted, rejected, discarded, and reformulated are situational. These intellectual performances are circumscribed by cultural beliefs and intersect with race. From this perspective, Wilson's role as master sociologist derives from how he has been able to both synthesize and clarify sociological controversies of race and poverty for the general public. His sociological prism is the bigger picture that transcends the racial divide. In his holistic sociological consciousness of race relations, there is a dualism which constrains him to experience and simultaneously interpret conflicting and often contradictory realities of the "insider" and "outsider." This is the holism of the intermediary who is the marginal man and buffer. The complexity in his holistic syntheses of race relations is also influenced by the diverse and competing collegial and personal associations of race and social class out of which his visions and opinions of society have developed. As the "man-in-the-middle," he is expected to be both a conciliator and reformer.

Other threads of a microsociology of race may be gathered from his interviews and discussions. The dualism in his presentation as a sociologist, however, has two layers of consciousness and experience that are in conflict and tension. On the one hand, there is a scholar whose broad, independent-minded, imaginative, and courageous perspectives have morally challenged sociologists by example and direction to seriously study the complexity of contemporary race relations, using analyses that recognize in changing conditions of capitalist industrial economies and politics the intersection of class, race, and political party. There is a public image of William Julius Wilson as a race relations leader, accomplishing the difficult intellectual tasks of paradigm building and consensus building and through his recognitions and successes rivaling and surpassing his peers. As a contemporary academic "race man," he has attempted to integrate the diversity of consensus and conflict perspectives of race relations into a pluralistic synthesis that constitutes a middle ground and common ground. While he is clearly sensitive to the invidious distinctions, constraints, and structures of race as a sociological problem, he apparently feels morally obligated in his perspectives to be free of the obligations and constraints of Black thinkers, Black solidarity, or ethnic chauvinism. This freedom to intellectually pursue scholarship, within, between, and transcending race, is necessary for the growth of the profession. Wilson's intellectual identification with the plight of the Black underclass or the "ghetto poor" indicates the sensitivity and courage to assist and help care for those Blacks who are most in trouble.

On the other hand, the breadth, independence, and insightfulness in his microsociological sensitivities of race and the "hidden agenda" approach at public policy derive from a vision of race relations in contemporary America that is torn between the possibilities of assimilation and persistent constraints of racial caste. While morally challenging sociologists to seriously study the complexity of contemporary race, he appears restrained, reserved, and closed in avoiding and evading important questions and implications of other theories that challenge mainstream theories and ideologies of racial integration. In developing a refocused liberal consensus, pluralistic synthesis, and middle ground, Wilson appropriates tenets of contemporary neoconservative, neoliberal, and social democratic perspectives of civil rights and race. Yet the limitations and dilemmas of these neoconservative, neoliberal, and social democratic agendas are not critically appraised and discussed as forthrightly as those advanced in his analyses of the most visible liberal, conservative, and Black solidarity perspectives.

It is more than ironic that in his quest to pursue scholarship free of the obligations and constraints of Black solidarity and transcending race, Wilson's scholarship has for the most part of thirty years been focused on African Americans and changing institutions. The scholarly freedom and independence in his microsociological perspectives are in tension and counterbalanced by professional expectations for recognition and affiliation. The intellectual identification with the plight of the Black underclass simultaneously involves significant degrees of intellectual independence, distancing and alienation with the Black middle class. Wilson's biography of upward mobility and the mobility of the new Black middle class, although sometimes advanced as analytically separable from the changing prospects of working- and lower-class Blacks, is actually more historically and empirically connected.

CHAPTER 10

━━━━━━

EPILOGUE

William Julius Wilson's journey, beginning from the poverty of a small, rural nonfarm community through strong extended family and supportive community relationships, the molding and tempering of his sociological imagination at Wilberforce, Bowling Green, and Washington State, and his ascendancy as the leading public intellectual in sociology at the University of Chicago occurs during several periods in American history—the years of the Great Depression, New Deal, World War II, post-World War II, and post-civil rights years. His biography of social and professional mobility symbolizes the larger post-World War II changes in American economic growth, the continuing aspirations of African Americans in the post-civil rights years, and the promise of sociology. The historic, sociological, and situational contexts in which Wilson's training, professionalization, and mobility in academic sociology occur have several points of convergence and divergence with the changing post-World War II social and economic conditions of African Americans in general and Black sociologists specifically that appear to bear on his racial prisms.

The continuities between Wilson's biography, the history of African Americans, and changing American institutions contribute to his sociological consciousness and increase his insights, voice, and symbolism. First, the changes in the post-World War II economy and opportunity structure leading to the growth of employment in industrial, governmental, and service activities and the continued migration and urbanization of African Americans in the largest metropolitan areas and central cities are the same macrosociological changes that influence his entry into sociological controversies of race, class, and the postindustrial city. Second, the higher education and training of the Black professional and administrative middle classes and Black leadership, which was traditionally based in Black colleges and Black community institutions through the early post-World War II years, become increasingly and strategically integrated into traditionally White universities, the government, corporations, and White institutions of the larger society during the post-civil rights years. Wilson's education, training, and professionalization

213

are influenced by both the Black college and White university contexts that parallel that of the new Black middle class and leadership classes. Third, the political changes and sociological controversies deriving from the civil rights and Black power movements and the cultural revolution in Black America during the 1960s are intellectually reflected and reproduced in Wilson's emerging interests in race relations through sociohistorical and power-conflict perspectives at the University of Massachusetts-Amherst. These draw significantly from both mainstream and critical theory. At the same time, the independence in his perspectives anticipate later developments within the Black community. His intellectual identification of the schism within the Black community and the Black lower class derives from theoretical sources and a biography of mobility that remains connected to its roots and has not forgotten where he came from. The continuities and ambiguities between Wilson's professional biography and the dominant sociological belief system reinforce these American values.

Wilson's scholarly role as a "middle-man" in sociological controversies of race relations is partly a consequence of his marginality as an "outsider" and African American. This marginality, however, through sociological controversies is turned into a strength. As an "outsider," he has the independence and freedom of utilizing numerous perspectives in clarifying and resolving sociological controversies and can arrive at syntheses that are sensitive to race and simultaneously go beyond race. This intellectual identity involves the development of a universal persona that is informed by philosophical considerations, theoretical possibilities, and social policy visions. The universalism in his sociological consciousness partly grows out of a dualism where Wilson is constrained to experience and interpret simultaneously the conflicting and often contradictory realities of the "insider" and "outsider" in race relations. This is the holism of the intermediary who is an intellectual centrist and buffer.

Through sociological and public policy controversies, Wilson's status as "outsider" becomes increasingly one of "insider." In moving toward an "insider" status, Wilson makes continuous attempts to construct a synthesis and higher ground among competing theoretical and social policy perspectives that are usually contentious, differentiated, and isolated. Many of these different theoretical and social policy perspectives represent different points or stages in Wilson's sociological journey and professional career. These are influenced by the competing collegial and personal associations of race and social class out of which his visions and opinions of society have developed. There are also expectations as an "insider" to play the roles of "philosopher-king," judge, "gatekeeper," and "executioner" with respect to sociological knowledge on race relations and urban inequality. Through his introductions, reviews, analyses, commentaries, and opinions, Wilson has come to exercise

considerable discretionary power and influence in the development of sociological knowledge. This involves influencing some perspectives inside and
directing that other perspectives be left outside.

At the same time, Wilson's intellectual connections with African Americans and the changing Black community are in tension and contradiction
with many of the theoretical and social-policy perspectives that constitute his
universal framework. These are reflected and reproduced in many of his
analyses and discussions of race, class, and the postindustrial city.

First, Wilson's assimilation-integration perspectives of contemporary
urban inequality, while consistent with the dominant American cultural
beliefs and the normative requirements of pragmatic social policy, are accompanied by large-scale social dislocations for the Black working class and poor
which understate many of the power conflicts of race and poverty. The
assumptions of economic growth, which structure his policy discussions of
the reintegration of the truly disadvantaged into the new economy, are based
on the normative requirements of a "long range" vision and consciousness
raising. However, the current social dislocations in Black communities are of
such a large magnitude that these may actually require more radical institutional changes.

Second, Wilson's contemporary sociological perspectives of Blacks in
cities are primarily theoretical and derive "from the armchair" and the "car
window." His liberal expectancy interpretation of assimilation among the
Black middle class is theoretical and actually captures the neoconservative
and neoliberal assessments of Black progress and the aspirations of the new
Black upper middle class. His analyses of postindustrial economic changes,
class schisms within the Black community, demographic analyses of the Black
community, and the moral and social order of the inner-city ghetto probably
say as much about leading social-policy discussions, the dominant American
sociological beliefs concerning race relations, and the cultural beliefs concerning African Americans as it does concerning the objective and complex
conditions of urban life among African Americans.

Third, the locus for Wilson's theorizing of race, class, and the postindustrial city is based largely on Chicago. Similar to the classic "growing
city" perspectives which universalized ecological processes in the internal
structure of the city, he has taken the historically specific patterns of Black
poverty within inner-city neighborhoods in Chicago and generalized these
nationally. This is not to argue that continuities do not exist between Chicago
and other cities. There are, however, important discontinuities. What
appears more serious is that in advancing selected relationships of urban
change as a universal or master model to other cities, there is the possibility
that the historic, regional, and localized complexities of these cities will
become reified as the Chicago model. As noted earlier, the analysis of the

inner-city Chicago Black community is regionally and historically specific. This postindustrial "city of the underclass" is decontextualized from macrosociological changes such as urban redevelopment and gentrification. Over time, Wilson delimits these generalizations as an industrial city model characterizing the largest cities of the northeast and Midwest.

Fourth, Wilson's handling of social policy questions such as affirmative action and continuing discrimination have often been independent of national Black leadership and Black public opinion. While he has had a continuing commitment to civil rights and universal economic rights policies, his perspectives have undergone shifts based on changing professional situations and public-policy controversies. At the University of Chicago, Wilson initially viewed affirmative action programs based on equality of individual opportunity and preferential group treatment as insufficient in addressing the truly disadvantaged (Wilson 1978, 112). In attempting to move beyond the race-based programs of the civil rights movement, he later proposed as an alternative universal and economic class-based programs based on the "principle of equality of life chances" (Wilson 1987, 117). While these universal programs constituted the primary thrust, affirmative action that was part of the "hidden agenda" remained necessary. At Harvard University, Wilson more strongly embraced race-based affirmative action and flexible standards alongside the importance of class-based standards and universal social rights. In *The Bridge Over the Racial Divide* he argued that "class-based affirmative action programs would fail to maintain anywhere near the levels of racial and ethnic diversity attained in the last several years" and "class-based policies, however justified, are not a substitute for race-based policies" (Wilson 1999, 96).

Fifth, his universal perspectives of American culture, changing institutions, and social policy have not seriously treated the role that African Americans have played, or might play in the future as active social agents, in affecting social change. Similar to Myrdal, who did not anticipate the role of the Black church in the southern civil rights movement, Wilson's analysis of changing institutions is focused largely on majority group White Americans and mainstream institutions. Although he expects African Americans to be a necessary part of the multiracial political coalition he envisions, the "common ground" of universal nonracial issues should precede Black solidarity and the more divisive race-specific issues.

Wilson's perspectives of integration, as reflected in his interviews, reveal no major personal incidents of racial antagonisms and discrimination in his professional academic career. This does not necessarily mean that his professional academic career has always been characterized by acceptance and security or free of racial prejudice, discrimination, and conflict. The "collegial misgivings" episode surrounding the editor's role suggests that he, like other Black scholars, has had to continually struggle to defy and rise above White gentlemen's agreements and presumptions of competence. And in producing scholarship that rises above these presumptions, there is a consciousness that the most direct, confrontational, radical, and controversial sociological discourses on race have usually been relegated to the margins and are to be carefully avoided. His personal memories and stories of race in interviews often appear diplomatic, cautious, guarded, reticent, and understated.

Wilson's sociological legacy is an unfinished and continuing intellectual journey. While his sociological perspectives address the challenges of postindustrial society by identifying the institutional changes and class and race inequalities that bear on the inner-city poor, his policy prescriptions and discussions for the cities essentially urge a reexamination of social democracy and liberalism in the United States. As a leading sociologist and public intellectual who has influenced the public understanding of sociology, Wilson recognizes that a most important intellectual task focuses on how to bring the sociological imagination into public-policy controversies and simultaneously refocus these. The pragmatism in this task, where sociological theory and political sociology converge, involves an appraisal of competing public-policy perspectives of liberalism and conservatism and their appropriation into a refocused, holistic and neoliberal vision for the future. The relevant social structures of politics and power, influencing the nation's changes in urban inequality and the inner-city poor, center on the institutional level public policy decision makers, social scientists, mainstream journalists and media, and public opinion. Mediating between these political relationships is the development of a multiracial political coalition that will help mobilize the issues of social rights and democracy.

Because contemporary racism is essentially viewed by him as an ideology of privilege and power associated with changing economic, political, and social situations and ultimately divisive, the contradictions of racism for democracy are ultimately addressed through macro-level economic and political institutions, multiracial social movements, and consciousness raising that emphasize economic common ground. For Wilson, universal policies that emphasize social class and disadvantage more than race-specific agendas are theoretically and morally most consistent with this higher ground. The liberal expectancy assumptions of assimilation and integration that initially structured his analyses and policy prescriptions did not frontally assault the continuing significance of race but rather treated it as part of a "hidden agenda." This "hidden agenda" while strategic is incomplete. As a practical matter, Wilson recognizes the need for race-based policies has continued rather than declined in significance.

Critics will continue to raise questions concerning the interpretations and significance of William Julius Wilson's sociological analyses of race, class, and the postindustrial city, his contribution to the public understanding of sociology, including his social policy discussions and recommendations, and his legacy as a sociologist and public intellectual.

There will be questions and criticisms raised concerning the subject matter or domain in contemporary race relations that Wilson has become a leading expert. His focus on African Americans and changing American institutions and questions of urban inequality and the underclass is delimited to a relatively narrow focus of historical and sociological problems which has been theoretically interpreted. When compared to the scholarship of sociological predecessors such as W. E. B. Du Bois, Charles S. Johnson, E. Franklin Frazier, St. Clair Drake, and Oliver Cromwell Cox, the range of institutional and organizational problems empirically researched on the African American community such as the family, church, work and business, politics, education, and community organization is limited. More than these classical sociologists, Wilson is explicitly concerned with bringing a theoretical interpretation of the post-World War II African American experience into a discourse with the leading sociological perspectives of race relations.

There will be several questions raised concerning how and why Wilson became the most recognized and visible sociologist in America at the end of the twentieth century. Many will point out that among the sociologists of his generation, his scholarship has not necessarily been the most productive or brilliant. Rather than his sociology, some critics note it is the manner in which he has conducted himself politically that has counted most. In advancing an argument that social class matters more than race, Wilson offered a public discourse and apologia for those social scientists and policymakers attempting to deny the continuing significance of racism and institutional discrimination. In crafting a macrosociological theory of urban inequality and managing to place a refocused liberal interpretation of poverty on the national agenda, Wilson captured the moral ground from conservatives in sociological controversies. Also, the manner in which he has crafted broad generalizations from sociological research, public-policy perspectives, and dominant cultural beliefs has added to the controversies.

There will be criticisms and arguments made that Wilson's contribution as a sociologist and public intellectual rests much less on the macrosociological theory, research, and concepts he has become associated with. Critics argue that Wilson's prominence derives not from the clear analyses and arguments he has provided explaining race, class, and the postindustrial city but from the absence of clear analyses and arguments. Instead of clear analyses and arguments, he has raised questions that are accessible to academic and public audiences. In most respects, he has summarized and incorporated other sociological, social policy, philosophical, and journalistic controversies and dramatically raised questions which other theorists and researchers will find the answers to. In refocusing the national debate on race relations and urban inequality, Wilson has continued to ask questions. The numerous hypotheses, which make up his research agenda, are questions.

There will also be questions and doubts concerning how Wilson has responded to his reviewers and critics in sociological controversies and integrated these perspectives and insights in his discussions, generalizations, and revisions. Among the criticisms viewed as constructive and serious, he uses these in revisions and elaborations of his arguments. Critiques and recommendations from the early editorial of the *Chicago Tribune*, scholars at the University of Pennsylvania Conference on the Declining Significance of Race, Kenneth Clark, Charles Willie, Herbert Gans, and Douglas Massey are among those which have been reflected in important revisions. More often, Wilson has responded to critics more symbolically and subtly by integrating different assumptions, concepts, and hypotheses into his microsociological discussions of intergroup relations while essentially retaining the macrosociological political-economy perspectives. Although Wilson has maintained a primarily macro-level, political-economy, and class-based analysis, his more explicit discussions of the racial attitudes of employers, statistical discrimination, and flexible standards in more recent scholarship may be viewed in part as a response to his critics. In his attempt to out flank the more conservative culture-of-poverty perspectives, he has integrated dimensions of these cultural analyses in his discussions of neighborhood "concentration effects" and "social isolation." In this centrist attempt of finding common ground between the situational outcomes of social structure and the culture-of-poverty, several critics see him as "straddling the fence" between liberalism and conservatism.

There will also be criticisms and arguments raised that Wilson's contributions to sociological theory and controversy have been more symbolic than substantive. In the sociological controversies related to *The Declining Significance of Race*, Wilson challenged and debated the leading Black and White social scientists. Although the points raised by him were not new and contained in the neoconservative perspectives of "Black progress" by scholars such as Edward Banfield, Daniel Patrick Moynihan, Nathan Glazer, Richard Scammon, and Ben Wattenberg, the force and conviction of his arguments provided a legitimation of the retreat from racial justice for American sociologists who wanted to believe that problems of institutional racism and discrimination were things of the past. In response to several Black sociologists that emphasized the importance of "insider viewpoints," "strengths of Black families," Black solidarity, and the salience of racism, Wilson's complex analyses which argued that the historic effects of discrimination, changing contemporary American institutions, and the intersection of social class and race offered a compelling alternative explanation. In the controversies related to *The Truly Disadvantaged*, Wilson offered a social democratic and liberal alternative to the most pernicious and pejorative culture-of-poverty arguments that was pragmatically couched in the conventional wisdom and dominant American beliefs. His normative theory, with value assumptions of the "liberal expectancy" offers the possibilities of optimism and progress.

At the beginning of the twentieth century, W. E. B. Du Bois warned that "the problem of the twentieth century is the problem of the color line" (Du Bois 1903, 23). While he recognized that the color line or race would constitute an important base of intergroup conflicts, Du Bois was aware that its resolution would, in many important respects, transcend racial groups and that it was inalienable from social, economic, and political justice. Decades later, he observed:

> I still think today as yesterday that the color line is a great problem of this century. But today, I see more clearly than yesterday that back of the problem of race and color lies a greater problem which both obscures and implements it: and that is the fact that so many civilized persons are willing to live in comfort even if the price of this is poverty, ignorance, and disease of the majority of their fellow men. (Du Bois 1961, xiv)

Du Bois' observations of the "problem of the color line" and its intersection in social class, derived from an intellectual career as sociologist, historian, propagandist, and activist. Through pioneering empirical research on several aspects of African-American conditions, institutions, and organized life, he set out on a search for truth through scholarship that he hoped would lead to social reform. Because Du Bois recognized that the continuing problem of the "color line" was not singularly affected by social science knowledge, the enlightened rationalism and optimism in the scholarship of his early years was accompanied by more pragmatism and activism in his maturing years.

The changing social conditions of race, class, and the postindustrial city that are reflected in the scholarship and perspectives of William Julius Wilson converge in part with the insights of the mature Du Bois. Yet it is from the seminal perspectives of the Chicago School that his analyses of urban inequality are continually refocused. From the classic theories of Robert Park and Ernest Burgess, Wilson derives concepts and hypotheses that influence his treatments of the ecological structuring of the city, the moral order of neighborhoods, and social isolation and concentration effects. In his analyses of industrialization, urbanization, and the changing class conditions of African Americans, Wilson's analyses draw from, in letter and spirit, the insights of E. Franklin Frazier's theories of industrialization, urbanization, and race relations and the Negro family specifically. Wilson's macrosociological perspective of social control, which brings together political, economic, technological, ecological, and other dimensions, has formal similarities with the macrosociological theories of Morris Janowitz (Janowitz 1970).

At the same time, in bringing together aspects of enlightened rationalism, pragmatism, liberalism, and the sociological imagination, Wilson's discussions draw from, inform, and refocus some of the leading analyses and commentaries relevant to sociologists in social policy and as public intellectuals. Similar to Gunnar Myrdal, Wilson advances a role of theoretical research in which the values in sociological research should be made explicit and resonate with influential policymakers and a role of practical research, which is focused on the sociologist clarifying the value assumptions relevant to policy choices and social planning. In his interpretation of contemporary race relations, Wilson has drawn from and highlighted the value assumptions of the dominant American belief system such as optimism, progress, integration, and the liberal expectancy that were initially identified by Myrdal. From Daniel Patrick Moynihan, there is a pragmatic model of using public-policy controversies to bring social science knowledge into national decision making through the use of public discourses. This includes a public intellectual model and strategy of how to raise questions, dramatize issues, and set agendas that appears in Wilson's later scholarship.

Simultaneously, the important consciousness raising and value clarifying roles that Wilson plays in formulating public issues, which are situated in changing institutional contradictions, approaches in part the intellectual and political challenges identified by C. Wright Mills. From Mills, there is a moral and political imperative, articulated by Wilson, which requires sociologists to increasingly translate private troubles into public issues while increasing the public's understanding of sociology. Relatedly, Wilson has attempted to negotiate in part the dualism of intellectual challenges charted by Harold Cruse in his book, *The Crisis of the Negro Intellectual* (1967). Not only has his analyses and discussions been attuned to the American political structure and cultural institutions and structural changes in economics, politics, and social class, but also through refocused liberalism he has redefined a role as public intellectual that combines cultural and political criticism and social reforms that includes programs and demands.

At the turn of the twenty-first century, the contemporary problem of the color line remains a continuing American dilemma. It is a more complex, sophisticated, and pressing problem than the one posed a century earlier by Du Bois. Globally, it can be seen in the increasing centralization of wealth among advanced industrial nations and the growing social inequalities among rich and poor in these same nations which are socially reproduced in the poverty, debts, and political struggles within most southern hemisphere nations in Africa, Asia, and Latin America. In the United States, the stronger intersection of social class and race with respect to African Americans goes beyond the issues of economic dislocation and the underclass and extends to contemporary issues such as the emerging prison industrial complex, drugs and violence, police harassment and brutality, imprisonment, political disfranchisement, miseducation, and death at an early age. The policy arguments of civil rights, empowerment, and economic justice raised by African-American leaders throughout the twentieth century have been recently accompanied by arguments for debt forgiveness within African nation-states and calls for reparations within the United States (Robinson 2000).

Although many sociologists view the development of modern postindustrial society as becoming increasingly rational and secular with the irrationalities of racism, racial solidarity, and racial group decreasing in significance, this is premature. With respect to informed public discourses on race relations, there is sufficient historical and sociological evidence that indicates that the increasing significance of class does not mean the declining significance of race, nor does the increasing significance of race mean the declining significance of class. When the historic and contemporary effects of social class and race are cumulative and interactive, the social pressures and boundaries constraining those "faces at the bottom of the well" will strengthen unless these are countered by sustained and organized struggles to clarify and change these inequities.

It is significant that while social scientists have undermined any biological bases of racial categorization, race as a sociopolitical and cultural category remains salient in cultural discourses, public policy, and everyday practices. For political purposes, the continued confusion of the biological and sociopolitical boundaries of race in contemporary public discussions, the continued denial of racism as an institutional and cultural problem and its reduction to individual acts of racism, and the possibilities of a more diverse and multicultural mosaic, characterizing racial and ethnic stratification and intergroup relations, suggest continuing social struggles and intellectual challenges. Contemporary racism is systematic, rational, sophisticated, covert, coded, layered, indirect, and impersonal.

The sociological controversies of race, class, and the postindustrial city are much larger than the analyses and discussions captured by William Julius Wilson. In addressing the unfinished intellectual challenges, scholars will be required to learn from the insights and directions of the big thinkers, clarify and focus the current debates, and through constructive criticisms, reanalyses, syntheses, and programs open new paths and possibilities for the future. The most effective of these intellectual projects, in their bold analyses and programmatic actions, will not only connect the academy with the community in its global, national, and localized contexts. In addressing the increasingly complex economic, political, and cultural issues bearing on race and class in global and national contexts, these will be informed and energized by grass roots urban struggles. These will be required to cut across the social boundaries of academics and political orientation. These scholars will be challenged to not only raise questions, but also provide clear arguments and programmatic action.

Although William Julius Wilson's sociological interpretations and policy analyses remain controversial and his contributions continue to be debated, his footsteps are embedded. Scholars in the twenty-first century will be challenged to address the questions raised by him, build on his analyses, develop strategies for bringing sociology into the public understanding of social issues, and help realize the promise of sociology that he has charted. To the extent that sociologists become increasingly committed to influencing policymaking that is focused on analyzing the causes and consequences of changing social institutions and the intersection of race, social class, and the postindustrial city, and energized by the sociological imagination, this promise will be actualized.

REFERENCES

Aaron, Henry, Thomas Mann, and Timothy Taylor, eds. 1994. *Values and Public Policy*. Washington D.C.: The Brookings Institute.

Abramowitz, Michael. 1990. "Fighting Old Notions, Sociologist William Wilson on the Grip of the Ghetto." *Washington Post*, 12 December.

Allen, Walter and Reynolds Farley. "The Shifting Social and Economic Tides of Black America, 1950–1980." *Annual Review of Sociology* 12 (1985): 277–306.

Andersen, Margaret and Patricia Hill-Collins, eds. 1998. *Race, Class, and Gender*. Belmont, CA: Wadsworth Publishers.

Anderson, Elijah. 1990. *Streetwise: Race, Class, and Change in an Urban Community*. Chicago: University of Chicago Press.

———. 1997. "Violence and the Inner City Street Code." In *Violence and Childhood in the Inner City*. Edited by Joan McCord, 1–30. Philadelphia: Temple University Press.

Anderson, Jervis. 1973. *A. Phillip Randolph: A Biographical Portrait*. New York: Harcourt, Brace, Jovanovich.

———. 1997. *Bayard Rustin: Troubles I've Seen: A Biography*. New York: Harper Collins.

Aponte, Robert. 1999. "Socioeconomic Inequality: Race and/or Class." Introduction of William Julius Wilson's keynote address at the Race in the 21st Century America Conference. Michigan State University, East Lansing, Michigan, April 8.

Auletta, Ken. 1982. *The Underclass*. New York: Random House.

Banfield, Edward. 1970. *The Unheavenly City: The Nature and Future of Our Urban Crisis*. Boston: Little, Brown, and Company.

Banks, William. 1995. *Black Intellectuals: Race and Responsibility in American Life*. New York: W. W. Norton and Company.

Bartelt, David W. 1993. "Housing the Underclass" In *The Underclass Debate: Views From History*. Edited by Michael B. Katz, 118–157. Princeton: Princeton University Press.

Becker, Gary. 1957. *The Economics of Discrimination*. Chicago: University of Chicago Press.

———. "Investment in Human Capital: A Theoretical Analysis." *Journal of Political Economy* 70 (1962): 9–49.

———. 1993. *Human Capital: A Theoretical and Empirical Analysis with Special Reference to Education*. Chicago: University of Chicago Press.

Bennett, Lerone Jr. 1979. "The Status of Race in American Culture." In *The Declining Significance of Race: A Dialogue Among Black and White Social Scientists*. Edited by Joseph Washington. Philadelphia: Afro-American Studies Program, University of Pennsylvania.

Berger, Peter and Thomas Luckmann. 1970. *The Social Construction of Reality*. Harmonsworth: Penguin Press.

Billingsley, Andrew. 1968. *Black Families in White America*. Englewood Cliffs, NJ: Prentice Hall.

———. "The Sociology of Knowledge of William J. Wilson: Placing the Truly Disadvantaged in its Sociohistorical Context." *Journal of Sociology and Social Welfare* 16, No. 4. (December 1989): 7–40.

Blackwell, James and Morris Janowitz, eds. 1974. *The Black Sociologists: Historical and Contemporary Perspectives*. Chicago: University of Chicago Press.

Blau, Peter and Otis Dudley Duncan. 1967. *The American Occupational Structure*. New York: John Wiley.

Blauner, Robert. 1972. *Racial Oppression in America*. New York: Harper Collins.

Blaylock, Hubert M. 1980. *Sociological Theory and Research: Critical Appraisal*. New York: The Free Press.

Bluestone, Barry and Bennet Harrison. 1982. *The Deindustrialization of America: Plant Closings, Community Abandonment, and the Dismantling of Basic Industry*. New York: Basic Books.

Bluestone, Barry and Mary Huff Stevenson. 2000. *The Boston Renaissance: Race, Space, and Economic Change in an American Metropolis*. New York: Russell Sage.

Blumenstein, Alfred. 2001. "Race and Criminal Justice." In *America Becoming: Racial Trends and Their Consequences. Vol. 2*. Edited by Neil Smith, William Julius Wilson, and Faith Mitchell, 21–31. Washington, DC: National Academy Press.

Blumer, Herbert. 1965. "Industrialisation and Race Relations," In *Industrialisation and Race Relations*. Edited by Guy Hunter. New York: Oxford University Press.

———. 1990. *Industrialization as An Agent of Social Change: A Critical Analysis*. New York: Aldine de Gruyter.

Bobo, Lawrence and Ryan A. Smith. 1994. "Antipoverty Policy, Affirmative Action, and Racial Attitudes" In *Confronting Poverty: Prescriptions for Change*. Edited by Sheldon H. Danziger, Gary D. Sandefur, and Daniel H. Weinberg, 365–395. Cambridge: Harvard University Press.

Bobo, Lawrence, Melvin Oliver, James Johnson, Jr., and Abel Valenzuela, eds. 2000. *Prismatic Metropolis: Inequality in Los Angeles*. New York: Russell Sage.

Bonacich, Edna. "A Theory of Ethnic Antagonism: The Split Labor Market." *American Journal of Sociology* 37 (October 1972): 547–559.

———. "Racism in Advanced Capitalist Society: Comments on William Wilson's The Truly Disadvantaged." *Journal of Sociology and Social Welfare* 16, No. 4 (December 1989): 41–56.

Bound, John and Harry Holzer. "Industrial Shifts, Skills Levels, and the Labor Market for White and Black Males." *Review of Economics and Statistics* 75 (1993): 387–396.

Bourdieu, Pierre. 1986. "The Forms of Capital." In *Handbook of Theory and Research for the Society of Education*. Edited by John Richardson. New York: Greenwood Press.

Boxill, Bernard. 1992. *Blacks and Social Justice*. Lanham: Rowman and Littlefield.

———. 1992. "The Underclass and the Class/Race Issue." In *The Underclass Question*. Edited by Bill E. Lawson, 19–32. Philadelphia: Temple University Press.

Bracey, John H., August Meier, and Elliot Rudwick, eds. 1971. *The Black Sociologists: The First Half Century*. Belmont: Wadsworth Publishing Company.

Brewer, Rose. "Neglected Issues in the Declining Significance of Race: A Comment." *The Black Sociologist* 7, Nos. 3, 4 (Spring/Summer 1978): 69–72.

Browne, Irene, Farley Reynolds, James Johnson, and Chris Tilly. 1993. *The Multi-City Study of Urban Inequality Analysis Plan*. Los Angeles: Center for the Study of Urban Poverty, Institute for Social Science Research, University of California, Los Angeles.

Bryce-Laporte, Roy. 1979. "Response to William Julius Wilson," In *The Declining Significance of Race: A Dialogue Among Black and White Social Scientists*. Edited by Joseph Washington, 27–33. Philadelphia: Afro-American Studies Program, University of Pennsylvania.

Bulmer, Martin. 1992. "The Growth of Applied Sociology After 1945." In *Sociology and Its Public: The Forms and Fates of Disciplinary Organization*. Edited by Terrance Halliday and Morris Janowitz, 317–346. Chicago: University of Chicago Press.

———. 1994. *The Chicago School of Sociology: Institutionalization, Diversity, and the Rise of Sociological Research*. Chicago: University of Chicago Press.

———. 1998. "Chicago Sociology and the Empirical Impulse: Its Implications for Sociological Theorizing." In *The Tradition of the Chicago School of Sociology*. Edited by Luigi Tomasi. Brookfield, VT: Ashgate Publishing Company.

Burgess, Ernest. 1925. "The Growth of the City: An Introduction to a Research Project." In *The City*. Edited by Robert Park, Ernest Burgess, and Roderick McKenzie, 47–62. Chicago: University of Chicago Press.

———. "Residential Segregation in American Cities." *Annals of the American Academy of Political and Social Science* 91 (November 1928): 105–117.

Bush, Roderick. 1999. *We Are Not What We Seem: Black Nationalism and Class Struggles in the American Century.* New York: New York University Press.

Butler, John Sibley. 1991. *Entrepreneurship and Self-Help Among Black Americans: A Reconsideration of Race and Economics.* New York: State University of New York Press.

———. 1997. "When Work Disappears: Mining Hidden Lessons of William Julius Wilson." Austin: University of Texas.

Carmichael, Stokely and Charles Hamilton. 1967. *Black Power: The Politics of Liberation in America.* New York: Random House.

Center for Budget and Policy Priorities. 1988. *Still Far From the Dream: Recent Developments in Black Income, Employment, and Poverty.* Washington, D.C.: U.S. Government Printing Office.

Chicago Tribune. 1986. *The American Millstone: An Examination of the Nation's Permanent Underclass.* Chicago: Contemporary Books, Inc.

Chicago Tribune. 1978. Editorial, 12 April, Sec. 2, p. 4.

Clark, Kenneth B. 1965. *Dark Ghetto: Dilemmas of Social Power.* New York: Harper and Row.

———. 1978. "No. No. Race, Not Class, Is Still at the Wheel." *New York Times,* 22 March, p. 22.

———. 1979. "Contemporary Sophisticated Racism." In *The Declining Significance of Race: A Dialogue Among Black and White Social Scientists.* Edited by Joseph Washington, 99–106.Philadelphia: Afro-American Studies Program, University of Pennsylvania.

———. 1980. "The Role of Race." *The New York Times Magazine,* 5 October 5, 25–33.

Cloward, Richard and Frances Fox Piven. "Race and the Democrats" *The Nation* (December 9, 1991): 737–740.

Cohn, Samuel and Mark Fossett. "What Spatial Mismatch? The Proximity of Blacks to Employment in Boston and Houston." *Social Forces* 75, No. 2 (1996): 557–572.

Coleman, James. "Social Capital in the Creation of Human Capital." *American Journal of Sociology* 94 (September 1988): 95–120.

———. 1994. "A Rational Choice Perspective on Economic Sociology." In *Handbook of Economic Sociology*. Edited by Neil Smelser and Richard Swedberg. Princeton: Princeton University Press.

Collins, Sharon. "The Making of the Black Middle Class." *Social Problems* 30, No. 4 (1983): 369–382.

———. "The Marginalization of Black Executives." *Social Problems* 36 (1989): 317–331.

Cooke, Thomas. "Proximity to Job Opportunities in African American Male Employment: A Test of the Spatial Mismatch Hypothesis in Indianapolis." *Professional Geographer* 45, No. 4 (1993): 458–467.

Coser, Lewis. 1971. *Masters of Sociological Thought: Ideas in Historical and Social Context.* New York: Harcourt Brace Jovanovich.

Cox, Oliver C. 1948. *Caste, Class, and Race: A Study in Social Dynamics.* New York: Doubleday.

———. 1959. *Foundations of Capitalism.* New York: Philosophical Library.

———. 1964. *Capitalism as a System.* New York: Monthly Review Press.

Cruse, Harold. 1967. *The Crisis of the Negro Intellectual.* New York: William Morrow.

———. 1969. *Rebellion or Revolution.* New York: William Morrow.

———. 1987. *Plural but Equal: Blacks and Minorities in America's Plural Society.* New York: William Morrow.

Danziger, Sheldon and David H. Weinberg, eds. 1986. *Fighting Poverty: What Works and What Doesn't.* Cambridge, MA: Harvard University Press.

Danziger, Sheldon, Gary D. Sandefur, and Daniel H. Weinberg. 1994. *Confronting Poverty: Prescriptions for Change.* Cambridge, MA: Harvard University Press.

Danziger, Sheldon and Peter Gottschalk. 1995. *America Unequal.* Cambridge: Harvard University Press.

Darity, William, Jr. "The Human Capital Approach to Black-White Earnings Inequality: Some Unsettled Questions." *The Journal of Human Resources* 17, No. 1 (1982): 72–93.

Darity, William, Jr., and Samuel Myers, Jr. "Does Welfare Dependency Cause Female Headship?: The case of the Black family." *Journal of Marriage and the Family* 46 (1984): 765–779.

Darity, William, Jr,. Samuel Myers, Jr., Emmet Carson, and William Sabol. 1994. *The Black Underclass: Critical Essays of Race and Unwantedness.* New York: Garland Publishers.

Denton, Nancy and Douglas Massey. "Residential Segregation of Blacks, Hispanics, and Asians by Socioeconomic Status and Gender." *Social Science Quarterly* 69 (1988): 797–818.

Dill, Bonnie Thornton. "Occasional Laborers and Chronic Want." *Journal of Sociology and Social Welfare* 16, No. 4 (December 1989): 69–76.

Drake, St.Clair and Horace Cayton. 1945. *Black Metropolis*. New York: Harper and Row.

Du Bois, W. E. B. 1899. *The Philadelphia Negro: A Social Study*. Philadelphia: University of Pennsylvania Press.

———. [1903] 1961. *The Souls of Black Folks: Essays and Sketches*. New York: Fawcett.

Dumont, Richard G., and William J. Wilson. "Aspects of Concept Formation, Explanation, and Theory Construction in Sociology." *American Sociological Review* 32, No. 6 (December 1967): 985–995.

Duncan, Otis Dudley. 1959. "Human Ecology and Population Studies" In *The Study of Population: An Inventory and Appraisal*. Edited by Phillip M. Hauser and Otis Dudley Duncan, 678–716. Chicago: University of Chicago Press.

Duneier, Mitchell. 1992. *Slim's Table: Race, Responsibility, and Masculinity*. Chicago: University of Chicago Press.

Durr, Marlese and John R. Logan. "Racial Submarkets in Government Employment: African American Managers in New York State." *Sociological Forum* 12, No. 3 (1997): 353–370.

Dyson, Michael Eric. 1993. *Rethinking Black: African American Cultural Criticism*. Minneapolis: University of Minnesota Press.

Early, Gerald Lynn. "William Julius Wilson: Interview." *Mother Jones* (September-October 1996): 20–23.

Edari, Ronald S. "The Concept of the "Urban Black Underclass": An Inquiry into Its Theoretical Status and Ideological Dimensions." *Nature, Society, and Thought* (January-April, 1991).

Edin, Kathryn. "What Do Low-Income Single Mothers Say About Marriage." *Social Problems* 47, No. 1 (2000): 112–133.

Edwards, G. Franklin, ed. 1968. *E. Franklin Frazier on Race Relations*. Chicago: University of Chicago Press.

———. 1974. "E. Franklin Frazier." In *The Black Sociologists: Historical and Contemporary Perspectives*. Edited by James Blackwell and Morris Janowitz, 85–120. Chicago: University of Chicago Press.

Edwards, Harry. Review of "The Declining Significance of Race." *Social Forces* 57, No. 3 (1979) : 991–993.

Eggers, Mitchell and Douglas Massey. "The Structural Determinants of Urban Poverty." *Social Science Research* 20 (1991): 217–255.

Ellwood, David. 1986. "The Spatial Mismatch Hypothesis: Are There Jobs Missing In the Ghetto?" In *The Black Youth Employment Crisis*. Edited by Richard Freeman and Harry Holzer. Chicago: University of Chicago Press.

Fainstein, Norman. "Race, Class, and Segregation: Discourses About African Americans." *Journal of Urban and Regional Research* 17, No. 3 (1993): 384–403.

Fainstein, Norman and Susan Nesbitt. "Did the Black Ghetto Have a Golden Age?: Class Structure and Class Segregation in New York City, With Initial Evidence for 1990." *Journal of Urban History* 23, No. 1 (1996): 3–19.

Faris, Robert E. L. 1967. *Chicago Sociology 1920–1932*. Chicago: University of Chicago Press.

Farley, John. "Disproportionate Black and Hispanic Unemployment in U.S. Metropolitan Areas: The Roles of Racial Inequality, Segregation, and Discrimination in Male Joblessness." *The American Journal of Economics and Sociology* 46, No. 2 (1987): 129–150.

Farley, Reynolds and Walter Allen. 1987. *The Color Line and the Quality of Life in America*. New York: Russell Sage.

Farley, Reynolds, Sheldon Danziger, and Harry Holzer. 2000. *Detroit Divided*. New York: Russell Sage.

Feagin, Joe R. "The Continuing Significance of Race: AntiBlack Discrimination in Public Places." *American Sociological Review* 56 (1991): 101–116.

Feagin, Joe R., and Melvin P. Sikes. 1994. *Living With Racism: The Black Middle Class Experience*. Boston: Beacon Press.

Featherman, David L. and Robert M. Hauser. "Changes in the Socio-Economic Stratification of the Races, 1962–1973." *American Journal of Sociology* 82 (November 1976): 621–649.

———. 1978. *Opportunity and Change*. New York: Academic Press.

Fischer, Claude S. "Toward A Subcultural Theory of Urbanism." *American Journal of Sociology* 80 (May 1975): 1319–1340.

Franklin, Raymond. 1991. *Shadows of Race and Class*. Minneapolis: University of Minnesota Press.

Frazier, E. Franklin. 1932. *The Negro Family in Chicago*. Chicago: Univeristy of Chicago Press.

———. "Negro Harlem: An Ecological Study." *American Journal of Sociology* 43, 1 (1937): 22–28.

———. 1957. *The Black Bourgeoisie: The Rise of A New Middle Class in the United States.* New York: Free Press.

———. "The Failure of the Negro Intellectual," *Negro Digest* (February 1962): 26–36.

———. [1939] 1966. *The Negro Family in the United States.* Chicago: University of Chicago Press.

———. 1968. "The Negro Family in America." In *E. Franklin Frazier on Race Relations.* Edited by G. Franklin Edwards, 191–209. Chicago: University of Chicago Press.

Freeman, Richard. 1976. *Black Elite: The New Market for Highly Educated Black Americans.* New York: McGraw Hill.

Freeman, Richard and Harry Holzer. 1986. *The Black Youth Employment Crisis.* Chicago: University of Chicago Press.

Gans, Herbert. 1962. "Urbanism and Suburbanism as Ways of Life: A Re-evaluation of Definitions." In *Human Behavior and Social Processes: An Interactionist Approach.* Edited by Arnold Rose, 625–648. Boston: Houghton Mifflin Company.

———. "Deconstructing the Underclass: The Term's Dangers as a Planning Concept." *Journal of the American Planning Association* 56, No. 3, (Summer 1990): 271–277.

———. 1991. *People, Plans and Policies: Essays on Poverty, Racism, and Other National Urban Problems.* New York: Columbia University Press.

Gershman, Carl. 1980. "A Matter of Class." *New York Times Magazine,* 5 October.

Gilder, George. 1981. *Wealth and Poverty.* New York: Basic Books.

Glasgow, Douglas. 1980. *The Black Underclass: Poverty, Unemployment, and Entrapment of Ghetto Youth.* New York: Random House.

Glazer, Nathan and Daniel Patrick Moynihan. 1963. *Beyond the Melting Pot: The Negroes, Puerto Ricans, Jews, Italians, and Irish of New York City.* Cambridge: MIT Press.

Glazer, Nathan. 1975. *Affirmative Discrimination: Ethnic Inequality and Public Policy.* New York: Basic Books.

Godfried, Enberson, Kees Schuyt, Jaap Timmer, and Frans Van Waarden. 1993. *Cultures of Unemployment: A Comparative Look at Long-Term Unemployment and Urban Poverty.* Boulder, CO: Westview Press.

Gomes, Ralph and Wanda Katz Fishman. "A Critique of the Truly Disadvantaged: A Historical Materialist Perspective." *Journal of Sociology and Social Welfare* 16 (December 1989): 77–98.

Gordon, Milton. 1964. *Assimilation in American Life.* New York: Oxford University Press.

———. "Models of Pluralism: The New American Dilemma." *Annals of the American Academy of Political and Social Science* 454 (March 1981): 189–206.

Gottdiener, Mark and Joe Feagin. "The Paradigm Shift in Urban Sociology." *Urban Affairs Quarterly*, December 1988.

Gouldner, Alvin. 1971. *The Coming Crisis of Western Sociology*. New York: Basic Books.

Greely, Andrew. 1978. "Racism fading, but poverty isn't." *Chicago Tribune*, 21 March 21, sect. 2, p. 4.

Green, Dan S. and Edwin D. Driver, eds. 1978. *W. E. B. Du Bois: On Sociology and the Black Community*. Chicago: University of Chicago Press.

Hamilton, Charles and Dona Hamilton. 1986. "Social Policies, Civil Rights and Poverty." In *Fighting Poverty: What Works and What Doesn't*. Edited by Sheldon H. Danziger and David H. Weinberg. Cambridge: Harvard University Press.

Hannerz, Ulf. 1969. *Soulside*. New York: Columbia University Press.

Harrington, Michael. 1962. *The Other America; Poverty in the United States*. New York: MacMillan.

Harris, Fred and Roger Wilkins, eds. 1988. *Quiet Riots: Race and Poverty in the United States: The Kerner Report Twenty Years Later*. New York: Pantheon Books.

Harrison, Bennett and Barry Bluestone. 1988. *The Great U-Turn: Corporate Restructuring and the Polarizing of America*. New York: Basic Books.

Hawley, Amos. 1950. *Human Ecology: A Theory of Community Structure*. New York: Ronald Press.

———. 1981. *Urban Sociology: An Ecological Approach*. New York: John Wiley.

Haymes, Stephen Nathan. 1995. *Race, Culture, and the City: A Pedagogy for Black Urban Struggle*. Albany: State University of New York Press.

Herring, Cedric. "Convergence, Polarization, or What?: Racially Based Changes in Attitudes and Outlooks, 1964–1984." *The Sociological Quarterly* 30 (1989): 267–281.

Herrnstein, Richard and Charles Murray. 1994. *The Bell Curve: Intelligence and Class Structure in American Life*. New York: The Free Press.

Hess, Steven. "The Effect of Employment and Welfare on Family Structure: Explaining the Time Trend of Female Headed Families." *American Economist* 34, 1 (Spring 1990): 76–82.

Hill, Robert. 1972. *The Strengths of Black Families*. New York: Emerson Hall.

———. 1978. *The Illusion of Black Progress*. Washington, D.C.: National Urban League Research Department.

Hill-Collins, Patricia. 1990. *Black Feminist Thought: Knowledge, Consciousness, and the Politics of Empowerment*. Boston: Unwin Hyman.

Hirsch, Arnold. 1983. *Making the Second Ghetto: Race and Housing in Chicago, 1940–1960*. New York: Cambridge University Press.

Hochschild, Jennifer. "Equal Opportunity and the Estranged Poor." *Annals of the American Academy of Politcal and Social Science* 501 (January 1989): 143–155.

Holzer, Harry. 1996. *What Employers Want: Job Prospects for Less-Educated Workers*. New York: Russell Sage.

Horowitz, Irving Louis, ed. 1963. *Power, Politics, and People: The Collected Essays of C. Wright Mills*. New York: Oxford University Press.

Horton, Hayward Derrick, Beverlyn Lundy Allen, Cedric Herring, and Melvin E. Thomas. "Lost in the Storm: The Sociology of the Black Working Class, 1850 to 1990." *American Sociological Review* 65, No. 1 (2000): 128–137.

Hout, Michael. "Occupational Mobility of Black Men: 1962–1973." *American Sociological Review* 49 (1984): 308–323.

Hughes, Mark Alan. "Misspeaking Truth to Power: A Geographic Perspective on the "Underclass Fallacy." *Economic Geography* 65 (1989): 187–207.

———. "Concentrated Deviance and the Underclass Hypothesis." *Journal of Policy Analysis and Management* 8 (1989).

Hunter, Guy. 1965. *Industrial and Race Relations*. New York: Oxford University Press.

Jackson, Kenneth. 1985. *Crabgrass Frontier*. New York: Oxford University Press.

Jackson, Thomas. 1990. *Gunnar Myrdal and America's Conscience: Social Engineering and Racial Liberalism*. Chapel Hill: University of North Carolina Press.

Janowitz, Morris. 1970. "The Logic of Political Sociology." In *Political Conflict: Essays in Political Sociology*. Edited by Morris Janowitz, 5–35. Chicago: Quadrangle Books.

———. 1970. *Political Conflict: Essays in Political Sociology*. Chicago: Quadrangle Books.

Jargowsky, Paul. 1997. *Poverty and Place: Ghettos, Barrios, and the American City*. New York: Russell Sage.

Jarrett, Robin. "Living Poor: Family Life Among Single Parent, African American Women." *Social Problems* 41, No. 1 (1994): 30–49.

Jaynes, Gerald D., and Robin M. Williams, Jr., eds. 1989. *A Common Destiny: Blacks and American Society*. Washington, D.C.: National Academy Press.

Jencks, Christopher. 1991. "Is the American Underclass Growing." In *The Urban Underclass*. Edited by Paul Peterson and Christopher Jencks. Washington, D.C.: Brookings Institution.

Jencks, Christopher and Susan Mayer. 1990. "Residential Segregation, Jobs Proximity, and Black Job Opportunities: The Empirical Status of the Spatial Mismatch Hypothesis." In *Inner City Poverty in the United States*. Edited by Lawrence Lynn and Michael McGeary. Washington, D.C.: National Academy Press.

Johnson, James and Melvin Oliver. "Economic Restructuring and Black Males Joblessness in U.S. Metropolitan Areas." *Urban Geography* 12 (1991): 542–562.

Jones, Butler. 1971. "The Tradition of Sociology Teaching in Black Colleges: The Unheralded Professionals." In *The Black Sociologists: Historical and Contemporary Perspectives*. Edited by James Blackwell and Morris Janowitz 121–163. Chicago: University of Chicago Press.

Jorgensen, Carl C. "On Being Misunderstood: A Review Discussion of William J. Wilson, The Declining Significance of Race: Blacks and Changing American Institutions." *The Black Sociologist* 7, Nos. 3 and 4 (Spring/Summer 1978): 58–68.

Kasarda, John. 1988. "Jobs, Migrations, and Emerging Urban Mismatches." In *Urban Change and Poverty*. Edited by Michael G. McGeary and Laurence E. Lynn. Washington, D.C.: National Academy Press.

———. "Urban Industrial Transition and the Underclass." *Annals of the American Academy of Political and Social Science* 501 (January 1989): 26–47.

Katznelson, Ira. 1973. *Black Men, White Cities: Race, Politics, and Migration in the United States, 1910–1930, and Britain, 1948–68*. London: Oxford University Press.

———. 1981. *City Trenches: Urban Politics and the Patterning of Class in the United States*. New York: Pantheon Books.

———. "Du Bois for the 1990s: A Review of William Julius Wilson's *When Work Disappears*." *Boston Review* 22, No. 1 (February/March, 1997).

Kaus, Mickey. "The Work Ethic State." *The New Republic*, July 7, 1986: 22–33.

———. 1992. *The End of Equality*. New York: Basic Books.

Kelly, Robin D. 1993. "The Black Poor and the Politics of Opposition in a New South City, 1929–1970." In *The Underclass Debate: Views From History*. Edited by Michael B. Katz, 293–333. Princeton: Princeton University Press.

———. 1997. *Yo' Mama's Disfunctional: Fighting the Culture Wars in Urban America*. Boston: Beacon Press.

Killian, Lewis M. 1968. *The Impossible Revolution: Black Power and the American Dream*. New York: Random House.

Kirkland, Frank. 1992. "Social Policy, Ethical Life, and the Urban Underclass." In *The Underclass Question*. Edited by Bill E. Lawson, 152–187. Philadelphia: Temple University Press.

Kirschenman, Joleen and Kathryn Neckerman. 1991. "'We'd Love to Hire Them, But . . .': The Meaning of Race for Employers." In *The Urban Underclass.* Edited by Christopher Jencks and Paul E. Peterson, 203–234. Washington, D.C.: Brookings Institution.

Kluegal, James R. and Eliot R. Smith. 1986. *Beliefs About Inequality: America's Views of What Is and What Ought to Be.* New York: Aldine de Gruyter.

Kristol, Irving. "The Negro Today Is Like the Immigrant Yesterday." *New York Times Magazine*, 11 September 1966, pp. 50–51, 124–142.

Krivo, Lauren and Ruth Peterson. "Extremely Disadvantaged Neighborhoods and Urban Crime." *Social Forces* 75 (December 1996): 619–648.

Krivo, Lauren, Ruth Peterson, and Helen Rizzo. "Race, Segregation, and the Concentration of Disadvantage, 1980–1990." *Social Problems* 45, No. 1 (February 1998): 61–80.

Kuhn, Thomas. 1970. *The Structure of Scientific Revolutions.* Chicago: University of Chicago Press.

Ladner, Joyce. 1971. *Tomorrow's Tomorrow: The Black Woman.* New York: Anchor Doubleday.

———. 1973. *The Death of White Sociology.* New York: Vintage Books.

Landry, Bart. 1987. *The New Black Middle Class.* Berkeley: University of California Press.

Lawson, Bill E. *The Underclass Question.* Philadelphia: Temple University Press.

Lemann, Nicholas. "The Origins of the Underclass." *Atlantic Monthly*, June 1986: 31–61.

———. 1991. *The Promised Land: The Great Black Migration and How It Changed America.* New York: Alfred A. Knopf.

Lieberson, Stanley. 1980. *A Piece of the Pie: Blacks and White Immigrants Since 1880.* Berkeley: University of California Press.

Loury, Glen. 1977. "A Dynamic Theory of Racial Income Differences." In *Women, Minorities, and Employment Discrimination.* Edited by Phyllis A. Wallace and Annette M. LaMond. Lexington: Heath.

———. "Beyond Civil Rights." *New Republic* (7 October 1985): 22–25.

Malthus, Thomas. [1798, 1830] 1985. *An Essay on the Principle of Population.* New York: Penguin Books.

Marable, Manning. 1980. "The Continuing Burden of Race: Wilson's *Declining Significance of Race.*" In *From the Grassroots: Social and Political Essays Towards Afro-American Liberation.* Edited by Manning Marable. Boston: South End Press.

———. 1980. *From the Grassroots: Social and Political Essays Toward Afro-American Liberation*. Boston: South End Press.

Mare, Robert and Christopher Winship. 1991. "Socioeconomic Change and the Decline of Marriage for Blacks and Whites." In *The Urban Underclass*. Edited by Paul Peterson and Christopher Jencks, 175–202. Washington, D.C.: Brookings Institution.

Marks, Carole. 1989. *Farewell, We're Good and Gone: The Great Migration*. Bloomington, IN: Indiana University Press.

———. "Occasional Laborers and Chronic Want: A Review of the Truly Disadvantaged." *Journal of Sociology and Social Welfare* 16 (December 1989): 57–68.

Marrett, Cora Bagley. "The Precariousness of Social Class in Black America." *Contemporary Sociology* 9 (1980): 16–19.

Martindale, Don. 1981. *The Nature and Types of Sociological Theory*. Boston: Houghton Mifflin Company.

Marx, Gary. 1971. *Radical Conflict: Tension and Change in American Society*. Boston: Little, Brown, and Company.

Massey, Douglas S. Review of William Julius Wilson's *When Work Disappears* in *Contemporary Sociology* 26, No. 4 (July 1997): 416–418.

———. 1990. "American Apartheid: Segregation and the Making of the Underclass." *American Journal of Sociology* 96, No. 2: 329–357.

Massey, Douglas S., and Mary Denton. "Hypersegregation in U.S. Metropolitan Areas: Black and Hispanic Segregation Along Five Dimensions." *Demography* 26, No. 3 (August 1989): 373–391.

Massey, Douglas S., and Nancy Denton. 1993. *American Apartheid: Segregation and the Making of the Underclass*. Cambridge, MA: Harvard University Press.

Massey, Douglas S., and Mitchell L. Eggers. "The Ecology of Inequality: Minorities and the Concentration of Poverty, 1970–1980." *American Journal of Sociology* 75 (1990): 512–529.

Massey, Douglas S., Andrew Gross, and Kumiko Shibuya. "Migration, Segregation, and the Geographic Concentration of Poverty." *American Sociological Review*, 1994: 425–445.

MacLeod, Jay. 1987. *Ain't No Making It: Leveled Aspirations in a Low Income Neighborhood*. Boulder: Westview Press.

McCord, Joan. 1997. *Violence and Childhood in the Inner City*. Philadelphia: Temple University Press.

McCudy, William. 1983. *Culture, Ethnicity, and Identity*. New York: Academic Press.

McFate, Katherine, Roger Lawson, and William Julius Wilson, eds. 1995. *Poverty, Inequality, and the Future of Social Policy*. New York: Russell Sage.

McLaughlin, Neil. "Beyond "race vs. class": the politics of William Julius Wilson." *Dissent* 40 (Summer 1993): 362–367.

Mead, Lawrence. 1986. *Beyond Entitlement: The Social Obligations of Citizenship*. New York: The Free Press.

———. 1989. "The Logic of Workfare: The Underclass and Work Policy." In *The Ghetto Underclass: Social Science Perspectives. Annals of the American Academy of Political and Social Science*. Edited by William Julius Wilson. Vol. 501 (January, 1989): 156–16?

Merton, Robert K. 1968. *Social Theory and Social Structure*. New York: Basic Books.

———. 1968a. "On Sociological Theories of the Middle Range." In *Social Theory and Social Structure*. Edited by Robert K. Merton, 39–72. New York: Basic Books.

———. 1968b. "The Bearing of Sociological Theory on Empirical Research." In *Social Theory and Social Structure*. Edited by Robert K. Merton, 135–155. New York: Basic Books.

———. 1968c. "Social Structure and Anomie." In *Social Theory and Social Structure*. Edited by Robert K. Merton, 185–214. New York: Basic Books.

Miller, Andrew. 1993. "Social Science, Social Policy, and the Heritage of African American Families." In *The Underclass Debate: Views From History*. Edited by Michael B. Katz, 254–289. Princeton: Princeton University Press.

Miller, Jerome G. 1996. *Search and Destroy: African American Males in the Criminal Justice System*. New York: Cambridge University Press.

Mills, C. Wright. 1951. *White Collar: The American Middle Class*. New York: Oxford University Press.

———. 1956. *The Power Elite*. New York: Oxford University Press.

———. 1959. *The Sociological Imagination*. New York: Oxford University Press.

———. 1963. "Situated Actions and Vocabularies of Motive." In *Power, Politics, and People: The Collected Essays of C. Wright Mills*. Edited by Irving Louis Horowitz, 439–452. New York: Oxford University Press.

Mincy, Ronald. 1994. "The Underclass: Concept, Controversy, and Evidence." In *Confronting Poverty: Prescriptions for Change*. Edited by Sheldon H. Danziger, Gary D. Sandefur, and Daniel H. Weinberg, 109–146. Cambridge, MA: Harvard University Press.

Morris, Aldon. 1984. *The Origins of the Civil Rights Movement: Black Communities Organizing for Change*. New York: Free Press.

———. "What's Race Got to Do With It?" *Contemporary Sociology* 25 (1996): 309–313.

Moss, Phillip and Chris Tilly. 2001. *Stories Employers Tell: Race, Skill, and Hiring in America*. New York: Russell Sage.

Moyers, Bill. 1989. "William Julius Wilson, Sociologist." In *A World of Ideas*. Edited by Bill Moyers. New York: Doubleday.

Moynihan, Daniel P. 1965. *The Negro Family: The Case for National Action*. Washington, D.C.: U.S. Government Printing Office.

———. "The Schism in Black America." *Public Interest* 27 (Spring 1972): 3–24.

Murray, Charles. 1984. *Losing Ground: American Policy 1950–1980*. New York: Basic Books.

Myrdal, Gunnar. 1944. *An American Dilemma: The Negro Problem in Modern Democracy*. New York: Harper and Row.

———. 1963. *Challenge to Affluence*. New York: Pantheon Books.

———. 1968. *Asian Drama*. New York: Twentieth Century Fund.

National Advisory Commission on Civil Disorders. 1968. *Report of the National Advisory Commission on Civil Disorders*. New York: Bantam Books.

Niemonen, Jack. 2002. *Race, Class, and the State in Contemporary Sociology: The William Julius Wilson Debates*. Boulder, CO: Lynne Rienner Publishers.

Nisbet, Robert. 1986. *Conservatism: Dream and Reality*. Minneapolis, MN: University of Minnesota Press.

Noel, Donald L. "A Review of William J. Wilson's Power, Racism, and Privilege: Race Relations in Theoretical and Sociohistorical Perspective." *Contemporary Sociology* 4 (May 1975): 285–287.

Orfield, Myron. 1997. *Metropolitics: A Regional Agenda for Community and Stability*. Washington, D.C.: Brookings Institution Press.

O'Conner, Alice, Chris Tilly, and Lawrence Bobo, eds. 2000. *Urban Inequality: Evidence From Four Cities*. New York: Russell Sage.

Park, Robert, Ernest Burgess, and Roderick McKenzie, eds. 1925. *The City*. Chicago: University of Chicago Press.

Park, Robert. 1950. "Nature of Race Relations." In *Race and Culture*. Edited by Robert E. Park. New York: The Free Press of Glencoe.

———. 1950. *Race and Culture*. New York: The Free Press of Glencoe.

Patillo-McCoy, Mary. 1999. *Black Picket Fences: Privilege and Peril Among the Black Middle Class*. Chicago: University of Chicago Press.

————. "Lecture on William Julius Wilson." Columbia University, New York, NY. June 1997.

Patterson, Orlando. 1997. *The Ordeal of Integration: Progress and Resentment in America's "Racial Crisis."* Washington, D.C.: Civitas Counterpoint.

Payne, Charles. 1979. "On the Declining—And Increasing—Significance of Race." In *Caste and Class Controversy.* Edited by Charles Willie. Dix Hills: General Hall.

Peterson, Paul and Christopher Jencks, eds. 1991. *The Urban Underclass.* Washington, D.C.: Brookings Institution.

Pettigrew, Thomas F. 1979. "The Changing—Not Declining—Significance of Race." In *Caste and Class Controversy on Race and Poverty.* Edited by Charles Willie. Dix Hills: General Hall, Inc.

Pinkney, Alphonso. 1984. *The Myth of Black Progress.* New York: Cambridge University Press.

Platt, Anthony. 1991. *E. Franklin Frazier Reconsidered.* New Brunswick, NJ: Rutgers University Press.

Popkin, Susan, James Rosenbaum, and Patricia Meaden. "Labor Market Experiences of Low Income Black Women in Middle Class Suburbs: Evidence from a Survey of Gatreaux Program Participants." *Journal of Policy Analysis and Management* 12 (1993): 556–573.

Portes, Alejandro. "Rationality in the Slum: An Essay on Interpretive Sociology." *Comparative Studies in Society and History* 14, No. 3 (1992): 268–286.

————. "Social Capital: Its Origin and Application in Modern Sociology." *Annual Review of Sociology* 241 (1998): 1–24.

Rose, Arnold. 1962. *Human Behavior and Social Processes: An Interactionist Approach.* Boston: Houghton Mifflin Company.

Record, Wilson. "A Review of *The Declining Significance of Race.*" *American Journal of Sociology* 85 (1980): 965–968.

Reed, Adolph. "The Liberal Technocrat: A Review of *The Truly Disadvantaged.*" *The Nation,* February 6, 1988: 167–170.

————. "The Underclass as Myth and Symbol: The Poverty of Discourse About Poverty." *Radical America 24* (January/March 1990): 21–42.

————. "Dissing the Underclass." *The Progressive* 60 (December 1996): 20–21.

Remnick, David. "Dr. Wilson's Neighborhood." *The New Yorker,* 29 April and 6 May 1996, pp. 96–107.

Reynolds, Gretchen. "The Rising Significance of Race." *Chicago,* December 1992: 81–85.

Richardson, John. 1986. *Handbook of Theory and Research for the Society of Education.* New York: Greenwood Press.

Riley, Matilda White. 1988. *Sociological Lives: Social Change and the Life Course.* Newbury Park: Sage Publications.

Robinson, Randall. 2001. *The Debt: What America Owes to Blacks.* New York: Dutton.

Rolison, Gary L. "Black Single Female-Headed Family Formation in Large U.S. Central Cities." *the Sociological Quarterly* 33, No. 3. (1992): 473–481.

Rose, Arnold. 1962. *Human Behavior and Social Processes: An Interactionist Approach.* Boston: Houghton Mifflin Company.

Rose, Peter. 1993. "White Liberal: Some Reflections on Personal and Professional Socialization and the Field of Race Relations." In *A History of Race Relations Research: First Generation Recollections.* Edited by John Stanfield, 210–232. Newbury Park: Sage Publications.

Rose, Peter. 1972. *Nation of Nations: The Ethnic Experience and the Racial Crisis.* New York: Random House.

Rose, Peter, Stanley Rothman, and William J. Wilson, eds. 1973. *Through Different Eyes: Black and White Perspectives on American Race Relations.* New York: Oxford University Press.

Rosenthal, Steven. "How Liberal Ideology Assists the Growth of Fascism: A Critique of the Sociology of William Julius Wilson." *Journal of Poverty* 3, No. 2 (1999): 67–87.

Rothenberg, Randall. 1984. *The NeoLiberals: Creating the New American Politics.* New York: Simon and Schuster.

Russell, George. " The American Underclass." *Time*, 29 August 1977, 14–16.

Rustin, Bayard. "From Protest to Politics: The Future of the Civil Rights Movement." *Commentary* (February 1965): 25–31.

———. 1971. "Black Power and Coalition Politics." In *Racial Conflict: Tension and Change in American Society.* Edited by Gary Marx, 193–200. Boston: Little, Brown, and Company.

———. "Are Blacks Better Off Today?" A Review of Alphonso Pinkney's *The Myth of Black Progress* in *The Atlantic Monthly*, October 1984: 121–123.

Sampson, Robert. "Urban Black Violence: The Effect of Male Joblessness and Family Disruption." *American Journal of Sociology* 93, No. 2 (1987): 348–382.

———. 1997. "The Embeddedness of Child and Adolescent Development: A Community-Level Perspective on Urban Violence." In *Violence and Childhood in the Inner City.* Edited by Joan McCord, 31–77. Philadelphia: Temple University Press.

Sampson, Robert and W. Byron Groves. 1989. "Community Structure and Crime: Testing Social Disorganization Theory." *American Journal of Sociology* 94, No. 4 (1989): 77–802.

Sampson, Robert and William Julius Wilson. 1995. "Toward a Theory of Race, Crime, and Urban Inequality." In *Crime and Inequality*. Edited by John Hagan and Ruth Peterson. Stanford: Stanford University Press.

Sawhill, Isabel V. "The Underclass: An Overview." *Public Interest*, Summer 1989.

Schermerhorn, Richard. 1970. *Comparative Ethnic Relations: A Framework for Theory and Research*. New York: Random House.

Schuman, Howard, Charlotte Steeh, and Lawrence Bobo. 1988. *Racial Attitudes in America: Trends and Interpretations*. Cambridge: Jarvard University Press.

Short, James F., ed. 1971. *The Social Fabric of the Metropolis: Contributions of the Chicago School of Sociology*. Chicago: University of Chicago Press.

Sjoquist, David. 2000. *The Atlanta Paradox*. New York: Russell Sage.

Small, Mario Luis and Katherine Newman. "Urban Poverty after the Truly Disadvantaged: The Rediscovery of the Family, the Neighborhood, and Culture." *Annula Review of Sociology* 27 (2001): 23–45.

Smelser, Neil and Richard Swedberg. 1994. *Handbook of Economic Sociology*. Princeton: Princeton University Press.

Smith, Dennis. 1988. *The Chicago School: A Liberal Critique of Capitalism*. New York: St. Martin's Press.

Smith, James P. "Affirmative Action and the Racial Wage Gap." *American Economic Review* 83, No. 2 (May 1993): 79–84.

Smith, James P. 2001. "Race and Ethnicity in the Labor Market: Trends Over the Short and Long Term." In *America Becoming: Racial Trends and Their Consequences-Volume II*. Edited by Neil Smith, William Julius Wilson, and Faith Mitchell, 52–97. Washington, D.C.: National Academy Press.

Smith, Neil, William Julius Wilson, and Faith Mitchell, eds. 2001. *America Becoming: Racial Trends and Their Consequences*. Vol. 2. Washington, DC: National Academy Press.

Smith, Robert C. 1995. *Racism in the Post-Civil Rigths Era*. Albany: State University of New York Press.

———. 1996. *We Have No Leaders: African Americans in the Post-Civil Rights Era*. Albany: State University of New York Press.

Smith, Stanley. 1974. "Sociological Research and Fisk University: A Case Study" In *The Black Sociologists: Historical and Contemporary Perspectives*. Edited by James Blackwell and Morris Janowitz, 164–190. Chicago: University of Chicago Press.

Son, In Soo, Sue Model, and Gene Fischer. "Polarization and Progress in the Black Community: Earnings and Status Gains for Young Black Males in the Era of Affirmative Action." *Sociological Forum* 4 (1989): 309–327.

Sowell, Thomas. 1983. *The Economics and Politics of Race.* New York: Quill.

Stack, Carol. 1974. *All Our Kin: Strategies for Survival in a Black Community.* New York: Harper and Row.

Stanfield, John, ed. 1993. *A History of Race Relations Research: First Generation Recollections.* Newbury Park: Sage Publications.

Steele, Shelby. 1990. *The Content of Our Character.* New York: St. Martin's.

Steinberg, Stephen. 1989. *The Ethnic Myth.* Boston: Beacon Press.

———. 1997. *Turning Back: The Retreat from Racial Justice in American Thought and Policy.* Boston: Beacon Press.

———. "The Role of Racism in the Inequality Studies of William Julius Wilson." *The Journal of Blacks in Higher Education,* Spring 1997.

Steinfels, Peter. 1979. *The NeoConservatives.* New York: Simon and Schuster.

Stokes, Randall and Albert Chevan. "Female-Headed Families: Social and Economic Context of Racial Differences." *Journal of Urban Affairs* 18, No. 3 (1996): 245–268.

Strauss, Anselm. "Blumer on Industrialization and Social Change." *Contemporary Sociology* 20, No. 2 (March 1991): 171–172.

Suro, Robert. "Income, Not Race, to Divide Chicago." *Chicago Tribune,* 17 March 1978, sec. 1: 1 and 16.

Swedberg, Richard. 1990. *Economics and Sociology: Redefining Their Boundaries.* Princeton: Princeton University Press.

Taeuber, Karl and Alma Taeuber. 1965. *Negroes in Cities: Residential Segregation and Neighborhood Change.* Chicago: Aldine Press.

Thomas, Melvin and Mark Hughes. "The Continuing Significance of Race: A Study of Race, Class, and the Quality of Life in America." *American Sociological Review* 51 (1986): 830–841.

Tilly, Charles. 1970. "Race and Migration to the American City." In *The Metropolitan Enigma: Inquiries into the Nature and Dimensions of the "Urban Crisis."* Edited by James Q. Wilson, 144–169. New York: Anchor Books. 1970.

"Time's 25 Most Influential Americans." *Time* 147, No. 9 (June 17, 1996): 52–58.

Tocqueville, Alexis de. 1969. *Democracy in America.* New York: Doubleday and Company.

Tomasi, Luigi, ed. 1998. *The Tradition of the Chicago School of Sociology.* Brookfield, VT: Ashgate Publishing Company.

U.S. Bureau of the Census. 1991. *The Black Population in the United States: March 1990 and 1989. Prepared by Current Population Reports, series p–20*, Washington, D.C.: U.S. Government Printing Office.

U.S. Bureau of the Census. 1994. *Characteristics of the Black Population. Prepared by* 1990 Census of Population. Washington, D.C.: U.S. Government Printing Office.

Van den Berghe, Pierre. 1967. *Race and Racism: A Comparative Perspective*. New York: John Wiley.

Ventura, S. J., S. C. Curtin, and T. J. Matthews. 1996. *Teenage Births in the United States, 1990–1996*. Hyattsville, MD: National Vital Statistics System, National Center for Health Statistics.

Wacquant, Loic J. D. 1994. "The New Urban Color Line: The State and the Fate of the Ghetto in Post-Fordist America." In *Social Theory and the Politics of Identity*. Edited by Craig J. Calhoun. Oxford: Basil Blackwell.

Wacquant, Loic J. D., and William Julius Wilson. "The Cost of Racial and Class Exclusion in the Inner City." *Annals of the American Academy of Political and Social Science* 501 (January 1989): 8–25.

Warren, Mark R. "Racism and the Underclass" *Research in Race and Ethnic Relations* 8 (1995): 77–97.

Washington, Joseph. 1979. *The Declining Significance of Race?: A Dialogue among Black and White Social Scientists*. Philadelphia: Afro-American Studies Program, University of Pennsylvania.

Wattenberg, Ben and Richard Scammon. "Black Progress and Liberal Rhetoric." *Commentary*, April 1973: 35–44.

West, Cornell. 1992. "Philosophy and the Urban Underclass." In *The Underclass Question*. Edited by Bill E. Lawson, 191–204. Philadelphia: Temple University Press.

———. 1993. "Nihilism in Black America." In *Race Matters*. Edited by Cornell West, 9–20. Boston: Beacon Press.

West, Hollie. "Getting Ahead and the Man behind Class-Race Furor." *Washington Post*, 1 January 1979, C1, C13.

Wilhelm, Sidney. 1971. *Who Needs the Negro?* Garden City: Anchor Books.

———. "Can Marxism Explain America's Racism?" *Social Problems* 28, No. 2 (1980): 98–111.

Williams, Walter. 1982. *The State Against Blacks*. New York: McGraw Hill.

Willie, Charles V. "The Inclining Significance of Race." *Society* 10 (July/August 1978): 12–15.

———. 1979. *The Caste and Class Controversy*. Dix Hills: General Hall.

———. 1989. *Caste and Class Controversy on Race and Poverty: Round Two of the Willie/Wilson Debate.* Dix Hills: General Hall.

Wilson, Frank Harold. "Rising Tide or Ebb Tide: Recent Changes in the Black Middle Class in the U.S., 1980–1990." *Research in Race and Ethnic Relations* 8 (1995): 21–56.

Wilson, Franklin D., Marta Tienda, and Lawrence Wu. "Race and Unemployment: Labor Market Experiences of Black and White Men, 1968–1988." *Work and Occupations* 22, No. 3 (1995): 245–270.

Wilson, George and Deirdre Royster. "Critiquing Wilson's Critics: The Declining Significance of Race Thesis and the Black Middle Class." *Research in Race and Ethnic Relations* 6 (1995): 57–75.

Wilson, James Q. 1970. *The Metropolitan Enigma: Inquiries into the Nature and Dimensions of the "Urban Crisis."* New York: Anchor Books.

———. 1994. "Culture, Incentives, and the Underclass." In *Values and Public Policy.* Edited by Henry Aaron, Thomas Mann, and Timothy Taylor, 54–77. Washington, D.C.: The Brookings Institution.

Wilson, William J. 1966. "Preference, Evaluation, and Norms: An Empirical Exploration in Measurement." Ph.D. Diss., Washington State University, Pullman.

Wilson, William J., Nicholas Sofios, and Richard Ogles. "Formalization and Stages of Theoretical Development." *Pacific Sociological Review* 7, No. 2 (Fall 1964): 74–80.

Wilson, William J. and Richard Dumont. "Rules of Correspondence and Sociological Concepts." *Sociology and Social Research* 52, No. 2 (1968): 212–227.

Wilson, William J. "New Creation or Familiar Death?: A Rejoinder to Vincent Harding." *Negro Digest*, (March 1970): 6–11, and 57–59.

———. 1972. "Race Relations Models and Ghetto Experience." In *Nation of Nations: The Ethnic Experience and the Racial Crisis.* Edited by Peter Rose. New York: Random House.

———, 1973. "The Significance of Social and Racial Prisms." In *Through Different Eyes: Black and White Perspectives on American Race Relations.* Edited by Peter Rose, Stanley Rothman, and William J. Wilson. New York: Oxford University Press.

———. 1973. *Power, Racism, and Privilege: Race Relations in Theoretical and Sociohistorical Perspectives.* Chicago: University of Chicago Press.

———. 1974. "The New Black Sociology: Reflections on the 'Insiders and Outsiders' Controversy." In *Black Sociologists: Historical and Contemporary Perspectives.* Edited by James E. Blackwell and Morris Janowitz. Chicago: University of Chicago Press.

———. 1978. *The Declining Significance of Race: Blacks and Changing American Institutions*. Chicago: University of Chicago Press.

———. 1979. "The Declining Significance of Race: Myth or Reality?" In *The Declining Significance of Race?: A Dialogue Among Black and White Social Scientists*. Edited by Joseph Washington. Philadelphia: Afro-American Studies Program, University of Pennsylvania.

———. 1980. *The Declining Significance of Race: Blacks and Changing American Institutions*. 2d Ed. Chicago: University of Chicago Press.

———. "The Significance of Race in America: A Rejoinder to Marrett and Pettigrew." *Contemporary Sociology*, January 1980: 21–25.

———. 1980. "Comparative Race and Ethnic Relations: Issues of Theory and Research" In *Sociological Theory and Research: Critical Appraisal*. Edited by Hubert M. Blaylock, 228–242. New York: The Free Press.

———. "The Black Community in the 1980's: Questions of Race, Class, and Public Policy." *Annals of the American Academy of Political and Social Science* 454 (1981): 26–41.

———. "Social Change and Racial Progress." *Contemporary Sociology* 15 (January 1986): 30–34.

———. 1988. "Academic Controversy and Intellectual Growth" In *Sociological Lives: Social Change and the Life Course*. Edited by Matilda White Riley, 79–90. Newbury Park: Sage Publications.

———. 1987. *The Truly Disadvantaged: The Inner City, the Underclass, and Public Policy*. Chicago: University of Chicago Press.

———. " A Response to Critics of the Truly Disadvantaged." *The Journal of Sociology and Social Welfare* 16 (December 1989): 133–148.

———. 1989. "Introduction to the Wesleyan Edition of Dark Ghetto" in Kenneth Clark. *Dark Ghetto: Dilemmas of Social Power. ix–xxii*, Middletown: Wesleyan University Press.

———. 1989. *The Ghetto Underclass: Social Science Perspectives. Annals of the American Academy of Political snd Social Science* 501 (January): 156–16?.

———. "Studying Inner City Dislocations: The Challenge of Public Agenda Research: 1990 Presidential Address." *American Sociological Review* 56, No. 1 (1991): 1–14.

———. "Race Neutral Policies and the Democratic Coalition." *The American Prospect*, Spring 1990: 74–81.

———. "Racism and Race-Conscious Remedies: A Response to Kenneth S. Tollett." *The American Prospect* 5 (Spring 1991): 93–96.

———. "The Truly Disadvantaged Revisited: A response to Hochschild and Boxill." *Ethics* 101 (April 1991): 593–609.

———. 1993a. *Sociology and the Public Agenda.* Newbury Park, CA: Sage Publications.

———. 1993b. "Can Sociology Play a Greater Role in Shaping a National Agenda." In *Sociology and the Public Agenda.* Edited by William Julius Wilson, 3–22. Newbury Park, CA: Sage Publications.

———. 1993c. Foreward to Godfried, Enberson, Kees Schuyt, Jaap Timmer, and Frans Van Waarden. *Cultures of Unemployment: A Comparative Look at Long-Term Unemployment and Urban Poverty.* Boulder, CO: Westview Press.

———. 1996. *When Work Disappears: The World of the New Urban Poor.* New York: Alfred A. Knopf.

———. 1997. "Jobs and Economic Prosperity." *Department of Housing and Urban Development, Community* 2020 Series. Washington, D.C.: Government Printing Office.

———. 1997. "Jobless Ghettos: The Impact of the Disappearance of Work in Segregated Neighborhoods." Paper presented at the plenary session of the Association of Black Sociologists, Toronto, Ontario, Canada, August 8.

———. "Engaging Publics in Sociological Dialogue Through the Media." *Contemporary Sociology* 27, No. 5 (1998): 435–438.

———. 1999. *The Bridge Over the Racial Divide: Rising Inequality and Coalition Politics.* Berkeley: University of California Press.

———. 1999. "The American Underclass: Inner-City Ghettos and the Norms of Citizenship." The Godkin Lecture, John F. Kennedy School, Harvard University. April 26.

———. "Rising Inequality and the Case for Coalition Politics." *Annals of the American Academy of Political and Social Science* 568 (March 2000): 78–99.

Winant, Howard. 1994. *Racial Conditions: Politics, Theory, Comparisons.* Minneapolis: University of Minnesota Press.

Wirth, Louis. "Urbanism as a Way of Life." *American Journal of Sociology* 44 (July 1938): 1–24.

Wolfe, Alan. "Not the Ordinary Kind in Politics or at Harvard." *New York Times*, 9 September 2000, A15 and A17.

Wong, Morrison and Charles Hirschman. 1983. "The New Asian Immigrants." In *Culture, Ethnicity, and Identity.* Edited by William McCurdy. New York: Academic Press.

Wood, Robert G. "Marriage Rates and Marriageable Men: A Test of the Wilson Hypothesis." *The Journal of Human Resources* 30 (Winter 1995): 163–193.

Woodson, Robert. 1987. *On the Road to Economic Freedom*. Washington, D.C.: Regency-Gateway.

Woolcock, Michael, "Social Capital and Economic Development: Toward A Theoretical Synthesis and Policy Framework." *Theory and Society* 27, No. 21 (1998): 151–208.

AUTHOR AND NAME INDEX

SUBJECT INDEX